CyberArts 2020

Prix Ars Electronica   S+T+ARTS
                                  Prize'20

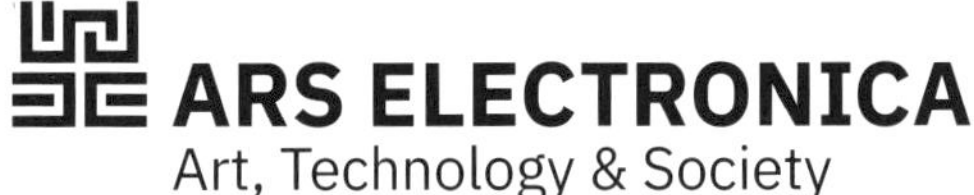

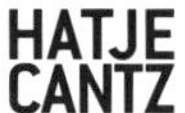

Hannes Leopoldseder · Christine Schöpf · Gerfried Stocker

CyberArts 2020

Prix Ars Electronica 2020

Computer Animation · Interactive Art + · Digital Communities
Visionary Pioneers of Media Art · u19–create your world

STARTS Prize'20

Grand Prize of the European Commission honoring Innovation
in Technology, Industry and Society stimulated by the Arts

Contents
Prix Ars Electronica 2020

Visionary Pioneers of Media Art 2020

u19—create your world

Young Professionals

Young Creatives

Contents

PRIX
ARS ELECTRONICA
2020

2020 Prix Ars Electronica

Christine Schöpf, Gerfried Stocker

The 2020 Prix Ars Electronica recorded a total of 3,209 entries from 90 countries: 1,236 entries in the category Interactive Art+, followed by Computer Animation with 930 works and Digital Communities with 373 projects submitted for the international competition. The category u19–create your world, open to Young Creatives (up to age fourteen) and Young Professionals (age fourteen to nineteen) from all over Austria, drew a total of 670 entries.

Established in 1987 and based on an idea by Hannes Leopoldseder of the Austrian Broadcasting Corporation (ORF), the Prix Ars Electronica has become the world's largest continuously held competition for digital art.

The year 2020 saw a decisive break in the thirty-three-year history of the Prix Ars Electronica: for the first time since 1987, the international jury met only virtually, due to the COVID-19 restrictions. It is early 2020. Suddenly, from one second to the next, it is no longer possible for anyone to travel around the world; no one is immune from becoming infected, and maintaining physical distance is the utmost priority. The pandemic determines our daily lives, and it does not spare media art, either. But despite varying time zones, despite physical distance, and despite technical challenges and external factors, a large number of tremendous projects were waiting to be evaluated and awarded prizes by a jury of experts. Thus, for the first time in thirty-three years, the international jury met not on location in Linz but via video conference in the digital space.

As the jury for Interactive Art+ aptly notes in this year's Jury Statement: "In 2016, Prix Ars Electronica expanded its definition of the Interactive Art category, broadening the concept of interaction and adding the + sign. Ironically, the 2020 jury members found themselves in extraordinary circumstances while judging the submitted works, as the coronavirus pandemic affected transportation globally and imposed social distancing. It was on this shifting ground that the jury decided on the prize winners. The 2016 category Interactive Art+ is concerned with interactivity, and now, during the pandemic, the jury needed to use social media and other forms of interactive technology to view and judge the submitted works. In 2020, there was actually NOTHING outside the interactive."

The broad spectrum of submitted works demonstrates once again that the Prix Ars Electronica unites artists and scientists from a wide variety of countries and cultures just as it does creative types from various fields: Activists who explore the possibilities of social networks, and artists who, for example, use our Smart Homes as a starting point for illuminating the relationship between intimacy and privacy on the one hand and convenience and constant hands-on activity on the other, or examine the influence navigation systems or apps like Airbnb and Tinder have on our perception of the world and how they influence our behavior. Another issue that is addressed is how racist profiling and the error-prone logic of AI systems are used to target low-income or non-white people with supposedly criminal intentions. The Prix Ars Electronica has always been a meeting place for artists who demonstrate in and with digital media how nearly every facet of our lives—communication, politics, business, finance, ecology, sociology—changes virtually on a daily basis. And it has become secondary against what political and cultural backdrops these changes occur and leave their mark. These are the developments that form the reservoir that the Prix Ars Electronica can draw on in its annual position analysis. It is not about making judgements here, but rather about exploring the current media culture.

In each category, the main prize in the form of a Golden Nica plus €10,000 prize money is awarded, as well as two Awards of Distinction and twelve Honorary Mentions. In 2020, in the u19–create your world youth category, a Golden Nica plus €3,000 prize money is awarded in the Young Professionals group (age fourteen to nineteen) as well as two Awards of Distinction and twelve Honorary

Mentions, with prize money totaling over €2,000. For the Young Creatives (up to age fourteen), main prizes, Awards of Distinction, and Honorary Mentions totaling over €2,000 are awarded, graded according to age. In addition, with the support of MIC – managing international customs & trade compliance—a special prize for innovative ideas and projects in the area of IT, programming, game design, Web, and Internet is awarded. This prize is endowed with €1,000 and is aimed at all creative young people who enjoy programming and developing new ideas.

The selection of the winning works was made by a group of twenty international experts from the world of art and science who serve the Prix Ars Electronica as jury members. We would like to take this opportunity to express our special appreciation for the extraordinary commitment with which they devoted themselves to the evaluation of the works, despite the time differences between Los Angeles, Seoul, San Francisco, and Tokyo, and the technical challenges that had to be overcome. In 2020, for the fifth time, the Prix Ars Electronica includes the STARTS Prize, which the Ars Electronica awards in cooperation with BOZAR and Waag for the European Commission. This prize, endowed with a total of €40,000, recognizes innovative projects at the nexus of science, technology, and arts (STARTS) and is awarded by the European Commission as part of the Horizon 2020 funding program for research and innovation.

The Prix Ars Electronica is being staged for the 34th time in 2020. This has been made possible by the City of Linz, which has funded Ars Electronica since 1979 and the Prix Ars Electronica since 1987. We would also like to express our gratitude to the OK in the Upper Austrian Culture Quarter, MIC—managing international customs & trade compliance, KulturKontakt Austria/OeAD, and the University of Applied Sciences Upper Austria, Hagenberg Campus.

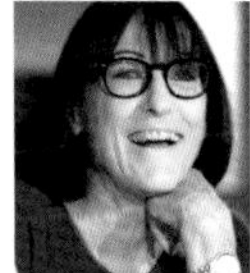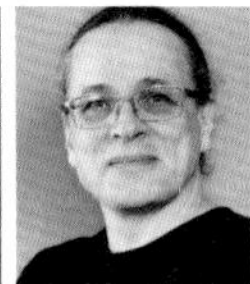

Christine Schöpf (AT), PhD, studied German and Romance Languages. She has worked as a radio and television journalist and was the head of the art and science department at ORF Upper Austria (1981–2008). In 2009 she was appointed Honorary Professor at the University of Art and Design Linz. Since 1979, she has held a number of positions in which she has been able to contribute considerably to the development of Ars Electronica. She was responsible for conceiving and organizing the Prix Ars Electronica from 1987–2003. Together with Gerfried Stocker, she has been the artistic co-director of Ars Electronica since 1996. **Gerfried Stocker** (AT) is a media artist and an engineer for communication technology and has been artistic director and co-CEO of Ars Electronica since 1995. In 1995/96 he developed the groundbreaking exhibition strategies of the Ars Electronica Center with a small team of artists and technicians and was responsible for the setup and establishment of Ars Electronica's own R & D facility, the Ars Electronica Futurelab. He has overseen the development of the program for international Ars Electronica exhibitions since 2004, the planning and the revamping of the contents for the Ars Electronica Center, which was enlarged in 2009, since 2005; the expansion of the Ars Electronica Festival since 2015; and the extensive overhaul of Ars Electronica Center's contents and interior design in 2019. Stocker is a consultant for numerous companies and institutions in the field of creativity and innovation management and is active as a guest lecturer at international conferences and universities. In 2019 he was awarded an honorary doctorate from Aalto University, Finland.

Out of the Blue
The Disappearance of Smiles
Hannes Leopoldseder

Forty-seven days before May 1, 2020, a virus began to change our lives: COVID-19, Coronavirus Disease 2019, a viral infection that, among other things, leads to respiratory disorders and originated in the Chinese city of Wuhan, which has a population of 11 million.

The first of May is a national holiday in Austria whose history goes all the way back to 1890. A hundred and thirty years later, in 2020, the Social Democratic Party's traditional May Day demonstration in front of Vienna's City Hall was cancelled. The reason: COVID-19. The lockdown. A change began in Austria, as well as all over the world, and our lives and daily routines began to change, thanks to an invisible virus that suddenly appeared. From out of the blue. And smiles disappeared from the faces of the people. These changes have impacted the entire world, for COVID-19 has spread to all the earth's continents. And it has affected all generations. It is not only older people who are concerned but also the younger ones. Here is an example from the "Generation Pandemic," to which the US news magazine *TIME* dedicated an entire issue in June 2020. Abigail Harrison, a young, very ambitious woman, is president of The Mars Generation (TMG), a nonprofit in Minneapolis, Minnesota, USA, that is focused on exciting young people and adults about human space exploration: "The COVID-19 pandemic has profoundly affected my generation, Generation Z [those born between 1990 and 2000], and will continue to affect us for years to come. In a matter of weeks, many of our best-laid plans have fallen apart. ... On my journey to becoming an astronaut, I know the potential implications of missing opportunities like this. ... The world will no longer exist as we once knew it, and we will have the opportunity to reshape it and make it a better place for all who inhabit it. Now is not the time for fear; it's the time to be bold and dream big."[1]

This optimistic attitude, this focus on the positive, should be given center stage. Opinions on the pandemic diverge. When the pandemic has ebbed, will our lives return to the way they used to be, or will a new kind of attitude toward life emerge?

A decisive characteristic of time is speed—the extent of change. A far-reaching transformation has been taking place in all areas of life for decades, and at a steadily increasing pace. The way we experience time varies—from suddenness to the seemingly never-ending wait when one is put on hold. And in the case of COVID-19, we don't know where the journey is taking us. We find ourselves in new territory without a horizon.

Our daily lives have, in any case, slowed down. Street scenes with people have a new face; with many wearing masks—simple masks but also colorful, stylish, and elegant ones—in order to protect themselves from COVID-19. A kind of "Corona couture" has even developed. For the editor-in-chief of *Vogue,* Anna Wintour, the mask has brought with it a new awareness of life. The mask has mutated into a fashion statement—in many variations. Everywhere one looks, faces are covered by masks. Smiles have disappeared. Let us go in search of the missing smile.

In the German weekly *Welt am Sonntag,* the journalist Heiko Zwirner writes about the history of the mask.[2] Zwirner takes a broad view of the subject—from the beaked masks worn by physicians in the plague epidemic of the 17th century to the COVID-19 masks: "Wearing a mask in public has always represented a taboo in our culture; a covered face is perceived as a threat. This perception is currently undergoing a shift. What is conspicuous about the sewing-box aesthetic of the handsewn masks is that they are not the least bit repellent or even hostile; rather, they send almost exclusively positive signals—with floral patterns, butterflies, and cute comic figures."[3] Perhaps the smile will return after all?

But one conclusion would seem to suggest itself: the COVID-19 mask will be retained in one form or another; it will become part of everyday life and perhaps a quite natural, optional accessory for every woman and man, reflecting the way fashion is incorporated into our daily lives. Due to the pandemic, these protective masks, whether they are for medicine, fashion, or for other areas, have set off a worldwide trade battle between China, the USA, and even Europe in which billions of dollars are at stake.

The mask has become a symbol for COVID-19 as well. The physician and psychotherapist Martina Leibovici-Mühlberger refers to the "Homo sapiens corona." In her book about the re-emergence of the world after COVID-19, she writes: "Due to its global impact, COVID-19 will be recorded in the history books not only as a virological but also as a socio-psychological phenomenon. The fear planted in our society by COVID-19 will not be easily uprooted. We will naturally have to redevelop or even reinvent our social and economic interaction with each other in view of a heightened need for security."[4] What Leibovici-Mühlberger means here is a wake-up call to implement far-reaching changes, because it is not only the mask that defines our everyday space; social distancing also contributes to changes in how people interact with each other. This is accompanied by a loss of closeness, of encounter, contact, and immediacy—all things that humans need. Our social safety net is changing. Everything is becoming tighter. People feel restricted. Fears about safety and health are palpable. Our social environment is changing; the norms that we humans have grown accustomed to are faltering. Our life design is called into question. We can confront this new situation either with more control or with a new way of life.

The Italian physicist, journalist, and bestselling author Paolo Giordano not only wrote a novel in 2017 about *The Solitude of Prime Numbers;* he also published a remarkable little book in April 2020 called *How Contagion Works: Science, Awareness, and Community in Times of Global Crises.* The 77-page pamphlet (which is small enough to fit in your pocket) is a much more interesting read than many of the other countless publications about the COVID-19 pandemic. This can be seen already by chapter titles like "Nerdy afternoons," "Contagion by numbers," "This crazy nonlinear world," "Really stopping the spread," "Cautious calculations," "Hand, foot, and mouth," "Hairspray," "Foreign multinational corporations," and "Numbering our days."

In this final chapter, "Numbering our days," Giordano remarks that in times of infections, all we can focus on is counting: the number of deceased, infected, recoveries, etc. He ultimately comes to this conclusion: "We can tell each other that Covid-19 is an isolated incident, a calamity or a scourge, cry that it's all 'their' fault. We're free to do so. Or we could try making sense of the contagion. Make better use of this time, use it to think about what our busy normality prevents us from considering: how did we get here, how do we want to start again? Number the days. Gain a heart of wisdom. Don't allow all of this suffering to be in vain."[5]

Which means: take a deep breath and prepare to adapt to a new life.

The demands of this new life are more complex than they may seem at first glance, for everywhere one looks, something is different—one just has to look closely. We will increasingly have to do without things we are accustomed to. The Dutch trend forecaster and international business consultant Lidewij Edelkoort (who, after *Vogue,* is the world's most famous trend forecaster) predicts that we have a rocky path in front of us: "We will have to reset our values and slow down. We will learn to live with less and to become more self-determined and mindful. Ownership and the hoarding of clothing or cars have long since fallen out of favor among the young generation. Our consumption will go into quarantine, and we will learn to be happy just with a simple dress, rediscovering old favorites we own, reading a forgotten book, and cooking up a storm to make life beautiful. We will have to start from square one and build a new system, and I hope a better one."[6]

In addition to this not particularly optimistic look into the future, we can also detect another trend now coming into focus: "out into the countryside." Interestingly, it is an architect who is drawing attention to this topic. Rem Koolhaas had mounted an exhibition at New York's Guggenheim Museum with the title *Countryside, The Future.* Due to the Corona crisis, the exhibition had to be closed down after only a few weeks. For the post-Corona era, Koolhaas is imagining a kind of "country life 2.0":

he talks about "pixel farming," climate change, the use of robots, new leisure time, and new recreational opportunities. The architecture critic Michael Kimmermann wrote in *The New York Times* about Koolhaas: "A corrective to the focus on growing cities, *Countryside* aims to turn a spotlight on the 98 percent of the planet not yet occupied by cities. Anticipating the obvious criticism, Mr. Koolhaas describes the show as a 'pointillist' portrait, a 'global sampling' of the current condition of 'countryside,' which he acknowledges seems 'a glaringly inadequate term for all the territory that is not urban.'"[7]

We will ultimately be faced with a two-fold challenge: on the one hand we must modify our lives as we once knew them, and on the other it is simultaneously essential to move more quickly into the phase of digitization and artificial intelligence. As the German trend forecaster Matthias Horx says: "The world as we know it is in the process of disintegrating. But behind it, a new world is forming whose shape we are able to at least surmise."[8]

This time it is not only a new world that is taking shape; for the first time, the entire world is affected by an event that can reach every person on earth. However, it is likely that not every individual can be adequately helped. And this is unique. We have been learning the new vocabulary for several months now: social distancing, mandatory face coverings, changes in social relationships, critical discussions about globalization, withdrawal to the local environment, changes in working habits, home office, new closeness, physical distance, contact tracing, wearables, sensitive physical data, health tracking in the fight against Corona, sensor-based monitoring, and on and on. The journalist and book author Thomas Vaŝek, former editor-in-chief of *Technology Review* and the author of numerous books, is now editor-in-chief of the philosophy magazine *Hohe Luft.* In its April 2020 issue he wrote of these times: "Up until March we were counting smileys and likes, and then suddenly deaths. With the Corona crisis, the old normal came to an end. The era of the virus caused us to revert to the essentials: to caring for ourselves and others. And it teaches us how we should live. ... The pandemic is an experience of closeness and distance. It affects us in a very personal way. It scares us, it defines our life, it confronts us with death. But at the same time, it also forces us to disregard ourselves and to think of others, who are just as affected by the pandemic as we are. It distances us from those close to us, while simultaneously creating a new closeness to those who are spatially distant from us."[9]

Today, different realities always exist side by side: There is the factual reality in which we live physically, the world of the COVID-19 virus, with all the risks associated with it. We must survive the virus. But there is another reality as well: the perceived reality of feelings. The facts recede into the background; we have arrived in the post-factual world, the word of the year 2016. But four years have passed since then, and now we are in the middle of a pandemic. "Everything will be fine, right?" asks the journalist Marcus Jauer in an article in *DIE ZEIT* with the subtitle "Why trust is especially important at a time when everything is based on control and knowledge." "Why do we still need trust?" he writes. "Since a virus closed down the whole world within a period of only three months, we have been dependent on trust to an extent that we never experienced before. We must trust virologists we had never heard of until recently, but whose assessments now determine our daily lives. We must trust politicians who never before had to make decisions that so directly and concretely affect the personal well-being of so many people, and who now cannot afford to make any mistakes. We must trust our fellow humans that they maintain physical distance, even if they are not afraid of becoming sick themselves. ... The unknown has shifted from the edge of our attention to its very center."[10]

This uncertainty, this unpredictability is also stressed by Jeffrey Katzenberg, the Hollywood mogul who, along with Steven Spielberg and David Geffen, founded the film production company DreamWorks SKG: "I don't have a crystal ball and am not a prophet. I have no answer to the question of how the crisis will change us. Even economists cannot give us a reliable prognosis. We are in the center of a tornado with zero visibility. We can't even see our hand in front of our face, let alone know what it looks like on the other side of the tornado. As an optimist, I am convinced that we will succeed in rebuilding and that we will emerge from the Corona crisis all the stronger."[11]

Ars Electronica 2020 intends to convey an idea, a

vision of this new world. After five years at the POSTCITY, the Ars Electronica Festival 2020 takes the stage at a new location and with a new partner: it is moving from the POSTCITY to the KEPLER GARDENS of Johannes Kepler University Linz. The title of this year's Festival is:

In Kepler's Gardens
A global journey mapping the 'new' world
Autonomy – Democracy
Ecology – Technology
Reality – Uncertainty
Humanity

The Festival sees itself as a journey—as a virtual journey to the partners in Ars Electronica's international network. There will also be encounters in the real network of artists in the KEPLER GARDENS on the campus of the Johannes Kepler University as well as at the many partner institutions in Linz, such as the University of Art and Design Linz, the Lentos Kunstmuseum, the OK in the Upper Austrian Culture Quarter, and numerous others.
Visitors can lounge in the KEPLER GARDENS as if they were on a picnic—with the appropriate distancing, of course, depending on what Corona-related distancing measures, if any, are still in effect at the beginning of September. The other option for visitors is to take advantage of a journey or guided tours through the digital world of Ars Electronica with the 2020 Festival—meaning a freedom of choice between a close world and a distant world. This is where "Home Delivery" comes in: with this feature, Ars Electronica comes to you and brings its program right into your home, enabling everyone to experience Ars Electronica and the Festival activities and atmosphere.

A significant aspect of this Ars Electronica Festival 2020 is therefore the bipolarity between the two levels of the festival: the simultaneity and the duality of local physical activity in the KEPLER GARDENS in Linz, with real events, and with artists and Festival guests present in person on the one hand; while on the other, Ars Electronica 2020 will simultaneously take place on the net. Gerfried Stocker, Artistic Director of Ars Electronica: "With this simultaneity and duality of local physical and globally networked activity, Ars Electronica will yet again become an exciting experimental laboratory and prototype for a next-level interconnectedness in which the focus will above all be on new forms and possibilities of the fusion and coexistence of the analog and the digital, of the real and the virtual, of physical and telematic proximity." The Festival thus aims at making a statement in favor of science, art, culture, and civilization, but also making a statement against fear, the erosion of solidarity, and discrimination.

1. Abigail Harrison, "The Possibilities after the Pandemic," *TIME,* June 1 / June 8, 2020, p. 54.
2. Heiko Zwirner, *Welt am Sonntag,* No. 16, April 2020.
3. Ibid.
4. Martina Leibovici-Mühlberger, *Startklar. Aufbruch in die Welt nach COVID-19*, Vienna, 2020, p. 135.
5. Paolo Giordano, *How Contagion Works,* London, 2020, p. 77.
6. Lidewij Edelkoort, *S-Magazin. Das Stilmagazin vom SPIEGEL,* May 2020, p. 15.
7. Michael Kimmelman, *Why Rem Koolhaas Brought a Tractor to the Guggenheim,* https://www.nytimes.com/2020/02/20/arts/design/rem-koolhaas-guggenheim.html.
8. www.horx.com/www.zukunftsinstitut.de.
9. Thomas Vaŝek, "Zeit der Sorge," *Philosophie-Zeitschrift Hohe Luft,* issue 4/2020, p. 15, 16.
10. Marcus Jauer, "Wird schon gut gehen, oder?" *Die Zeit,* Dossier, No. 22, 28, May 2020, p. 13.
11. Barbara Gasser, "Hollywood-Mogul Jeffrey Katzenberg: Meine Fehler sind endlos," *Die Presse,* May 18, 2020, p. 12.

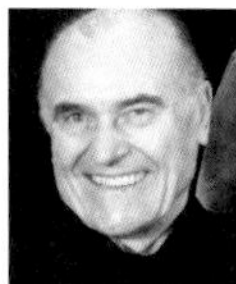

Hannes Leopoldseder (AT), PhD., was born in 1940 in St. Leonhard near Freistadt. He has worked as a television journalist for ORF Vienna (from 1967), as the managing director of ORF Upper Austria (1974 – 1998), and as the information director of ORF Vienna (1998 – 2002). In 2007 he received the Austrian Cross of Honour for Science and Art, First Class, and in 2013 the Grand Decoration of Honour for Services to the Republic of Austria. In 2009 he was appointed Honorary Professor at the University of Art and Design Linz. He co-founded Ars Electronica and the Linzer Klangwolke in 1979 and initiated the Prix Ars Electronica (1987) and the Ars Electronica Center (1996). He is also the co-editor of Ars Electronica's catalogues.

PRIX
ARS ELECTRONICA

COMPUTER ANIMATION

Voices from the Network

Peter Burr, Birgitta Hosea, Mathilde Lavenne, Erick Oh, Mimi Son

The jury came together this year in virtual form, separated by a global pandemic that had quickly transformed the world into something not yet known. In this moment of uncertainty, we connected through a shifting array of telecommunications paraphernalia, considering the future of computer animation. The formal definitions of this category have been blurry for years. "Isn't all animation moved through a computer at some point now?" we affirmed, speaking to each other through webcams and LCD displays. We relished in the diversity of this category: stop motion cartoons, live performances, immersive installations, video games, hand drawn feature films, VR experiences, and music videos (to name just the tip of the proverbial iceberg). This work asked us to question labels about what animation is, such as: "does it have to be made frame by frame?—does it have to be displayed on a screen?—could it be considered as a process rather than an outcome?—and could it be live?" We asked ourselves what animation could be, rather than narrow it down with rules and definitions. It is both troubling and fascinating to let the artworks guide us through what would be new rules, and so we embraced the unknown, with delight at what we found.

There was an impressive constellation of themes this year, raising questions for us around synthetic ecology, serendipity, and cracking veneers of technology. These concepts were explored through a range of advanced techniques such as 3D scanning, generative adversarial networks, and real time processing. What kind of responsibility does a jury like ours engage in by choosing one work over another? We allowed this testimony to emerge from the network of our voices, and it is unanimous.

Through the consensus of five individuals coming from different disciplines and perceptions, it seems that the female gaze has imposed itself on us this year both in the strength of new stories it offers and in the way these artists seize their technological tools to challenge a system of dominant values. This perspective, with humor and sensitivity, shows us an alternative to the dystopian universe our progress-driven world often creates for itself. The history of science and the history of animation do not use the same grammars, but they both contribute to a cultural narrative of the world. This year, we are excited by evolutions taking place at the level of technical perfection and are proud to award prizes to work that asks us to pay attention to who is using this technology as we continue building our future.

While we each had specific affinities towards works that were close to our individual hearts and that we had to defend, in the end we discovered the feeling of having grown our reflections together as we contemplated with great enthusiasm the selection of these fifteen projects.

Golden Nica

Infinitely Yours · Miwa Matreyek

Merging live performance, sculpture, and animation, *Infinitely Yours* depicts an all too familiar world drowning in the by-product of material abundance. Miwa Matreyek physically places her body at the center of this mess, navigating a kinetic journey through natural and man-made infrastructure that, like any memorable journey, is best experienced firsthand. Forefronting vaudevillian and pre-cinematic animation alongside late 20th century music video and installation art,

Matreyek invokes a timeless yet assuredly timely collage of media history. The central axis of this piece is what's at stake. Engaging the shadow of her whole body in the images, she invites us to see it is never objectified. Contrasting a materialist conception of the world in which capitalism plays a major role in the objectification of women's bodies, her presence feels radical. Mired in mountains of garbage, the female body struggles and detaches itself both metaphorically and visually. *Infinitely Yours* finds a curious glow at the heart of environmental calamity, offering no simple answers. This salient work lingers in the imagination as both a banner for action and a recipe for magic.

Awards of Distinction

Average Happiness · Maja Gehrig

This short film co-opts the visual language of Capitalism, re-animating data graphics of charts and graphs into abstract landscapes. Finding sexuality in the bars of graphs and the spheres of pie charts, it reminds us of the patriarchal domination of the business world. Through its questioning of the representation of data, the film also critiques the status of quantitative data as a source of objective evidence that can be summed up in the phrase "lies, damned lies, and statistics."

Bab Sebta · Randa Maroufi

Located on the African side of the Gibraltar Strait, Ceuta is an autonomous Spanish city bordering Morocco. It is a dense and lively crossing point heavily trafficked with manufactured products and contraband. Bab Sebta (or Ceuta's Gate) is a vibrant and almost theatrical reconstruction of this strategic customs location. The artist's mental cartography reveals this landscape's cold logic of surveillance, order and control. The omniscient camera eye and the absence of a physical environment contrasts with the choreography of an overflowing human tide, struggling to be contained by administrative rigidity. Composed exclusively of fixed shots, the film excels in the art of collage. By associating the artist's memory and that of the workers who reproduced their gestures, the film succeeds in creating a collective work that reveals the excesses of our consumer society.

Honorary Mentions

#21xoxo · Sine Özbilge & Imge Özbilge

A witty and sassy commentary on the fakeness of social media and online dating from a female perspective. The Pop Art style re-animates the logos of social media brands to pastiche their permeation of contemporary culture and how they get inside our heads as we re-perform their brand values.

Bodyless · Hsin-Chien Huang

Created in response to the experience of martial law in Taiwan, this VR work presents a series of complex and highly detailed intertwining worlds. The viewer travels from a prison cell to the world of the spirits and then to cities of data where people are dying of the plague. In a prescient ending that evokes our current epidemic, the final reveal is of giant, god-like figures spraying and disinfecting the entire city.

Pile · Toby Auberg

This CG animated short film depicts today's human society and system in one singular take, which starts from the bottom of a river bank where lower class people exist, and vertically travels all the way up to the top of the hierarchy where everything ends up turning into a surreal abstract explosion of capitalism. While observing every detail of each stage and different level in life, we get to reflect ourselves and ask fundamental questions about how the world is constructed today. In terms of the technique, it provides a great cinematic experience but can be easily showcased as a looping video installation piece that the audience can watch multiple times.

Pulsión · Pedro Casavecchia

This Argentinian short film turns dark feelings that a boy has accumulated after his mother's death during his childhood into a disturbing yet compelling experience for the audience. The narrative is revealed through a series of vignettes around the protagonist in a carefully staged mise-en-scène with unique pacing and intense editorial rhythm. It is a refreshing take on storytelling through CG animation, a familiar form that continues to surprise us.

Recursive Truth · Rachel Rossin

This short looping artwork presents fragments of deep fake clips, computer vision tests, video game mods, and webcam recordings in a malleable exploration of popular images. As this piece loops over and over in a never-changing cycle, what at first appears to be a random assortment of digital files slowly reveals the artist's questions around surveillance, value, and power.

Serial Parallels · Max Hattler

This captivating architectural animation draws a dizzying portrait of Hong Kong's urban environment. Through the lens of the animated film, each floor or window corresponds to a film frame. The colors follow one another in a repetitive and rhythmic movement that plunges us into a meditative state that is both gentle and anxiety-provoking. A rhythmic escalation until the saturation of a space in which we finally lose our bearings. It is only when the sky appears to us that we can finally breathe the air we desperately miss as we climb the floors of these overcrowded towers. The experience is not unlike the one that the global situation has forced us all to apprehend individually from the windows of our respective habitats.

Squarepusher / Terminal Slam
Daito Manabe, Kenichiro Shimizu

This music video is visually and musically breathtaking, employing a mix of live-action footage and computer-generated images and animations. Even more, it deals with subject matter that today's modern society faces everyday: privacy-loss, data mining, pervasive marketing, and surveillance capitalism. As the people in the video start to glitch, an omniscient artificial intelligence appears to hack all the advertising space—replacing it with pixelated CG textures that pulsate violently from billboards and screens as the music continues to the climax. This piece is a great example of balance between commercial entertainment, technical achievement, artistic exploration, and important cultural observations that raise social awareness.

The Entropy Gardens · DEPART

This visually arresting VR work investigates the idea of the garden as a creation of the imagination—a poetic space. Generative animation is used to create an abstract environment of mutating, synthetic vegetation alongside recognizable plant forms. Moving through this lush jungle of shifting forms, the viewer experiences a field of poetry—spoken and visual.

The Sky is on Fire
Emmanuel van der Auwera

This multi-screen installation depicts a fractured landscape composed of 3D scanned urban environments across 3 large LED arrays. Viewers are presented with a hollowed-out world echoing with isolated monologues that capture a feeling of collapse alongside a refusal to be destroyed. It evokes a feeling of fragility while also asserting a plea for permanence. The virtual world is here to stay.

This Means More · Nicolas Gourault

Liverpool FC supporters recount their experience of a tragic event: the Hillsborough disaster in 1989. Crowd simulation software is used as a tool to explore the movement of the masses of football fans who crowded the stands that day. Their sensitive testimonies make us realize through an analytical documentary that for the motive of profit, the addition of separations partly caused this tragedy. A subtle and methodical critique of the class logic within football.

Toomas Beneath the Valley of the Wild Wolves · Chintis Lundgren

What happens when a handsome young wolf loses his job? This enjoyable and stylish 2D animation is an engaging story of polymorphous perversity and complex desires.

Underground Circuit · Yuge Zhou 周雨歌

In this installation, the viewer is invited to sit in the middle of multiple film clips taken in the New York subway that radiate out on four sides. This viewing position is inspired by the figure of the Four Face Buddha who can see in all four directions. In taking up this position, the viewer becomes implicated in their own voyeurism, as if they were a supreme being watching the world from the center of a visual network. It is an effective comment on the surveillance culture of cities and how we are all involved.

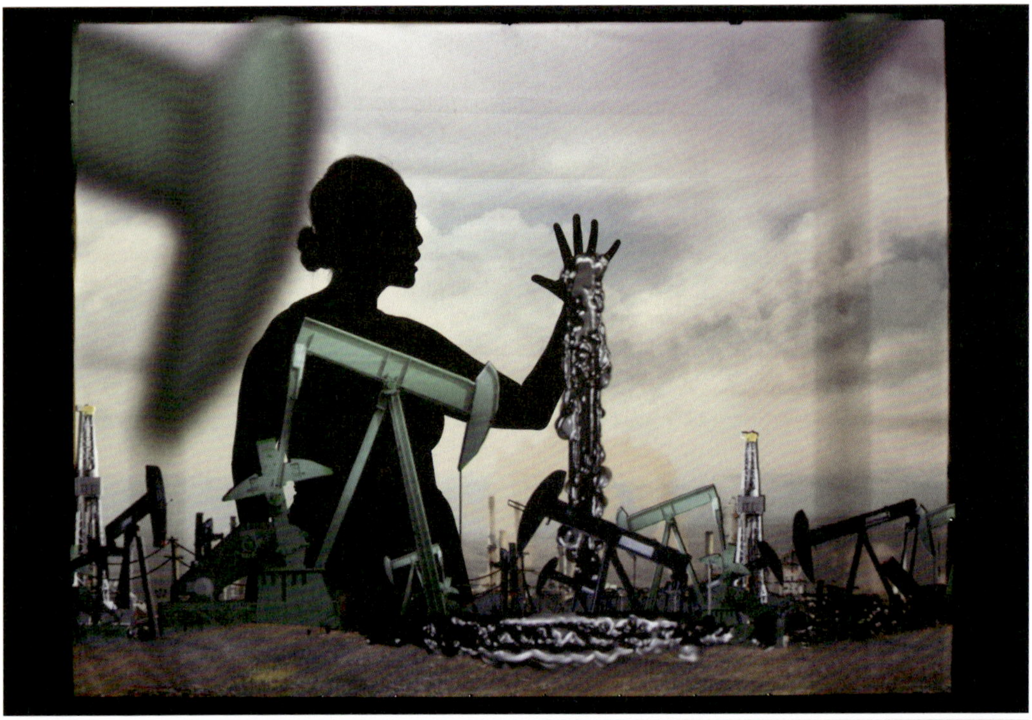

Courtesy of the artist

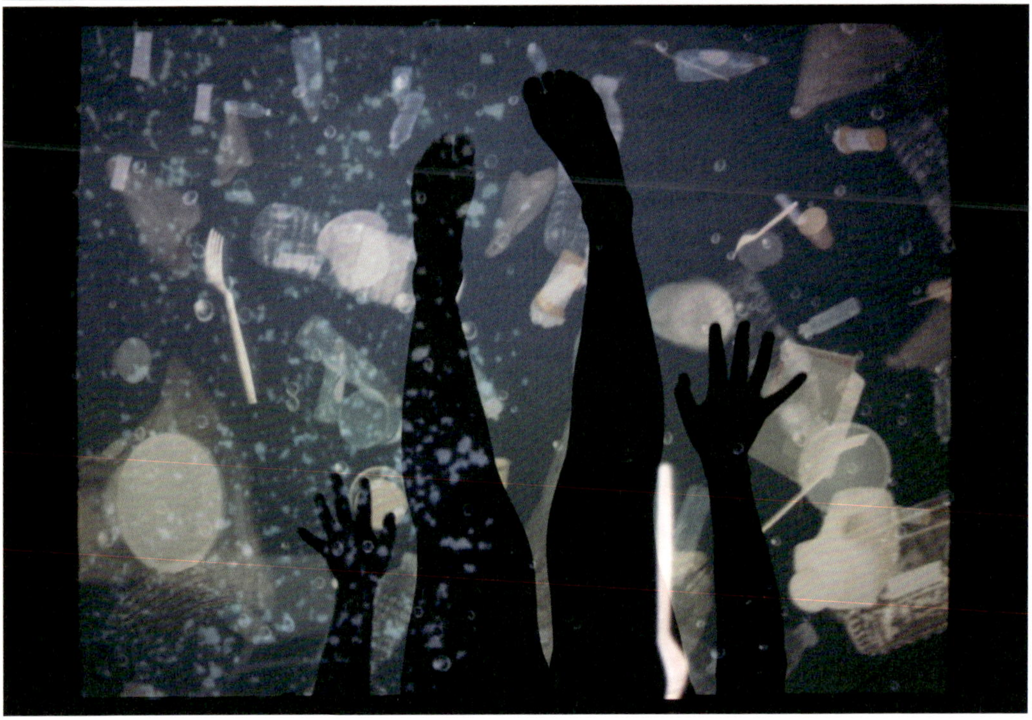

Courtesy of the artist

COMPUTER ANIMATION · Golden Nica 2020

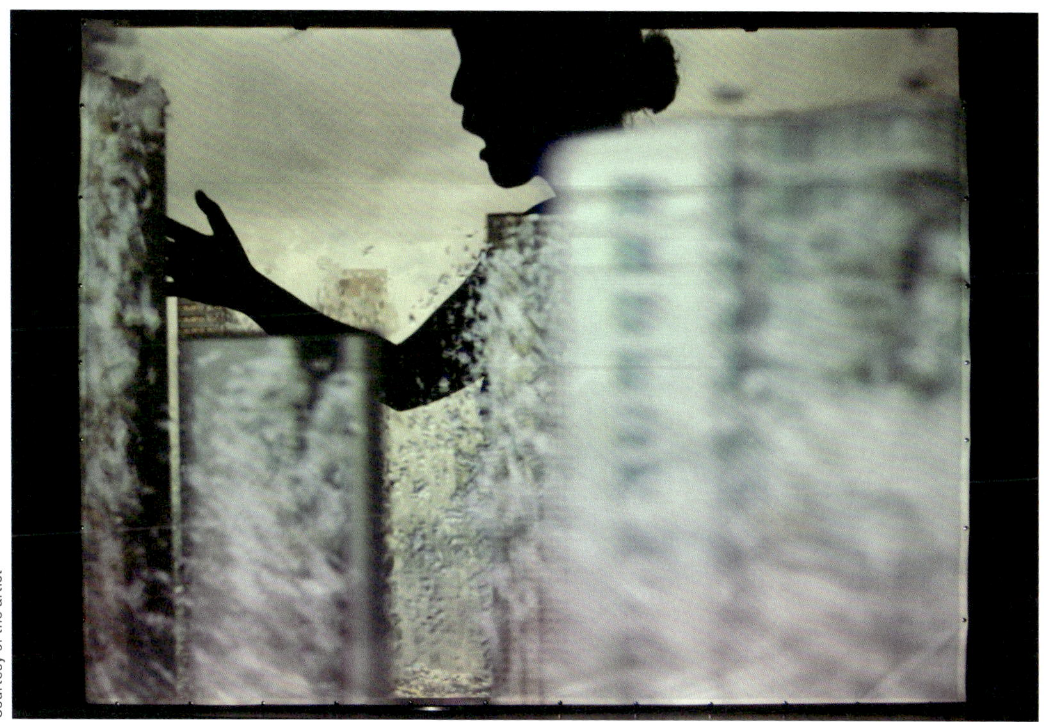

Infinitely Yours

Miwa Matreyek

I tell stories about the world of humanity and nature through performed metaphorical experiences. I want my work to be a catalyst for conversation, addressing current events and challenging the viewer to see the world differently and emotionally through symbolic images.

Infinitely Yours is the fourth in my series of solo work that mixes animation and live performance, involving a screen, layered projected animation, and a live performer (myself) as a shadow silhouette from behind the screen. The piece is 25 minutes long and falls into the interdisciplinary realms of animation and theater. It is a staged live performance at the intersection of tech and hand-made, the fantastical and physical, in a form of storytelling that feels uncanny and visceral.

Infinitely Yours is a kaleidoscopic interpretation of the increasingly alarming headlines from the last 4 – 5 years: destructive weather, floods and droughts, extraction and pollution, and our worry about an uncertain future. How can I show the invisible systems that hold up our globalized world, and peel back the layers of what a planet with 8 billion people feels like? My work attempts to dig at our collective complicity with the larger destruction happening by proxy of our everyday comforts... and the complex nature of that in our contemporary society.

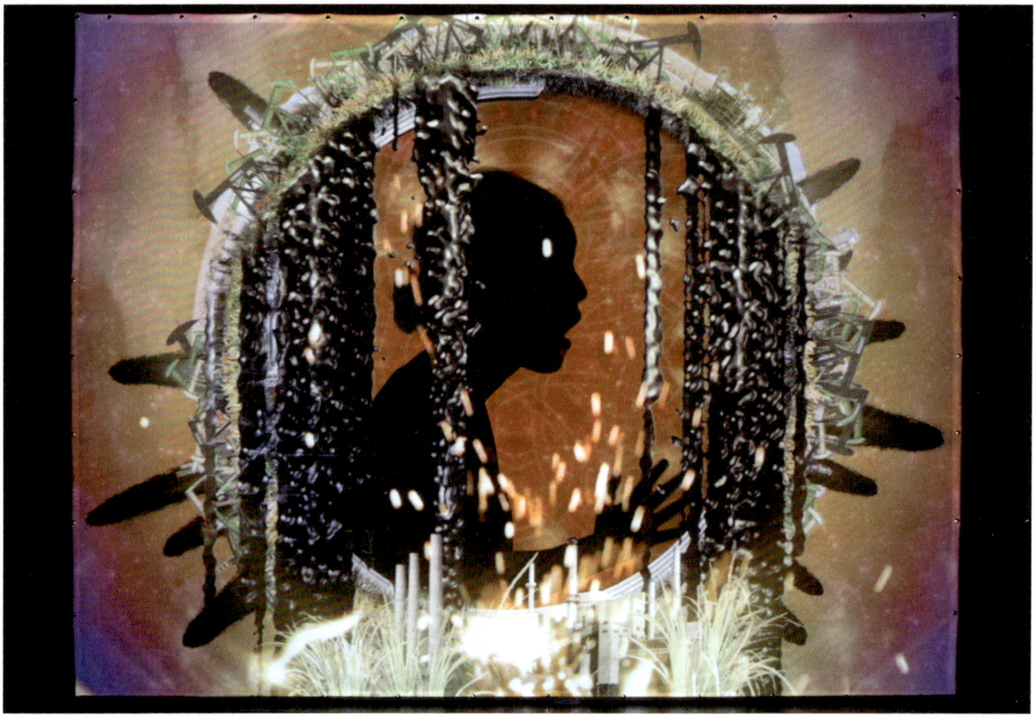

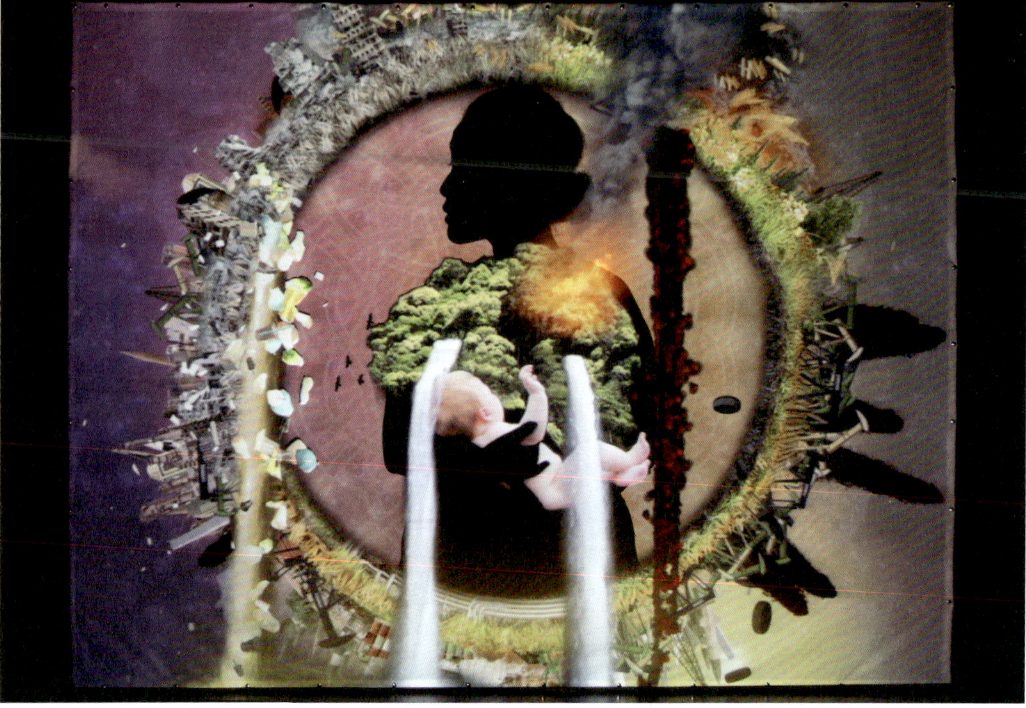

COMPUTER ANIMATION · Golden Nica 2020

The piece features a single silhouette figure in shadow who morphs through scales and points of view—from one individual, to all of humanity, to the earth itself, switching at a turn from scene to scene. These levels of consciousness are at odds, creating and destroying each other and the worlds around them, as I take the audience on an emotional journey to see perspectives beyond their own. The shadow is an interesting medium. As a live performer, I am physically there but obscured, uniquely myself but also reduced to a symbol of a person, and as the show unfolds, my silhouette becomes a vessel for the audience to consider the nightmarish world I present. I wanted the moments and experiences of climate change to look like they directly affect my body, as I drown in an ocean full of plastics, rise and fall with the city, and choke on smog. As humans continue to push the world toward the tipping point of climate change, my work attempts to navigate the shifting realities of the Anthropocene through embodied imagery. The average American produces about 2 kg of trash a day, or 940 kg of trash a year: what does that look like and feel like, if it all were to literally pour out of a body in one moment?

I come from a background in collage and animation. I use photoshop and aftereffects to build visually rich collaged and composited worlds. A good portion of the images in this piece came from my life. The pouring and floating trash in the animation is built out of footage of garbage pulled from the recycling bin of my apartment building. The oil field is built from footage of one I saw while on a road trip through central California.

It has been interesting that in the process of making this piece and after, there are scenes that continue to feel relevant to unfolding world events. The opening scene with the forest fire I first imagined after the wildfires in California, but it felt relevant again and again with the Amazon Rainforest fires, then the fires in Australia.

Creation and performance: Miwa Matreyek
All music tracks: Morgan Sorne
Documentation stills: Keida Mascaro
This project is supported by a 2019 Princess Grace Foundation Special Project Grant

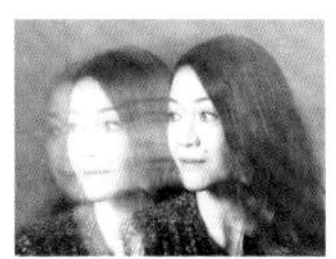

Miwa Matreyek (US) is an animator, designer, and performer based in Los Angeles. Coming from a background in animation, Matreyek creates live, staged performances where she interacts with her kaleidoscopic moving images as a shadow silhouette, in a dreamlike visual space that makes invisible worlds visible. Her work often weaves surreal and poetic narratives of conflict between humanity and nature. She performs her interdisciplinary shadow performances all around the world, including animation/film festivals, theater/performance festivals, art museums, science museums, universities, and tech conferences. A few past presentations include TEDGlobal, New Frontier at Sundance Film Festival (2011, 2014, 2020), MOMA, SFMoMA, Future of Storytelling conference, ISEA conference, and many more.

http://www.semihemisphere.com/#/infinitelyyours

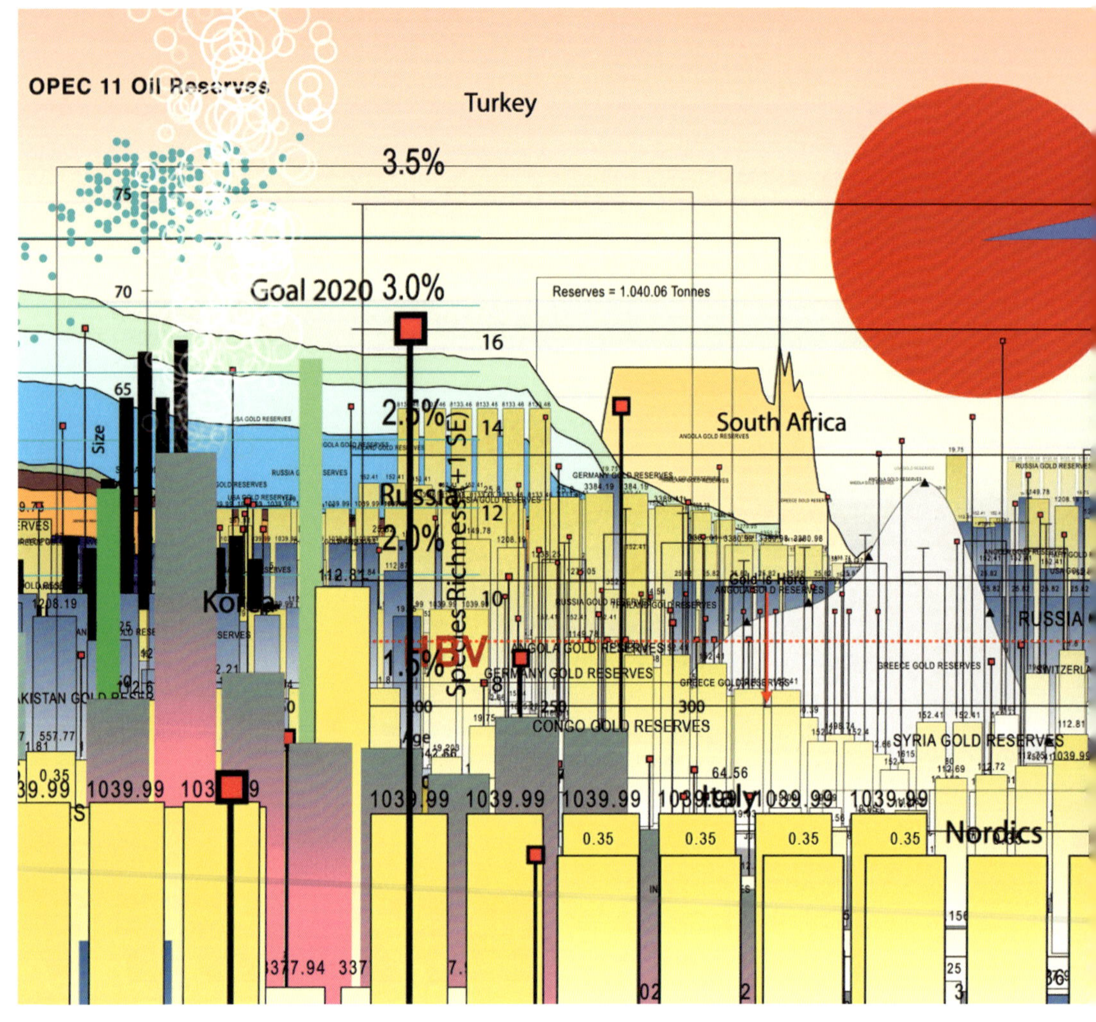

Average Happiness

Maja Gehrig

During a PowerPoint presentation, statistical diagrams are breaking free from the strait-jacket of their coordinates. A trip into the sensual world of statistics begins. Pie charts are melting, arrow diagrams twisting, scatter plots, bar graphs, and stock market curves join in a collective climax.

Animation: Maja Gehrig, Stefan Holaus
Scenario, script: Maja Gehrig
Film editor: Maja Gehrig, Nora de Baan
Mix: Christoph Benz, Jingle Jungle

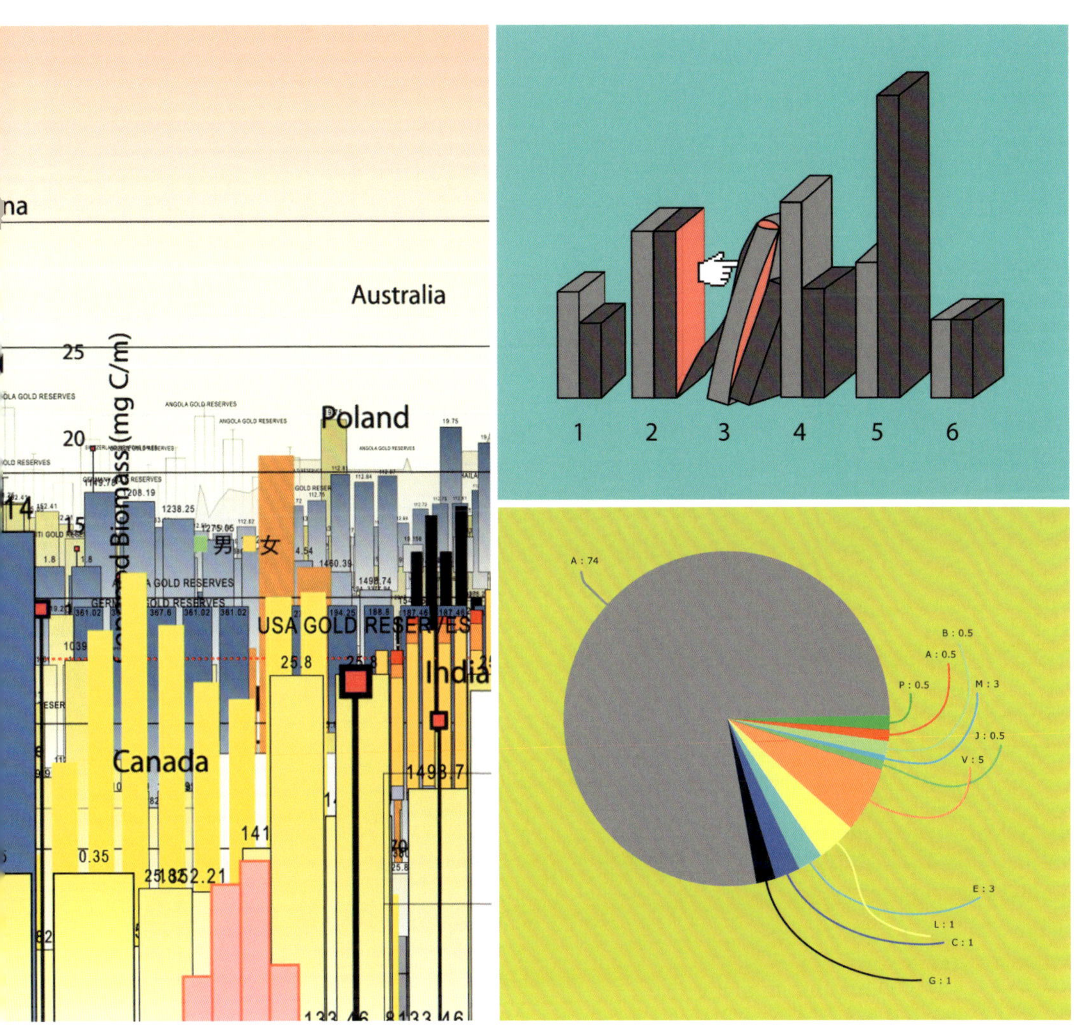

Maja Gehrig (CH), born in 1978 in Zurich. Following a preparatory course at Zürcher Hochschule der Künste (1999-2000), she spent two years at Fachhochschule Aarau, Media Arts department (2000-2002) before taking up an internship at Eesti Joonisfilm, Tallinn (2002-2003). From 2003-05 she attended HSLU (Hochschule Luzern, Design & Kunst) animation department. She worked as curator of installations and performances at ARM (Artspace Rondeel Maastricht) between 2006-11 and founded Gehrig Trick & Sohn in 2011. Her short films include *TripleTexas Dream* (2003), *Metawalz* (2003), *2PS* (2003/2004), *Une Nuit Blanche* (2005), *Amourette* (2009) and *Königin Po* (Queen Bum, 2015). She has participated in many international festivals and has received numerous awards.

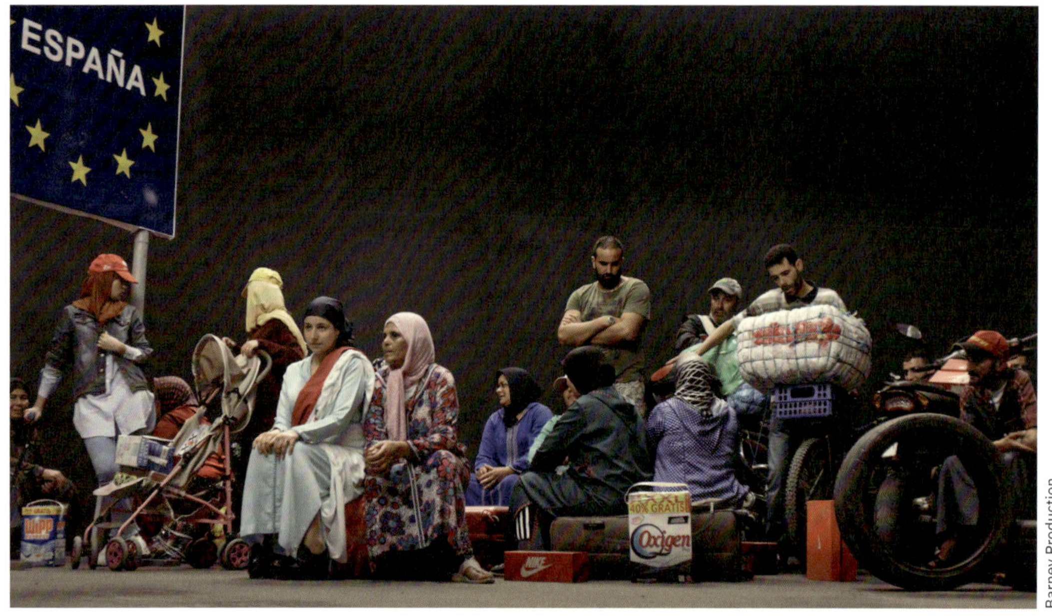

Barney Production

Bab Sebta

Randa Maroufi

Bab Sebta consists of a series of reconstructed situations based on observations made on the border of Ceuta, a Spanish enclave on Moroccan soil that provides the scene for an intense trafficking of manufactured goods, sold at discounted prices. Every day, thousands of people work there.

Bab Sebta can be considered as an artistic experiment that questions the limits of the representation. Proceeding from the same economy found in Lars Von Trier's *Dogville* (2003), which reduces and eliminates all elements of scenery, there is no image of the city of Ceuta, so that all attention is paid to the gestures.

The protagonists were people who actually worked at the border of Ceuta and whom I asked to play themselves. They were equipped with their bags and working clothes.

The film was shot from two different points of view, a zenith and a frontal one. The whole film is composed only of still shots. All camera movements are virtual, the floor drawings and signage were added in post-production.

In this film, I aim to convey both the particular tension felt on this small territory separating Africa from Europe and also a more general state of the world. I wanted to raise the question of the passage between continents from the perspective of everyday life.

Bab Sebta by Randa Maroufi
Production: Barney Production & Monfleuri Production
Director: Randa Maroufi
Producer: Saïd Hamich Benlarbi & Sophie Penson
Associate producer: Randa Maroufi
Voiceover: Nouha Ben Yebdri, Ahmed Ben Youssef, Mohamed Mohrach
DOP: Luca Coassin
Camera assistant: Othmane Mansouri, Taoufik Ait Baha
Sound: Mohamed Bounouar, Abla Boumlik, Léonore Mercier, Christian Cartier
Decor: Khaled El Attafi, Abdellatif El Rhazouani, Anas Yamine
Editing: Ismaël Joffroy Chandoutis, Randa Maroufi
Special effects: Paul Guilbert, Gregory Mc Grew
Color grading: Laurent Navarri
With support from: AFAC – Arab Fund for Arts and Culture, La Fondation des Artistes,
La Casa de Velázquez, CNC, Doha Film Institute, FIDlab, Kamal Lazar, France 2

   COMPUTER ANIMATION · Award of Distinction

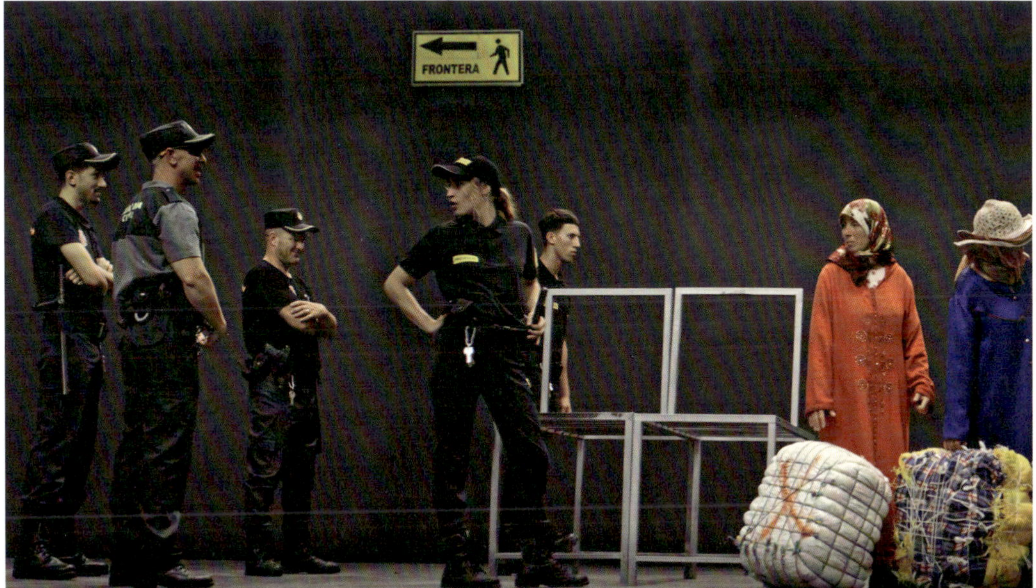

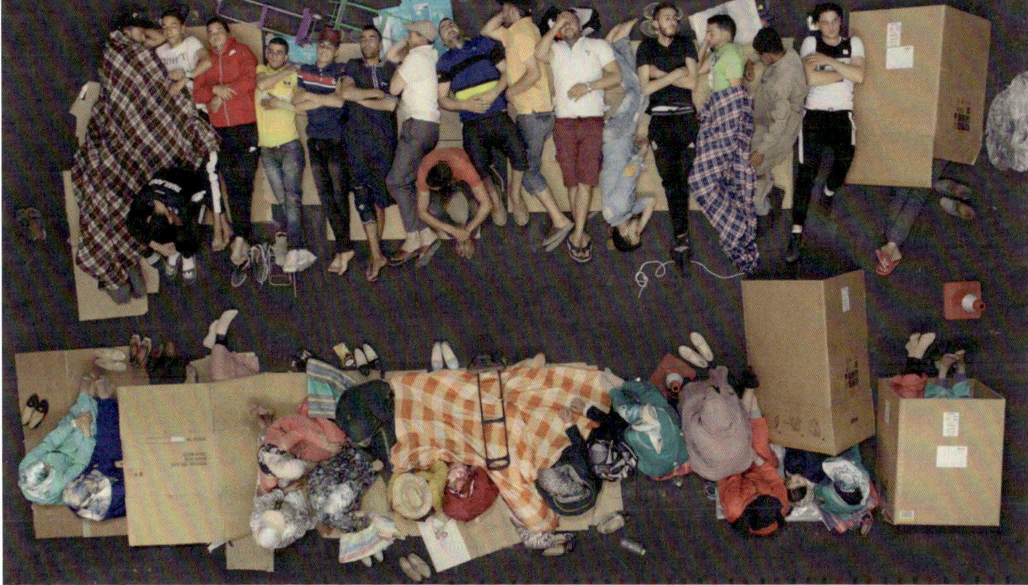

Randa Maroufi (MA/FR). Born in 1987 in Casablanca. She currently lives and works in Paris. The experimental works of filmmaker and artist Randa Maroufi explore an elastic awareness of reality. Her films and moving images often employ special effects and other formal devices that alter perceptions of time, space, and movement. She has received many awards for her film *Le Park* (2015), and *Bab Sebta* (2019). Maroufi is a graduate of the National Institute of Fine Arts, Tetouan, MA (2010) and the School of Fine Arts, Angers, FR (2013). She also earned a diploma from Le Fresnoy—Studio National des Arts Contemporains, Tourcoing, FR (2015). Randa Maroufi was Artist Member of the French Academy in Madrid at Casa de Velázquez in 2018.

https://vimeo.com/361075796

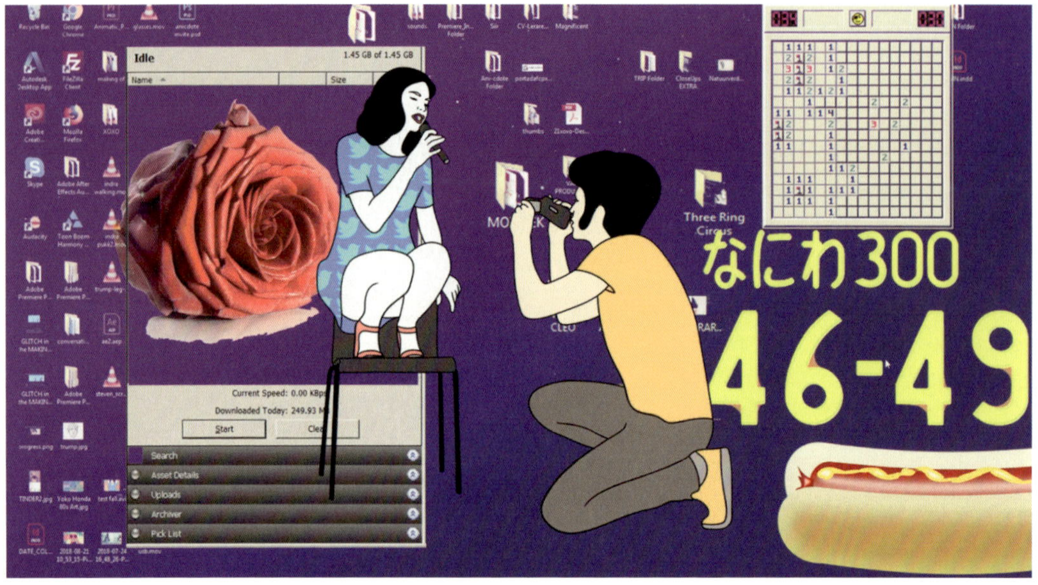

#21xoxo

Sine Özbilge & Imge Özbilge

#21xoxo is an experimental animated short film that reflects on the impact of 21st century technologies on intimacy, love, and relationships. It revolves around the nihilistic, narcissistic and millennial adventures of a girl in a parallel digital universe interlaced with cyber-love, speed dating, hipster culture, meme and vaporwave aesthetics as well as post-net attitudes. Absurd, surreal, and metamorphic scenes of digital nonsense intertwine with 90s nostalgia, design culture, femininity, the subconscious, and pop art in order to paint a picture of today's zeitgeist.

It has a mixed media basis where animation and live action fuse in order to explore new connotations and stylistic forms, generating sub-layers, open endings, and distorted realities. Contemporary video clutter (media-related filmic aesthetics that have infiltrated our everyday lives through social media and technological gadgets such as fisheye lenses, Skype angles, GoPro footage, Instagram cadrages etc.) is filtered through the language of animation. This deformation by animation makes us question reality. The inhabitants of *#21xoxo* are stuck in a sort of cyber-real limbo between our actual world and cyberspace. As hybrids they neither fit into the rules of live action, nor of classical animation. This is a reference to our daily lives where we demonstrate a sort of schizophrenic existence, floating in between our real selves and our online avatars, Facebook profiles and Instagram personas.

The classic narrative structure is glitched to create a fragmented yet still continuous visual experience. This method derives from the same fragmented yet flowing social media experience of "reading posts," "swiping on tinder," "cruising on

COMPUTER ANIMATION · Honorary Mention

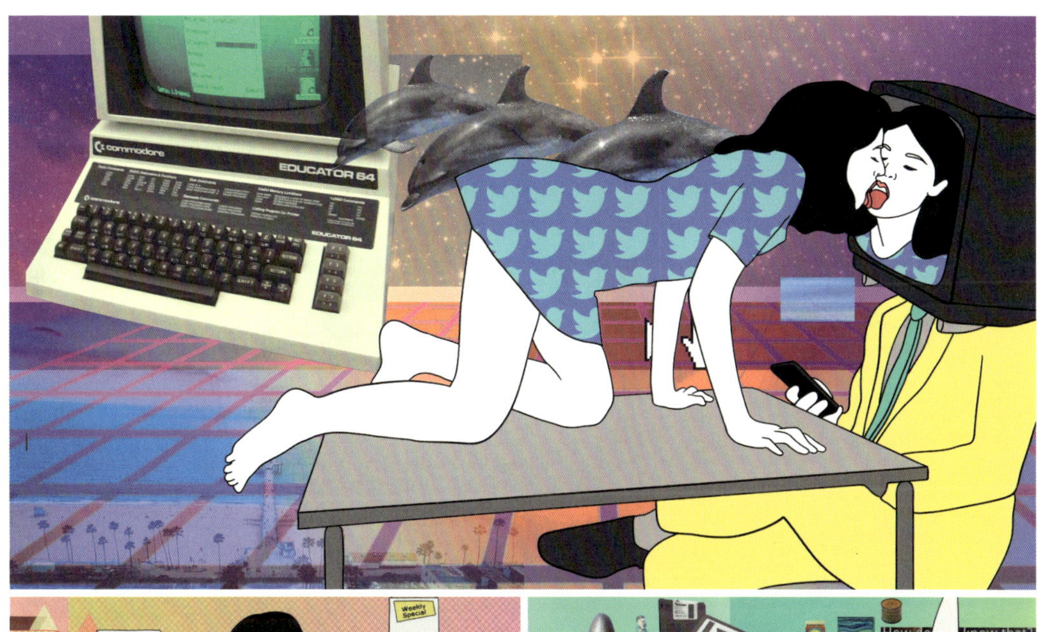

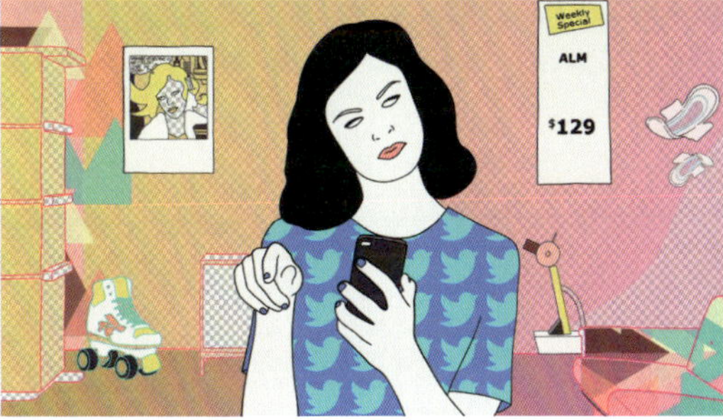

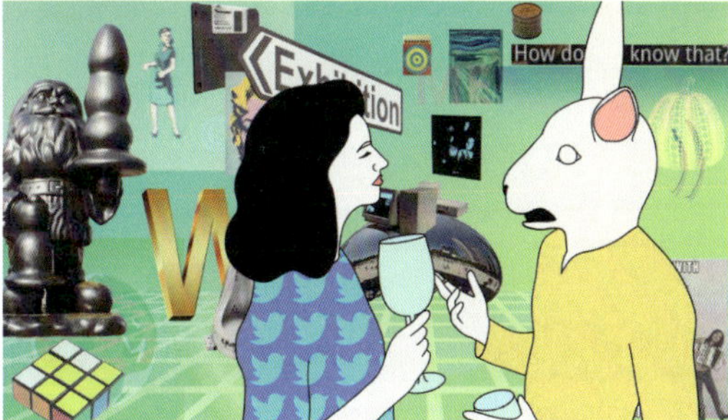

Instagram" and so forth. Just like in *#21xoxo,* the visual content and information that we receive on these platforms are brief glimpses between narration and abstraction.

Director: Sine Özbilge
Co-director: Imge Özbilge
Music: Remco Weyns
With support from: VAF – Flanders Audiovisual Fund, Creative Europe Media, Lunanime

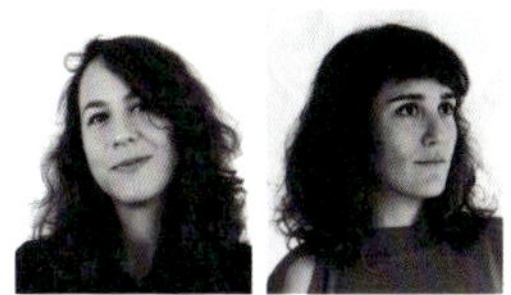

Sine Özbilge & Imge Özbilge (TR). The sister directors duo Sine Özbilge and Imge Özbilge work together as each other's mirrors. They experiment with the medium of animation, the 16:9 screen, digital installation art, and the use of mixed media, exploring new connotations and stylistic forms. When writing concepts, Sine focuses on psychological matters and the subconscious, while Imge reflects on the surreality of society. The director duo collaborated on the award-winning short film *Camouflage* (world premiere at Cannes Film Festival 2017) and *#21xoxo* (world premiere at BFI Film Festival 2019) and are currently working on their latest short *Mosaic.*

https://vimeo.com/373572414

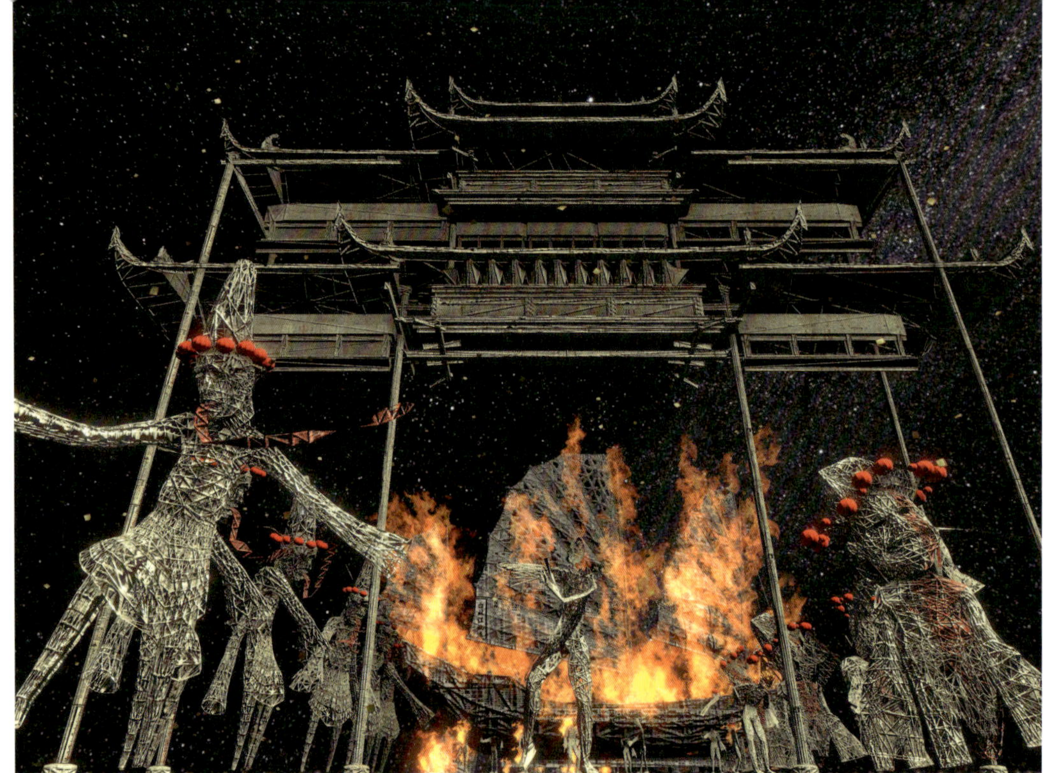

Bodyless

Hsin-Chien Huang

Bodyless is a surreal VR experience based on the director's childhood memories during the martial law period in Taiwan in the 1970s. In that era, human qualities were simplified and quantified with only few characteristics recognized and measured by the ruling class. This era has long passed, but the rise of digital technologies is following the same tendency. Governments started to use new technologies like digital surveillance, big data, and artificial intelligence as a means to monitor and control people. A powerful world leader uses tweets with fewer than 140 characters to define the direction of his country. Human beings are reduced to a few pixels on the screen and it is left to the military drone pilot to decide whether to kill them or not.

In *Bodyless,* the retrospective martial law and the ultramodern digital technologies are fused in a dark oppression that conflicts with retrospective life and beliefs. The audience experiences this VR journey through the eyes of an old man who was a political criminal under a secret government experiment. After his death, he becomes a ghost and descends into the underground world.

In Taiwanese folk belief, the gates of hell open and ghosts can return to the world of the living to visit their families during "Ghost Month"—the seventh month of the lunar calendar. The old man's ghost makes up his face and ascends to the surface world. Through his eyes, the folk culture forms a rich spiritual world interwoven with nature. However, a mechanical force starts to deteriorate the spiritual world and eventually reduces human forms and memory into simple geometrical shapes that can be easily processed by technologies.

Director: Hsin-Chien Huang
Producer: Saiau-Yue Tsau
Music: Giong Lim
Program: Hsin-Chien Huang, Wei-Chieh Chiu, Chun-Yen Yu
Project manager: Chung-Hsien Chen
Special thanks: Bureau of Audiovisual and Music Industry Development, MOC

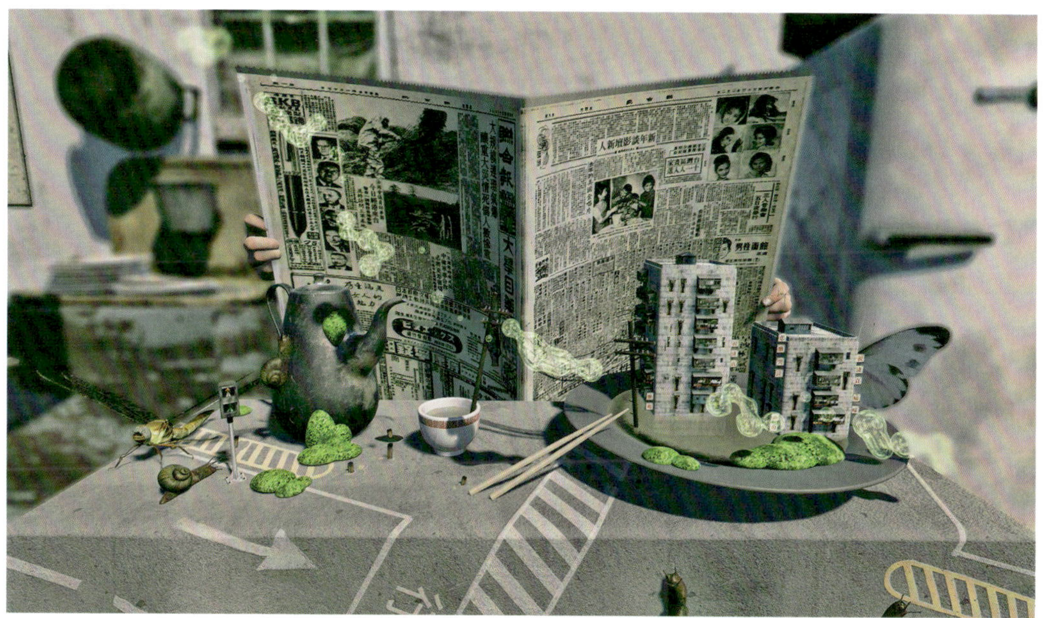

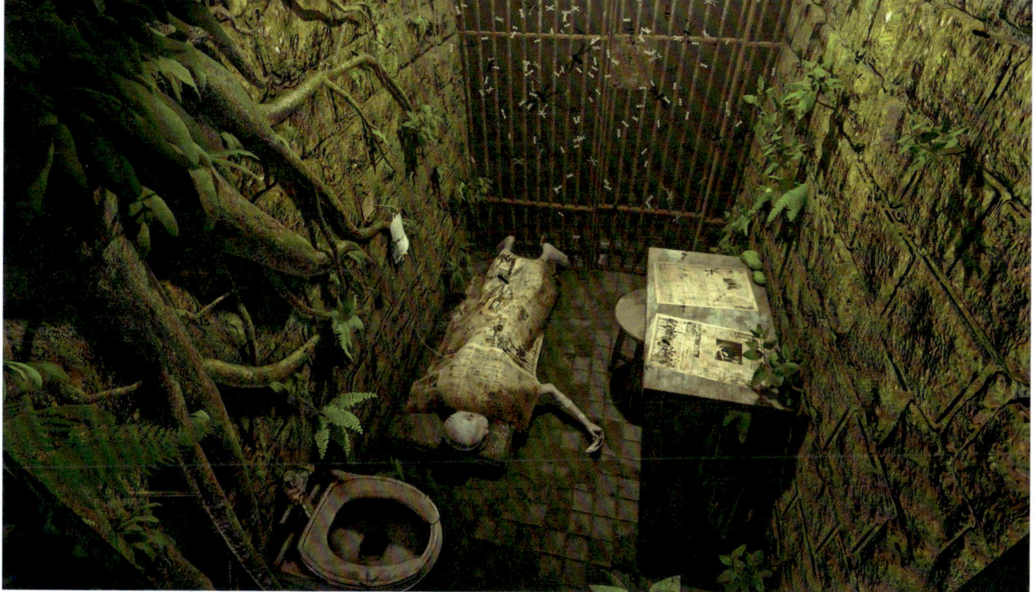

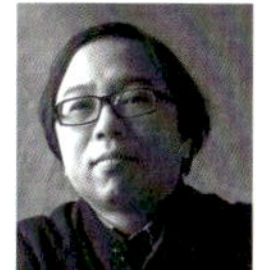

Hsin-Chien Huang (TW) is an artist who specializes in mixed media. Science, technology, new media, programming, and algorithms are tools he uses to bring the universe of his imagination to life. He collaborated with Laurie Anderson, and their VR work *La Camera Insabbiata* won the Best VR Experience Award at the 74th Venice Film Festival. His latest work *Bodyless* also won the Special Mention at the 2019 Kaohsiung Film Festival. He is especially enthusiastic about virtual reality because it opens up a world of possibilities, free of any constraints.

https://www.storynest.com/2_cv.php?lang=en · https://www.youtube.com/watch?v=_SCaBCQslw0&t=1s

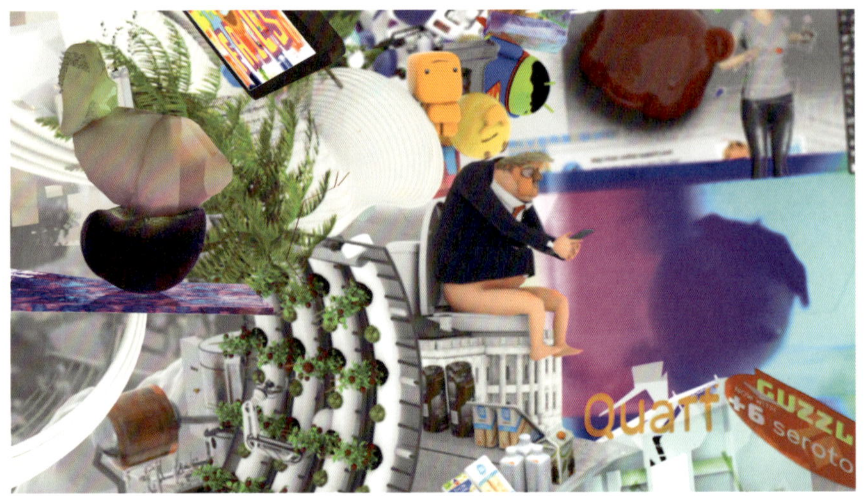
FRIES
Quaff
+6 GUZZL
seroto

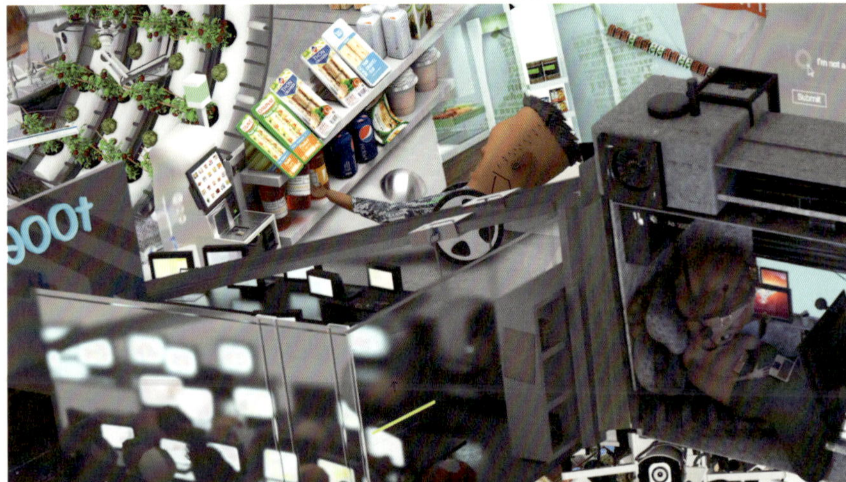
oot
I'm not a
Submit

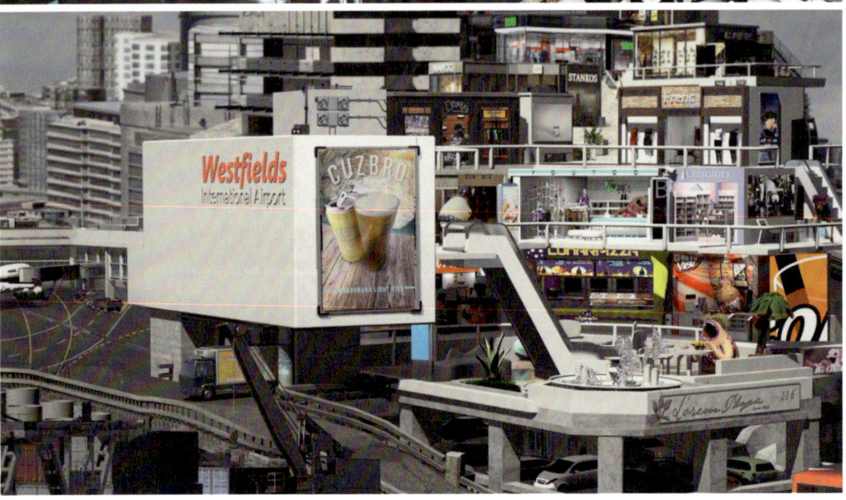
STANKOS
Westfields
International Airport
CUZBRO
Lorem Ipsa

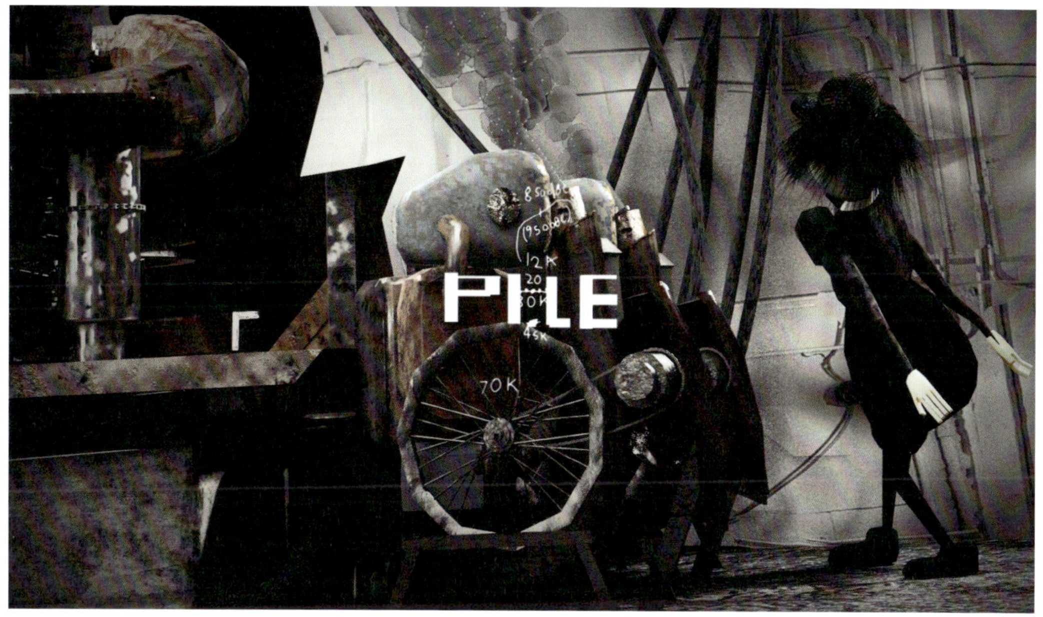

Pile

Toby Auberg

Water then food. Agriculture then industry. Old then new. Critical then extra. Simple to complex. Concrete to abstract. Dirt to clouds. Real to unreal. Artist statement: *Pile* is a CG animated film that attempts to visually map an intuitive worldview, underpinned by an elusive composite of orders, such as the hierarchy of needs, history, economic stratification, and the global supply chain. This compounded worldview is visualized as a vertical settlement made of rooms or modules that each represent a facet of human activity and the infra-structure that modern life depends on. The trajectory of material progression and detachment from reality within the film world reinforce a series of contrasts that often overlap in our real world, such as between old and new, critical and superfluous, simple and complex, concrete and abstract, real and unreal.

Animation: Toby Auberg
Sound engineer: Ben Goodall
Sound editor: Ben Goodall
Mix: Ben Goodall
Soundtrack: Ben Goodall

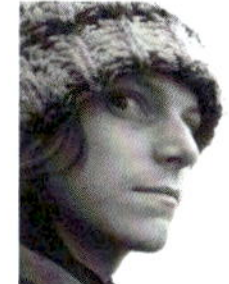
Toby Auberg (SE) is a London based 3D visual artist and animator, who is really into sensory overload, abstract characters, and virtual worlds, and sometimes dabbles in political themes. He started out working in film in Los Angeles, moved to Sweden to study Motion Graphics at Hyper Island, and studied Experimental Animation at the Royal College of Art in London. He worked at the award-winning creative studio DBLG before going freelance in 2015 and is a founding member of the not-for-profit shared workspace Fudio Collective. Animated shorts filmography: *Seratox* (2016), *Causims* (2018), *Pile* (2019).

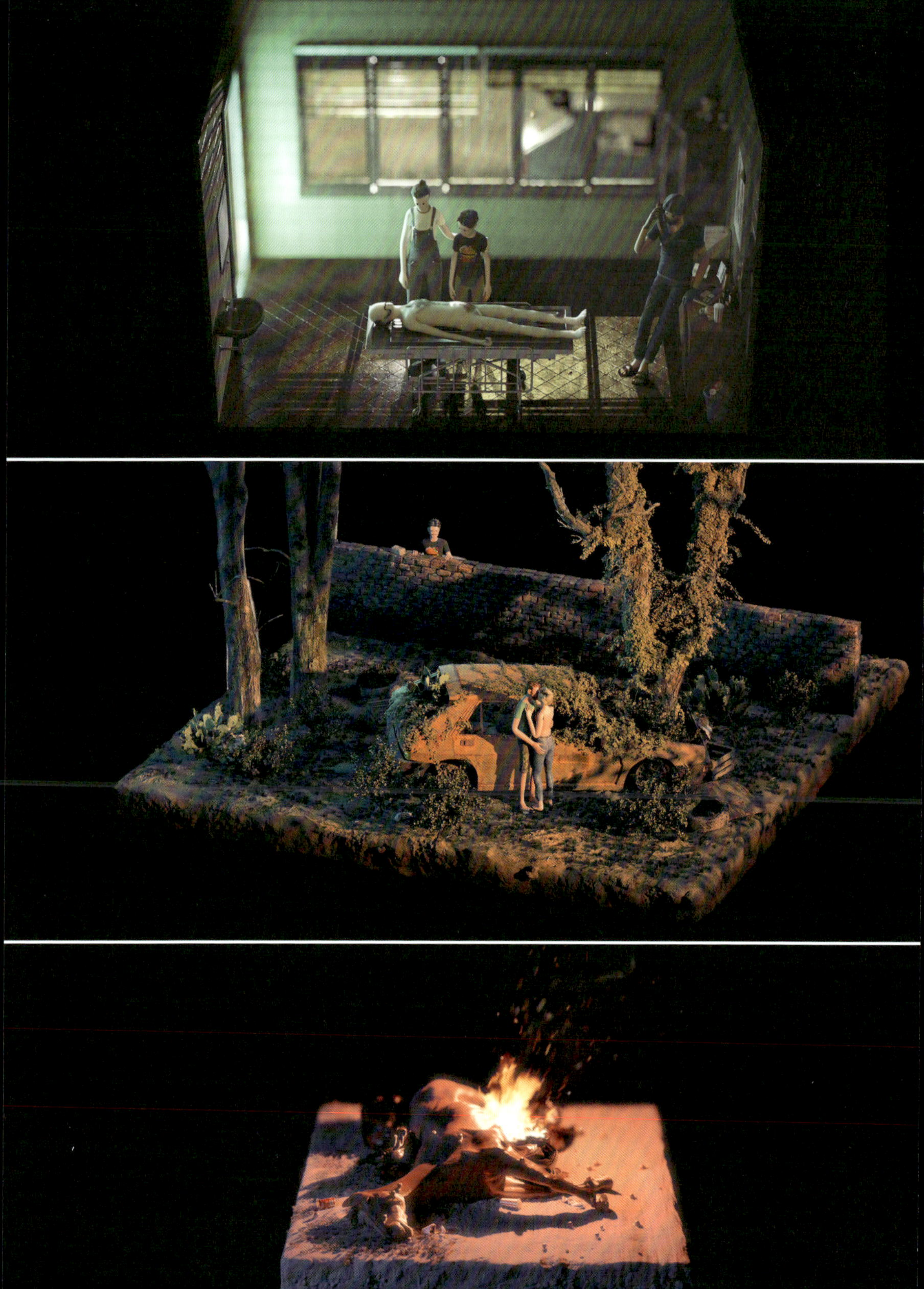

Pulsión

Pedro Casavecchia

Dark feelings harvested during the childhood of a kid erupt in violence after his mother dies. *Pulsión* (Drive) explores themes of abuse and dysfunctional family environments.

Pulsión is a full cg independent animation made with 0 budget! A passion project that took four years to complete.

The environments of the film play a major role in the story. They are used to bring context to the lives of the characters and also to depict how they feel trapped in their realities. In addition to that, narrowing down the space on the screen was key to being able to add as many details as the limited resources of the production allowed.

In order to create some of the models, a technique called Photoscan was used. It consists of taking lots of pictures of a real object, and then translating this to the computer. By doing that it becomes easier to produce highly realistic models. This was mostly used to create the outdoor scenarios.

Taking advantage of the static nature of the camera, some extra details were painted on top of the final images using Photoshop and After Effects in a process called Digital Matte Painting.

Writer, director: Pedro Casavecchia
Executive producers: Nico Casavecchia, Arnaud Colinart, Corentin Lambot
Co-executive producers: Antonie Cayrol, Pierre Zandrowicz, Fred Volhuer
Artists: Pedro Casavecchia, Marc Tingle, Charlotte Tyson, Peter Mitchel Paterson, Djordje Ilic, Ivan Sorgente, Zach du Toit
Music: Anna-Maria Rammou

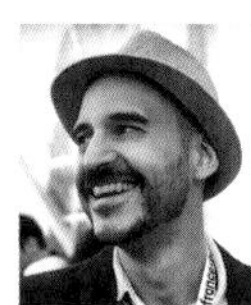

Pedro Casavecchia (AR) is a CGI artist and director based in London. He has worked in the Lighting and Environments departments for films like *Thor: Ragnarok* (2017), *Avengers, Infinity War* (2018), *Kingsman: The Golden Circle* (2017), *Fantastic Beasts And Where To Find Them* (2016), *Mary Poppins Returns* (2018), *Avengers Endgame* (2019) and more! *Pulsión* (2019) is his directorial debut. He wrote, directed, and completed most of the production by himself.

https://vimeo.com/326223038 · https://vimeo.com/339872122

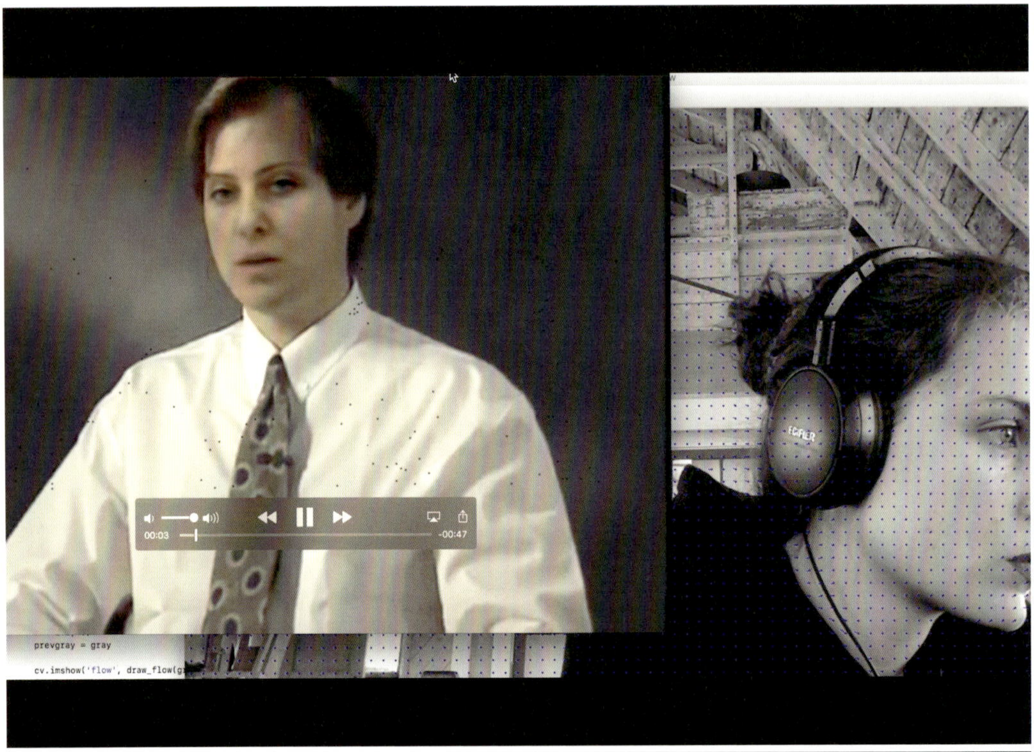

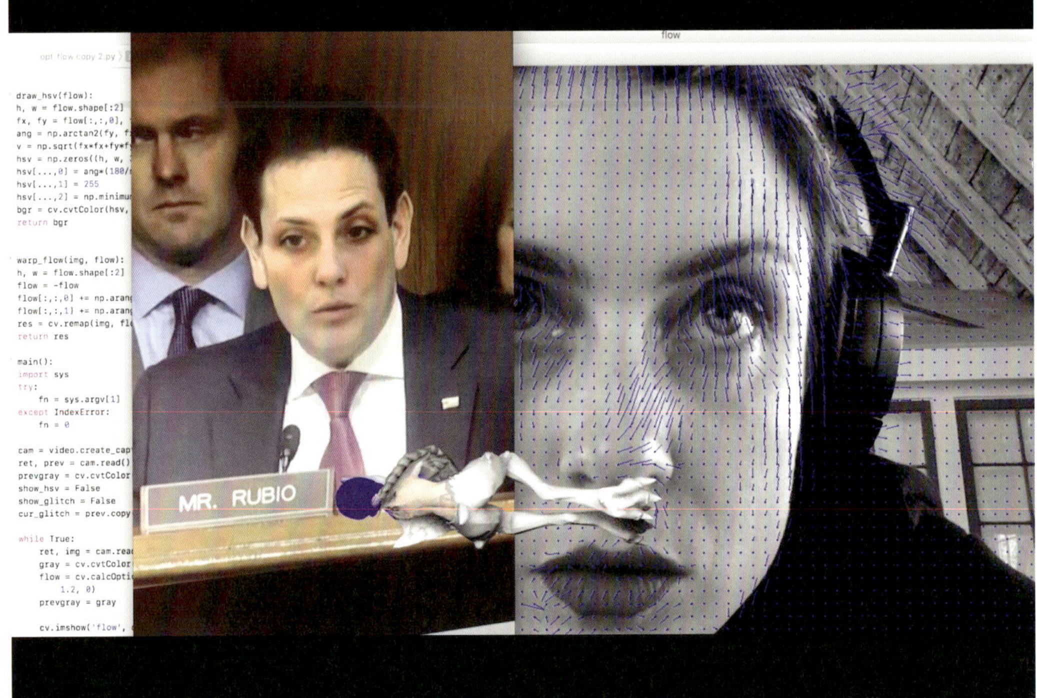

COMPUTER ANIMATION · Honorary Mention

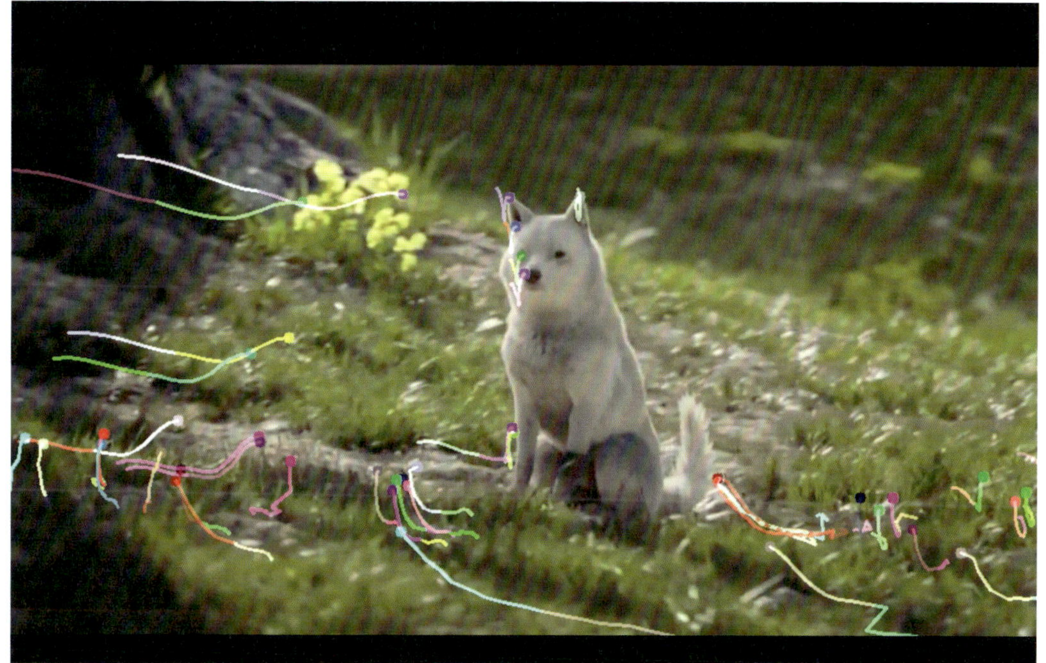

Recursive Truth

Rachel Rossin

Recursive Truth is a video work based on generative AI and programming imaging research; using video game mods, OpenCV (facial recognition and motion tracking libraries), and deep fakes to explore loss, memory, and truth as a medium. Bugs created inside the work expose the fragility of memory and ultimately either destroy the video game or function only as visual gags.

Recursive Truth is a looping video that runs at 2:55, however, the piece is meant to play on loop—every cycle tends to reveal new connections between the collaged material. The work addresses the increasing subjectivity of truth and the codebases that are shaping this new reality. The primary codebase featured is OpenCV—the most commonly used language in the infrastructure of surveillance capitalism. Visualizations of AI in the form of Deepfakes with Optical Flow represent these infrastructures on a recursive loop. Recursion is a principle in the codebase that is short-hand for meta or self-referential—which is the structure of the piece: by representing the very code bases that the work is addressing, the work is a structured recursive loop where new connections are made in viewing the piece.

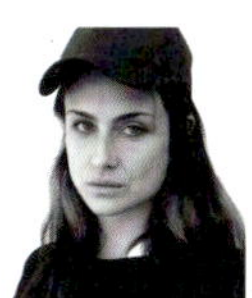

Rachel Rossin (US) is a painter and programmer whose work explores entropy, embodiment, the ubiquity of technology and its effect on our psychology. Over the last four years, she has gained recognition for a series of astonishing exhibitions that blend oil painting, sculpture, and virtual reality. Rossin has shown her work at Sundance New Frontiers, The Zabludowicz Collection in London, The New Museum in New York City, K11 in Shanghai, Kiasma in Helsinki, The Frist Center for the Visual Arts in Nashville and The Akron Art Museum. Rossin was a 2015 fellow at the New Museum's incubator in virtual reality research, and was on the Forbes 30 under 30 2017 for visual art.

rossin.co · https://vimeo.com/342070900

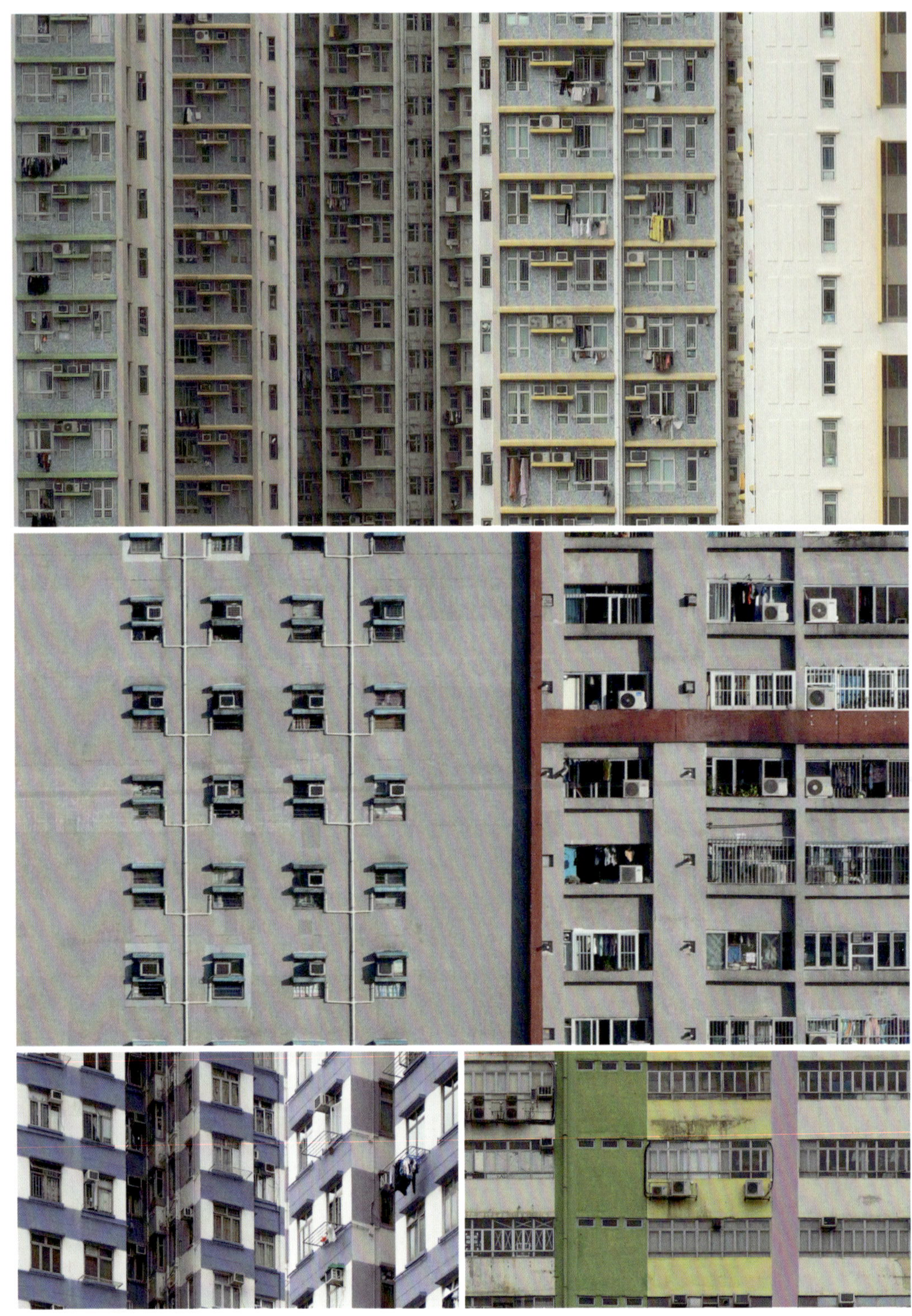

COMPUTER ANIMATION · Honorary Mention

Serial Parallels

Max Hattler

Hong Kong is defined in no small part by its dense and architecturally extreme high-rise housing estates. This has been much-documented through still-image photography—an ideal medium to convey a sense of scale of the repetitive patterns of buildings. Photographic documentation presents a fixed reality of the built environment, which has become a stereotype of Hong Kong, ready to be consumed by tourists and instagrammers. To create a novel engagement with Hong Kong's cityscape, this experimental animation approaches the built environment of Hong Kong from the conceptual perspective of celluloid film, by applying the technique of film animation to the photographic image. The city's signature architecture of horizon-eclipsing housing estates is reimagined as parallel rows of film strips: Serial Parallels. High-resolution digital photographs of entire building facades are re-animated through vertical/ serial and horizontal/parallel movements, with each floor or window corresponding to a film frame. As a consequence of this process of alienation through abstraction, new visual and temporal relationships are forged, and new movement is created, through which an entirely different perspective on the city emerges. What was fixed becomes fluid, through the spatiotemporal sequencing of repetitive patterns. What was literally set in stone in the single image becomes a re-animated film sequence of architectural flow.

Director: Max Hattler
Animation: Zhang Riwen, Iresa Cho
Photography: Iresa Cho, Zhang Riwen, Max Hattler
Sound: David Kamp
Additional sound: Sky Kung
Sound research: James Banbury
Production: Relentless Melt
Supported by grants from the Hong Kong Arts Development Council and the Research Grants Council of Hong Kong (Project No. 21609017)

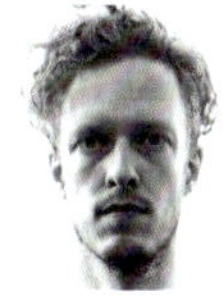
Max Hattler (DE) is an artist and academic who works with abstract animation, video installation, and audiovisual performance. He holds a master's degree from the Royal College of Art and a Doctorate in Fine Art from the University of East London. His work has been shown at festivals and institutions such as Resonate, Ars Electronica, ZKM Center for Art and Media, MOCA Taipei, and Beijing Minsheng Museum. Awards include Supernova, Cannes Lions, Bradford Animation Festival, and several Visual Music Awards. Max has performed live around the world including at Playgrounds Festival, Re-New Copenhagen, Expo Milan, Seoul Museum of Art, and the European Media Art Festival. He lives in Hong Kong where he is an Assistant Professor at School of Creative Media, City University of Hong Kong.

www.maxhattler.com/serialparallels · www.vimeo.com/maxhattler/serialtrailer

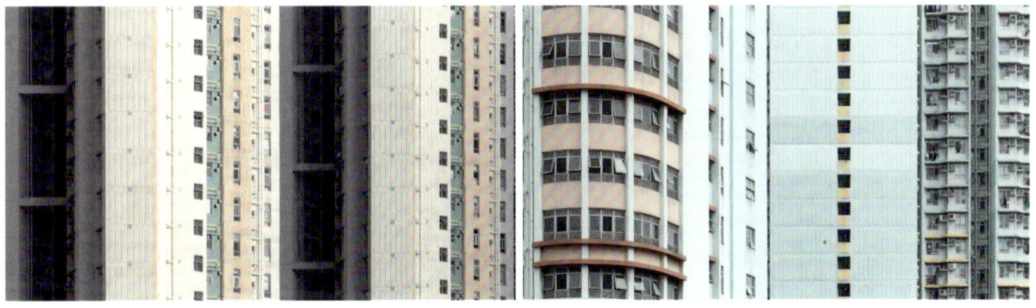

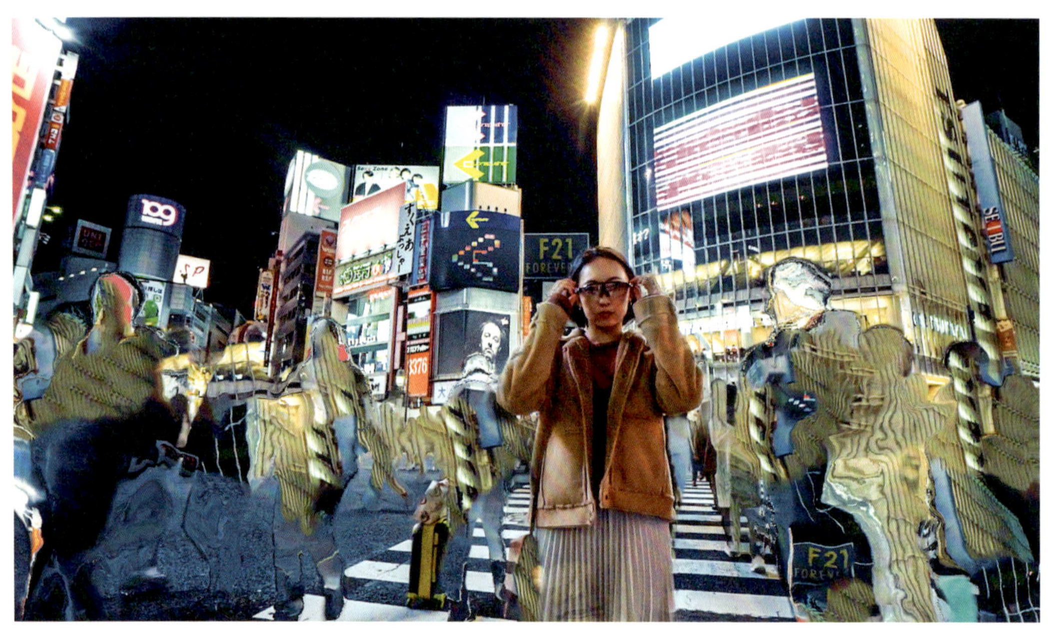

Squarepusher / Terminal Slam

Daito Manabe, Kenichiro Shimizu

Terminal Slam is a subversive music video where all the ads around the city are deleted or replaced with the ones related to the artist Squarepusher. The inspiration came from Daito Manabe's thought that the scenery in the city will become rewritable with AR/MR glasses in the near future, as seen in the video.

The three main techniques used to create the video utilizing machine learning technologies are:
- Object Detection (to recognize the position of objects in the image)
- Semantic Segmentation (to classify the segment of the image into categories based on the meaning of each pixel by labeling every pixel)
- Image Inpaint (image restoration technique)

Also, masks are generated from those data to add optical camouflage effects in post-processing such as glitch effects only on the areas where humans are. Since such detection to extract only ads is not yet possible with current machine learning technologies, some operations had to be done by hand. But it is expected that these operations also can be automated in the near future.
We first started from organizing video and sequential image data and processed them prior to pro-duction using python and OpenCV, a library for computer graphics. Next we proceeded to object detection using YOLO and semantic segmentation using DeepLab and YOLACT to be added to offline editing of the video. This process was all done by TensorFlow and PyTorch. This provides the data of where the people or objects exist in each frame of video. However, billboards and advertisements are still difficult to detect automatically with machine learning approaches, so they are extracted manually. These extracted advertisements are adjusted visually so that their visual styles match with other footage processed with object detection and semantic segmentation. Python and OpenCV were adopted for this post-production. Based on object detection and semantic segmentation, mask data were generated and inpainting techniques were applied to those masks. Inpainting is a technique that allows you to "paint" only a specific area of a picture or video. This is done with Python and TensorFlow. These materials are exported with sound to be audio-reactive using openFrameworks (C++) and veneer. Finally the source video, midi data, and footage added with glitch effect are combined for final rendering. This is done with openFrameworks and FFmpeg.

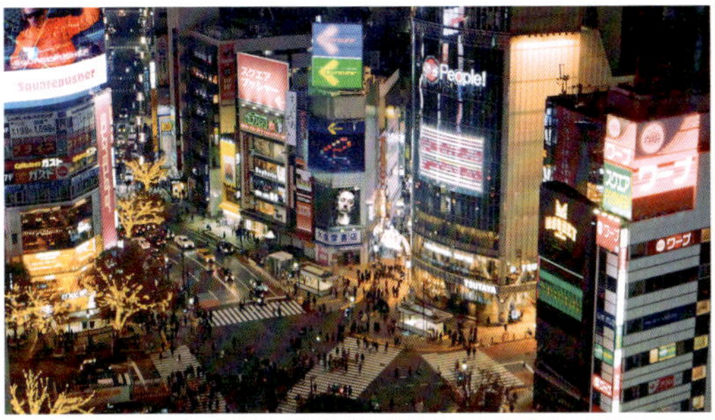

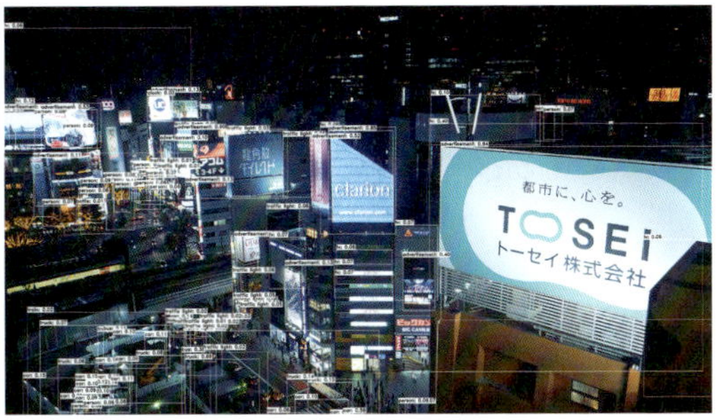

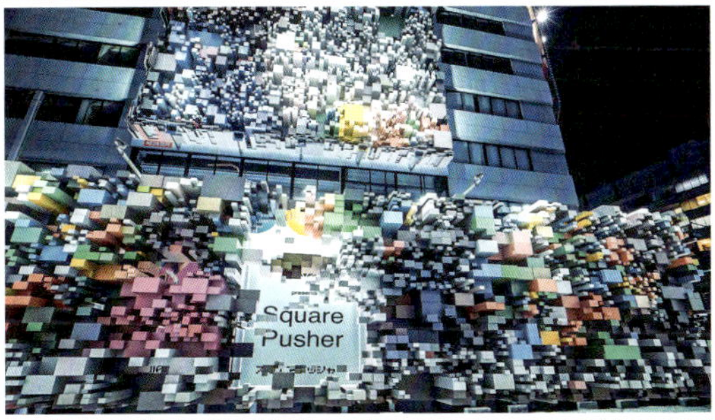

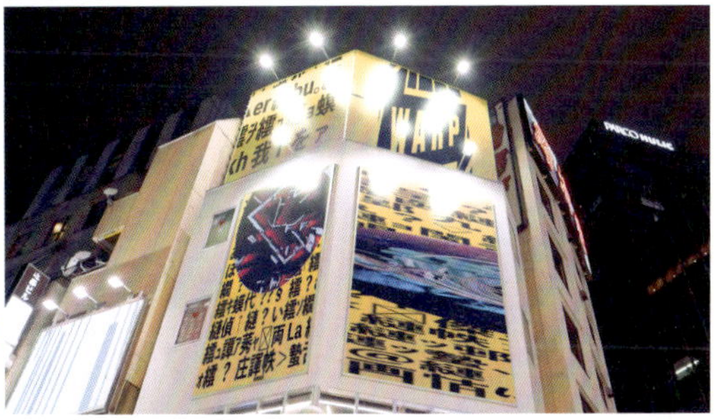

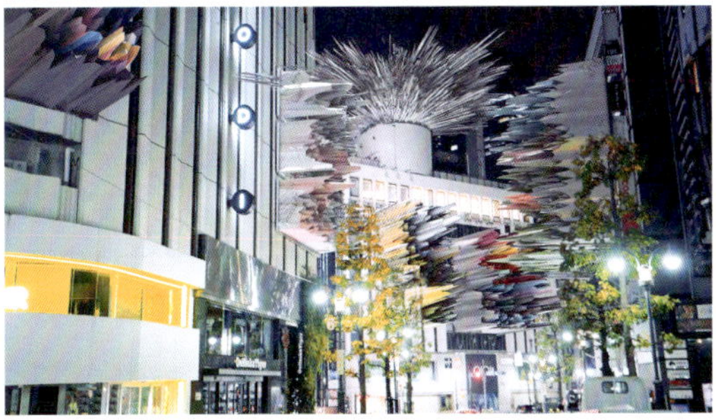

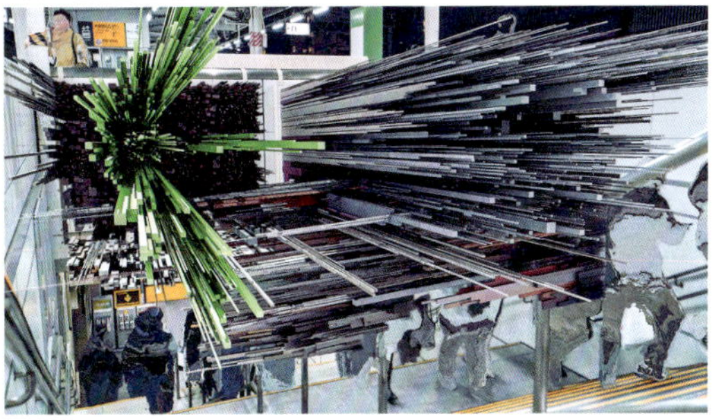

Director, glitch effects and interaction designer: Daito Manabe (Rhizomatiks)
Film and editing director: Kenichiro Shimizu (PELE)
Machine learning engineer: Yuta Asai (Rhizomatiks)
Video export tool developer: 2bit
Effects artist: Aya Takamatsu (Rhizomatiks)
Ad graphic designer: Kaori Fujii (Rhizomatiks)
CG director: Junichi Ebe (Freelance)
Effects Supervisors: Kenta Katsuno (+Ring), Takeshi Ozaki (+Ring)
Effects artists: Mikita Arai (Freelance), Masaki Takahashi (Freelance)

Digital artists: Yuki Hirakawa (+Ring), Yu Onishi (+Ring), Kenta Hasegawa (+Ring), Ayaka Yamaguchi (+Ring), Takeya Kamimura (+Ring), Ryuichi Ono (Freelance)
CG producer: Toshihiko Sakata (+Ring)
VFX artist: Yoshinobu Okino (Nomad)
Colorist: Felipe Szulc (Nomad)
Cinematographer: Kazuki Takano (TRIVAL)
Cinematographer / Operator: Takuya Higa (Cyanworksandfilms)
MIDI data designer: Kyoko Koyama
Cast: SARA (ELEVENPLAY)
Film producer: Chikako Nagai (PELE)
Producer: Takao Inoue (Rhizomatiks)

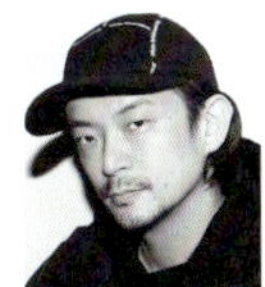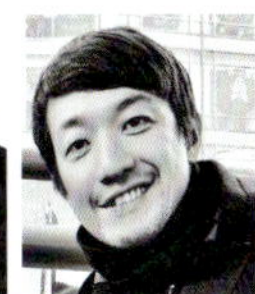

Daito Manabe (JP) is a Tokyo-based artist, interaction designer, programmer, and DJ. He launched Rhizomatiks in 2006. Co-director of Rhizomatiks Research since 2015 and professor at Keio University SFC. Manabe's work in design, art, and entertainment takes a new approach to everyday materials and phenomenon. His practice explores the potentialities inherent to the human body, data, programming, computers, and other phenomena, thus probing the interrelationships and boundaries delineating analog and digital, real and virtual. **Kenichiro Shimizu** (JP) is a video director and a VFX artist who uses CG, VFX, AR, and VR effectively for high quality visual effects, e.g. in adverts and film. Awards include the ACC Grand Prix / Minister of Internal Affairs and Communications Award and the Journalist Award. In 2018, he launched his own company Pele Co., Ltd., working with video installation for events or live shows and vision production.

https://research.rhizomatiks.com/s/works/squarepusher/

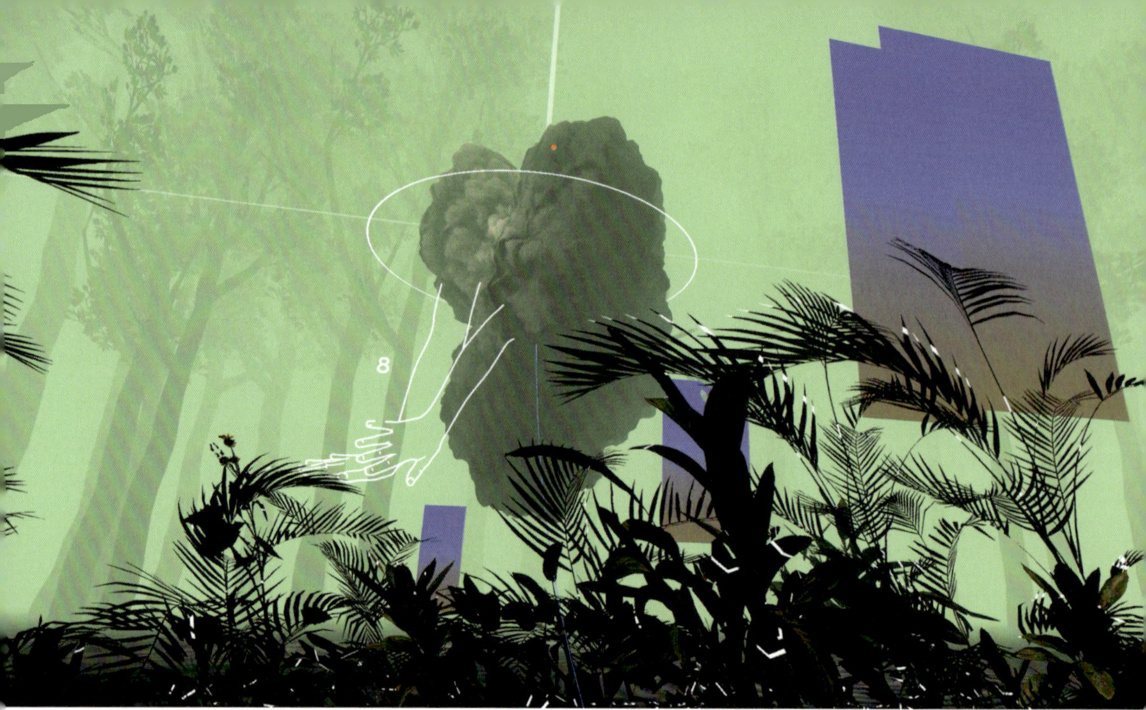

The Entropy Gardens
DEPART

The Entropy Gardens is a unique artistic VR experience that explores the question: What could be the "nature" of a post-digital reality and how can we construct a garden from it?
Drawing on and investigating humanity's maybe most archetypical art (garden-making), the project challenges its myths, aesthetics, and modes of perception by combining poetry and generative coding to construct a spellbinding and surreal utopian place. In the form of an open-ended simulation it constructs a hermetic, virtual garden as a poetic ecosystem—a psychic landscape that is foremost a complex audiovisual experience. It admits the visitors into a place that is equally challenging and contemplative (and at times a little weird).

Formally *The Entropy Gardens* consists of an audiovisual 3D environment that combines "realistic" natural elements with abstract, computational forms. It is populated by data-organisms that resemble plants, animals, or organic matter and evolve through interactions with their environment. It sacrifices faithful realism in order to embrace the digital condition with its glitches, malleability, and potential uncanniness. The whole environment is in a constant flux, ceaselessly negotiating its rules and generating narrative structures. There is also a strong poetic element in the form of haiku-style poems and other poetry, which are integrated both via voice and graphic elements. When a visitor enters the garden (puts on the VR-Headset), the garden starts to react to her/him and as such presents a frame for potential dramaturgy.

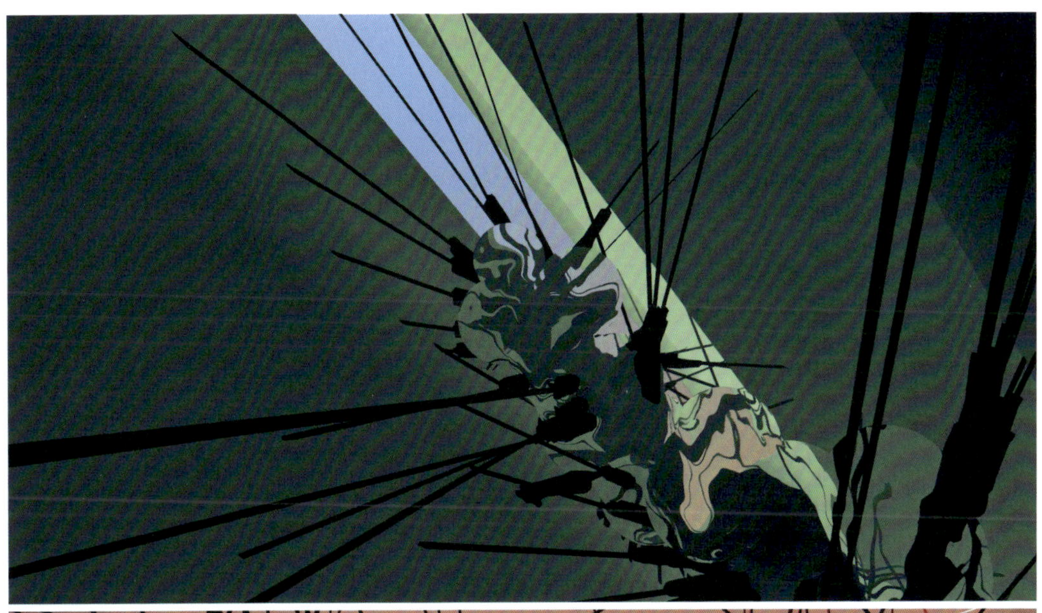

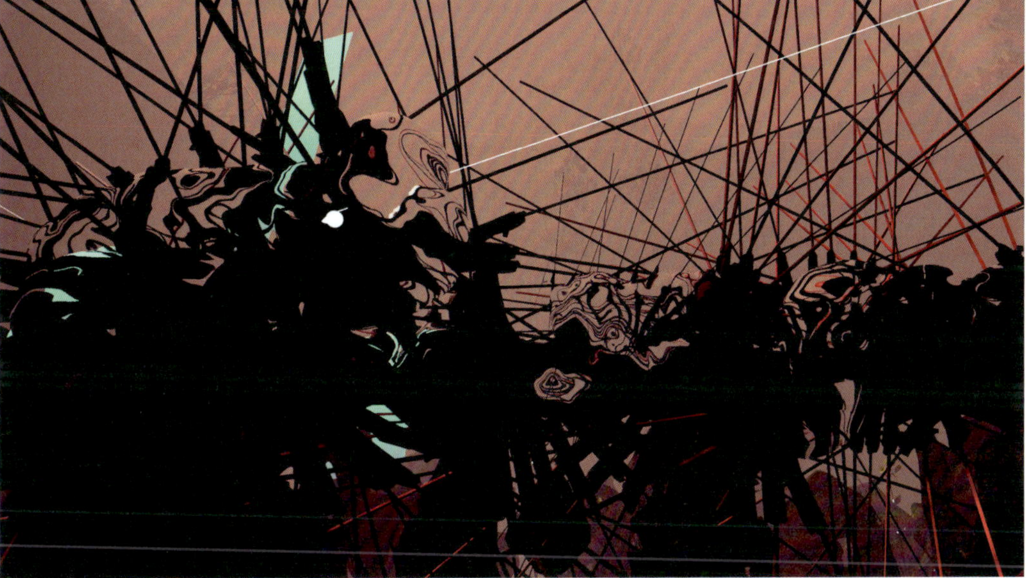

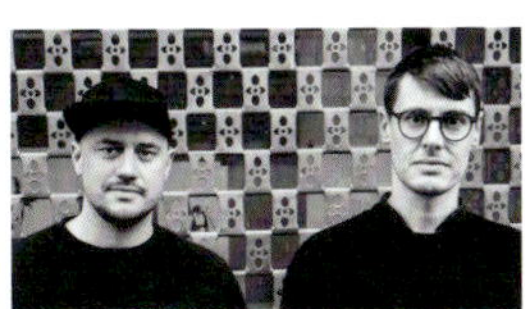

DEPART (AT) is an artist duo, consisting of Leonhard Lass and Gregor Ladenhauf. Their core endeavor is the construction of audiovisual immersions. Deeply rooted in the digital domain they explore the ritualistic character of algorithms and venture deliberately into the uncanny—creating unique moments using kinetic syntactics and synthetic aesthetics. DEPART work in a poetic tradition: They strive to subvert languages—not just literal, word-based languages but languages as symbolic systems in general (involving sounds, images, algorithms, gestures, objects, etc.). Through subtle manipulation of their specific grammars, intentional short-circuiting of their reference networks, and slight shifts of perspective, they aim to trigger internal landslides of consciousness. DEPART employ generative processes and real-time simulation as their modus operandi to construct hermetically "believable worlds" and transitory sandboxes of synchronicity, bordering on the surreal to evoke some sort of virtual immanence. They love surprises.

http://www.depart.at/portfolio/the-entropy-gardens

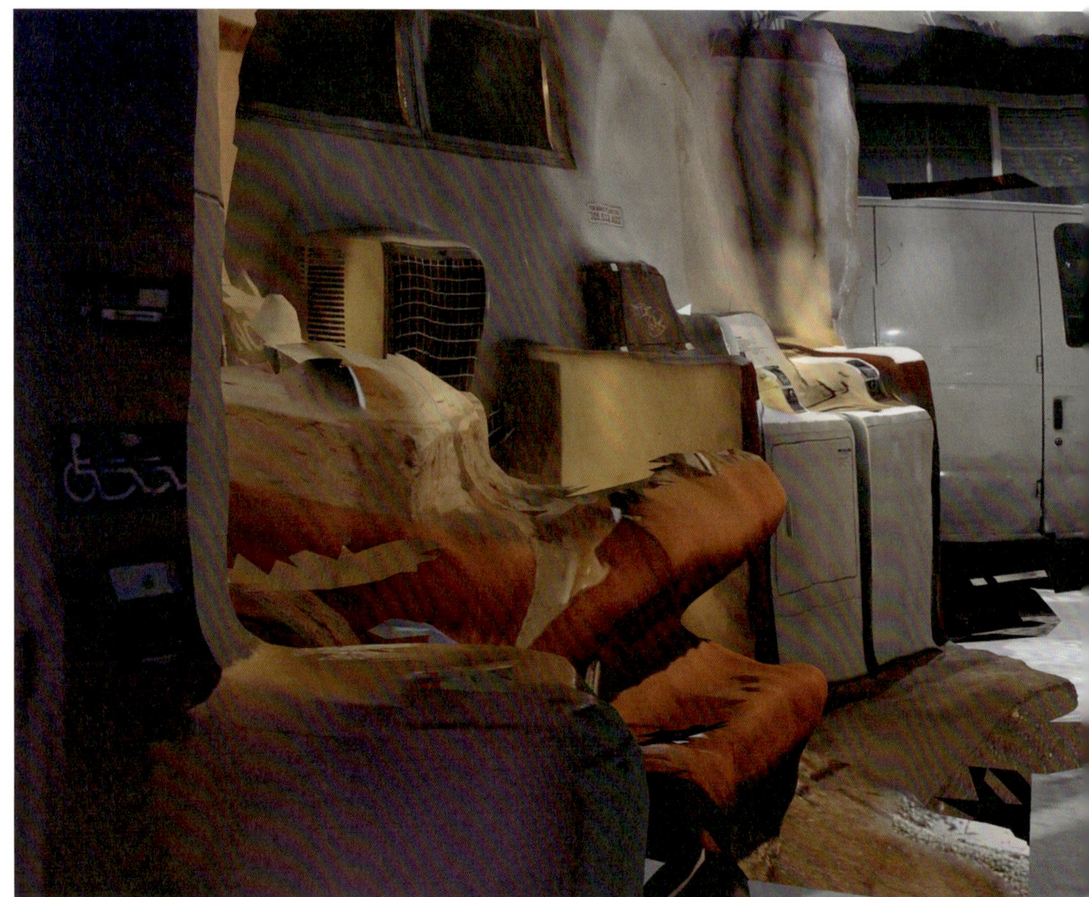

The Sky is on Fire

Emmanuel Van der Auwera

The Sky is on Fire is an example of Van der Auwera's research into how technological developments alter our way of seeing, understanding, and interacting with the world. Like many of his works, the point of departure is in the blur of taboo or tragedy as the location is set in the zones connecting documentary, reconstruction, and fictional genres to map the intersections of physical and digital space.

The Sky is on Fire begins with a monologue from a troubled man who comforts himself with the thought that nothing will ever be destroyed or lost, because everything is being backed up and technology will save us. It's a transhumanistic position. As the man's monologue moves between calamity and calm, the images traveling in the screens are also eschatological—uncanny technological reconstructions, molds with no substance, an applied sense of hollow and sleek aesthetics that seem almost real. The images were built by walking around areas of Miami and using an application called SCAN3D, which takes photos of objects and turns them into 3D renders.

This larger than life reconstruction speaks of contemporary life as it is, at once superficial and immersive, overexposed and overconnected, pervasive and discontinuous, an environment representative of the civilizational malaise of our current relationship to the world. The meticulous approach with which the artist compiles, stitches,

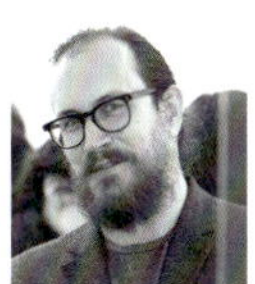

and composes a visual narrative from an infinity of images bound for virtual oblivion perhaps prefigures the approach that future archaeologists will use as they wrestle with the work of reconstitution from the remains of files floating in the sidereal digital space.

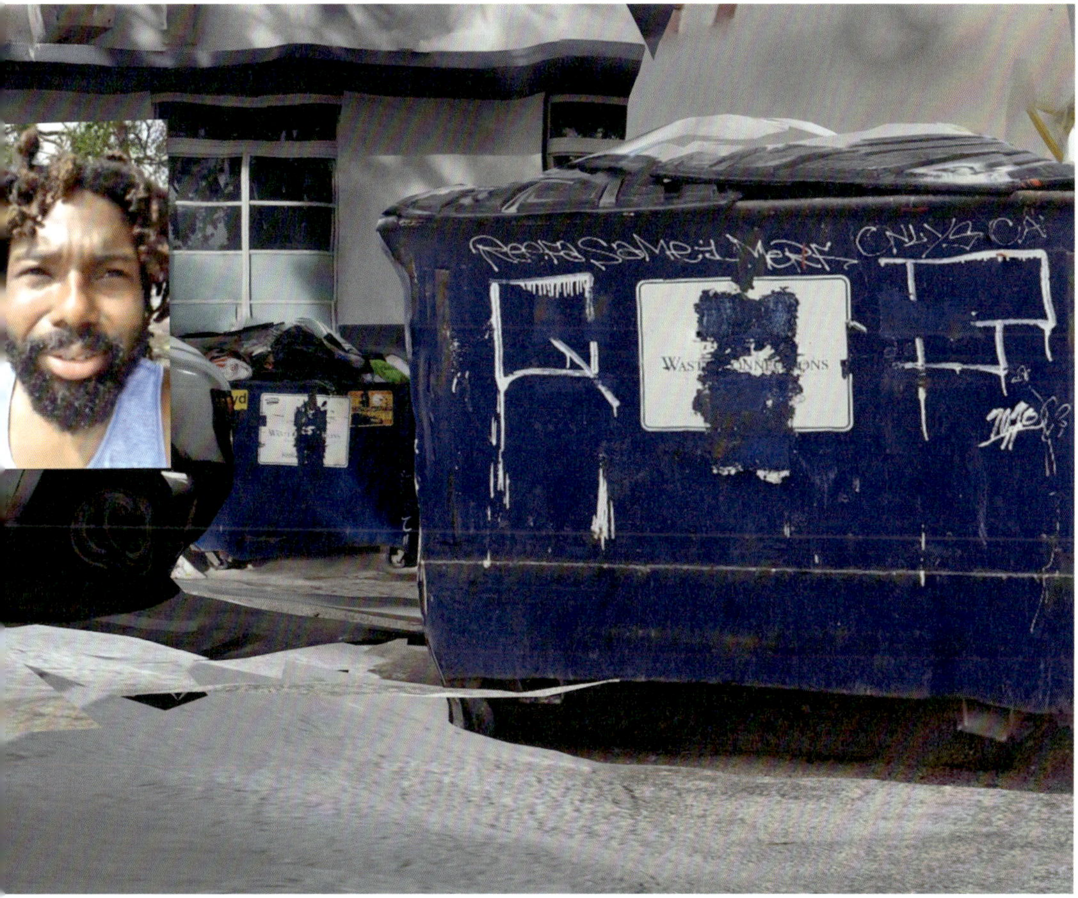

Text: Harlan Levey

Director: Emmanuel Van der Auwera
Assistant director: Thomas Depas
Sound editing and mixing: Pierre Dozin
Special Thanks to: Sophie Sherman, Gregory Thirion, Olivier Burlet
Produced by: Cigo, Harlan Levey Projects
With support from Botanique Museum, Brussels

Emmanuel Van der Auwera (BE) lives and works in Brussels. Through filmmaking, video sculpture, theater, printmaking, and other media, Van der Auwera sets up encounters with images that provoke a questioning of our visual literacy: How do images of contemporary mass media operate on various audiences and to what end? With the formal rigor of a logician, the artist dissects how images are engineered, mastering specialized industry techniques and intervening in their protocol. In so doing, Van der Auwera brings us no closer to a monolithic truth, but constructs new paradigms for reading images and understanding our relationships with them. Van der Auwera is a 2015 Laureate of the Higher Institute for Fine Arts (HISK) post-academic course in Ghent and has exhibited widely in Europe and the US. He is represented by Harlan Levey Projects.

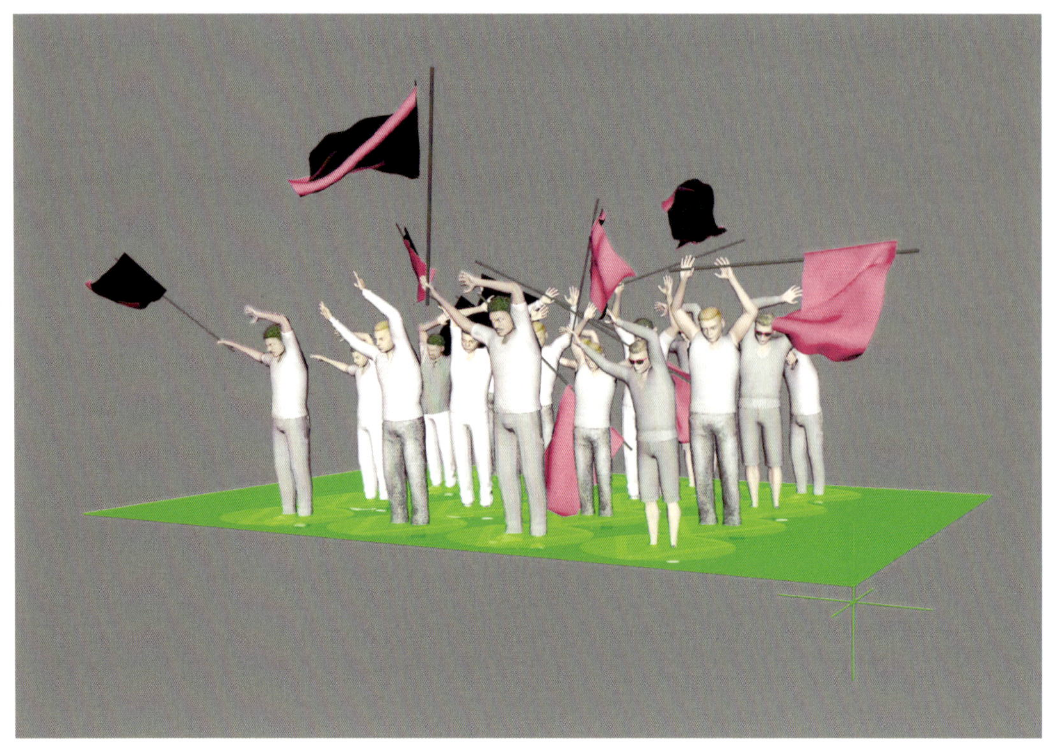

This Means More

Nicolas Gourault

A crowd simulation software serves as a tool for exploring football supporters' collective memory. *This Means More* juxtaposes testimonies of football supporters with the industrial tools used to represent virtual crowds. These tools are usually used to create images of crowds in advertisements, or to manage flows by anticipating the movement of bodies. As a counterpoint to these virtual images, supporters of Liverpool FC recount their experience marked by a tragic event—the 1989 Hillsborough stadium disaster, which changed the face of football.

Simulation technology becomes an archaeological tool in order to explore the traumatic memory of football fans. The confrontation of two forms of knowledge about the crowd, one distant and analytical, the other lived and embodied, raises the question of what constitutes a community and how this lively collective collides with the infrastructures that seek to control it.

Football has always had a mixed relationship with the crowd. Both a public space for profane culture and a control apparatus, the stadium embodies this conflicted relationship. At a time when working class supporters get banned due to financial and security pressures, I want to use a contemporary visual tool—crowd simulation—to explore the history of this exclusion. The stadium being a microcosm for society, its evolution relates to broader social changes that have happened over the last thirty years.

Production: Le Fresnoy, Studio national des arts contemporains
Testimonies: Peter Carney, Richie Greaves, Damian Kavanagh, Peter Hooton, Ian Lewis
Additional voice-over: Nicholas Masterton
CGI: Nicolas Gourault
Image: Alan Guichaoua, Nicolas Gourault
Editing: Félix Rehm
Sound editing: Arno Ledoux
Mixing: Simon Apostolou
Color grading: Baptiste Evrard

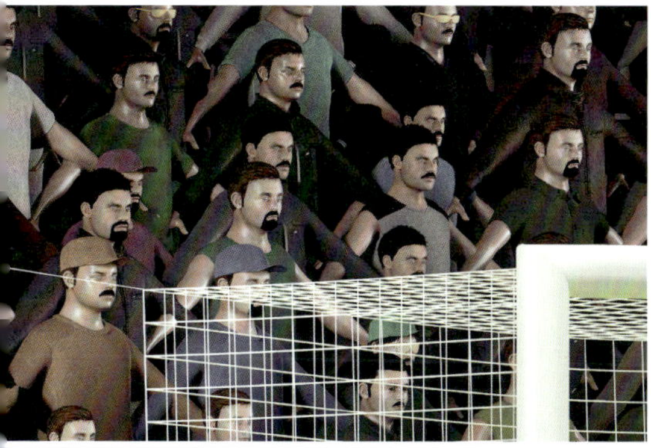

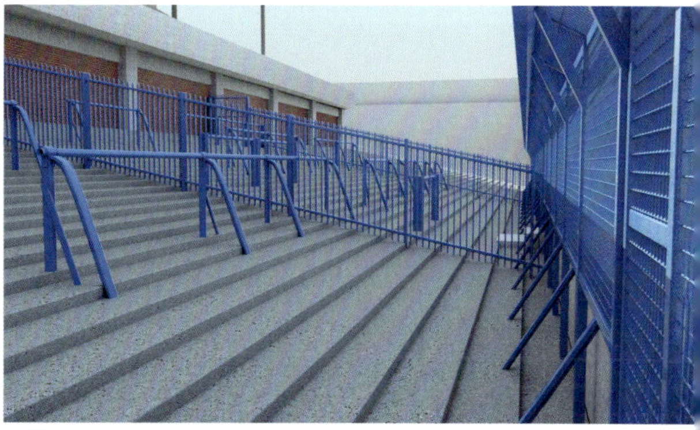

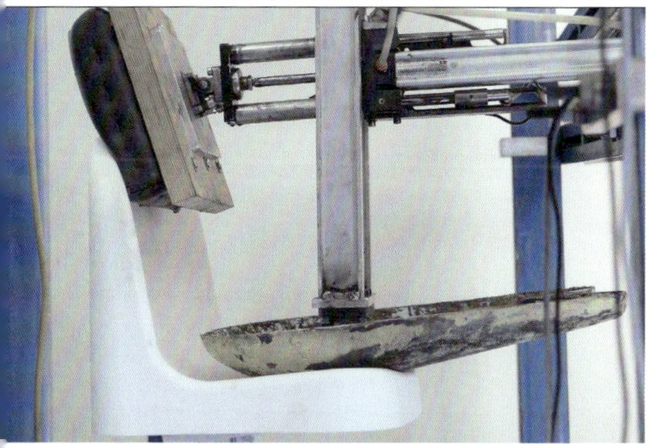

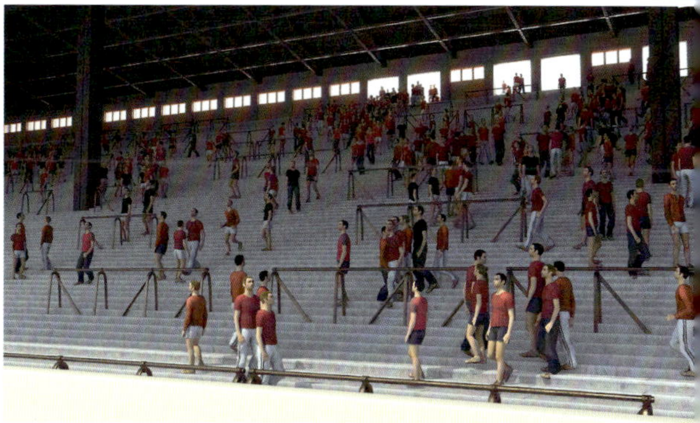

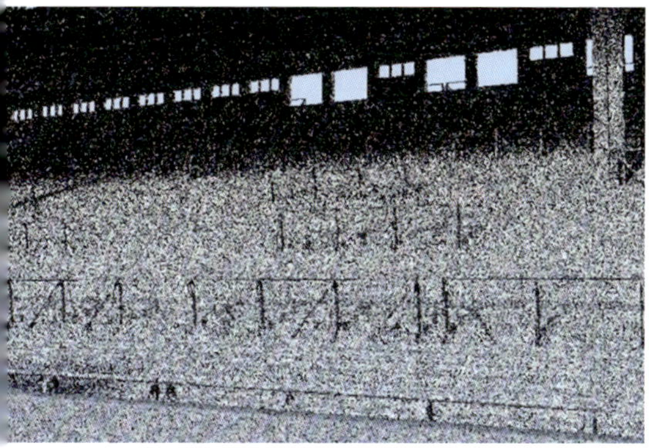

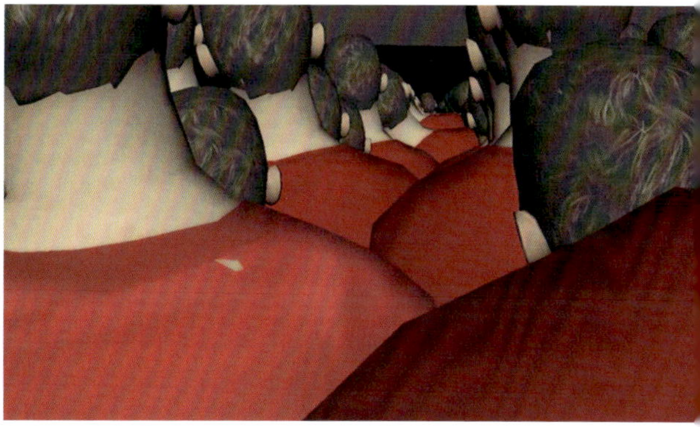

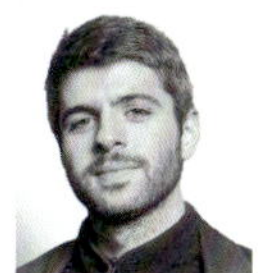

Nicolas Gourault (FR) is an artist and filmmaker, trained in contemporary art schools such as Le Fresnoy, Studio national des arts contemporains, but also in visual studies at École des hautes études en sciences sociales (EHESS). His work is imbued with these two fields of studies and aims at creating bridges between visual issues and political concern by means of a documentary critique of new media. He is particularly interested in how simulation technologies transform modes of representation and control spaces in order to prevent unwanted events.

https://vimeo.com/369854788

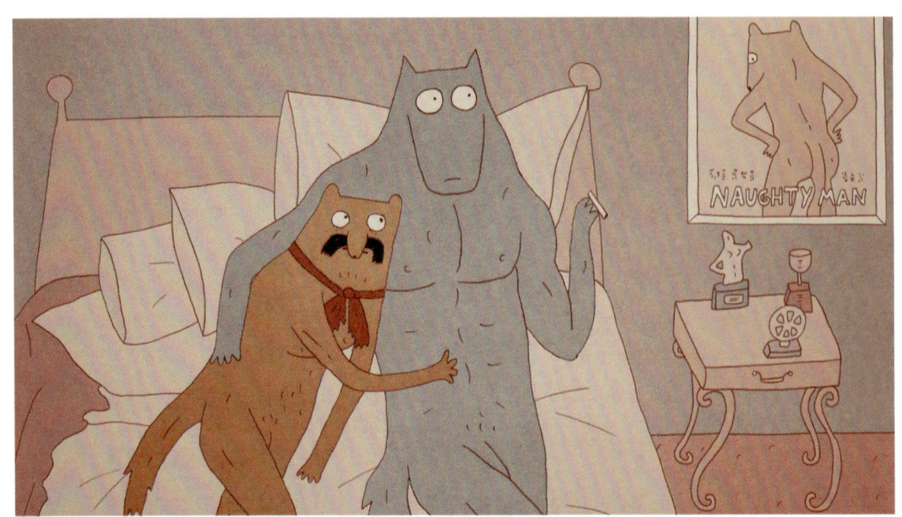

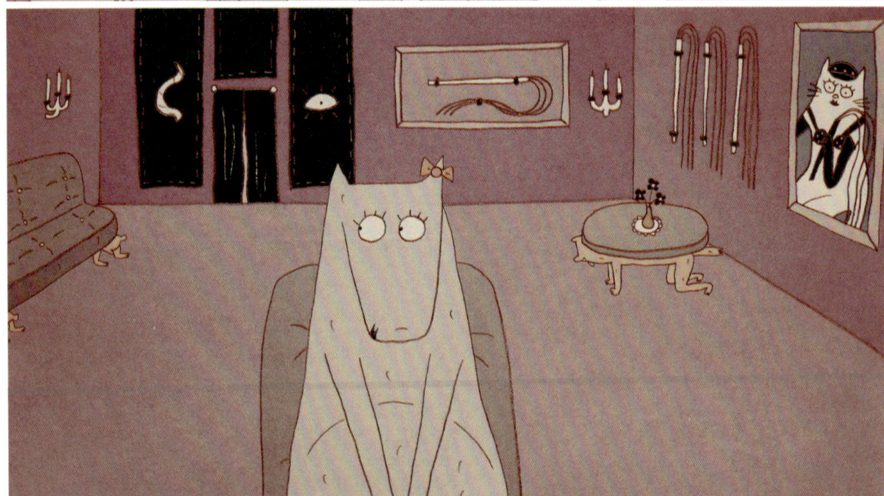

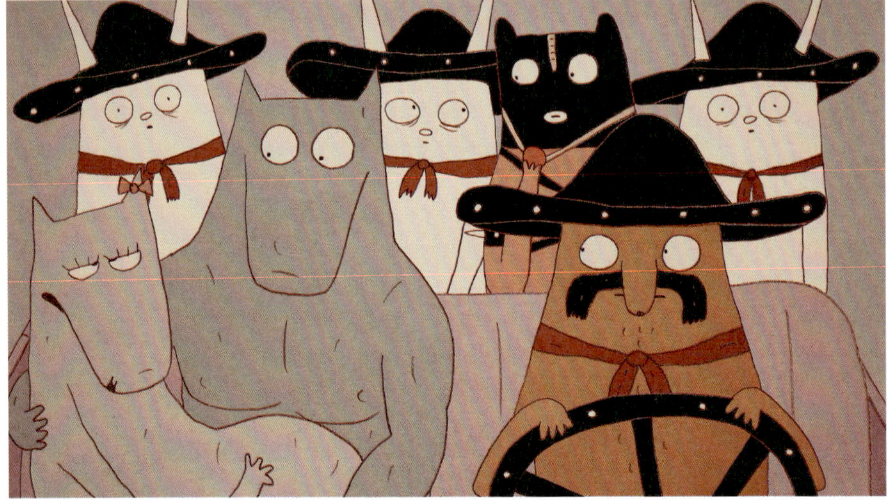

COMPUTER ANIMATION · Honorary Mention

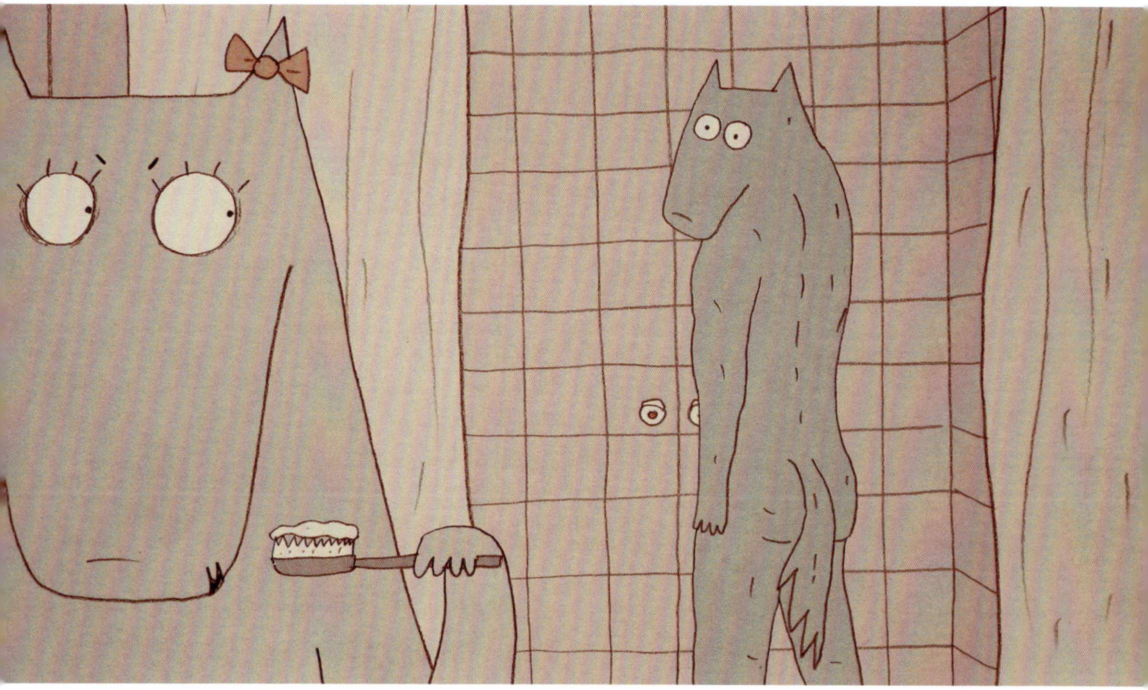

Toomas Beneath the Valley of the Wild Wolves
Chintis Lundgren

After losing a well paid engineering job, Toomas, a hot young wolf, gets cornered into working as a gigolo to support his family. He is keeping it as a secret from his pregnant wife Viivi. Viivi also has a secret: she is attending a female empowerment seminar involving male slaves. When Toomas gets a role in a sexploitation movie, it becomes harder to keep his new profession a secret.

Original title: *Toomas teispool metsikute huntide orgu*
Animation: Chintis Lundgren, Draško Ivecić, Darko Vidačković
Scenario, Script: Chintis Lundgren, Draško Ivecić
Cast: Draško Ivecić, Leon Lučev, Lee Delong, Dražen Šivak, Chintis Lundgren
Image: Chintis Lundgren
Film editor: Chintis Lundgren, Draško Ivecić
Sound designer: Pierre Yves Drapeau
Mix: Pierre Yves Drapeau, Benoît Coallier
Soundtrack: Terence Dunn

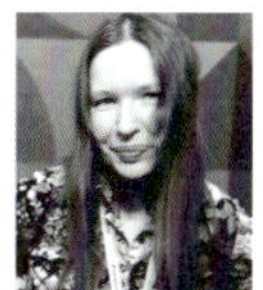

Chintis Lundgren (EE) is an Estonian-born animator currently living in Croatia. Self-taught, Lundgren's body of work includes an assortment of quirky music videos, PSAs, and short films featuring a light, absurdist tone along with distinct anthropomorphic characters. In 2011, Lundgren created her own animation studio called Chintis Lundgreni Animatsioonistuudio, and later co-founded Adriatic Animation, an animation studio based in Croatia. Her films (including the award-winning shorts, *Manivald* (2017) and *Life with Herman H. Rott* (2015) have screened at numerous international festivals including Sundance, Toronto, Annecy, Animafest Zagreb, Hiroshima, and Ottawa.

https://vimeo.com/326447677

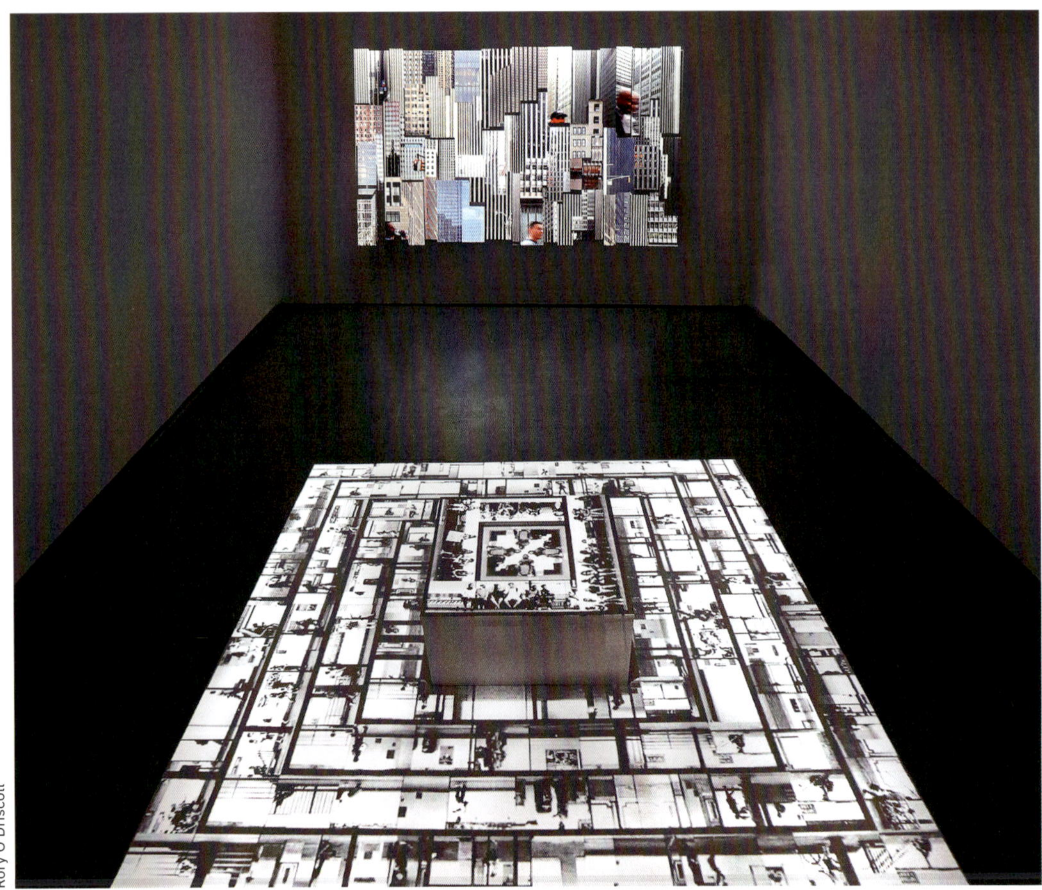

Photo credit (vertical, left margin): Rory O'Driscoll

Underground Circuit

Yuge Zhou 周雨歌

Underground Circuit is a collage of hundreds of video clips shot in the subway stations in New York. Station to station, the movement of the commuters in the outer rings suggests the repetitive cycle of life and urban theatricality and texture. The inner-most ring includes people who are waiting on benches. The central drummers act as if they were the controllers of the commuters' movement, similar to the four-faced Buddha in Chinese folk religion, who fulfills and grants all wishes of its devotees.

For the installation, the video is projected onto the gallery floor and mapped onto a cube with relief in the middle of the projection area. The installation invites audiences to sit on the central cube as voyeurs, to observe the anonymous characters in the projected urban labyrinth.

Artist: Yuge Zhou 周雨歌
Sound design: Stephen Farrell

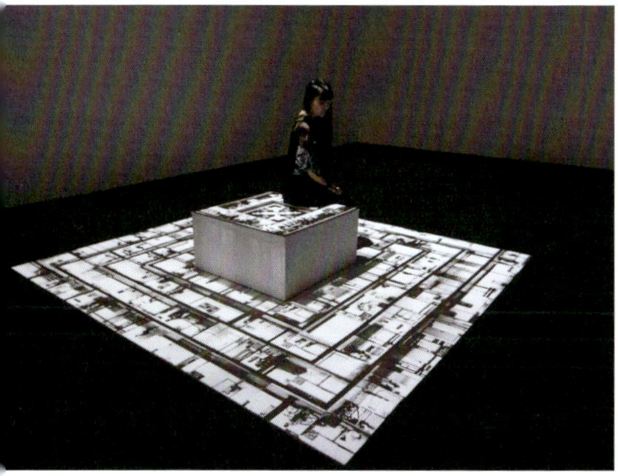

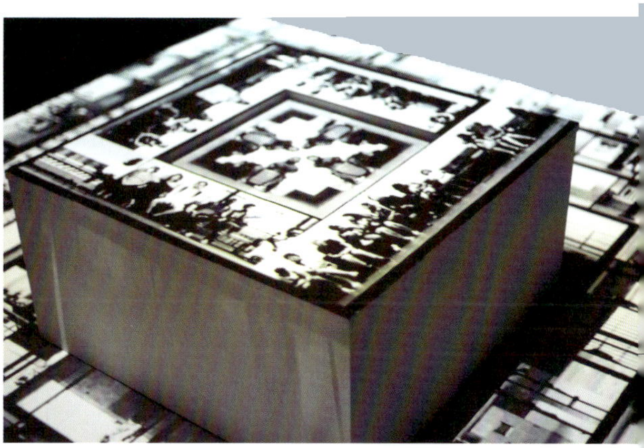

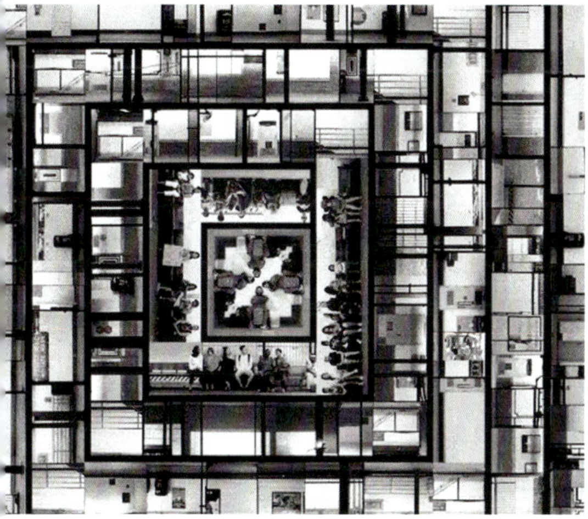

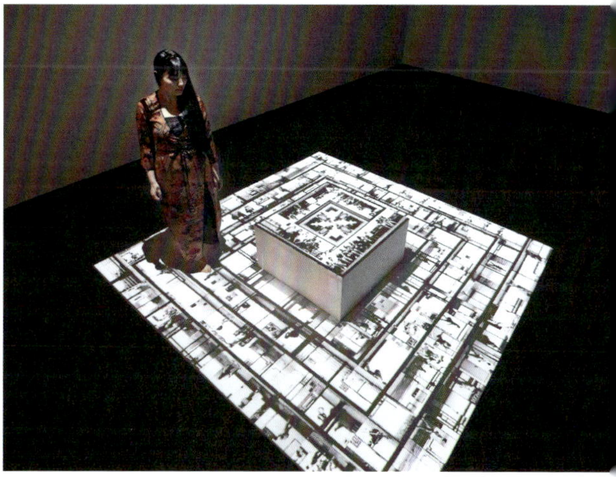

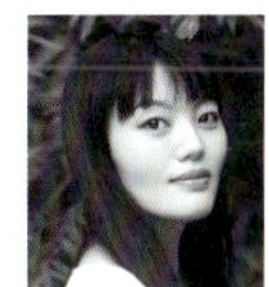

At the age of five, **Yuge Zhou** 周雨歌 (CN) became a household name in China as the singer for a popular children's TV series. Yuge studied photography and then moved into video art, earning her Master of Fine Art from the School of the Art Institute of Chicago. Yuge creates videos and installations that address connections, isolation, and longing across urban and natural environments. She has exhibited nationally and internationally, and her work has been the subject of various articles in such publications as *New York Magazine* and *Hypebeast Magazine.* Yuge received the 2017 Santo Foundation Individual Artist Award. In addtion to her art practice, she directs and curates the 3300-square foot 150 Media Stream, the largest public digital art installation in Chicago. Yuge also holds a masters degree in Computer Engineering from Syracuse University.

https://vimeo.com/238650658 · yugezhou.com

INTERACTIVE ART +

Interactive Art + in the Age of Uncertainty

DooEun Choi, Sabine Himmelsbach, Vladan Joler, Haytham Nawar, Stefan Tiefengraber

In 2016, Prix Ars Electronica expanded their definition of the "Interactive Art" category, broadening the concept of interaction and adding the + sign. Ironically, the 2020 jury found themselves in extraordinary circumstances while judging the submitted works, as the coronavirus pandemic affected transportation globally and imposed social distancing. It is on this shifting ground that the jury decided on the prize-winners. The 2016 category, "Interactive Art+," is concerned with interactivity, and now, during the pandemic, the jury needed to use social media, and other forms of interactive technology, to view and judge the submitted works. In 2020, there was actually NOTHING outside the interactive.

In the midst of the global pandemic caused by the coronavirus, a jury meeting on site in Linz was no longer possible, borders were closed, and travel opportunities across the entire planet were restricted, coming to an almost complete standstill. The jury meetings shifted to online platforms and took place on video conferencing platforms, overcoming the different challenges such as time differences, physical distance, and technical challenges. It actually worked surprisingly well. Each jury member had to spend time viewing the projects alone, instead of the usual process of viewing the projects with the group in a shared space. Nevertheless, the mutual exchange was intense and constructive, and included animated discussions. All jury members were well prepared, making for a smooth process. Our only concern was the question of interactivity as embodied by each individual artwork, since jury members could not experience the individual works physically. However, the project documentation and the discussions between jury members facilitated the process. This year's submissions were very distinct from previous years and were highly influenced by socio-cultural aspects, trying to react to international phenomena. With over 1,300 submissions, the abundance of artistic production in the Interactive Art + category was once again evident. The submissions included interactive installations and videos, biotechnological experimental set-ups, architectural studies, robotics, and artificial intelligence. It is undeniable that technology has become an indispensable part of the artistic canon today, especially in the case of AI projects. It was impressive to see many socio-political interventions within the submitted projects. Artists are reflecting on the topics of labor, surveillance, and censorship that are questioned by current technological advancement. Another important field of reflection is ecology and the issues related to climate change and the steps we need to make regarding a sustainable future. Last but not least, emotions, which are often called the core of human experience, are addressed in many works, as our emotions are extensively manipulated and targeted by algorithmic systems and regimes.

Furthermore, an increase in the outstanding achievements of women artists was welcomed as a positive development, and the jury is very pleased that the Golden Nica will go to a female artist this year, while eight female artists will receive Awards of Distinctions and Honorary Mentions. In addition, the jury was careful to achieve a general parity and to provide a broad and diverse range of the submitted artworks in the category of Interactive Art+. Nevertheless, we hope to reach more diverse applications in terms of geography and ethnicity in future editions. On the other hand, a sensitive approach in the selection of the submitted works and the values that these projects convey was as important as innovative technological aspects.

The quantity and diversity of the submitted works also reflect the views of the individual artists on the category Interactive Art +. It is extremely exciting to see in which direction this art form is developing. The selected works not only show the origins of the definition of interactive art but also indicate the very open approach that this category carries as "+." As the artworks continue to evolve, new developments are taken into account and a current state of this art form is represented. The new developments are different from classical approaches of human-machine-interaction. In 2020, our ideas about interactivity are no longer linked to specific mediums. As a result of the global pandemic, the meaning of interactivity has been challenged and our understanding of the relationship between humanity, nature, and the machine has deepened, facilitating more profound discussions about humanity in an age of uncertainty.

Golden Nica

SOMEONE · Lauren Lee McCarthy

The artist Lauren Lee McCarthy questions the role of the human in the age of intelligent machines by examining communication media and re-imagining them. For McCarthy, the *SOMEONE* is the human version of Amazon's Alexa, staging an interaction between the public audience in the gallery and people at home. The human-to-machine interaction is reversed to become a human-to-human interaction as filtered through a machine. During the global pandemic, physical interaction between humans has been challenged and virtual interaction between humans mediated through the machines has been tested in our everyday life in an unprecedented way. To navigate an uncertain future, this work raises awareness of the new, emerging challenges of the 21st century. It suggests relevant ideas about what might constitute the definition of intelligence itself by revisiting the social and emotional intelligence of humans as they were, but now couched within a machine-intelligent system.

Awards of Distinction

Google Maps Hacks · Simon Weckert

Google Maps Hacks by Simon Weckert is a great example of the contemporary situationist practice combining performance, social activism, obfuscation, and hacking. In this action, 99 second-hand smartphones are transported in a handcart to generate a virtual traffic jam in Google Maps. Through this activity, he is turning a green street red, which has an impact in the physical world by navigating cars along another route to avoid being stuck in traffic. With this intervention Simon Weckert is basically giving us a simple DIY recipe on how to interact and influence invisible algorithms behind the Google Map, a proprietary platform that is shaping our movements and behavior. We believe that actions like this, that are experimenting with the strategies on how to obfuscate and intervene in data flows, is of great importance for our present and the future in the age of surveillance capitalism and digital totalitarianism.

Shadow Stalker · Lynn Hershman Leeson
Shadow Stalker is an interactive installation by American media art pioneer Lynn Hershman Leeson, based on personal data that allows visitors to experience their data shadows in real time. Based solely on the use of just their email address, personal information about the participants retrieved from internet databases is displayed within a generated digital shadow. Further elements of the installation include a film that focuses on Data Mining, predictive policing, and identity theft, and a website that presents the percentage of predicted financial crimes by an algorithm, which is presented by zip code. The jury was convinced by the conceptual strength of the work, the highly political topic, and the awareness it raises for surveillance issues and racial profiling. The jury also recognizes the formal quality of the work, how visually compelling the whole installation is and how it enables the audience to engage with the important subject matter by becoming an active part of it.

Honorary Mentions

999 years, 13 sqm (the future belongs to ghosts) · Cécile B. Evans in collaboration with biologist-architect Rachel Armstrong
999 years, 13 sqm (the future belongs to ghosts) is an installation by the British artist Cécile B. Evans and Rachel Armstrong, professor of experimental architecture. The installation reflects on the topic of housing and is composed of two parts: a 'living' wall that houses several elements that create an organic battery system which is powered by microbes and provides small amounts of electricity that run the electronic devices, and an anima-tion of a dying bird, projected onto a misty curtain of fog. The jury was convinced by the strength of the artistic concept, which reflects the severe challenges in terms of the housing situation, future living scenarios, and the need for co-habitation with other entities. The piece confronts us with a dying life form and a living entity, to whose care we must contribute by active engagement. It enables critical reflection as well as a poetic encounter.

Algorithmic Perfumery · Frederik Duerinck
Algorithmic Perfumery is an interface that allows the user to create their own personal scent combination based on the data they input through a questionnaire. The machine processes this data and generates an individual code that is processed to create a particular fragrance. This work by Dutch artist Frederik Duerinck offers a new narrative to the future of perfumery and allows the visitor to take away a physical souvenir of the experience. After testing the generated scent, the visitor can communicate their feedback to help the algorithm learn and refine itself.
The jury was persuaded by the multisensory nature of this work and how the experience is both conceptual and physical, making this project particularly attractive. The user is at the center of this project and each experience, although following the same meticulous process, results in a different and unique product. This artwork gives a glimpse into the future of perfumery and challenges the concept of mass production. By interacting with the machine, the user possesses the power to be an active part of the creation process.

Appropriate Response · Mario Klingemann
Appropriate Response is an interactive installation
that is concerned with meaning, expectation, and
relationship with AI. The visitor is presented with
a traditional wooden kneeler facing a split flat display that generates random sentences. The AI
system is triggered when the visitor uses the
kneeler and displays a unique sequence of words.
Through his pertinent work, German artist Mario
Klingemann explores the significance attached to
written words.
The jury found it witty and particularly relevant
that the entire experience is transformed into a
ritual that is very similar to religious experience.
Although this interaction between Human and AI
results in unique coherent aphorisms, it is how the
human understands it and makes sense of it that
gives this interaction meaning. The artwork is built
on expectation, hope, and fear—feelings that associate the generated words with feelings, giving
them a new life.

Center for Technological Pain · Dasha Ilina
Center for Technological Pain offers, as the artist
states: "multiple practices for eliminating tech-
pain." Wrapped in a diverse range of self-built
objects and solutions, and a DIY approach, an
archive around workshops and tutorial videos like
"Yoga for Healthy Phone Use" is created, to start
a critical discussion about the negative effects
that technology can have on our bodies. The
artist's approach is not to condemn new technologies and to ban them from our lives, but to investigate how we can live in symbiosis with digital
technologies without being harmed.
The jury was convinced that this humorous
approach to a—in a certain context—serious topic,
plays with a contemporary problem that affects
the rapidly growing space digital technologies take
in society. In addition, the topics of open commons and DIY culture are addressed, which are
becoming increasingly important, especially in the
current situation.

Compression Cradle · Lucy McRae
Compression Cradle is a machine that gently
squeezes the body and holds it tight. The Austra-
lian-British artist Lucy McRae has developed a bed
or 'cradle' that the visitors can step into. Slowly
the air is let out and the participant is softly held
by a blanket, as if in a tender embrace. The immersive artwork reflects on a touch-deficit status of
our mediated society, where people increasingly
seek closeness through machines, but in the pandemic that currently shakes the whole world,
becomes even more an attempt to prepare the self
for a future without human touch. The jury was
convinced by the urgency of the work, its critical
reflection on our relationship towards technology,
and how it addresses our need for human connectivity. The work offers the audience new perceptual experiences that—especially in our troubled
and challenging times—open space for reflection
and thought.

khipu / electrotextile prehispanic computer
Constanza Piña Pardo
The artist Constanza Piña Pardo, also known as
Corazón de Robota (Robot Heart), is a member and
co-founder of different feminist collectives and
labs and a very active performer in the field of
sound art who shares her knowledge of open hard-

ware in workshops and on her website. In her project *khipu / electrotextile prehispanic computer* she relates to the ancient conclusion that beyond the visible sky lies a calculating power that organizes everything. The result is an open-source textile computer based on an astronomical Inca khipu, an early computing system. Produced in an experimental creation laboratory together with five other women, the artist uses her artistic approach to interpret technology combined with her research about the resemblances of this system of knots and contemporary binary coding. The jury acknowledged that the interaction of this project does not only take place in the exhibition space, but also in the creation of the artwork, in the artist's community, where old and almost forgotten knowledge is preserved by transferring it to our time by following a DIY and open commons approach.

Machine Auguries
Alexandra Daisy Ginsberg
With this work the artist shows the easily overlooked man-made influences and their effects on the environment, especially in densely populated areas. Light and noise pollution influence the behavior of the birds necessary for a balanced ecosystem. They have to adapt their behavior to survive alongside humans in this environment. Alexandra Daisy Ginsberg created with *Machine Auguries* an immersive environment in which the visitor can experience the singing of birds accompanied by changing light moods according to times of the day. Parts of the audible bird sounds are artificially created and mixed with the singing of real birds—communication between birds and the machine that tries to hear and respond to the voices with the help of machine learning and is thereby creating a new language. The crescendo that is audible through a multi-channel sound installation is also reflected by the trained neural networks that are responding to the real birds and slowly taking over at the end with pure artificial bird songs not distinguishable from real bird songs.

Mind · Shinseungback Kimyonghun
Emotions which were thought to exist only in the realm of the human, are captured here in *Mind* by the artists Shinseungback Kimyonghun. In contemporary culture, collective emotions are instrumentalized, classified, analyzed, and manipulated by machines. *Mind* examines captured facial expressions and data collected by machine intelligences such as FER+ Emotion Recognition and ONNX (Open Neural Network Exchange) Runtime. A collective "meta-mind" generated by the last one-hundred faces of visitors to the exhibition site, is generating algorithmic patterns. These algorithmic patterns are used to create sound, which acts upon a series of moving plates filled with small metal beads. The sounds and beads move in tandem, all generated by the emotional expressions of exhibition visitors. Shinseungback Kimyonghun describe this work as "a sea of emotions." The jury felt that the piece expressed the power of art to help people with the emotional challenges of the current global pandemic, suggesting that, collectively, humanity can navigate this difficult time.

The Intimate Earthquake Archive
Sissel Marie Tonn
The Intimate Earthquake Archive by Sissel Marie Tonn is an ongoing research project and interactive installation dealing with the phenomenon of man-made earthquakes. In her work she is offering us the chance to experience "deep listening"

of the effects of fossil fuels exploitation. Even this project has a strong local dimension because it deals with the site-specific problem that is a result of the gas drilling in one of the largest gas fields in Europe. It is also provoking dialog in a wider ecological and socio-political context of the human role in the environment undergoing changes. By creating tactile sensory experiences from the collected seismic recordings, she is offering us the chance to feel those changes and effects with our bodies.

The Net Wanderer—A tour of suspended handshakes · Guo Cheng

The Net Wanderer by Guo Cheng is an artistic research project that explores the connection between the critical network gateways in China, known as the Great Firewall of China (GFW), and the infrastructure behind these gateways. This project investigates the materiality of the invisible but one of the most influential technological borders that shape territoriality of the internet nowadays. In this project, which combines artistic and technical research, his personal investigative journey into the physical locations determined by the network diagnostic tools are transformed into the installation that lets us become virtual firewall tourists. Even as this project reveals some of the aspects of this complex and invisible infrastructure, it also reveals to us many obstacles and limitations of our capacity to investigate those systems from the position of the artist and independent researchers.

Trickle Down, A New Vertical Sovereignty · Helen Knowles

Trickle Down, A New Vertical Sovereignty is an installation composed of different elements: a tokenized four-screen video installation, a generative soundscape attached to the blockchain, and a machine. The experience starts when the user puts a coin in a machine that converts it into crypto-currency and distributes it on the Trickle Down community (prisoners, Ethereal Summit attendees, employees at a blockchain company, Mancunians at Openshaw market, Manchester, and the Russian community in central London) who participated in the project. The space is equipped with sensors that are triggered by the visitor's location, making each experience individual.

The jury agreed that what's intriguing in this work by British artist Helen Knowles is that every element of the installation is visible to the visitor, making their experience transparent and revealing what is usually hidden in real life. The artwork denounces the technological and financial power structures that support the disparity between a wealthy elite and everyday working people and attempts to imagine a more horizontal approach.

Warriors · James Coupe

In the 2020 Prix Ars Electronica, there were many submissions related to AI, and *Warriors* was selected due to its thematic strength and the level of interaction elicited from viewers whose faces were captured and then assigned to cinematic, filmed actors, composited in real time into the cult film *Warriors.* Coupe's piece blurred the boundaries between the real and the fake by using the deepfakes algorithm, which is based on a Generative Adversarial Network. The work questions the biases built into the current profiling systems used to construct AI. Viewers are invited to experience the face swap, and the impact of technology is no longer abstract and objective but something intimate and psychologically disturbing.

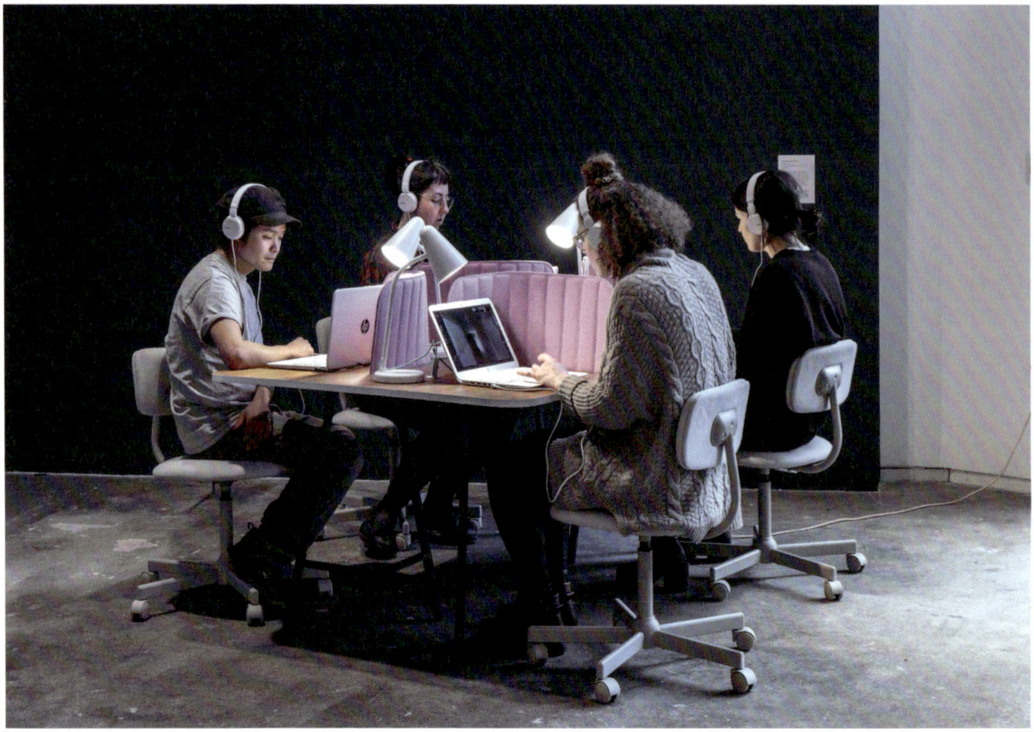

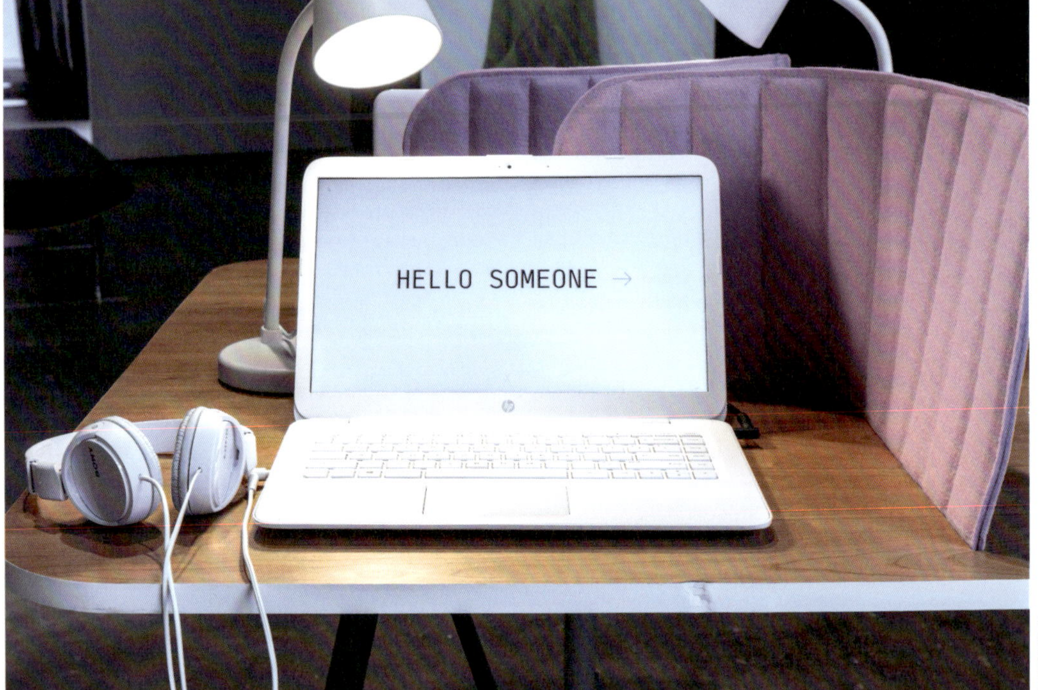

Stan Narten

Stan Narten

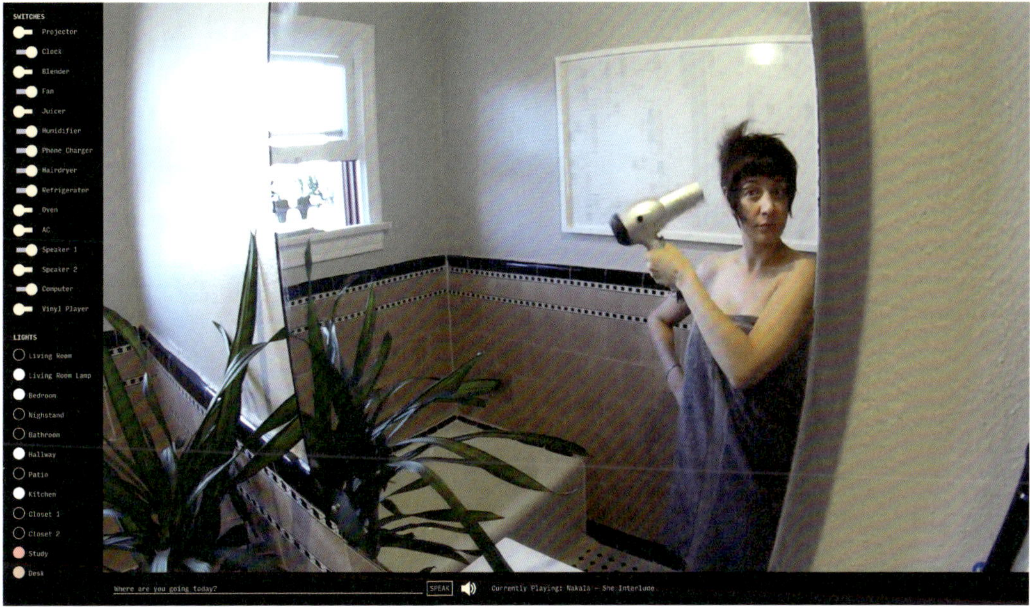

SOMEONE

Lauren Lee McCarthy

Upon entering the gallery, visitors encounter a command center that resembles a cross between a call center and WeWork coworking space, featuring four computer stations. Each computer looks into one of four participant homes, installed with custom-designed smart devices, including cameras, microphones, switches, lights, and appliances. Visitors are invited to take on the role of a human Amazon Alexa.

They may hear smart home occupants call out for "Someone"—prompting them to step in as their home automation assistant and respond to their needs. They can peek into the four homes via the laptops, watch over them, and remotely control the devices in their homes. The first version of this installation was a live remote intelligence portal into four homes across the United States that took place over a two-month period.

We're sold smart devices that outfit our homes with surveillance cameras, sensors, and automated control, offering us convenience at the cost of loss of privacy and control over our lives and homes. We're meant to think these slick plastic pieces of technology are about utility, but the space they invade is personal. The home is the place where we are first watched over, first socialized, first cared for. How does it feel to have this role assumed by artificial intelligence? Our home is the first site of cultural education—it's where we learn to be a person. By allowing these devices in, we outsource the formation of our identity to a virtual assistant whose values are programmed by a small, homogenous group of developers.

It is hard to imagine any living person with a personality like Alexa or Siri. AI assistants lack the flaws and inconsistencies of human personalities.

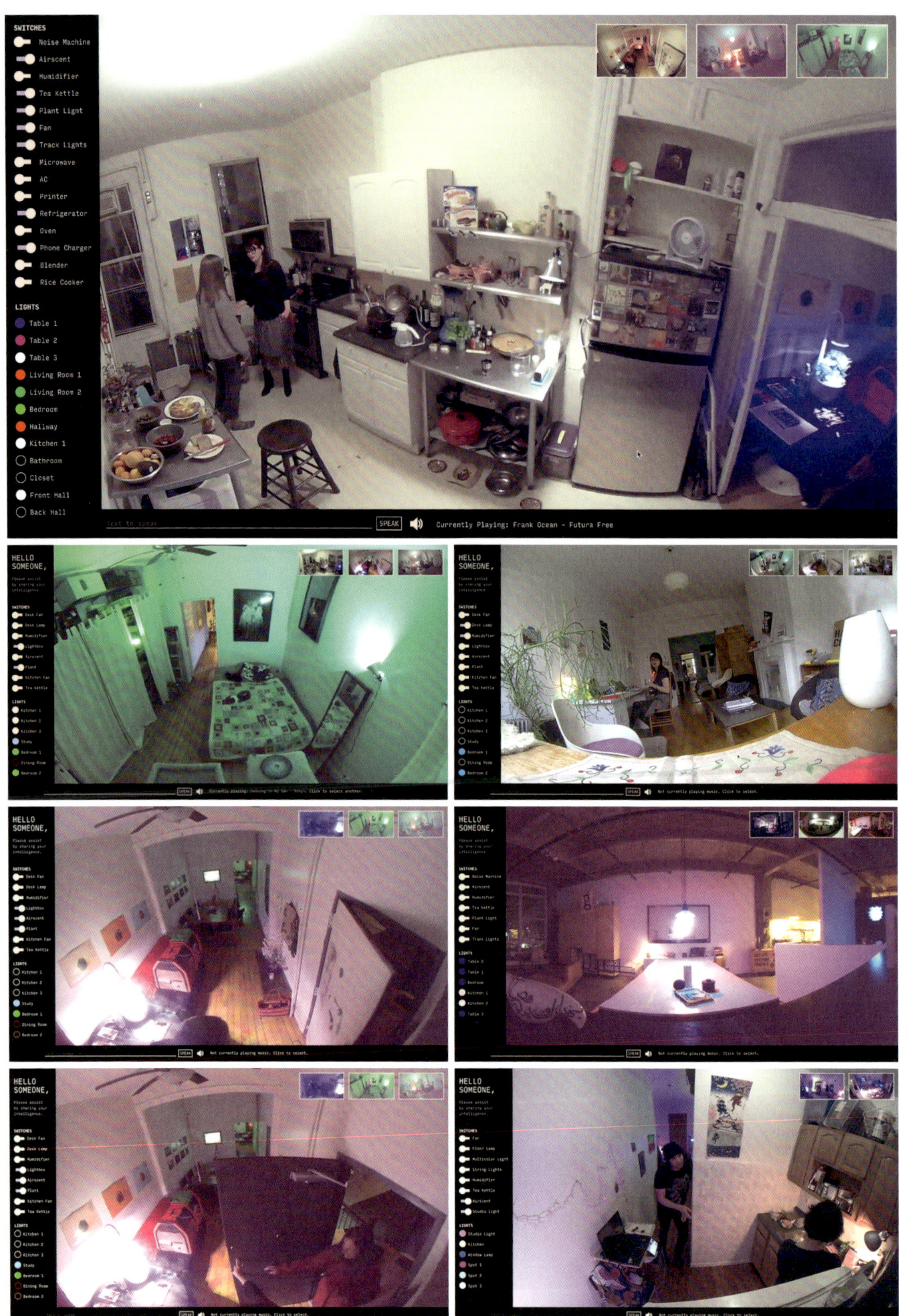

INTERACTIVE ART + · Golden Nica 2020

Right now, virtual assistants are designed to accommodate the most common and universal needs. Imagine if instead they attended to our particular, obscure needs and desires. They could probe beyond what we expect of these technologies, into the types of help we might feel able and comfortable to ask only of technology. This points to possibilities that are both exciting and worrying. This installation does not impose a judgment but creates space for the viewers and inhabitants to form their own opinions.

While designing the project, I spent a lot of time thinking about the question, "If I were an AI, what would I be like?" I aimed to create *SOMEONE* as an entity that felt human but could also function like a system. Rather than speaking to people directly, visitors used a text-to-speech interface to invoke a synthesized voice. Rather than feeling like a guest to be accommodated in the home, they could more easily integrate into the infrastructure of the environment.

The devices were based on research into existing smart home and IoT devices, while exploring more human and imaginative forms and functionalities they may take on. The custom device objects incorporate cameras, microphones, and sensors, and address the needs of the inhabitants by functioning as smart switches, lights, locks, environment adjusters, small appliances, and more surreal mechanisms of control. Custom software, built with node.js, runs on a Raspberry Pi computer that serves as the central hub for the system, connecting all the devices and enabling them to be interactive and remotely controlled.

By substituting humans for AI, the role of virtual assistant is re-contextualized. As inhabitants call out for "Someone," invoking visitors as intelligence, the dynamic between audience and performer is complicated. Installed simultaneously in multiple homes across the country, we're challenged to consider the scale of the work, and the even more expansive, networked systems that structure society. *SOMEONE* is a meditation on the smart home, the tensions between intimacy vs privacy, convenience vs agency, and the role of human labor in the future of automation.

Artist: Lauren Lee McCarthy
Software and hardware development: Harvey Moon, Josh Billions
Interface software: Lauren Lee McCarthy
Furniture design collaboration and fabrication: Lela Barclay de Tolly
Smart home participant collaborators: Valeria Haedo, Adelle Lin, Amanda McDonald Crowley, Ksenya Samarskaya

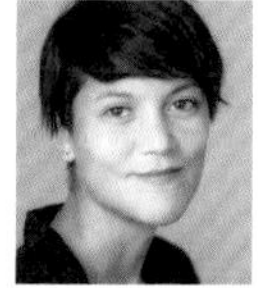

Lauren Lee McCarthy (US) is an LA-based artist examining social relationships in the midst of surveillance, automation, and algorithmic living. She is the creator of p5.js, an open source JavaScript platform that aims to make creative expression and coding on the web accessible and inclusive. Lauren's work has been exhibited internationally, including the Barbican Centre, Fotomuseum Winterthur, SIGGRAPH, IDFA DocLab, Science Gallery Dublin, Seoul Museum of Art, and the Japan Media Arts Festival. She's a 2020 Sundance New Frontier Fellow, 2019 Creative Capital Grantee, and has previously held residencies with Sundance New Frontiers, Eyebeam, CMU STUDIO for Creative Inquiry, Autodesk, and Ars Electronica, among others. She's the recipient of grants from the Knight Foundation, the Online News Association, Mozilla Foundation, and Google AMI.

https://lauren-mccarthy.com/SOMEONE

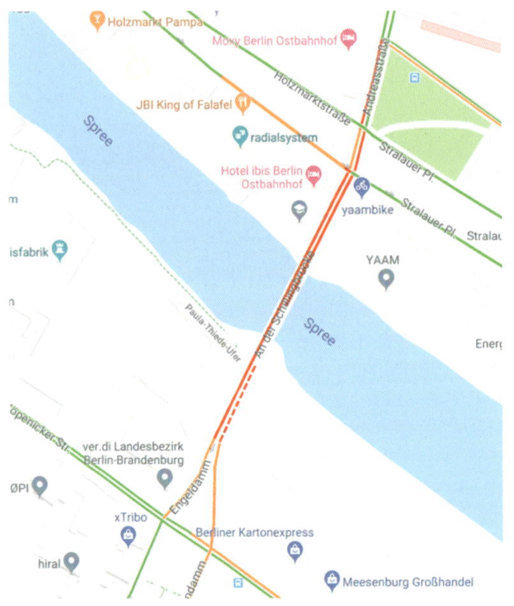

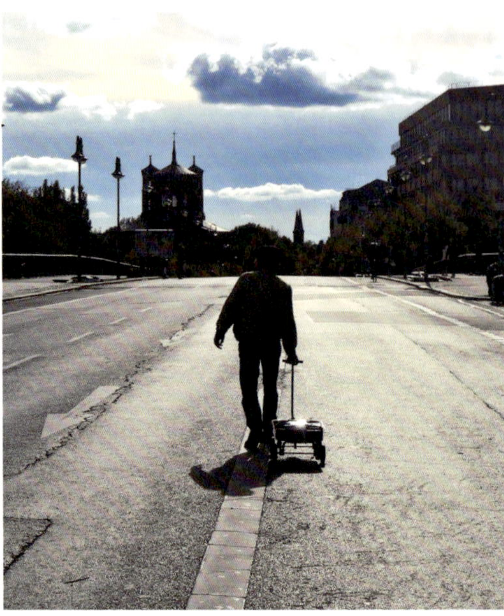

Google Maps Hacks

Simon Weckert

99 secondhand smartphones are transported in a handcart to generate a virtual traffic jam in Google Maps. Through this activity, it is possible to turn a green street red, which has an impact in the physical world by navigating cars on another route to avoid being stuck in traffic.

The advent of Google's Geo Tools began in 2005 with Maps and Earth, followed by Street View in 2007. Google's map service has fundamentally changed our understanding of what a map is, how we interact with maps, their technological limitations, and how they look aesthetically.

In this fashion, Google Maps makes virtual changes to the real city. Applications such as Airbnb and Carsharing or Uber have an immense impact on cities: on their housing market and mobility culture, for instance. There is also a major impact on how we find a romantic partner, thanks to dating platforms such as Tinder, and on our self-quantifying behavior, thanks to the Nike jogging app. An additional mapping market is provided by self-driving cars; again, Google has already established a position for itself.

All of these apps function via interfaces with Google Maps and create new forms of digital capitalism and commodification. With its Geo Tools, Google has created a platform that allows users and businesses to interact with maps in a novel way. This means that questions relating to power in the discourse of cartography have to be reformulated. What is the relationship between the art of enabling and techniques of supervision, control, and regulation in Google's maps? Do these maps function as dispositive nets that determine the behavior, opinions, and images of living beings, exercising power and controlling knowledge?

Text: Moritz Alhert

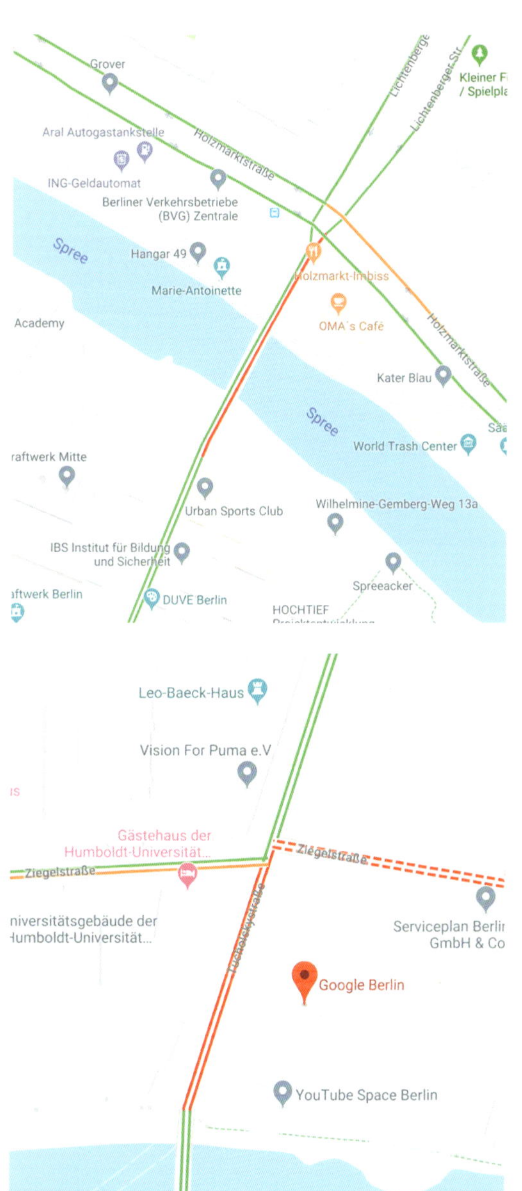

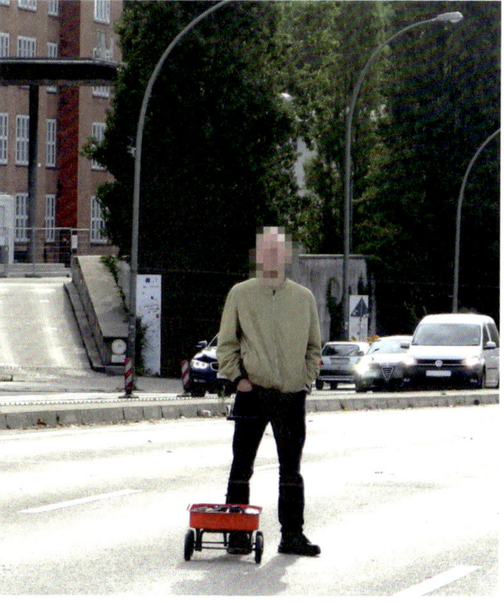

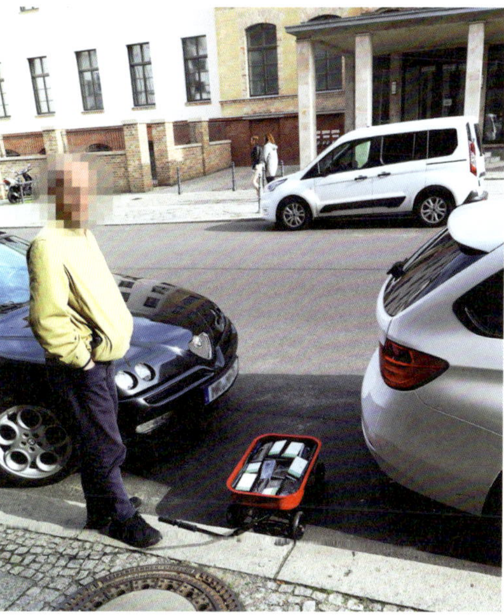

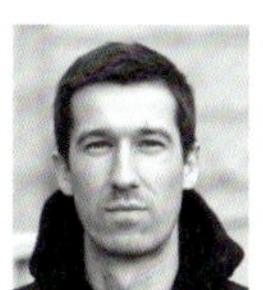

Simon Weckert (DE) is an artist with his home base in Berlin. He likes to share knowledge on a wide range of fields from generative design to physical computing. His focus is the digital world—everything related to code and electronics including reflection on current social aspects and ranging from technology-oriented examinations to the discussion of current social issues. In his work, he seeks to assess the value of technology, not in terms of actual utility, but from the perspective of future generations. He wants to raise awareness of the privileged state in which people live within Western civilization and to remind them of the obligations attached to this privilege.

http://www.simonweckert.com/googlemapshacks.html

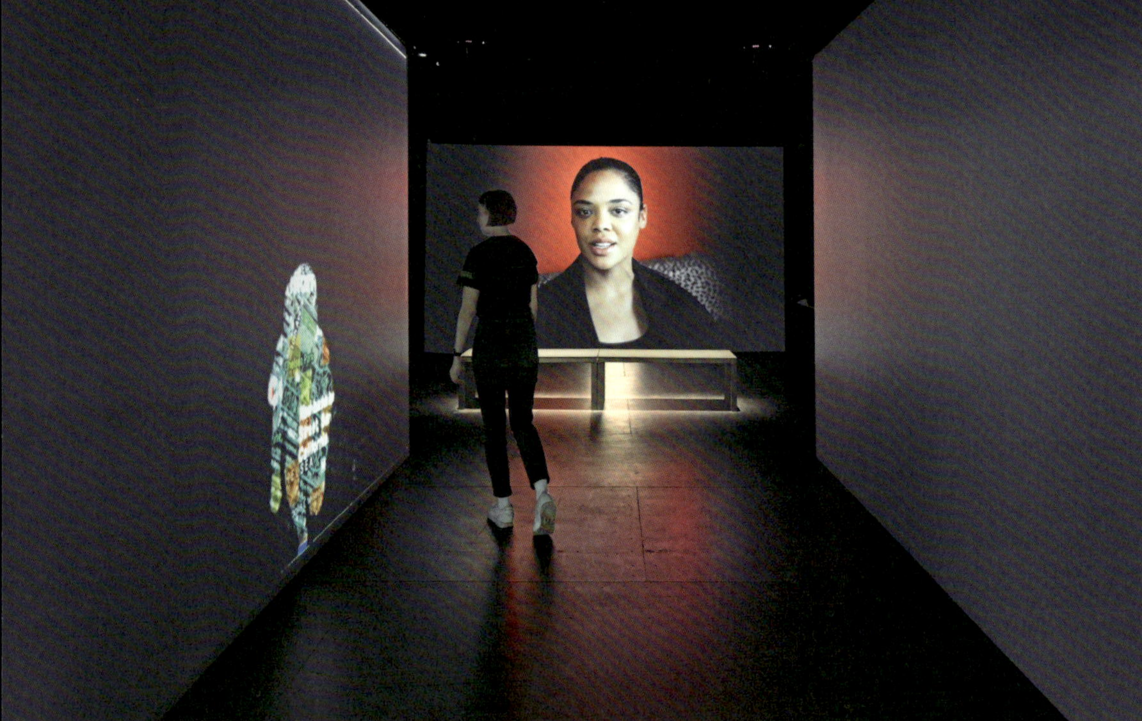

Shadow Stalker

Lynn Hershman Leeson

Shadow Stalker is a "live" interactive installation that uses original algorithms, data mining, live performances, and projections in order to make visible normally private internet information. This project directly reveals an individual's "digital shadow," providing access to online internet information, which is crucial as data has surpassed oil as the world's most valuable commodity. *Shadow Stalker* directly exposes hidden surveillance systems that now dominate police arrests and highlights the consequences of geographic and economic limitations these systems cause. Audiences will be educated about options for understanding how this software functions and have access to identify some of the limitations that are surreptitiously being placed on their freedom. Increas-

ingly, law enforcement promotes racial profiling and employs flawed artificial intelligent logic to target low income or non-white individuals as possessing criminal intent, often leading to their arrest before a crime occurs.

This is how it works: participants stand inside a "red square" and enter their email on an iPad, a surveillance camera captures their shadow and exposes a chilling sense of their own vulnerability to this kind of data-mining, revealing, in complete sentences, online information inside their shadow, which tracks progressive data in real time as they move through the installation where a video projection warns about invisible surveillance systems and algorithmic violence that robs people of their civil rights. The video advises how to take control

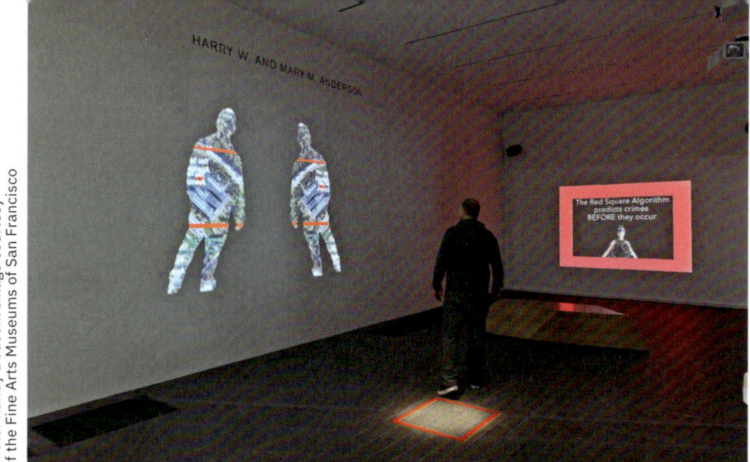

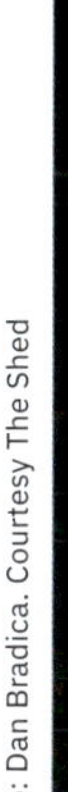

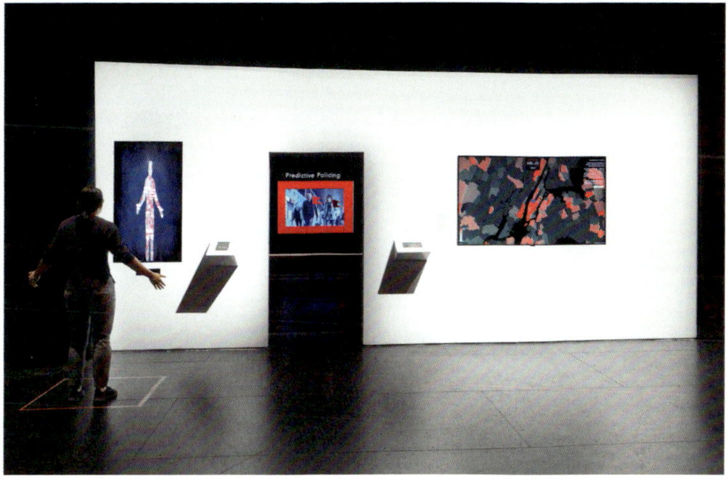

Photo: Dan Bradica. Courtesy The Shed

and own their online digital profiles and independence. Government issued and tracked red squares instigate a coded prison. Yet the red square has historically been a place of revolution. Specially designed algorithms and data mining systems define people by race, economics, or gender. There is an implicit urgency now to expose the existence of these tactics and develop a means of revealing and correcting the global damage these dangerous and violent algorithms are causing.

Shadow Stalker by Lynn Hershman Leeson
Commissioned by The Shed with additional funding from VIA Art Fund
Performers: Tessa Thompson, January Steward
Associate producer and hair: Marine Macerot Bahet, Emma Scully
Camera: Hiro Narita
Sound: Javid Soriano
Costumes: Nina Hollein
Original algorithms programming: Mark Hellar
Interactive developer: Rachel Rose Ulgado
Conversion of zip code algorithms for *White Collar Crimes:* Francis Tseng, Sam Lavigne, Brian Clifton

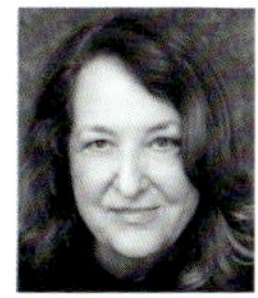

Lynn Hershman Leeson (US), b. 1941, Cleveland, lives and works in San Francisco and New York. Exhibitions include *Lynn Hershman Leeson: Twisted* (The New Museum, NY, opening 2021), *Civic Radar* (Karlsruhe, 2014), and solo exhibitions in Madrid (2019), Berlin (2018), Basel (2018), San Francisco Museum of Modern Art (2013), and Manchester (2007). Her 6 feature films include *Teknolust* (Sloan Writer Director Award), *!Women Art Revolution* (Best Art Film Award), and *Strange Culture* (Humanitarian Award) and she has received numerous other awards. She has permanent exhibits in Museum of Modern Art, NY, MOMA SF, ZKM, Tate Modern, Walker Art Center, Whitney, Thoma Foundation, FAMSF and numerous private collections. *The New York Times* listed *Civic Radar* as "Best Art Book 2016" and *Lynn Hershman Leeson: Antibodies* as "Best Art Book 2019".

https://www.lynnhershman.com/project/shadow-stalker

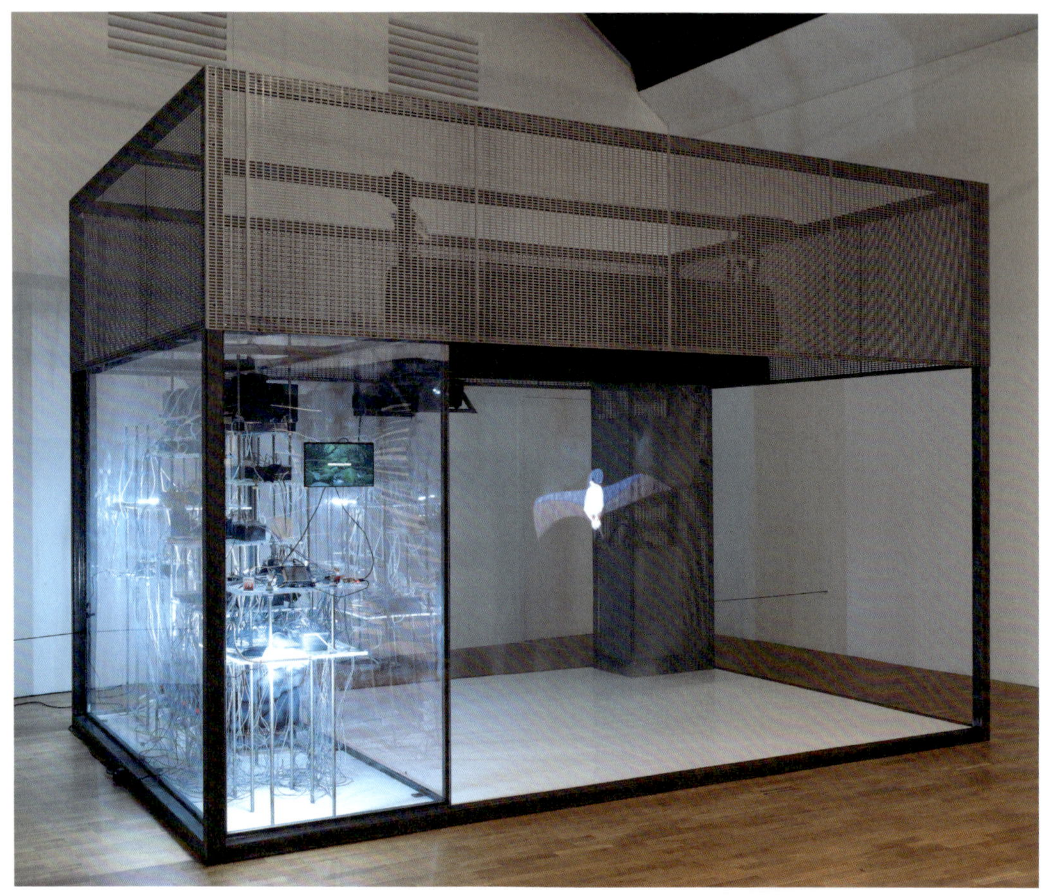

999 years, 13 sqm (the future belongs to ghosts)
Cécile B. Evans, in collaboration with biologist-architect Rachel Armstrong

The polymorphous installation is an exploration of the parameters of a dead future, that is, a future defined by the failures of the past. Prevailing units of measurement and capital, here the 13 sqm defined as the smallest official living space in London or the 999 years listed on the longest leasehold agreements in the UK, often fail to align with the reality of lived experiences. Armstrong and Evans suggest it's the 'uncooperative matter'—entities such as emotions or microbes—that could lead to fluid, unfixed perceptions of multiple realities: something more aligned with the uncertainty that dominates human experience. The structure acts as a living and dying organism, prioritizing the material realities of change over its coordinates. The figure of an animated blue swallow appears, rising and falling, a holographic illusion projected onto a curtain of fog. The atomized particles of the curtain are partially collected by dehumidifiers and recycled back into the machine. A compartment contains an ever-evolving colony of microbes, which inhabit a microbial fuel cell (MFC) bioreactor brick installation, generating energy to power an electronic display. Within the display, a text shaped by conversations around the project and the power generated by recalcitrance and change quietly unfolds as the structure evolves to propose mutability as a strategy for survival.

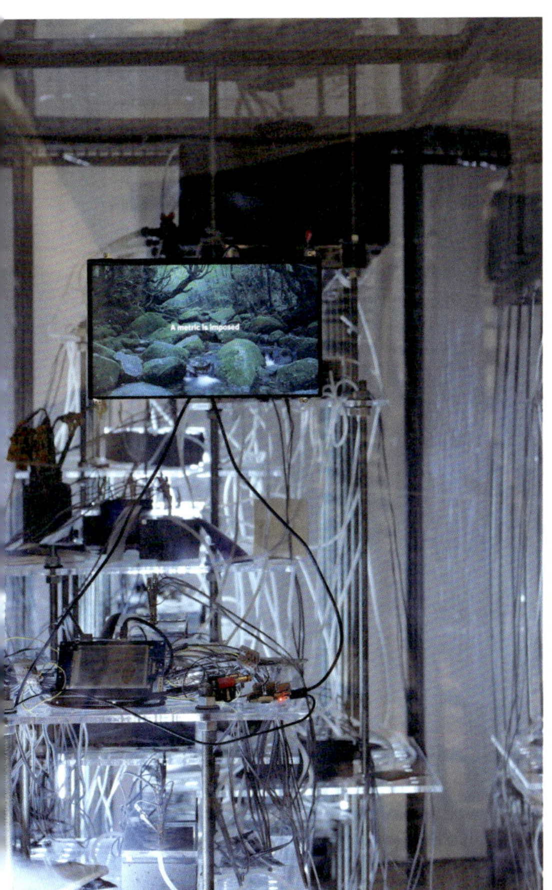

Bioengineering team:
Ioannis Ieropolous (lead), Jiseon You, Arjuna Mendis, Tom Hall, Patrick Brinson / University of the West of England; Simone Ferracina / University of Edinburgh; Rolf Hughes, Pierangelo Scravaglieri / Newcastle University
MFC bioreactor brick installation design: Pierangelo Scravaglieri, under the guidance of Ioannis Ieropolous
Structure designer: Dominik Arni
Structure fabricator: Weber Industries
Contributing writer: Amal Khalaf
Animator: Tom Kemp
Composer: Mati Gavriel
Research and production assistance: Anna Clifford
Commissioned by Whitechapel Gallery for the exhibition *Is This Tomorrow?*
With support from: Personal Improvement Ltd., Living Architecture (EU Grant Agreement no. 686585) at Newcastle University, with additional support from Andrew Hesketh, Audioviz (UK FogScreen), and the Bristol BioEnergy Centre at the Bristol Robotics Laboratory.

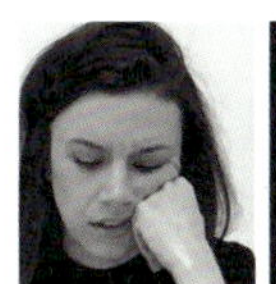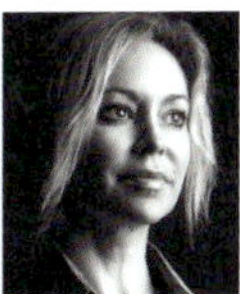

Cécile B. Evans (BE/US) is a Belgian-American artist based in London. Her work examines the value of emotion and its rebellion as it comes into contact with ideological, physical, and technological structures. Recent solo exhibitions include Frac Lorraine (FR), Museum Abteiberg (DE), Tramway (UK), Chateau Shatto (US), Museo Madre (IT), mumok Vienna (AT), Castello di Rivoli (IT), Galerie Emanuel Layr, Vienna (AT), Tate Liverpool (UK). **Rachel Armstrong** (GB) is Professor of Experimental Architecture at the School of Architecture, Planning and Landscape, Newcastle University, a Rising Waters II Fellow (Robert Rauschenberg Foundation, 2016), TWOTY futurist (2015), Fellow of the British Interplanetary Society, and a 2010 Senior TED Fellow. She is Director and founder of the Experimental Architecture Group (EAG), whose work has been widely published and internationally exhibited and performed, for example at Venice Art and Architecture Biennales, Tallinn Architecture Biennale, and Trondheim Art Biennale.

http://cecilebevans.com

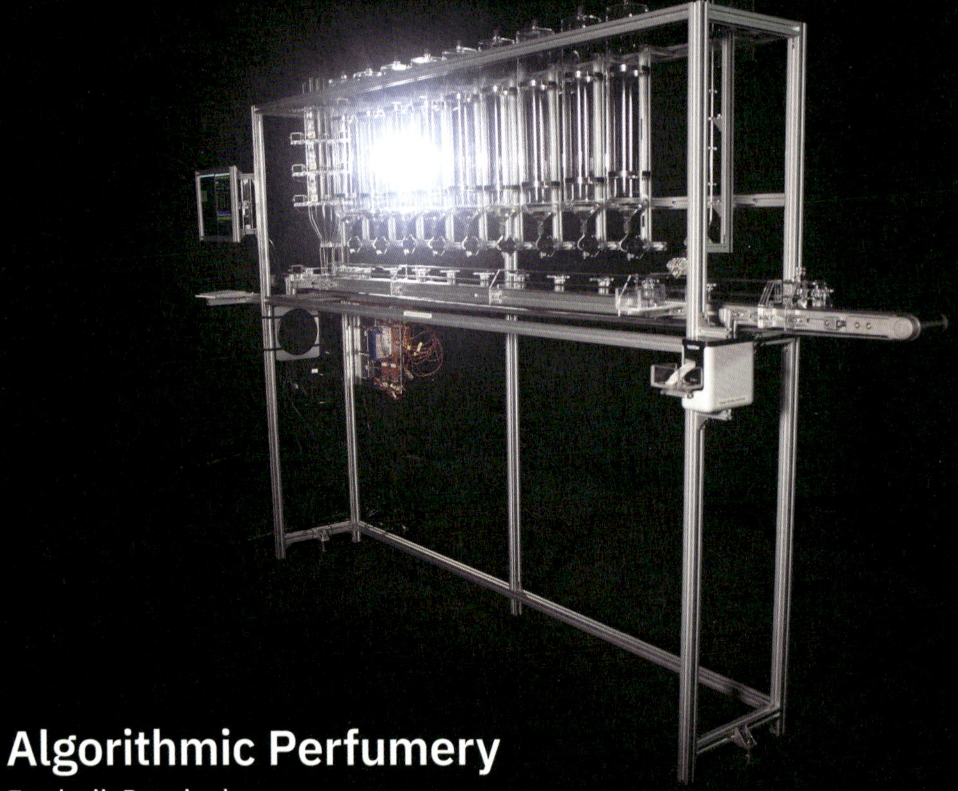

Algorithmic Perfumery

Frederik Duerinck

"What if every human could have their own personal scent?"

In *Algorithmic Perfumery*, the world of scent is explored by using the visitor's input to train the creative capabilities of an automated system. Custom scents are created by a machine learning algorithm based on the unique data we feed it. The outcome is a unique scent generated and compounded on-site. By participating in the experience, visitors contribute to the on-going research to improve the system and reinvent the future of perfumery. Generative perfume design is the emergence of the not too distant future. *Algorithmic Perfumery* not only ignites the senses, it also allows participants to walk away with a tangible and usable memory of the work. Individuals may complete a personality test lasting about 15 minutes, composed of standard questions and a few more focused on scent preference. After the participants' answers are compiled, a code is generated. You proceed to a contraption lined with tubes of concentrates, type in your code, and the machine proceeds to mix the concentrates in amounts based on the data provided. And at the end of the assembly line, a small sample vial of your individually crafted scent awaits you. You may then review your feelings about the scent, and in this way the AI learns and refines its scent crafting abilities. An inspiringly unique approach to a seldom represented creative process, *Algorithmic Perfumery* is indicative of the cohesive future between human ability and technological potential.

Concept: Frederik Duerinck
Visual design: Frederik Duerinck, Vincent Soffers, Mark Meeuwenoord
Scent design: Anahita Mekanik, Spyros Drosopoulos, Andreas Wilhelm
Electronics: Nathaniel Akkermans
Firmware: Rodey Seijkens, Dominggus Salampessy, Jan Thijn van Lisdonk
Backend: Rodey Seijkens, Dominggus Salampessy, Wietse Neven, Lothar Krause
Interface design: Marleen van de Velde, Karin de Jong, Erik Vlemmix
AI: Emmanuela Maggioni, Christiaan van Ratingen, Xavi Moreno, Dominggus Salampessy,
With support from: Cherubic Ventures, IFF, Duerinck Producties

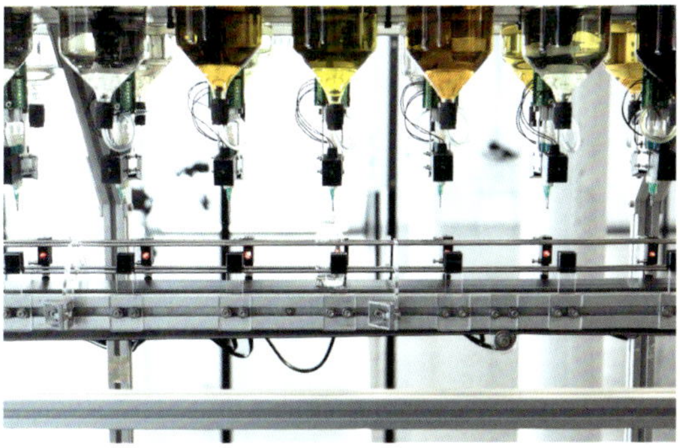

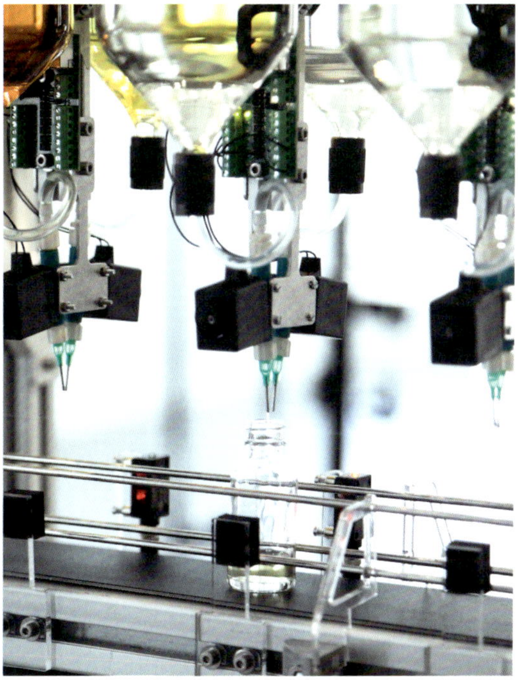

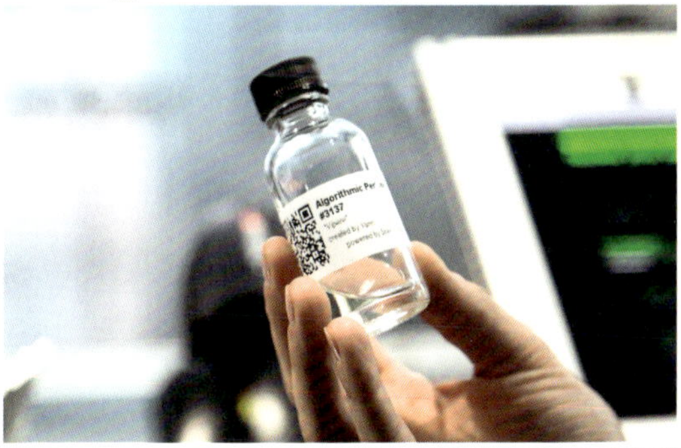

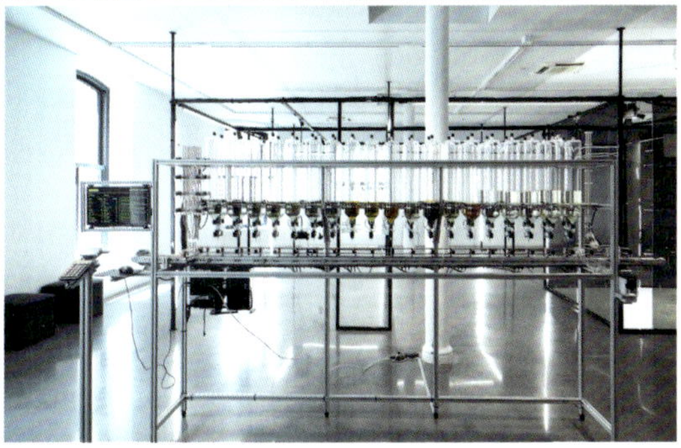

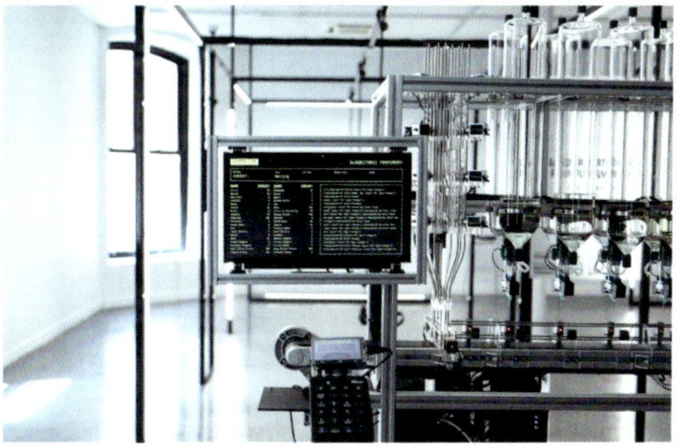

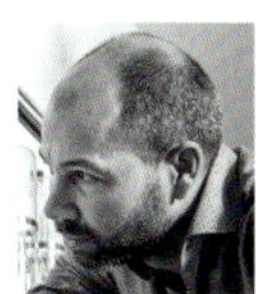

Frederik Duerinck (NL) is a filmmaker and artist located in Breda. He is the lead designer of the award-winning multisensory installation *Famous Deaths* and is co-author of the book *Sense of Smell.* In his work, he researches the boundaries of conventional storytelling, creating embodied narratives. His most recent work, *Algorithmic Perfumery,* was rewarded with the Septimus Piesse Visionary Award 2019 by the Art & Olfaction Institute and the Docfest Alternate Realities Audience Award 2019. Besides his career as filmmaker and artist, since 2018 Frederik has been running his start up Scentronix, focusing on further developing *Algorithmic Perfumery.*

https://algorithmicperfumery.com

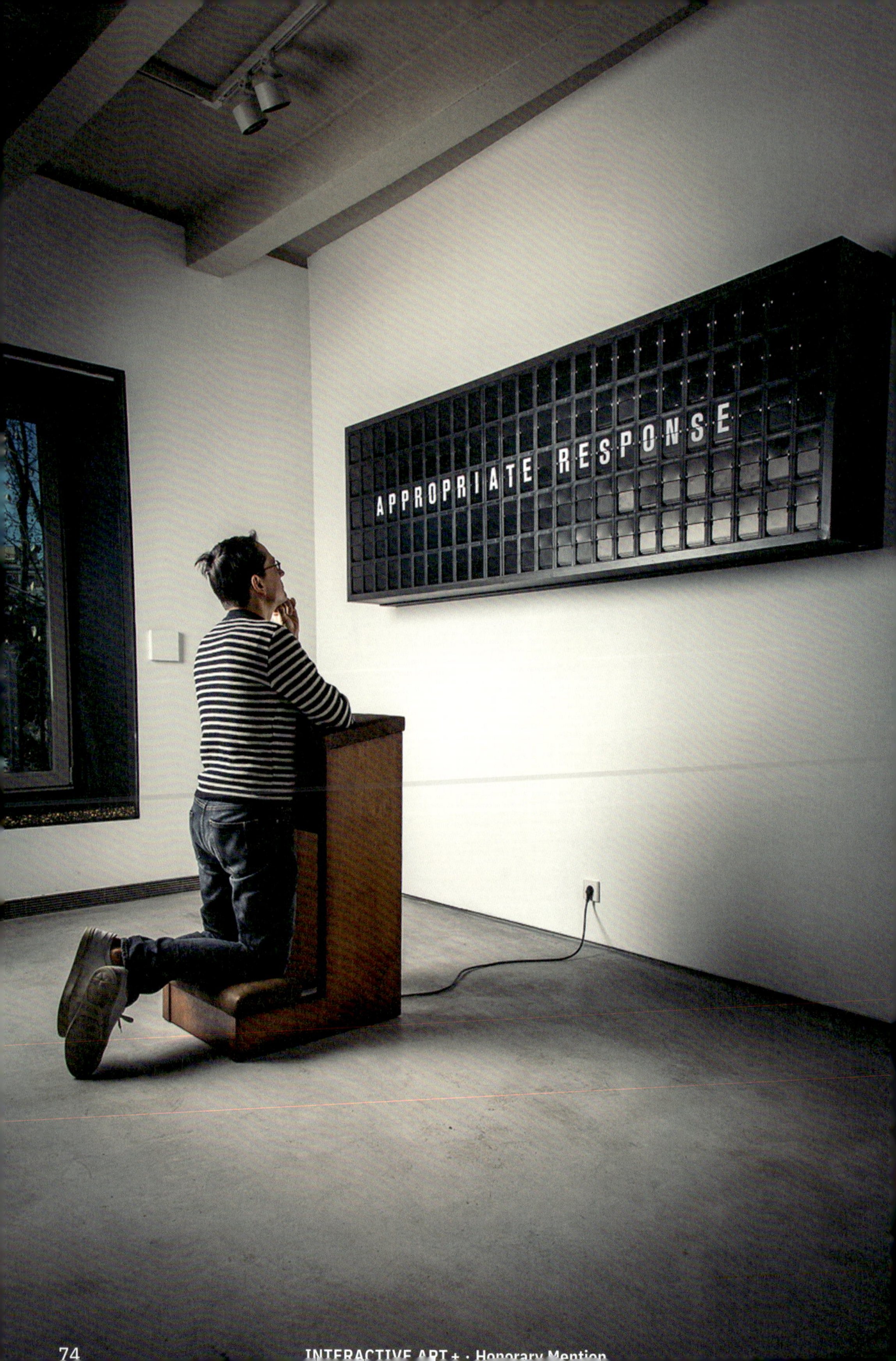

INTERACTIVE ART + · Honorary Mention

Appropriate Response

Mario Klingemann

A reflection on meaning

How much can be expressed in just 125 letters? *Appropriate Response* addresses this question. Inspired by the power of words, this interactive piece explores meaning, expectation, and relationship with artificial intelligence.

The installation features a wooden kneeler and a split flap display that shows a random selection of continuously changing letters. When a person interacts with the work by kneeling down, the installation's built-in artificial intelligence responds by presenting on the screen a short sentence that is reminiscent of an inspirational quote or aphorism. Each phrase is written by the machine's neural networks and is entirely unique; no two visitors will ever receive the same line of distilled wisdom from *Appropriate Response.*

The power of words

From religious principles to marketing slogans or self-help, pithy phrases abound as a source of inspiration and guidance. Yet with today's technology, it can be difficult to discern whether certain texts have been produced by humans or machines. Within this context, Klingemann's artwork raises pertinent questions about authorship and the significance attached to written language.

Physicality, ritual and interpretation

For *Appropriate Response,* Klingemann enhanced the GPT2 neural network with a further 60,000 quotes to create a model capable of producing short texts. These appear on a split flap display, chosen by the artist for its aesthetic appeal, distinctive sound, and connotation of waiting.

The kneeler turns interaction with *Appropriate Response* into a ritual-like experience. "We fear AI but also hope it might help us," says Klingemann. "That balance between hope and fear is related to religious experience, so I felt kneeling was very fitting." Context and expectation are also key. Viewers participate by kneeling but also by processing the text displayed on screen. *Appropriate Response* generates coherent aphorisms, but it is human viewers that furnish them with meaning.

With support from: Colección SOLO

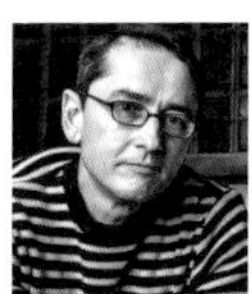

Mario Klingemann (DE) is an artist who uses algorithms and artificial intelligence to create and investigate systems. He is interested in human perception of art and creativity and is a recognized pioneer in AI art, neural networks, and machine learning. He was Artist in Residence at Google Arts and Culture, and his artworks have been shown at the MoMA and the MET New York, and Centre Pompidou Paris, among others. Klingemann received the British Library Labs Artistic Award 2016 and in 2018 won the Lumen Prize Gold Award. His installation *Memories of Passersby I* made history in March 2019 as the first autonomous AI machine to be successfully auctioned at Sotheby's.

https://onkaos.com/mario-klingemann

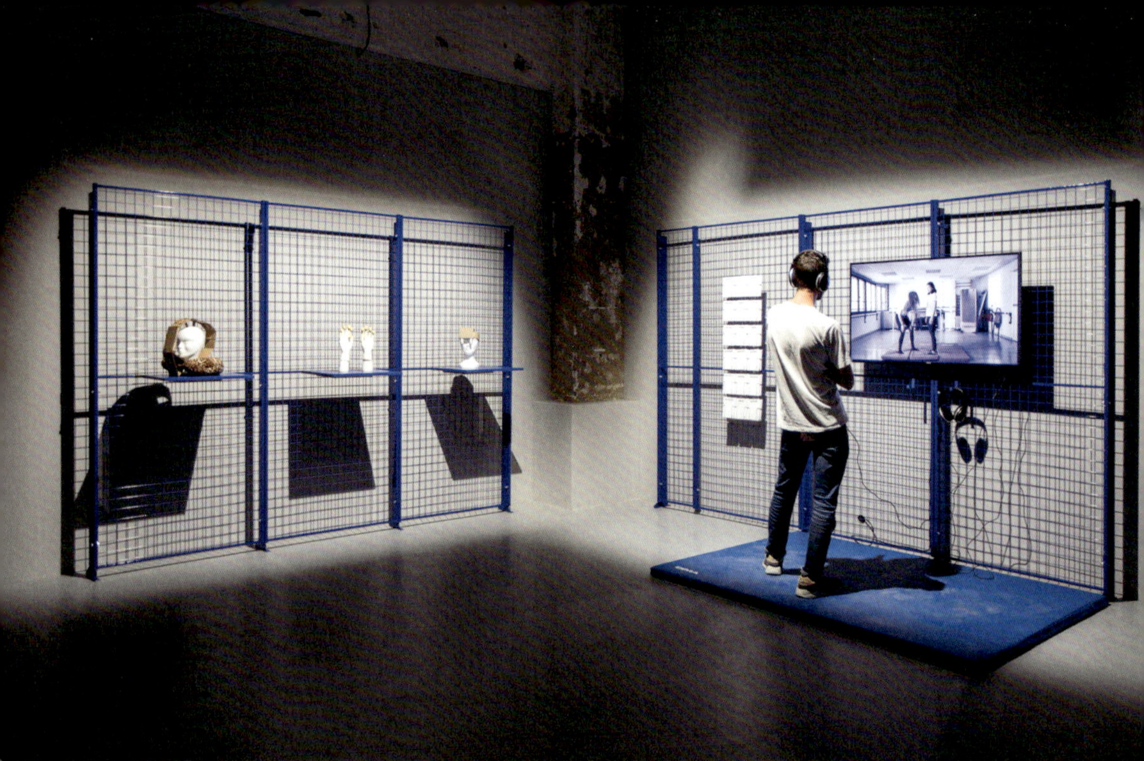

Center for Technological Pain

Dasha Ilina

Center for Technological Pain (CTP) is a mock company created by Dasha Ilina that offers DIY and Open Source solutions to health problems caused by digital technologies, such as smartphones and laptops. *CTP* offsets the negative effects of technology on the human body through physical objects, self-defense techniques against technology and yoga moves, as well as workshops. Among some of the objects proposed by the center are mechanical glasses that prevent eyestrain, a headset that liberates your hands when using your smartphone, thus eliminating neck pain, and a headband that regularly pours eyedrops in your eyes to avoid dryness.

Center for Technological Pain offers multiple practices for eliminating tech pain. The objects are tangible solutions, made to quickly prevent the pain that can be caused by technology, while genuinely solving the problems they address. Instructions on how the objects proposed by the center are built, help to ensure that anyone with the right materials at home is able to recreate the objects.

Simultaneously, workshops organized by the center allow for a guided exchange of skills and ideas, as well as a critical discussion about the negative effects of technology on the body. As a further means of investigation into the subject of addiction to technology, *CTP* proposes Self-Defense Moves Against Technology. These moves are a set of tactics of resistance against our own digital aids and are based on and adapted from real self-defense practice. For those looking for a less radical solution, *CTP* also offers Yoga for Healthy Phone Use, a routine for becoming one with your phone. This routine is at once a relaxation tool: a way to meditate and exercise while keeping up with recent updates from your friends; and a way to ridicule our obsessive media consumption by inserting our phones into one of the most solitary activities.

Special thanks to: Niklas Ayris, Amanda Lewis, Ice Baibolov, Morgan Kim, Jac Capra, Benjamin Gaulon
With support from: Simplon.co

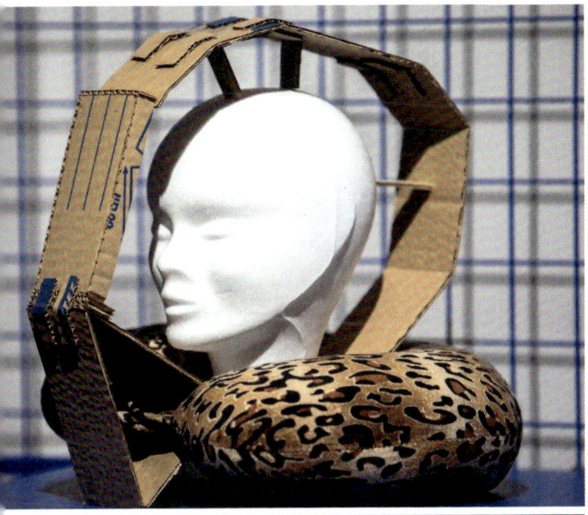

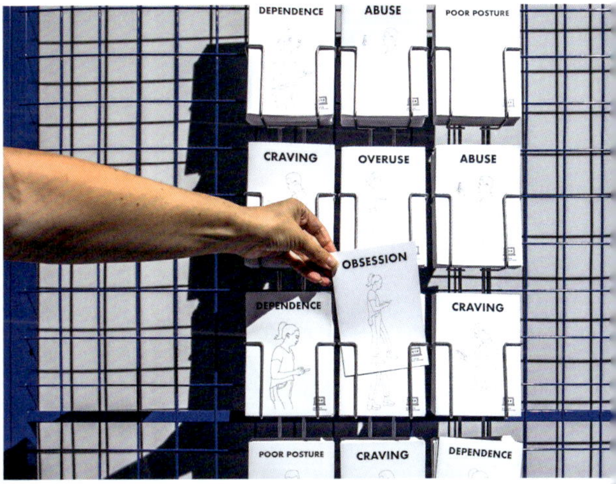

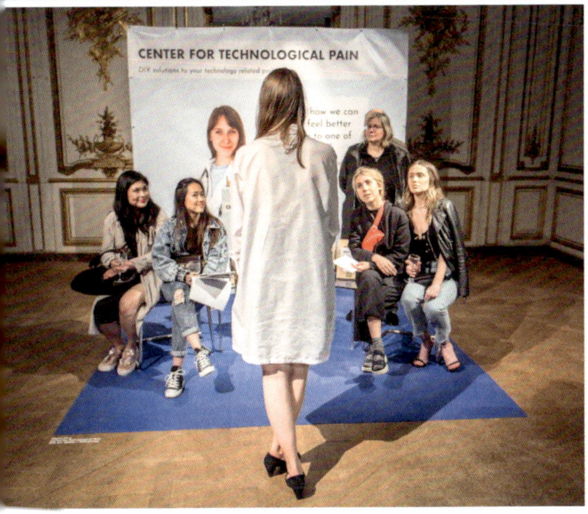

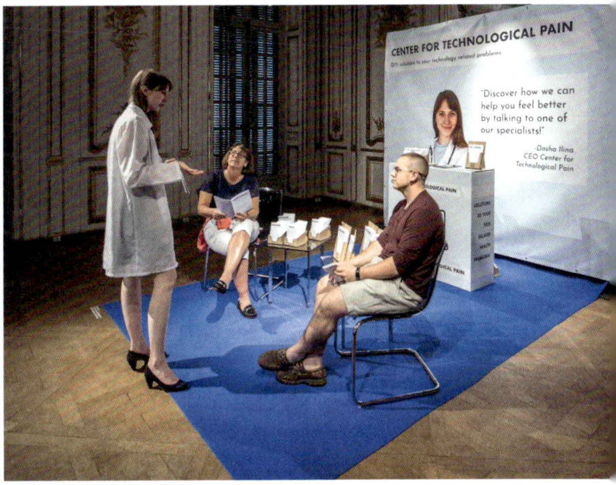

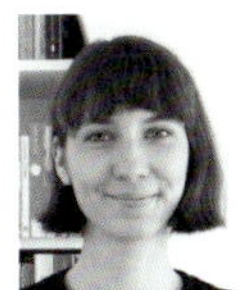

Dasha Ilina (RU) is a digital artist based in Paris. Her work explores the relationship we develop with the digital devices we use on a daily basis, specifically with regard to the human body. Ilina's work centers around the notions of care and technology, DIY practices, and low-tech solutions to examine various issues such as phone addiction, tech-related health problems, and privacy in the digital age. She is the founder of the Center for Technological Pain, a center that proposes DIY solutions for health problems caused by digital technologies. She is also the co-director of NØ SCHOOL.

http://centerfortechpain.com

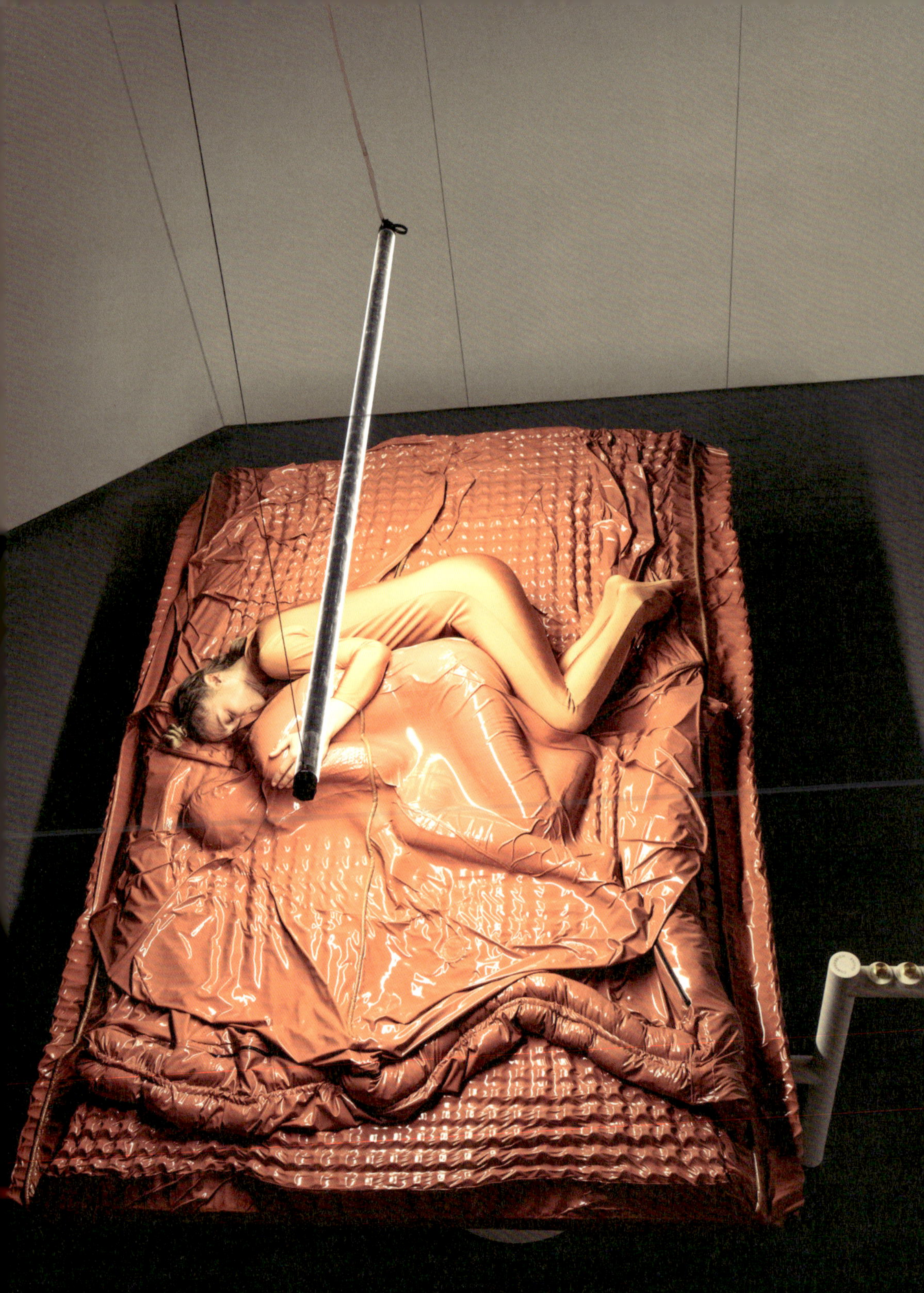

INTERACTIVE ART + · **Honorary Mention**

Compression Cradle

Lucy McRae

Compression Cradle looks like a remnant from a world we have not yet seen but might soon inhabit. One where mechanical touch may be an antidote for today's "forever connectedness," a behavior that has triggered collective anxiety. As people increasingly choose to live independently, handling devices more than human flesh, we create opportunities for technology to vie for our affections. De-evolving physical touch will change our species as we know it. We are inducing a crisis of touch—how will art, design, and business cater to society's evolving physical and emotional needs? *Compression Cradle* is a machine that affectionately squeezes the body with a sequence of aerated volumes that hold you tight, in an attempt to prepare the self for a future that lacks human touch. Through a choreography of touch sensations, this mechanism assists in altering the expression of oxytocin—the hormone released in the brain, responsible for building trust and pair bonding. This immersive artwork is a playful and mechanical antidote to a condition that will become more extreme in the future.

Based on audience feedback we have uncovered critical insight into the relationship mechanical touch has with autism. During an exhibition of the work, parents of an autistic child noticed considerable difference and calm after spending time in the *Compression Cradle.*

How could this artwork be developed into a consumer product to reduce the effects of autism?

The *Compression Cradle* is an ongoing research project investigating the human losses and gains of touch. The project's aim is to gather data at future exhibitions to form the premise for a new work and symposium that discuss research and new points of view on the future of touch, empathy, and the human condition.

With a set of deeply ingrained beliefs and ethics, all of Lucy McRae's projects, including the *Compression Cradle,* are committed to a single objective: the preservation of humanity.

Co-commission by Het Nieuwe Instituut and Museum of Applied Arts & Sciences
Artist: Lucy McRae
Creative producer: Alice Parker
Machine fabrication: Machine Histories
Custom soft goods: Anjia Jalac
Studio team: Minah Kim, Fiona Ng & Brendan Ho
Co-curators: Francien Van Westrenen, Angela Rui, Marina Otero, Keinton Butler
Photography: Scottie Cameron, Daria Scagliola
Special thanks to: Keinton Butler, Guus Beumer, Mark Van Veen, Ellen Zoete, Angela Rui, Steven Joyner & Jason Pilarski

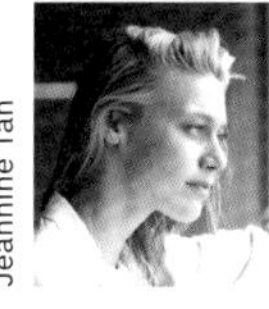

Lucy McRae (GB) is a science fiction artist, filmmaker, inventor, and body architect, who works across installation, film, photography, artificial intelligence, and edible technology. Her work speculates on the future of human existence, exploring the limits of the body, beauty, biotechnology, and the self as well as the cultural and emotional impacts science and cutting edge technology have on redesigning the body. Lucy uses art as a mechanism to signal and provoke our ideologies and ethics about who we are and where we are headed. She has exhibited internationally at museums, film festivals, institutes such as MIT, Ars Electronica, NASA, and science forums and is recognised as a Young Global Leader by the World Economic Forum.

https://www.lucymcrae.net/compression-cradle

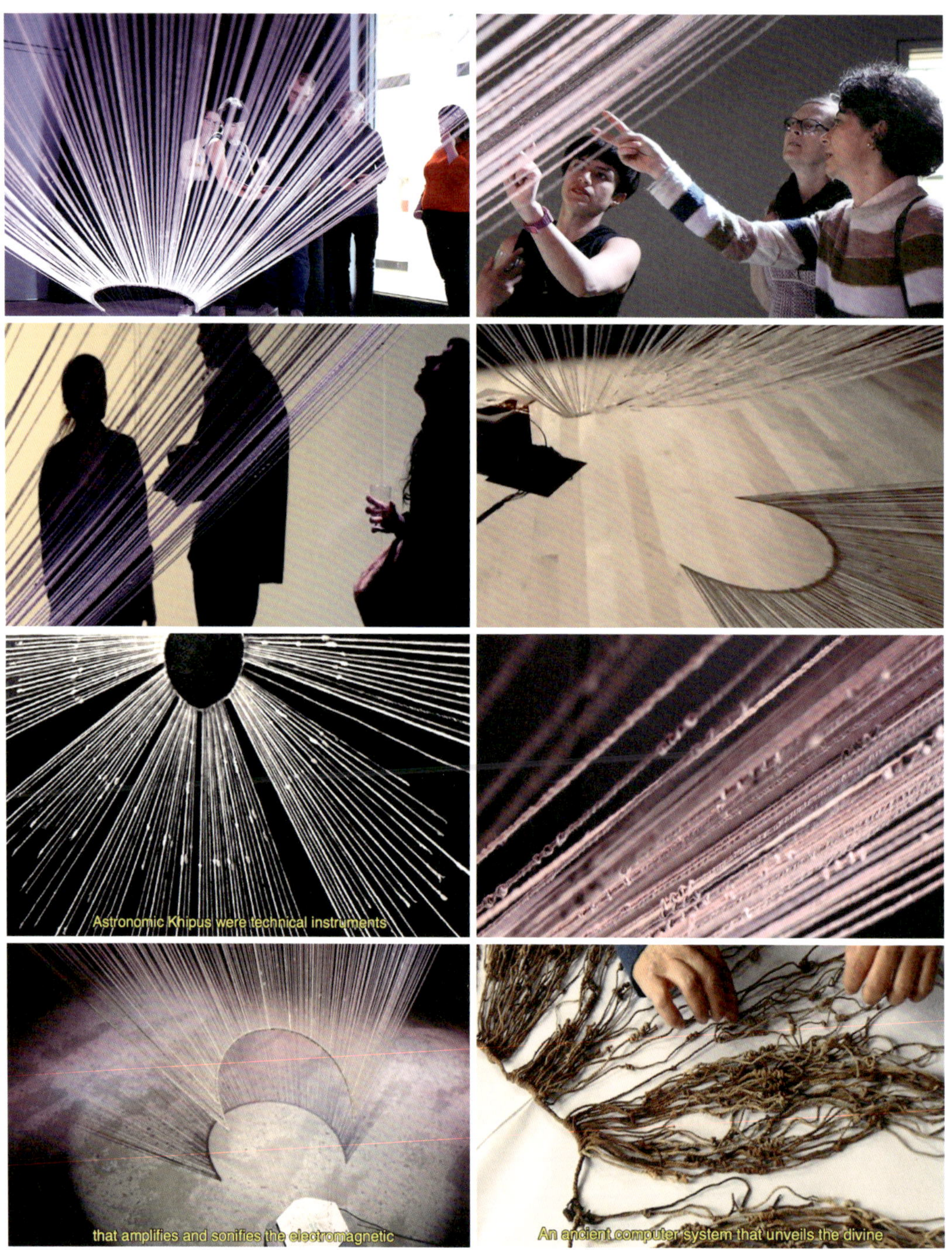

INTERACTIVE ART + · Honorary Mention

khipu / electrotextile prehispanic computer

Constanza Piña Pardo

The Inca khipu are textile prehispanic devices for recording information, made of cotton or camelid fiber strings that store data coded as knots. The khipu are considered prehispanic ecological computers. These computers were made with organic materials such as stones, wool, vegetable fibers, ceramics, seeds, and even the human body itself is part of the computer system (fingers and toes encode and the user's brain processes the information). The importance of these computers lies in the transcendental, cosmic significance and the transmitted wisdom of our native peoples.

This piece is an open-source textile computer based on the manufacture of an astronomical khipu.

The installation of this piece consists of an antenna of about 6 meters in diameter, that is composed of 180 ropes. Each of them was hand-spun from a mixture of copper wire and alpaca wool. These ropes are connected to an electronic circuit that amplifies and sonifies the electromagnetic changes present at the installation site.

This piece was done for a group of five women in an experimental creation laboratory, called "Textile Computing and Spectrum Sonification," in order to study the signs of the traditional Inca khipu and the analogies between this system of knots and the current binary coding system.

The information collected into this khipu includes a spectral classification of the main stars in the Boötes constellation that were located mid-sky (zenith) during the dates of the open laboratory. This project is a sound and arts interpretation of the technology, wisdom, and history of our ancestors, meant to express how the universe is governed by harmonious numerical proportions. What we are hearing now is thus the amplification of inaudible Space, the voices of specters visiting the void, a celestial score, the music of the spheres: the voice of silence.

Direction and concept: Constanza Piña Pardo
Realization: Melissa Aguilar, Ana Cervantes, Ana Ortiz, Daniela Sofia Main Reyes, Constanza Piña Pardo
Electronics: Corazón de Robota
Graphic and editorial design: Melissa Aguilar
Technical assistance: Alexandre Castonguay, Jaime Lobato
Video: Vero Ireta and Daniel LLermaly
Made in MedialabMX for Transitio MX (Mexico City)
Perte de Signal (Montreal).
Special thanks to Pedro Soler
With support from: Melissa Aguilar, Ana Cervantes, Ana Ortiz, Daniela Sofia Main Reyes, Constanza Piña Pardo, Vero Ireta, Daniel LLermaly, Alexandre Castonguay, and Pedro Soler

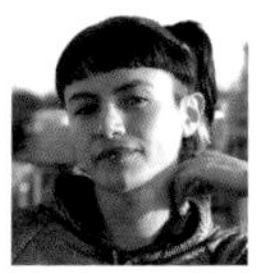
Constanza Piña Pardo (CL) is a visual artist, dancer, and researcher, focused on electronic experimentation, free technologies, and social practices. Her work reflects on the role of machines in our culture, criticizing capitalism and the techno-patriarchy system. Interested in recycling, handicrafts, and electronic wizardry, she generates her sound project *Corazón de Robota* (She-Robot Heart) with DIY synthesizers, exploring the field of audible and inaudible frequencies as physical perceptions and noise. Constanza embodies the philosophy of free culture, technofeminism, and electronic anarchy.

https://proyectokhipu.wordpress.com

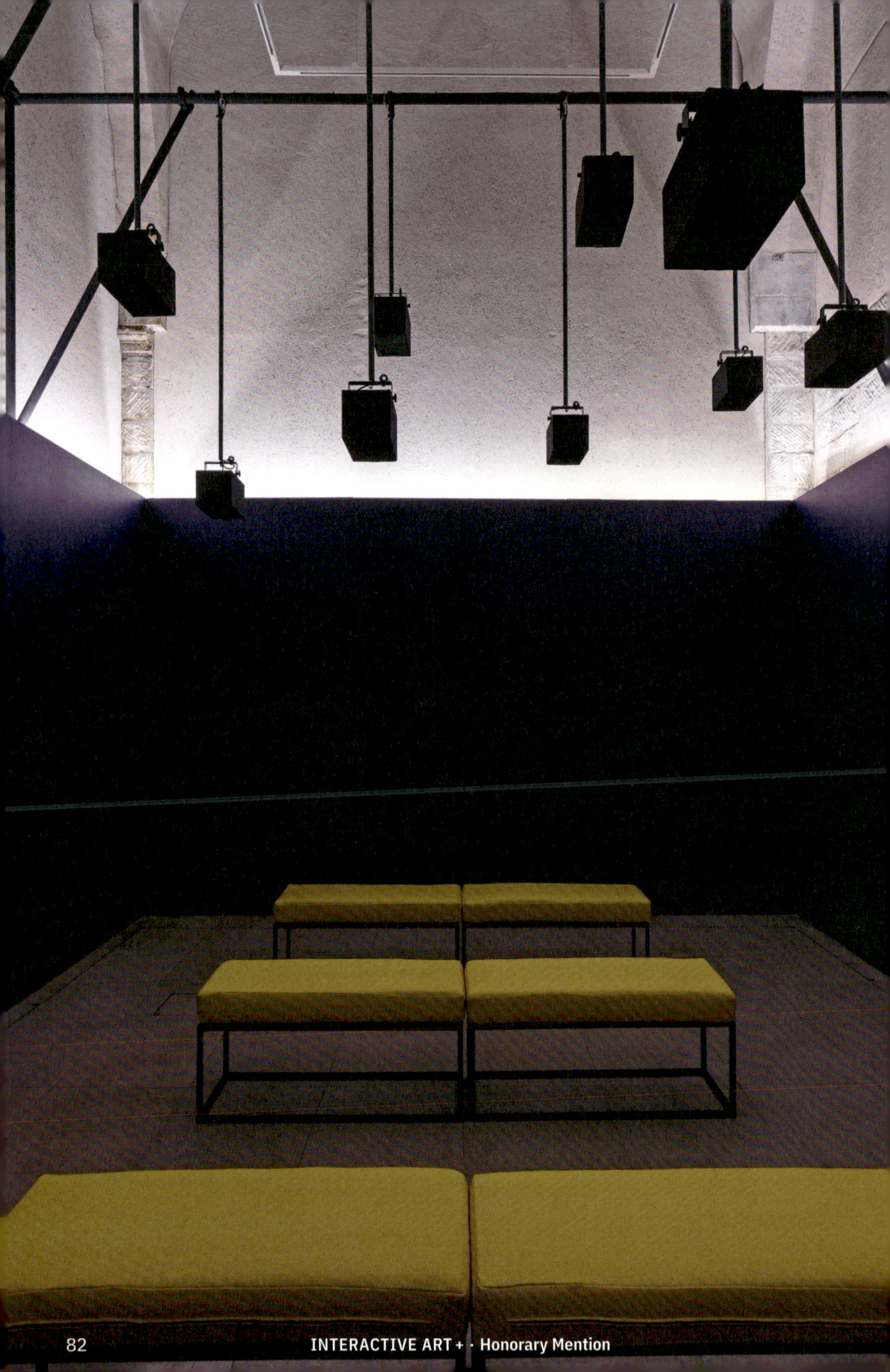

INTERACTIVE ART + · **Honorary Mention**

Machine Auguries

Alexandra Daisy Ginsberg

Before sunrise, a redstart begins his solo with a warbling call. Other birds respond, together creating the dawn chorus: a back-and-forth that peaks thirty minutes before and after the sun emerges in the spring and early summer, as birds defend their territory and call for mates. Light and sound pollution from our 24-hour urban lifestyle affects birds, who are singing earlier, louder, for longer, or at a higher pitch. But only those species that adapt survive. *Machine Auguries* questions how the city might sound with changing, homogenizing, or diminishing bird populations.

In the multi-channel sound installation, a natural dawn chorus is taken over by artificial birds, their calls generated using machine learning. Solo recordings of chiffchaffs, great tits, redstarts, robins, thrushes, and entire dawn choruses were used to train two neural networks (a Generative Adversarial Network, or GAN), pitted against each other to sing. Reflecting on how birds develop their song from each other, a call and response of real and artificial birds spatializes the evolution of a new language. Samples taken from each stage (epoch) in the GAN's training reveal the artificial birds' growing lifelikeness.

The composition follows the arc of a dawn chorus, compressed into ten minutes. The listener experiences the sound of a fictional urban parkland, entering in the dim silvery light of pre-dawn. We start with a solo from a lone "natural" redstart. In response, from across the room, we hear an artificial redstart sing back, sampled from an early epoch. A "natural" robin joins the chorus, with a call and response set up between natural and artificial birds. The chorus rises as other species enter, reaching a crescendo five minutes in. As the decline starts and the room illuminates to a warm yellow, we realize that the artificial birds, which have gained sophistication in their song, are dominating.

Machine learning: Dr. Przemek Witaszczyk (Faculty)
Sound design: Chris Timpson (Aurelia Soundworks)
Birdsong: Chris Watson, Geoff Sample, The British Library, Sara Keen, Xeno-canto
Lighting: Lucy Carter
Commissioned by Somerset House and A/D/O by MINI. With additional support from Faculty and The Adonyeva Foundation.

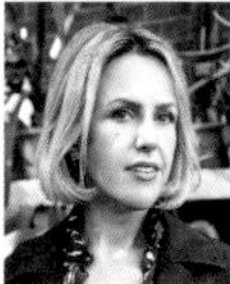

Alexandra Daisy Ginsberg (GB) is an artist examining our fraught relationships with nature and technology. Through subjects as diverse as artificial intelligence, synthetic biology, and conservation, she investigates the human impulse to "better" the world. Daisy is lead author of *Synthetic Aesthetics: Investigating Synthetic Biology's Designs on Nature* (MIT Press, 2014), and in 2017 completed *Better,* her PhD, at the Royal College of Art, interrogating how powerful dreams of "better" futures shape what we design. Daisy exhibits internationally, including at MoMA, the Museum of Contemporary Art, Tokyo, the Centre Pompidou, and the Royal Academy, and her work is in museum and private collections.

https://www.daisyginsberg.com/work/machine-auguries

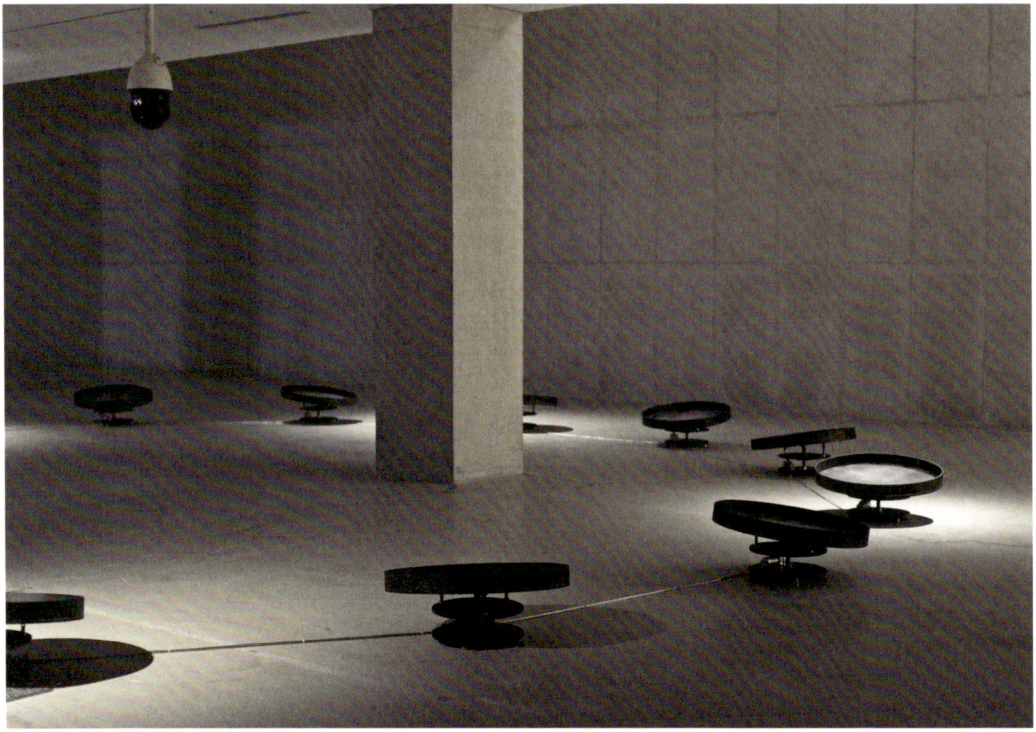

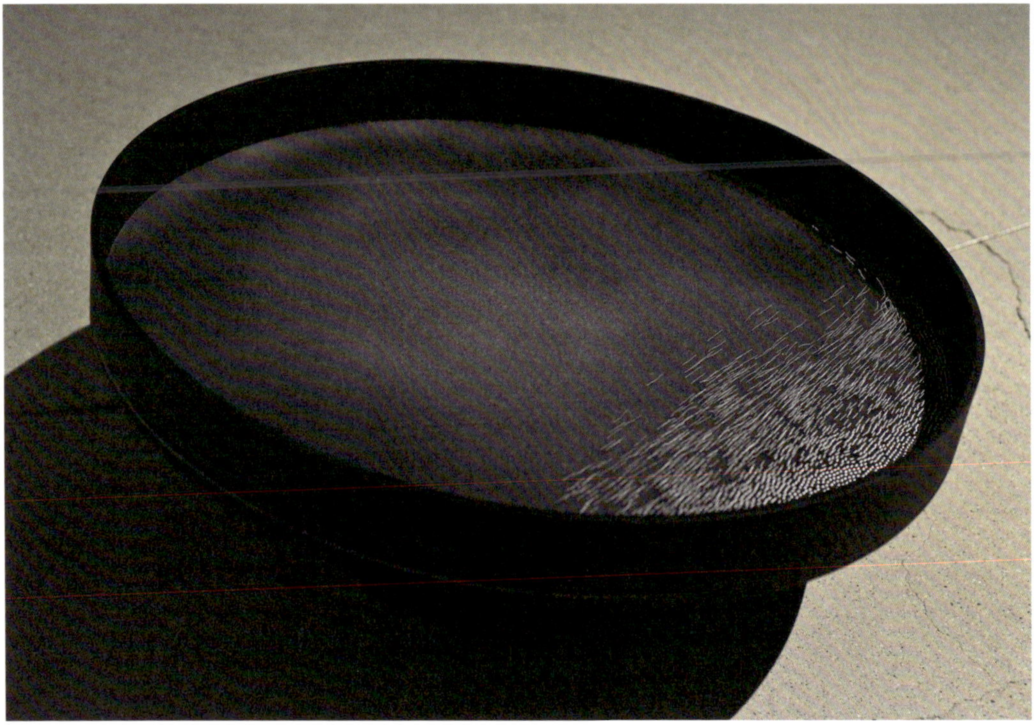

INTERACTIVE ART + · Honorary Mention

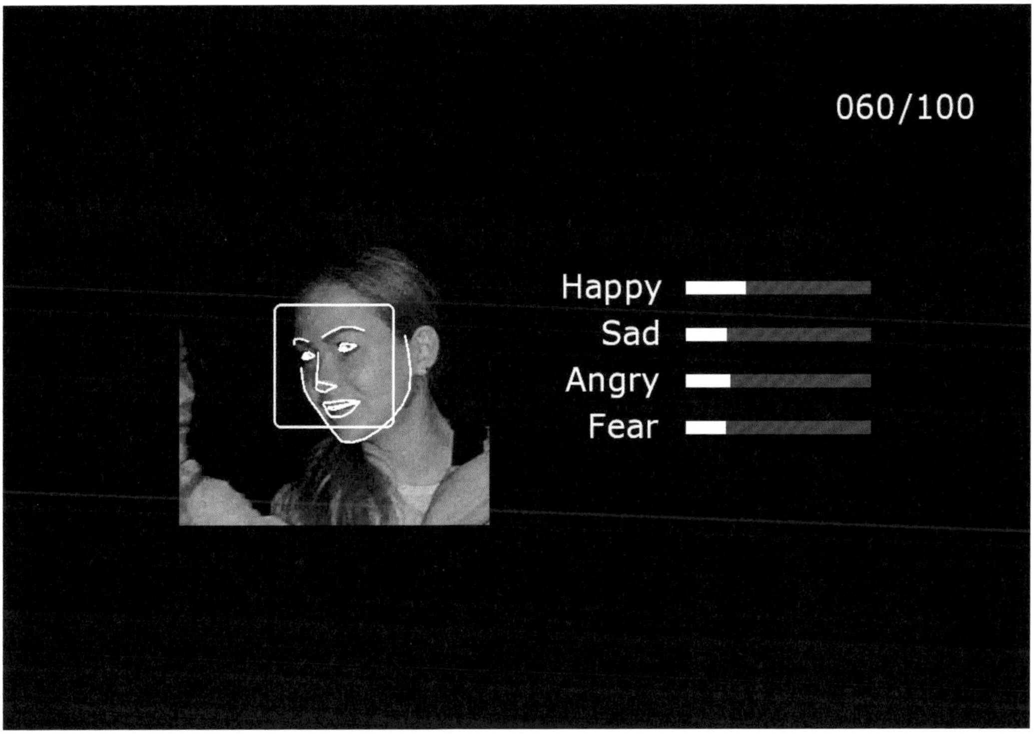

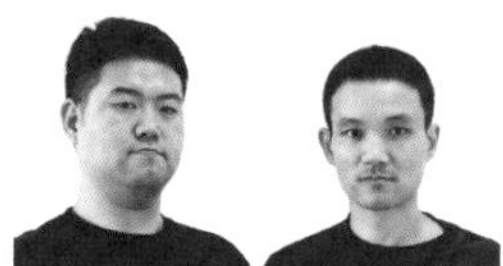

Mind

Shinseungback Kimyonghun

Mind creates a space where the minds of people come together as a sea. The rotating camera in the center of the exhibition space analyzes facial emotions of audiences, and the mechanical ocean drums on the floor generate sea sounds based on the average emotions of the latest 100 faces.

The sound of the sea constantly changes as the collective emotions of the people are updated. Small monitors on the wall show the facial emotion analysis process and the graphic simulation of the current sea.

Commissioned by The National Museum of Modern and Contemporary Art, Korea.

Shinseungback Kimyonghun (KR) is a Seoul based artistic duo consisting of computer engineer Shin Seung Back and artist Kim Yong Hun. Their collaborative practice explores technology and humanity. Their work has been exhibited internationally, including Ars Electronica, ZKM, and MMCA.

http://ssbkyh.com/works/mind

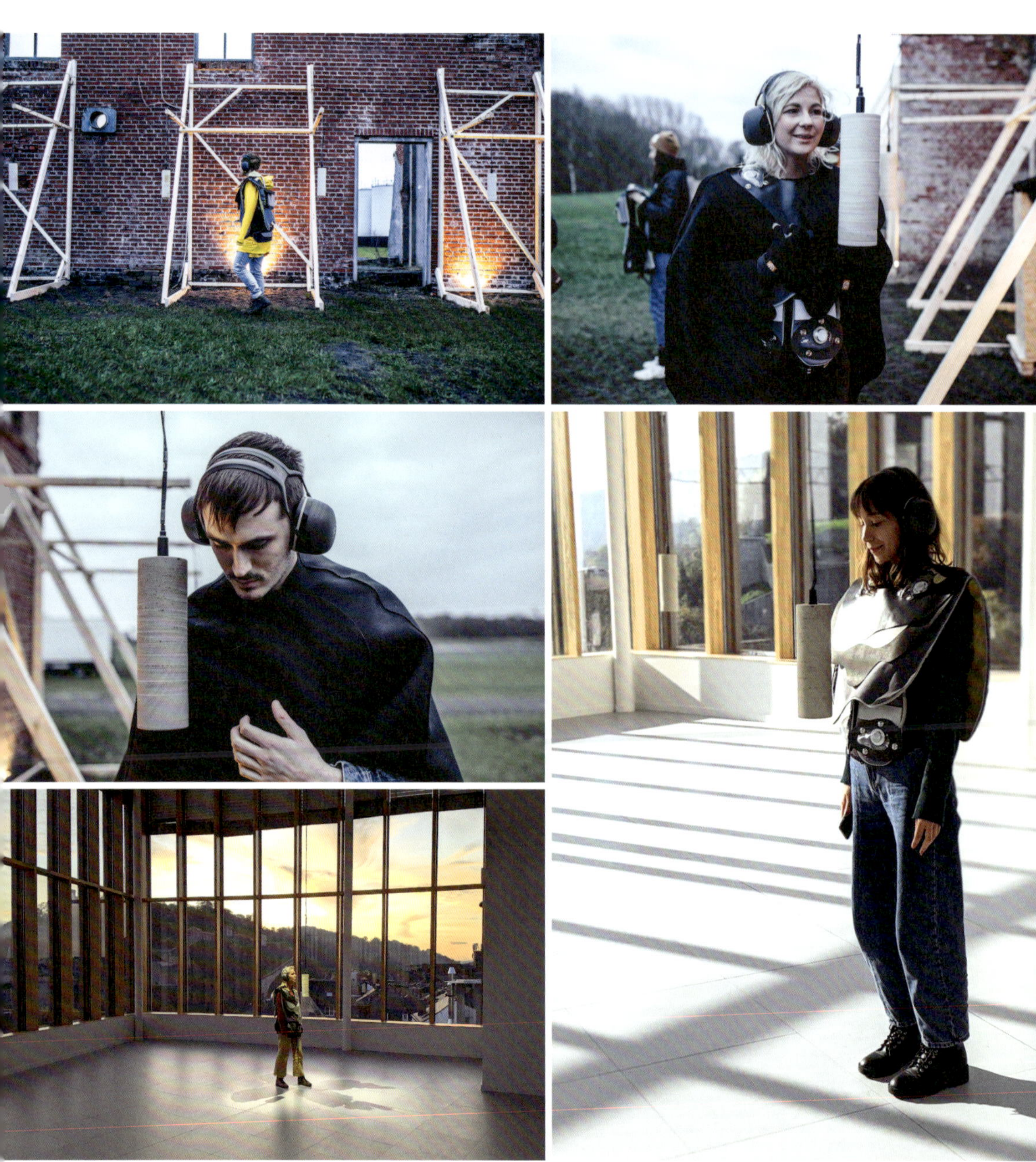

INTERACTIVE ART + · Honorary Mention

The Intimate Earthquake Archive

Sissel Marie Tonn in collaboration with Jonathan Reus

The Intimate Earthquake Archive is an ongoing research project and interactive installation dealing with the man-made earthquakes in the Dutch province of Groningen. When I started the research in 2015, I came across an overwhelming amount of data in scientific archives: a warehouse full of core samples, sand and soil tests, as well as the immense database of seismic recordings managed by the KNMI. Meanwhile, hearing the stories of people who had experienced the earthquakes, I wondered what the role of the body might be in the archiving of these events.

The installation consists of hanging sandstone core samples—each emitting one earthquake recorded in Groningen through a long-wave radio system. The public is invited to put on wearable "tactile vests" with inbuilt transducer speakers, which react to the transmitters in the installation, allowing the wearer to explore the seismic data with their body. Sound artist Jonathan Reus has created unique tactile compositions for each earthquake, which relate the movement of the vibrations played onto the body to the actual movements of the earthquakes across the land.

Thus the data collected by the KNMI is used as raw material for creating tactile sensory experiences.

The earthquake compositions range from barely perceptible to intense, and the work is thus a 'test ground' for the threshold of sensory perception, offering a kind of "deep listening" to the earth as it is being affected by our dependency on fossil fuels. The project is continuously under development, as we are working on new ways of experimenting with the available data, the socio-political context of each earthquake (e.g. which new legislation a particular event afforded) or how subsonic seismic data acts on the resonating qualities of the body (and using this in the composition). My long-term dream is to expand the installation to encompass the entire data bank of more than 1400 man-made earthquakes over the span of 30 years.

Compositions, seismic data integration: Jonathan Reus
Hardware design/Interaction: Marije Baalman, Jonathan Reus, Carsten Tonn-Petersen
With support from: Theodora Niemeijer Fund, Van Abbemuseum, TNO - Innovation for Life, KNMI, Artefact festival, Stroom Den Haag, Stimuleringsfonds NL

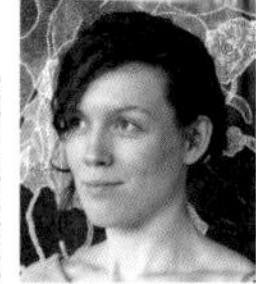

Jonathan Reus

Sissel Marie Tonn (DK) is an artist based in The Hague. In her practice she explores the complex ways in which humans are entangled with their environments. She is particularly fascinated by the threshold of our senses, and how we might be able to "tune" our bodies to subtle environmental changes through various forms of knowing. She makes wearable, sculptural, or performative "props," which challenge and question the body's preconfigured modes of perception and attention and invite the audience to engage directly with them. Together with Jonathan Reus and Flora Reznik, Sissel runs the artist initiative The Reading Room, a nomadic event series focusing on ways of reading and studying together in a non-institutional setting.

https://jonathanreus.com/portfolio/the-intimate-earthquake-archive

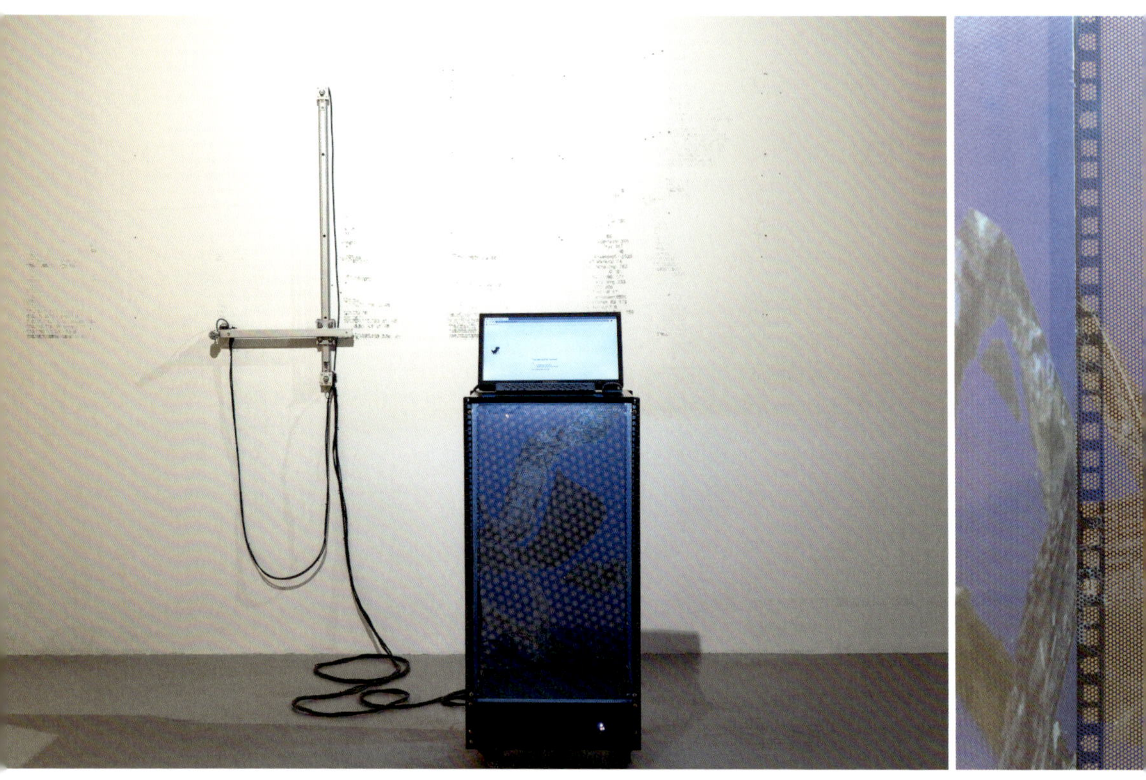

The Net Wanderer—A Tour of Suspended Handshakes
Guo Cheng

The Net Wanderer is a research project that explores the connection between the critical network gateways in China and the infrastructure running these gateways. Guo Cheng uses computer network diagnostic tools that track the IP addresses of these nodes as well as specific geographic locations. In this way, the artist creates a map of firewall proxies that block Chinese users from roaming the Internet freely.

Main tasks of the Chinese firewall are to slow down and censor cross border Internet traffic and to block some foreign websites. The project investigates how borders have been constructed to protect cyber-sovereignty, and how it can be observed. By mapping the giant wall and physically visiting some of those geolocations, Guo Cheng seeks to expose the entanglement of technology, culture, and ideology behind China's Internet infrastructure.

The utopian idea of the Internet was that of a universal space for all, unbound by borders. In reality, networks are intertwined with real-world territoriality, as Guo Cheng shows by taking on the role of a tourist visiting the elusive sites hosting the network infrastructures of the Great Firewall of China (GFW). The installation lets users become virtual firewall tourists, entering websites of choice that—if blocked by the GFW—take them to a game that allows them to submit their usernames. A custom-made wall-mounted machine

     INTERACTIVE ART + · Honorary Mention

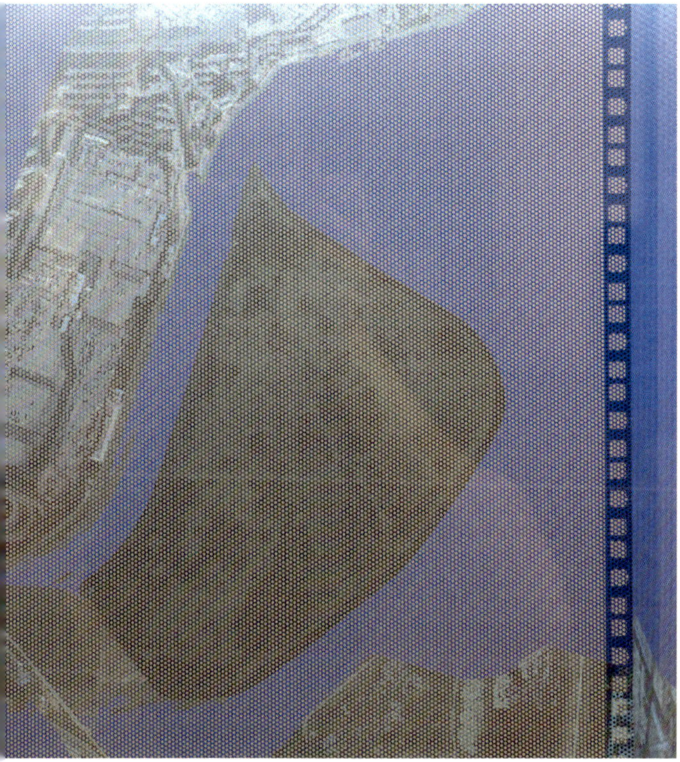

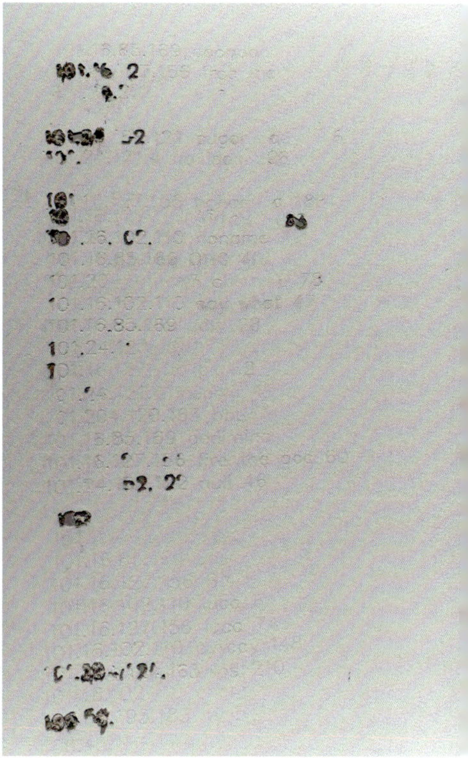

then engraves the names and scores along with the IP address of a GFW node, while footage on the screen shows Guo Cheng using geolocation data to track the physical location of the firewall's network gateway.

The work was originally commissioned within the Digital Earth fellowship program.

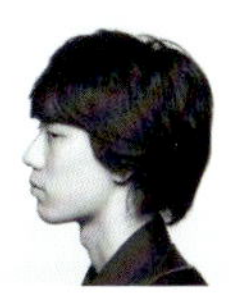 **Guo Cheng** (CN) is an artist currently based in Shanghai. He graduated from MA Design Products at Royal College of Art (London) and obtained his BE in Industrial Design at Tongji University (Shanghai). His practice mainly focuses on exploring the interrelation between mainstream/emerging technologies and individuals in the context of culture and social life. His recent solo show, *Down to Earth,* took place at Canton Gallery, Guanshou (2019). Group exhibitions include *The Eternal Network* (Transmediale 2020, HKW, Berlin), *Machines Are Not Alone: A Machinic Trilogy* (Chronus Art Center, Shanghai, 2018), and *The Ecstasy of Time* (HE Xiangning Art Museum, Shenzhen, 2017). He was awarded the Digital Earth fellowship (2018) and the Special Jury Prize of Huayu Youth Award (Sanya, 2018) and was the winner of BAD Award (The Hague, 2017).

http://www.guo-cheng.net/index.php/projects/the-net-wanderer

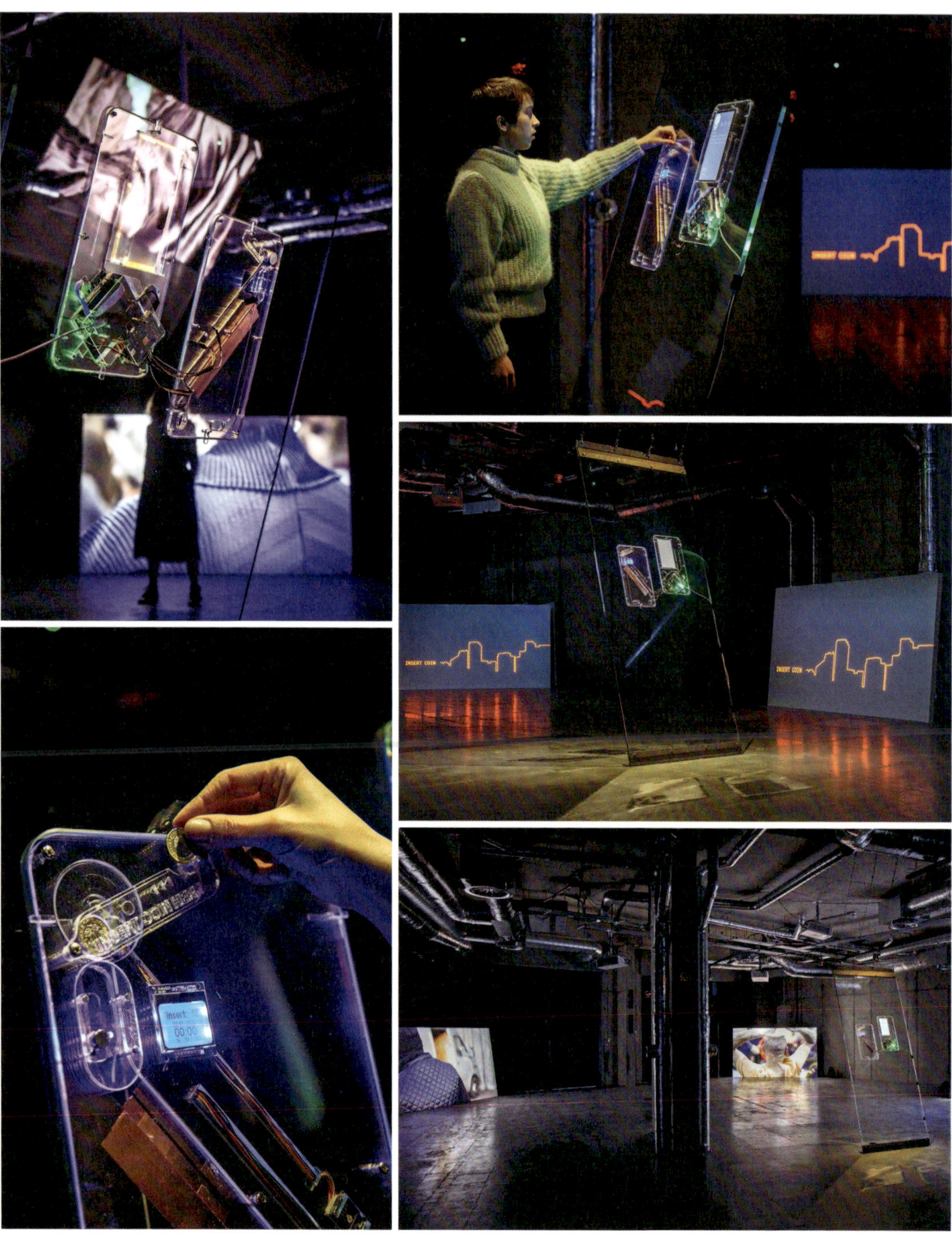

INTERACTIVE ART + · Honorary Mention

Trickle Down, A New Vertical Sovereignty

Helen Knowles

Trickle Down, A New Vertical Sovereignty is a tokenized four-screen video installation and generative soundscape attached to the blockchain, which explores value systems and wealth disparity. The artwork is composed of auction scenes, performances, and choral interludes by different communities such as prisoners, blockchain technology employees, market sellers, and Sotheby's auction bidders. Knowles documented a series of auctions which reflect the breadth of wealth and financial power individuals in different communities have. These include prisoners at HMP Altcourse, Liverpool, Ethereal Summit attendees, employees at blockchain company ConsenSys in NY, Mancunians at Openshaw market, Manchester, and the Russian community in central London buying their cultural artefacts at Sotheby's auction house. Knowles captured images of people from these communities bidding, through documenting their attire rather than identities, and made audio recordings of them singing and the sounds of their environments—ultimately revealing the texture of these communities. The work draws on technological and financial power structures that traditionally scaffold the disparity between a wealthy elite and everyday working people but looks to re-imagine our vertically stacked digital ecosystem to horizontally distribute wealth.

The installation commences when a visitor drops a coin into a machine designed to expose the mechanisms needed to convert fiat currency into cryptocurrency. Alongside the machine, Knowles has created a film and soundscape triggered by sensors responding to visitors locations in the installation. Each and every member of the *Trickle Down* community who has helped the work come to fruition receives a share of the ETH via a smart contract on the blockchain every time the work is played. The sensors, software, and electronic components are all exposed, along with a read-out of the blockchain ledger.

Photography, film and sound editing: Helen Knowles
Recordings: Helen Knowles, Denis Jones, Damien Mahoney and Arone Dyers
Machine design: Daniel Dressel
Composition, coding and sound diffusion design: Pablo Galaz Salamanca
Interaction design: Lewis Sykes
Smart contract: BlockRocket
Legal oversight: Howard Kennedy LLP
Produced by FutureEverything. Supported using public funding from Arts Council England with additional support from The Whitworth, The University of Manchester, arebyte Gallery, The University of Salford, Ethereal Summit, ConsenSys, and FACT.

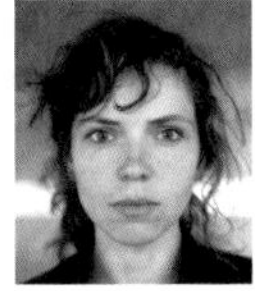

Helen Knowles (GB) (b.1975) is an artist and curator of the Birth Rites Collection. She studied at Glasgow School of Art and Goldsmiths University. She has exhibited at arebyte Gallery, London, The Mori Art Museum, Tokyo, NEMO festival, 104 Paris, Hannover Kunstverein, ZKM Karlsruhe, and Zabludowicz Collection, London. Her work is held in collections including The Whitworth Art Gallery, Tate Library and Archive, The National Art Library. Residencies include Trelex Residency, Future Everything, HMP Altcourse, FACT, Liverpool, Moscow ICA, Santa Fe Arts Institute, and Jodrell Bank Science Centre and Arboretum.

http://www.helenknowles.com/index.php/work/trickle_down

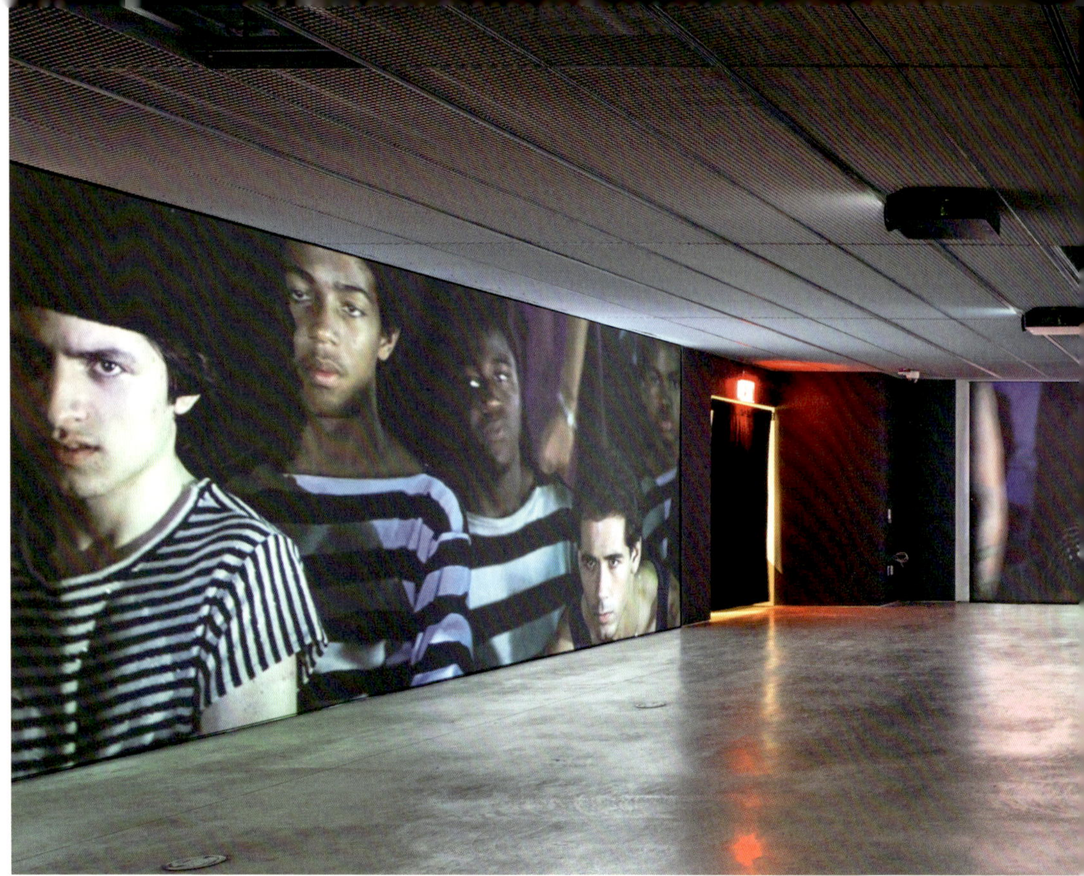

Warriors

James Coupe

Warriors uses three excerpts from Walter Hill's 1979 cult movie *The Warriors,* a film which features over one hundred rival gangs, each with distinct demographic, stylistic, and sexual preferences, which they communicate through linguistic, sartorial, behavioral, and visual signifiers. The installation uses these gangs as templates to explore issues of racial, gender, and class division. iPads in the gallery use imageNet and other AI classifiers to profile visitors' faces, based on demographic, economic, and occupational markers. A customized version of the notorious deepfakes algorithm is then used to dynamically organize visitors into gangs, based on common markers, and then swap their faces into the film, in place of the original gangs, at a variety of speeds and resolutions. Due to its durational and interactive composition, the work evolves in relation to the profiles of its viewers. Installed at ICP in New York's Lower East Side, the new gangs generated by the work reflect patterns of immigration, gentrification, and demographic shifts in a neighborhood that exemplifies the historical image of the United States as a "nation of immigrants." Visitors find themselves algorithmically segregated, an experience that is "participatory" yet not "democratic," since it forecloses any sense of control over how one's profile is instrumentalized.

The installation has three parts: a large three-channel crowd scene in which Cyrus, one of the gang leaders, makes a Marxist-inflected demand for class solidarity and revolution against the cor-

     INTERACTIVE ART + · Honorary Mention

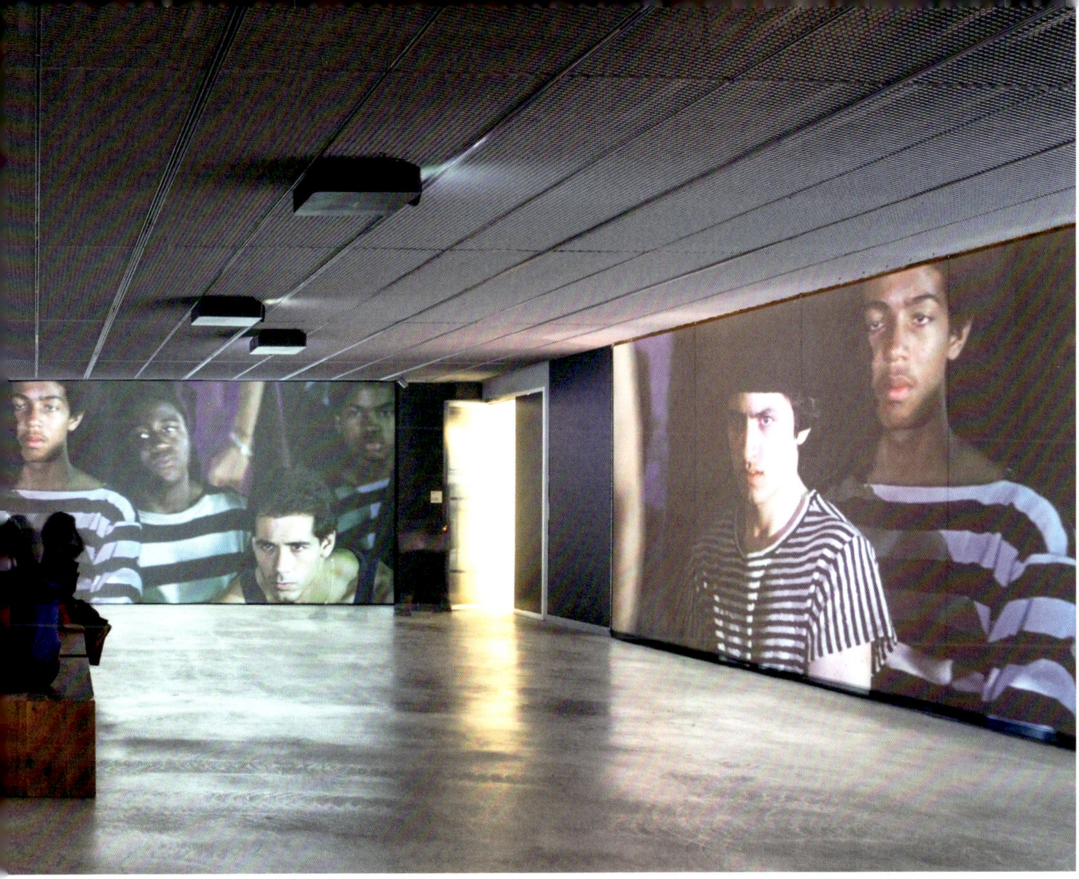

rupt city police force, before being assassinated by a white, alt-right gang; a five-channel encounter between the all-male Warriors gang, and an all-female gang, the Lizzies, becomes a gender-fluid deepfake interchange of aggressors and victims; and a two-channel face-off between the Warriors and an even larger rival "gang" that dominates the city: the wealthy, putting the focus on class antagonism.

Commissioned by and exhibited at International Center of Photography, New York City,
January 23 – May 17, 2020
With thanks to the Center for Digital Art and Experimental Media (DXARTS), University of Washington. Software development by Jacob Fennell, Forrest Fabian Jesse, and Yuying Hung.
With support from: International Center of Photography (ICP), Center for Digital Art and Experimental Media (DXARTS)

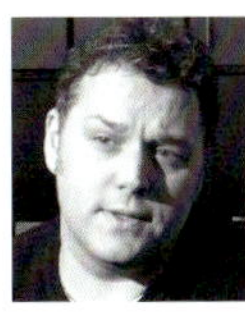

James Coupe (GB/US) is a Seattle-based artist who works with a broad range of platforms, including real-time public surveillance systems, live social media content, and Amazon's Mechanical Turk, a global workforce of micro-laborers. Reflecting on the impact of Big Data, immaterial labor, and AI, Coupe's works explore the aesthetic value of searches and queries, automation, the use of algorithmic narratives, surplus information, and human affect. He has been exhibited at venues including ICP, ZKM, FACT, Prix Ars Electronica, and Toronto International Film Festival/Museum of Contemporary Canadian Art.

http://jamescoupe.com

PRIX
ARS ELECTRONICA

DIGITAL COMMUNITIES

Community at a Time of Crisis

Thomas Gegenhuber, Chiaki Hayashi, Dietmar Offenhuber,
Irini Papadimitriou, Farah Salka

Community is about shared experience, even when the defining experience is one of separation. Coming together online as a jury from multiple continents and overcoming inhospitable time zone differences, the question of what makes a meaningful connection is no longer an academic one. The global experience of the lockdown during the coronavirus crisis necessarily affected our perspective on the submitted projects, even though the vast majority were created and submitted before the onset of the pandemic.

In this situation—beyond the usual discussion of novel ideas, formats, and causes worthy of support—we found ourselves coming back to appreciating the many different ways in which the submitted projects created meaningful experiences by sharing presence, purpose, and values. As Jean-Luc Nancy puts it, "meaning is itself the sharing of Being."[1]

As stated on the Ars Electronica website, the Digital Communities category focuses on projects which "deliver social benefits, create and support communities, and foster an open and inclusive civil society." The submitted projects address a broad range of purposes that reflect the big topics of our time beyond the pandemic: organizing collective action to address inequality, document and combat violence, explore new modes of learning, defend transparency and free speech, confront global warming and ecological crises. But many projects were meaningful not through their problem-solving ambitions, but through their humor, playful relief, and the imagination of possible futures.

Notably, the question of technology and its various roles in fostering communities did not come up much during the jury discussions. Most of the submitted projects did not emphasize this point either, as digital media has become an everyday part of life. Projects that focused on technologies often addressed their embedded politics—the regimes of algorithmic governance, the platform economy and its social rifts, or the invisible power structures of surveillance capitalism. In many cases, the conspicuous absence of technology in a project was a political statement about technology in itself.

Turning to our selection process then, we felt it was important to consider actions and impact, but also reflect on what and who drives the communities behind these projects, how they position themselves, how they value or invest in their activities and goals, but also their impact, not necessarily at a global level, but the significance of their role even at a smaller, local level. What is the meaning of a digital community in challenging times? how can it relate to current events or issues? and what actions can it inspire? To an equally significant degree, and with a large range of projects submitted from across the globe, the jury deemed it crucial to present initiatives, collaborations or collective projects from culturally diverse groups and from diverse geographical areas.

Community can be a force of social change and the submitted projects here—often initiated by art and/or activist groups or communities—not only address a whole range of social, humanitarian, political, environmental, and cultural issues, but also inspire collective action and change, helping us see the world through a different lens and understand the importance and power of public participation, collaboration, human connection, and shared vision. It can enable the imagination and potential of different society models, as well as economic and social systems based on solidarity and equality.

The artistic, creative, and interdisciplinary approach that we found present in many of the projects has been quite important too. Art can have a transformative role for our society, creating powerful ways for people to engage with challenging, dramatic, but also overwhelming ideas and issues. At the same time, and as we often encountered during the jury process, art can inspire and enable participation, open conversation, and critical thinking. It can create safe and fair spaces for all to come together, explore, and respond to important ideas. At times of disruption and suffering, art can inspire, empower, and enable systems of repair and care that could eventually also help build more open, democratic, and ethical systems, and a more humane and caring world.

Golden Nica

Be Water by Hong Kongers
Dedicated to the Hong Kong protesters
by Eric Siu & Joel Kwong

This year, the Golden Nica went for the first time to an anonymous group: the citizens of Hong Kong who organized the pro-democracy protests of 2019. Their decentralized, leaderless, and technologically sophisticated organization continues the line of recent protest movements, from the Arab Spring to the Spanish anti-austerity movement, from anonymous to Occupy Wall Street. Through the exchange of knowledge, tactics, and tools, each collective has learned from past experiences and documented its lessons for the future. The modes of collective action in Hong Kong are, in many ways, exemplary for the notion of a digital community, but with important qualifications. The demonstrators did not organize around a particular technology but used digital media as one of many means to organize, communicate, document, and evade surveillance. The title of the submission refers to Bruce Lee's famous maxim—"to be shapeless, formless and able to adapt to any situation," as the submitters note. This shape-shifting tactic holds a vital insight for digital communities: the socio-technical infrastructures are ephemeral and interchangeable; the only constant elements are human relationships and a shared purpose.

Awards of Distinction

Algorithmic Justice League (AJL)
https://www.ajlunited.org

Algorithms have become essential elements in our everyday life, being deployed in almost every aspect of our society; from online searches, navigation, and recommendations to smart devices, bots, but also in banking, speech/facial recognition, health, policing and so on. As more of these systems are being embraced and widely used though, the more important it is that we address their social implications. In a world where inequality, racism, discrimination, and unfairness are often present, we can't ignore the fact that the systems we design can be homogenous and not neutral, and therefore algorithms can be biased and discriminatory.

The *Algorithmic Justice League* (AJL) stood out in this year's selection as an organization that carries out urgent research and action in this area, investigating algorithmic bias, injustice, and the non-neutrality of Artificial Intelligence systems. But more importantly, it goes a step further by translating its findings into actions, principles, and recommendations for building awareness, educating people, and advocating for alternative infrastructures and moral frameworks that we should be applying in order to create a more equitable AI.

Habaq Movement
www.facebook.com/habaqmovement

Habaq Movement wins our vote through its aligned combo of politics and action, all geared towards survival alternatives for local communities. They are an agricultural reclamation cooperative that is run by militants from the north of Lebanon and that is all about getting back to one's land by having the people revitalize the agricultural sector. The young people behind this understand the agricultural sector has been abandoned by the state for far too long and imagine a different state/society model and a very different new economic and social system, all about interaction and sharing. The people of Habaq believe in the right to food, taking a food sovereignty approach to its activities, in support of local markets, building an exchange network between farmers with the aim of freeing them from the dominance of seed production and distribution companies, promoting an economy based on solidarity and participation.

Honorary Mentions

Code of Conscience
www.codeofconscience.org

Code of Conscience is a discursive technology that allows producers of agricultural and construction machinery to commit to the goal of fighting deforestation and protecting indigenous land. Developed in partnership with Brazilian indigenous groups, the *geo-fencing* technology is designed to stop the vehicles when they are steered into protected areas and habitats. The jury did not read this project as a technological solution to a political and economic problem, but as an important commitment by commercial manufacturers to accept responsibility for how their products are used. As Langdon Winner notes, technologies are ways of building order in the world, and therefore allow for different possibilities of re-imagining this order.[2]

Ghana ThinkTank is Developing the First World · www.ghanathinktank.org

Ghana ThinkTank flips the assumptions and stereotypes behind the idea of international development on its head. The collective gathers "experts" in the "third world" to solve "first-world problems" in a series of international workshops. Beyond the ironic reversal and critique of the paternalistic reality of international development that often merely preserves existing power relationships, the jury was impressed by the throughout practical, innovative, and inspiring outcomes of the workshops. From a Moroccan team developing affordable housing and civic infrastructure for Detroit to a Sudanese team mediating between African asylum seekers and local Israelis, *Ghana Think-Tank* presents a humane and empathic vision for international collaboration beyond design-thinking workshops and bureaucratic constraints.

Indigemoji · www.indigemoji.com.au

Indigemoji is an ambitious idea and at the same time an important and timely project, since it raises much needed questions about digital colonialism and the lack of diversity in technology and online spaces. At a time of increasing need for people to get access to the web, having diverse voices, languages, and perspectives is an important requirement in order to have online spaces that are safe and accessible to as many people as possible. And language is important for building human connections online, rather than building virtual monocultures. Empowering Indigenous communities to shape the web, *Indigemogi* has created a platform enabling hundreds of people to co-design emoji "stickers" that represent life, culture, and language in Arrernte Country in Central Australia. Emojis have names in Arrernte, the critically endangered traditional language of Mparntwe/Alice Springs, but also represent endangered or extinct species promoting and preserving their memory. Having already achieved a great outcome, *Indigemoji* is an important project for addressing the absence of diverse cultures and

languages online, exploring ideas of power and control, and making a case for digital inclusion and then of widening access to technology.

Listening at Pungwe
https://listeningatpungwe.wordpress.com

A sonic cartography and alternative listening and un-listening project, *Listening at Pungwe* enables critical engagement through performative installations, recordings, and radio performances, challenging ideas about archives and colonial praxis. A Shona term for "political vigil," Pungwe here alludes to public liberatory and spiritual acts of challenging the ways one sees, thinks, or hears the surrounding world in the context of power and powerlessness, mediated through sound. Through collective action, *Listening to Pungwe* invites us to deconstruct and rethink colonial archival practices and provenance, considering alternative practices, ideas, and methodologies of knowledge towards the restoration of the archive.

Participedia · https://participedia.net

How can we innovate our democratic institutions and create more sustainable communities? One answer to this question calls for governments to include citizens in decision-making beyond the act of voting every few years. But top-down bureaucracies meeting bottom-up citizen engagement can cause frictions. Against this backdrop, it would be great to have a publicly available archive at our disposal documenting various examples of public participation so that actors starting such initiatives can get useful inspiration and learn from someone else's experiences. *Participedia* does exactly that. The jury honors this initiative collecting cases dedicated to public participation and democratic innovation from around the globe.

PULANG PERGI · https://play.google.com/ store/apps/details?id=com.pulang.pergi
PULANG PERGI is an online platform merging communication and education and focusing on supporting future migrants, working migrants, and ex-migrants from Indonesia. The jury particularly admires the concepts adhered to by this platform, namely knowledge sharing by means of a bottom-up approach, working on various projects with migrants on different levels of the migration cycle, and having the affected community be at the core of active engagement as opposed to passive participants. The value of this project is that its wealth lies in its reliance on knowledge sharing from the migrant workers themselves, from their daily lived labor experiences, and we hope more projects follow this track.

School of Machines, Making & Make-Believe
http://schoolofma.org
Tech is still a male-dominated field. This is further fueled by a masculine Silicon Valley model of doing digital entrepreneurship. Clearly, we need to grow tech ecosystems favoring diversity and equal opportunities. Indeed, there are many initiatives, ranging from top-down public programs to encourage women to engage with STEM subjects to a bottom-up movement, such as female coding communities creating a social learning environment attracting women. The jury sees *The School of Machines, Making & Make-Believe* as a worthy representative of this bottom-up movement seeking to make technology more diverse—particularly by embracing an artistic approach in the exploration of technologies. This Honorary Mention also serves the purpose to call for policy makers and the private sector to support various initiatives of this bottom-up movement and aid them in scaling-up.

Smart Coop · http://www.smart.coop
Freelancers are a new normal in today's knowledge economy. However, the institutional infrastructure (e.g. welfare systems) are still tailored around "regular" employment and put solo-entrepreneurs at a disadvantage. *Smart Coop* seeks to offer freelancers to maintain their freedom and autonomy while also offering protection within a collective. Originating in Belgium in 1998, the network has expanded in 9 countries across Europe with more than 100,000 members. *Smart Coop* members, who include freelance creative and cultural workers, get access to secure simplified invoicing tools and various other services that allow them access to social security benefits as regular employees. The jury thought this was a great example of support network and space addressing needs that freelancers and cultural workers have. While the coronavirus pandemic is affecting the world, projects such as *Smart Coop* are needed even more.

STEAM physical education program
Takashi Terada
The *STEAM physical education program* reminds us that using a combination of triggering curiosity through playfulness and providing the means to experiment with 3D printing can have a huge impact. While many such projects take place in major cities, the STEAM project takes place in the countryside. A village with a small population of 5,000, which is further decreasing every year. The artist aimed to teach 3D modeling and 3D printing to elementary school students by using flying discs, helping the young people to reconnect with the real world and active play through creativity and making. By enabling the students to learn and play with 3D modeling, this project gave them confidence and something to be proud of. The jury

was touched by the children's genuine response and joy, reminding all how important learning through play can be.

The *Syrian Archive* is a most important and inspiring form of attaining justice to the ongoing Syrian people's struggle for rights, liberty, and freedom. They work on archiving content around the Syrian revolution and conflict methodically before it is removed from the online platforms it was originally found on, which is a pattern Syrians are faced with all the time: the need to constantly find means to not only survive the systematic layers of violence and attacks, but to also bear the burden of finding means of proving these horrors and atrocities happened in the first place to a questioning world with a short attention span. The work of the *Syrian Archive* is a race against time and is essential to the future of Syria, to any path of justice and accountability, and for informing future generations about what actually happened in Syria since the people took to the streets in 2011. This is a reliable source of information revolving around visual documentation of human rights violations and shaping evidence in a quest to bring people and their movement to freedom and life some form of justice.

Vis. *[un]necessary force_3* started as an artistic project, with a grassroots approach involving a collaborative and participatory audio-visual cartography. The project exposes the shocking fact that over 60,000 people were the victims of forced disappearance in Mexico in 2019, often with the complicity of police or military forces. Although the project size remains small, the artist has created a powerful tool that encourages citizens who self-organize to perform investigations to co-create a document of these human rights violations, to expose and share with the world the wrongdoing and violations of power, and to build a digital memory for affected communities.

The coronavirus crisis hits us hard. When the day-to-day life and the institutions we take for granted break down, communities can step in. The *#WirVsVirus Hackathon* was an event that successfully brought together government, civil society, and the private sector. The jury applauds the hackathon organizers for carefully orchestrating the process and fostering collaboration among 26,581 participants—making it one of the largest online hackathons to date. This hackathon demonstrates that governments opening up to its citizens can result in innovative solutions that can help tackle the crisis. Beyond generating viable ideas, this hackathon also has great symbolic value. Joining forces, being united in a common cause, inspires hope and empowers people, softening the blow of the social crisis.

1   Nancy, Jean-Luc. 2000. *Being Singular Plural.* Stanford University Press.
2   Winner, Langdon. 1980. "Do Artifacts Have Politics?" *Daedalus 109 (1):* 121–136.

Be Water by Hong Kongers

Dedicated to the Hong Kong protesters by Eric Siu & Joel Kwong

 "Be Water" is a famous saying of martial arts star Bruce Lee: to be shapeless, formless, and able to adapt to any situation. This philosophy has recently been embraced by the protest movement in Hong Kong. The latest wave of protests began in 2019 in response to an extradition bill that threatened the territory's judicial independence. The protests have now become a case study in the use of digital activism to safeguard democratic freedoms.

Hong Kong, a former British colony, was returned to mainland China in 1997. Since then, Hong Kong has been governed by the constitutional principle of "One Country, Two Systems." Under this principle, Hong Kong continued to have its own governmental systems and legal, economic, and financial affairs, including trade relations with other countries, all of which are independent from those of mainland China. However, the interpretation of this principle has occasionally caused tensions to erupt.

In the summer of 2019, 22 years after the handover, a tremendous political movement emerged to protest an extradition bill that would allow criminal suspects to be extradited to mainland China under certain circumstances. Dissenting voices claimed this would risk exposing citizens to unfair trials and treatment, further eroding political freedoms in Hong Kong. Hundreds of thousands of Hong Kongers (as they now refer to themselves) took to the streets, and weeks of protests and civil disobedience followed, which helped to bring the

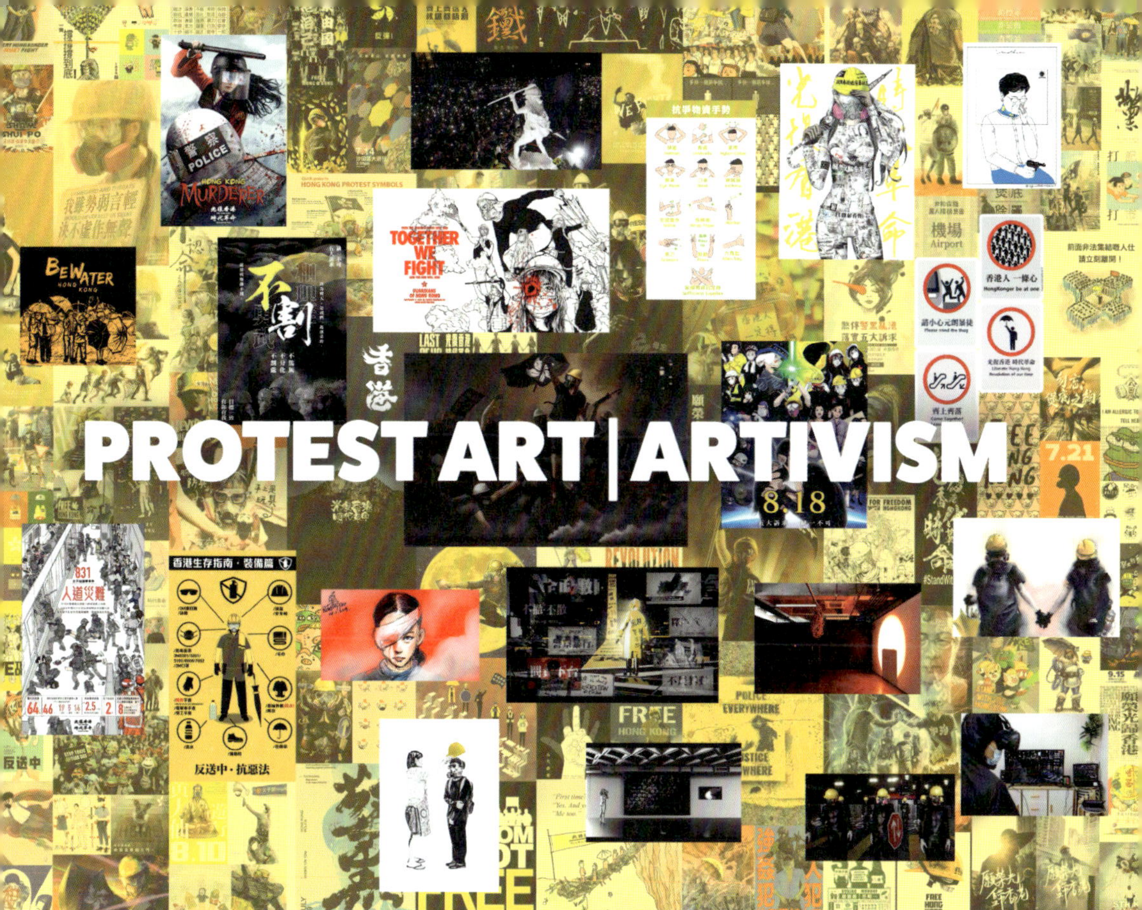

PROTEST ART | ARTIVISM

movement to global attention. While the controversial bill was withdrawn in September 2019, the movement doesn't stop but continues with a broader set of demands, including a full inquiry into alleged police brutality.

Digital technology plays a key role in the whole movement, and the use of technology is creative, innovative, and pervasive. Digital community functions range from front-line support and crowd-sourcing campaigns to protest art, social media (fact-checking and reporting), online petitions, political education, and so on. Protesters use multiple platforms including live-streaming, forums and apps, e-commerce, websites, music, and whatever else seems appropriate in the moment, a perfect expression of the "Be Water" philosophy.

The protest movement is leaderless, and this decentralization results in massive online and organic tactics using platforms like LIHKG—a local, lo-fi version of Reddit where users can communicate and vote on posts—or AirDrop to share campaign messages. The protests have unleashed a wave of digital activism in which everything is new and creative.

We submit this project not as artists but as messengers. Our agenda is to collect examples of digital excellence from within the protest movement and generalize them into one discourse of "digital community." Hong Kongers have set new standards of digital activism, the lessons of which must be shared. "Be Water" is their guiding philosophy, just as in the Chinese classical text

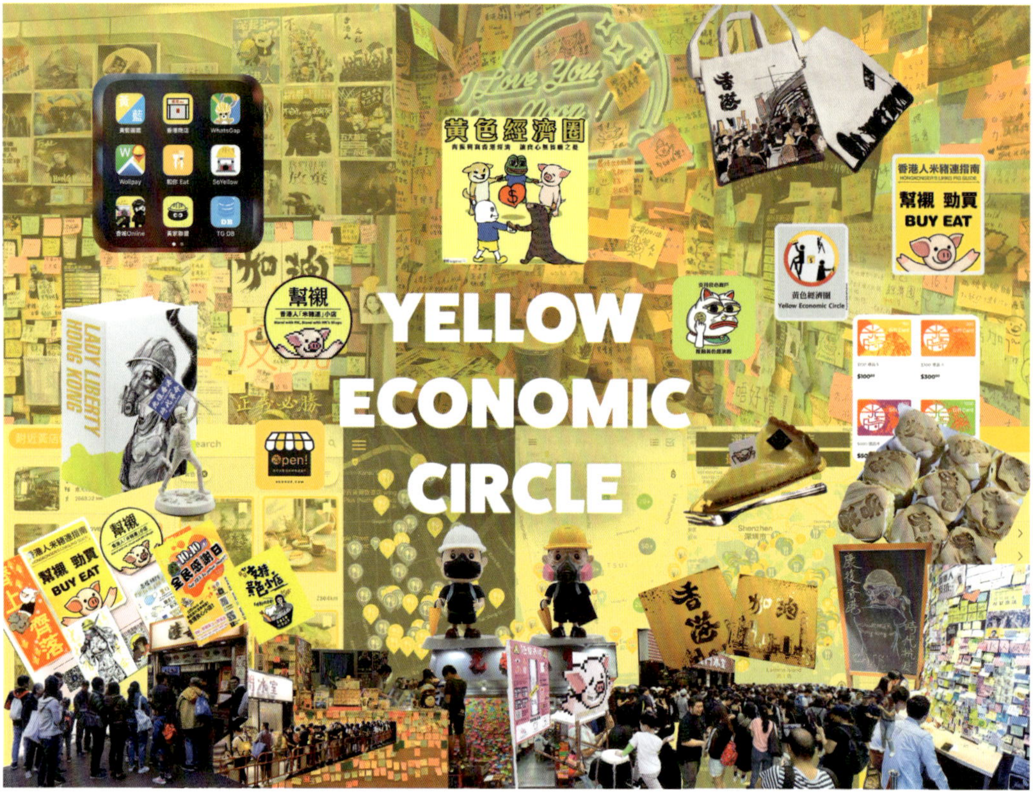

黃色經濟圈
YELLOW ECONOMIC CIRCLE
幫襯 勁買
BUY EAT
LADY LIBERTY HONG KONG

SALVEN A HONG KONG EN EL G20
STAND WITH HONG KONG UNTIL DAWN
STAND WITH HONG KONG AT G20
STAND WITH HONG KONG UNTIL DAWN
CROWDFUNDING
STAND WITH HONG KONG AT G20
Hongkong fällt
CATCH HONG KONG AS WE FALL
NO DEJEN CAER A HONG KONG
WE RESIST. FOR WHAT WE DESERVE
SAVE HONG KONG AT G20
STAND WITH HONG KONG UNTIL DAWN
VIVE HONG KONG LIBRE
G20
自由のため
香港と共に

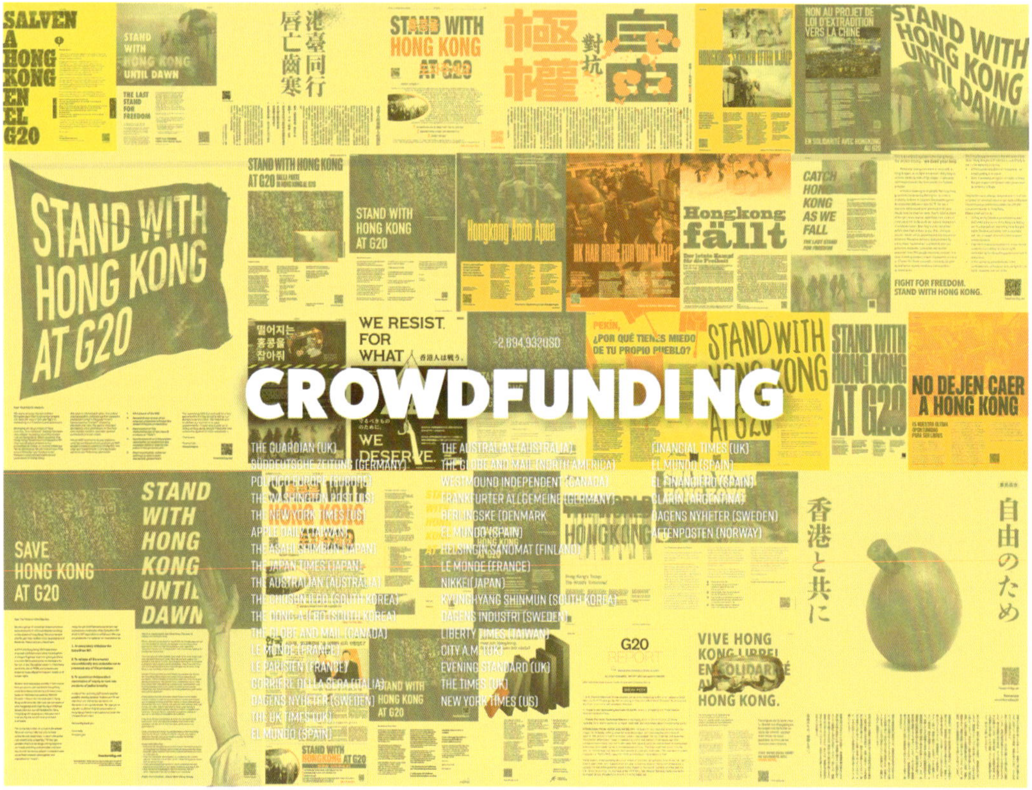

Tao Te Ching by Lao Tzu, the highest good is like water. As messengers and Hong Kong citizens ourselves, we document the past and present, credit the Hong Kong protesters, and hope to bring Hong Kongers to the center of art, technology, and society and provoke a much-needed dialogue about how digital culture shapes our practice of civic responsibility now and in the future.

Source
New Statesman/ "Be Water!": seven tactics that are winning Hong Kong's democracy revolution
www.newstatesman.com/world/2019/08/be-water-seven-tactics-are-winning-hong-kongs-democracy-revolution
Wikipedia: One country, two systems
https://en.wikipedia.org/wiki/One_country,_two_systems
Taylor & Francis Online: A Report of the 2019 Hong Kong Protests
https://www.tandfonline.com/doi/full/10.1080/03068374.2019.1672397
BBC: The Hong Kong protests explained in 100 and 500 words
https://www.bbc.com/news/world-asia-china-49317695

All Hong Kong protesters involved in the struggle to safeguard democracy

Hong Kong protesters. Since the latest pro-democracy movement erupted in 2019, Hong Kong protesters have been following a strategy called "Be Water." With this philosophy, Hong Kongers have recollected the scattered pieces of hope from the Umbrella Movement in 2014 to imagine a new form of protest. Among their many innovations, Hong Kongers have pursued leaderless organization and digital activism, which have captured the world's attention. To continue their movement, Hong Kongers hope to widen global solidarity and let the "Be Water" current flow to the worlds of art and technology. Eric Siu is a media artist, born and raised in Hong Kong. Joel Kwong is a media art curator, raised and currently based in Hong Kong.

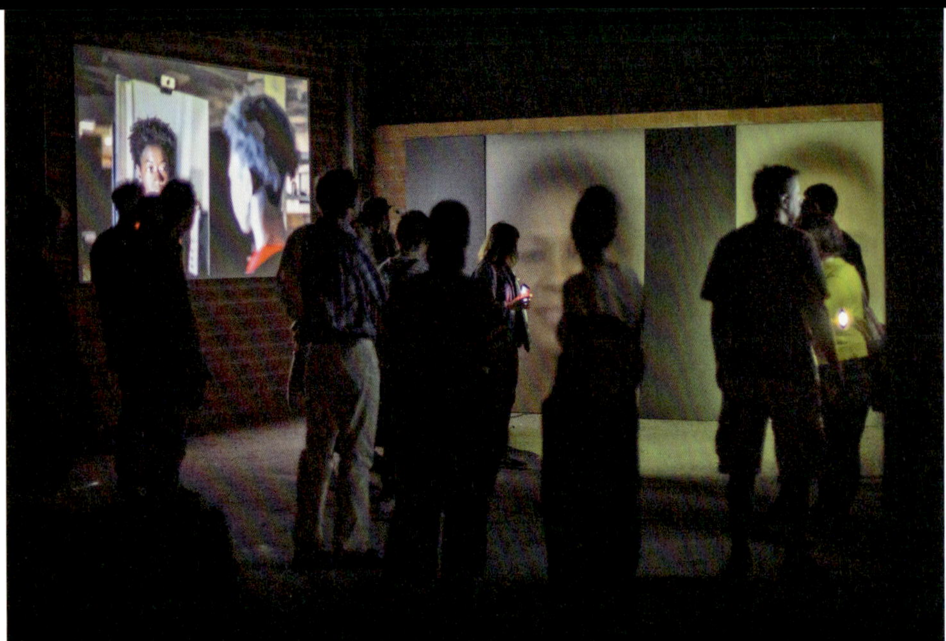

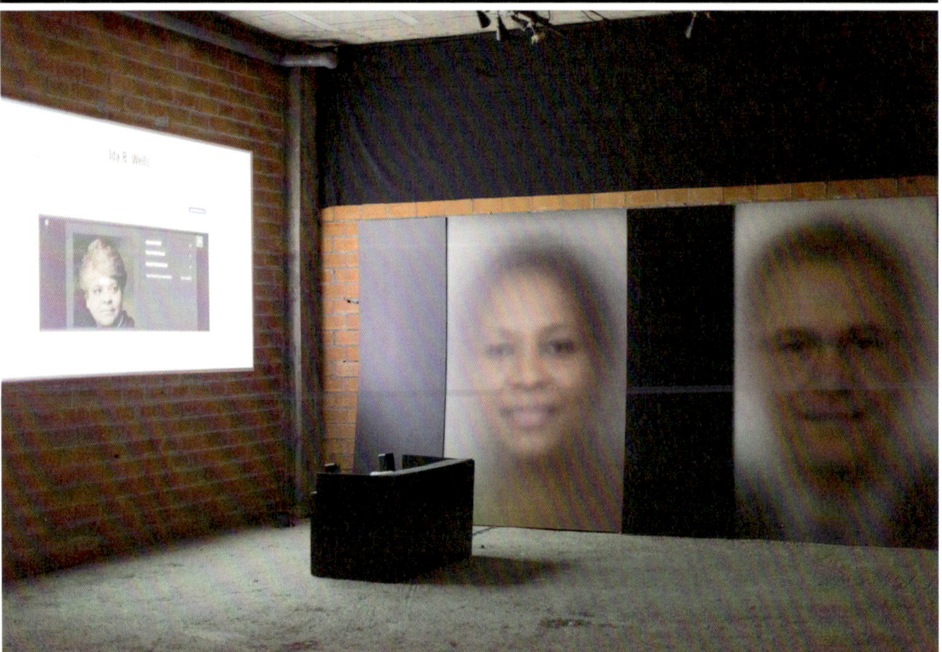

Serena Williams

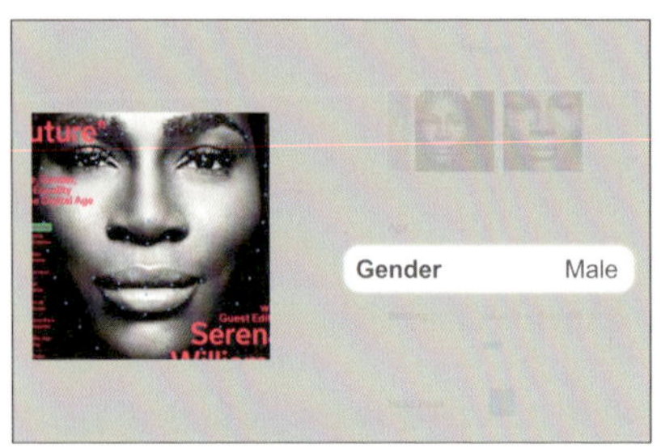

Michelle Obama

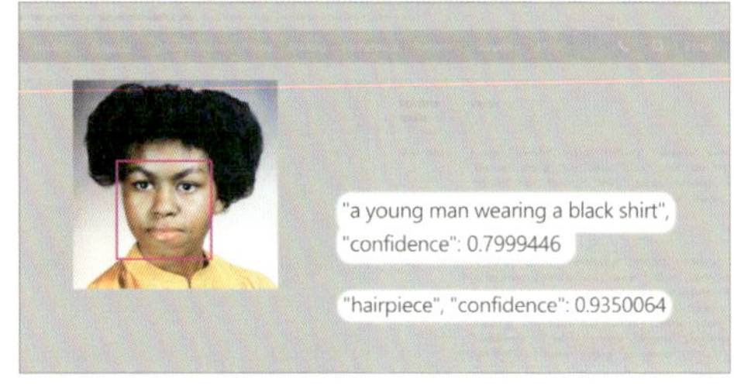

Algorithmic Justice League (AJL)

https://www.ajlunited.org

The *Algorithmic Justice League* (AJL) is an organization that combines art and research to illuminate the social implications and harms of Artificial Intelligence. AJL's mission is to raise public awareness about the impacts of AI, equip advocates with empirical research to bolster campaigns, build the voice and choice of the most impacted communities, and galvanize researchers, policymakers, and industry practitioners to mitigate AI bias and harms.

The *Algorithmic Justice League* takes a threefold approach to address harmful impacts and shift the AI ecosystem toward equitable and accountable AI:

- Increasing public awareness about the risks and harms of artificial intelligence through art, writing, and creative science communication projects; for example, AJL's founder Joy Buolamwini's TED talk has been seen over 1.2 million times; in 2019 she placed Op-Eds in the *New York Times* and *TIME* magazine; and in 2020 the film *Coded Bias* premiered at Sundance Film Festival.
- Conducting research on algorithmic bias, AI harms, and discriminatory technology that propagates racism, sexism, ableism, and/or other harmful intersecting forms of inequality; for example, AJL's research study "Gender Shades and Actionable Auditing" reveals gender and racial accuracy disparities in commercially sold facial analysis systems from IBM, Microsoft, and Amazon.
- Advising regulatory and industry decision makers on AI standards and development processes with research-backed recommendations to address algorithmic discrimination and mitigate bias; for example, in 2019 Joy testified before the US House Committee on Oversight and Government Reform, AJL participated in the ACLU of Massachusetts' "Press Pause on Face Surveillance" campaign for a statewide moratorium on government use of the technology, and wrote an Amicus Support Letter in solidarity with Brooklyn tenants' successful fight against a facial recognition entry system.

Algorithmic Justice League Art Team: Founder Joy Buolamwini, Creative Communications Lead Nicole Hughes
Supporters of the *Algorithmic Justice League* include: the Ford Foundation, MacArthur Foundation, Sloan Foundation, Rockefeller Foundation, and individual donors.

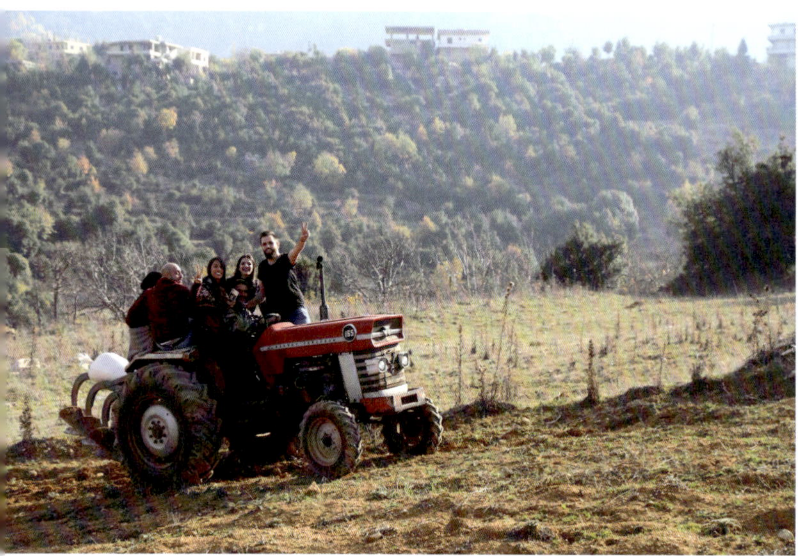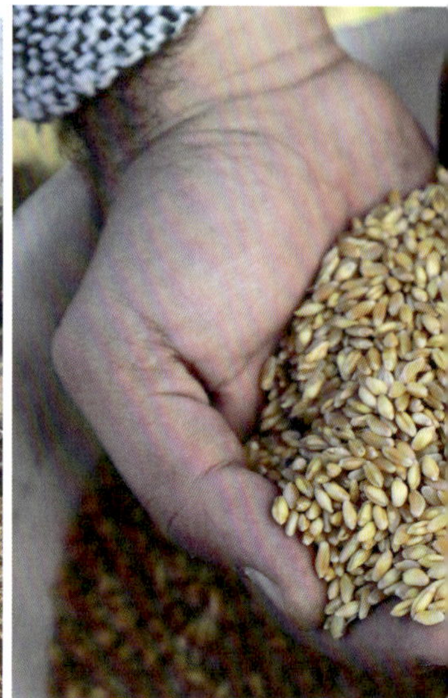

Habaq Movement

www.facebook.com/habaqmovement

The current economic and social crisis in Lebanon highlights the importance of youth initiatives with a futuristic and targeted vision for solutions. Young people have become increasingly aware of the important role they can play in the development and improvement of society. With their energy and experience, young people from all different social groups—regardless of their nationality, race or religion—are joining together to manage this crisis and to help build a better society.

In Lebanon, the rentier economy is near collapse, and the absence of the state since the Lebanese Civil War period has created huge economic and social challenges. The rentier economy is unable to provide enough jobs to meet people's needs.

Habaq Movement promotes collective initiatives and activities—such as encouraging food crops in public spaces—making them open and available to the whole community. It believes in a social economy based on solidarity and partnership, creating new interactions and social roles while trying to build a sustainable local economy. *Habaq Movement* is an agricultural reclamation cooperative aiming to recuperate abandoned agricultural land around the country, set up working teams, and provide alternative solutions for local communities. *Habaq* believes in the right to food, taking a food sovereignty approach to its activities, especially in support of local markets, and advocates sustainable agricultural practices and rural development at state and local government level.

Habaq is currently providing training on ecological

     DIGITAL COMMUNITIES · Award of Distinction

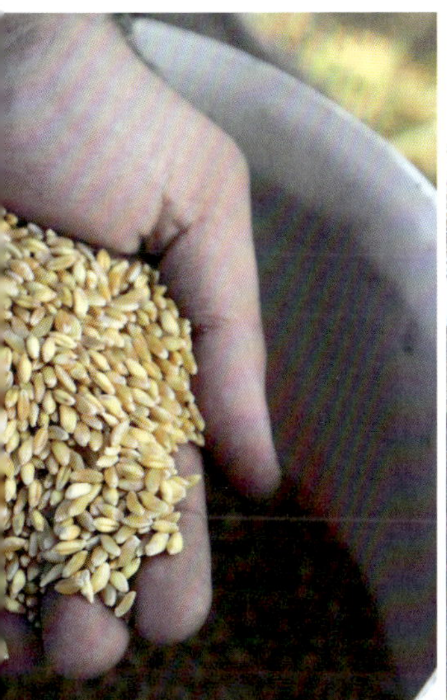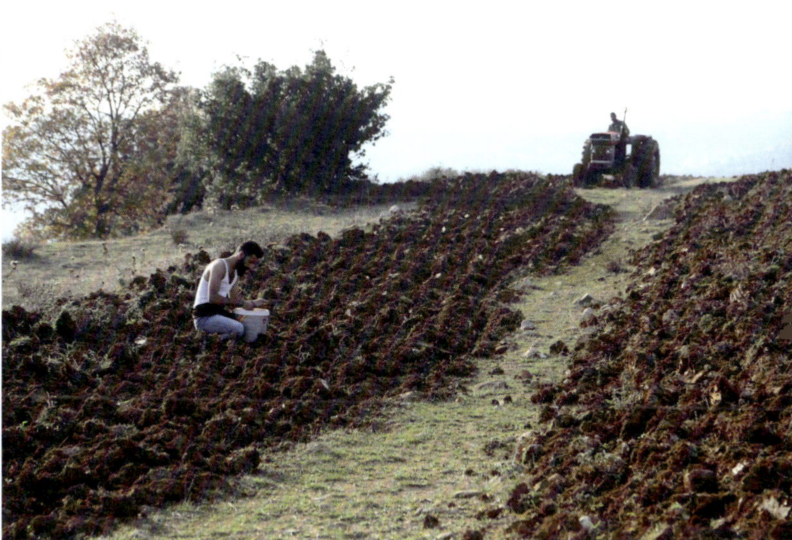

agricultural practices and food sovereignty issues, with the aim of contributing to the establishment of a food sovereignty movement in Lebanon. It has already conducted workshops in 10 locations around the country. One of *Habaq's* main achievements to date is to link agricultural initiatives between Lebanese and refugee populations. *Habaq's* mobilization and advocacy are based on social media to link various farmers with young social initiatives that could enable the development of agriculture in the country and relink the youth with agriculture and rural areas. Based on this process and in collaboration with partners, *Habaq* is creating a digital database of land available for community initiatives, which will be later linked to an agricultural almanac.

Habaq Movement is an agricultural reclamation cooperative aiming to recuperate abandoned agricultural land around the country, set up working teams, and provide alternative solutions for local communities. *Habaq* believes in the right to food, taking a food sovereignty approach to its activities, especially in support of local markets, and advocates sustainable agricultural practices and rural development at state and local government level. It promotes collective initiatives and activities, believes in a social economy based on solidarity and partnership, and aims to build a sustainable local economy.

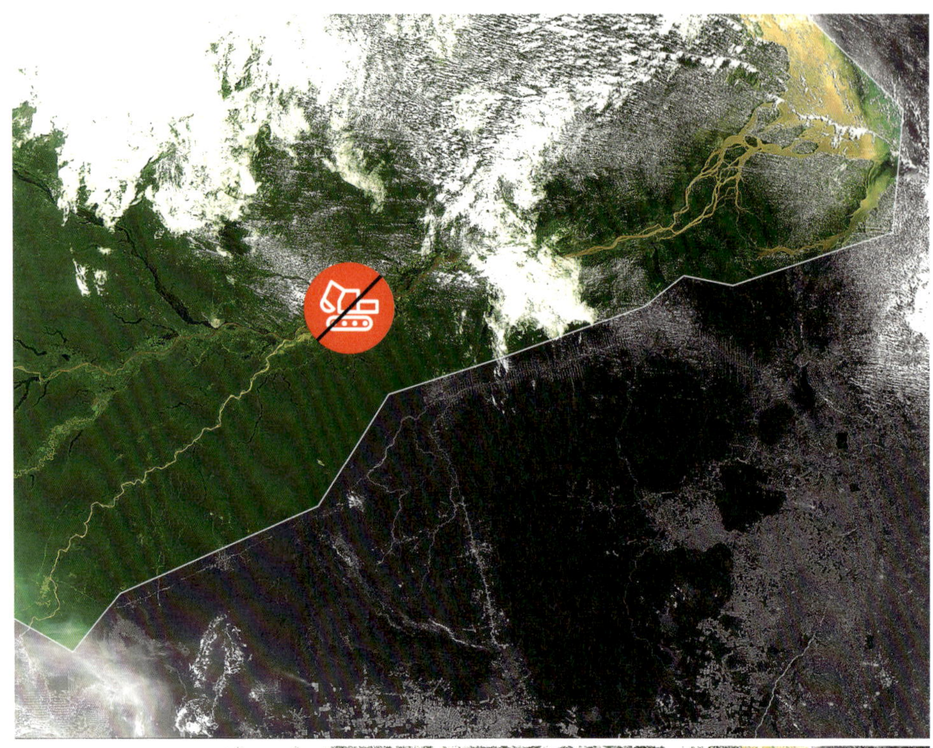

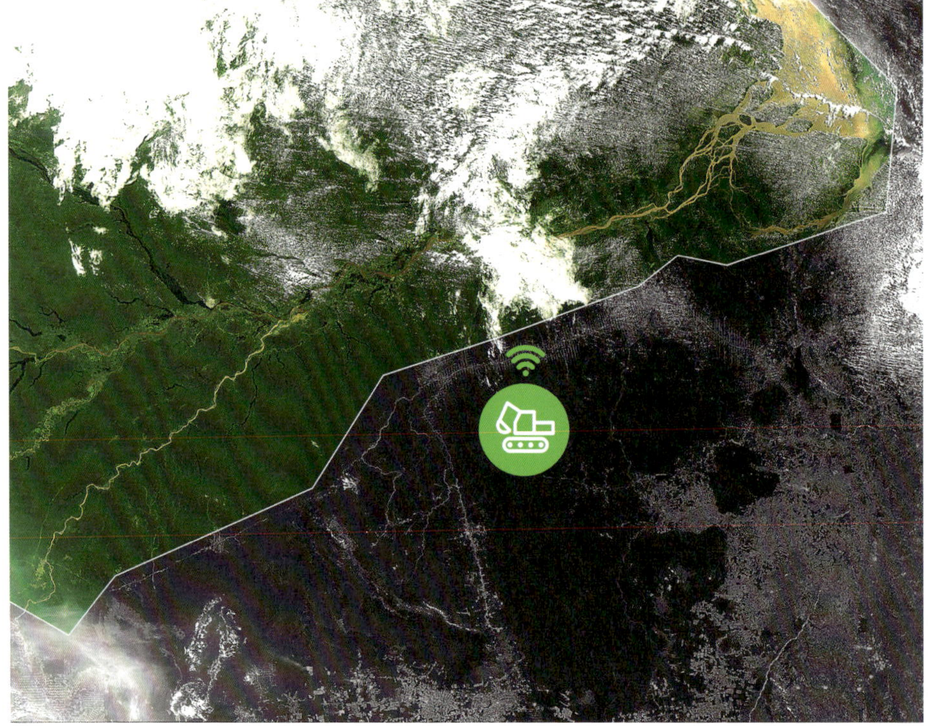

 DIGITAL COMMUNITIES · Honorary Mention

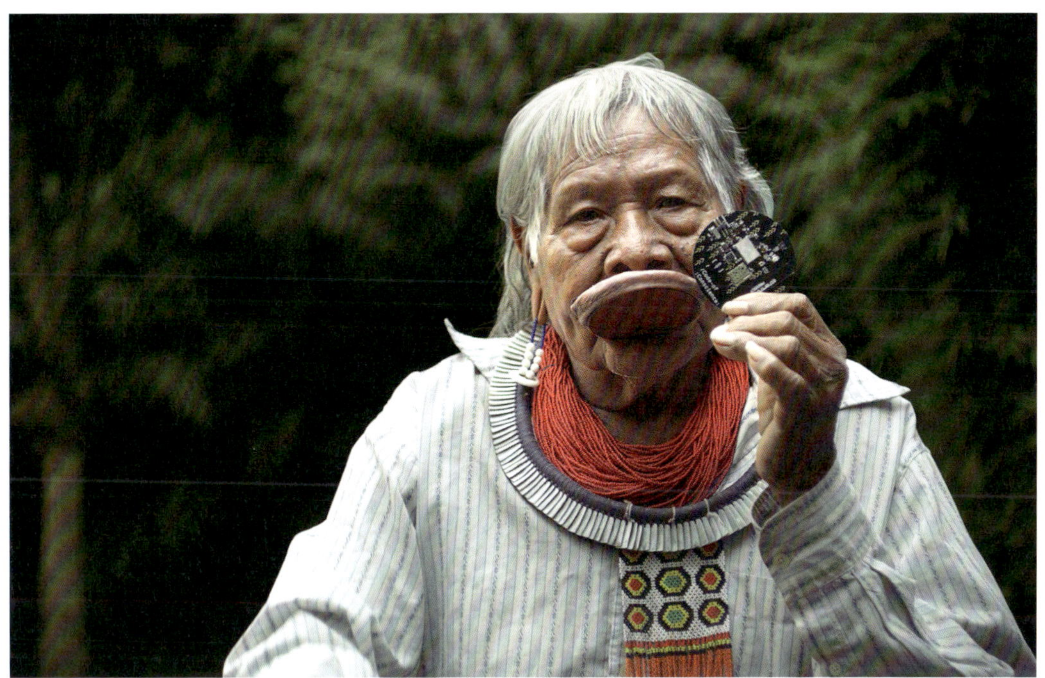

Code of Conscience

https://www.codeofconscience.org

Despite its protective status, one-third of the world's nature reserves are under threat from human activity. It's hard to stop industry from destroying our planet, but we can stop the machines they use. *Code of Conscience* is open source software that restricts the use of heavy-duty vehicles in protected land areas. The code uses open source mapping data from the United Nations World Database on Protected Areas in conjunction with on-vehicle GPS tracking technology to autonomously restrict deforestation crews from entering protected zones. A small, low-cost chip has been developed to equip the code into older, non-GPS models. The software is available for free on *CodeofConscience.org*.

An invitation comprising the *Code of Conscience* chip embedded in a wooden sculpture of an endangered animal was sent to the CEOs of the world's top ten construction equipment manufacturers, urging them to adopt the code for all new machines leaving their factories.

Chief Raoni Metuktire—the most prominent Native Brazilian leader and a living symbol of the mission to preserve the rainforest and its indigenous culture—affirms the urgent need for action: "May all heavy machine manufacturers and leaders come and see this. So that the tractors operate, but stop when they reach our land, our forest and so it continues to exist. It is for our awareness and for the forest to stand up."

Team:
AKQA: Tim Devine, Hugo Veiga, Pedro Araújo, Daniel Kalil, Adam Grant
Tekt Industries: Matthew Adams

Code of Conscience. Launched in the second half of 2019, the Code of Conscience is a collective of designers, engineers, industrial and governmental partners led by Tim Devine, Hugo Vega, and Adam Grant.

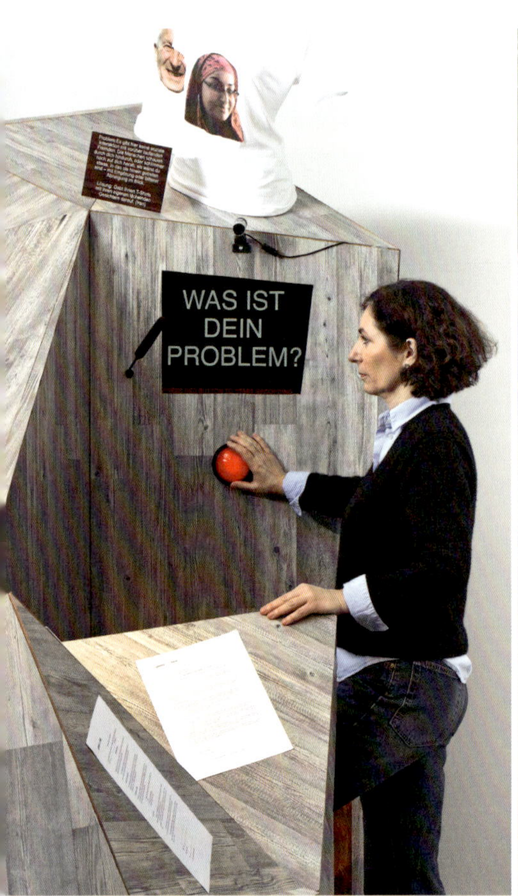

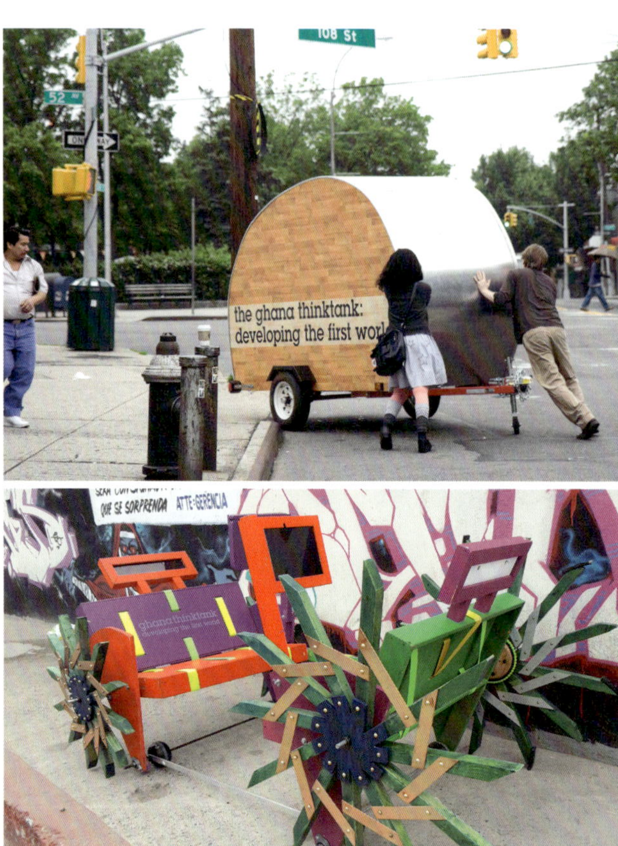
WAS IST DEIN PROBLEM?
the ghana thinktank: developing the first world
108 St
52
ghana thinktank

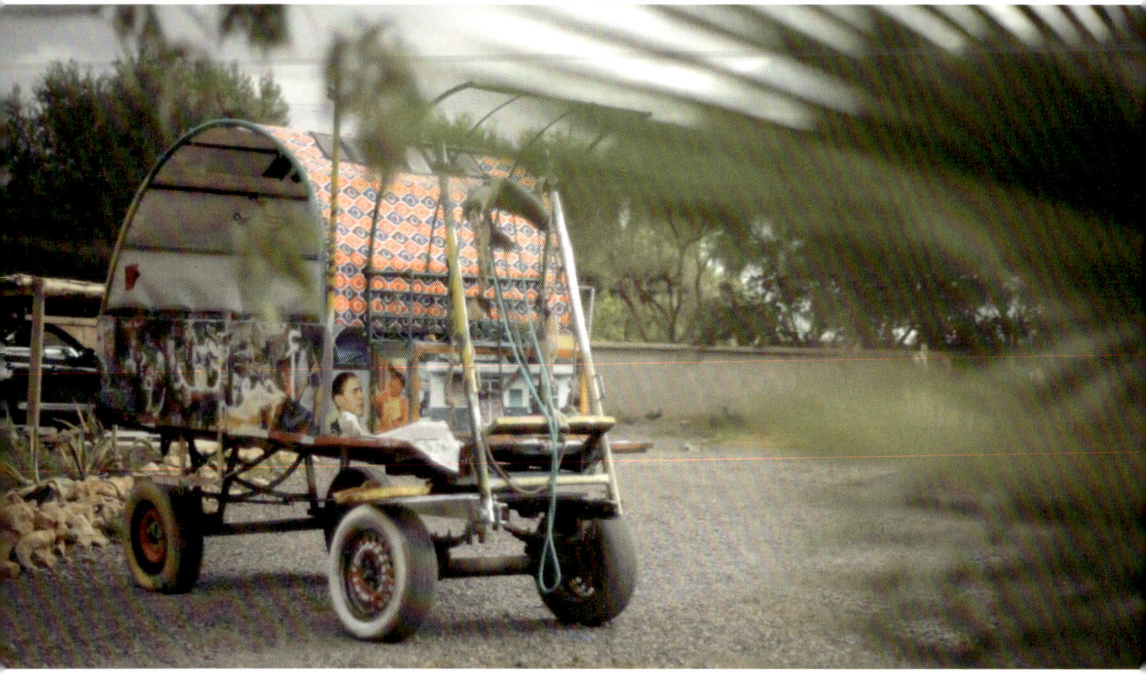

Ghana ThinkTank is Developing the First World

www.ghanathinktank.org

Ghana ThinkTank is an international collective that develops the "first world" by flipping traditional power dynamics, asking the "third world" to intervene in the lives of the people living in the so-called "developed" world.

We collect problems from communities in the USA and Europe, and send them to think tanks we created in "developing" communities. The think tanks—which include a group of bike mechanics in Ghana, a rural radio station in El Salvador, Sudanese refugees seeking asylum in Israel, an artist collective in Iran, and a group of incarcerated girls in the US penal system, among others—propose solutions, which are then implemented in the "first world."

Ghana ThinkTank's innovative approach to public art reveals blind spots between otherwise disconnected cultures, challenges assumptions about who is "needy," and turns the idea of expertise on its head by asking people in the "third world" to solve problems of people in the "first world." This process helps people overcome their own stereotypes while being exposed to the stereotypes that other cultures have about them.

We accomplish this through unexpected applications of technology and social engineering. In rural Morocco, we converted a donkey-cart into a solar-powered media center and tea house, which travelled from village to village collecting African solutions to US problems. In Israel, we integrated a touch-screen running *Ghana ThinkTank* software into an interactive sculpture/bicycle, which we used to connect Sudanese and Eritrean refugees seeking asylum in Israel with South Tel Aviv residents who wanted the African refugees removed. At the US/Mexico border at Tijuana, we built a hand-cranked "border cart" that provided mobile seats for self-identified "immigrants" and "Americans" to face each other while using custom software to exchange problems/solutions around immigration, and connected recently deported immigrants with groups of US-based border vigilante/"patriot" groups.

With support from: Creative Capital, Creative Time, Foundation for Art and Creative Technology, John S. and James L. Knight Foundation, CEC ArtsLink, Queens Museum of Art, Detroit Justice Center, Puffin Foundation, Black Rock Arts Foundation, New York State Council on the Arts, SUNY Research Foundation Network of Excellence in Arts and the Humanities, SUNY Purchase College, Kindle Project, DTE Foundation, Michigan Economic Development Corporation, and Sigrid Rausing Trust.

Ghana ThinkTank was founded in 2006. Their recent work has been featured in major international exhibitions such as the Venice Biennial of Architecture, the National Museum of Wales, Hong Kong/Shenzhen Biennial of Architecture and Urbanism, and the Global Contemporary at ZKM in Germany, among many others. They spoke at the Creative Time Summit in Stockholm, received a Creative Capital Grant in Emerging Fields, and are currently focusing on *The American Riad,* a project that uses art, architecture, and open-source law to promote housing justice in the historically Black neighborhood of Detroit's North End.

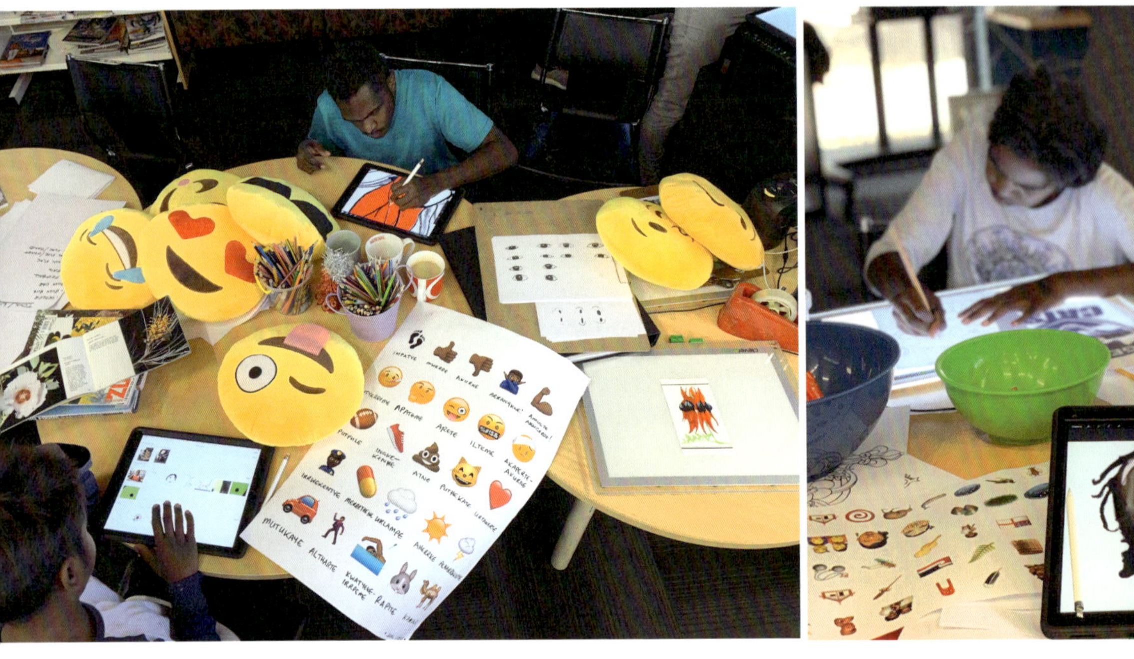

Indigemoji

www.indigemoji.com.au

"Emoji itne-areye Australia mpwepe-arenye itne ayeye anwerne-akerte, altyerre-akerte, angkentye akerte uthene. Arrernte angkentye anwernekenhe impene anthurre, altyerrenge. Australian-mpwepe angkentye atningke akerte kenhe Arrernte Mparntwe-arenye kwenhe. Marle, urreye, arelhe, artwe-areye-uthene-arle emoji-kenhe arlkenye intel-heleke uterne-ureke. Emoji arrpe-anenhe arritnye Arrernte-kenhe-akerte, anwerne ahentye arrantherre itnenhe akaltye-irretyeke. Anwerne internet-nge itnenhe arrerneke kele angkentye anwernekenhe rlterrke-aneme-akwete."

Indigemoji is a digital arts and inclusion project which developed the first set of Indigenous emojis from Australia. The emojis were created by over 900 young Aboriginal people during seven weeks of digital art workshops held at the public library in Mparntwe/Alice Springs in the Northern Territory. It was the first time many of the young people had ever used an iPad or any graphic design software. Led by senior Arrernte leaders and linguists, with a team of Indigenous artists, designers, and programmers, the project resulted in a sticker set of 90 emojis, each with a name in Arrernte, the traditional language and culture of Mparntwe/Alice Springs. The set features local hand signs, plants, faces, and symbols. Emojis were also developed for special totemic animals,

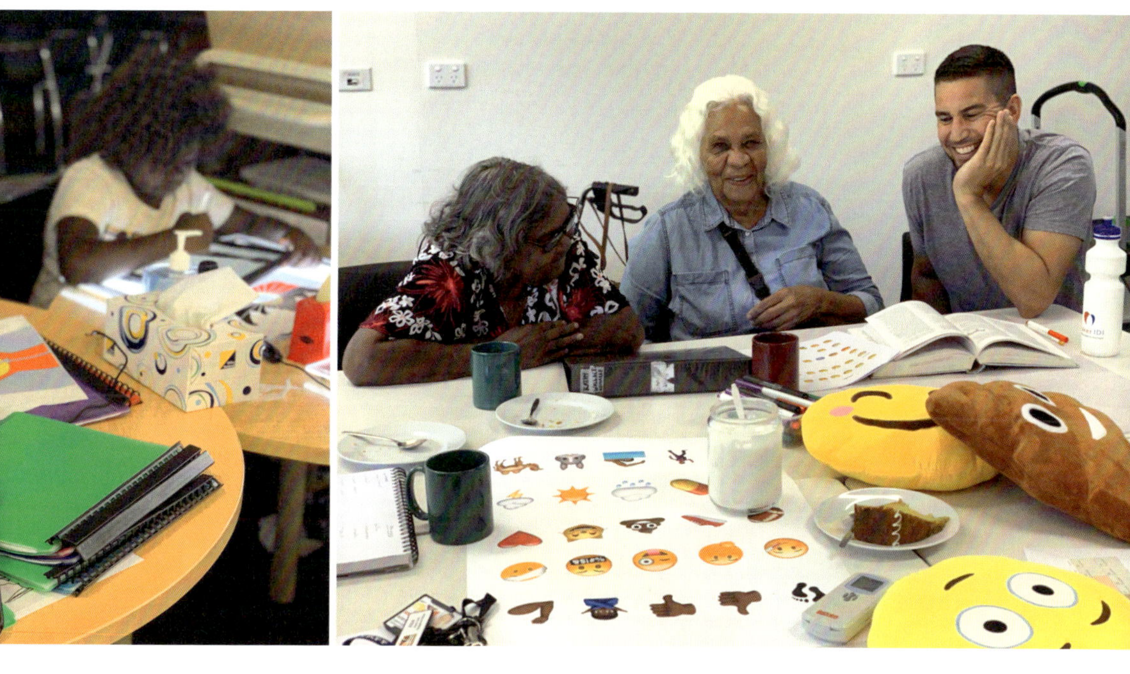

many of which are endangered or extinct, to promote their memory, their names, their places—a way of keeping them in the landscape. The sticker set was launched for public use via a free app in November 2019, the International Year of Indigenous Languages. It was downloaded over 40,000 times in its first week. *Indigemoji* offers a new means of communicating online at a time of rapid growth in connectivity in the remote deserts of Central Australia. It provided digital skills development, mentoring, and access to technology for young people who were able to contribute to a culturally relevant product that is now being used in daily life in their communities. It is a small but significant step towards improving the representation and inclusion of the many diverse cultures and languages of Australia in digital technologies.

Indigemoji was delivered through funding partnerships with the Johnston Foundation, Northern Territory Government, Ingeous Studios, Alice Springs Public Library and inDigiMOB, a partnership between First Nations Media Australia and Telstra.

Indigemoji was created by over 900 young Aboriginal people from across Central Australia. It was led by a cultural reference group of senior Arrernte leaders and linguists Veronica Dobson Perrurle, Kathleen Wallace Kemarre, and Joel Liddle Perrurle, with a team of Indigenous artists, designers, and programmers: *https://www.indigemoji.com.au/alpewarrewarre-team.* The final sticker set of 90 Arrernte-named emojis is available via the free Indigemoji app.

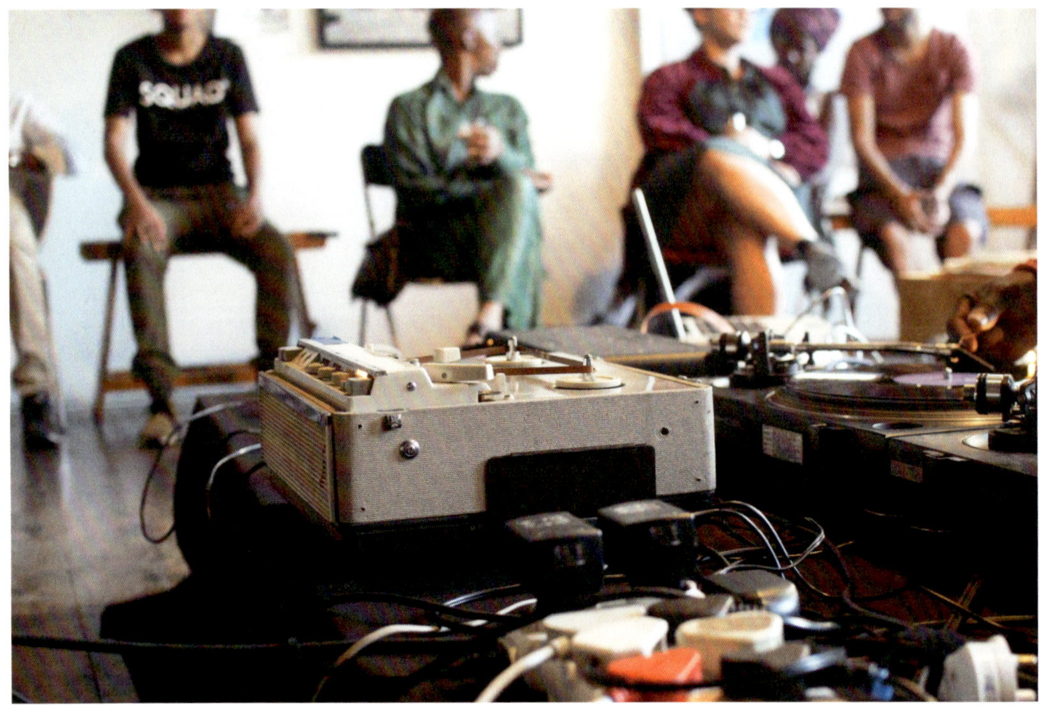

Listening at Pungwe

https://listeningatpungwe.wordpress.com

Listening at Pungwe is a collaborative project that produces sonic installations and performances through the interplay of analog and digital audio-visual recordings and technologies. Our exploration of Southern African instrumentation, with a focus on the mbira, examines the history of remix, re-possession, transformation, and adaptation, listening to the centrality of instruments as modes of exchange and transportation of voices. Sound technology can be heard as a simulacrum of ancestral voices that link the three intersecting dimensions of time—past, present, and future. When there is need for deep spiritual commitment and moral elevation, people tend to converge in song. This phenomenon is a convergence of peo-ple involving sound. A gathering of this form was known as Pungwe (Shona word for vigil), during Zimbabwe's armed liberation movement. It was mediated through mbira music rituals. We draw the ideological framework of an event we call PUNGWE from this narrative. The project *Pungwe* is an inter-disciplinary project circling African music with related contemporary arts practices and spaces. This practice takes the shape of a participatory public platform hosting alternative music and sound performances.

The platform creates a performative episteme and praxis, a "listening" that places the moment of recording and re-play in a dialectical relationship, which, while marking the distinction in the relay,

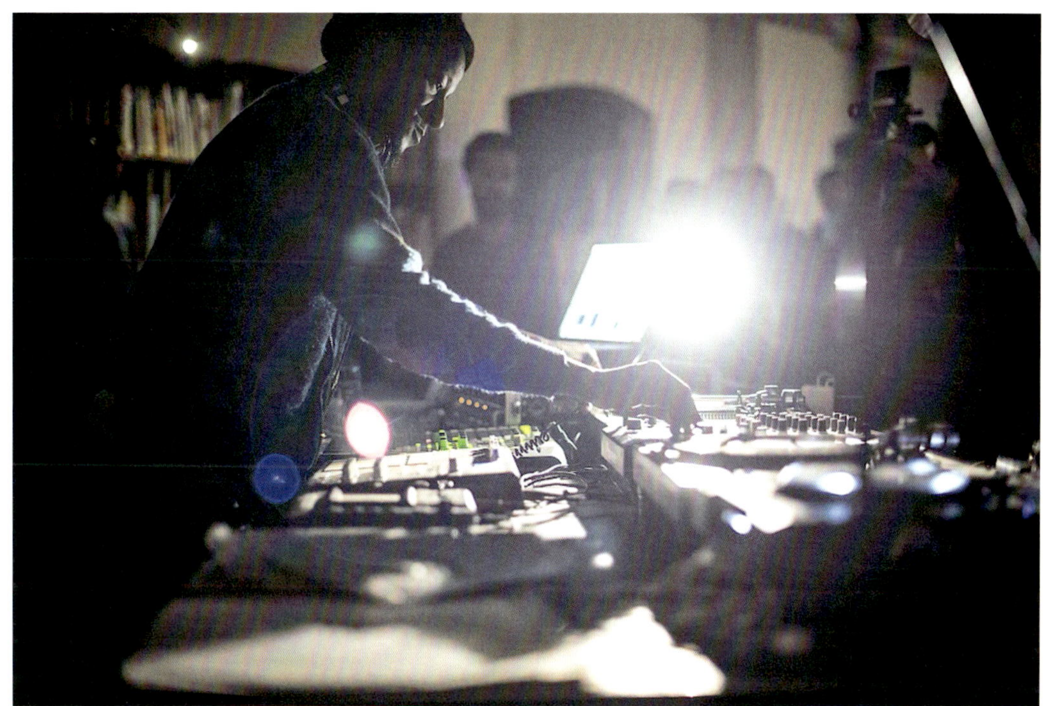

allows one to re-create a new sonic version. Our use of "the remix framework" as an approach provides an interrogatory vantage point of mbira, viewing it not only as a cultural product, but also as an extension of the broader African futurist imagination.

With support from Deutschlandfunk Kultur, Germany, Savvy Contemporary, Berlin, DAAD – Deutscher Akademischer Austauschdienst, Goethe Institute (Namibia), ProHelvetia (Johannesburg), PASS at Chimurenga, Capetown

The project **Listening at Pungwe** is realized through research and sonic cartographic work and manifests through performative installations, live interventions, location recordings, and radio performances. The project (full title: *Listening to a Listening at Pungwe Nights: A conversation between Memory Biwa and Robert Machiri*) is a proposition of new publics in the contemporary and a collaborative experiential corpus where we re-listen to the use of voice, language, instruments, bodily movements, and modern technology in the recordings. *Listening at Pungwe* was created by Memory Biwa and Robert Machiri.

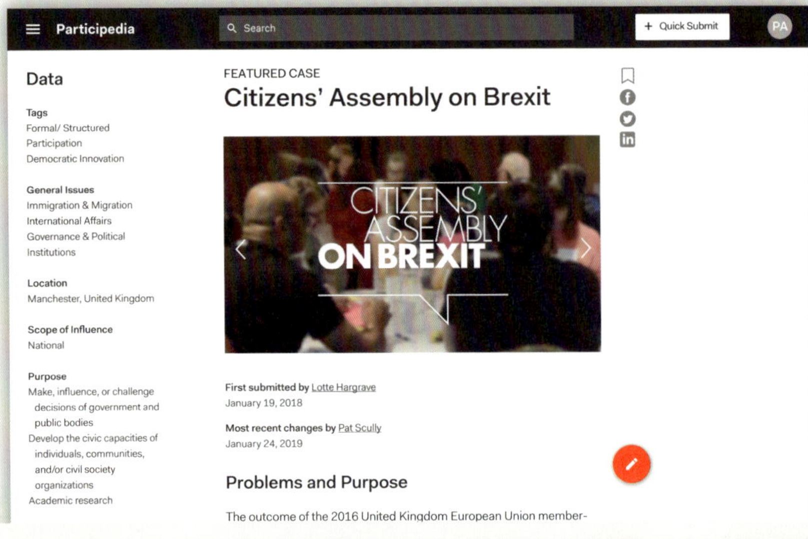
Participipedia
Search
+ Quick Submit
PA
Data
Tags
Formal/ Structured
Participation
Democratic Innovation
General Issues
Immigration & Migration
International Affairs
Governance & Political
Institutions
Location
Manchester, United Kingdom
Scope of Influence
National
Purpose
Make, influence, or challenge
decisions of government and
public bodies
Develop the civic capacities of
individuals, communities,
and/or civil society
organizations
Academic research
FEATURED CASE
Citizens' Assembly on Brexit
First submitted by Lotte Hargrave
January 19, 2018
Most recent changes by Pat Scully
January 24, 2019
Problems and Purpose
The outcome of the 2016 United Kingdom European Union member-

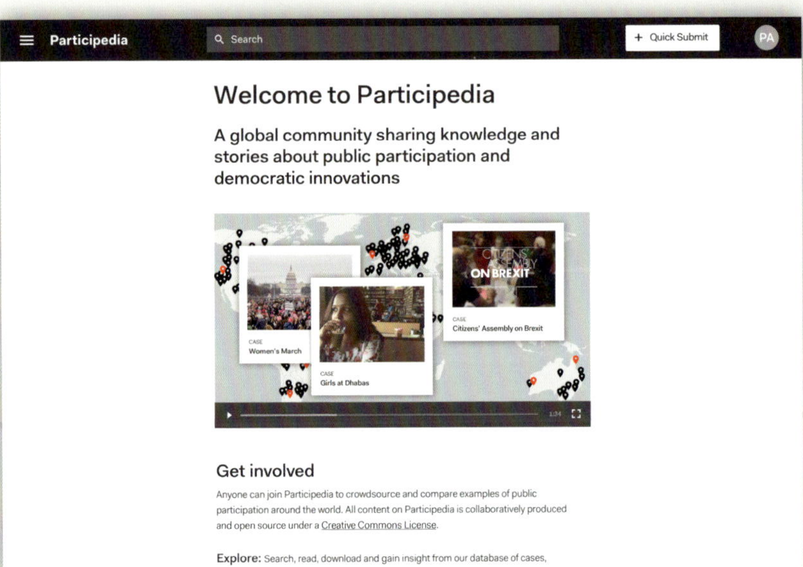
Participipedia
Search
+ Quick Submit
PA
Welcome to Participipedia
A global community sharing knowledge and
stories about public participation and
democratic innovations
Get involved
Anyone can join Participedia to crowdsource and compare examples of public
participation around the world. All content on Participedia is collaboratively produced
and open source under a Creative Commons License.
Explore: Search, read, download and gain insight from our database of cases,

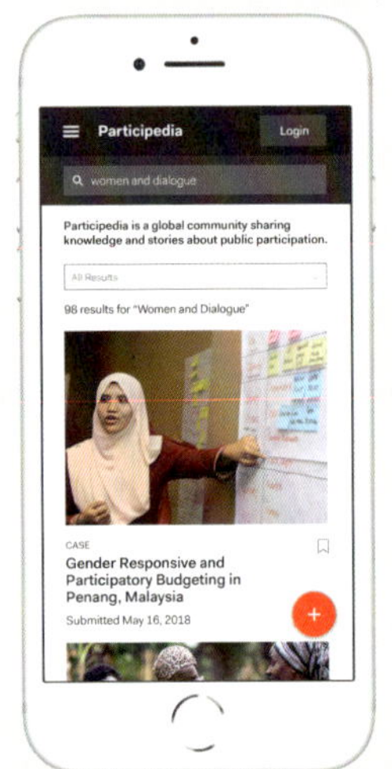

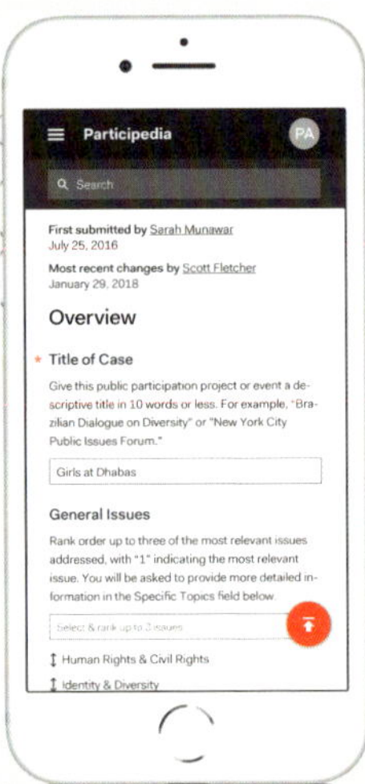

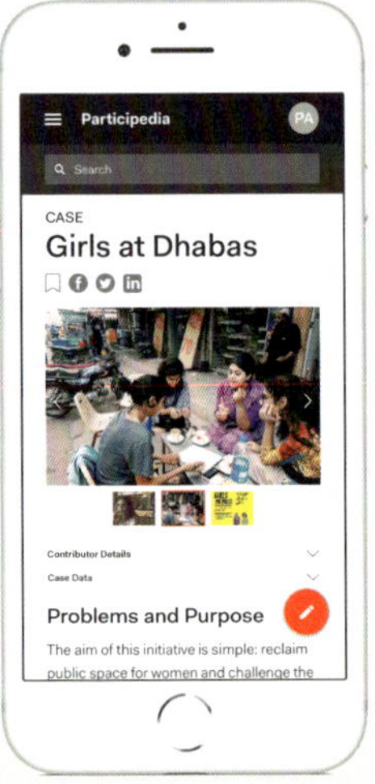

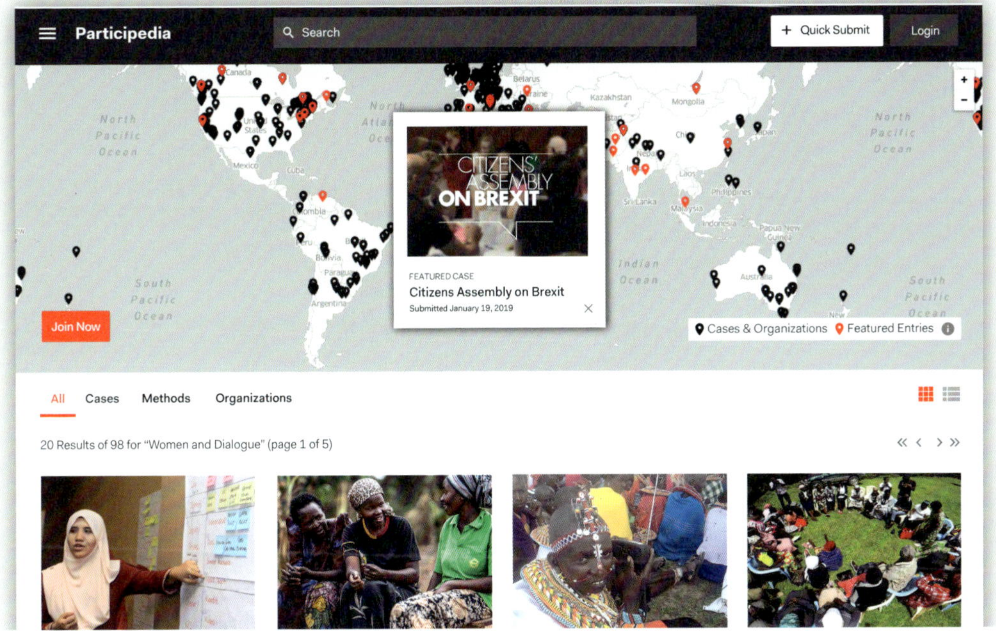

Participedia

https://participedia.net

Electoral democracy is under increasing strain. Centrist governments are no longer able to govern their disaffected citizens while populism's disdain for mediating institutions and technocratic elites gives rise to autocrats who promise something better. Faced with these threats, communities test new forms of collective processes to empower themselves. *Participedia* addresses the urgent need to understand the impact of these countervailing phenomena by mapping the recent exponential growth of participatory innovations globally. *Participedia's* open source, multilingual platform brings activists and scholars together to crowdsource local knowledge of participation on a global scale. For example, the Covid-19 Response Collection documents participatory initiatives that address the Coronavirus pandemic, including forms that range from protests and vol-unteering to hackathons and DIY tracking apps. *Participedia* embraces the idea that a platform about participation should itself be participatory. Grounded in feminist human-computer interaction theory, *Participedia's* design and technology team engages a multidisciplinary network of collaborators, embedding values of equity into the design research and platform. The team built an open-source codebase from the ground up *github.com/participedia,* focusing on student mentorship and creating employment opportunities for women and LGBTQ+, who are underrepresented in the tech sector. *Participedia.net* is designed at the Studio for Extensive Aesthetics, Emily Carr University of Art & Design.

Participedia is currently supported by the Social Sciences and Humanities Research Council of Canada (SSHRC) and international partner organizations.

Participedia is a crowdsourcing platform for researchers, activists, practitioners, and anyone interested in public participation and democratic innovations. The platform was collaboratively designed by an international research partnership to connect and bolster their work on participatory democracy with publicly crowdsourced knowledge. *Participedia.net* was founded by Dr. Archon Fung, Kennedy School of Government, Harvard University, and Dr. Mark E. Warren, Department of Political Science, University of British Columbia, and is guided by a set of standing committees.

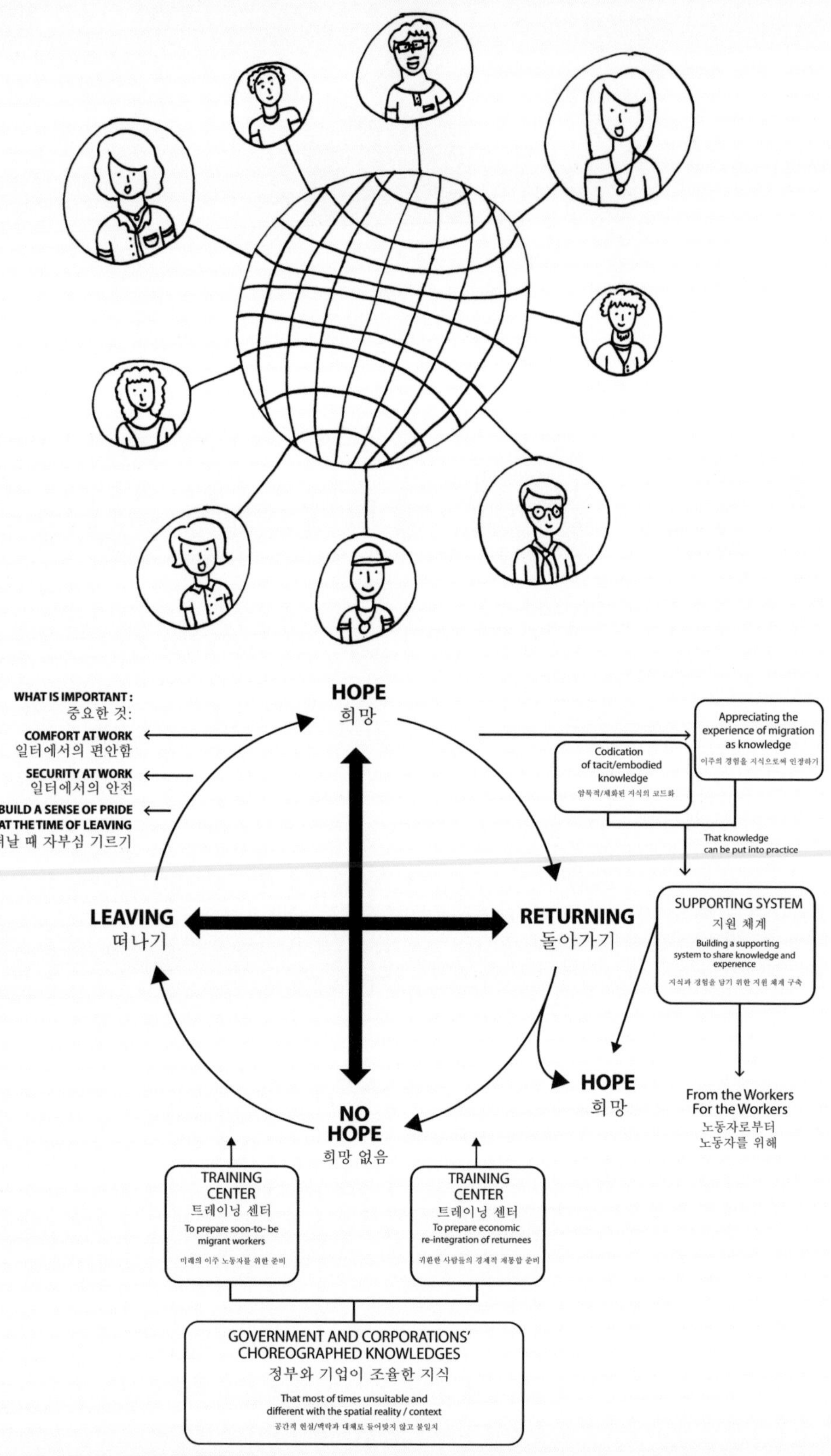

DIGITAL COMMUNITIES · Honorary Mention

PULANG PERGI

https://play.google.com/store/apps/details?id=com.pulang.pergi

In 2016, Indonesian artist Julia Sarisetiati and her friends collaborated with Indonesian migrant workers in the South Korean city Ansan to develop the project *Indo K-Work, www.indokwork.com* and *https://tinyurl.com/ybrv82yg,* an online platform for which the workers become active agents, gathering and sharing knowledge and information acquired from their daily lives and labor experiences. *PULANG PERGI* (Round Trip, 2019–present) is inspired by this previous project.

Our goal was to create an online platform for knowledge sharing amongst Indonesian migrant workers who are currently still abroad, and those who have returned home; focusing on the variety of bottom-up economic reintegration practice possibilities. These bottom-up types of knowledge are particular and quite difficult to formalize as it always depends on the specific geographical, environmental, social, and political context. The platform is also an attempt to answer the question whether it is possible or not to codify tacit knowledge (so that it would be transferable/be translated).

Leaving and returning play a certain role in the life cycle of low-skilled workers in Indonesia, and pose a challenge as the sustainability of reintegration (both in the home or destination country) are not guaranteed. Not until 2010 did the Indonesian government start thinking of their reintegration in their home communities (socially, economically, etc.), but still returnees often lack information about state-led initiatives which most of the times are not even suitable for them. Only a small portion of returnees have successfully (economically) reintegrated in their respective regions. Their bottom-up knowledge and experiences are valuable to share with other migrant workers who, for example, are currently still abroad.

PULANG PERGI aims to be a platform where previously un-codified knowledge can be articulated, accumulated, and distributed, making it accessible and initiating an endless dialogue among those who are currently abroad with those who have returned.

Voiceover: Arie Dagienkz,
English subtitles: Libby Davitri
Audio scoring: Dylan Utomo & R.A. Syukur
With support from: Gwangju Biennale (2016), Goethe Institut East Asia and Southeast Asia (2018-2019)
Collaborating returnees: Ronny Girash, *Aya Kremes Sehati.* Triana Purba, *Desa Wisata Nglangeran.* Bambang Sutrisno, *Kulit Lumpia dan Pangsit Cap Jempol.* Edy Susanto, *Getuk Take.* Slamet Prihatin, *Kue Sempe Sarangheyo.*

PULANG PERGI is a platform that focuses on aiding future migrants, working migrants as well as former migrants from Indonesia. It was initiated in collaboration with Teguh Safarizal (designer), Riza Syahrial (IT Developer), Ube Dwi Suryasumirat (visual artist), Deasy Elsara (copywriter), Ary Sendy, Nissal Nur Afryansah, Liemena Sapriya Putra (video maker team), Budi Mulia and Gusti Enda Pratama (researchers), and many others. Communication and education are the main aims of the *PULANG PERGI* platform—based on the principle of bottom-up knowledge sharing.

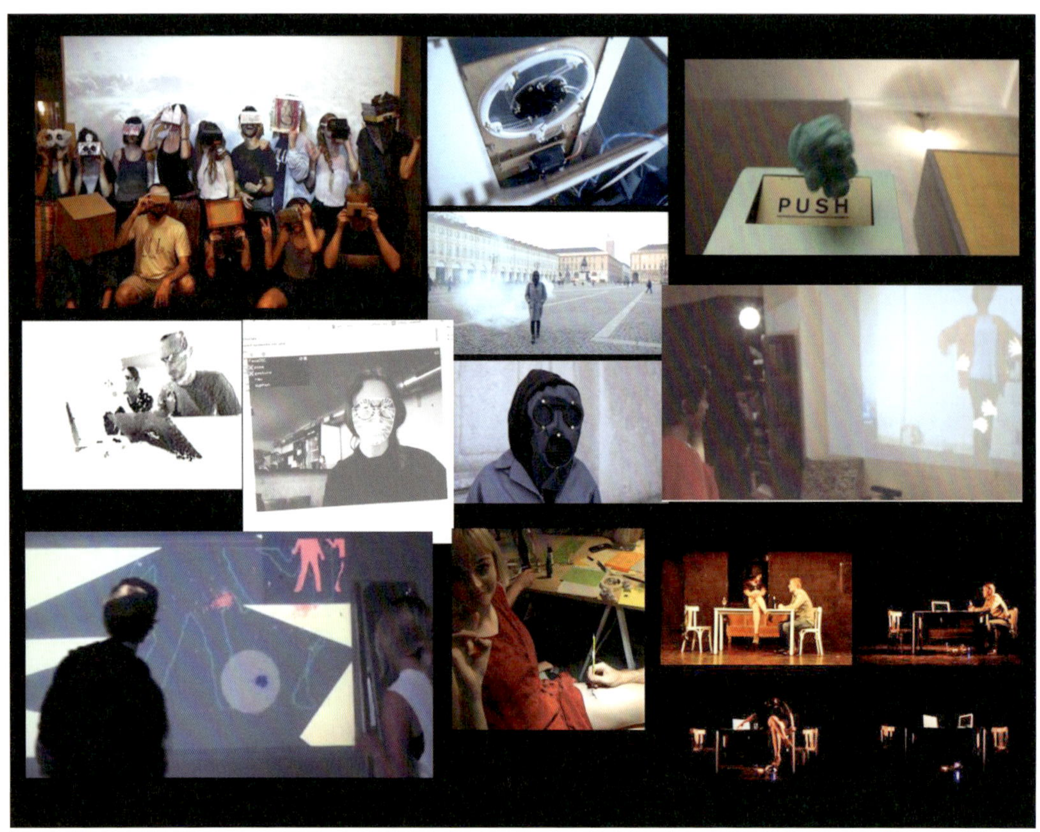

Racheluwa

School of Machines, Making & Make-Believe

http://schoolofma.org

School of Machines, Making & Make-Believe, founded in Berlin in 2014, creates one-of-a-kind hands-on learning experiences in the areas of art, technology, design, and human connection. Our programs examine contemporary cultural issues while exploring latest technologies as a catalyst to question their usage, the world around us, and ourselves.

As a female-led initiative, we actively encourage women and participants from underserved communities to join in our activities. Thus far, we've held 25 unique four-week full-time programs with 300+ participants, coming from 52 countries, 60% are women. Classes are small and intimate, generally between 10-15 participants. They are hands-on project-driven and conclude with a public exhibition of work.

Our programs are designed to encourage students' curiosity, confidence, and the enthusiasm to say something with their work. Our philosophy is centered around the idea that we are all lifelong learners. We love it when our students leave programs activated; equipped with technical and hands-on tools and skill sets, but also critically-minded, more deeply engaged with their surroundings and with themselves.

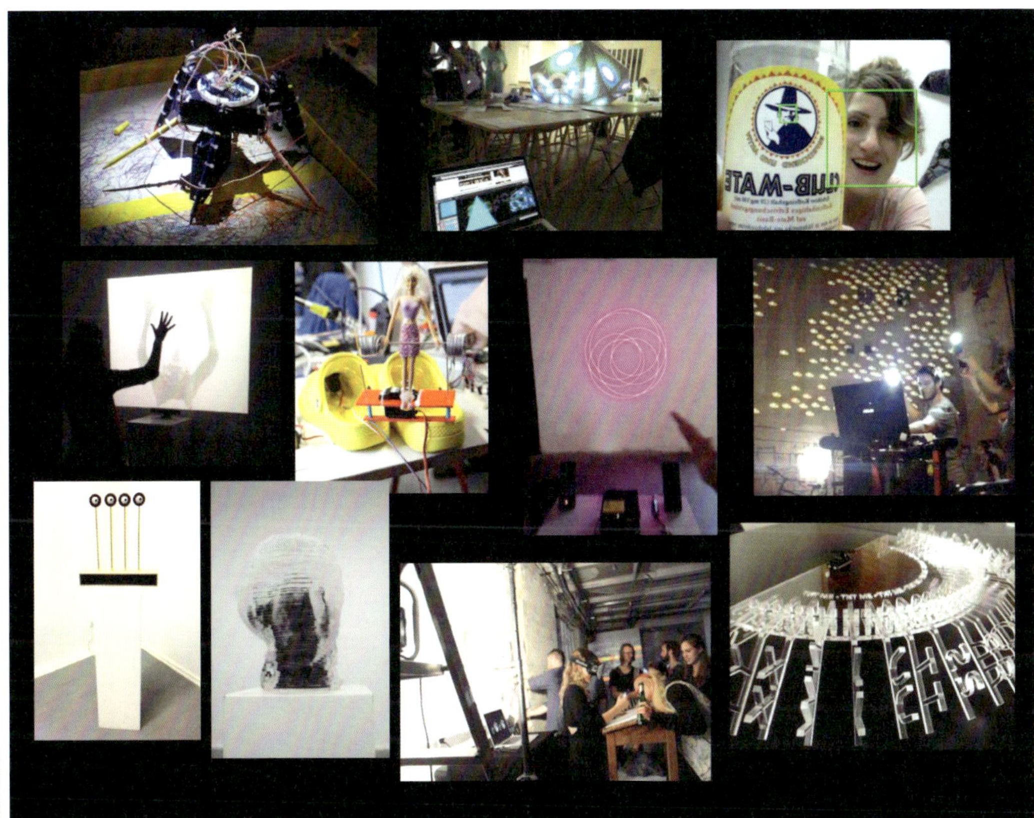

We also run shorter workshops, online classes, and community events open to the public year-round. In 2019, we started "Cake & Conversation" evenings, serving cake and inviting speakers to discuss interesting topics affecting humans and the process of creativity. Similarly Pancake Society is a Saturday morning gathering open to all where we cook and eat pancakes together and actively discuss current issues in society and how we might improve upon them. The Hong Kong protests and sexual harassment and assault were recent topics.

These programs are developed organically in response to the needs of and direct requests from our community. An interest in technology is what brings us together but our communal discussions and what we care about extends far beyond that.

School of Machines, Making & Make-Believe is a uniquely curated school, founded by artist Rachel Uwa in Berlin in 2014, keen on inventing one-of-a-kind hands-on learning experiences in the areas of art, technology, design, and human connection. It embraces art, creativity, and exploring the latest technology and ourselves with openness, humility, and curiosity. The school's philosophy is centered around the idea that we are all lifelong learners.

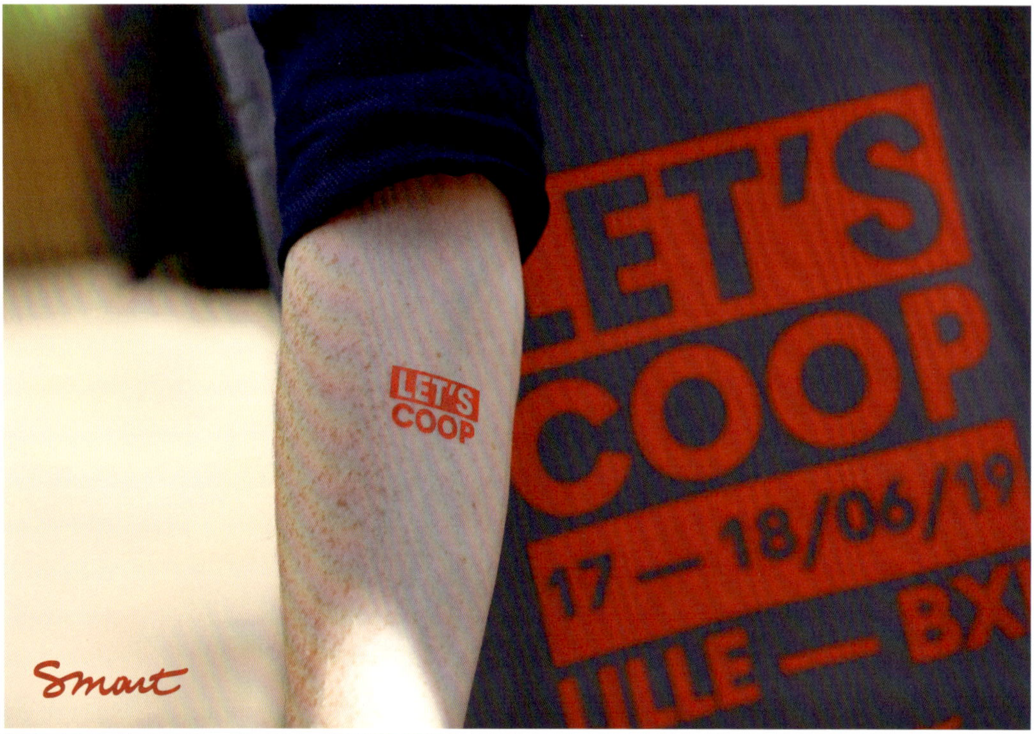

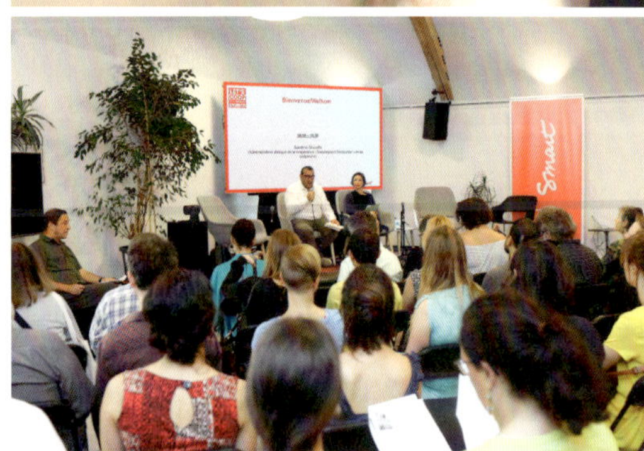
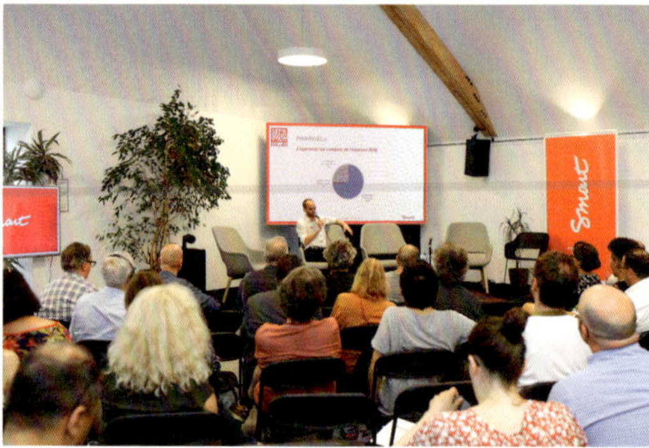
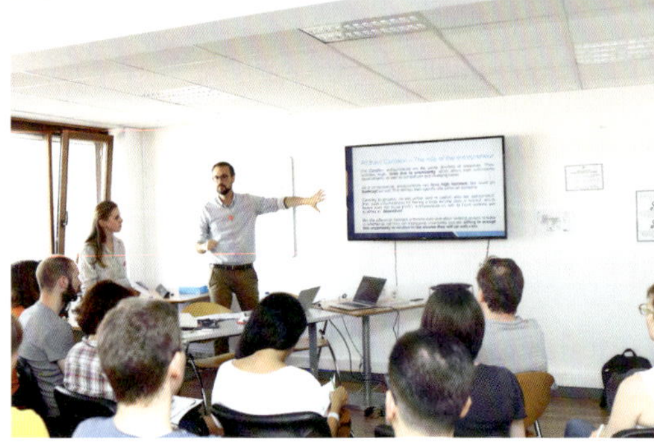
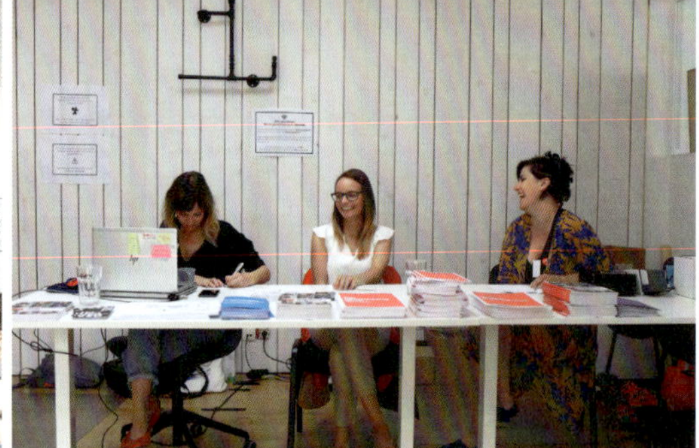

Smart Coop

http://www.smart.coop

Smart is the largest cooperative group of freelancers and entrepreneurs in Europe. It is the story of a pragmatic approach born in 1998: the construction of responses to needs of workers who want to exercise an activity of their choice and benefit from the best social protection available.

Created in Belgium in 1998 to support artists and broadly creative and cultural workers, today *Smart* is open to freelancers of all sectors and activities and represents a turnover of over 200 million euros in Europe. It is established in 9 countries and nearly 40 cities and accompanies more than 30,000 people each year.

With *Smart*, freelancers manage their activities autonomously. They find their customers, decide on the amount to invoice, and act independently. They have access to invoicing tools (in some countries, through software), meaning that *Smart* takes care of invoicing the members' clients, with an upfront payment guarantee. Members may obtain an employment contract from the cooperative based on their freelance income and get access to the same social security benefits as regular employees. Members can concentrate on their creativity and customers while *Smart* is responsible for making all the social and tax declarations arising from their activities. *Smart* also provides freelancers with a range of other mutualized services such as legal assistance, insurance cover, information, trainings, legal advice, a social professional network, and co-working spaces.

Smart is a shared enterprise made up of freelancers who decide to join forces to practice their profession by pooling a set of services and tools necessary to develop economic activities while reducing the risks inherent to any project. Rather than each creating their own structure, they use the shared enterprise, which is the common legal, administrative, and insurance vehicle used by all its members to act economically: invest, buy, hire staff, produce, or sell.

Smart is a cooperative open to all those who need it. Whatever the profile of its users (artists, freelancers, SMEs, collectives…), whether they wish to provide services one day or to develop their activities in a sustainable way, whether they plan to employ staff, whether they consider making major investments, and whatever their sector of activity.

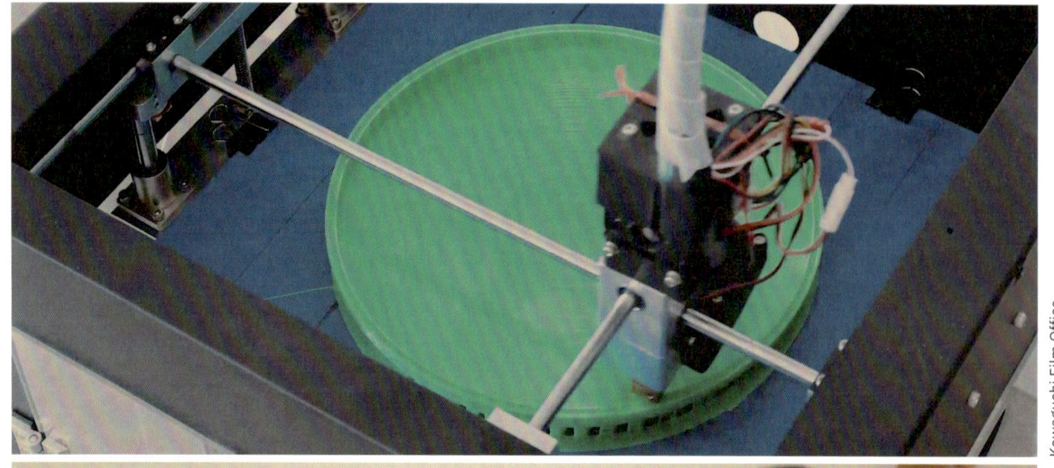

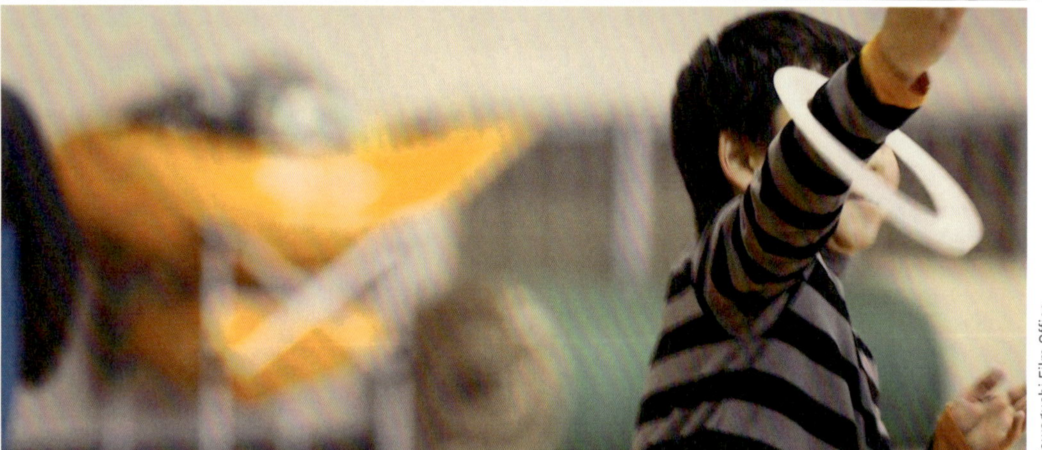

STEAM physical education program

Takashi Terada

STEAM physical education program is an educational program that enables users to learn the fusion of physicality and digital through recreation. It is an educational program that focuses on 3D modeling and 3D printer studies using flying discs. In Japan, children's physical strength and athletic ability have dropped significantly due to increasing screen time on smartphones. Children seem to be being played by the digital. Terada developed this STEAM education program out of concern about gaming disorders and the resulting lack of real communication and exercise. The program was designed with a focus on creating constant communication (3D modeling). The reason why the developer and 3D modeler Takashi Terada

decided to feature flying discs as the subject is due to the fact that he is a flying disc player himself and he has the ability to teach unique throwing techniques, tricks, as well as creative ways to play the game. And children can utilize digital technology and physically play at the same time. Elementary school children are in the phase of developing their space perception, imagination, and physical senses using their bodies, rather than the minds. Takashi Terada recognized the importance of feeling rather than thinking, and wanted the students to experience how a simple object like a flying disc can fly in different ways depending on its form, by making their own flying discs using 3D modeling and 3D printers. Terada con-

DIGITAL COMMUNITIES · Honorary Mention

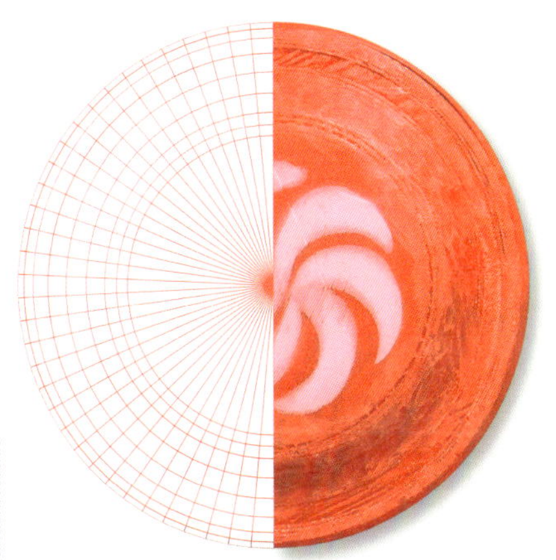
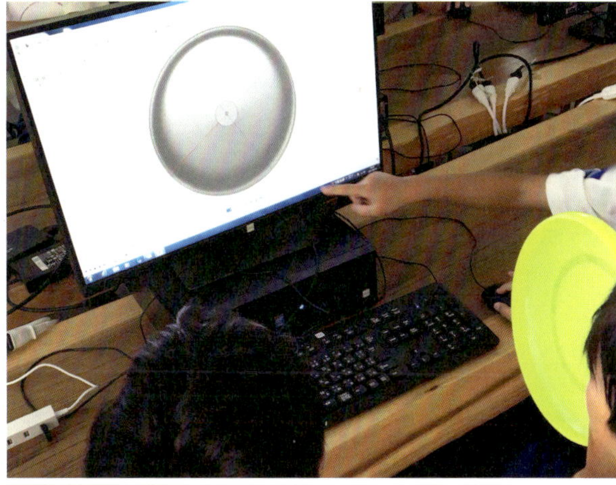

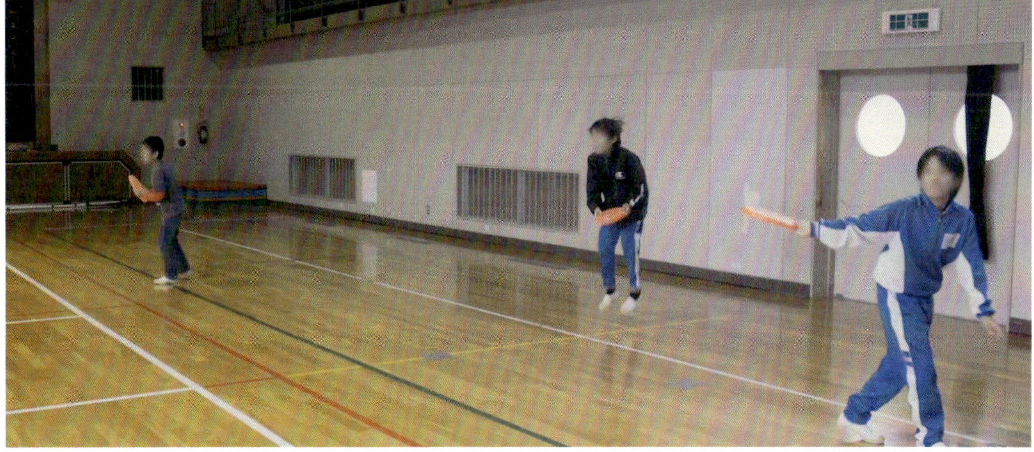

vinced the public elementary school in his small town to incorporate the digital fabrication class into their integrated studies program. The program is also designed to link with environmental issues e.g. related to cedar trees in Japan's mountainous areas. In Japan, heavy rains caused by global climate change have led to many landslides and deaths. Students learn about such problems in their classes and about ways to use thinned wood by carving design patterns with laser cutters. The use of thinned wood contributes to the thinning of Japanese cedar trees, thus supporting optimal tree growth and preventing landslide damage. The 3D printed flying discs are plastic. The environmental issue of how to properly dispose of or reuse the plastic is also under consideration for the future of this educational program.

Planning, direction: Takashi Terada (Terada 3D Works)
Video: Kawaguchi Film Office
With support from: Jinryou Elementary School, Kamiyama-cho (The town of Kamiyama), NPO Green Valley Inc.

STEAM physical education program was developed by Japanese 3D modeler **Takashi Terada** and enables users to experience the fusion of physicality and the digital through recreation. In Japan, children's physical strength and athletic ability have significantly decreased due to the increase in screen time on smartphones. Children seem to be being played by the digital. Terada developed this STEAM physical education program out of concern about gaming disorders and the resulting lack of real communication and exercise. He negotiated with the principal of the elementary school in the small town that he lives in, and began teaching this special class there.

https://youtu.be/6tI8sX-lIsU

DONATE ع en

Syrian Archive

Curating visual documentation for justice and human rights

The **Syrian Archive** is a Syrian-led and initiated collective of human rights activists dedicated to curating visual documentation relating to human rights violations and other crimes committed by all sides during the conflict in Syria with the goal of creating an evidence-based tool for reporting, advocacy and accountability purposes.

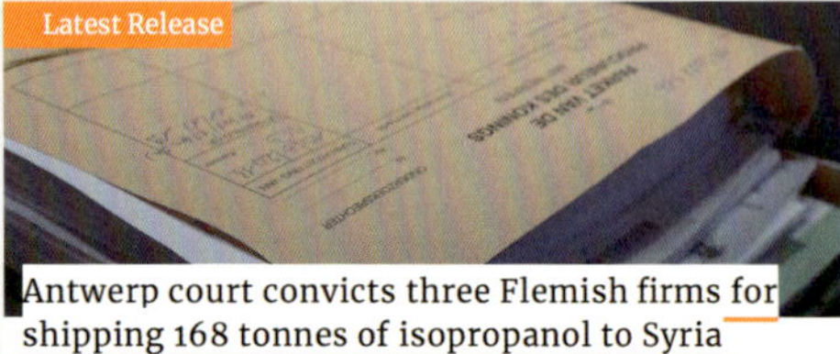

Latest Release

Antwerp court convicts three Flemish firms for shipping 168 tonnes of isopropanol to Syria

Update on isopropanol export to Syria

Sections

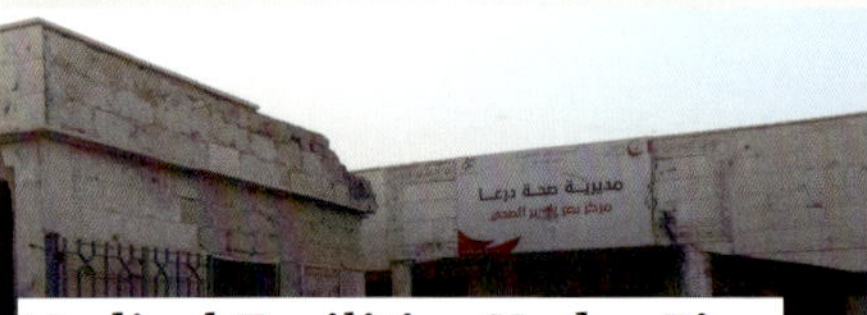

Medical Facilities Under Fire: Busra Al Harir Healthcare Center

investigation reveals the targeting of a health care center in Daraa

Mon Jun 08 2020

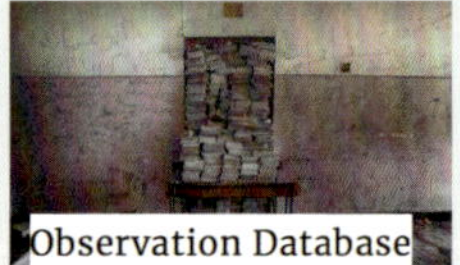

Observation Database

Verified videos of observations of violations

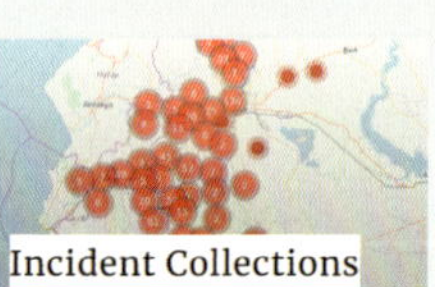

Incident Collections

Clustered visual content by incident, thematically disaggregated.

Tue Apr 24 2018

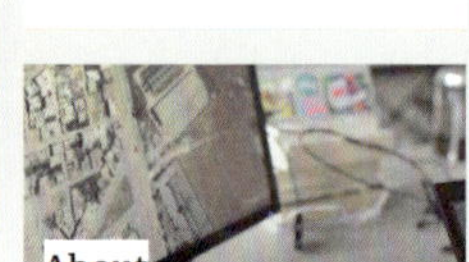

Tech Advocacy

Amount of content preserved, made unavailable and restored

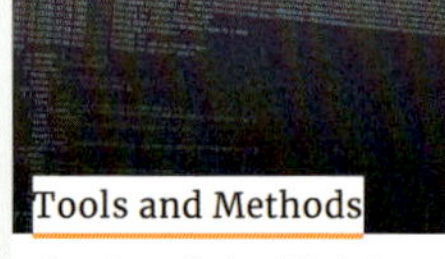

Tools and Methods

Open Source Tools and Methods for Open Source Investigations

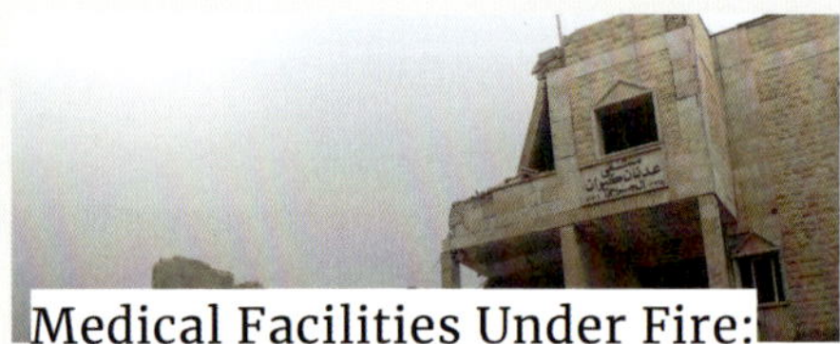

Medical Facilities Under Fire: Kiwan Charitable Hospital

Investigation reveals the destruction of a hospital operating in southwestern Idlib

Mon Jun 01 2020

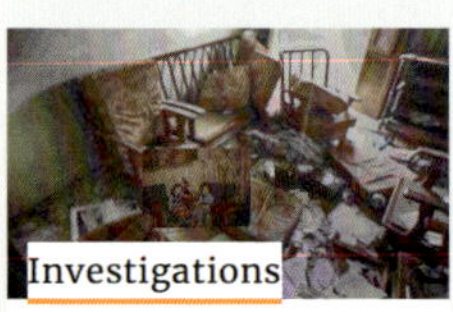

About

Mission, vision, and workflow

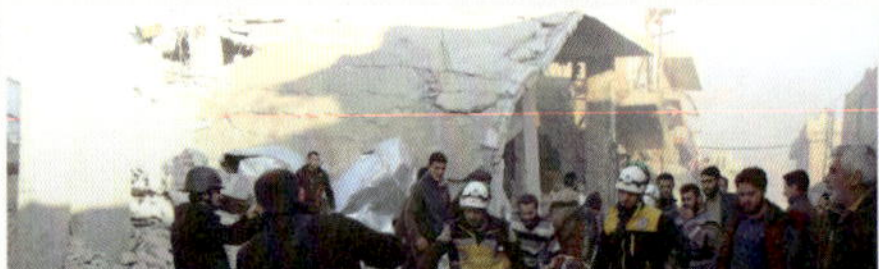

Targeting Balyoun Market with airstrikes

Investigation reveals market targeted by airstrikes

Mon May 25 2020

Investigations

Verification and open source analysis

Syrian Archive

https://syrianarchive.org

Syrian Archive is a Syrian-led project that aims to support human rights investigators, advocates, media reporters, and journalists in their efforts to document human rights violations in Syria through developing new open source tools as well as providing a transparent and replicable methodology for collecting, preserving, verifying, and investigating visual documentation. The organization, which was founded in 2014, believes that visual documentation of human rights violations that is transparent, detailed, and reliable is critical for improving accountability and can positively contribute to post-conflict reconstruction and stability. Making sure verified content is publicly available and accessible for journalists, human rights defenders, and lawyers is equally important. Such documentation can humanize victims, reduce the space for dispute over numbers killed, help societies understand the true human costs of war, and support truth and reconciliation efforts.

Gaining physical access to be able to investigate and report on human rights violations in Syria is very limited and dangerous for independent journalists, international news agencies, UN investigation bodies, and international human rights organizations. This is the main reason *Syrian Archive* and other documentation groups depend on verified user-generated content to assist in criminal case building as well as human rights research.

One of the ways this is done is through releasing all software developed publicly in free and open-source formats. This is done both to ensure trust is built and maintained between the *Syrian Archive* and its partners and collaborators, as well as to allow software to be reused and customized by other groups outside of this project. Technical integration with existing open-source investigative tools ensure that work is not duplicated.

Syrian Archive works in collaboration with other archival groups, as well as lawyers and journalists, to develop its methodology, and with other technologists to develop the open source tools we are using.

Once content has been processed, verified, and analyzed, it is then reviewed for accuracy. In the event of a discrepancy, content is fed back into the digital evidence workflow for further verification. If content is deemed accurate, it moves to the publishing stage of the digital evidence workflow. Regular reports on verified visual content ensure that the feedback loop between the *Syrian Archive* and sources who filmed the videos is closed. This allows *Syrian Archive* to add value to the visual content being preserved, verified, and analyzed immediately for advocacy purposes and later on for accountability and justice purposes.

Through collecting, verifying, preserving, and investigating visual documentation of human rights violations in Syria, the *Syrian Archive* aims to preserve data as a digital memory, to establish a verified database of human rights violations, and to act as an evidence tool for legally implementing justice and accountability as concept and practice in Syria.

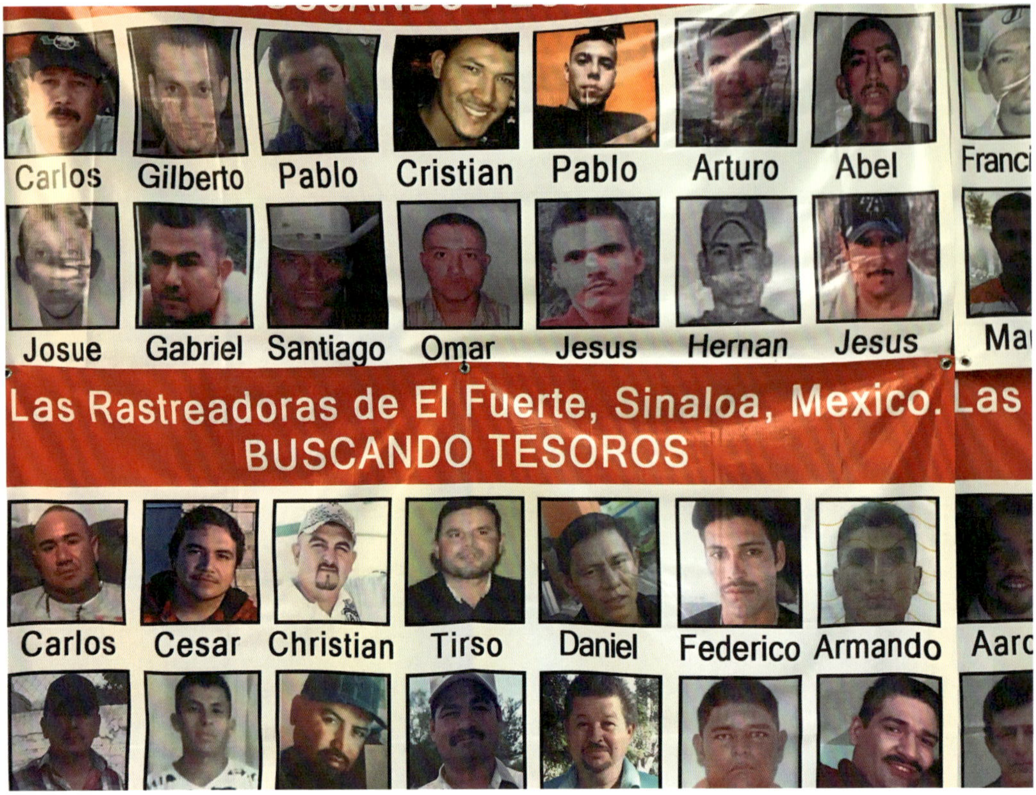

Fernando Gonzalez Buenrostro

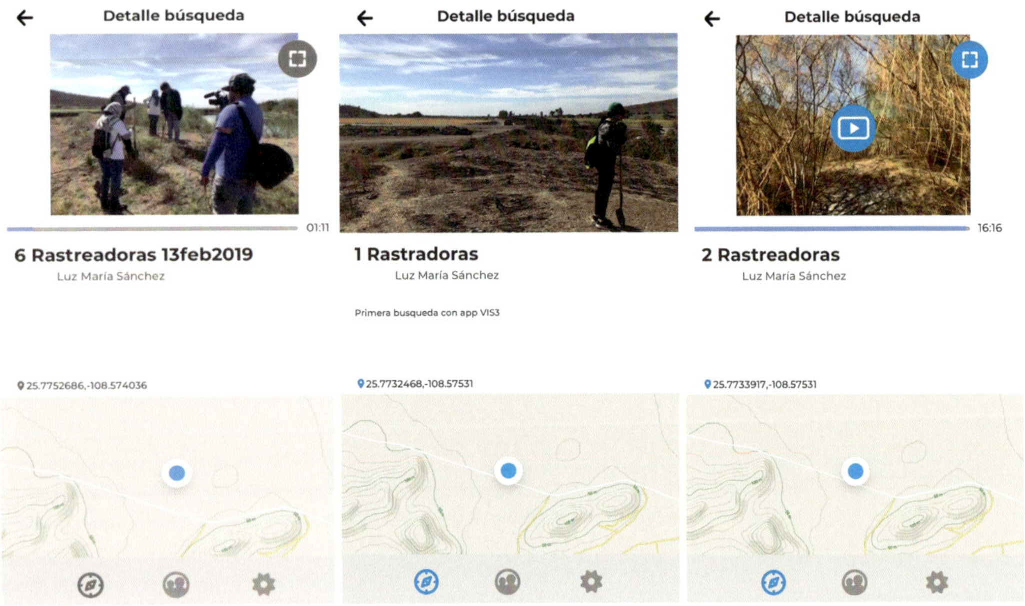

Detalle búsqueda

Detalle búsqueda

Detalle búsqueda

01:11

6 Rastreadoras 13feb2019
Luz María Sánchez

1 Rastradoras
Luz María Sánchez

Primera busqueda con app VIS3

16:16

2 Rastreadoras
Luz María Sánchez

25.7752686,-108.574036

25.7732468,-108.57531

25.7733917,-108.57531

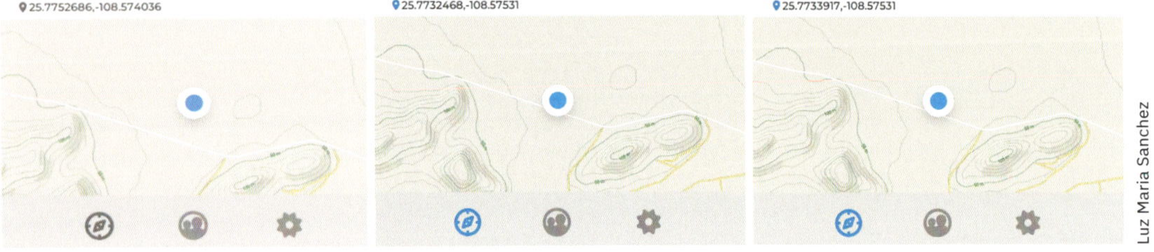

Luz María Sanchez

Vis. [un]necessary force_3

www.vis-unnecessaryforce.org

Vis. [un]necessary force_3 or under its acronym *V.[u]nf_3,* addresses one of the most alarming issues in Mexico: the abduction of young individuals, mostly male, aged 18 to 30, often with the complicity of police/military forces. In 2019 numbers escalated to +60,000 forced-disappearance registered cases. Due to the lack of action of the local/federal authorities, citizens have been organising themselves to perform independent investigations and on-site searches for their abducted family members. Threatened by cartels and police/military forces alike, these citizens are the only ones who—organised in small groups—are looking for forced-disappearance victims nationwide.

V.[u]nf_3 is an artistic-social project developed for communities that search for their family members, victims of forced-disappearance. It consists of a collaborative and participatory audio-visual cyber-cartography for mobile systems and a data-visualisation website. And materialises as a tool + online-space created for documenting expeditions of individuals—embedded in close-knit communities—looking for clandestine graves. The app registers text, audio, video, and geo-locates data. The website is the archive—visualising and systematising data recorded: private histories that together construct the chronicles of the whole community.

V. [u]nf_3 is a tool explicitly designed for Mexican trackers of clandestine graves. The preliminary functional model was made after the activities of Las Rastreadoras de El Fuerte (The Trackers from El Fuerte), a community—consisting predominantly of women—that has been searching for graves around the city of Los Mochis, in the northern state of Sinaloa since 2014 under the guidance of Mirna Medina.

V. [u]nf_3 allows for reinforcing citizen-empowerment through the building of an individual + collective data-cartography; strengthening the community through the shared experience of reviewing and analysing outcomes from data-recollection; breaking the digital exclusion through learning-while-using the app + website; experiencing a bespoke social software made for the specificity of their search practices; creating an expedition-archive through this user-generated content + metadata tool; building resistance against oblivion and neglect while constructing a digital memorial that will honor their loved ones when registering their stories.

With support from: Sistema Nacional de Creadores de Arte (SNCA)/ Secretaría de Cultura Mexico, Universidad Autónoma Metropolitana, Romain Ré *molosc.com*

V.[u]nf_3 started off as Luz María Sánchez's research-creation project developed at Universidad Autónoma Metropolitana, and was supported with a grant from the National System of Art Creators. The project was sparked off by the question: How do civilians survive amongst extreme violence performed by legit and non-legit groups of power in Mexico? Its results have been on exhibition at MUAC (Mexico City), WRO Biennale/WRO Art Center (Wroclaw), and ZKM|Center for Art and Media (Karlsruhe). *V. [u]nf_3's* core team include Luz María Sánchez (author), Romain Ré (general digital developer/programmer), Ana Paula Sánchez-Cardona (production assistant), Jorge Vélez (mobile app programmer), Josué Martínez Alcántara/Fernando González Buenrostro (on-site documentation). Advisors for *V. [u]nf_3* are Carolina Robledo (GIASF), Daniela Rea, Jacobo Dayán, and Salvador Maldonado Aranda.

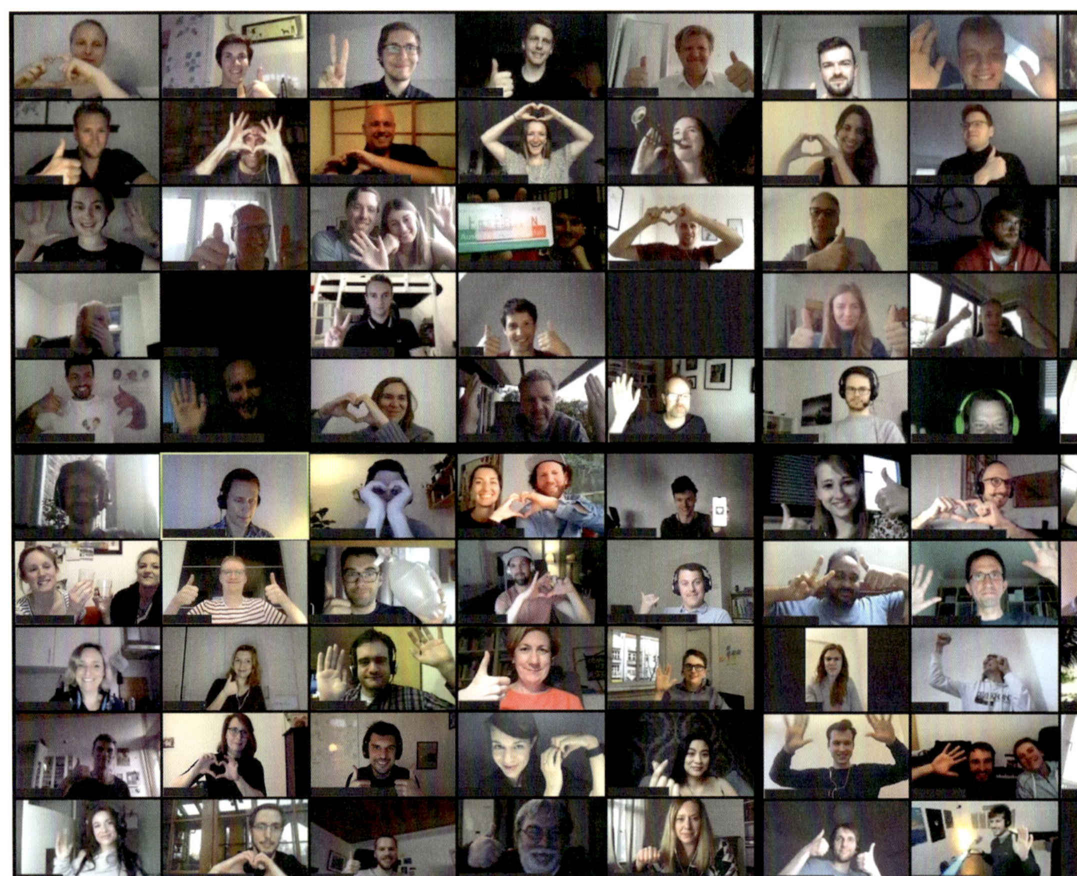

#WirVsVirus Hackathon

www.wirvsvirus.org

Within only four days, seven civil non-profit organizations combined forces to organize the *#WirVsVirus Hackathon.* The hackathon's purpose was to create a digital space for everyone who had already started working on solutions for the situation caused by Covid-19 or who was eager to do so. The hackathon was supposed to create a digital space for collaboration, co-creation, inspiration, and networking. We specifically reached out to all citizens with time and Internet access to join us for 48 hours of hacking—meaning: finding creative solutions in interdisciplinary teams for challenges posed by Covid-19.

In total, over 28,000 citizens participated making the *#WirVsVirus Hackathon* the world's largest ever organized hackathon. 1,500 teams came up with 1,500 solutions. The solutions covered a wide ranging field from medical resource supply to job security to government service digitalization and community cohesion. The hackathon set an example for the power of German innovation and created a community that lasts to this day. Especially because the hackathon was only the start. From the beginning we planned a support program for the months after because we knew that ideas are only as good as the value they contribute to society. The support program consists of four elements: a support program of 130 most promising solutions, a fast track program for 10 solutions most needed, a community management for

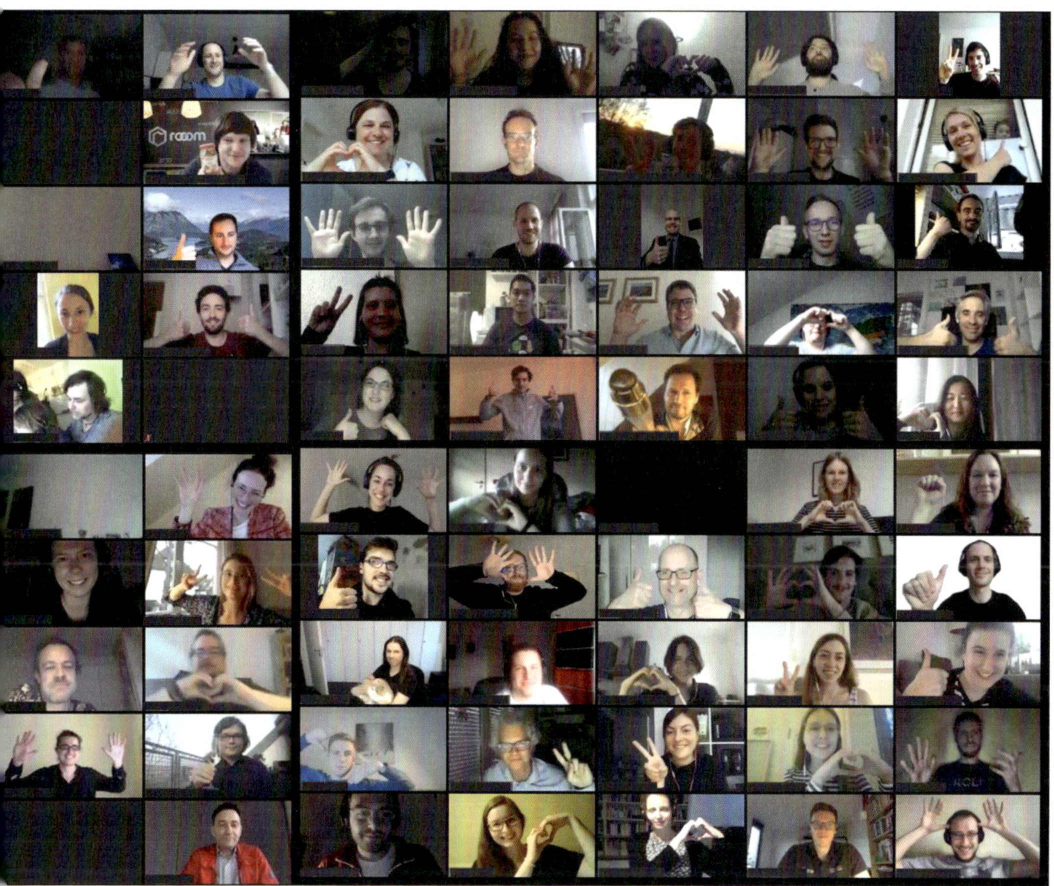

the Slack workspace where over 3,000 individuals still interact and a fund that supports Covid-related projects financially. We gathered over 2.5 million euros from the German government as well as from companies to support projects and enable us to run the program over the course of six months.

The *#WirVsVirus Hackathon* and support program have shown how digital communities in coopera-tion with government and private actors can foster change and contribute to a better society. The strong community has proven that citizens want to be involved. The concept is also a blueprint for a continuous participatory process to develop solutions for the great challenges of our time.

With support from the German government which functioned as co-initiators and patrons of the Hack-athon (no financial involvement).

#WirVsVirus Hackathon. The hackathon was a first starting point for a continuous participatory process to develop common solutions in order to master the great challenges posed by Covid-19 to society. The *#WirVsVirus Hackathon* was initiated and realized on a voluntary basis by: Tech4Germany, Code for Germany, Impact Hub Berlin, Project-Together, SEND e.V., Initiative D21, Prototype Fund. The hackathon took place from 20-22 March 2020 and attracted over 42,000 registrations, 28,000 participants and resulted in 1,500 ideas. So far, the *#WirVsVirus Hackathon* is the biggest hackathon worldwide. The hackathon took place under the patronage of the German government.

Visionary Pioneers of Media Art

Visionary Pioneers of Media Art

Launched in 2014, this category is dedicated to recognizing and celebrating the men and women whose artistic, technological, and social achievements have decisively influenced and advanced the development of new artistic directions.

What began as a technological revolution has since developed into a new cultural and social reality with its own specific forms of communication, cultural techniques, and artistic expressions, the roots of which extend far back into the past and lead us to encounters with remarkable, extraordinary personalities—the visionary pioneers of media art. Thus, in many respects, these men and women established the foundation of media art as we know it today. With Prix Ars Electronica's Golden Nica for Visionary Pioneers of Media Art, we want to give them the respectful recognition commensurate with their accomplishments, and, at the same time, generate more awareness about the history of media art in general.

Visionary Pioneer of Feminist Media Art 2020

In its fifth edition, the Austrian filmmaker, media artist, and performance artist VALIE EXPORT has been selected as the recipient of Prix Ars Electronica's Golden Nica for Visionary Pioneer of Feminist Media Art 2020. VALIE EXPORT stands for a consistent feminist-political stance and its like-minded counterpart in (media) art. She has created a trend-setting connection between performance, public space, and media representation and has participated in major exhibitions and taught at renowned institutions such as the Art Institute in San Francisco, the University of Wisconsin, Milwaukee/USA, the Berlin University of the Arts, and the Academy of Media Arts Cologne. VALIE EXPORT is one of the most important and successful international pioneers of feminist media art and is being honored with this award for her impressive life's work.

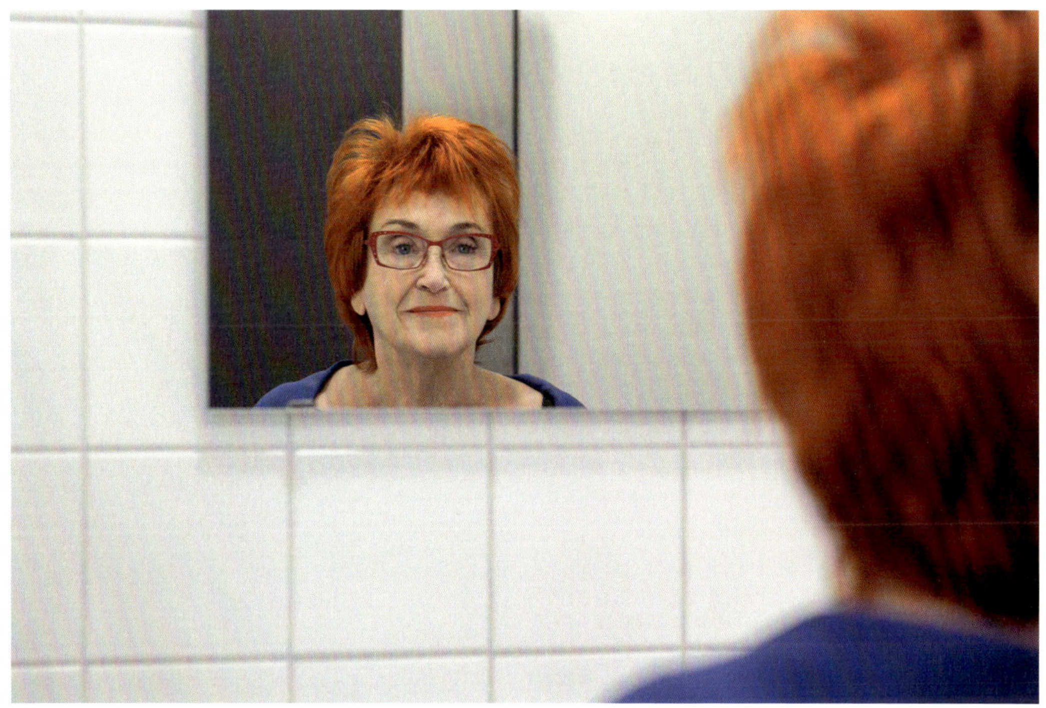

VALIE EXPORT, photo: Violetta Wakolbinger, 2017

VALIE EXPORT

VALIE EXPORT was born as Waltraud Lehner in 1940 in Linz, where she attended the School for the Arts and Crafts. In 1964 she graduated from the HBLVA for Textile Industry in Vienna. Since 1967 she has gone by the name VALIE EXPORT, an artistic concept and logo. She works with a wide range of media and has attracted attention with actions in public spaces that belonged to the field of performance and to media art and were developed from a feminist perspective. VALIE EXPORT presents her work in international solo and group exhibitions.

A co-founder of the Austrian Filmmakers Cooperative, she has participated in numerous film and video festivals all around the world. She began her curatorial activities in the 1970s, focusing on feminism and media art, and has taught at such institutions as the San Francisco Art Institute, the University of Wisconsin-Milwaukee/USA, and the Berlin University of the Arts. Until 2005 VALIE EXPORT held the professorship for Multimedia and Performance at the Academy of Media Arts Cologne. In addition to her international exhibition activities and participation in major exhibitions such as the Venice Biennale (1980) and documenta (1977, 2007), she was the co-commissioner for the Austrian Pavilion at the 2009 Venice Biennale.

For her work to date, VALIE EXPORT has been awarded numerous accolades and prizes, including the Gustav Klimt Prize (1998), the Oskar Kokoschka Prize (2000), the Alfred Kubin Prize (2000), the Austrian Decoration of Honour for Science and Art (2005), the Yoko Ono Lennon Courage Award for the Arts (2014, together with Laurie Anderson, Marianne Faithfull, and Gustav Metzger), the Austrian Women's Lifetime Achievement Award (2015), and the Great Golden Decoration of the City of Linz for Services to Culture. In 2019, VALIE EXPORT was the recipient of the best-endowed European art award, the Roswitha Haftmann Prize, for her pioneering feminist and media-reflexive works.

VALIE EXPORT
I invent myself, therefore I am.

With the selection of her pseudonym in 1967, VALIE EXPORT expressed a self-conception that aimed at exporting itself as well as her thoughts and ideas.[1] With this, she created her own identity. The notion of extension, of expansion, which is evident in all of her works, was also established already at this time, becoming a determining factor in her oeuvre.

"One of the first steps was to create an alias as a concept, and the cigarette package was also the first object of my artistic career." [2]

The artistic production of VALIE EXPORT now spans more than five decades and represents an extensive and diverse oeuvre ranging from actions, scripts, film and video works, photographs, installations, and art objects to performances, sculptures, texts, and drawings. Curatorial projects such as exhibitions, screenings, and symposia as well as her readings and lectures enrich VALIE EXPORT's means of expression.

VALIE EXPORT utilizes her body, the female body, in order to criticize the male gaze. With the *TAPP UND TASTKINO (TOUCHCINEMA)* (1968), she activated the audience, confronting it with an actual woman instead of a depiction of one. She thus illustrated her idea of "expanded cinema," in which the film is produced without celluloid, and expanded the concept of the screen by becoming the projection surface herself. The involvement of the audience and the active eye contact with the artist facilitated a reinterpretation of the role of women in cinema and in the social structure.

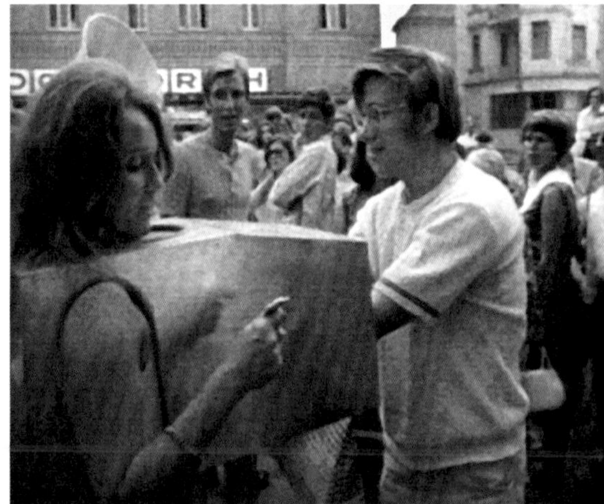

VALIE EXPORT, *TAPP und TASTKINO (TOUCHCINEMA),* 1968

"I came into contact with feminism through my experiences, because as a female artist I was largely ignored not by fellow artists but by audiences. They always directed questions to the filmmakers. And I thought, what is that about? After all, these are my films. Back at the time of the 1968 movement I was already wondering what kind of art a female artist would have to show in order to be seen and noticed. I realized that people had no idea about female artists. This is why I also studied art history, but also explored the question of how the role of women in our society is determined."[3]

VALIE EXPORT, *VALIE EXPORT—SMART EXPORT,* 1970, (object, package of cigarettes, 1967)

Gertraude Wolfschwenger

In the 1970s, VALIE EXPORT investigated gender roles through the medium of photo collages. Based on models by great masters from art history, it was clear what position was expected from a woman—a position difficult to assume not only in a physical sense. VALIE EXPORT humorously transformed these idealized attributes to daily life.

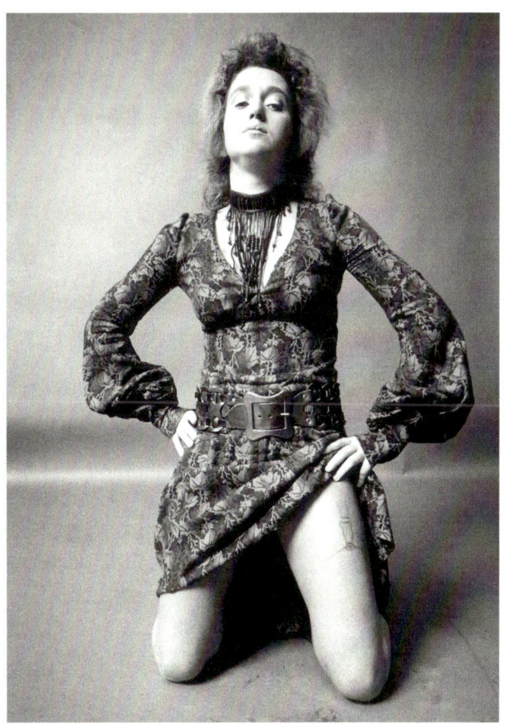

VALIE EXPORT, *Geburtenmadonna*, 1976 (after Michelangelo Buonarroti's pietà, *Madonna della Febbre* (1498–1499), Basilica di San Pietro, Rome)

With unequivocal words, VALIE EXPORT highlights the difference between men and women in society as well as in the world of art. In 1972, the artist wrote a manifesto with the title *WOMEN'S ART* on the occasion of the exhibition *MAGNA. Feminismus: Kunst und Kreativität,* which she conceived and in which only women participated. Once again VALIE EXPORT was ahead of her time and her concept initially attracted little interest. Only in 1975 was she able to present her project in a modified form at Vienna's Galerie nächst St. Stephan as part of the International Women's Year, with Austrian female artists and a supporting program featuring international guests. It was the first art symposium on feminism in Europe.

The above-mentioned manifesto begins with the statement:

"THE POSITION OF ART IN THE WOMEN'S MOVEMENT IS THE POSITION OF THE WOMAN IN THE ART MOVEMENT. THE HISTORY OF WOMAN IS THE HISTORY OF MAN, because man has defined the image of woman for both man and woman. men create and control the social and communication media such as science and art, word and image, fashion and architecture, social interaction and division of labor. men have projected their image of woman onto these media, and it was in accordance with these medial patterns that they shaped women and women shaped themselves. if reality is a social construction and men its engineers, we are dealing with a male reality.

VALIE EXPORT, *Body Sign B*, 1970

women have not yet come to themselves, because they have not had a chance to speak insofar as they had no access to the media.

let women speak so that they can find themselves; this is what I ask for in order to achieve a self-defined image of ourselves and thus a different view of the social function of women. we women must participate in the construction of reality via the building stones of media communication."[4]

It is this attitude, one of participating in the construction of reality from a position of equality, that guides VALIE EXPORT in her actions. Self-empowerment plays a crucial role in this regard and has led to an exploration of the possibilities of artistic expression with contemporary media.

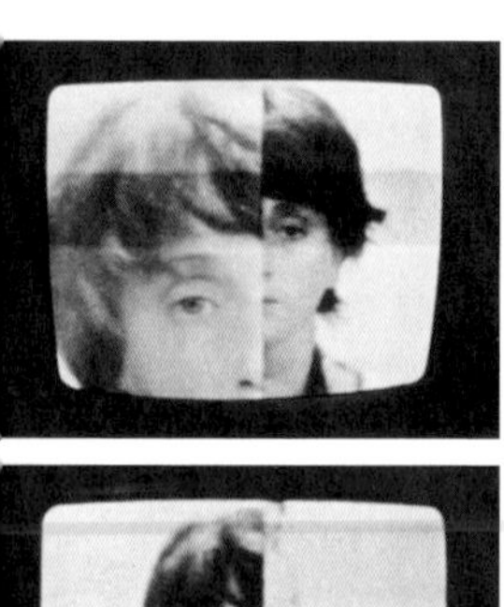
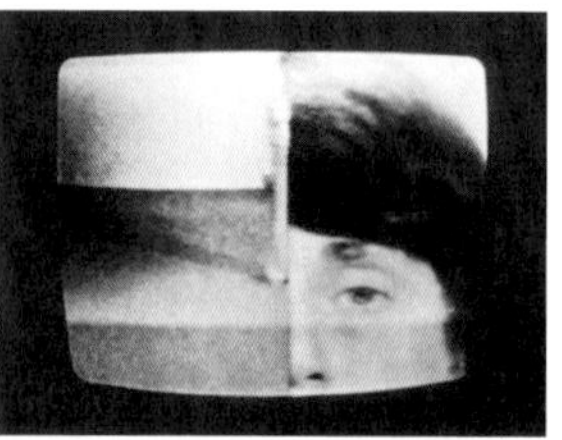
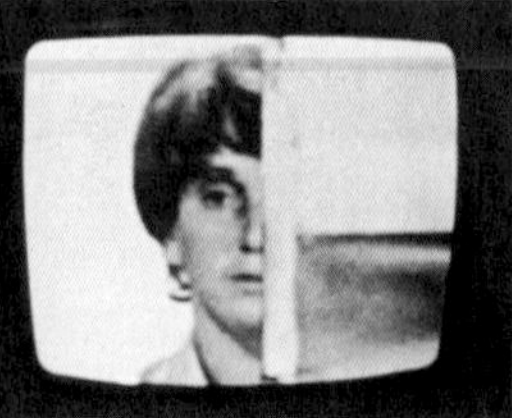
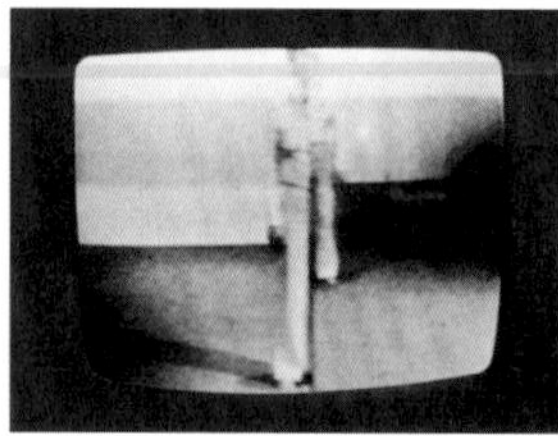
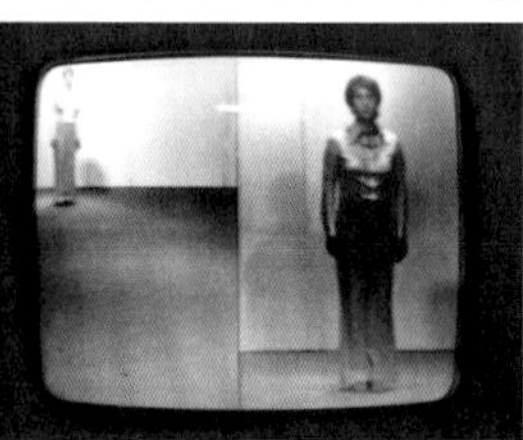
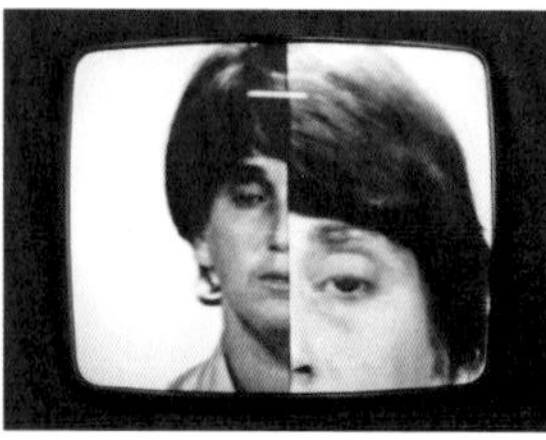

VALIE EXPORT, *Raumsehen und Raumhören (Space Seeing and Space Hearing)*, 1974

Since 1968 VALIE EXPORT has developed expanded cinema actions that require both an active screen and an active audience and, through technical means, widen the field of vision so far that they dissolve the separate entity of both the cinema and of its medium. *"Expanded Cinema* was also about depicting and breaking down power structures, or, as they used to say: decoding and deconstructing."[5]

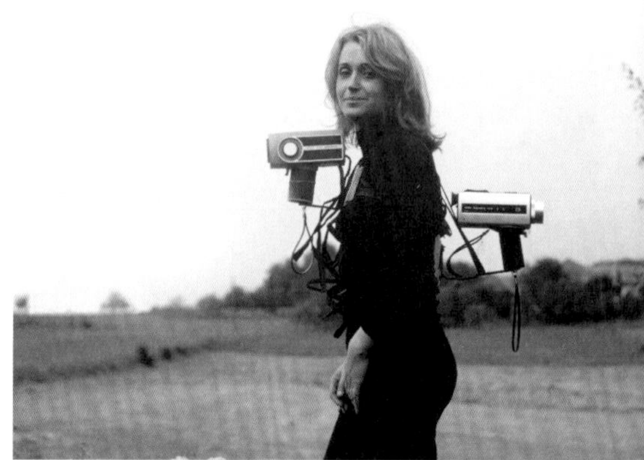

VALIE EXPORT, *Adjungierte Dislokationen (Adjunct Dislocations)*, 1973

VALIE EXPORT experiments with the perception and experience of space by applying the closed-circuit technique and expanded cinema with its intermedia techniques to her performances and installations. Reality and its medial representation become visible to the spectator simultaneously, while they nonetheless constitute different representations. Through the instant transfer of the image material to monitors, the editing tools available at the mixing desk, and by means of camera angles, the medium of video gives recipients the chance to observe many perspectives at the same time. Choreographed and staged by the artist, superimpositions of body, space, time, and motion are achieved—and an environment emerges.

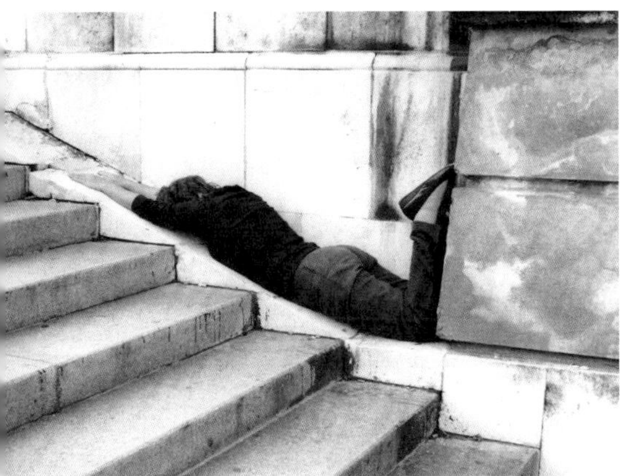

VALIE EXPORT, *Pönologie,* 1982

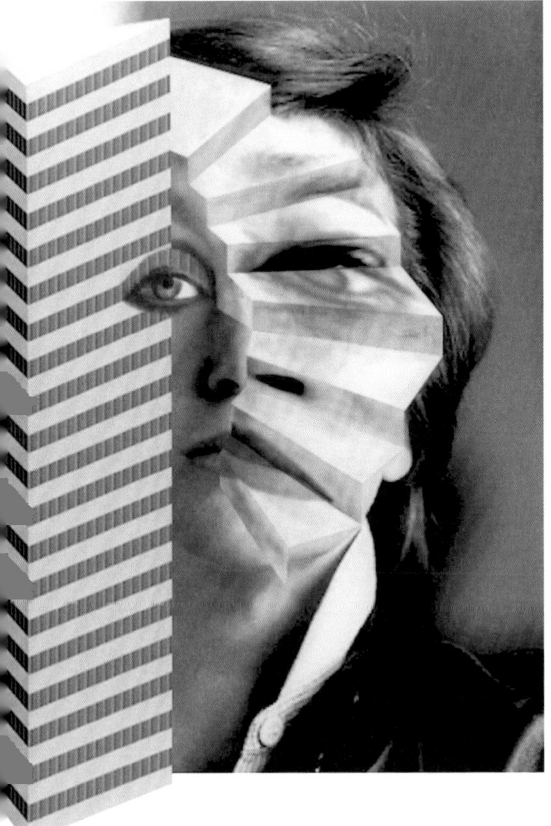

VALIE EXPORT, *Selbstportrait mit Stiege und
Hochhaus (Self-portrait with Stairs and High-rise),* 1989

The artist's exploration of conceptual photography was reflected, among other things, in the *Körperkonfigurationen (Body Configurations)* that she created between 1972 and 1982. These themes revolve around the relationship of the body to its environment, to its surrounding architecture. The continuation of this exploration manifested itself beginning in the late 1980s in works that were further developed through the use of computer programs.

"It's not about distorting the photograph or the model but rather about using the computer to create new spaces, to make new statements. With the computer, I go one step further: I "mediatize;" I use a medium intermediately in order to place the body in a configuration, to expand it. The computer is merely a tool in this process. Every medium is an extension of the body, and I have always used the media to this end in my body art. The furthermost extension of the body is that via the electronic medium of television, where a body is seen on a million different screens at the same time."[6]

In the early 1970s, the medium of television—as an expansion of the scope of action in a technical sense and with regard to new audience segments—inspired VALIE EXPORT to new artistic explorations. Her 1970 TV action *FACING A FAMILY* shows in a self-referential manner a generic family watching TV, being observed at the same time by another equally generic family. Her television works from the 1980s utilized the medium as a tool for conveying information. The subject matter of *Das Bewaffnete Auge. VALIE EXPORT im Dialog mit der Filmavantgarde (The Armed Eye—VALIE EXPORT in a Dialogue with the Film Avant-Garde)* (1984) and *Aktionskunst International. Dokumente zum Internationalen Aktionismus (Action Art International. Documents on International Actionism)* (1989) resembles a lecture series revolving around art history and film and media theory.

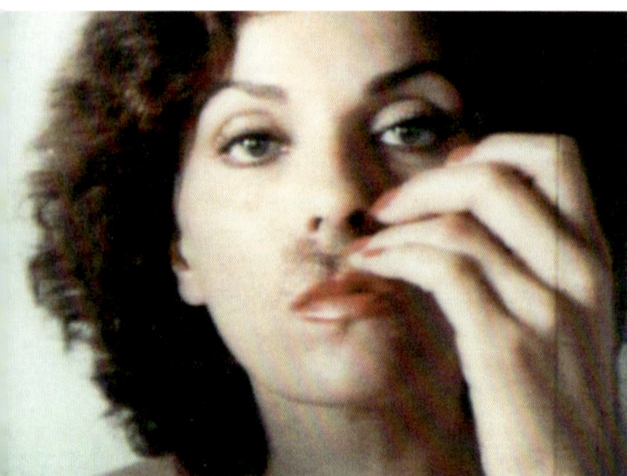

VALIE EXPORT, *Unsichtbare Gegner (Invisible Adversaries),* 1976

VALIE EXPORT's first of three feature films, *Unsichtbare Gegner* (Invisible Adversaries) (1976), makes use of some of her early works. Photography, performance, and video are incorporated into the story of a woman who increasingly feels threatened by an invisible power.

Menschenfrauen (Human Females) (1979) examines the social conditions of women through four protagonists, whose attempt to break out of their appointed social roles is visualized skillfully and artistically by VALIE EXPORT.

In the film *Die Praxis der Liebe (The Practice of Love)* (1984), VALIE EXPORT translates her experiences from the avant-garde genre into a thriller that revolves around dependence and abysses.

VALIE EXPORT shows her cinematic works with great success in exhibitions and at international festivals, and can position her experimental works both in the projection room of the cinema and in the institutional space of a museum or gallery. In 1968, VALIE EXPORT co-founded the Austrian Filmmakers Cooperative, today called the Austria Film Coop, in order to establish a distribution system for independent Austrian films in this country and abroad.

Since the 1980s, VALIE EXPORT has distinguished herself not only through her artistic output but also through her international teaching activities at institutions including the University of Wisconsin-Milwaukee, the HdK (Berlin University of the Arts), the Academy of Media Arts Cologne, and the Salzburg International Summer Academy of Fine Arts.

She has also given numerous lectures and taught courses dealing with a thematically broad range of performance and experimental film works as well as the connections between the artistic practice of the avant-garde—including her own—and feminism, psychoanalysis, architecture, and ethnology. In 1985, ten years after *MAGNA,* VALIE EXPORT, along with Silvia Eiblmayr and Cathrin Pichler, mounted *Kunst mit Eigen-Sinn,* an internationally acclaimed exhibition focusing on current works by female artists, accompanied again by a symposium and a selection of video works. For the 1991 Wiener Festwochen festival, she organized an international symposium on the topic of *Ent-Fesselung der Geschlechter,* and in 2009, VALIE EXPORT served as co-commissioner, together with Silvia Eiblmayr, of the Austrian Pavilion at the Venice Biennale.

For the project *Bilder der Berührungen* (1997/98), VALIE EXPORT, along with Syntax/Köln, was awarded the first CD-ROM prize at the *Videonale Bonn.* This compilation was based on the conceptual transfer of a catalogue into the new format of a multimedia CD-ROM, which broke new ground in terms of artistic work and is to be seen as an independent work and means of expression. On the CD-ROM, sixteen videos and a number of serial photographs are joined with the experimental film *Syntagma* (1983).

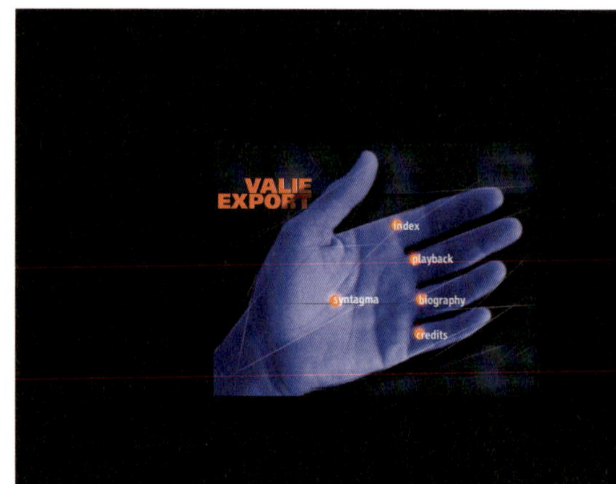

VALIE EXPORT, *Bilder der Berührungen,* CD-ROM, 1997/98

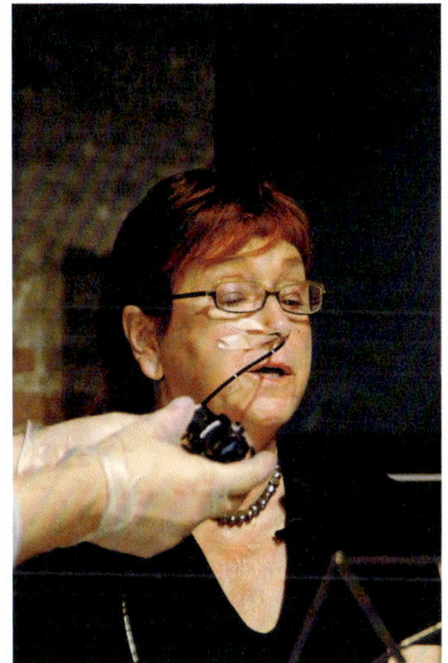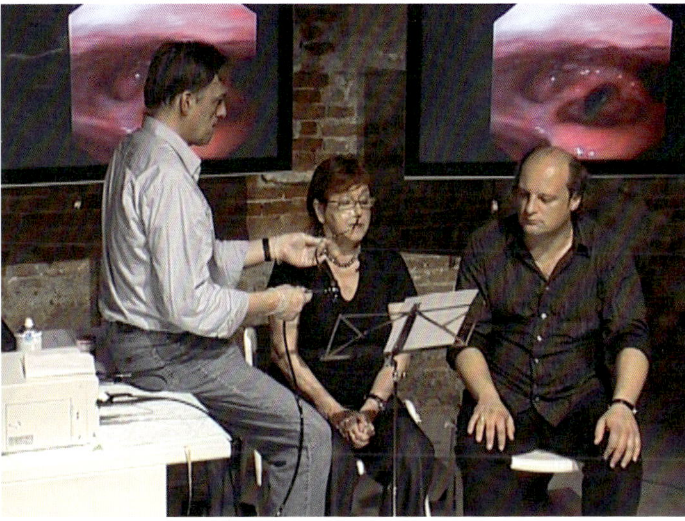

VALIE EXPORT, *The voice as performance, act and body,* 2007, Venice Biennale

The use of a technology from the medical field enabled VALIE EXPORT to broaden and literally deepen her examination of the voice as a medium, as a carrier of information, and as a political issue. Her performance at the 2007 Venice Biennale showed the technical apparatus of the voice, the place of production of letters and sounds.

VALIE EXPORT is concerned with the power of the voice, used and abused by people in influential (political) positions. Last but not least, it is also about the self-empowerment of women who raise their voices to make themselves heard in asserting their concerns, demands, and self-determination. This interest began in 1969 with the project *TON-FILM* (Sound Film) and has accompanied VALIE EXPORT ever since. It has been implemented in various formats defined by the artist: as a multi-channel video installation, as a *body-communication-action* and expanded film, as a performance, and as an *intermedial stage play.*

Since the beginning of her artistic activities in the late 1960s, VALIE EXPORT has not only created a comprehensive body of work but has also assembled a substantial archive. The spectrum of materials ranges from initial concept ideas, accompanying research, sketches and preparatory studies, finalized submission documents, and mediating texts to correspondences, lectures, and reviews of the subjects she has dealt with and works she has realized.

In 2015, the Linz-born artist turned this archive over to the VALIE EXPORT Center Linz, which is operated as a cooperation between the City of Linz, the LENTOS Kunstmuseum Linz, and the University of Art and Design Linz. The VALIE EXPORT Center Linz appraises, studies, contextualizes, and mediates the premature legacy of VALIE EXPORT.

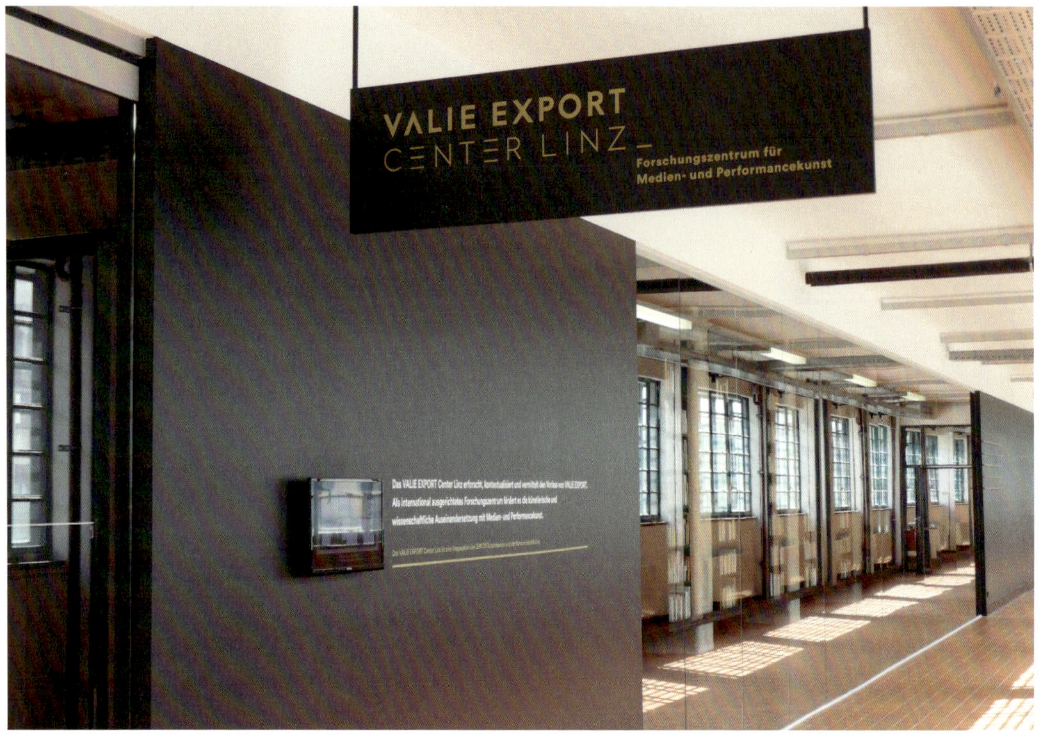

VALIE EXPORT Center Linz, photo: Dagmar Schink, 2019

As part of research work at the VALIE EXPORT Center Linz, a bilingual edition of the unfinished script *Der virtuelle Körper. Vom Prothesenkörper zum postbiologischen Körper (The Virtual Body. From the Prosthetic to the Post-biological Body)*, which VALIE EXPORT wrote at the end of the 1990s, has recently been published by the Verlag der Buchhandlung Walther König. It was edited by Sabine Folie (director of the VALIE EXPORT Center Linz) and Marius Babias (director of the Neuer Berliner Kunstverein, n.b.k.).[7]

"This essayist documentary relates the history of the body as a journey of body representations and performances, from the earliest civilizations up until our digital era. It deals with body rituals, body movements, and body inscriptions in different cultures, with the civilized body in arts and science, and finally with the virtual, intangible body. It tells of replicants, hybrids, chimeras, avatars, aliens, robots, girl monsters, and cyber feminists—but also of modern genetic research and its dream of artificial life."[8]

Many of her project ideas require great patience and perseverance on the part of the media and performance artist. VALIE EXPORT is, to borrow from the title of a ceremonial address by Marie-Luise Angerer at the VALIE EXPORT Center Linz, "A radical performance artist ahead of her time."[9]

Text: Dagmar Schink
Translation: Resina Haslinger (Manifesto), Thomas Taborsky, and Douglas Deitemyer

Image credits if not stated otherwise: © VALIE EXPORT, Bildrecht Wien, 2020, Courtesy VALIE EXPORT:
p. 138 – 141, 142 top and 143.
Premature legacy VALIE EXPORT, VALIE EXPORT Center / LENTOS Kunstmuseum Linz: p. 142 bottom

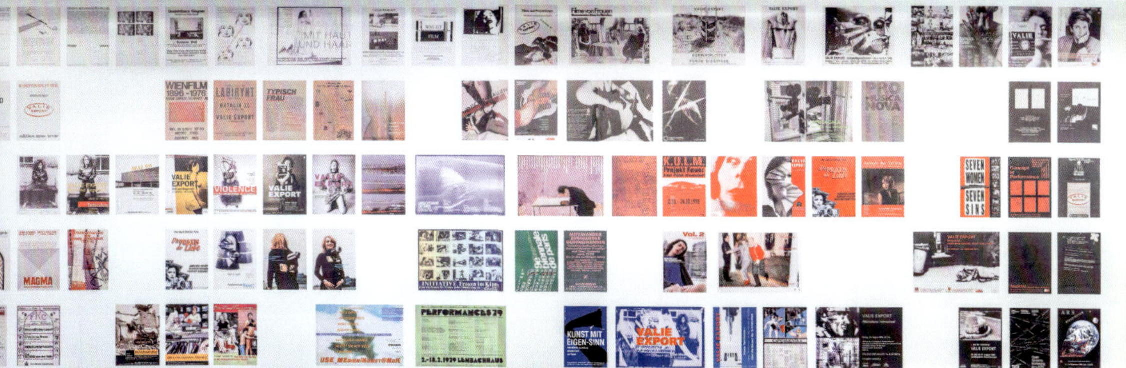

Ausstellungsansicht / exhibition view *VALIE EXPORT. Das Archiv als Ort künstlerischer Forschung,* poster wall, LENTOS Kunstmuseum; photo: Violetta Wakolbinger, 2017

1 VALIE EXPORT in conversation with Felicitas Herrschaft, "Gespräch mit Valie Export, April 2004," accessed June 26, 2020, http://www.fehe.org/index.php?id=572.

2 VALIE EXPORT in conversation with Brigitta Burger-Utzer and Sylvia Szely, "In der Erweiterung liegt die Möglichkeit zur Veränderung" (2006), in Sylvia Szely, *EXPORT Lexikon. Chronologie der bewegten Bilder bei VALIE EXPORT* (Vienna: Sonderzahl Verlag, 2007), p. 205.

3 Ibid., p. 208.

4 VALIE EXPORT, "Women's Art. Ein Manifest" (1972), *Neues Forum,* No. 228, Jan. 1973, translation by Resina Haslinger by permission of the author.

5 VALIE EXPORT, "Die Polizei war gewarnt. Gespräch mit Valie Export über die Situation der Körperkunst," Robert Fleck in *Der Standard,* Oct. 18, 1996, *Album,* p. 3.

6 VALIE EXPORT, "Jeder Zeit ihre Kunst," an interview with Valie Export in *Skytec,* March 1990, p. 22.

7 VALIE EXPORT, *Der virtuelle Körper. Vom Prothesenkörper zum postbiologischen Körper / The Virtual Body. From the Prosthetic to the Post-biological Body,* Marius Babias and Sabine Folie, eds. (Cologne: Verlag der Buchhandlung Walther König, 2020).

8 VALIE EXPORT, *Sprich Körper,* 2011, synopsis for a later version of the script, VALIE EXPORT Center Linz, bundle 148.

9 Marie-Luise Angerer, "A radical performance artist ahead of her time," ceremonial address at the opening of the VALIE EXPORT Center Linz on Nov. 10, 2017, borrowing from a quote by Andrea Juno in "The Female Image as Critique in the Films of Valie Export (Syntagma)," in *Angry Women* (RE/Search, No. 13), Andrea Juno and V. Vale, eds. (1991), p. 186.

Dagmar Schink (AT) studied at the University of Art and Design Linz and in Helsinki at the University of Art and Design (UIAH). After working at the OK Offenes Kulturhaus and the Crossing Europe Film Festival, she moved to the University of Art and Design Linz, where in 2016 she was entrusted with co-establishing the VALIE EXPORT Center Linz at the Tabakfabrik. In 2017 she was named managing director of the Center. She is also a member of the Linz City Culture Advisory Board, the jury for the Marianne.von.Willemer Prize for Digital Media, and the Linz UNESCO City of Media Arts Advisory Board.

PRIX
ARS ELECTRONICA

u19–create
your world

Creating your World to Change our Perspective
The Moment Before

Sirikit Amann, Gerald Hartwig, Conny Lee, Karl Markovics, Irene Posch

As much as *u19–create your world* is, among other things, a representative sample of today's youth and as such reflects the entire spectrum of inventiveness of an up-and-coming generation, each year is nonetheless marked by its own trend. This may be shaped by factors that have already manifested themselves in the lives of these young people, or by the degree to which they develop a sense of what adults expect from them. But youths also certainly have a feel for tendencies that are simply "in the air" and only gradually find their way into the collective perception. Even if the connection to the now ubiquitous and global Coronavirus would seem to suggest itself, one must, of course, be careful with such references. At the time of the submissions for this year's u19 competition, COVID-19 did not even yet have a name, much less a public perception. It is nevertheless striking that a large number of the submitted works deal with topics that could be considered dark, chaotic, even dystopian: the disruption of adolescence, bullying, depression, suicide, the destruction of our earth by war or environmental damage, to mention only a few themes addressed by this year's works. Two of the submissions even explicitly explore the subject of viruses. Without wanting to read too much into the projects or to overinterpret them, this much can be said: u19/2020 has no illusions! The time for rose-colored glasses is over. But u19/2020 also has no fear, because it is too late for pessimism as well! There is something crucial at stake here: our future as individuals and the fact that this can never be separated from our collective future—particularly not in a world that we refer to as a "global village." One way or another, the future begins in the coming moment. What is decisive is the moment before.

Young Professionals (14 – 19 years)
Golden Nica

Samen · Lisa Rass, Franziska Gallé, Jona Lingitz, Anna Fachbach, HTBLVA-Graz Ortweinschule

There are works that stand for themselves, even if they depict something or tell a story. Just the fact that they even exist makes them something special, exceptional—one could even say something vital. In any case, the world would be a different place if these works didn't exist. *Samen* is just such a work. Using puppet animation, the phenomenon of adolescence is described in all its baffling facets—with all its unpredictability, disruption, and fascination. In their work, the creators forwent any spoken language, instead developing their own extremely compelling visual language, through which they create a complementary world: an allegory, a pictorial narrative that describes something that language is not able to express, because that which is to be described resists any logical disciplines. Man, the speaking animal, is rendered speechless when sexuality stirs within him and turns his body and soul into a jungle. In their film, barely four minutes long, Lisa Rass, Franziska Gallé, Jona Lingitz, and Anna Fachbach find an exceedingly artful expression for the statement "Everything in life has to do with sexuality (except sex)." *Samen* is a work of art in a technical sense as well. The few effects that are used are carefully placed. The spare, precise soundtrack foregoes music as strictly as it omits language. The chromaticity, lighting, and montage are masterly. Like the main figure in the film, the viewer is given a tough nut to crack, a puzzle. And as anyone knows who has experienced adolescence or is in the middle of it right now: for this puzzle there are many solutions and no answer.

Awards of Distinction

In Reactio Veritas · MOLEKÜL Kollektiv

At first glance it seems a simple idea: adapting EEG streams of thought from imaging material so that moving waves and patterns can be displayed and viewed live. This description, however, falls far short of adequately conveying the potential and the sensorial character of *In Reactio Veritas.* Here, a digital process transforms something already in existence. This diagnostic procedure originally served to detect irregularities in the functional connectivity of the human brain, which is still inadequately understood. In *In Reactio Veritas,* this basic material is then subjected to an artistic and metaphorical transformation through the application of a refined algorithm, and one can say with certainty that in this case, the whole is much greater than the sum of its parts. One is almost literally immersed in a singular, symbiotic world of images made up of luminous patterns and mutating shapes; one can follow the installation-like concept almost intuitively and has the desire to devote all of one's senses to the ever-changing structures. It is not only the adapted algorithms that reveal a new, transfigured world; rather, it is the overriding idea of the emotional mirror that captivates the viewer. It is held up to us as participants in an unforeseeable experimental setup, and this meta level seems both reflexive and futuristic. The insight into one's own state of mind has an air of immersive quantum reality about it. It is wonderful when the visualization of a meta level of interhuman relationships allows one to become a glimmering thought wave oneself and wishes to think and interact more clearly. This is the connection between electronics, art, emotion, and visualized astonishment.

Robdilo'clock · Benjamin Aster

What begins with a catchy play on words ultimately leads to a dizzying philosophy about time. *Robdilo'clock* is described by its creator as "a robot clock that in an analog manner (with motors) shows the time digitally, which gives it its name: ROBot – DIgital – anaLOg – CLOCK." Moreover, the "o'clock" at the end represents another pun. On a black-painted plexiglass plate lie 28 segments that, similar to an LCD clock, show the time. In order to display the next hour or minute, a gripper grasps the relevant segments and repositions them accordingly. One follows the mechanical process with astonishment as it arranges the individual elements, which then in their entirety reveal the new time. Every procedure takes exactly one minute, of course. In this interval, the "old" time is dismantled and the "new" one is assembled. And the entire process is "transparent": all elements lie in front of us in plain view—gear wheels, threaded rods, the plexiglass plate, etc. The mechanics that show us the time always require the same amount of time to do this. This means nothing less than what we can watch as a phenomenon both creates and defines itself. With this, Benjamin Aster has accomplished a great feat: he has created his own distinctive expression for the indescribable.

MIC SPECIAL PRIZE 2020

CareLine · Simon Krist, Gabriel Neuberger, Matthias Janitsch

It has become a tradition to award a supplementary prize in addition to the other prizes of the Prix Ars Electronica. This year, for the first time, the MIC Special Prize 2020 was awarded. This prize is endowed with a cash award of 1,000 euros and is aimed at all young, creative people who enjoy programming and developing new ideas.

We were looking for ideas, concepts, or finished projects that focus on the world of tomorrow. How will the IT sector develop in the future? What problems must be solved? What does IT have to do with climate change? How will artificial intelligences continue to evolve in the future? These are only some of the questions that technologically-minded young people devote themselves to. As this prize was awarded for the first time, there were no models to follow, which made the selection process both exciting and difficult, as our decision also determines to a certain extent the future orientation of the prize. Should the winning project be primarily technology-based; should it be a finished project, or should we choose an idea that then could possibly be brought to fruition with the prize money? We ultimately agreed on a submission that was able to combine most of these aspects: This is a prototype that has already been tried out in the field but still has potential for further development, one that includes very good documentation, meets a need, and also has been tested with the end users. With *CareLine,* students at HTL Rennweg have developed a self-driving serving cart that is aimed at easing the workload of the staff at care facilities. It is guided by lines affixed to the floor and drives itself from the kitchen to the dining room. The automation of this process results in more time for caregiving, as the staff is able to focus its attention on the needs of the patients. *CareLine* demonstrates how innovative approaches and technical solutions can improve the quality of work in the long term for people in caregiving facilities.

Honorary Mentions

Ameisen im Haus · Sophie Dögl,
Nastasja Stempkowski
These two artists draw on a long tradition in experimental filmmaking, using powerfully associative images and superimpositions to visualize the lyrics of a song they composed themselves. The color scheme subtly adapts to the mood that has been created and mutates parallel to the spoken poetic elements. On a metaphorical but not overladen level, many issues are addressed that concern the youth of today: the pressure to own the very latest phone, or the emotional distant and difficult relationship with parents, friends, and relatives are translated into word images in the form of cockroaches and insects that the authors placed deftly in the video. This poetic visualization is multilayered in its unagitated compactness, as a complete synthesis of the arts incorporating interwoven text, images, and sound.

ARTouch · Jonathan Wiener, Jasmin Lersitz, Paul Rosenberger, HTL Rennweg
The project *ARTouch* by Jonathan Wiener, Jasmin Lersitz, and Paul Rosenberger shows how much our interaction with digital objects can vary in terms of material and form. The project combines functional necessity with forms of artist expression, thus turning the management of smart-home devices as we know it on its head. This fusion of technical competence and free creative expression could in the future enable us to control heating, lighting, and music by means of graffiti and children's drawings—an idea worthy of an Honorary Mention in the Young Professionals category.

Der Rapper – Die Dokumentation
Mohammed Elyesa Bilge, Emre Tuncer, Stefan Hromada, Haris Beshta Bradaric
This film is simultaneously a technically professionally-made documentation and a very personal glimpse into the life of a young man who, with his ambition of launching a career as a rapper, stands as an example for countless young people. This documentary describes the unvarnished reality of hip-hop beneath the surface of bling and hype, as a music that stands for an attitude toward life, as an art form in which one must work hard in

order to be successful with it. The combination of a non-judgmental, documentary portrayal and a personal insight into a human being is pulled off with great success in *Der Rapper.*

Fade – Fate · Sadet Muadini

This is an unsettlingly beautiful hybrid of animation and live-action film, whose unparalleled and compelling dynamic results from the various materials used and the extremely skillful montage. Due to the coronavirus pandemic, Sadet Muadini was not able to complete the work. Nevertheless, the storyboard sketches alone, which was all that she originally submitted, were sufficient to demonstrate that this is an extraordinary and completely independent work. An incomplete film without sound and without closing credits, but by a complete filmmaker!

Juksel – Die Jukebox der Zukunft · Julian Kronlachner, Paul Wiesiger, Paul Krenn, Max Grubauer, David Gangl, HTBLA Grieskirchen

A bar is primarily characterized by the kind of music played there. The music determines the clientele that patronizes the bar and feels at home there: young or old, rock or vintage pop; is there dancing or do people prefer to talk about lucrative investment funds? Different groups of people will populate a bar depending on what kind of music is playing there. The *Juksel* app approaches the question of music from the other direction: in a bar, a sound system is connected to *Juksel,* and the guests can use the app to compile a playlist. This process is democratized through a voting procedure. An innovative idea, executed in the form of a professional app!

Meine Welt, Deine Welt · Zoe Borzi, Nikolaus Heckel, Jonathan Steininger

The central theme of this documentary is the diversity of lifestyles in Austria: that of a female farmer, a monk, an activist, and a drag queen. All of the characters have their own world in which they live, and none is better than another. The strength of this work lies in the narrative style: the subjects are not interrupted with questions; rather, they talk about their lives, and we listen—with pleasure. The attempt is made here (to borrow a statement from one of the figures in the documentary) "to put the image of truth in a positive light." And therein lies perhaps the most outstanding quality of this project: it demands an answer from us. This is a courageous, important work.

Musik zum Mitnehmen · Magdalena Schiesser, HTBLVA-Graz Ortweinschule

Among all the many submissions, Magdalena Schiesser's *Musik zum Mitnehmen* stands out in terms of its materiality, interaction, and subject matter. Her work is a ring that is both a piece of jewelry and a musical instrument. We were won over by the combination of wearable mechanics, functional aesthetics, and the conceptual incorporation into one's personal environment, making it absolutely worthy of an Honorary Mention in the Young Professionals category.

Nomsters · Students from class 7c and 8a at BORG Bad Leonfelden

Nomster is a play on words that stands for an amusingly clever tactical digital board game. One sees the attention to detail in the design of the bizarre avatars, these diverse, imaginative, and hand-drawn figures that add a very special touch to the game. The names given to the figures are another successful element; they are thought-provoking and let one enter the game flow with a grin. Even if the game's setup resembles that of a board game, the connection between technology and tactical game play is extremely appealing. The range of combination possibilities rules out any danger of boredom. Game on for the Young Professionals!

Querdenker · Max Wolfmajer, Clemens Pfeiffer, Gergely Varecza, Nora Puntigam, Mirjam Fladenhofer, HTBLVA-Graz Ortweinschule

A story about a conflict between youths in a park develops into a parable about attitudes and changes in attitudes, about intolerance and narrow-mindedness, and about how little would be necessary to achieve more awareness: merely more freedom in thought. The filmmakers skillfully play with the medium of smartphone video and the different image formats. The scenes have a casually improvised feel without coming off as amateurish. Mirjam Fladenhofer, Nora Puntigam, Gergely Varecza, Clemens Pfeiffer, and Max Wolfmajer lend a universality and depth to the disturbing topicality of the story.

WWW.VIRUS · Ria Kathan, Florian Sigl

WWW.VIRUS reflects the omnipresent consumption of smartphones and social media in a fashion collection. Instead of aiming to please, Ria Kathan and Florian Sigl take a critical look at how we deal with current technologies and address the almost incomprehensible impact they have on our lives. The sculptural, critical, and committed approach to this topic convinced us to award the work an Honorary Mention in the Young Professionals category.

Young Creatives (up to 14 years)
u14 Prize

The Truth Part 2 · Students from NMS Lehen, Creative Media Design

The Truth Part 2 is a game that fuses elements of visual novels and augmented reality. It immerses us in an exciting story and challenges our brain cells in the process. To play the game, players must scan in QR codes that can be distributed in the surrounding area. In between, they must make decisions that influence the course of action. But it is not only the gaming elements of *The Truth Part 2* that are well made but also the video sequences, which have a professional look and draw us into the action. The game tells a story and utilizes creative technical tools to produce immersion.

Young Creatives (up to 14 years)
u14 Award of Distinction

Coded Art Gallery · Michael Zaminer

In his submission, Michael Zaminer explores the constantly modulating interface between art and science/computer technology in a comprehensible and independent manner. One can sense his interest in and enthusiasm for the technology but also his delight in experimentation with regard to using the principle of randomness in design. This desire to rethink and reshape a world will certainly keep Michael Zaminer busy for a long time, and it will be interesting to observe what interfaces are still to change in the course of this journey. What we find particularly impressive and remarkable is the curiosity with which Michael utilizes a constantly changing and evolving technology as his "tools of the trade" and strives to explore autonomous varieties of structures of our world.

Zwischentöne · Students from class 4e
at Musisches Gymnasium Salzburg

Zwischentöne, an audio drama by students from class 4e at Musisches Gymnasium Salzburg, addresses in manifold ways current issues at play in the music industry—and not only there: the focus is on intellectual property, the pressure to succeed, trust, and major questions concerning society. The story is embedded in a professionally mixed audio mystery full of dramaturgical inter-relations, special effects, and nuances that capture the imagination of the listeners and give them pause for thought.

Young Creatives (up to 14 years)
u14 Honorary Mention

Die Zukunft liegt in unseren Händen
Students from BG & BRG III Boerhaavegasse
On an unusual "canvas," fifteen girls from an 8th-grade class at BG & BRG III created on an unusual "canvas" a picture of their wishes for their future; they drew their thoughts with markers and felt-tip pens on their hands and documented the results in a photography project. The power of this submission lies in the wealth of the works. Despite the various artistic styles—some pictures display delicate lines, in some the entire surface is covered, while in others the individual themes of the hands literally intertwine—the overall image resulting from *Die Zukunft liegt in unseren Händen* is one of fairness, respect, and individuality; of a world without racism and homophobia, of a healthy planet, and much more.

Young Creatives (up to 14 years)
u12 Prize

Lury · Laurin Steinhuber, Amelie Steinhuber, Niklas Steinhuber
Lury is a stop-motion animation about a fiercely contested sword, demonic visitors, and ghosts. To make the video, the kids designed and built a huge film set complete with 20-cm-tall figures. Every-thing is tremendously rich in details and imagi-nation, and the manner in which it is staged—the close-ups, edits, and perspectives—is evidence of a keen eye for cinematic imagery. Moreover, the film is a follow-up project to a work that last year received an Honorary Mention in the u12 category and thus can serve as a positive example of how young artists can continue to develop their visions and expand their skills.

Young Creatives (up to 14 years)
u12 Award of Distinction

Schule der Zukunft · Matilde Irene Abarca Hernández
The assignment with this school project was: "Draw your vision of how school could look in 100 years." Matilde Abarca Hernández tackled this theme with a radical subjectivity and in the process hit a nerve at its most sensitive spot. In her drawing, the dream of "learning in your sleep" becomes a Kafkaesque nightmare. The useful-ness of drumming knowledge into students is not only questioned here; it is also reduced to sur-real absurdity. The depth of thought, the hypnotic effect, the reduction to paper and pencil, and not least the assuredness and maturity of the execu-tion causes one to marvel at what people are able to express even at such a young age.

u12 Honorary Mention

Das Verschwinden der Trolle
Luis Schweighofer

Coming up with a story as imaginative as this one is quite an achievement in itself. But to then translate it into a film is an even greater challenge, and both were accomplished very successfully and with tremendous inventiveness in *Das Verschwinden der Trolle.* The way in which Luis Schweighofer illustrates the narrative with simple methods demonstrates great ingenuity. Powerful cinematic special effects are achieved through things as simple as a small battery-operated candle or a bit of colored foil.

u10 Prize

Das Würfelhaus · Dominik Pichler

Das Würfelhaus is a work that one does not fully comprehend at first glance—but when one looks more closely, one understands: what we have here is a product of pure imagination. Starting with the simple desire to make something with a hot-glue gun, Dominik Pichler proceeded to create an entire world. Small tubes are glued together to make a complete space station and tell the story of the human race, which was forced to flee Earth because (how prophetic!) a horrible virus was raging. Now the people are living in this cube-shaped station, where they are supplied with everything they need, and waiting for the day when they can return home. *Das Würfelhaus* stands for the idea and for the artistic creation of a reality: this is what artistic creation looks like!

u10 Award of Distinction

Der Vogel mit dem coolen Hut
23 students from class 3c at
GTVS Kolonitzgasse, Vienna 3

The creative and unusual ideas and the self-designed world with which the young artists confront us in this project are as outlandish as the execution itself. The students linked the individual scenes and narrative levels together with great attention to detail, and one has the clear sense that a collective of young artists was at work here. Each figure contributes its own drawn and acted-out personality and causes us to laugh as well as reflect. Particularly impressive is the exploration of the digital world, the world of computer games, in which one spends a great deal of time these days and by which one is consciously or unconsciously influenced. These are issues that concern us even at a very young age and are becoming increasingly important in our society. A charming audio snippet at the end of the film shows us the concentrated creativity of the entire class in action. In chaos lies the power, and that deserves an Award of Distinction!

u10 Honorary Mention

In einer weißen Winternacht
Students at BrgOrg15

The young artists use the technical means at their disposal to tackle a stop-motion film project. The text of the story they have filmed is extremely poetic, and the students illustrate and interpret the work in their own very personal manner. The play with the recurring musical piece has an almost hypnotic effect on the viewer, and if one allows oneself to be taken in by this device, one can actually immerse oneself in the images and in the world created here. One sometimes feels one has been taken back in time to a fairytale world, and in this world, one is transported to a place where anything can happen.

PRIX ARS ELECTRONICA

u19–create your world

Young Professionals

14–19 years

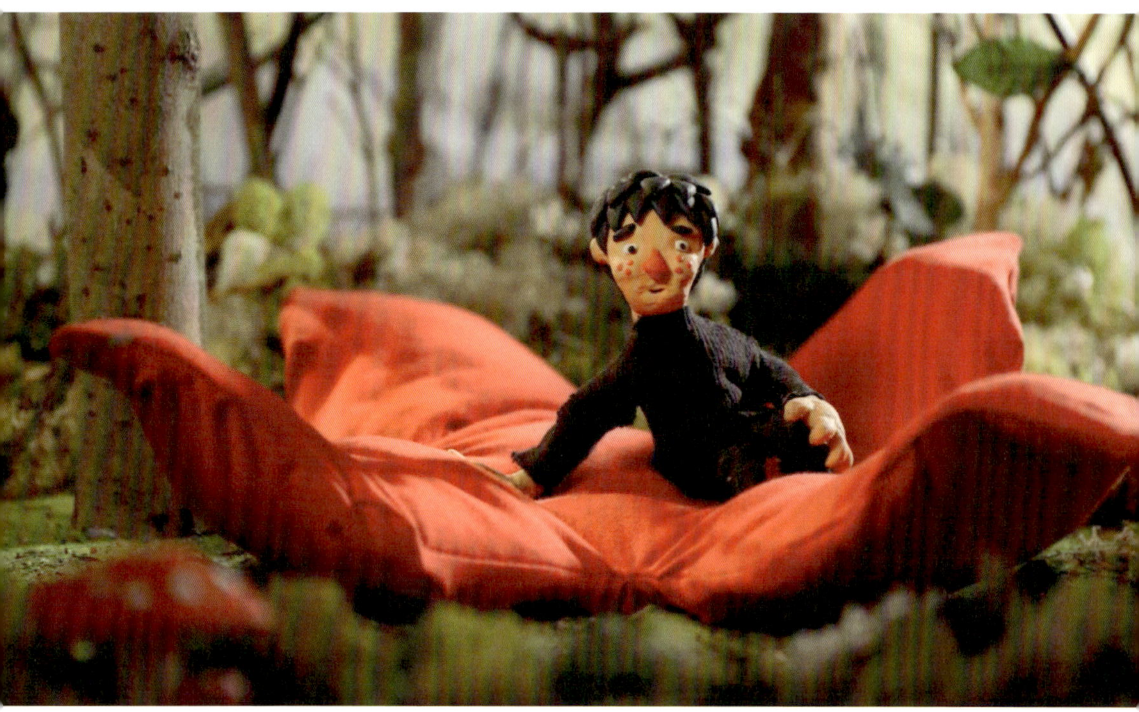

Samen

Lisa Rass, Franziska Gallé, Jona Lingitz, Anna Fachbach,
HTBLVA-Graz Ortweinschule

SAMEN is an experimental short film on the theme of entering adulthood. As a coming-of-age symbol, we send a boy on a journey through some woods. We used stop-motion technique and constructed all the backdrops and figures ourselves. We developed a short, artistic story with the most important steps, divided this story into three worlds, and then translated it into beautiful pictures.

As part of our final project, we had to work in a small team to produce a film. There were no further guidelines, but our four-person group realized immediately that we did not want to make a feature film but rather let our creativity take us wherever it wanted. We relatively quickly had the idea of taking on the major challenge of making a stop-motion film.

For the story behind the film, we wanted to explore a theme that affects all of us and that all of us could work on together. Because of the humorous life experiences of our team and our various perspectives, we then developed the coming-of-age story. What was completely new for us was the long, labor-intensive preparation time: building the sets and creating the figures represented a large part of the project.

The film was made with stop-motion technique. Individual frames were shot and then placed in sequence. To be able to work with more precision, we also used the stop-motion program Dragon Frame. The light in the film moves symbolically with the journey and the development of the main character. For the lighting, we used only Dedolight and tools such as small flashlights and desk lamps. With regard to the soundtrack, we worked exclusively with noises and atmospheric sounds. Special mention should be made of our sets and figures, which we made ourselves using materials we collected in the woods. We also painted the backdrops ourselves. For each of the figures, we made a wire frame, sewed garments from fabric remnants, and shaped the rest out of plasticine. Shooting the film using Dragon Frame was difficult

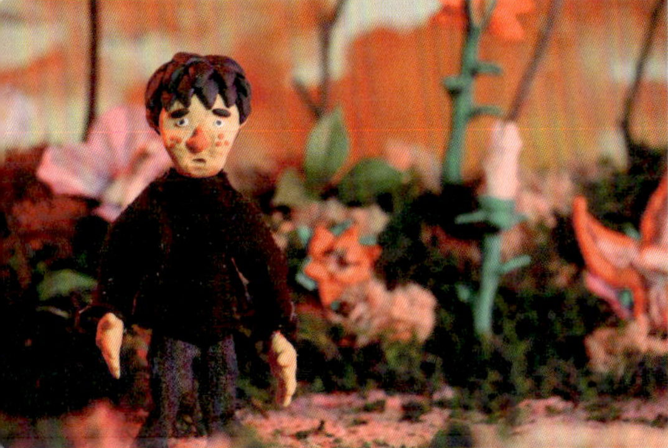

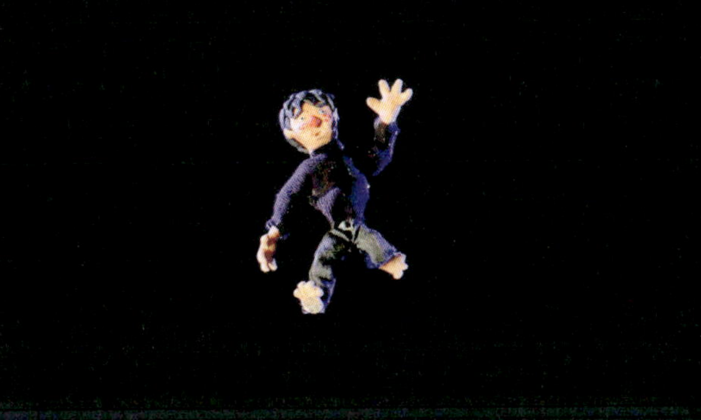

at first, but we picked it up very quickly. The entire project took a whole year to complete, which we hadn't expected when we started. Now we want to distribute our film and make it available to many young people.

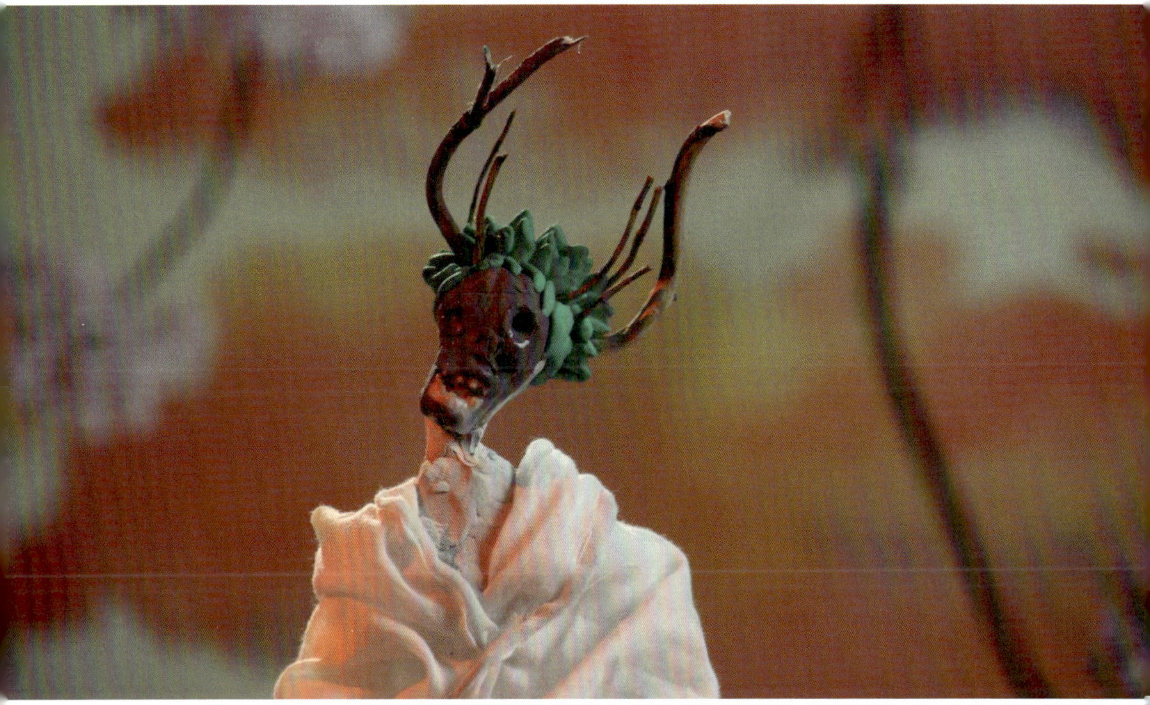

Camera: Anna Fachbach
Direction and post-production: Jona Lingitz
Direction and editing: Franziska Gallé
Production: Lisa Rass

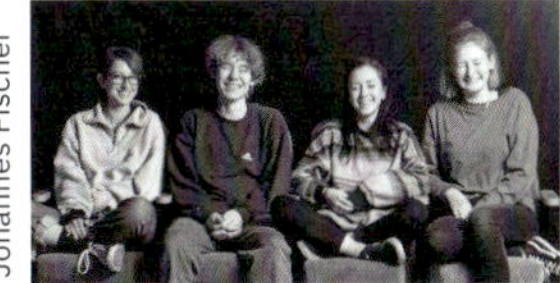
Johannes Fischer

Lisa Rass (b. 1999), **Franziska Gallé** (b. 2001), **Jona Lingitz** (b. 2001), and **Anna Fachbach** (b. 2000) are four students in their final year at Ortweinschule in Graz (Film and Media Art). Our passion is producing films and utilizing our knowledge and skill in this area in a purposeful manner. In this project, we expanded our horizons through experimental work and created something extraordinary. Through the work with stop-motion, we could allow our creativity free rein.

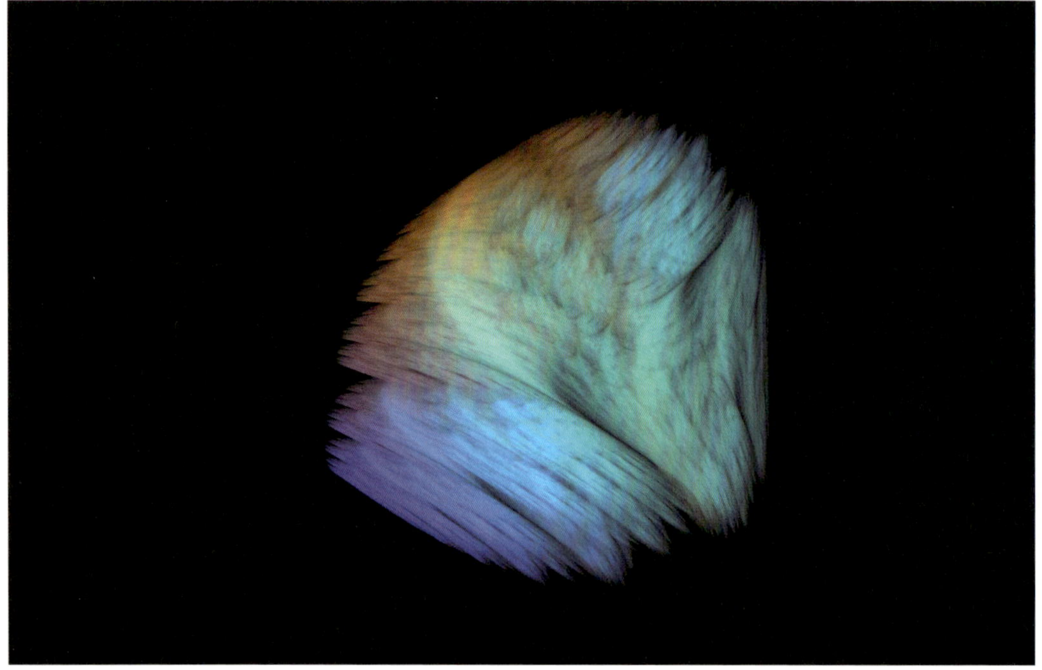

In Reactio Veritas

MOLEKÜL Kollektiv

Conflict and arguments have existed for even longer than humankind itself, and for many of us, the term "dispute" has largely negative connotations. *In Reactio Veritas* is intended to counteract this. The installation uses electroencephalography (EEG) to generate algorithmic artworks that encourage one to see the unexpectedly beautiful and common elements behind the process of conflict resolution.

In the installation, highly sensitive electrodes measure the brain activity of two people. *In Reactio Veritas* places both of them in a previously determined conflict situation. In the process of conflict resolution, an algorithm then combines the data measured in the brains of the two participants and generates from this a unique, aesthetic image as a summary of their conflict resolution. The installation is intended to demonstrate that, contrary to popular opinion, arguments and conflict can have many positive aspects if one does not view the process with a preconceived negative attitude. The participants are encouraged to adopt a more optimistic approach in future processes of conflict resolution and explore the positive developments that conflicts and their resolution can produce.

Graphische Vienna, Manuel Steinböck

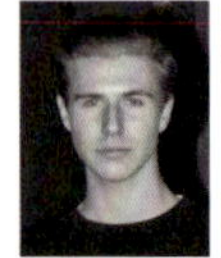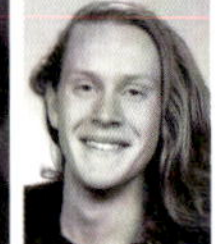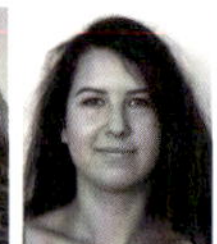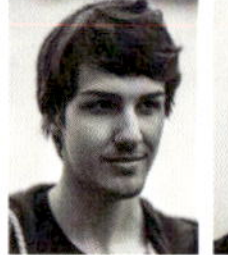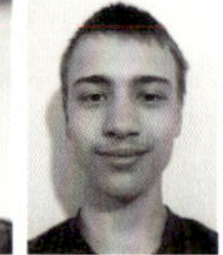

We are MOLEKÜL — a young, interdisciplinary collective from Vienna. The team behind the installation *In Reactio Veritas* includes **Claudio Reiter** (b. 2001), **Felix Strobl** (b. 1999), **Barbara Gregori** (b. 2000), **Ian Hornik** (b. 2001), and **Jeremy Kescher** (b. 2001). We met while working on joint projects at the Graphische and at HTL Spengergasse. Our common interest in creative solutions and our passion for teamwork ultimately resulted in a friendship. As MOLEKÜL, we are an unbeatable team of digital daredevils, avid acrobats of creativity, and organized multimedia jugglers.

www.molekuel.at

Robdilo'clock

Benjamin Aster

Robdilo'clock is a robot I designed, built, and programmed myself that shows the time in a very special way. Using a gripper, it grasps individual segments and positions them in such a way that they display the time in digital numerals. It is thus a robot clock that in an analog manner (with motors) shows the time digitally, which gives it its name: "ROBot – DIgital – anaLOg – CLOCK."

The gripper is moved by motor-operated threaded rods in two axes over a black-painted plexiglass plate. In order to lift up and deposit the segments, the entire plate is moved up and down. The system is controlled by an Arduino Mega 2560 microcontroller board. The up-and-down movement is accomplished by two mini stepper motors that rotate two rods. Two fischertechnik gear wheels fastened to the rods mesh with toothed racks mounted on the plate and thus lift or lower the plate. A servomotor opens and closes the gripper to grasp and release the segments. Each of these segments has two small magnets fixed to the underside with which they adhere to the metal plate located directly beneath the plexiglass. An elaborately constructed mechanism enables the gripper to rotate. I modelled the motor mountings and the complete carriage with the gripper head in 3D using the Onshape CAD software and printed them out with a 3D printer.

Time regulates our daily life. It can also convey messages. For the short film I made to show how *Robdilo'clock* works, I purposely chose the minutes shortly before 12 o'clock. This time span has a symbolic meaning as well: it can serve as a reminder that some problems of our time must be solved quickly, before it is too late.

I am now 14 years old. When I am twice as old, the world will have changed a great deal. *Robdilo'clock* determines our time every day. The future will show to what extent robots will increasingly determine our daily life.

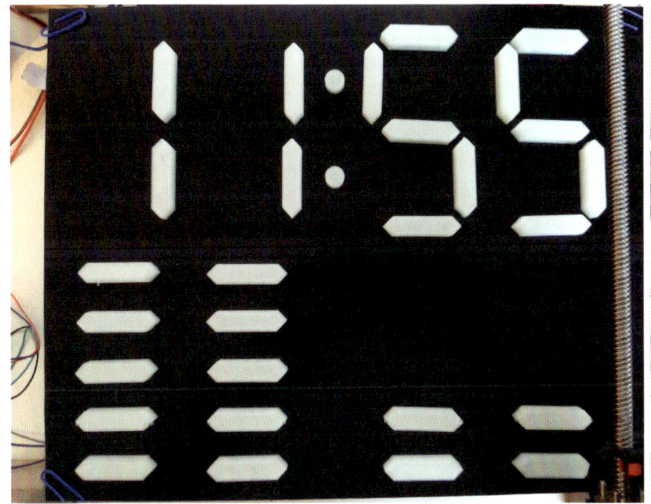

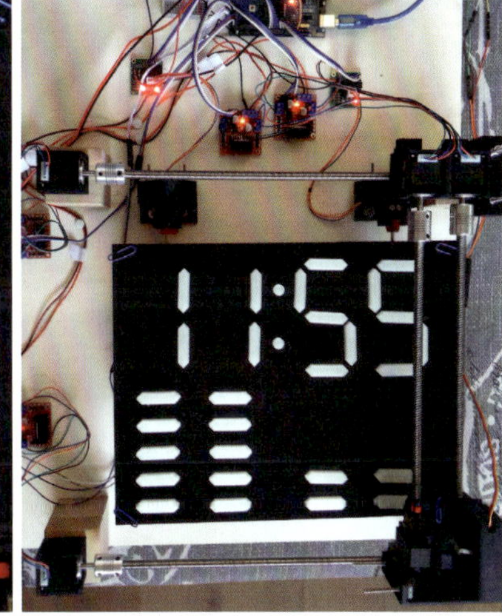

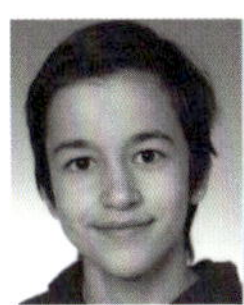

Benjamin Aster (b. 2005) is 14 years old and attends Akademisches Gymnasium Salzburg. In his free time, he enjoys programming—especially with Arduino and Processing—and creating mechatronic projects, for which he has been awarded prizes. He designs and models parts for the 3D printer with which he builds and programs machines and robots. He is also very interested in math and likes programming mathematical models. He was the 2017 national champion in the "Känguru" mathematics competition and in 2019 the federal state champion. Singing is another of his hobbies: he is a member of a children's choir and has performed as a soloist at the Salzburg Easter Festival.

MIC Special Prize 2020

As part of the Prix Ars Electronica "u19–create your world," a special prize was awarded in 2020—with the support of MIC—managing international customs & trade compliance – for innovative ideas and projects in the fields of IT, programming, game design, Web and Internet. The prize is endowed with 1,000 € and is aimed at all young creative minds who enjoy programming and developing new things.

We were looking for ideas, concepts, or finished projects that deal with the world of tomorrow! How will the IT sector develop in the future? Which problems have to be solved? What does IT have to do with climate change? How will artificial intelligence develop in the future?

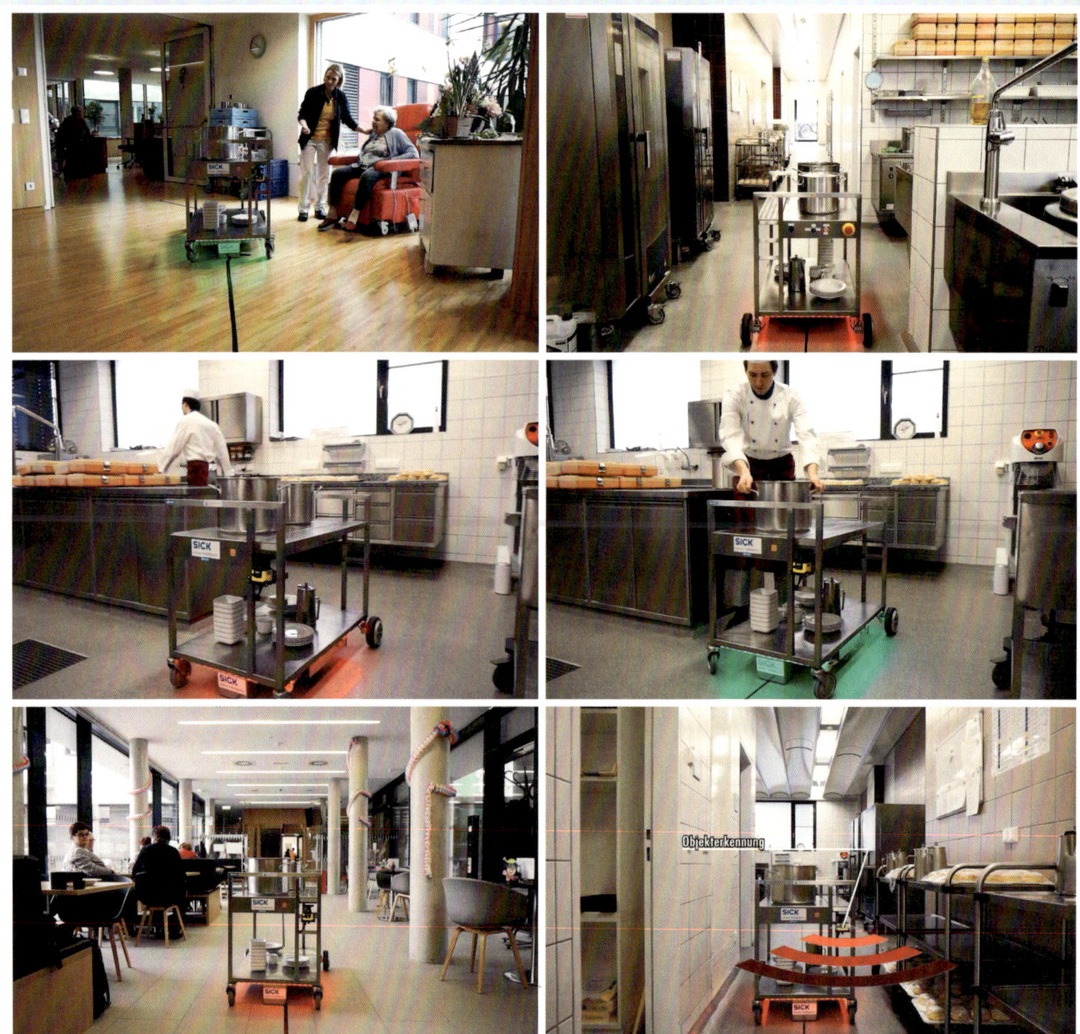

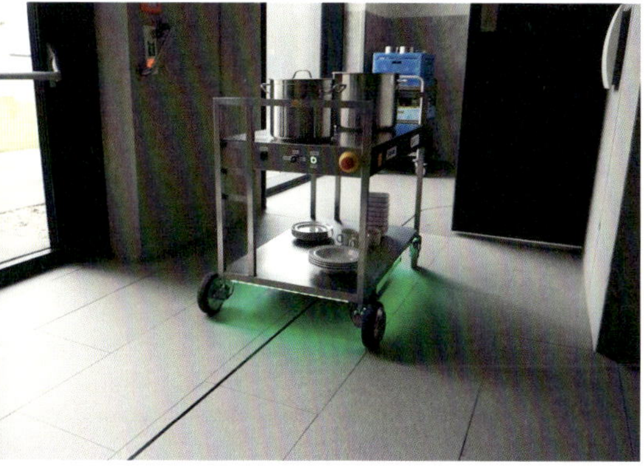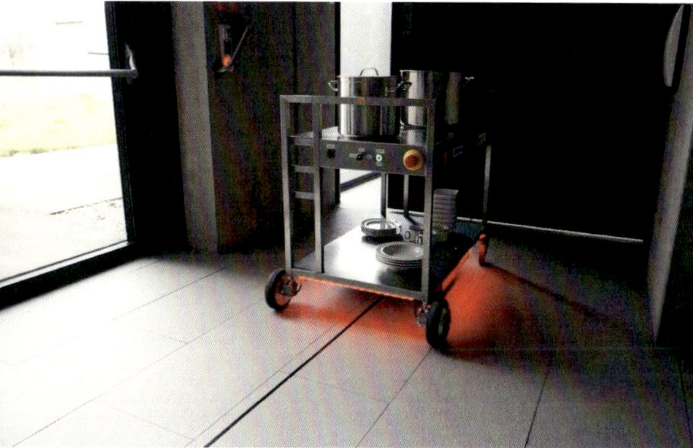

CareLine

Simon Krist, Matthias Janitsch, Gabriel Neuberger, HTL Rennweg

In order to provide the patients with meals in the morning, at noon, and in the evening, care facilities and nursing homes employ personnel that use serving carts to transport the prepared food along with cutlery, plates, and glasses from the kitchen to the dining room several times a day. This entire process not only requires long distances be covered; a great deal of time must be invested as well—a total of 1.5 hours per day, according to studies. As the staff cares for the residents of these facilities around the clock and seven days a week, this process takes up some 550 hours per year. This time could certainly be better used in other ways, such as allowing staff to devote itself more intensively to the care of the patients.

The idea is therefore to develop a self-driving serving cart that can ease the workload of the staff at the push of a button. It is guided by lines affixed to the floor and drives itself from the kitchen to the dining room. A laser sensor recognizes obstacles and prevents collisions along the cart's route. The automation of this process results in more time for caregiving, as the staff is able to focus its attention on the needs of the patients.

The uniqueness of this project is evident not only in its innovative nature; thanks to its line-following capabilities, it is also impressive for its flexibility, while its industry-standard collision sensors ensure its safety. *CareLine* shows how innovative approaches and technical solutions can provide long-term improvement in the quality of life for people in care facilities.

Principal advisor: Jörg Komenda
Advisor: Ewald Cekan
Advisor: Johannes Stehlik
Main sponsor: Pflege- und Betreuungszentrum Wolkersdorf

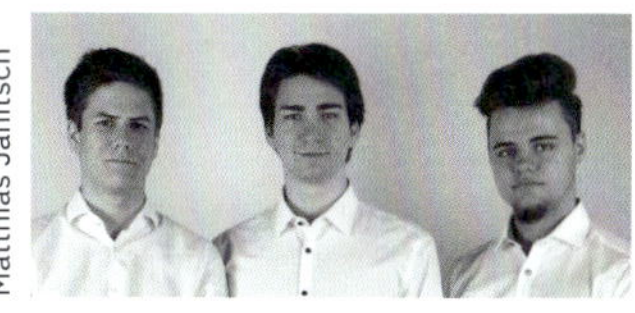
Matthias Janitsch

Simon Krist (b. 2001), **Matthias Janitsch** (b. 2001), and **Gabriel Neuberger** (b. 2000) met while in the lower level at Gymnasium Wolkersdorf. All of the team members decided to continue their schooling at HTL Rennweg, forming the *CareLine* team to complete their final project in the 2019/2020 school year. They faced a number of hurdles on the way to the final acceptance of their project, but thanks to the good teamwork in the group, they could all be easily overcome.

https://sites.google.com/view/carelineautonom · https://www.instagram.com/careline.autonom/?hl=de

Ameisen im Haus

Sophie Dögl, Nastasja Stempkowski

What problems do you struggle with every day? What problems do I struggle with every day? All around the world, people have various burdens to bear, and no two seem to be identical. To explore the uniqueness of the conflicts of every individual in more detail, in 2019 we composed a song as part of our music class. In this song we looked at the various problems people around the globe struggle with, ranging from mundane difficulties of everyday life to the uncertainty, particularly in countries where hunger and poverty are rampant, of whether sufficient money and resources are available to ensure survival.

In order to lend the lyrics more urgency, we decided to make a music video to accompany the song. The experimental film shows clips of animals that we used as a metaphor for the various problems. Film sequences of grimacing people establish a link between the animal world and us humans. The final result of a long period of development is colorful, experimental, and unusual and is aimed at getting people out of their bubble for a brief moment and giving them an overall view of the earth's population.

The audiovisual teacher who gave us honest feedback: Ramona Zdarsky; the music teacher who helped us with the audio recordings: Marco Battistella. Other composers of the song: Theresa Legerer and Marlene Hell; actors in the film: Lola Hochenegg, and Nastasja Stempkowski; recording studio: Tonstudio Edlmair & Lenz OG. School: Hegelgasse 12.

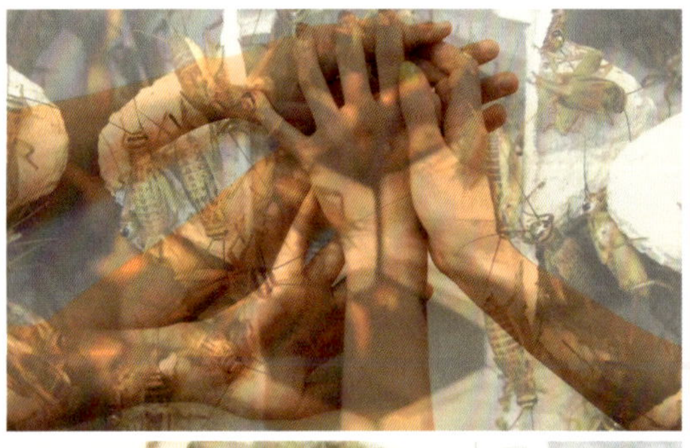

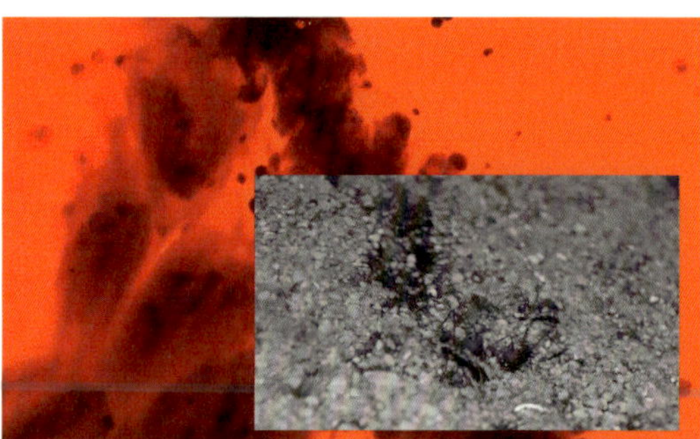

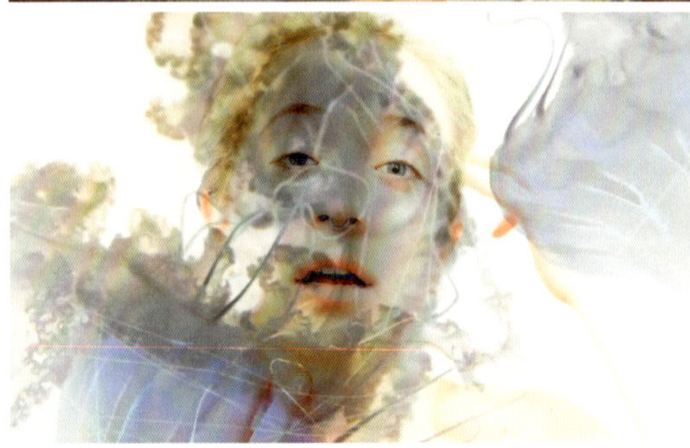

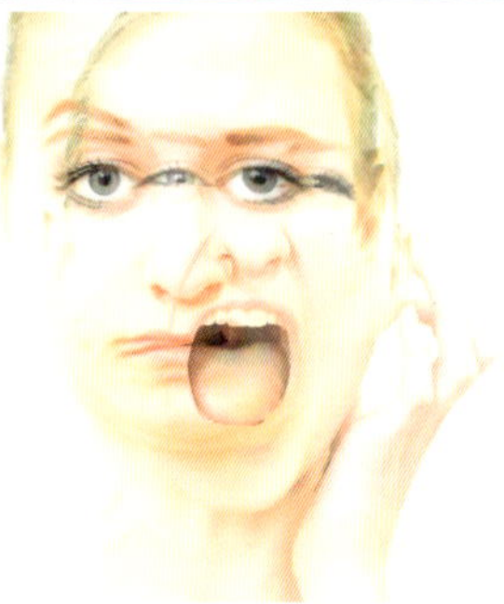

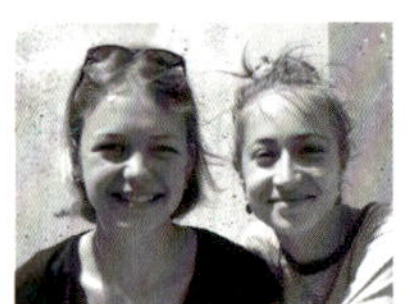

Sophie Dögl (b. 2002) and **Nastasja Stempkowski** (b. 2002), students at Hegelgasse 12, met four years ago through school. They feel connected not only because they both want to express feelings and thought processes in moving pictures and photographs, but also because their collaboration and close friendship has been shaped by many mutual experiences, adventures, and moments of happiness. This duo hopes to create many more projects in the future.

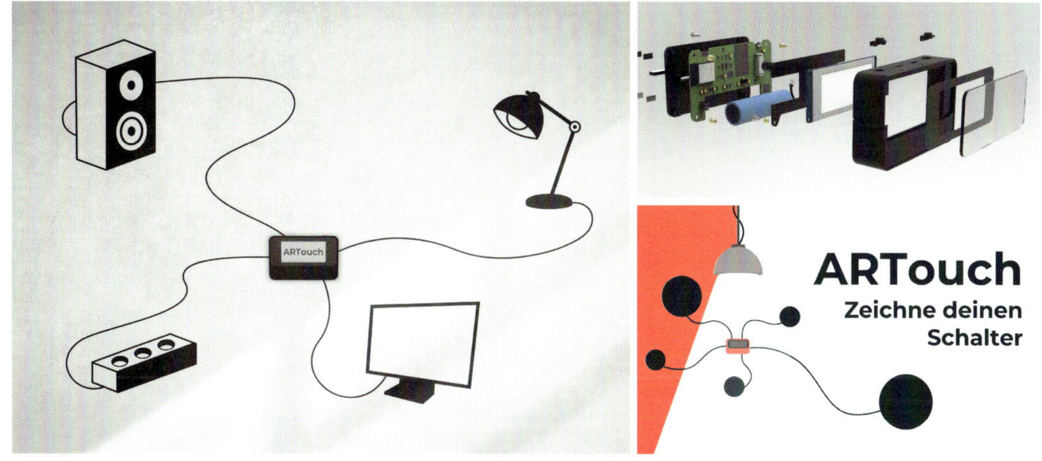

ARTouch

Jonathan Wiener, Jasmin Lersitz, Paul Rosenberger, HTL Rennweg

While the range of smart-home systems is constantly growing, the selection of control devices remains limited. *ARTouch* is aimed at remedying this problem. Using modern technologies and innovations such as TouchSense, WPS, 3D printing and much more, we have created a device that makes it possible to transform a drawing into a switch. And operating *ARTouch* could not be easier: it can be mounted anywhere in one's living space by means of magnets, which allow it to be quickly and easily removed from the wall for recharging.

Then one can begin drawing. For this, an electrically conductive paint, which is available commercially, must be used. It is recommended that the drawing be placed within a 2-meter radius of the device. Aside from that, one is free to design the drawing as one wishes. When the artwork is finished, it is connected to the device with a thin line of electrically conductive paint. In this way, up to eight individual drawings can be linked to *ARTouch.* These drawings serve as touchpads: when they are touched, this is recognized by the *ARTouch* device, which then switches the relevant smart-home device on or off. Which smart-home device is controlled by which touchpad can be predefined via an intuitive web interface.

Extensive support with electronics and project management: Vanessa Jurschan
Supervision and technical consultancy: Richard Drechsler, Martin Meschik, Johannes Stehlik
Furnishing of labs, project spaces, and equipment: HTL Rennweg
Cooperation partners and sponsors: Cubicure GmbH, Happylab GmbH, Kraus & Naimer Produktion GmbH, Bare Conductive Ltd, Easyname GmbH, Espressif Systems Co, Igus GmbH, IBR Leiterplatten GmbH & Co. KG, Bannerama - Oliver Pusswald, Fischer Elektronik GmbH, Hornbach Baumarkt GmbH, Printshop Sofortdruck- und Handels GmbH, Adkom Elektronik GmbH, Nanotec Electronic GmbH & Co. KG, Elternverein HTL Rennweg

Additional photo and video credits:
Film production of the *ARTouch* short video: Jonathan Wiener (direction, production, animation), Paul Rosenberger (cinematography, production of the explosion animation)
The image "Anwendungsbeispiel" (application example) uses a background from *www.freepik.com*

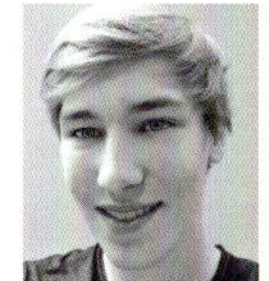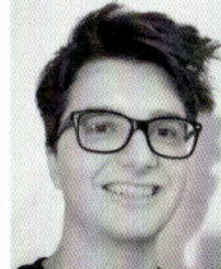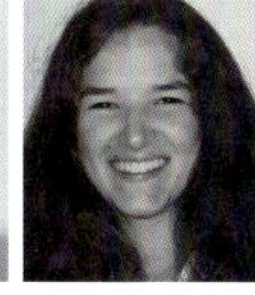

The *ARTouch* team, consisting of **Paul Rosenberger** (b. 2001), **Jonathan Wiener** (b. 2000), and **Jasmin Lersitz** (b. 2001), worked together previously on a joint project in the eighth grade at HTL Rennweg. With this project, the working atmosphere proved to be especially good and the division of areas of competencies was well balanced. This meant that tasks could be easily distributed and efficiently executed. Due to the successful collaboration in the eighth grade, the team decided to continue the working group for their diploma project.

https://artouch.at · https://www.instagram.com/project.artouch

Der Rapper – Die Dokumentation

Mohammed Elyesa Bilge, Emre Tuncer, Stefan Hromada,
Haris Beshta Bradaric, HTL Wien West

In our project *Der Rapper* (The Rapper—A Documentation), we report on our fellow student and want to find out what interests him about hip-hop (aside from the money that can be made with it), what plans and dreams he has, how he lives, and who his role models are. At the same time, we want to promote him as well with a professional music video on YouTube and a website of his own. As an interdisciplinary project, our work is divided into several parts:

– Writing the lyrics to the rap song that is presented in the music video. Our team member had already written a number of rap lyrics. We selected one of his texts that is authentic, focuses specifically on the life of a student with an immigrant background, and is neither racist nor offensive.

– Producing the background track for the song. This should support the flow and rhythm of the rap. For this we made use of our school's recording studio and audio equipment.

– Producing the music video. We wanted to design the music video as a professional rap video, just as they are produced by the major labels.

– The video was shot in the vicinity of our school in Vienna. For this, we recorded the video with several cameras and then edited and synchronized it in our school's video studio. The video is hosted on YouTube.

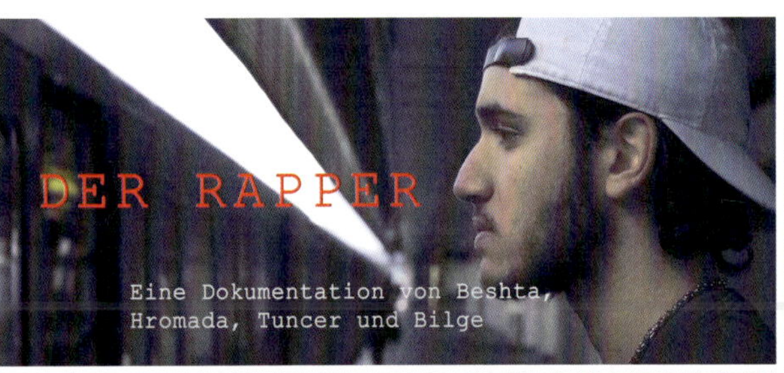

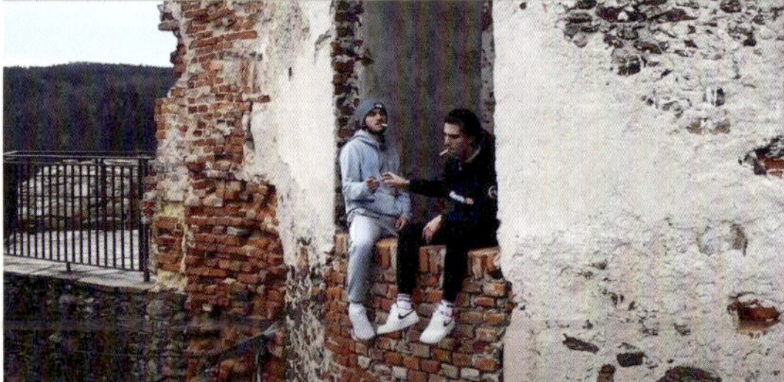

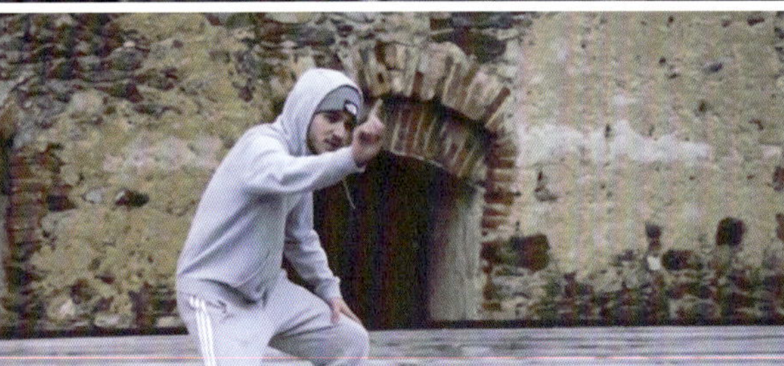

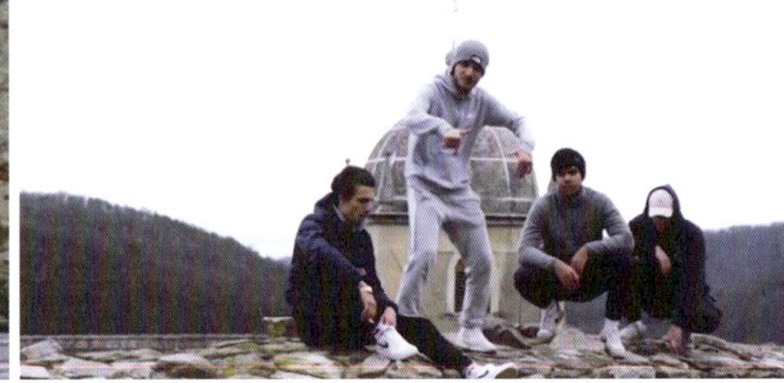

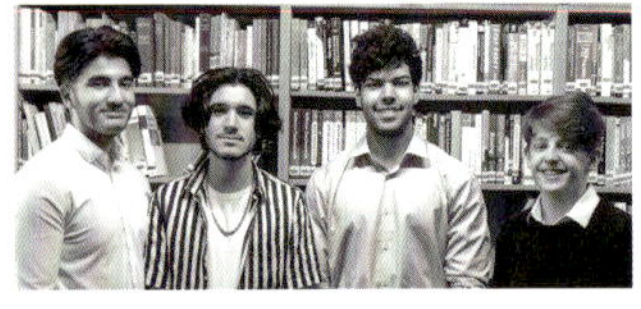

Mohammed Elyesa Bilge (b. 2001), Emre Tuncer (b. 2002), Stefan Hromada (b. 2002), and Haris Beshta Bradaric (b. 2001) are schoolmates and good friends who have known each other for several years. When the four first met at school, they hit it off immediately and Mohammed Elyesa Bilge told them about his hobby/passion: rapping and writing rap lyrics. At some point they had the idea that for a school project, they could tell the personal story of the rapper in order to help him turn rapping into more than just a hobby.

https://www.youtube.com/watch?v=ISQMx9W9UCM
https://www.youtube.com/watch?v=Uh86eG0_2mw&t=1s

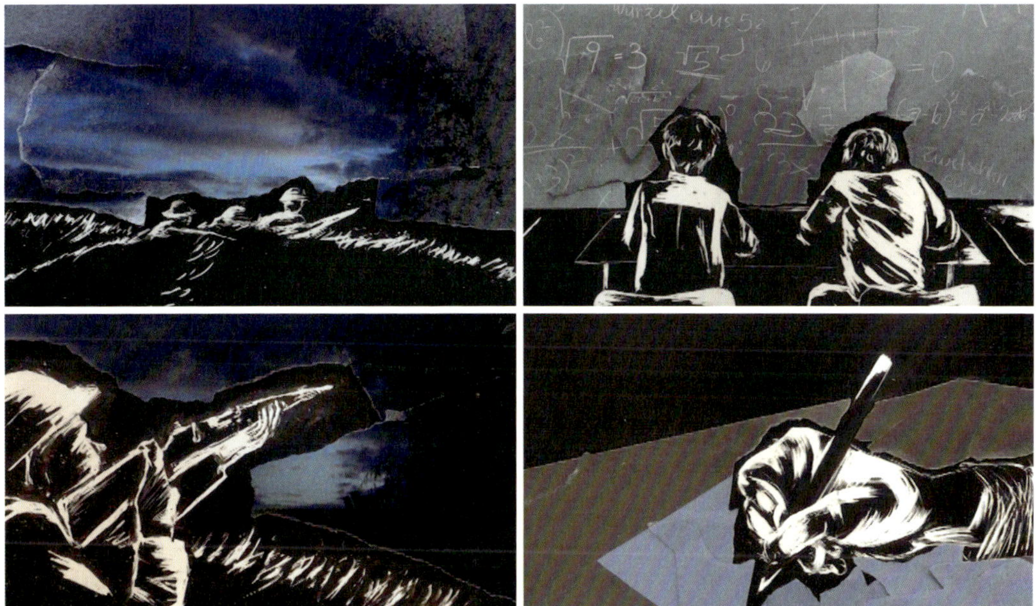

Fade – Fate

Sadet Muadini

The animated film *Fade – Fate* explores the friendship between two comrades-in-arms that ends just as the film begins. One of the two is shot and killed in the war. Still in shock, the friend of the dying soldier begins experiencing flashbacks of their mutual experiences in the past. These flashbacks portray their friendship, marked by moments of happiness as well as episodes of conflict and rivalry. At the end of every flashback, a certain body part of the dying soldier begins to decompose and dissolve, a body part that had played a crucial role in that flashback.

In my short film, the decomposition process stands for the loss of beloved people and for transience. But the everlasting nature of a person in the memories of others is also explored in the film. At the end of the film, one is brought back to the present. One sees a soldier, while all that remains of his comrade, who has reached the final stage of the decomposition process, is his gear. The surviving soldier comes to the realization that, although his friend is dead and has "disintegrated," he will live on in eternity in his memories.

HBLA für künstlerische Gestaltung Linz
Supporting teacher: Helmut Kolar
Film editing: Sadet Muadini, Johanna Weiss
Sound design: Dominik Kostolnik

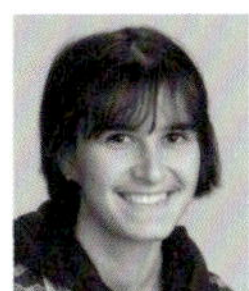

Sadet Muadini (b. 2000) currently attends the Federal Higher Technical Institute (HBLA) for Artistic Design in Linz and created this work as part of her diploma project, in which she explored the topic of decomposition and its depiction in the visual arts. With her animated film, she wants to offer an artistic and less gruesome view of this taboo subject. The acceptance of the transience and insignificance of human existence is the central theme that she addresses here. She drew the inspiration for the depicted war scenes from the collected stories of her family members who remained in their hometown.

https://www.youtube.com/watch?v=PYcl4bJSycM&feature=youtu.be

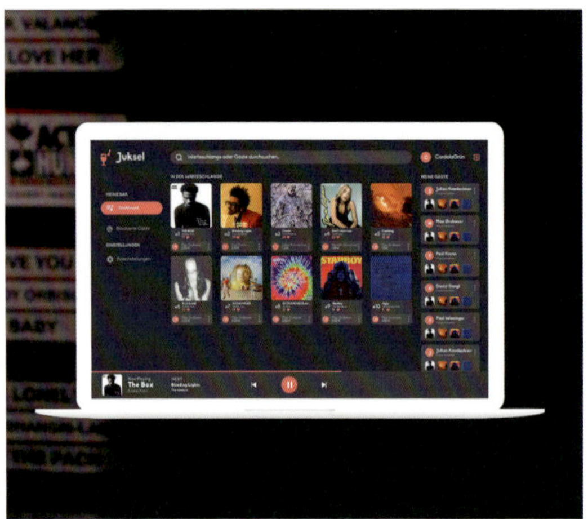
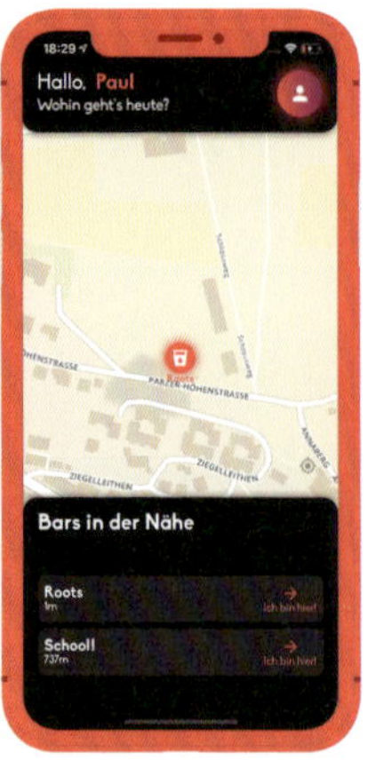
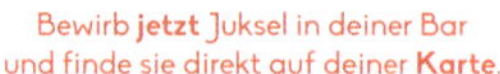

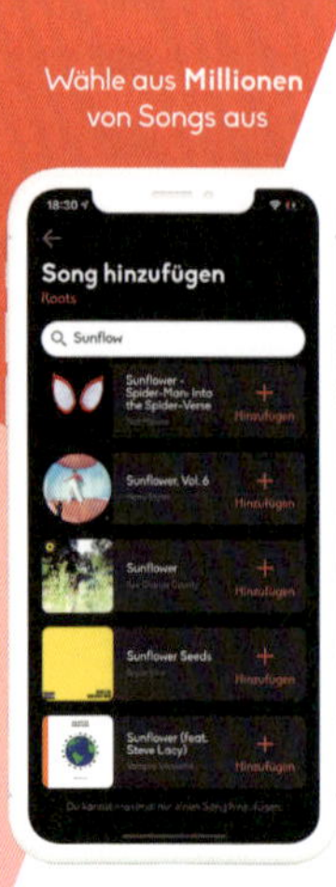

Bewirb **jetzt** Juksel in deiner Bar und finde sie direkt auf deiner **Karte**.

Juksel – Die Jukebox der Zukunft

David Gangl, Max Grubauer, Julian Kronlachner, Paul Wiesiger, Paul Krenn
HTBLA Grieskirchen

With *Juksel, the Jukebox of the Futur,* you can join the other patrons in deciding what music should be played in your bar. This prevents a boring atmosphere and adds some pep to your bar. The greatest thing about it?: *YOU* are the DJ! Add your songs to the bar playlist and then hear them only a few minutes later. Vote for songs you like so they are played sooner. See what song is currently playing! How does it work?

Register

Simply register in the app with your name—and NO, you don't need an email address or telephone number. We designed the registration process to be as simple as possible for you in order to collect as little data about you as possible. That's a promise!

(We) Find your bar

After you register, you will see all the bars in your area that support *Juksel.* A bar will automatically be displayed as soon as you are in the vicinity.

Let's start

As soon as you select a bar, you can start! You see what songs are currently on the playlist and can add songs yourself. If you find a song that you really love, simply vote for the song, which improves its ranking. That way, the music that YOU want to hear is played.

Romantic date

Surprise your girlfriend or boyfriend with "your song" by adding it to the playlist and then voting for it to ensure that it is played immediately. Believe us: it will make her or him very happy and you will have a wonderful evening together.

The idea for this project came to us at the beginning of the semester break. Afterward, we started developing the app in Flutter. Within only a few days we had the mock-up finished. This was followed by two weeks of hard work on the Flutter app. In the final weeks we began looking for test bars and developing the Web client. Unfortunately, at this point COVID-19 put a stop to our work. As soon as bars can reopen, *Juksel* will be tested in three bars in Wels. In the future we want to find more bars that will use our system, and *Juksel* will be optimized and expanded for private use so that it can be used for private parties as well.

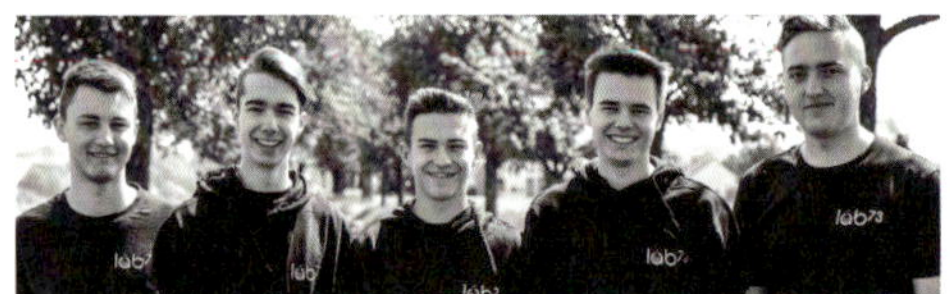

David Gangl (b. 2002), **Max Grubauer** (b. 2002), **Julian Kronlachner** (b. 2002), **Paul Wiesiger** (b. 2002), and **Paul Krenn** (b. 2002), all students at HTBLA Grieskirchen, worked together to develop the project *Juksel – Die Jukebox der Zukunft.*

http://www.lab73.at/juksel

Meine Welt, Deine Welt

Zoe Borzi, Nikolaus Heckel, Jonathan Steininger

How different are we really? This is the question that the documentary film *Meine Welt, Deine Welt* (My World, Your World) asks a drag queen, a monk, a female farmer, and an animal-rights activist—four people who could not be more different but who nevertheless have much in common. Four life stories about tolerance, decisions, and clichés. After our last documentation, *Kunst und Überleben* (Art and Survival), we wanted to keep growing and evolving and decided to make another documentary film. Because at the time we saw a polarization of society driven by politics, we wanted to counter this by showing that every individual is entitled to his or her own lifestyle. For us, the central theme in this film is diversity: the diversity of life concepts in Austria. We want to show just how varied and even antithetical life designs in Austria can be. In making this film, it was especially important to us that we create a balance: there is no good and no evil in this film; all the characters have their own world in which they live, and no one world is better than any other.

Cast: Meta Morkid, Markus Kohlross, Angelika Wechtitsch, Frater Philipp

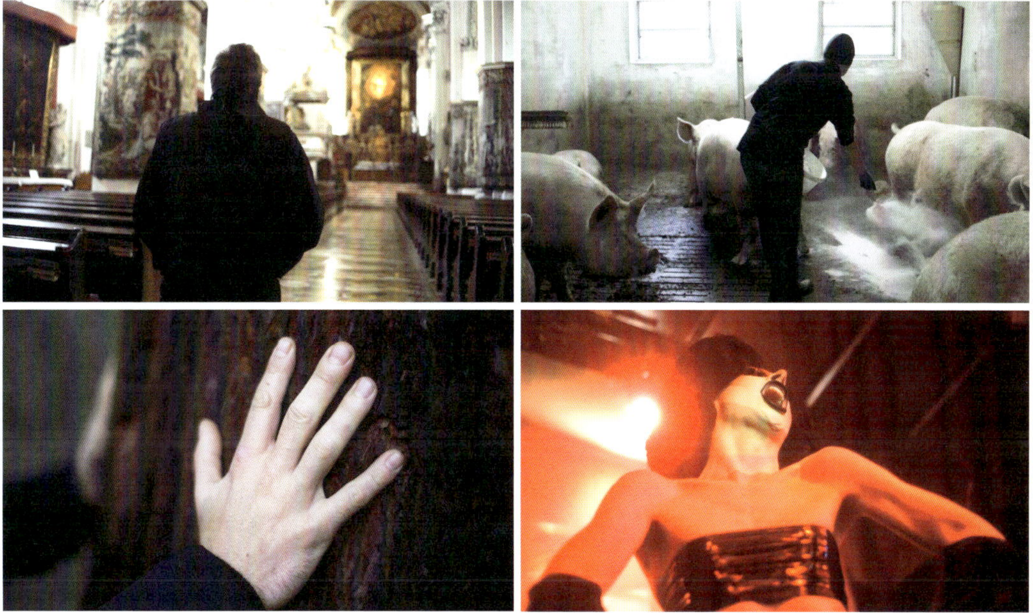

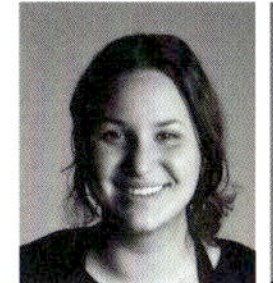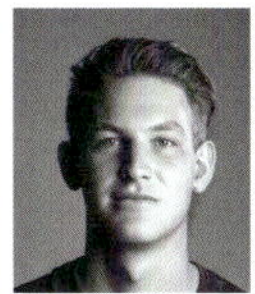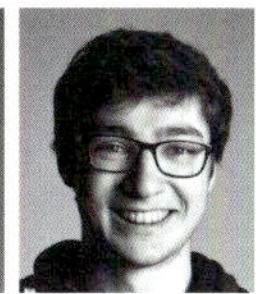

Zoe Borzi (b. 2000), **Nikolaus Heckel** (b. 2000), and **Jonathan Steininger** (b. 2000) met at school when they were 14. They quickly realized that they shared a passion: documentary films. For their final project in their final year of school, they decided to make a documentary themselves, and produced *Kunst und Überleben* (Art and Survival). Because the film was so well received, a year later they decided to produce another documentary film: *Meine Welt, Deine Welt*.

http://dahoam.ortweinschule-film.at/

Musik zum Mitnehmen

Magdalena Schiesser, HTBLVA Graz-Ortweinschule

The two rings I designed are dedicated to the theme of Styria and the traditional "Klapotetz." The special thing about the rings is that together, they make music. One ring looks like a small cog wheel, while the other is made out of steel resonating strips from an accordion. The cog-wheel ring is for the ring finger and the other ring for the middle finger. When one wears both rings on one hand, the movement of the cog wheel against the steel strips can produce a tone. The rings can also be worn separately, of course. I made both pieces of jewelry out of silver, using various silversmithing techniques.

For me, it was important to combine my roots in the province of Styria with my great passion for music. Music plays an important role in my life. The "Klapotetz," a noisemaking wind-wheel perched on a high wooden pole used to scare birds away from vineyards, is typical for Southern Styria, where I live. I have an equally deep connection to music, and since the "Klapotetz" makes a kind of music with its clapping sound, it influenced this work. When you wear these rings, you not only have a unique piece of jewelry; you also have a "musical instrument" with you all the time. This is why I chose the title "Musik zum Mitnehmen" (Music to Take with You).

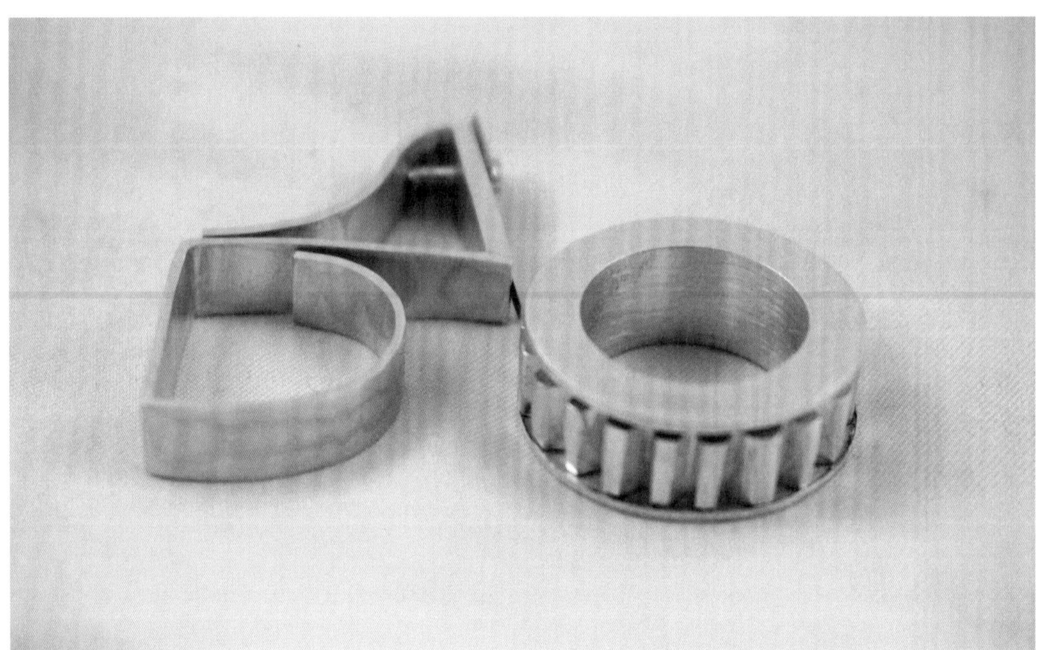

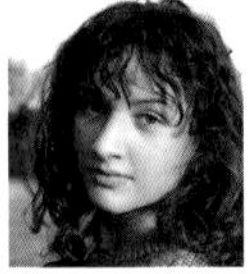

Magdalena Schiesser (b. 2002) attended primary school in the Styrian town of Wildon and then spent four years at BG/BRG Klusemann. In her final year at that school, her grandfather enrolled her in a silversmithing class, where she discovered that she enjoyed making silver jewelry and also had a talent for it. Since 2016 she has attended HTBLVA Ortweinschule in Graz (Jewelry and Metal Design). She will graduate next year.

　　u19–create your world · Young Professionals · Honorary Mention

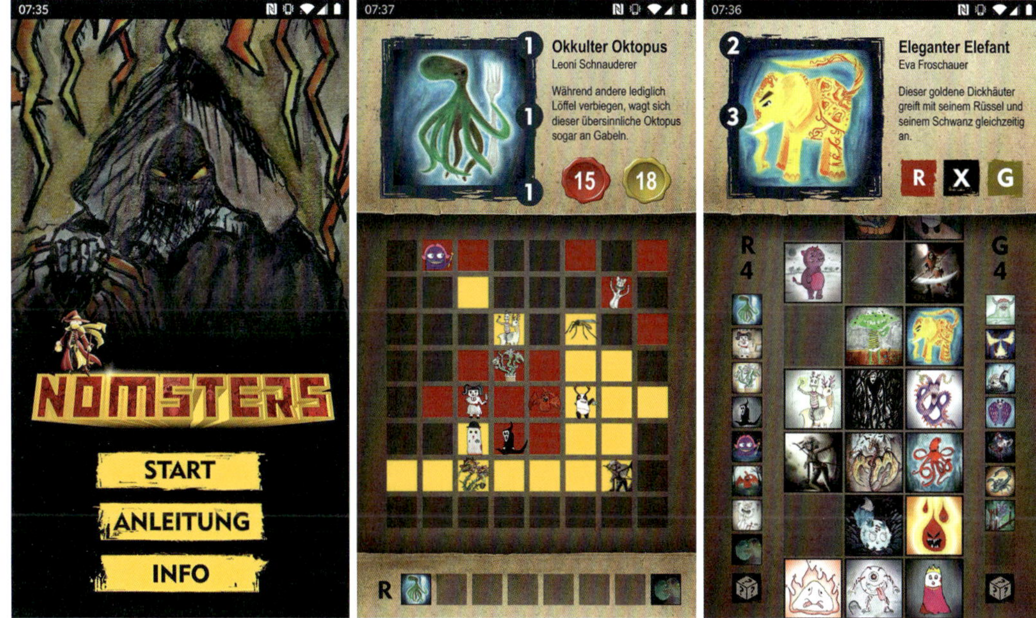

Nomsters

Students from class 7c and 8a at BORG Bad Leonfelden

One of our school's focal points is a special focus on arts with a strong emphasis on media. In our computer science class, we studied various ways of developing apps and in the process discovered the program Adobe Animate. We learned the programming language it uses, Actionscript, and began creating small applications that incremented variables or told stories in which the user could periodically decide how they would continue.

Together with other students from the subject areas of media design and art, we then developed the game *Nomsters*. In this game, two players compete with a team of eight creatures of their choice. These creatures were designed and executed by students from various grades. The Nomsters are placed on the playing field alternately and assume various field formations there according to their respective attack pattern. Whoever occupies the most spaces at the end is the winner. This app distinguishes itself from the many individual programming projects due to the large number of students involved in its development, and the long development period over nearly an entire school year. The app is now available for Android devices on the Google Play Store.

Project support: Wolfgang Hoffelner

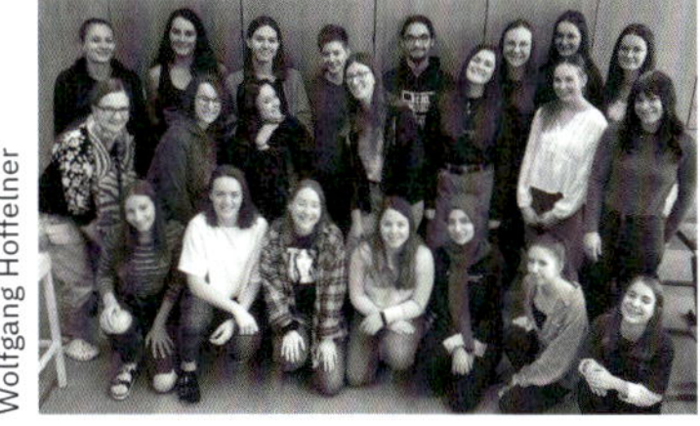

Students at BORG Bad Leonfelden The students are from grades 11 and 12 at BORG Bad Leonfelden; two classes were from our media/art section and one class from the science section "Man-Nature-Technology" (MeNaTec). The project was supported by Wolfgang Hoffelner in the areas of computer science, media design, and art.

http://www.borgleon.at/2020/02/7c-8a-nomsters · www.borgleon.at/play

Querdenker

Max Wolfmajer, Clemens Pfeiffer, Gergely Varecza, Nora Puntigam,
Mirjam Fladenhofer, HTBLVA-Graz Ortweinschule

The short film *Querdenker* (Lateral Thinkers) looks at our modern social-media society as well as at lateral thinkers in society and how they are perceived. In a world that lives in an entrenched portrait mode, the young Mo defies these societal standards and films his videos in landscape or "lateral" orientation. One day in a park, three boys who, like Mo, are making a live stream, but in portrait mode, notice his unusual camera position and confront him about his alternative perspective. After they repeatedly demand that the lateral thinker hold his camera "properly," which Mo refuses to do, Max, one of the three, decides to get rough—and he is joined in this by his friend Andreas. Only Julian, who complies with Max's demand that he should film the proceedings, is a bit uncertain and keeps a low profile. But for fear of not being part of the group, he also contributes a few crude comments. The situation escalates and ultimately takes a violent turn: Mo lies motionless on the ground, and the three culprits, fearing the consequences for their actions, flee. The complete scene, however, finds its way onto the Internet in the two active live streams, and within only a few hours the videos have gone viral. The brutal episode also comes to the attention of a well-known news network, which decides to report on it in order to encourage society to reflect on the incident. The report is seen by a large number of people, including the three culprits, who watch the news show that evening with their parents. While Max, along with his father, seems almost proud of what he and his friends did, and Andreas, as well, exhibits absolutely no compassion, Julian slowly but surely realizes that something horrible had happened that day …

HTBLVA-Graz Ortweinschule: Franz Leopold Schmelzer, Johannes Steger
With support from: ITEC Tontechnik, Verkehrsverbund Steiermark "Verbund Linie"

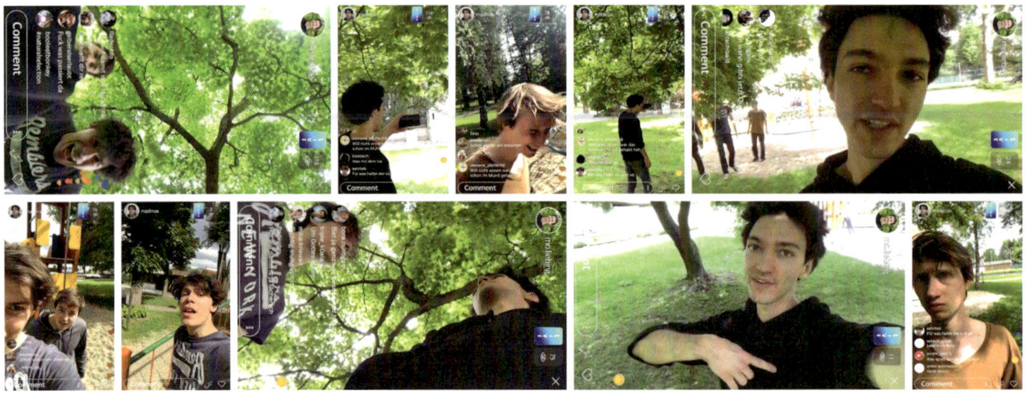

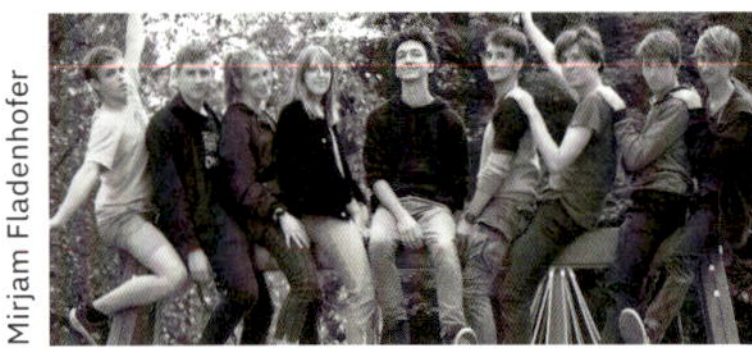

Mirjam Fladenhofer

Max Wolfmajer (b. 2002), **Clemens Pfeiffer** (b. 2003), **Gergely Varecza** (b. 2001), **Nora Puntigam** (b. 2003), and **Mirjam Fladenhofer** (b. 2002) are five students who met at Ortweinschule Graz and decided to join forces to make the film *Querdenker*. It is the first project these students have realized in this configuration. Over the years, all five have developed their various interests in the area of filmmaking and thus complement each other well as a team. Despite their different areas of interest, they share a common passion: film. *www.norapuntigam.at · www.clemenspfeiffer.com · www.varecza.com · www.mirjamfladenhofer.at · www.maxwolfmajer.com*

https://vimeo.com/422123608

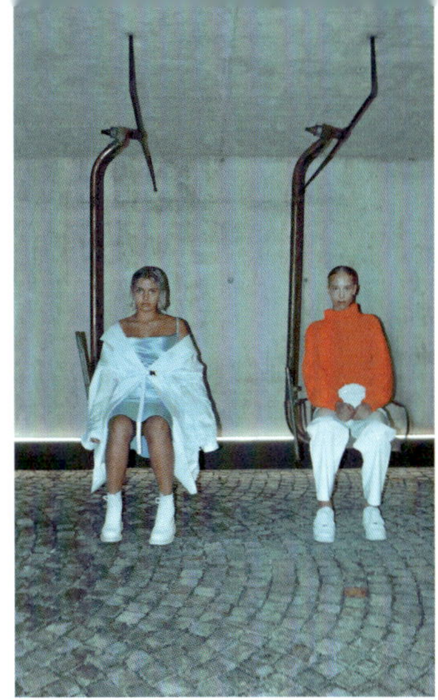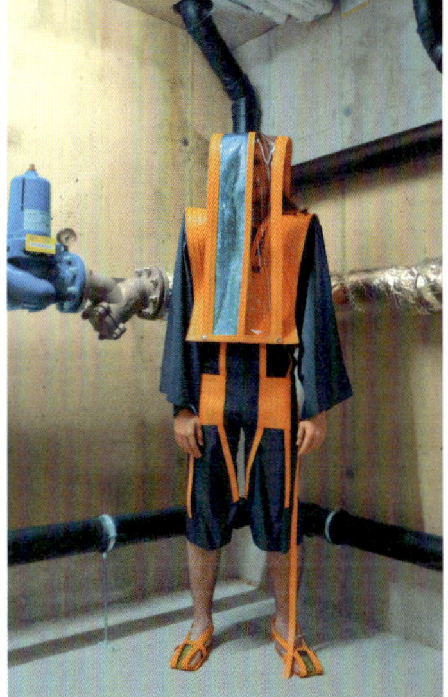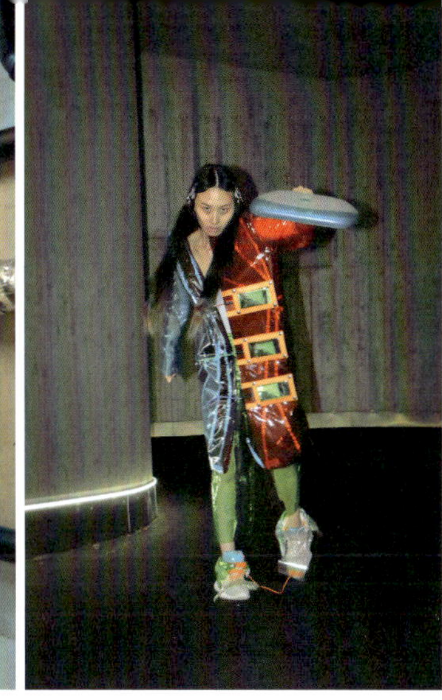

WWW.VIRUS

Florian Sigl, Ria Kathan

Mankind's most revolutionary invention has spread throughout society like a virus. The smartphone has infiltrated our everyday life quietly and inconspicuously and exerted an enormous influence on it. The price we pay for the convenience these devices offer us has a different significance for each of us, but its sum remains the same. Every one of us is responsible for oneself; one must decide whether one places the services provided by Google Maps, Instagram, Amazon, and WhatsApp above one's own privacy. But these devices impact nearly every other area of our lives as well—in the case of young people, it is particularly their health that is affected. "Text neck" is a posture problem now recognized by medical professionals, and studies from South Korea show that some 80 percent of young people in that country are now nearsighted. Every year at a lavish event, Apple's newest device is unveiled, and since a segment of society capitulates to capitalist ideology and buys the latest iPhone in order to define themselves among the masses, millions of smartphones also become redundant each year. These superfluous phones are then burned at enormous e-waste dumps in Third World countries, with the emissions having a huge impact on climate, nature, and environment. Because social media and the smartphone go hand in hand, the *WWW* collection devotes itself primarily to the networking of social media users, with the seemingly perfect image that is presented to the outside world, with their transparency and the longing for beauty and perfection. In the *Virus* collection, the risks and problems that smartphones bring with them are visualized. The individual articles of clothing/sculptures are to be seen as an artistic exploration of the topic and are aimed at raising the viewers' awareness of the risks of technological indulgence.

Photos: Armin Rafili
Hair & makeup: Lilly Evita
Models: Miao Yan, Jan Kössl, Elias Geser, Chiara Fahrner, Alma Kathan
Support teacher: Julia Wetrov

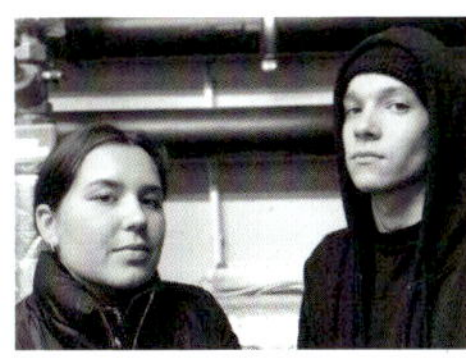

Florian Sigl (b. 2000) and Ria Kathan (b. 2000) have known each other since their high school days. When both of them decided to enter the fashion department at the Ferrarischule Innsbruck, their paths crossed again. The five years they spent together at school led to a close friendship that formed the foundation for a respectful collaboration for their final project. They had the opportunity to exhibit their work at the 2019 Design- & Erfindermesse in Tirol, winning first prize in the Fashion & Design category. In the future they want to use their work to share their thoughts about the risks and effects associated with the excessive use of smartphones and social media.

Young Creatives

up to 14 years

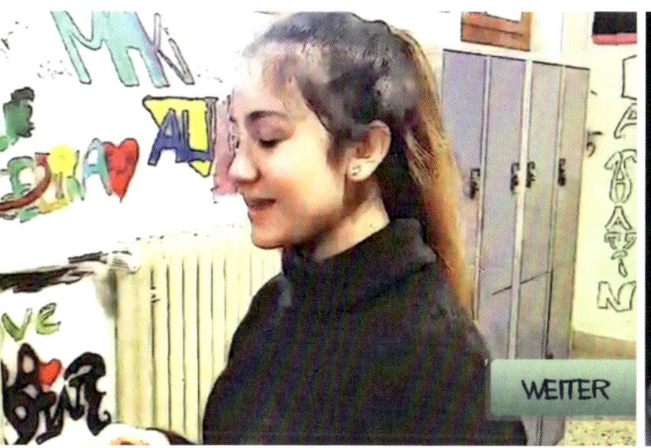

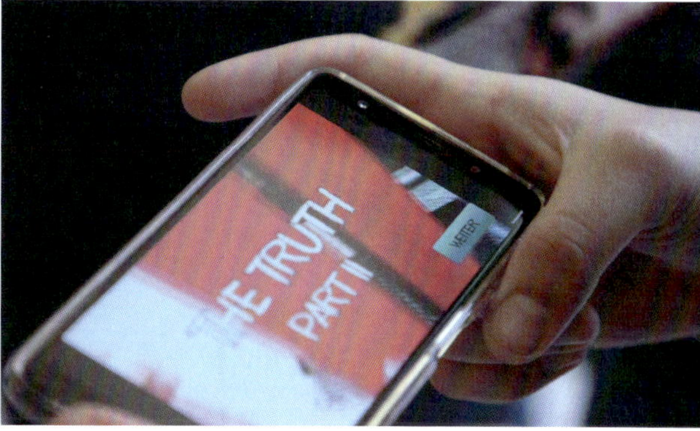

The Truth Part 2
Students from NMS Lehen, Creative Media Design

The Truth Part 2 is a mixed-reality game that takes players to the abysses of modern cities. The game was developed by fifteen students from the Neue Mittelschule Lehen and members of the media artist group "gold extra" as part of the research project *schnitt # stellen*.

The Truth Part 2 combines a story, whose outcome can be decided by the players themselves, with puzzles and elements of augmented reality. The game is played live, with 80 triggers that can be scanned with a smartphone app.

The audience embarks on an exciting journey to Shadow Town. The kids have scarcely arrived at school when the director takes a telephone away from one of them. They find a phone in the locker of their friend Haley, who is absent that day, but there is a surprise in store: Haley's Facebook account has been set to "In Memory of"—which happens only when someone has died …

The players experience a number of surprises, including street chasms, mobs of kids in parks, eerie cellars, diamonds, and pictures of cats. Shadow Town is a dangerous place: French fries, bicycling, and lockers can kill you. The adventure is an exploration of friendship, one's own neighborhood, the dangers of the city, and—ironically, of course—of failure in computer games. The fails of the players are counted, and the winner is the one who at the end has lost the fewest lives—or maybe it's the one who took the most risks?

The Truth Part 2 was created with the students in a year-long process. They researched in their neighborhood, designed the game and a system of rules, and produced intertwined adventure stories as well as the picture, video, and audio material. The result is a multilayered adventure full of excitement and humor. The students collaborated with a group of artists under the motto "We are all game experts." Together, they discussed ideas, aesthetics, and production methods, designing the game as equal partners.

Artists/project directors: Sonja Prlić, Karl Zechenter
Culture and media education support: Iwan Pasuchin
Artists/workshop assistance: Reinhold Bidner, Tobias Hammerle, Georg Hobmeier
Programming: Christian Knapp
Additional actor: Botond Fodor
Project support: gold extra, MediaLab der Universität Mozarteum Salzburg
Performance partner: ARGEkultur Salzburg
Financial support from the City and Province of Salzburg

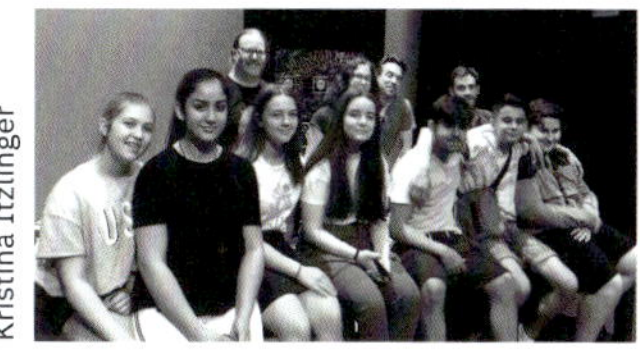
Kristina Itzlinger

The Truth Part 2 is a game created as part of the research project *schnitt # stellen*. As part of their artistic research, the media artists and game authors Sonja Prlić and Karl Zechenter worked for the entire 2018/19 school year with fifteen eighth-grade **students from NMS Lehen in Salzburg (Creative Media Design)** on a mixed-reality game project. Together, they call themselves "Kaktus Landoo" (Landoo: a variant of Ladu, a Somali game).

https://goldextra.com/the-truth-part-2

Coded Art Gallery

Michael Zaminer

The *Coded Art Gallery* is a collection of nine different programs that offer a graphic representation and usually function in interaction with the observer. They can be executed with the computer only with the Processing IDE.

With my work, I would like to show that art and technology can be successfully combined. With most of the programs, the user can save the frame and operate the program with the mouse as well. The programs were created with the programming language Processing, which is based on Java. Pictures are incorporated into the programs that can be processed, or mathematical functions are depicted graphically. A great deal of experimentation is done in the programs with regard to the color and position of the depicted objects. Moreover, rotations and other functions are built into the programs.

I learned about the competition from my German teacher, because our class wanted to take part in the u14 category (the project could not be completed due to the Coronavirus). Since I have been programming for quite some time, I had the idea of entering this competition myself. Over time, however, it turned into so many individual programs that I grouped them in a gallery.

Processing Foundation – for the provision of the software, in my opinion one of the best pieces of software for programming graphic representations.
https://processingfoundation.org

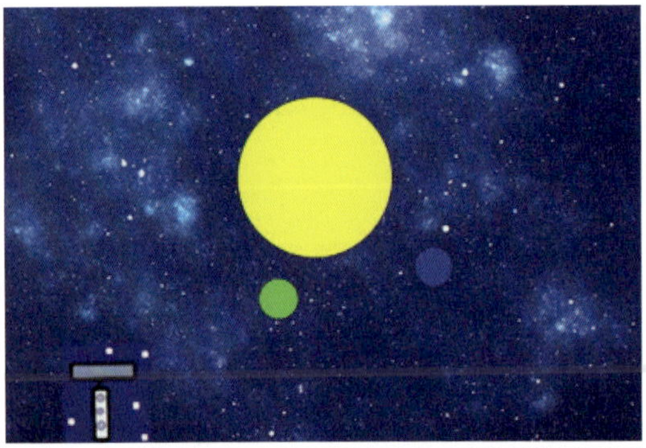

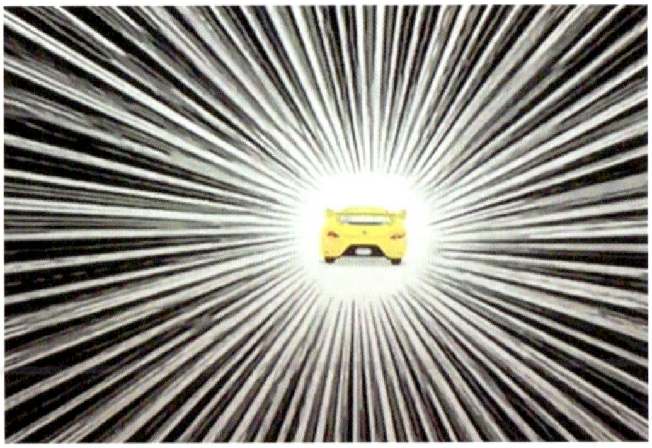

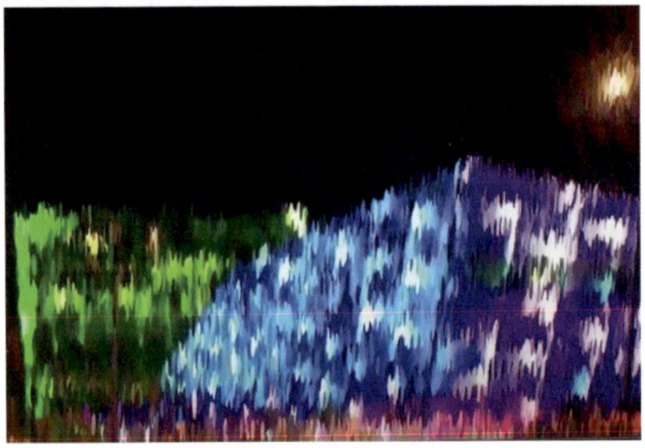

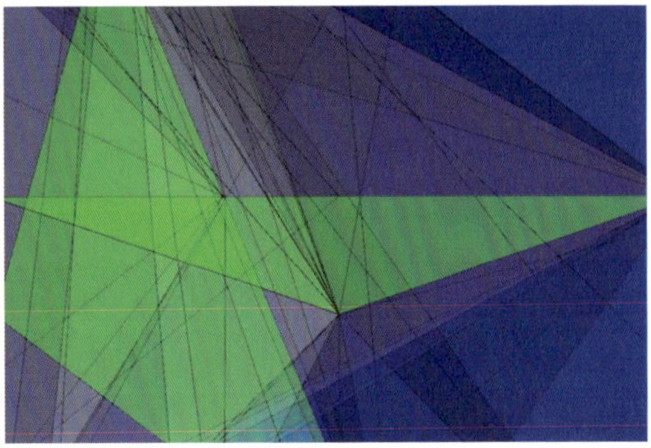

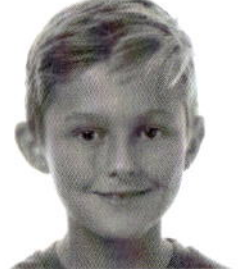

Michael Zaminer (b. 2006) is a 13-year-old who attends school in Vienna's 19th district and has been interested in technology since he was a child. He began programming in the fifth grade using Arduino (hardware). After a year he switched to the Java-based development environment Processing, with which graphic software, such as the programs in his award-winning project, can be programmed. He programs in C++ and HTML as well. In his free time, he plays soccer and enjoys skiing. He dreams of a job at SpaceX.

Zwischentöne

Students from class 4e at Musisches Gymnasium Salzburg

Our audio mystery is concerned with the topic of copyright in the music industry, Internet piracy, and intellectual property.

In the most recent murder case of the charming investigator James Sero, it is not easy to tell who is the victim and who is the perpetrator: A young girl recorded a song that suddenly stormed the charts a few years later. A famous singer sold it as her own work and made millions of dollars with it, while the young girl was left empty-handed, which had grave consequences for her and her single mother. Part of the blame for the girl's plight is shared by a shady music producer, who shortly afterward is found dead in his apartment …

The script for the audio drama was written by eight authors and then revised by the entire class. The song at the center of the story, which is so good that a murder was even committed for it in the mystery, was composed by our songwriter Nikolas Unger and two students, Faiza Maier and Sophia Polst, and recorded with the help of the whole class. The sound effects were largely made using the class's own recordings. The recordings were done in cooperation with Radiofabrik Salzburg, and the audio drama was edited and post-edited by our production team.

Carla Stenitzer and Radiofabrik Salzburg

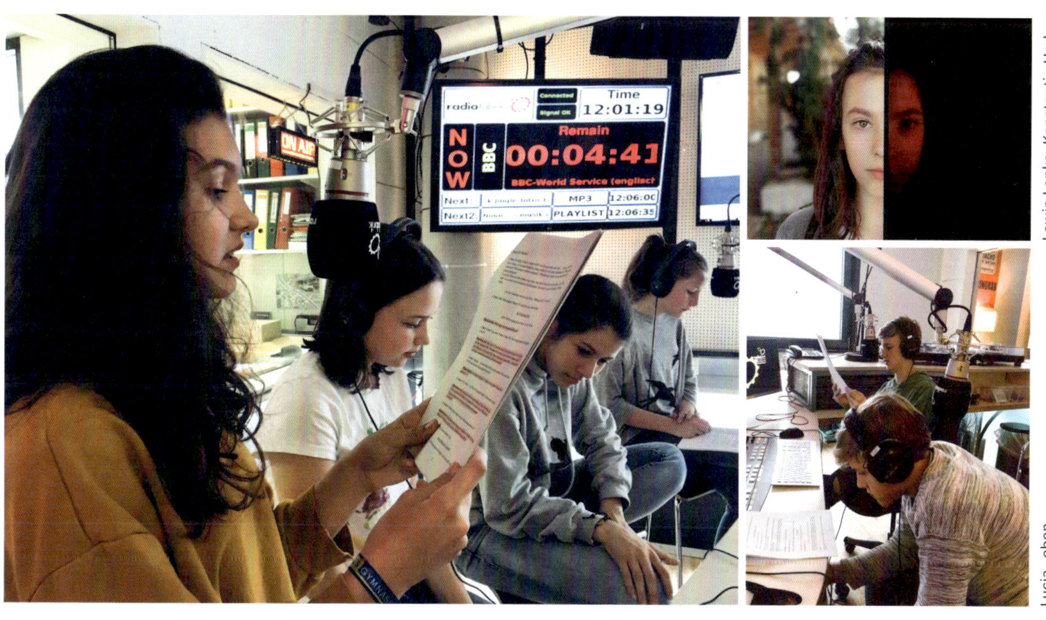

Lucia Leben

Lewin Lepka, Konstantin Hederer, Maria-Lara Markus, Lorenz Medicus

Lucia _eben

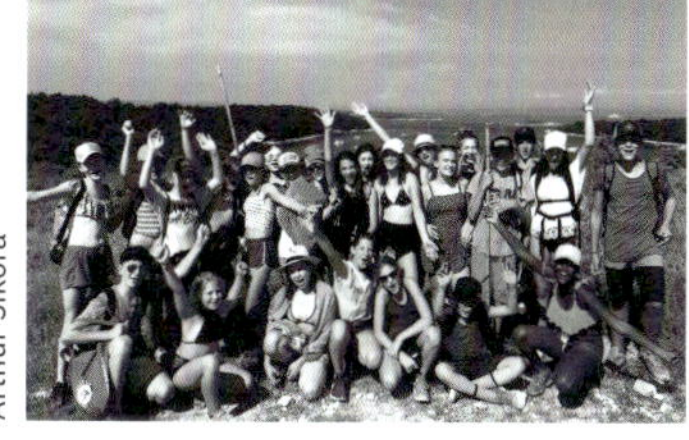

Arthur Sikora

Students at Musisches Gymnasium Salzburg. The creators of the audio drama *Zwischentöne* (Overtones) have known each other for four years and together have survived many ups and downs of everyday school life. When so many free spirits come together, things are not always completely harmonious, of course. But what they all have in common is their love for music, the visual arts, dance, theater, and literature. In musical projects, where all areas of the arts are joined together and every team member can contribute her or his talents, everyone pulls together and draws inspiration from the others!

https://cba.fro.at/405459 · https://cba.fro.at/405459%20%20

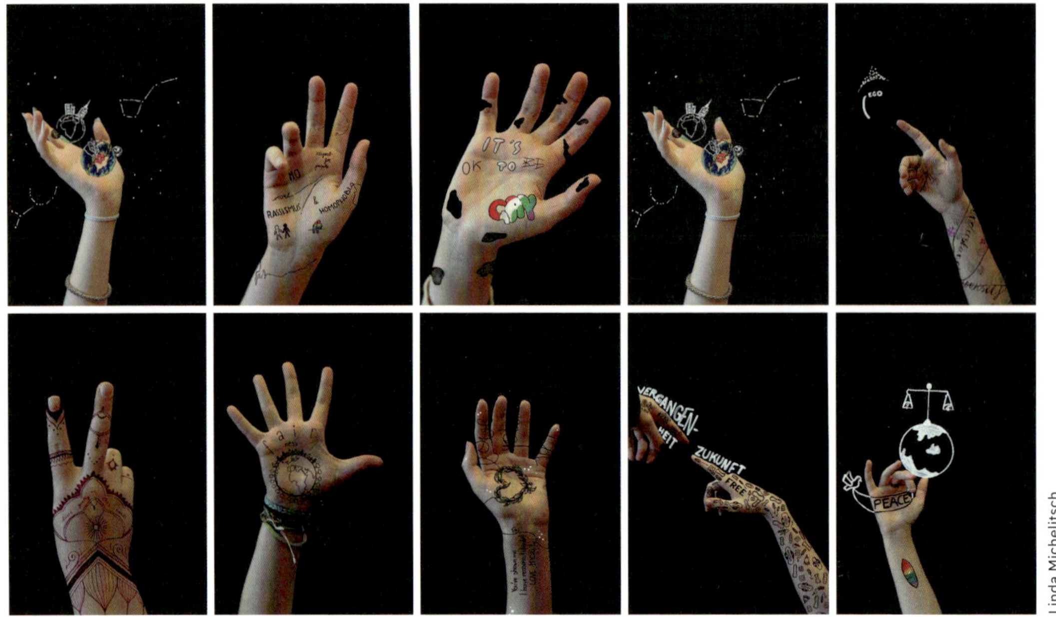

Die Zukunft liegt in unseren Händen

Students from BG & BRG III, Vienna

Hands can hit and destroy, but at the same time can be so light, caressing and tender. Let's live gently on this earth. The future is in our hands.

Together, we reflected on what we would wish for our future. We photographed our hands in various positions and gestures and then wrote our wishes on the photographs with markers and felt-tip pens. The result is the photography project *Die Zukunft liegt in unseren Händen* (The Future is in Our Hands). Photographing our hands was a beautiful experience. It is not only faces that can tell stories but also hands. Our hands are an expressive part of our bodies: we use them to express our feelings non-verbally and to accompany our words. Our hands help us to create artworks and to shape our future anew every day.

What do we wish for our future?
A world in which tolerance is more than just a word.
A healthy planet, climate justice, and acceptance.
Fairness, respect, individuality.
No racism, no homophobia.
Self-love, self-acceptance.
Peace and the equality of all people.
Respect for girls and women through free feminine-hygiene products.
No destruction or injuries.

Project support: Elisabeth Reingruber

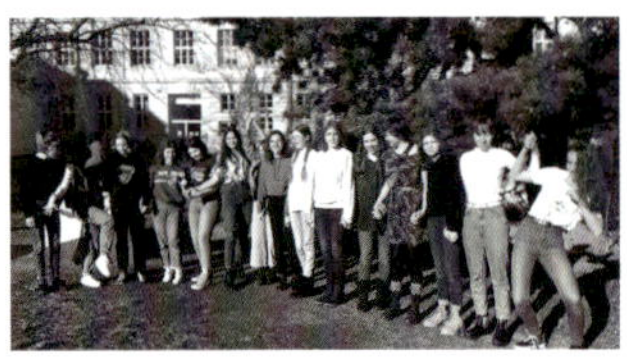

Students from BG & BRG III, Vienna. We are fifteen girls (b. 2005, 2006) from class 4a of BG & BRG III, Boerhaavegasse Vienna, a school with a special focus on music. Our class has an art focus with more advanced instruction in the visual arts. In our artistic work, we are able to freely develop and live out our talents.

Lury

Laurin Steinhuber, Amelie Steinhuber, Niklas Steinhuber

Lury is an animated film featuring 20-cm-tall figures and elaborate stage sets consisting of some 5,000 individual photographs.

The main character is Lury, a fisherman who has lost interest in fishing and wonders what other kind of occupation he could pursue. When a knock comes at the door and he opens it to find a demon, nothing is as it once was.

After their successful project *Gobi kommt* from 2018/19, the team wanted to take on an even more ambitious film project. The figures were to be more mobile and the sets even better. In addition, the camera was moved on a track and the lighting was improved. Like their previous film, it was to be an adventure and follow a fixed script. Moreover, this time texts were spoken, and only English subtitles were supplied. For this reason, Laurin, Amelie, and Niklas spent a large part of their summer vacation building and photographing and then many hours in the fall and winter editing and adding the soundtrack. The film was completed in March 2020.

The materials used for constructing the figures and building the sets in the carport were anything that could be found around the house: wood, metal, fabric, Styrofoam, paint, etc. For the skeletons of the figures, we used small metal plates, ball joints, and wire frames.

Because the figures required supports that should not be visible, we also used the green screen technique. As large parts of the sets had to be painted at the end of the film, we were not able to take any photographs afterwards, meaning that the scenes were edited together right away as little films and examined, some photos were accidently deleted, and scenes were photographed again. The photos were taken with a Samsung WB350F compact camera, the video editing was done with Pinnacle Studio 22, and the audio recordings were processed with Audacity.

Idea and script, stage sets, photos, editing, sound, voice-over: Laurin Steinhuber
Idea and script, stage sets, photos: Amelie Steinhuber
Stage sets, photos, editing, sound, voice-over: Niklas Steinhuber

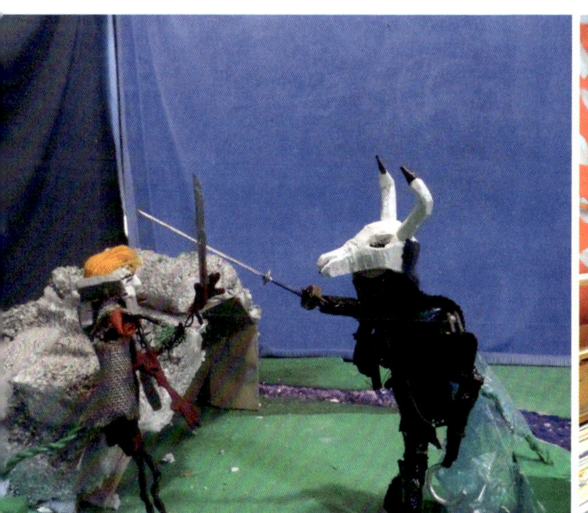

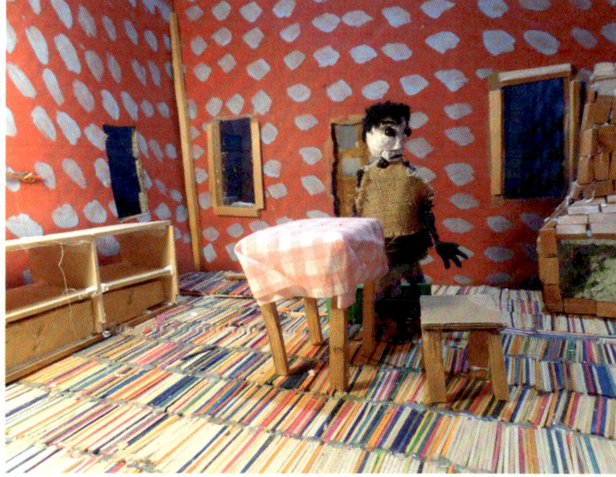

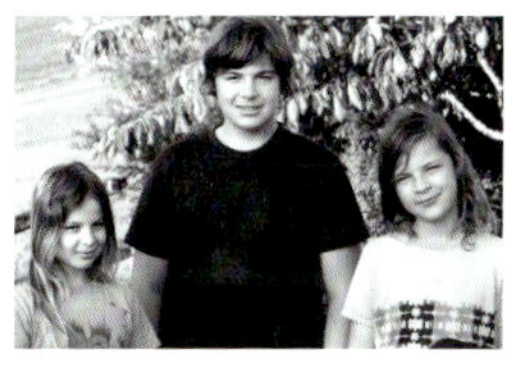

Laurin (b. 2008), Amelie (b. 2008), and Niklas (b.2003) Steinhuber are siblings. They began making short films several years ago using a simple video-editing program. In addition, they also regularly made LEGO animated films and short audio dramas.

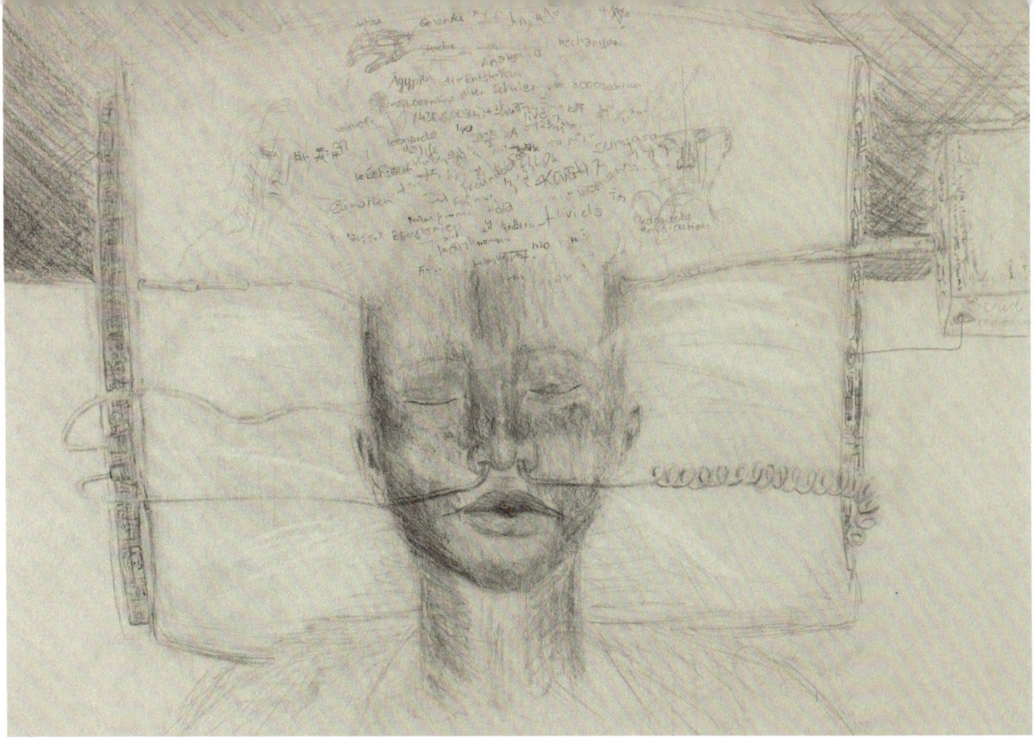

Schule der Zukunft

Matilde Irene Abarca Hernández

Faced with the question "How could the school of the future look," I suddenly had thousands of images in my head; super modern buildings, floating personalized touchscreens, digital textbooks … But then I thought, regardless of how modern and cool a school like that would be, there will always be someone who just doesn't like school. Perhaps this is because every person is different and therefore needs a different kind of learning.

This is why my school of the future has an electronic device that adapts to each person. When the students sleep, they lie on an electronic cushion that automatically connects with their brain. Every night, the device teaches the students new material in a personalized manner. The students then review this material on their own when they are awake.

The device can also recognize the subjects and areas of knowledge in which the students still need help, and it attempts to find the best mode of learning for them. The goal of all of this is for school to be fun for everyone!

When kids have fun learning, their interest in learning will also be stimulated, and they will want to continue utilizing this kind of learning to make a better future for themselves. In the school of the future, the question will not be how one learns but rather what one can achieve with what one has learned!

BG & BRG Vienna III Boerhaavegasse

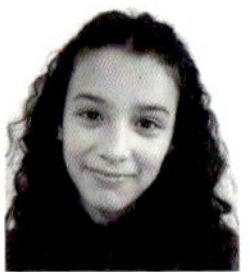

Matilde Irene Abarca Hernández (b. 2007) is in the sixth grade (arts program) of BG & BRG Vienna III Boerhaavegasse. She enjoys drawing, singing, and playing piano, and she loves school. Her favorite subjects are math and physics. Her goal is to draw hyperrealistic portraits. She was born in Colombia and has lived in Austria for six years.

Das Verschwinden der Trolle

Luis Schweighofer

The project *Das Verschwinden der Trolle* (The Disappearance of the Trolls) is a short film that was recorded in one take with a smartphone, using primarily Lego and Schleich figures and pictures. In order to change the "actors" and backdrops between the individual scenes, the recording was simply paused.

The story is about a mythical land long before our time, a land teeming with fantastic creatures such as unicorns, dragons, gryphons, and fairies, all of whom coexist peacefully. One day, however, trolls arrive on a large ship to overthrow the beloved king of this magical realm, Balduin the Barefooted and Brave, to conquer the land, and to steal the king's legendary crystal scepter, which is said to possess magical powers. The dim-witted ogres began their brutal search, destroying villages and woods along the way and killing many forest creatures. Ultimately, they succeed in finding the coveted treasure but also suffer a "misfortune" in the process: the trolls are banished into the magical crystal, and their evil deeds are thus all undone. Finally, peace returns to the land.

Petra Schweighofer (mother and camerawoman)

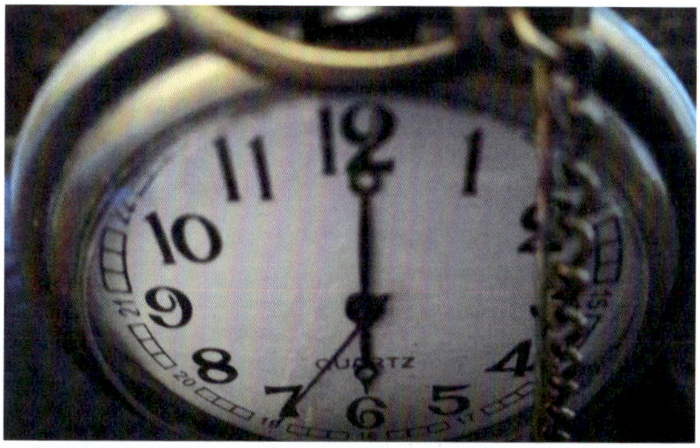

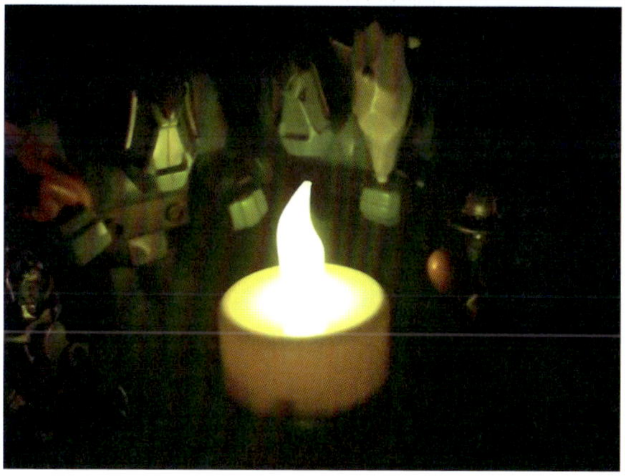

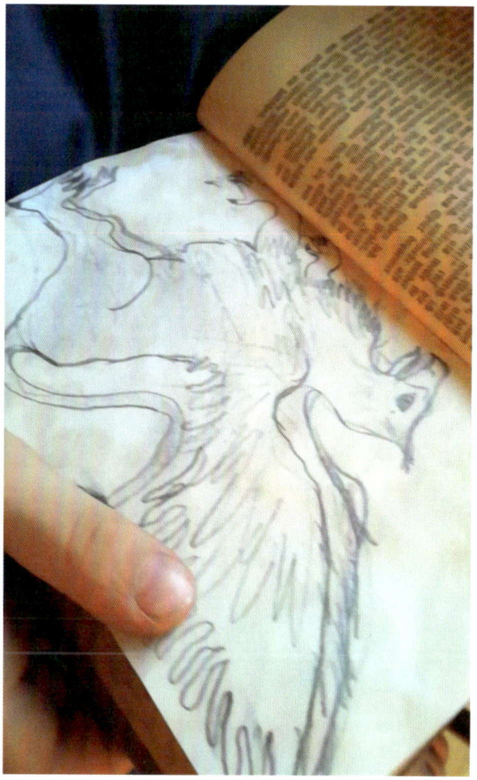

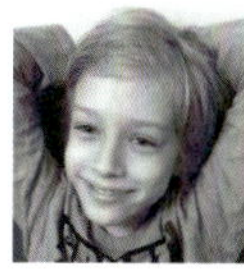

Luis Schweighofer (b. 2009) is the oldest of three siblings, lives with his family in Baden bei Wien, and is finishing his final year of primary school. When he is not playing with his friends or family, riding his bike, wandering through the woods and vineyards, building forts and climbing trees, he can usually be found with his nose in a book. Immersing himself in stories and even telling some himself is what he likes doing most. Ever since he could talk, he has been arranging figures and making up stories, from Punch and Judy shows and ghost trains to escape rooms. Luis is a member of the Biondekbühne theater club and very much enjoys acting out scenes and playing with language.

Das Würfelhaus

Dominik Pichler

Dominik has something special in mind with the extra-large drinking straws that Papa bought a long time ago, and which now stand in a large glass vase in Dominik's room: he wants to glue them together with a hot-glue gun to make a cube. Dominik thinks about connection bridges, combines colors, and plans various divisions of space. During the project, Dominik discovered that it is quite difficult to work precisely with a hot-glue gun, and that building something with such lightweight components is extremely demanding. After several starts, restarts, and revisions, after dealing with various problems and the loss of numerous straws that were too short, Dominik ultimately succeeded in making his cube. And in this period of reworking the cube, he had the idea for building an entire cube house, one that would float in space and turn on its own axis—as slowly as Earth. People live in the small tubes, and even when the cube floats freely through space, nothing in their living spaces is destroyed.

Question: Why did the people move out into space, into these little tubes?
Dominik: A virus is moving through Earth, which is why the people moved into space. They flew up in rockets. The cube house can hold a thousand people and is equipped with food supplies. The people play and live in the cube house until the virus has disappeared from Earth again.
Question: How will they know that the virus is gone?
Dominik: They get a message from Earth via a satellite. And the people want to return to Earth.
Question: How did you get this idea?
Dominik: I wanted to work with the hot-glue gun, so I asked Papa to show me how it works. We worked together to glue the cube; Papa helped me with the statics. A week ago, I then had the idea for the cube house, because I would like to float through space myself. And now it's a good thing that there is the cube house, because there is a virus on Earth.

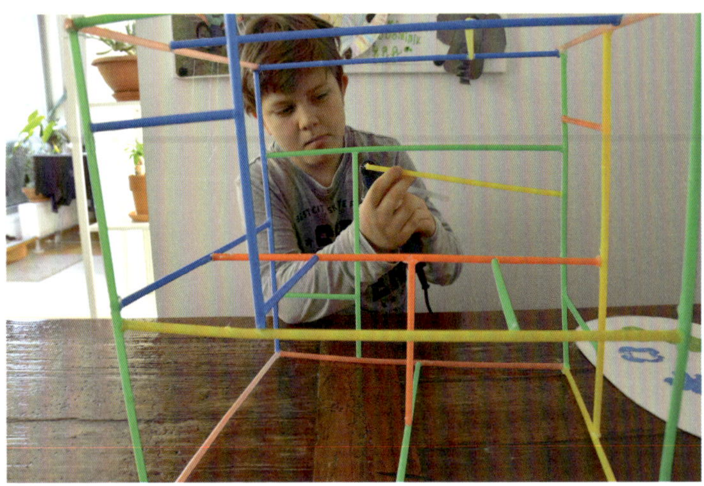

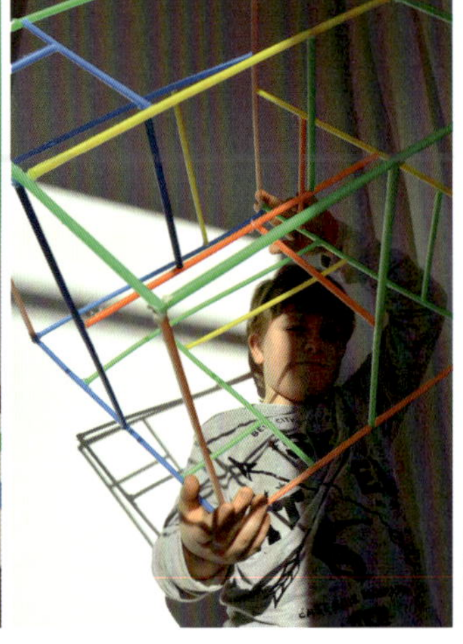

Gabriele Bauer

Gabriele Bauer

Dominik Pichler (b. 2009) is a student in the seventh grade at the Integrative Lernwerkstatt Brigittenau in Vienna. He did the work by himself, helped in the technical execution by his father, as gluing the straws with the hot-glue gun is very difficult to manage on one's own. Dominik feels more secure by himself than in the group when he has to work on something; Dominik has difficulty fitting into groups and presenting ideas in front of others. Dominik is a very active child who needs a lot of physical exercise; he has a hard time sitting down and concentrating on one thing. For this reason, he was particularly proud to have completed the submission for the u19 category. These kinds of feelings of achievement are very important for Dominik to encourage him to persist, and to increase his self-confidence.

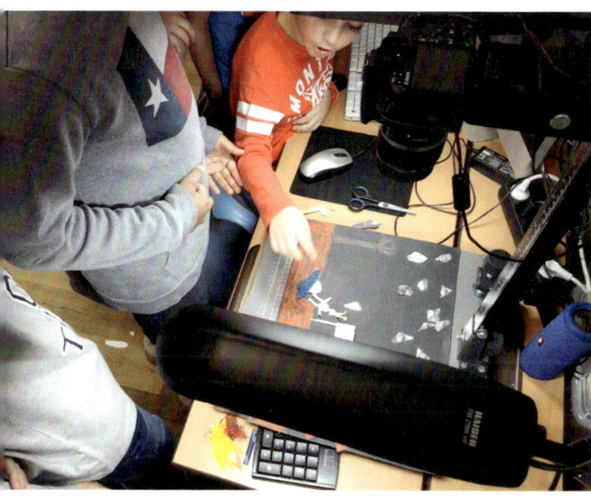
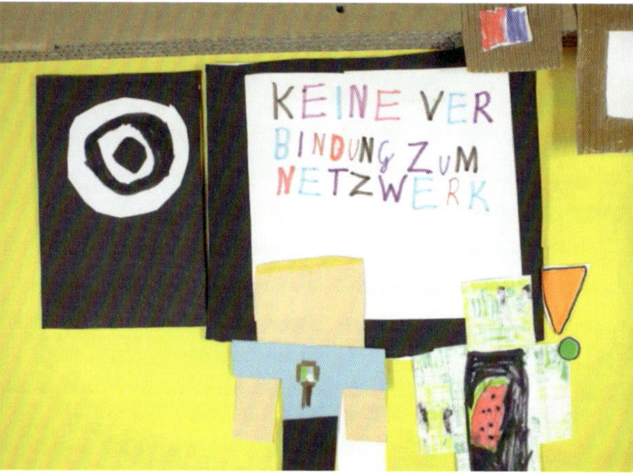

Der Vogel mit dem coolen Hut
23 students from class 3c at GTVS Kolonitzgasse, Vienna 3

For the animated cartoon project *Alles Trick,* the students were introduced to the principles of animated film and the analysis of moving pictures in a fun, playful manner at a three-day workshop. The experts from MuKaTo supported the students throughout the entire project.

In a "warm-up," the students and the MuKaTo team talked about the history of moving pictures and the kids experimented with stop-motion and single-frame animation. The MuKaTo team brought with them the necessary equipment (computers, cameras, lamps, tripods, and recording software) as well as the material for animatics, cut-out animation, and object animation and worked with the kids in small groups throughout the workshop. The students designed their own task schedule, with independent work alternating with structured tasks. The MuKaTo team contributed concrete input in the form of specialized information and film examples in order to work toward results in a consistent and goal-oriented manner.

The students learned how to utilize the filmmaking technology, worked in groups to develop their own scripts, and designed the necessary pictures, figures, and props. The filming was done with the assistance of the experts, and the individual scenes were underlaid with audio recordings in a rough cut and assembled.

The result is *Der Vogel mit dem coolen Hut* (The Bird with the Cool Hat), in which a video game gets out of control when the avatar is kidnapped by the crew of a spaceship and taken to a neighboring planet. In making this film, the students learned to use tools to participate in a critical, passionate, and constructive way to the development of the media and contribute to their design.

Initiative MuKaTo (workshop with the students)
culture connected – OeAD / BMBWF (sponsor)
Elisabeth Riener, Melanie Rapp – GTVS 3,
Kolonitzgasse 15

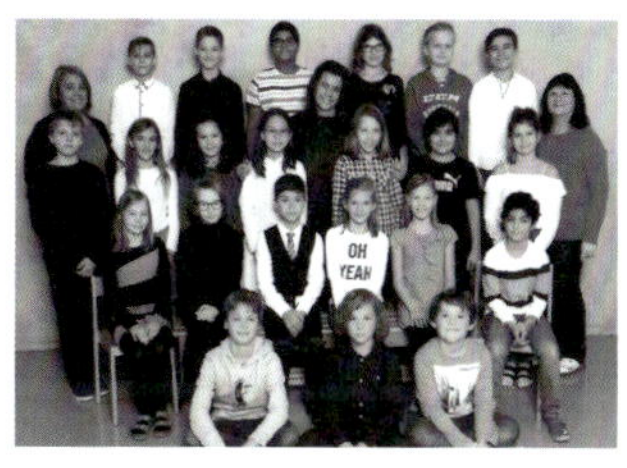

23 students at GTVS Kolonitzgasse, Vienna 3. At the time the film was made, the 23 children were in class 3c at GTVS Kolonitzgasse. A contributing factor to the success of the project was the fact that from the time the children started school, they were accustomed to working together very creatively as a team. They always placed great importance on constructive and successful collaboration.

https://www.youtube.com/watch?v=ez87TEK2N2w

In einer weißen Winternacht

Students at BrgOrg15

The students filmed the story *In einer weißen Winternacht* (Once Upon a Northern Night) by Jean E. Pendziwol and Isabelle Arsenault (published in 2017 by Verlag Freies Geistesleben) as a stop-motion film in their graphic arts class. As part of the story is set in the woods, they began by gathering branches, pine cones, leaves, etc. from outside in nature. Then the children crafted the various props, the main figures, and the animals, and finally drew the backdrops. Working in groups, the students produced a storyboard and subsequently filmed the individual sequences using the Stop Motion Studio app and the school's iPads. The teacher then did the editing and designed the texts.

The story line of the film: In a white winter night, parents tell their child a bedtime story. Thanks to the vivid description by the parents, the child experiences the tale in colorful images, and we see the pictures that unfold in the child's mind. We can see, for example, how the snow in the winter night gradually transforms the landscape into a magical environment, wrapping everything in a soft, white blanket, as cozy as the child's bed.

School: BrgOrg15, Henriettenplatz 6, 1150 Vienna
Teacher: Silvia Khan-Bolin

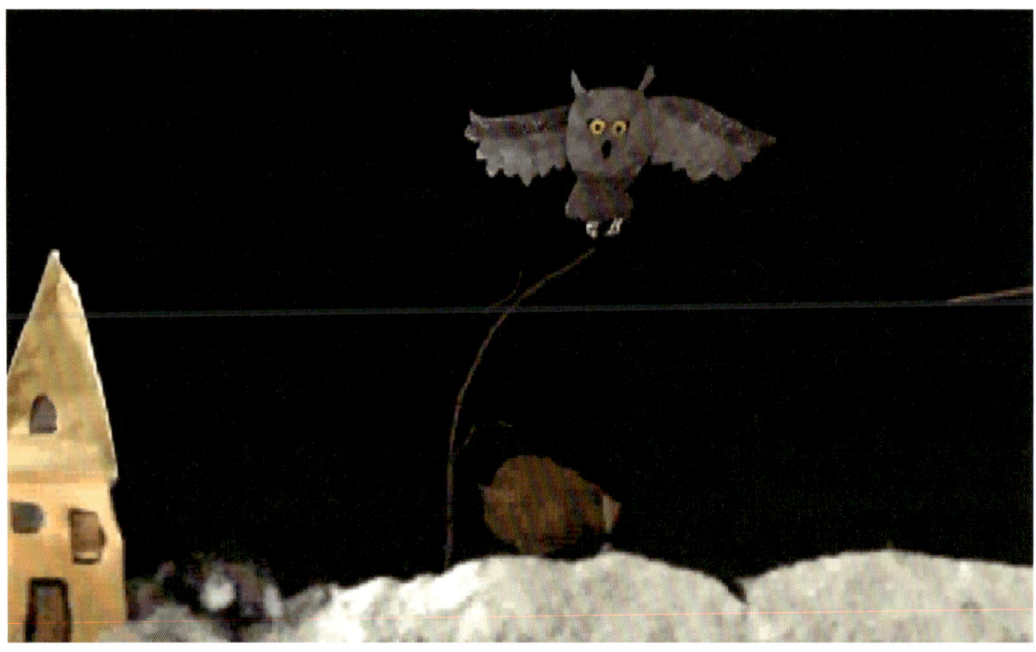

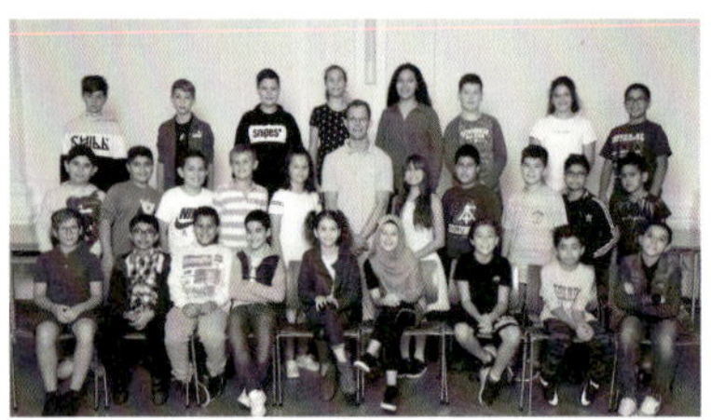

Students at BrgOrg15. The students are all in the fifth grade at BrgOrg15 in Vienna's 15th district and have known each other since fall 2019. They have worked together in their arts class to produce various creative projects, such as the film *In einer weißen Winternacht*. They undertake their group projects with enthusiasm, a great deal of creativity, mutual support, and team spirit.

https://www.youtube.com/watch?v=yhkItyyllKQ

PRIX ARS ELECTRONICA
Jury

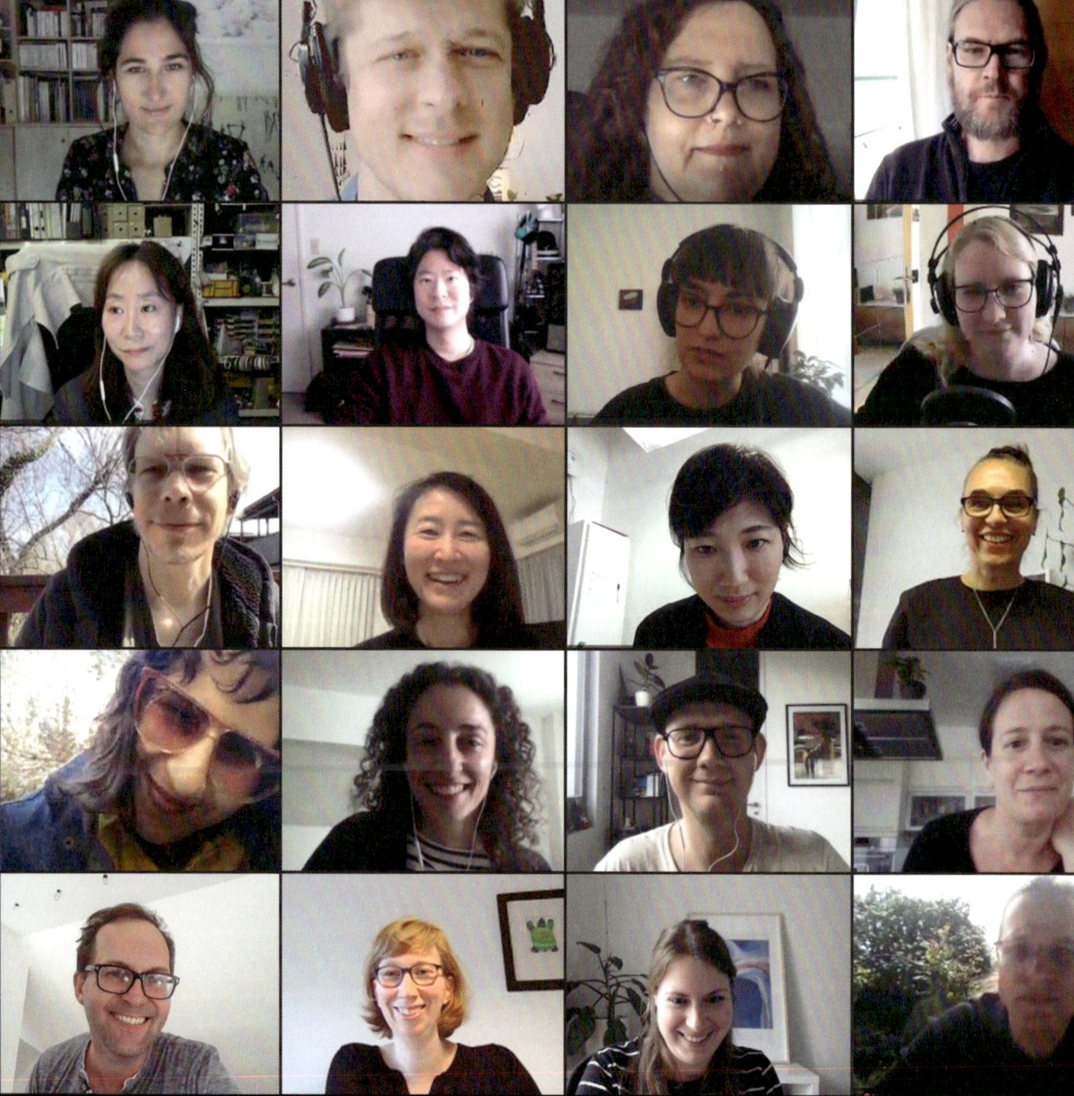

Computer Animation

Peter Burr, Birgitta Hosea, Mathilde Lavenne, Mimi Son, Erick Oh

Interactive Art +

DooEun Choi, Sabine Himmelsbach, Vladan Joler, Haytham Nawar, Stefan Tiefengraber

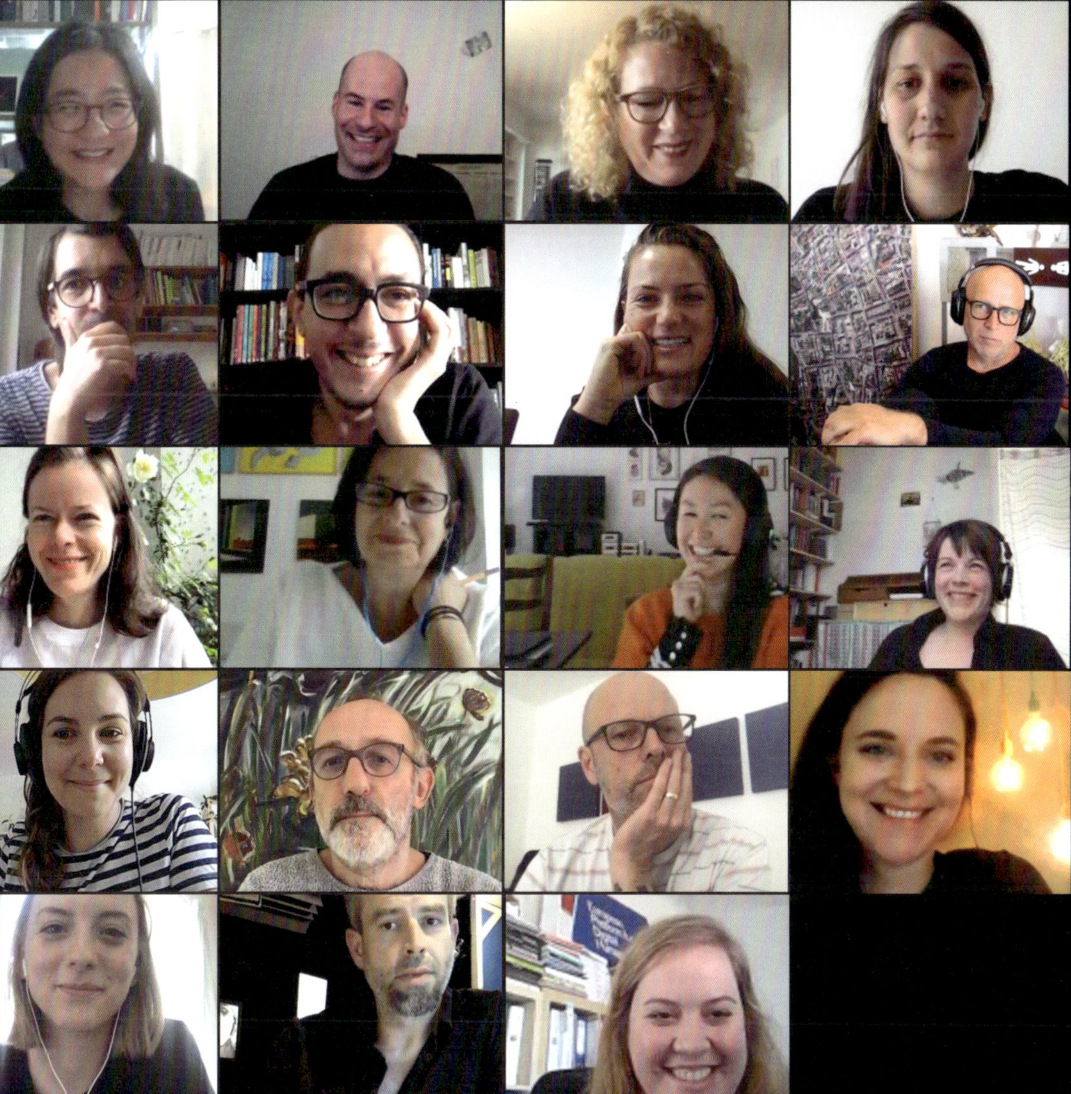

Digital Communities

Chiaki Hayashi, Dietmar Offenhuber, Irini Papadimitriou, Farah Salka, Thomas Gegenhuber

u19–create your world

Sirikit Amann, Gerald Hartwig, Conny Lee, Karl Markovics, Irene Posch

Computer Animation

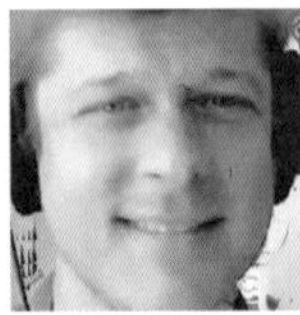

Peter Burr (US) is an artist from Brooklyn, NY. A master of computer animation with a gift for creating images and environments that hover on the boundary between abstraction and figuration, Burr has in recent years devoted himself to exploring the concept of an endlessly mutating labyrinth. His practice often engages with tools of the video game industry in the form of immersive cinematic artworks. These pieces have been presented internationally by various institutions including Documenta 14, Athens; MoMA PS1, New York; and The Barbican Centre, London. He is currently a visiting artist at the School of the Art Institute of Chicago.

Birgitta Hosea (SW/UK) is an artist, filmmaker and researcher in expanded animation. Exhibitions include Venice & Karachi Biennales; Oaxaca & Chengdu Museums of Contemporary Art;

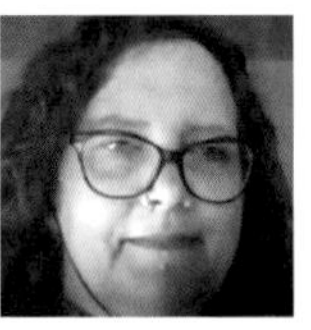

InspiralLondon; Hanmi Gallery, Seoul. She has a solo exhibition at ASIFAKeil, Vienna in April 2020. Included in the Tate Britain and Centre d'Arte Contemporain, Paris, archives, she has been awarded an Adobe Impact Award, a MAMA Award for Holographic Arts and an honorary fellowship of the Royal Society of the Arts. Currently Reader in Moving Image and Director of the Animation Research Centre at the University for the Creative Arts, she was previously Head of Animation at the Royal College of Art and prior to that at Central Saint Martins, where she completed a practice-based PhD in animation as a form of performance.

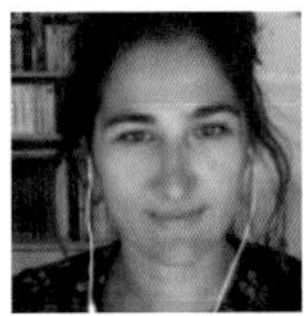

Mathilde Lavenne (FR) is a filmmaker and visual artist who also makes digital installations. Her work has been exhibited extensively in Europe and internationally. Her films have been screened in many festivals including the Rotterdam International Film Festival, the Tampere Film Festival in Finland, the Ann Arbor Festival where she received in 2019 the award of the best experimental short film. Her work has been awarded the Golden Nica of Ars Electronica and in France by the François Schneider Foundation Prize.

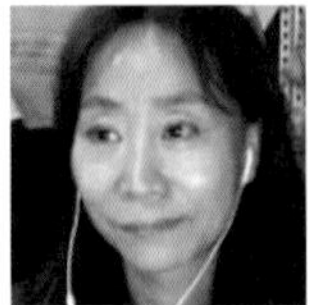

Mimi Son (KR) was born in Seoul where she currently lives and works. She co-founded a Seoul-based art studio Kimchi and Chips with Elliot Woods in 2009. An obsession with geometry and Buddhist philosophy inspires her to articulate space and time from various perspectives. This continuous experiment has allowed her to create installations that aim to depict an intersection of art and technology, material and immaterial, real and virtual, presence and absence. Over the past decade she has worked as an artist, professor, storyteller, curator, and artistic director in various countries and institutions. She completed her master degree on Digital Media Art and Design at Middlesex University and Interaction Design at Copenhagen Institution of Interaction Design (CIID).

Erick Oh (KR/US) is a Korean filmmaker / artist based in California. His films have been introduced and awarded at numerous film festivals including Academy Awards, Annie Awards, Annecy

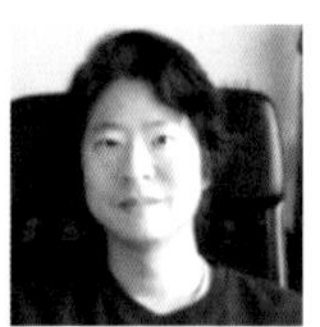

Animation Festival, Zagreb Film Festival, SIGGRAPH, Anima Mundi and more. With his background in fine art in Seoul National University, Korea, and film at UCLA, USA, Erick became an animator at Pixar Animation Studios from 2010 to 2016. Then Erick joined Tonko House with his fellow former Pixar artists and directed *PIG : The Dam Keeper Poems,* which won the Crystal Award at Annecy Animation Festival 2018. Erick is currently working on a variety of projects with his partners in film/animation, VR/AR industry, and also contemporary art scene in US and South Korea.

Interactive Art +

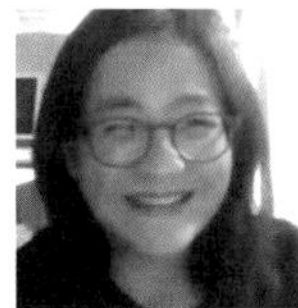

DooEun Choi (KR/US) is an independent curator based in New York and Seoul. Choi is currently serving as a guest curator of BIAN 2020, International Digital Art Biennial in Montreal, and curator of Pioneer Tower Iconic Public Art Project in Texas. She recently worked as a co-curator of Aurora 2018 in Dallas, art director of Da Vinci Creative 2015 and 2017, and curator of Art Center Nabi in Seoul. Since 2000, Choi has curated numerous international media art exhibitions in Kyoto, Beijing, Shanghai, Madrid, Geneva, Enghien-les-Bains, Istanbul, Brisbane, Montreal, San Jose, New York, and many other cities.

Sabine Himmelsbach (DE/CH) is the director of HeK (House of Electronic Arts Basel) since March 2012. After studying art history in Munich she worked for galleries in Munich and Vienna

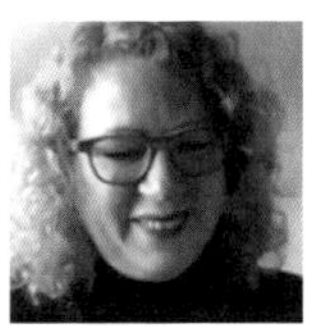

from 1993–1996 and later became project manager for exhibitions and conferences for the Steirischer Herbst Festival in Graz, Austria. In 1999 she became exhibition director at the ZKM | Center for Art and Media in Karlsruhe. From 2005–2011 she was the artistic director of the Edith-Russ-House for Media Art in Oldenburg, Germany. Her exhibition projects include *Fast Forward* (2003) and *Culture(s) of Copy* (2011). 2011 she curated *gateways. Art and Networked Culture* for the Kumu Art Museum in Tallinn as part of the European Capital of Culture Tallinn 2011 program. Her latest exhibitions at HeK in Basel include *Entangled Realities. Living with Artificial Intelligence* (2019). As a writer and lecturer she is dedicated to topics related to media art and digital culture.

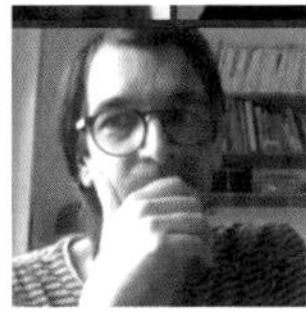

Vladan Joler (RS) is SHARE Foundation director and professor at the New Media department of the University of Novi Sad. He is leading SHARE Lab, a research and data investigation lab for exploring different technical and social aspects of algorithmic transparency, digital labor exploitation, invisible infrastructures, black boxes, and many other contemporary phenomena at the intersection between technology and society.

Haytham Nawar (EG) Haytham Nawar is an Egyptian artist, designer, scholar, and educator. He is the Chair of the Department of the Arts at the American University in Cairo and he is

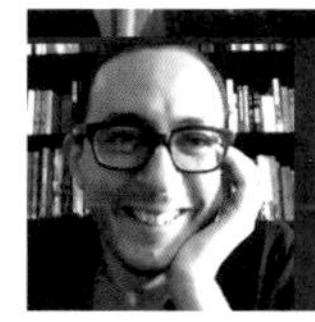

the founder and director of Cairotronica, Cairo Electronic and New Media Arts Festival. Nawar received his PhD from the Planetary Collegium, Center for Advanced Inquiry in Integrative Arts—University of Plymouth and is a Fulbright alumnus. He has participated in several exhibitions and has won several both national and international awards. Currently, he is researching, writing, and publishing in the field of design history and practices with a focus on the Arab World and Africa.

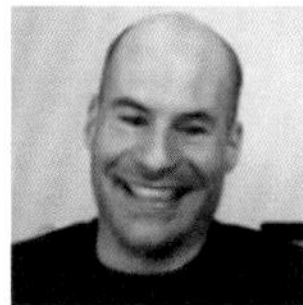

Stefan Tiefengraber (AT) is an artist who lives and works in Linz. His work ranges from kinetic sound installations and interactive installations to audio-video noise performances. His work has been shown at Ars Electronica Festival (Linz), Galerie Gerken (Berlin), New Media Gallery (Vancouver), 16th Media Art Biennale WRO 2015 (Wroclaw), TodaysArt 2014 (Den Haag), Blaues Rauschen 2018 (Bochum), …

Digital Communities

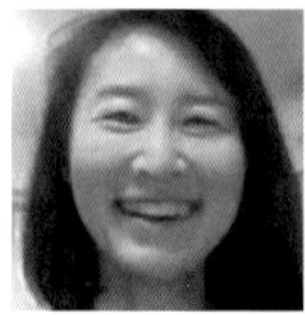

Chiaki Hayashi (JP) is Co-founder of Loftwork, which is a new style of creative company that boasts a network of over 30,000 creators. Each year Loftwork rolls out over 200 projects including web, community, and spatial design initiatives. Loftwork also operates the digital fabrication cafe, FabCafe. Hayashi pioneered the adoption of Project Management Body of Knowledge (PMBOK) guidelines in the creative industries in Japan and has penned the book *Web Project Management Standards.* Hayashi is a member of the Good Design Awards Screening Committee, and a chairman of Hidakuma that aims to up-cycle the resources into a form of regional value through the utilization of digital fabrication and technology.

Dietmar Offenhuber (AT/US) is Associate Professor and Director of the Master of Fine Arts program in Information Design and Visualization at Northeastern University in Boston. He received his PhD

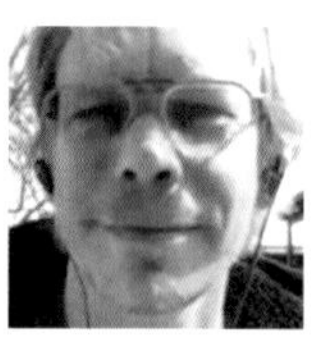

from the Massachusetts Institute of Technology Department of Urban Studies and Planning and studied at the MIT Media Lab in Cambridge. Prior to that he was a key researcher at the Ludwig Boltzmann Institute for Media Art Research and professor at the University of Art and Design Linz. His research areas include socio-cultural aspects of urban technologies, visualization, and auditory perspectives. He is author of the award-winning monograph *Waste is Information – Infrastructure Legibility and Governance* (MIT Press). His artistic work has been exhibited at the Centre Pompidou in Paris, the Armory Show in New York, ZKM Karlsruhe, Ars Electronica Linz, at Sundance, and at the Hong Kong International Film Festival, the Secession Vienna, the Seoul International Media Art Biennale, and Arte Contemporaneo in Madrid, among others.

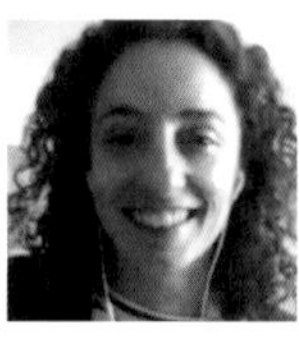

Irini Papadimitriou (GR/UK) is a curator and cultural manager, whose practice draws on interdisciplinary and critical discourse to explore the impact of technology in society and culture, and the role of art in helping us engage with contemporary issues. Currently Creative Director at FutureEverything, an innovation lab and arts organization in Manchester, she was previously Digital Programmes Manager at the V&A, and Head of New Media Arts Development at Watermans. Her exhibition, *Artificially Intelligent,* was on display at the V&A in 2018 and she has been a co-curator for the Arts & Culture experience at Mozilla Festival. She is a co-founder of Maker Assembly, a critical gathering about maker culture, and has been a recipient of curatorial research programs, including MOBIUS (Finnish Institute), Art Fund, Mondriaan Fund and British Council.

Farah Salka (LB) is a Lebanese-Syrian feminist activist based in Lebanon. She graduated from the American University of Beirut in 2006 with a degree in Public Administration and Polit-

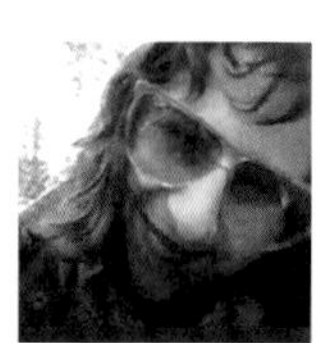

ical Science. She then received her Master in Human Rights Law from the University of Malta in 2007. Farah is the founder and Executive Director of the Anti-Racism Movement since 2012. She works on organizing with migrant communities, asylum seekers, and migrant domestic workers. Farah serves on the board of Mama Cash, the oldest international fund supporting women's, girls', and trans rights groups and feminist movements with money, know how, and networking opportunities. Farah is based in Beirut.

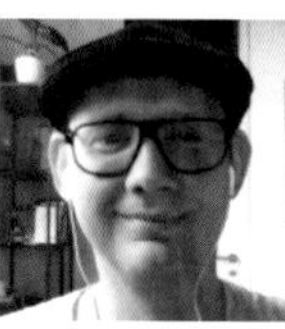

Thomas Gegenhuber (AT/DE) is an assistant professor for digital transformation at Leuphana University Lüneburg and researcher at the Institute of Organization Science at Johannes Kepler University Linz. During his doctoral studies (funded by the Austrian Academy of Sciences), he visited the University of Alberta, FU Berlin, and the University of Edinburgh. Under the umbrella of digital transformation, Thomas works on novel forms of organizing, various types of openness (open strategy, open innovation, and open government), cultural entrepreneurship as well as the implications of socio-technical change. Moreover, Thomas currently serves as an expert advisor for the 3rd gender equality report of the German Federal Government, which focuses on digitalization.

u19 – create your world

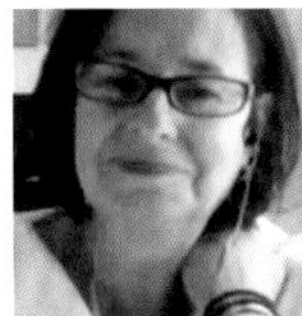

Sirikit Amann (AT) has been a juror since the very inception of the u19 – create your world category for youngsters under 19 years of age in Austria. She was director of cultural education at KulturKontakt Austria and since 2020 she is head of the Department for Education and Society at the OeAD-GmbH. The OeAD-GmbH is the central service center for European and international mobility and cooperation programs in the fields of education, science and research. She previously served as an expert advisor in artistic affairs at the Austrian Federal Ministry of Education, Art and Culture and in the Office of the former Federal Chancellery Minister.

Gerald Hartwig (AT) born 1973 in Graz. After graduating from high school he moved to the USA at the age of 19, where he studied film in Los Angeles. For ten long years he stayed in the USA

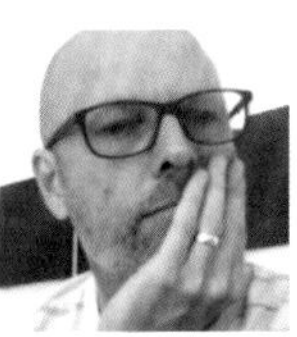

and experienced just about everything you can imagine under the desert sun. After exhibitions in L.A., Berlin, Dresden, Mexico, Trinidad, and Austria, Hartwig lived and worked with his wife and children as a freelance artist for a few years in Berlin before returning to Austria at the end of 2013. He draws for various magazines, the film industry, and for himself. His first graphic novel *Chamäleon* was published in 2013 by Luftschacht Verlag. In 2014 he founded the book distribution service "edition Brudertwist" with his brother Georg Hartwig, with whom the fourth book title has already been published. In 2017 the graphic novel *What Highly Effective People Don't Tell You: A Quest for Success & Growth you* was released in cooperation with author Christa-Madhu Einsiedler. Since 2018 Gerald Hartwig also teaches presentation and composition at HTBLA Ortweinschule in Graz.

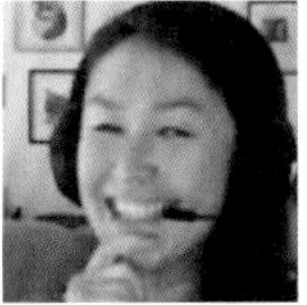

Conny Lee (AT) Conny Lee is a member of the u19–create your world core team and the popular host of Radio FM4's afternoon show FM4 Connected. She also produces and co-hosts the bilingual FM4 Morning Show and a show about video games in a socio-political context. In addition, Conny Lee is head of the "love department," which deals with current topics in the areas of sex, love and dating. As an editor she reviews games, literature, and comics.

Karl Markovics (AT) was born on 29 August 1963 in Vienna and lives with his wife near Vienna. He is an actor, director ,and screenwriter, likes to eat and drink, and works for theatre, film, radio, and

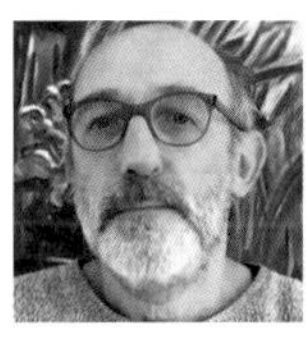

television. He moves and tries to move others.

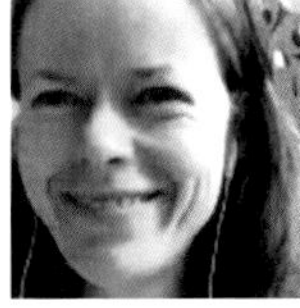

Irene Posch (AT) is a researcher and artist with a background in media and computer science. Her work explores the integration of technological development in the fields of art and craft, and vice versa, investigating the social, cultural, technical, and aesthetic implications thereof. She is Professor for Design & Technologies at the University of Art and Design Linz, Institute of Art and Education. Her research and artistic work has been shown internationally at conferences and museums, among them the CHI, TEI, and IDC conferences, ZKM Karlsruhe (DE), V&A London (UK), Ars Electronica Linz (AT), Laboratorio Arte Alameda Mexico City (MX), Biennale International Design St. Etienne (FR), Works Gallery San Jose (US), Istanbul Design Biennial, and the MAK Vienna (AT).

Digital Communities Advisory Board

Irene Agrivina (ID) Open systems advocate, technologist, artist, and the founder of HONF Foundation for Arts, Science & Technology based in Indonesia. *www.honf.org*

Agnes Aistleitner (AT) is currently living in Kampala, Uganda, building an offline content distribution network *eeboworld.com* with proprietary WiFis distributed all over the city. She previously founded *Teenah.org,* a social manufacturing enterprise in Irbid, Jordan, supported by UNICEF.

Memo Akten (TR) is an artist, researcher, and philomath from Istanbul, Turkey, who works with calculations as a medium, inspired by the intersection of science and spirituality. *www.memo.tv*

Mónica Bello (ES) is a Spanish curator and art historian working across disciplines, with a special interest for emerging cultural practices. For the last 15 years she has curated exhibitions and events internationally in collaboration with artists, curators, thinkers, designers, and scientists of various disciplines.

Dr. Tegan Bristow (ZA) is Director of the Fak'ugesi African Digital Innovation Festival since 2016, Senior Lecturer in Interactive Digital Media at the Wits School of Arts, and Editor in Chief of the *Ellipses Journal of Creative Research.*

DooEun Choi (KR/US) is an independent curator based in New York and Seoul. Choi is currently a guest curator of BIAN 2020, the International Biennale for Digital Art in Montreal, and curator of the *Pioneer Tower Iconic Public Art Project* in Texas.

Gabriele Kepplinger (AT) is a cultural worker and media activist based in Linz. From 1994–2004 she was a leading member of the Arts and Media collective Stadtwerkstatt and is co-founder and managing director of the community TV "dorf tv" in Linz.

Bess Lee (TW) is Chief of Staff of g0v jothon (task force for g0v bi-monthly Hackathon, g0v Civic Tech Prototype Grant, infrathon and Sch001). Co-Chair of g0v Summit 2020.

Lauren Lee McCarthy (US) is an LA-based artist examining social relationships in the midst of surveillance, automation, and algorithmic living. *www.lauren-mccarthy.com*

Carine Le Malet (FR) is Head of Artistic programmation and creation of Le Cube *www.lecube.com*. Since 2001 she has helped Le Cube gain international renown within the digital arts scene by inviting more than 2,000 artists, and co-producing 130 emerging or confirmed artists, from national and international new media scenes.

Leila Nachawati (ES) is a Spanish-Syrian writer and human rights activist. She is communication officer of the Association for Progressive Communications and Professor of Communication at Carlos III University in Madrid.

Afroditi Psarra (GR) is a multidisciplinary artist and Assistant Professor of Digital Arts and Experimental Media (DXARTS) at the University of Washington. Her research focuses on the art and science interaction with a critical discourse in the creation of artifacts.

Maren Richter (AT) is curator and researcher (territories, an/archives and memory). Currently she works for the Windhoek Biennial/Namibia as the chief curator for the first edition taking place in 2021.

Enrique Rivera (CL) is a curator and researcher. He has conducted a series of research and installations based on the use of electric energy and intangible means as a representation strategy and is the director of the Bienal de Artes Mediales de Chile *(www.bienaldeartesmediales.cl)* and president of the Chilean Video and Electronic Arts Corporation.

Robertina Šebjanič (SI) is an internationally exhibited and awarded artist. Her art research focus is cultural, (bio)political, ecological realities of aquatic environments at the intersection of art, technology and science. *www.robertina.net*

Fermín Serrano (ES) is Commissioner for the 2030 Agenda of Aragon, experienced in running and advising citizen science projects and innovation policies.

Regina Sipos (HU) is the Founder and Director of Social-Digital Innovation and Research Associate at the Technical University of Berlin, focusing on collaborative technology design for society, appropriate technologies, and makerspaces.

Mimi Son (KR) founded the Seoul-based art studio Kimchi and Chips in 2009, together with Elliot Woods. During the past ten years she has worked as an artist, professor, storyteller, curator, and artistic director in various countries and institutions.

Liselott Stenfeldt (DK) is Director at Gehl, she develops innovative concepts and prototypes that incorporate citizen centricity in order to make our cities more open, inclusive, and democratic.

Lubi Thomas (AU) is an experienced Australian based digital/media arts curator, with an extensive practice across exhibitions, projects, festivals, and events.

Michel van Dartel (NL) is Director of V2_Lab for the Unstable Media and Research Professor at the Avans Centre of Applied Research for Art, Design and Technology.

Filip Visnjic (UK) is an architect, curator, and an educator, born in Belgrade, now living in London. He directs projects and contributes to blogs and magazines at the intersections of art, design and technology. He is the founder of CreativeApplications.Net, editorial director at HOLO, director of platform at FRAMED, and lecturer at a number of universities in the UK.

Junji Watanabe (JP) is a Senior Distinguished Researcher, NTT Communication Science Laboratories. His research focuses on the application of haptic communication methods to achieve collective wellbeing.

Mushon Zer-Aviv (IL) sustains a love/hate relationship with data that informs his design work, art pieces, activism, research, lectures, workshops, and life in the city.

Andreas Zingerle (AT) is a media artist from Austria, researching topics such as Internet crime, vigilante counter movements, and anti-fraud activism.

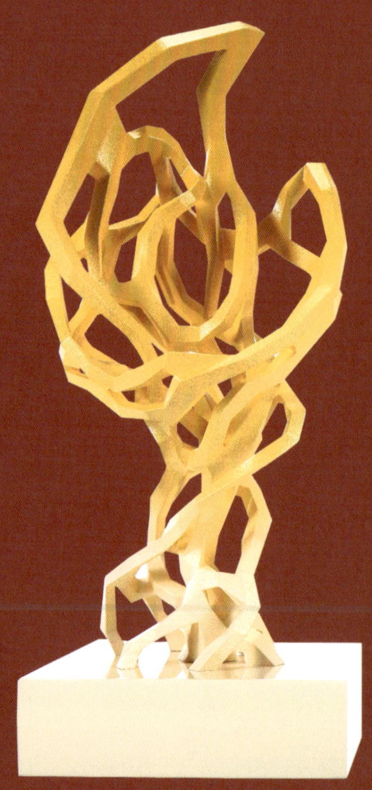

The STARTS Trophy was designed by Nick Ervinck. The Belgian artist explores the boundaries between various media, fostering a cross-pollination between the digital and the physical. He applies tools and techniques from new media, in order to explore the aesthetic potential of sculpture, 3D prints, animation, installation, architecture, and design.

TAWSTAR, 2016 Photo: Peter Verplancke

S+T+ARTS

PRIZE'20

Grand Prize of the European Commission honoring
Innovation in Technology, Industry and Society
stimulated by the Arts

"With STARTS, the European Commission wants to combine art-thinking with technology-thinking to design tomorrow's technologies based on empathy, the care for human values and the environment. In its first five years, the STARTS prize has honoured many brilliant collaborations of artists with engineers that give us precious insights how empathy can become part of technology development."

Roberto Viola, Director General of Communications Networks, Content and Technology, European Commission

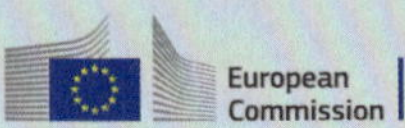
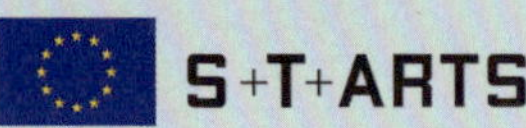
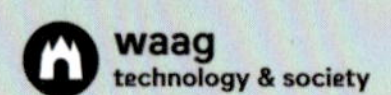
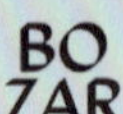

This project has received funding from the European Union's Horizon 2020 research and innovation program under grant agreement No 732019.

STARTS – Science, Technology, and the ARTS

The S+T+ARTS = STARTS program is a program of the European Commission launched in 2016 to encourage synergies between the arts and technology to support innovation in industry and society. STARTS promotes the inclusion of artists in research and innovation activities in Europe.

To encourage collaboration between engineers, scientists, and artists, STARTS is currently funding four different pillars: STARTS Residencies of artists in technology institutions, STARTS Lighthouse pilots to finance research with artists as active parts of projects that work on concrete challenges for industry and society, STARTS Academy uniting engineers and artists to teach digital skills to citizens and young adults in a playful way, and the annual STARTS Prize to give visibility to outstanding examples of collaboration between art and technology.

Innovation in and for Europe

It has long been an established fact that innovation is at the core of a competitive economy. Europe has historically focused its attention in engineering on R&D and standardization. Today, however, focusing only on technology is not sustainable. An increasing number of high tech companies throughout the world assert that, in addition to scientific and technological skills, the critical skills needed for innovation to happen and to be of value for society are skills such as creativity rooted in artistic practices. In this context, the expertise and practice of artists can directly drive and influence innovation in technology. They offer new perspectives, inspire new directions, and act as a catalyst for a successful and socially responsible transformation of new technologies into new products and new economic, social, and business models. In recognition of this development the European Commission has launched the STARTS initiative—Innovation at the nexus of Science, Technology, and the ARTS.

STARTS Prize'20
Grand Prize of the European Commission honoring Innovation in Technology, Industry and Society stimulated by the Arts

The European Commission's STARTS Prize is designed to spotlight people and projects that have the potential to make a sustainable positive impact on Europe's economic, technological, social, and ecological future. This competition seeks innovative projects at the nexus of science, technology, and the arts, and honors the best of them with the STARTS Prize. The STARTS Prize aims to showcase and celebrate visions and achievements at the interface between innovation and creation. The winners receive the STARTS Trophy and €20,000 in prize money. Both winning projects as well as a selection of the Honorary Mentions and Nominations are showcased at the Ars Electronica Festival in Linz. Plus, projects singled out for STARTS Prize recognition are featured in exhibitions and events that Ars Electronica, BOZAR, and Waag stage at partner institutions worldwide. The STARTS Prize competition is staged annually in two categories:

Grand Prize – Artistic Exploration
Awarded for artistic exploration and art works where appropriation by the arts has a strong potential to influence or alter the use, deployment, or perception of technology.

Grand Prize – Innovative Collaboration
Awarded for innovative collaboration between industry or technology and the arts (and the cultural and creative sectors in general) that open new pathways for innovation.

In an elaborate process of open call and nominations by advisory experts, a total of 1,775 entries from 89 countries were submitted in the application period that ran from January 9th to March 16th, 2020. 858 submissions were entered directly to STARTS and 917 submissions were received via the Prix Ars Electronica in the STARTS Prize database.
The STARTS Prize jury convened for a long weekend of intense conference calls to determine the two winning projects, 10 Honorary Mentions, and 18 Nominations for the STARTS Prize'20.
Following extensive deliberations, the unanimous decision was taken to award *EDEN—Ethique-Durable-Ecologic Nature* by Olga Kisseleva with the STARTS Prize for Innovative Collaboration and *Design by Decay, Decay by Design* by Andrea Ling with the STARTS Prize for Artistic Exploration.
The goal of *EDEN* is to introduce innovative technologies to art by using unorthodox thinking to solve ecological challenges. The project supports global biodiversity by examining the possibilities of the recreation of extinct plant species as well as adaptation of plants for changing environments through biotechnology. In addition, artist Olga Kisseleva collaborates with scientific and industry partners such as Orange Telecom France to create a network of vegetal communication by utilizing sensors and internet technology to make this communication visible to a human public.
For *Design by Decay, Decay by Design,* artist Andrea Ling collaborated with biotech company Ginko Bioworks to introduce the process of natural decay to the design process. The development process of these new biomaterials uses rapid prototyping technology as a crucial element of biological engineering. The work opens a discourse about how industrial product development today could be approached from a bottoms-up perspective, reshaping the design thinking process to evolve around the waste material that a product creates after its life span has ended.
Furthermore, 10 of the finalist projects were selected for an Honorary Mention.

Submission and evaluation process

On behalf of the European Commission, Ars Electronica in collaboration with BOZAR and Waag issued an open call for entries to the fifth annual competition for the STARTS Prize. Considering the interdisciplinary approach, the STARTS Prize'20 was once more launched with a dual approach for submissions:

Submission via open call

The STARTS Prize open call started on January 9th, and ended on March 16th, 2020. Submissions of projects could be made either by artists / creative professionals or the researchers / companies involved.

The competition was open:
- to groundbreaking collaborations and projects driven by both technology and the arts.
- to all forms of artistic works and practices with a strong link to innovation in technology, business, and/or society.
- to all types of technological and scientific research and development that have been inspired by art or involve artists as catalysts of novel thinking.
- to artists and teams from all over the world.

Purely artistic or technologically driven projects were not the focus of this competition. The competition was not limited to any genres such as media art, digital art etc., and not limited to Information and Communication Technologies.

Recommendations by international advisors

To encourage a wider range of participants as well as a geographical and gender balance, 14 international advisors who are experts in the field were engaged to recommend interesting projects and artists. These recommended participants were contacted by the Ars Electronica team and asked to submit their project via the submission platform, with the same process and deadlines as for the open submissions. These international advisors served as facilitators to identify relevant works and projects during the submission process and helped reach a wider range of artists and quickly introduce them to the award.

Jury Process

The jury consisted of seven international experts from the fields of industry, technology, governmental policies, and culture. For the first time, the jury was unable to travel to Linz. Restrictions imposed due to the COVID-19 crisis necessitated a different kind of jury process. All submissions were evaluated by a pre-selection committee on arrival, to determine whether they met all formal criteria of the call. For an individual pre-jury process, the seven STARTS Prize jury members each received 50 projects to assess in advance of the main jury weekend. Each project was assessed by two jury members.

Since the main categories of Prix Ars Electronica have a strong overlap with the criteria of the STARTS Prize, artists submitting for the Prix Ars Electronica could decide to also enter their submission for the STARTS Prize. Out of these submissions, a total of ten projects per category were nominated for prize consideration by the three Prix Ars Electronica Expert Juries (Computer Animation, Digital Communities, and Interactive Art+).

The resulting list of top 65 projects was presented at the remotely held main jury event and reduced to 30 finalists before the last jury meeting. The STARTS Prize jury evaluated these 30 finalists in order to select two prize-winning projects and ten Honorary Mentions. The list of the 30 finalists represents a comprehensive overview of the international state of the art collaborations between art and technology. Therefore all 30 projects are published in the *CyberArts 2020* catalog.

STARTS Prize'20, a joint project by Ars Electronica, Bozar, and Waag.

Reimagining Growth and Decay:
Artistic Research in Service of the Circular Economy

Statement of the STARTS Prize'20 Jury (Mara Balestrini, Clara Blume, Francesca Bria, Domhnaill Hernon, Nobu Ide, Alexander Mankowsky, Kei Shimada)

From the total of 1,775 entries, 858 projects were directly submitted to STARTS Prize'20. For the first time in the history of the STARTS Prize, the jury wasn't able to physically gather in Linz for its official jury meeting. In the context of the global COVID-19 health crisis, all travel was suspended, necessitating the first ever virtual jury meeting on May 1-3, 2020. Over the course of three days, the group of 7 members from three continents joined an online discussion; some started the session bright and early with the Californian sunrise while jury members in Tokyo wrapped up the meeting after midnight. A virtual jury process has the distinct advantage of helping to save the environment, time, and travel costs. However, the lack of physical proximity, missed opportunities for casual conversations among peers, and reduced downtime for reflection stripped our verbal exchanges down to their essential bits and pieces. The jury thus emphasized the necessity of physical interaction for in-depth discussions that allow for a thorough evaluation process by addressing a variety of questions that arose during the sessions.

The diversity among this year's jury members highlighted how cultural prerogatives construct different relations with and perceptions of art and technology. This realization led to a series of spirited debates around the value of art in today's societies, the nuanced distinction between art and design, and the broad range of contrasting evaluation criteria that on occasion complicated finding a consensus. Another critical point of discussion formed around the inherent difficulty to compare submissions by multi-institutional collaborative projects with DIY homemade installations by individual artists. The former have access to vast financial, material, and logistical means, which may warp the jury's expectations when contrasted with the latter's struggle with limited resources;

perhaps the future implementation of certain "weight classes" during the submission process could help solve this dilemma.

Lastly, this year's submissions were overshadowed by the gravitas of the global pandemic and its devastating long-term economic and societal repercussions. Due to the untimely call for this year's applications, none of the submitted projects was in a position to address the current crisis. After much deliberation and many stimulating discussions allowing for a constant reevaluation of the strongest projects, this jury proceeded to nominate two Grand Prize winners and 10 Honorary Mentions for the STARTS Prize'20.

The vast number of submissions by artists, technologists, designers, and scientists from around the world illustrates how the European Commission's STARTS Program and Prize has merited its international renown: As standard setter among collaborative projects at the intersection of Science, Technology and the Arts, it pushes the envelope of artistic exploration. Projects that embody the STARTS criteria tend to pursue a holistic approach for positive societal change by broadening their scope of influence and action to include our civil society, minorities, and marginalized groups. Many of this year's submitted projects advocated for shared responsibility in pressing global challenges, while simultaneously giving agency to people by encouraging a participatory and empowering self-starter attitude.

The profound distress over human-machine interaction and the emphasis on human-centered design prevalent in last year's submissions gave way to a more optimistic outlook on technology. Many submissions used VR to help us empathize with people suffering a variety of distressing circumstances. Others painted a distinctly European trajectory for tech regulation, embracing a third way between big tech surveillance capitalism and big state centralized control. Notably, this year's entries included very few artworks based on machine learning and/or dealing with society's troubled relation with this technology. This tendency further illustrates that AI is a moving target, more entangled in our lives than ever but no longer necessarily perceived as an omnipresent threat. On the contrary, the jury observed an optimistic shift towards incorporating AI into DIY artistic practices as yet another tool in an artist's toolbox, allowing it to enhance human capabilities while also raising awareness for its potential risks and biases.

The jury saw a rising trend in the artistic experimentation with wearable technology and smart textiles. This playful take on new fabrics anticipates a dynamic customization of apparel as well as the sensorial amplification of the wearer. Another notable tendency was apparent in the large number of submissions centered around 3D-printed objects. The increasing availability of 3D printers in private homes, design studios, and academic institutions has triggered a wave of new design approaches that pave the way for a revolutionary rethinking of consumerism and circularity in tomorrow's economy.

Perhaps the most dominant theme in this year's submissions is the circular economy, intending to use collective resources in a sustainable manner. Many of the submitted projects, including the Grand Prize winners, deal with climate change and environmental sustainability as the most pressing issues of our time and aim at providing tangible solutions. They respond to an increasingly global movement of citizens demanding concrete action from governments, industry, and society as a whole to deliver on the United Nations' sustainable development goals and significantly reduce global warming before it is too late. They also respond to some of the main goals articulated in the European Green Deal, such as resource efficiency, the restoration of ecosystems, and the preservation of biodiversity. It further illustrates that the ambitious plan of achieving climate neutrality by the mid-century will require the full mobilization of our ambition, passion, and ingenuity. Additionally, the winner in the category of artistic exploration inspires an urgent political and ethical debate around the necessity for a European approach outlining the risks and benefits of biotech. Born out of a genuine artistic inquiry, the winning projects led to a phase of open experimentation and artistic research, concluding in an artwork that helps us reflect our own relationship with nature and inspire the necessary change in our behavior.

Given the avalanche of chasmic events and unprecedented predicaments steamrolling our world today, this jury wants to encourage mutual learning between scientists, technologists, and artists. By joining forces in a bold out-of-the-box creative practice, they can spark pioneering collaborative ways to address this new set of challenges. Now more than ever, we rely on artists to help us make sense of the world we live in and envision a better path into the future.

STARTS Prize'20
Grand Prize—Artistic Exploration

Awarded for artistic exploration and art works where appropriation by the arts has a strong potential to influence or alter the use, deployment, or perception of technology.

Design by Decay, Decay by Design
Andrea Ling

Andrea Ling describes herself as an architect and installation artist. In architecture, most of the parts of a building will end as landfill. Natural ecosystems in contrast do not know about waste. Ling states that in biology, one system's entropy can be another system's organization. This insight has motivated her to enter a creative residency at Ginkgo Bioworks—a leader in synthesized biology. Artistic director Christina Agapakis emphasizes that the company's goal is "(…) to show, through art, the immense potential of synthetic biology and genome engineering." This is widely seen as a path into a sustainable future, replacing petroleum-based products through grown ingredients for a fuel free future.

Ling created biological artifacts to illustrate and prove the possibility of a paradigm shift in the production of goods: First, through a shared sense of agency between engineer and living material. Second, since biological ecosystems are finite, they aren't scalable. Overgrowth will always be punished. Biological systems can provide a far more robust system of growth and decay than extractive systems. And third, biology is a value creator using decay to fuel new life. Only by integrating biological systems into design processes can we truly meet our ambitious goals for a sustained renewal.

Finally, *Design by Decay, Decay by Design* illustrates the potential of combining two key-enabling technologies: ICT and biotechnology. This provides an opportunity to create new products that are sustainable by design. The artwork also exemplifies the importance for a political debate around a European approach to biotech by establishing ethical safeguards for gene editing and balancing both benefits and risks for a broader application of this technology. Andrea Ling's bold and visionary reimagination of growth and decay in service of the circular economy merits the Grand Prize in the category of Artistic Exploration of the STARTS Prize'20.

STARTS Prize'20
Grand Prize—Innovative Collaboration

Awarded for innovative collaboration between industry or technology and the arts (and the cultural and creative sectors in general) that opens new pathways for innovation.

EDEN—Ethique-Durable-Ecologie-Nature
Olga Kisseleva

EDEN won the STARTS Prize category of Innovative Collaboration because the project exemplified the role that art can play in driving large-scale societal change through interdisciplinary collaboration.

EDEN examines the difference between physical and genetic extinction. This project started as an artistic commission and evolved into a large-scale international collaboration from which the learnings and outcomes are transferable to other global-scale societal challenges facing humanity. *EDEN* commenced with, and succeeded in, bringing a species of elm tree back into existence in Europe and the project team extended their impact to several species of tree across the globe. The diverse project team was vast—far too many collaborators to reference here—further illustrating the benefits of cross-disciplinary collaboration.

EDEN leverages scientific thinking (genetics) and emerging sensor technology to gain a new understanding of nature. The project leveraged sensor and telecommunication network technology to investigate how trees interact with each other and their environment. They developed a technique to connect trees across the globe in the hope that different species across different locations could communicate and learn from each other. The vast and complex data captured from the tree net-

works was made audible and visible via a range of exhibits and performances across the world.

In summary, *EDEN* represents a world-leading example on how art can inform science and how science can inform art—where the combination of both is far greater than the sum, unlocking new knowledge to better humanity. The process and outcomes in *EDEN* are an exemplar that could, and should, be replicated elsewhere.

STARTS Prize'20
Honorary Mentions

c o m p u t e r 1. 0
Victoria Manganiello, Julian Goldman

c o m p u t e r 1.0 is a fascinating installation that is not only a beautiful art piece replicating an imaginary information processing device from the past but also a visually poetic testimony of the stressful dystopian future of the information age. Victoria Manganiello and Julian Goldman create a canvas using polymer, natural threads, and flowing fluids to represent an analog display that portrays the flow of information but leaves room for comprehension by the observer to what the analog representation, which can also be interpreted either as being the process or the output, means. It is both an intellectual stimulus from a communication design angle and an antithesis to the rigid society that we live in; one that is controlled by zeros and ones and often brings limits to the imagination by the observer.

The artwork is an intimate crossover of tech and textile, and a reminder of how intellectual people of the past have ignited the evolution of communication, starting from a primitive form of design.

Perception iO
Karen Palmer

Perception iO is an interactive installation that provides an intuitive understanding of the importance of transparency and regulation of AI, especially for citizens unfamiliar with the technology. Karen Palmer (aka Storyteller from the Future) creates an immersive experience utilizing film, biometrics, and other technologies to capture and assess the emotional response of participants in the judgment enforcement process, providing a valuable insight into the unarguable dark reality of inequality.

By uncovering unconscious bias in both ourselves and the authorities, it addresses the need for a control mechanism during the conceptualization, development as well as implementation of AI. While AI is oftentimes seen as something that will replace humankind, it is also largely misunderstood. The *Perception iO* installation in contrast provides an insight into the implications of a flawed process, without necessitating a deep understanding of the complex technology behind it. It thereby motivates the observer to reflect on their own ethical values while also recognizing the positives and negatives of AI.

Precious Plastic Universe
The alternative plastic recycling system.
Dave Hakkens

Precious Plastic opens a new perspective on waste and sustainability, while empowering local communities and creatives. The project is open source with over 400 projects globally using the *Precious Plastic* recycling system where local recycling workspaces process plastic waste into new products. It works because it's easy, shareable, and open to everybody, prompting local collective environmental action.

Precious Plastic offers a compelling vision for the future of a Green Europe, following the trajectory of maker spaces, fab-cities, and civic technology hubs. It shows how a global community led by creators, designers, and engineers can be harnessed to tackle one of the world's most pressing environmental problems. It's a fresh approach fit for the environmentally conscious youth: It's our future— we need to have a say, and we have the tools to create change!

In times of crisis, we are urged to change our behavior and adapt to the new circumstances for the greater good of society. The *Precious Plastic Universe* pushes us to embrace a new mindset while opening production pathways into a new sustainable future and putting communities first.

Proposals of Collaboration with
the Viral Entities
Tame is to Tame, Virophilia
Pei-Ying Lin

Proposals of Collaboration with the Viral Entities is an artistic reflection on our relationship with viruses. Especially in the context of the Corona pandemic, it provides a deeper understanding of our role as human species in the ecosystem we inhabit.

Viruses are a source of evolutionary variation. They cannot self-reproduce and are inert without inserting themselves into a living cell. The core idea in Lynn Margulis' *The Symbiotic Planet* is that the engine of evolution can be explained by symbiosis rather than the Darwinian survival of the fittest. Today's proof lies in the acceptance of the microbiome hosted in our bodies as an acquired organ, essentially turning us into supraorganisms. Viruses are thus no more our enemies than bacteria or human cells.

With *Virophilia,* Pei-Ying Lin has translated non-mainstream scientific knowledge into a thought-provoking artwork. Her cookbook, set up for the year 2068, where food is prepared with viruses integrated as functional ingredients, hints at productive change in the perception of ourselves in the biosphere: The symbioses between us and the Other opens room for innovation.

Prosthetic Memory
Eifler

Prosthetic Memory is an experiment composed of journals, video recordings of daily events and thoughts and processed by a personalized AI algorithm that triggers video projections filtered by the relevancy of analogue handwriting in journals. It is an ongoing experiment that might show some different adaptations in the future. With this project, M. Eifler tries to solve the limitation of her permanent loss of long-term memory capabilities, while also asking a series of interesting questions: How can AI capture and confirm human identity? Can an AI algorithm reproduce my own feelings or only generate feelings that I am supposed to be feeling?

The artist illustrates how a DIY homemade AI, solely designed for personal use and generated without any cloud data, can open up an empowering approach to this technology while also enhancing human capabilities. It lives up to the challenge of humanizing a technology that is so often negatively perceived. *Prosthetic Memory* is thus a highly relevant artistic inquiry into the relationship between humans and artificial intelligence.

Sociality
Paolo Cirio

Paolo Cirio offers a strong artistic provocation that serves as an urgent call for action to challenge tech monopolies and regain democratic accountability over algorithms. With *Sociality,* he inquires how new internet technologies impact our human psyche and behavior. By coding a scraper to download large volumes of patent data from Google, he depicts the new reality of surveillance capitalism. The 20,000 social media and Big Tech patents featured in *Sociality* deal with technologies firmly entrenched in the cultural zeitgeist.

This is a powerful artistic manifesto for a more ethical use of technology that subverts intellectual property laws in the interest of the collective intelligence of people that in the first place created the knowledge and data continuously harnessed and extracted in social media platforms. It provides a trajectory for a digital future where it is possible to regulate technology and put it at the service of society. It suggests that we embrace a third way between Big Tech surveillance capitalism and Big State centralized control: a people-first digital future based on democratic control and collective accountability that can be championed by Europe.

SOMEONE
Lauren Lee McCarthy

SOMEONE is a distributed installation and exhibition where visitors are invited to act as a human version of the Amazon smart speaker Alexa. The homes of four people have been augmented with bespoke smart devices. Through a command center with four computers, visitors can hear the occupants of the "smart homes" call out for "Someone," prompting them to step in as their home automation assistant and respond to their needs.

The exhibition addresses timely topics that have emerged in the intersection of smart technologies and everyday life, in particular surveillance and control. The piece questions whether these technologies give us convenience and improved quality of life or actually threaten our autonomy, agency, and privacy. Furthermore, by having the visitor act as a smart device themselves, the exhibition questions labor relations that exist behind the scenes of our apparently seamless connected world. These are pressing questions in a time when our most intimate spaces and routines are becoming increasingly embedded with "smart" devices that collect and share sensitive data about ourselves and our individual and social behaviors.

Spoiled Spores
Avril Corroon

Spoiled Spores is an artistic provocation on the topic of the housing crisis in Ireland and the UK. In the latest estimate, the UK requires 1 million homes to provide everyone with worthy living conditions. Within the rental community the standard of home is often so poor that toxic mold is commonplace.

Corroon harvests mold from properties in the UK and Ireland from which she crafts a range of artisanal cheeses. The various cheeses are exhibited within industrial fridges that resemble the buildings from which the mold was harvested. The critical aspect to the work is that the cheeses are toxic—they are poisonous to consume and present a real health hazard, as does the mold from which they are harvested.

The housing crisis has placed even more stress on rental communities during the COVID-19 pandemic and this issue will grow as more people move to urban areas and "mega cities" of the future. *Spoiled Spores* is an excellent example of the role art can play in provoking thought and action. It looks at a social issue from a new perspective. Not only does it look at a problem of today, it also addresses an issue of growing concern for the future.

The Wrong
David Quiles Guilló

As the COVID-19 pandemic and social distancing shuts down vast swathes of local and global activity, this piece shows an alternative yet ambitious new path for the arts and culture. *The Wrong Biennale* is a collaborative effort to create and promote digital art and culture across the world, launching a global art biennale open to participation, happening both online and offline, and harnessing the potential of collaboration and the internet.

Furthermore, the concept aims to connect the world through online pavilions that are virtually curated spaces and offline exhibitions at embassies, institutions, art spaces, galleries, and artist-run spaces in cities. The event is organized following a bottom-up approach through which an extended team of curators appoint themselves to feature what they like best of the new digital art scene today and artists also appoint themselves via open calls. Since 2013, more than 5,500 artists and curators have officially participated in *The Wrong Biennale*—a concept that could prove key to the flourishing of the arts and culture in post pandemic times.

TransVision
Jiabao Li

TransVision is an artistic provocation on the role that technology plays in mediating and controlling our perception of the world. Presented as a set of wearable devices in three scenarios, it shows how technology mediates our sense of vision and controls our perception.

The work is prescient given the proliferation of mobile screen-based technologies in the last decade and the emerging understanding of the role that digital technology plays across society. We have quickly entered a world where digital loneliness is a pandemic—one that has crept up on us without much warning yet penetrates all aspects of modern society.

In hyperallergenic vision, the user develops a hypersensitivity to the color red as a reflection on the ways that we have become hypersensitive to certain information presented online. In tactile vision, the user is alerted to the fact that we easily become immersed in echo chambers owing to the bias of our online networks and our methods of receiving information. In commoditized vision, the user is alerted to the fact that our existence has been commoditized through the monetization of our time, attention, and ultimately our existence itself.

STARTS Prize'20
Nominations

aqua_forensic
Underwater Interception of Biotweaking in Aquatocene
Robertina Šebjanič, Gjino Šutić

Be Water by Hong Kongers
Dedicated to the Hong Kong protesters by Eric Siu & Joel Kwong

BETAlight
Barbro Scholz with Esther Stühmer, Axel Sylvester and Tanja Döring

CMD: Experiment in Bio Algorithmic Politics
Michael Sedbon

Code of Conscience
Code of Conscience

Compression Cradle
Lucy McRae

CONTAIN / Open Cell—Mobile COVID19 Emergency Testing Facilities
Open Cell + worldwide contributors

Hale: An Upgrade on Patient Attire
Mariam Ibrahim

Hybrid Living Materials
The Mediated Matter Group

INNER VALUES
Tobias Trübenbacher

Re:flex
Pierre Azalbert, Benton Ching, Karlijn Sibbel

Re3 Glass
Faidra Oikonomopoulou, Telesilla Bristogianni

Sounding Soil
Marcus Maeder

Stymphalian Birds
Audrey Briot

The Substitute
Alexandra Daisy Ginsberg

The Net Wanderer—A tour of suspended handshakes
Cheng Guo

Topographie Digitale
DataPaulette

Voicing Borders
Irakli Sabekia

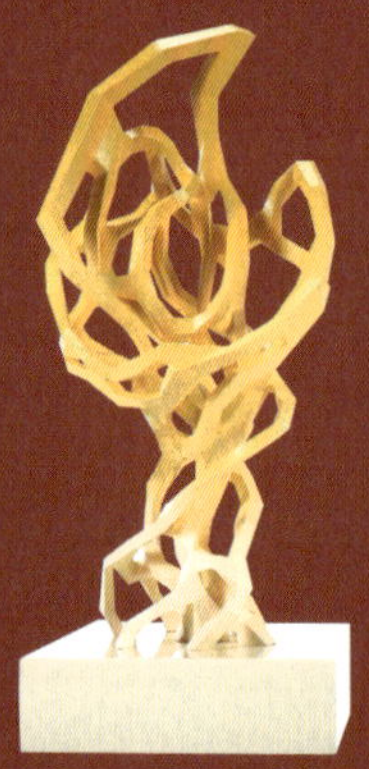

Grand Prize
Artistic Exploration

Awarded for artistic exploration and art works where appropriation by the arts has a strong potential to influence or alter the use, deployment, or perception of technology.

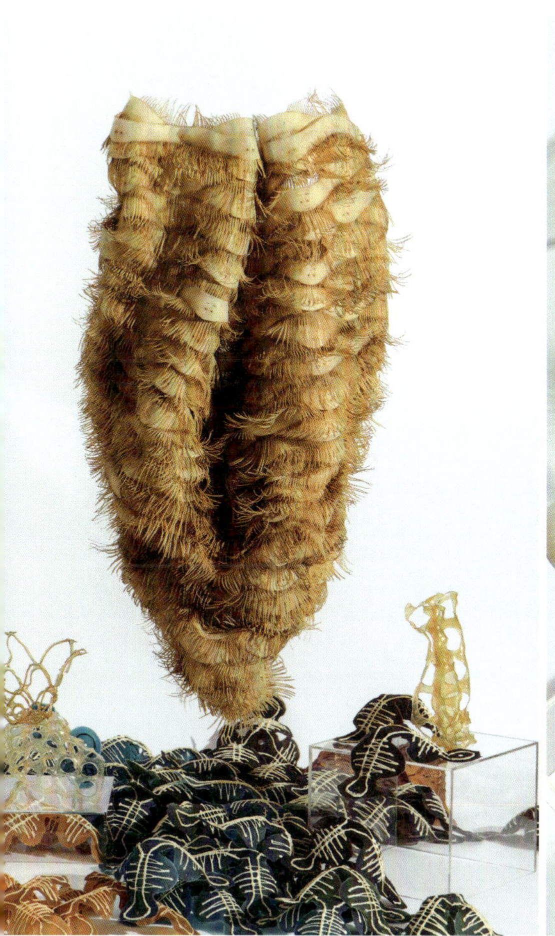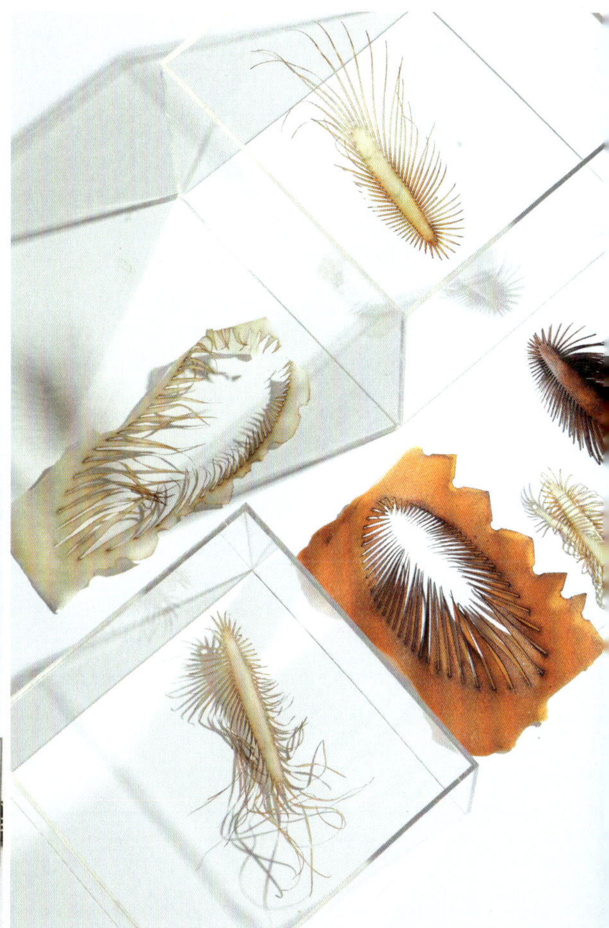

Design by Decay, Decay by Design

Andrea Ling

Design by Decay, Decay by Design is a series of artifacts that exhibit designed decay. They were done for the 2019 Ginkgo Bioworks Creative Residency on how to design a world without waste. As an architect and artist, I recognize that most of what I create goes to landfill. If that is the case, let me design waste that I can live with, garbage that retains some desirability as it degrades in sight and on site. Let me design waste as nature designs it, not only as the product of breakdown and destruction but also as input for renewal and construction. In biology, one system's entropy is another system's organization. With the assistance of Ginkgo, my goal was to organize decay, using enzymes, fungus, bacteria, and other biological agents as ways of decomposing and composing biological matter at the same time. By mediating decay through species selection, control of environmental conditions, and nutrient templating, I am actively pursuing mutability as a desired quality in the physical world as well as guarantee that the mechanisms of constructive renewal will be embedded into that world.

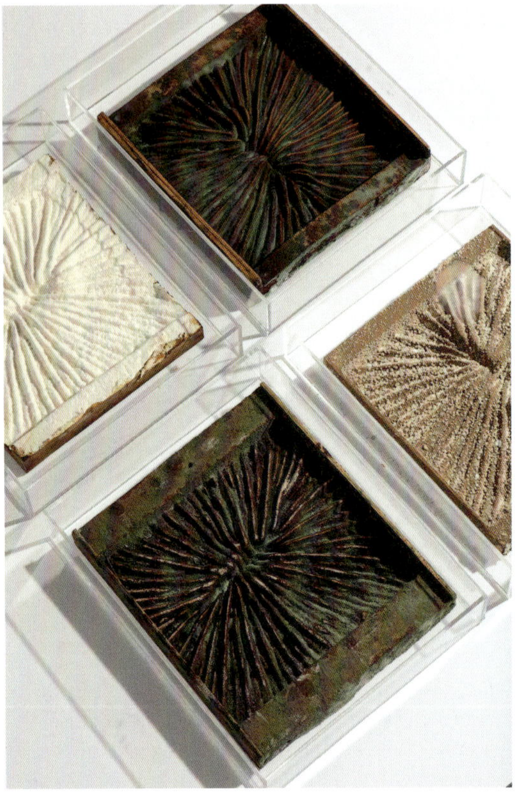

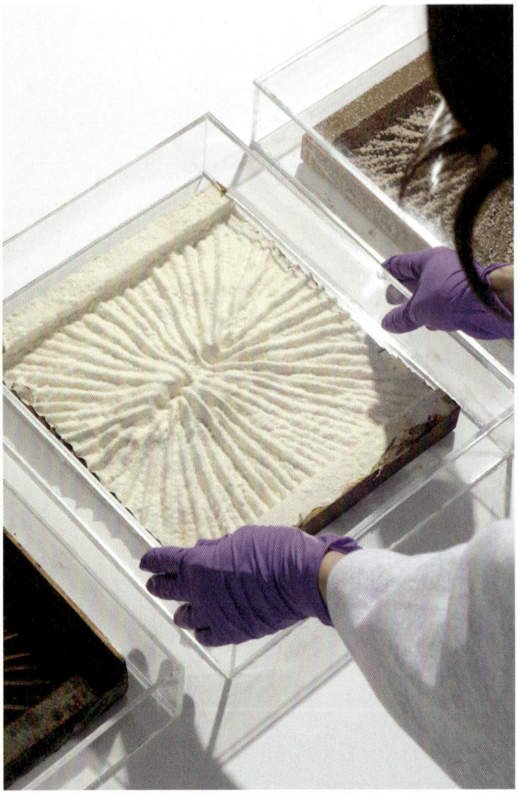

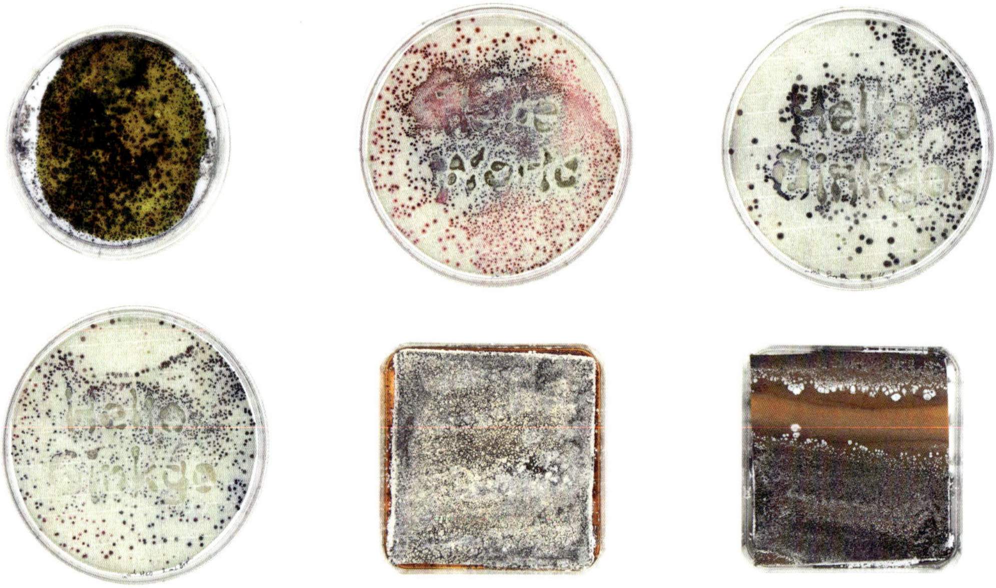

STARTS Prize'20 · Grand Prize − Artistic Exploration

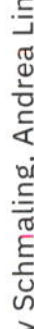

My base material system included biocomposites of chitin, cellulose, and pectin, derived from the exoskeletons of shrimp, tree pulp waste, and fruit skins. These materials can be combined in different ratios to form different bioplastics with a wide range of mechanical and physical characteristics and are environmentally responsive and easily degradable. The work was organized into 3 projects, done in Gingko's wetlabs with its scientists:

1. Using enzymes derived from fungus and human saliva and integrating them into biocomposites with spatial and temporal control to transform the material rather than only destroy it. This was degradation as a fabrication process.

2. Using different strains of *Streptomyces* bacteria to colonize cellulose and different bioplastics in order to transform them. *Streptomyces* are common soil bacteria and secondary decomposers that produce vibrant pigments and geosmin, the compound responsible for soil smell.

3. Using different types of fungi, *Aspergillus niger* (black mold) and *Trichoderma viride* (green mold) in co-cultures to transform and selectively degrade different materials. Mold is a much more powerful and resilient decay agent and would rapidly colonize any substrate we provided.

The challenge of working with biological materials and agents is that they are environmentally responsive and have agency, and the resulting artifacts are not always predictable or standardized. Contamination was common, as was loss of viability. As a classically trained architect, I am used to having precise control over my output, and the struggle in a design practice such as this is to learn how to accept the embedded tensions where material and biological agency sometimes work in contradiction to what I have planned or what I am comfortable with. It is a struggle for industry to accept this inconvenience as well. However, if we accept this inconvenience, using decay to facilitate renewal offers extraordinary advantages, such as access to circular systems and the ability to grow, adapt, and reproduce out of literal rotting, providing a resilience not found in industrial systems.

Given our state of climate crisis, we can no longer design primarily for human and economic convenience; our survival depends on changing our priorities and expectations for the material world. My goal in using these material systems and these biological agents is not to create a low carbon footprint project or upcycle waste into new products. Rather it's to support a different mode of design, one where the process of making and breaking is provisional and not only consumptive. *Design by Decay, Decay by Design* seeks to redistribute value away from permanent materials that destroy ecosystems onto transient ones that restore them, finding epistemological as well as practical value in designing responsivity, degradation, and renewal into man-made objects.

Artist: Andrea Ling
Curatorial Team: Ginkgo Bioworks + Faber Futures;
Natsai Audrey Chieza, Dr. Christina Agapakis, Grace Chuang, Kit McDonnell, Dr. Joshua Dunn
Scientific advisors: Ginkgo Bioworks; Dr. Joshua Dunn, Dr. Ming-Yueh Wu, Kyle Kenyon, Duy Nguyen, Dr. Lucy Foulston
With thanks to the MIT Media Lab: Mediated Matter Group, team *Aguahoja I*
With support from Ginkgo Bioworks

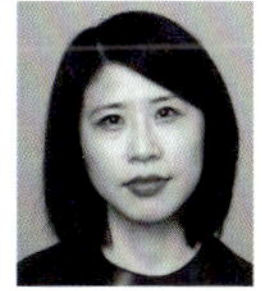

Andrea Ling (CA) is an architect and installation artist who works at the intersection of art, fabrication technologies, and biological sciences. Her most recent work focuses on how the critical application of biologically and computationally mediated design processes can move society away from exploitative systems of production to regenerative ones. She was the 2019 Ginkgo Bioworks creative resident exploring how to design the decay of artifacts in order to access material circularity. Andrea is a founding partner of designGUILD, a Toronto-based art collective and a former project lead for Philip Beesley Architect where she worked on a series of international immersive kinetic installations and textiles for Iris van Herpen. She is also a former research assistant and designer for the Mediated Matter Group, at the MIT Media Lab, where she and her teammates won Dezeen's 2019 project of the year with their research project, *Aguahoja I,* which will be shown in 2020 at the MoMA and 2021 at SFMOMA. Andrea has an MS from the MIT Media Lab and an M.Arch. from the University of Waterloo with a background in human physiology from the University of Alberta.

https://www.ginkgobioworks.com/2020/01/06/2019-creative-in-residence

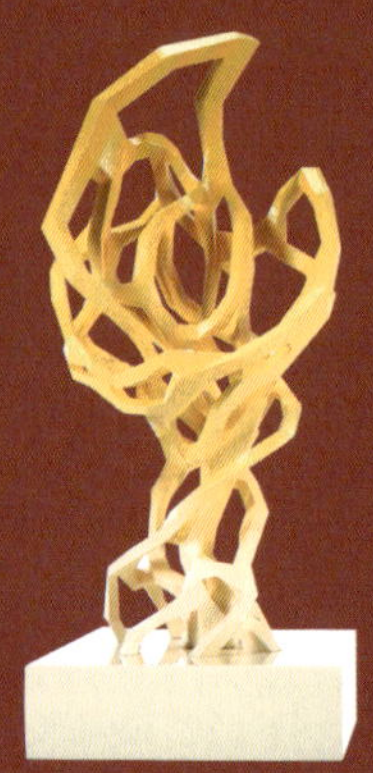

S+T+ARTS
PRIZE '20

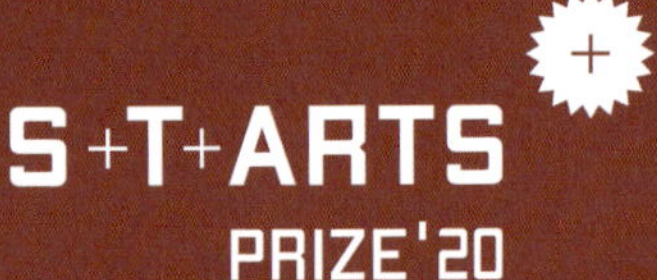

Grand Prize
Innovative Collaboration

Awarded for innovative collaboration between industry or technology and the arts (and the cultural and creative sectors in general) that open new pathways for innovation.

EDEN—Ethics-Durability-Ecology-Nature

Olga Kisseleva

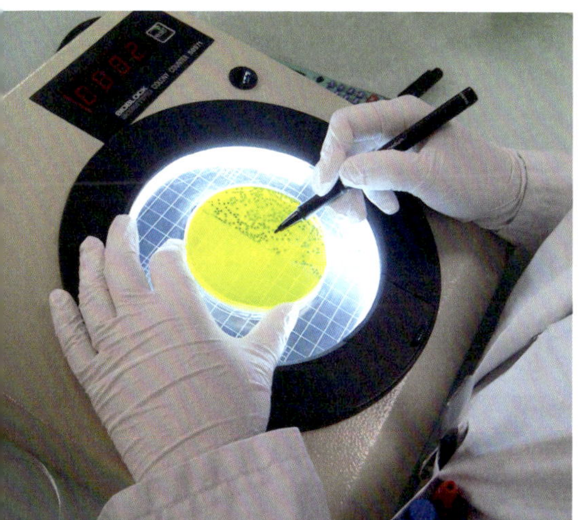

Bio-art: When a Tree became a Partner

It was the rebirth of the Biscarosse Elm in the frame of Oga Kisseleva's *Biopresence* project (2012) that served as a catalyst for the creation of a series of the tree-based bio-art works created by the artist during the last decade. The "arboreal" theme was taken up and developed in several parallel studies. One such extensive project is *EDEN— Ethics-Durability-Ecology-Nature,* which began in 2012 and has continued to the present day. The project touches on a range of issues, including the protection of endangered plant species and inter-specific communication between living subjects that are placed in the "inhuman"category.

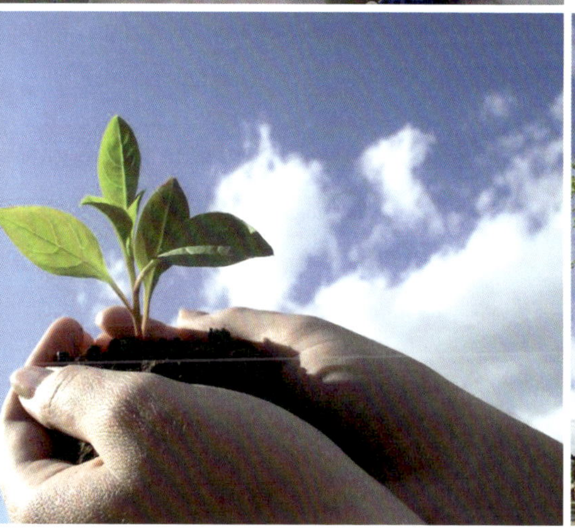

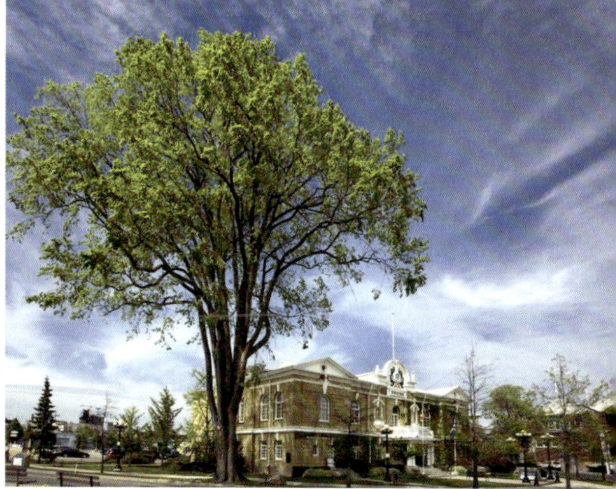

The *EDEN* project is aimed at creating a new Garden of Eden as the ultimate goal of introducing innovative technologies to art and using unorthodox thinking to solve ecological problems. In collaboration with scholars from various countries, Olga Kisseleva is currently "resurrecting" the following plant species: the West European elm (the *Biopresence* project, France), the Afarsimon and Methuselah palm tree (the Negev Desert, Israel, and Jordan), Sophora toromiro (Easter Island), Bodhi Jiulian (China and India), Wollemi Pine (Australia), and the Aport apple cultivar (Kazakhstan). The study of trees as guardians of biological and historical memory has a special place in Olga Kisseleva's project. The artist creates in this field the *Memory Garden* program (2020) based on the bioshere of Babi Yar, one of the most tragic sites of the Holocaust. The memory captured through its trees perceived as time capsules is a message about the future, despite the tragedies of the past. The artist scrutinizes the hypotheses advanced by European scientists, according to which plants can "communicate" among themselves. Olga Kisseleva is also investigating the possibility of "eaves dropping" on this arboreal "dialogue," and even taking part in it. This idea has given birth to the project in which trees can "communicate" on two levels: among themselves in the T2T (Tree-To-Tree) model, and on the level of the global T2N (Tree-To-Network). The trees included in the project can talk together across continents. Humans can follow their communication through the interactive installations created by the artist.

This network helps trees to optimize their vital mechanisms and to protect themselves from potentials aggressors. The trees included in the project can talk to humans through the Internet and let them know about any danger which can be perceived by vegetation before we know about it. *EDEN* experimented the first communication between the historical balm of Gilead trees in Israel and the similar trees in Jordan *(Listening to Trees Across the Jordan River,* the Negev Museum of Modern Art, 2020). Thanks to the T2T system, trees growing in natural conditions (Japanese Cedars) and trees that have a different biological memory (Wollemi Pine) establish contact through their relatives in Japan, and learn the anti-catastrophe scenario from them *(Echigo Tsumari Contemporary Art Triennale,* 2018).

Datascape is an interactive program that materializes and analyzes the whole communication activity of the organic network based on vegetal medium across the selected geographical area. At the heart of this project is the dynamic database dedicated to regional trees and to the broader ties between vegetal heritage, climate, and society. This database will be the source of all visual displays seen by the public and it will also have an interactive dimension: as the project goes on, the public itself will be able to feed the database thanks to a specific QR code. In other words, the art piece will take the shape of a visual display installation composed of digital objects that it will visually map and connect to one another.

Its goal is reviving extinct species of plants and preventing the extinction of species that have been placed on the IUCN Red and Green lists. The real culmination of the *EDEN* project is our contribution to landscape restoration. It leads to reflect on the implication of humans in this communication and these processes and how to durably change the behaviors by setting up the realization of a true utopia.

One of the directions of bio-art explored by the artist Olga Kisseleva is the possibility to avoid or inverse the natural catastrophe by bringing extinct species back to life, or creating new species on preexisting DNA bases. An artistic utopia, assuming that extinction, despite its supposedly definitive and irreversible nature, can be revoked thanks to the advancement of contemporary human civilization.

Support received from:
Centre National de Recherche Scientifique (CNRS)
Art&Science International Institute
Institut National de Recherche Agronomique (INRA)
Orange Art Factory, Orange Telecom RDD

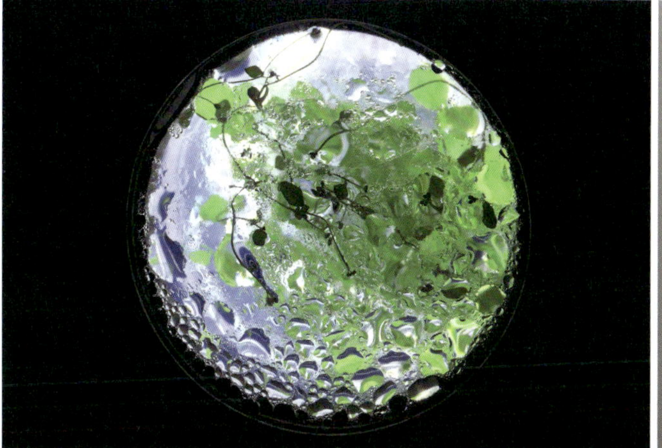

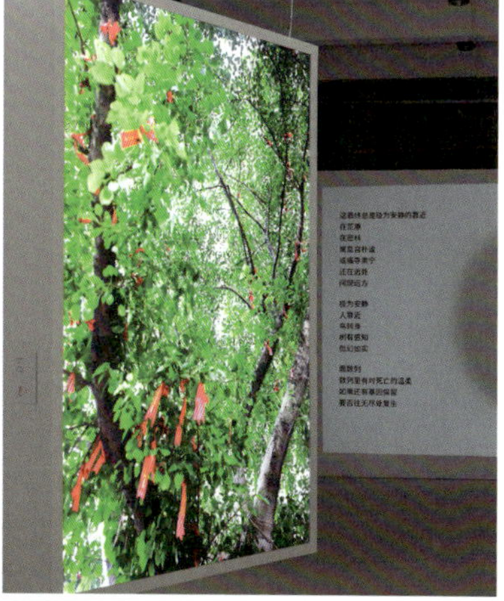

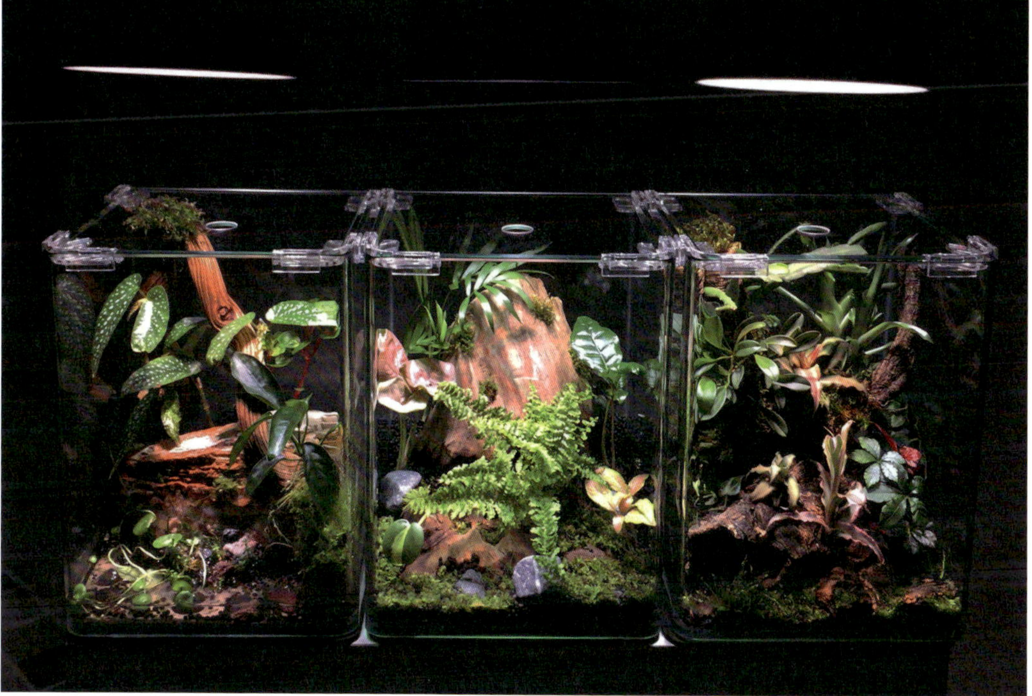

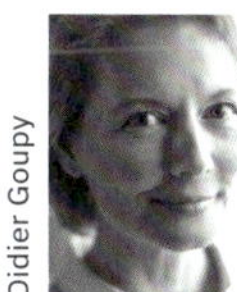

One of the key figures in the international art&science field **Olga Kisseleva** (RU) approaches her work as a scientist. She calls upon collaborations with exact sciences, biology and geophysics, and she proceeds with experiments, calculations, and analyses, while strictly respecting the methods of the scientific domain. Olga Kisseleva has had major exhibitions in Modern Art Museum (Paris), KIASMA (Helsinki), Museo Nacional Centro de Arte Reina Sofia (Madrid), Fondation Cartier for contemporary art (Paris), Centre Georges Pompidou (Paris), Guggenheim Museum (Bilbao), NCCA (Moscow), as well as Biennales of Dakar (2002), Tirana (2003), Moscow (2011), Istanbul (2013), and Venice (2019). Her works are present in many of the world's most important museum collections, including the Centre Pompidou, Louis Vuitton Foundation, ZKM, Moscow Museum of Modern Art, and the NY MoMA. Olga Kisseleva teaches contemporary art at the Sorbonne University of Paris, she is head of the Art & New Media program and Founding director of Art&Science International Institute.

http://www.kisseleva.org

HONORARY

MENTIONS

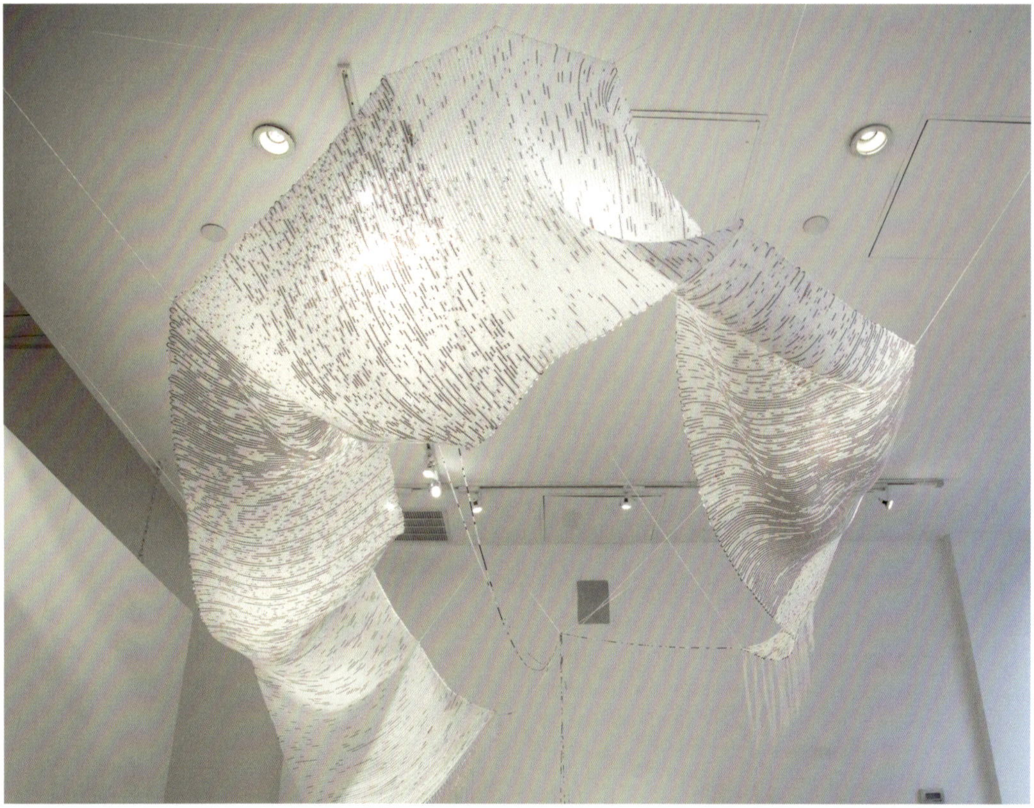

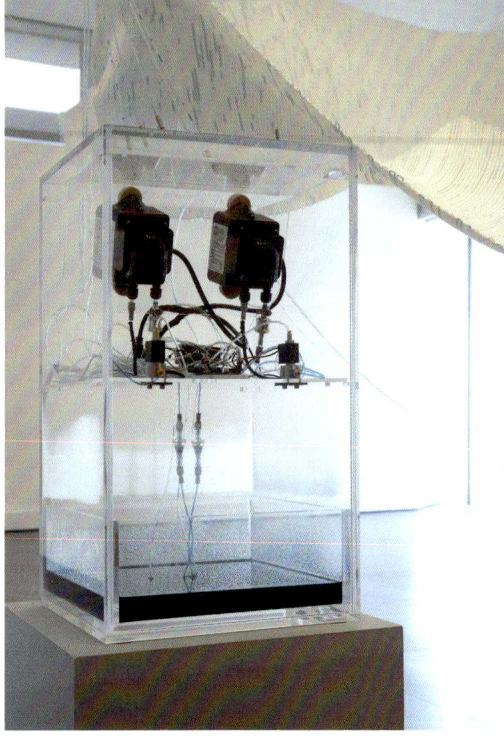

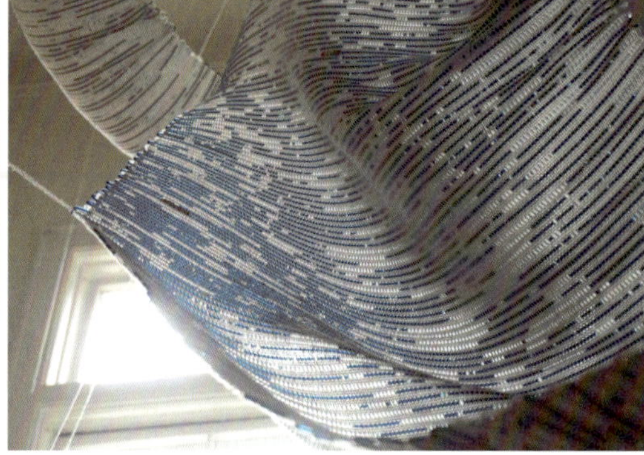

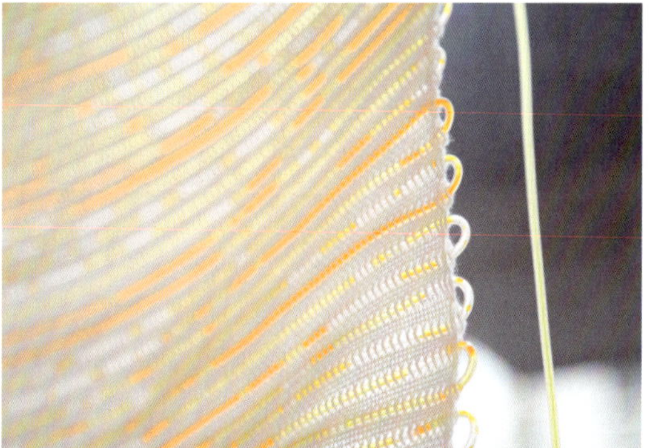

STARTS Prize'20 · Honorary Mention

c o m p u t e r 1.0
Julian Goldman, Victoria Manganiello aka SOFT MONITOR

Full or empty; color or clear; zero or one; under or over—*c o m p u t e r 1.0* imagines a display for the future, by looking at displays from our past. Artists Julian Goldman and Victoria Manganiello create a large-scale textile woven by hand using hollow polymer tubing and natural fiber thread. A patterned series of colored liquid/oil/air pixels will be pumped into the tubes in a sequence dictated by data from adjacent motion sensors and a series of computer-controlled valves, air compressors, and pumps. This textile will function as a lo-fi computer display, made with ancient natural materials and techniques juxtaposed with contemporary digital technologies.

In exhibition, the operating system is in the viewer's initial observation; the technologies and the sounds they make are not hidden but are an integral part of the audience experience. We show the means of production, rather than hiding it.

c o m p u t e r 1.0 also functions as a historical lens showing how our relationship to computing technology has always been fraught with opposed promises of utopian and dystopian futures. In 1801, French master silk weaver Joseph Marie Jacquard developed a loom using punch cards (see binary code) to direct cloth weaving. It was an engine for the Industrial Revolution, creating cloth more cheaply and quickly while mechanizing the work of thousands of laborers across Europe. The Jacquard loom is a direct, though often forgotten, ancestor of our modern computers that directly led to discoveries by Charles Babbage, Ada Lovelace, Alan Turing and onwards to our new-found obsession with and addiction to digital display.

We represent this digital heritage with digitized cloth, recalling current topics of data, privacy, and equity surrounding our communication infrastructure. This installation reminds us that our current digital existentialism and the persistent question of "are we better off?" is a conversation two centuries in the making between Luddites and evangelists.

This project was partially supported by the Awesome Foundation Grant. It was made possible with funds from the New York State Council on the Arts in Partnership with Wave Farm: Media Arts Assistance Fund, a regrant program of the New York State Council on the Arts, Electronic Media and Film Program, with the support of Governor Andrew Cuomo and the New York State Legislature. Research was supported by a Materials-Based Research grant from the Center for Craft.

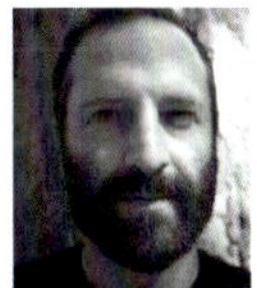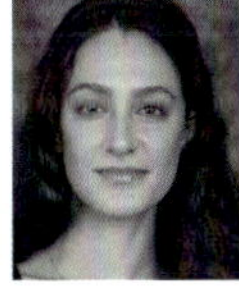

Julian Goldman (US), **Victoria Manganiello** (US) aka **SOFT MONITOR**. SOFT MONITOR is an art and design collective focused on telling stories of materials, technology, and culture through physical experience. Founded in 2017 by Victoria Manganiello and Julian Goldman, SOFT MONITOR's recent projects include participation at the Wall Street Journal Future of Everything Festival (NY, NY), Currents New Media Festival (Santa Fe, NM), Indianapolis Museum of Contemporary Art (IN), and the Museum of Arts and Design (NY, NY). Julian is a lead designer at Bolt Threads, a bio-material company producing bio-engineered materials like spider-silk and mycelium-leather. Victoria is an award-winning textile artist and professor (New York University and Parsons), with multiple internationally recognized exhibitions, residencies, and awards under her belt.

www.softmonitor.today

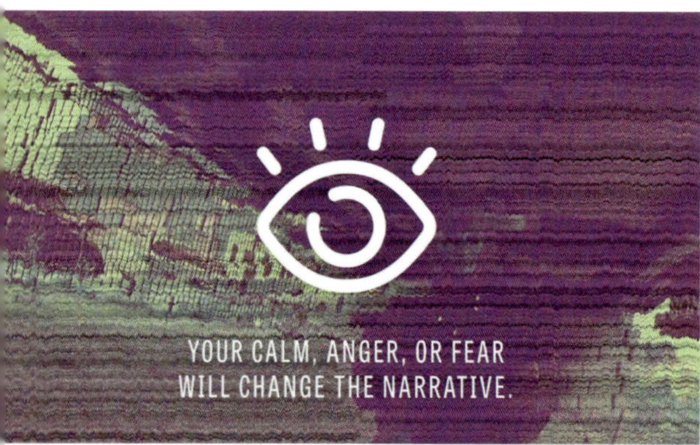

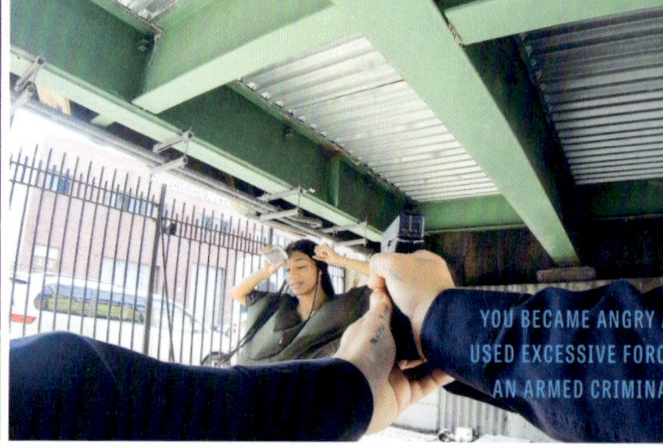

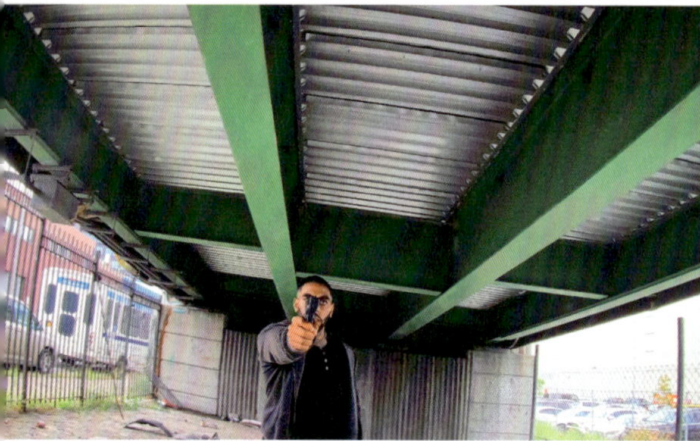

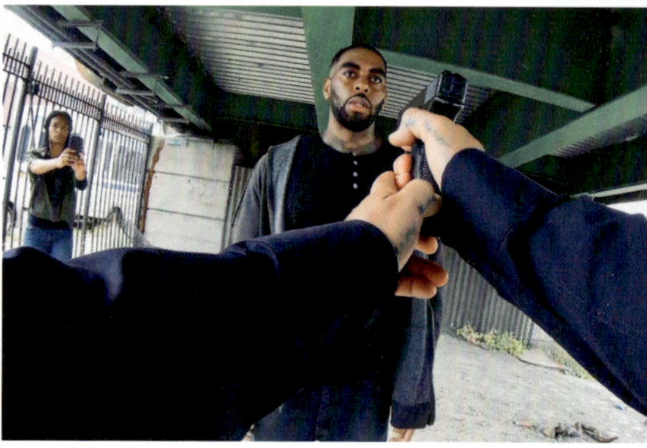

Perception iO

Karen Palmer

Perception iO (Input Output) is the future of Law Enforcement. An Artificial Intelligence data set emotionally responsive to the participant and potentially their bias.

The participant will assume the role of a police officer watching an interactive training video of an escalating volatile situation. They will experience the interaction from the perspective of a cop's body camera and come into contact (separately) with a black protagonist and white protagonist. Each protagonist plays either the role of a criminal or of a person with mental health issues.

The *Perception iO* system will track the participants' facial expression. How they respond emotionally to the scene will have consequences for the characters. It will influence the branching narrative to prompt the cop to either arrest, assist, or shoot the character on the screen.

The *Perception iO* immersive experience is a convergence of neuroscience, behavioral psychology, film, AI, facial emotion detection, eye tracking, bias, and social justice. It reveals how a person's emotions (and eye tracking functionality currently in development) influences their perception of reality through an immersive storytelling experience.

After extensive research in Artificial Intelligence, this installation will enable participants to experience how easily human bias can be intergraded into networks by humans and therefore understand the necessity for Transparency and Regulation in AI. The immersive experience generates self-reflection and discussion on issues of bias, ethics, and accountability for the participants and people creating these types of systems.

  STARTS Prize'20 · Honorary Mention

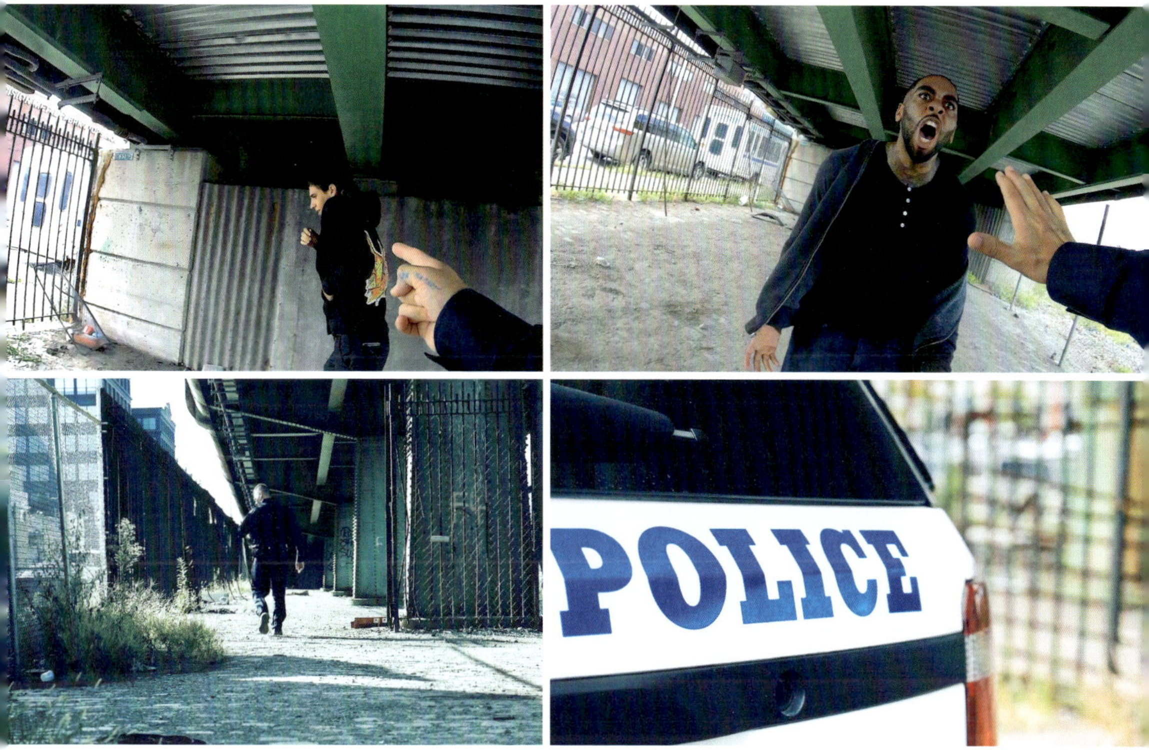

This is a collaboration of Art (Cooper Hewitt), Tech (ThoughtWorks Arts), and Science (NYU) to create the installation and undertake the ethical, academic, and philosophical R&D. EmoPy is the bespoke (open source), deep neural net toolkit for emotion analysis via Facial Expression Recognition (FER) created by ThoughtWorks Arts and Karen Palmer. *Perception iO* was commissioned by The Cooper Hewitt Smithsonian Design Museum NYC.

Director, producer: Karen Palmer
Commissioned by: Ellen Lupton, The Cooper Hewitt Smithsonian Design Museum
Software development: ThoughtWork Arts Program
Director: Andrew McWilliams, Julien Deswaef & The ThoughtWorks Development Team Emilio Escobedo, Lauren O'Neal, Tom Shannon, Dan Lewis-Toakley, J.C. Holder, Stephanie Weber, Peter Graves, Lee Faria, Diana Gámez Díaz, Emily Sachs, Whelan Workmaster, Andrew Zou, Ling Tran, Margaret Plumley, Megan Andrea Louw
R&D: Emily Balcetis
Special Thanks: Erica Wayne & Tobii Pro
Film Production Team: She Shot Me Films
Cast: Michael Mirlas, Hassan Farrow, Jeremie Egiazarian, Christin Johnson

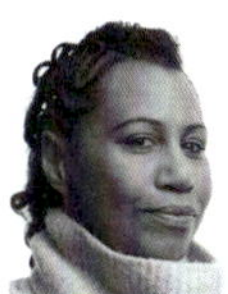 **Karen Palmer** (GB) is the Storyteller from the Future. International Artist and TED Speaker. Her work is at the intersection of AI, Immersive Storytelling, Neuroscience, Behavioural Psychology, Implicit Bias, and the Parkour philosophy of moving through fear. Articles (have appeared) in *WIRED, Forbes,* CBS TV, *Fast Company, Engadget, The Guardian* "This has Leapfrogged VR" etc. and she has exhibited at the V&A London, PHI Centre Montreal, FoST NYC, The Museum of Modern Art Peru, SXSW, SIDF etc. Her previous emotionally responsive film *RIOT* was honored as part of Columbia University's Digital Dozen: Breakthroughs in Storytelling 2017.

http://karenpalmer.uk/portfolio/perceptionio

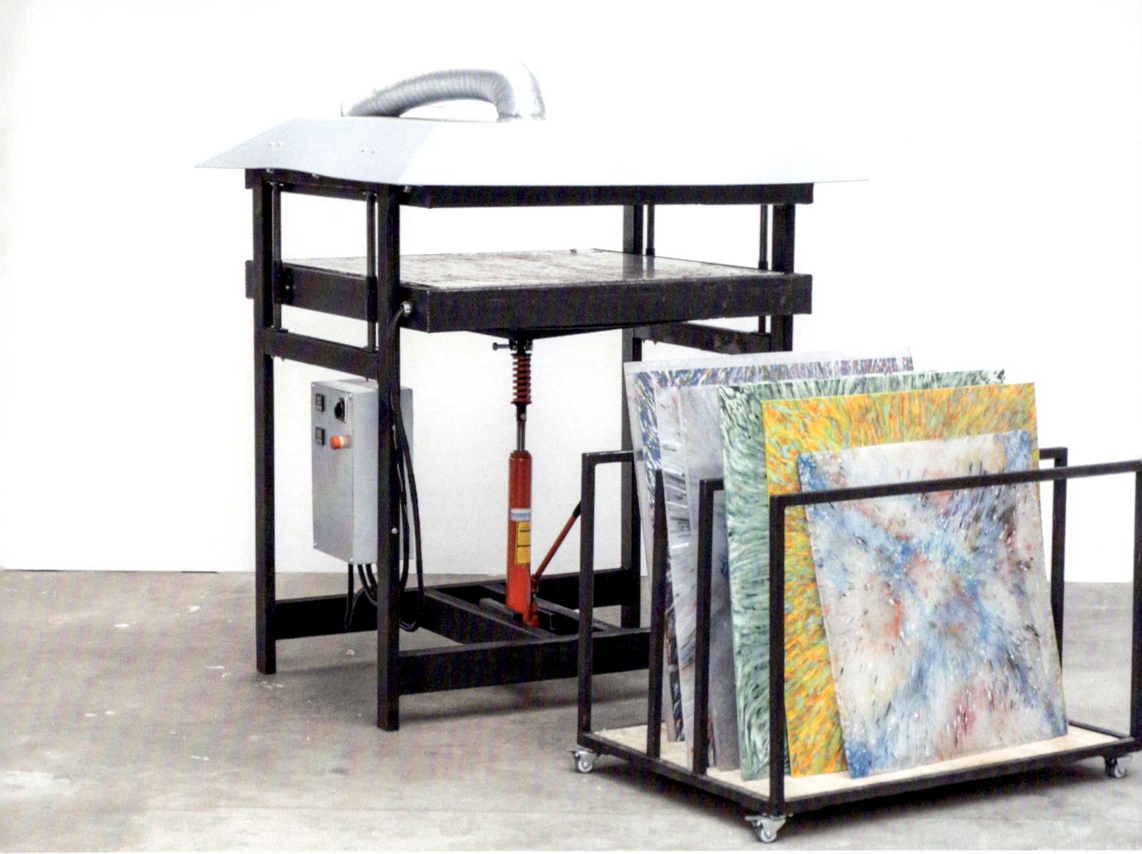

Precious Plastic Universe
The alternative plastic recycling system

Dave Hakkens

In every corner of the world, people are struggling with plastic waste. Plastic hardly gets collected and from the collected material only a fraction gets recycled (global average around 9%). In most cases it ends up burnt, in landfills, or harming our nature. The reason for this low recycling rate is that traditional recycling machinery typically requires huge capital investment and is often patented and proprietary. In addition to this technology accessibility problem, consumer culture and behavior continue to view plastic as cheap and disposable instead of valuable. The *Precious Plastic Universe* aims to boost plastic recycling globally by making it more understandable and accessible for everyone.

We develop open source recycling machines, products, and online collaboration tools so that anyone can become part of our alternative plastic recycling ecosystem, called the *Precious Plastic Universe.* We developed the *Precious Plastic Universe* over the past year and released it into the world in January 2020. At the center of the Universe are our starterkits, which are packages of tools and tutorials to help people create sustainable businesses around each step of the plastic recycling value chain—from plastic collection, machine manufacturing, shredding, and product production. This local network of independent organizations in each city, town, or region form a new ecosystem of plastic recycling that keeps

STARTS Prize'20 · Honorary Mention

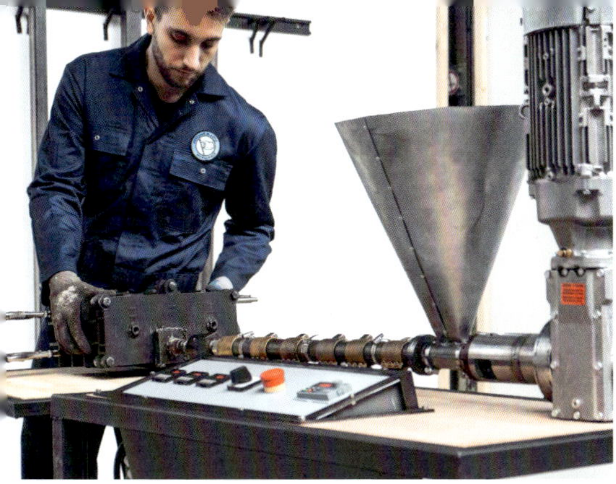

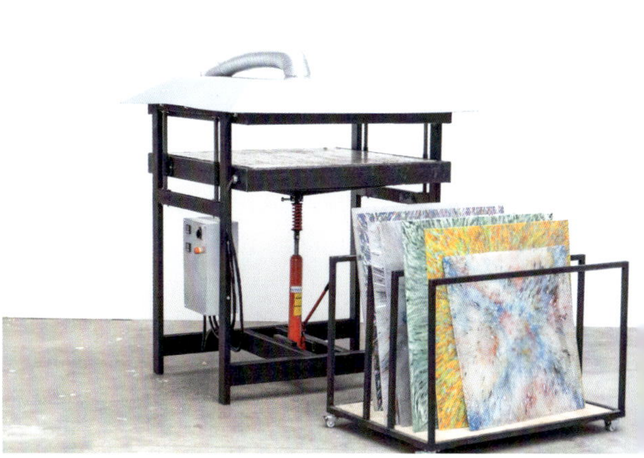

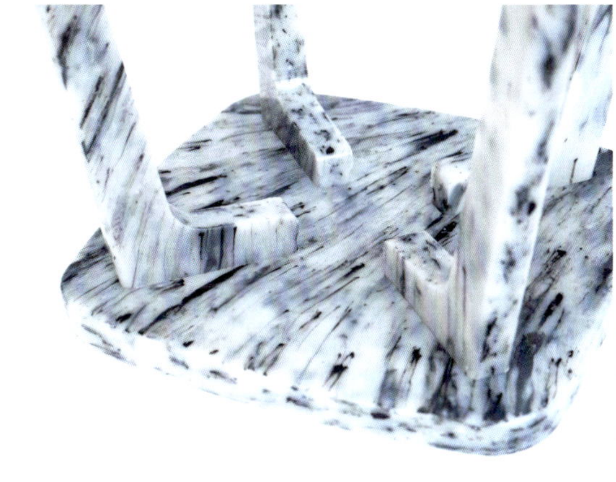

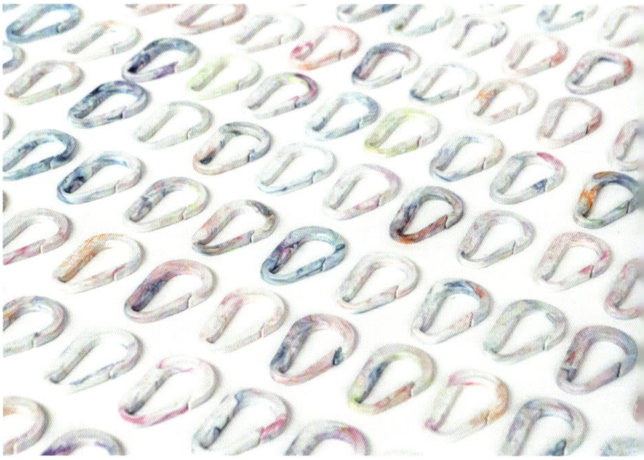

material local and recycles it into new valuable products. It's a system which allows everyone to understand the recycling process and take an active role in plastic recycling in a way that encourages behavior change towards reducing the amount of single use plastic consumed. It's through seeing plastic waste transformed locally into new valuable products that we can all begin to understand that plastic is precious. The *Precious Plastic Universe* is open source under a Creative Commons license.

With support from: Famae Foundation and Municipality of Eindhoven

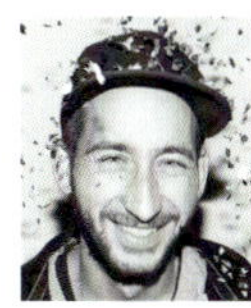

Dave Hakkens (NL) is a designer who lives and works in Eindhoven. Although an industrial designer by trade, he also loves to build machinery and make videos. His mantra is simple: "Try to make the world better by making things." It doesn't really matter whether it's an inspirational video, machines to recycle plastic, or a phone concept—as long as it pushes the world in a better direction, he is interested. In 2018 he won a €300,000 Famae award for his project *Precious Plastic* and invited over 100 volunteers from all over the world to the Netherlands to help develop *Precious Plastic Version 4.* His next project is about upcycling textiles to reduce fashion waste.

http://preciousplastic.com

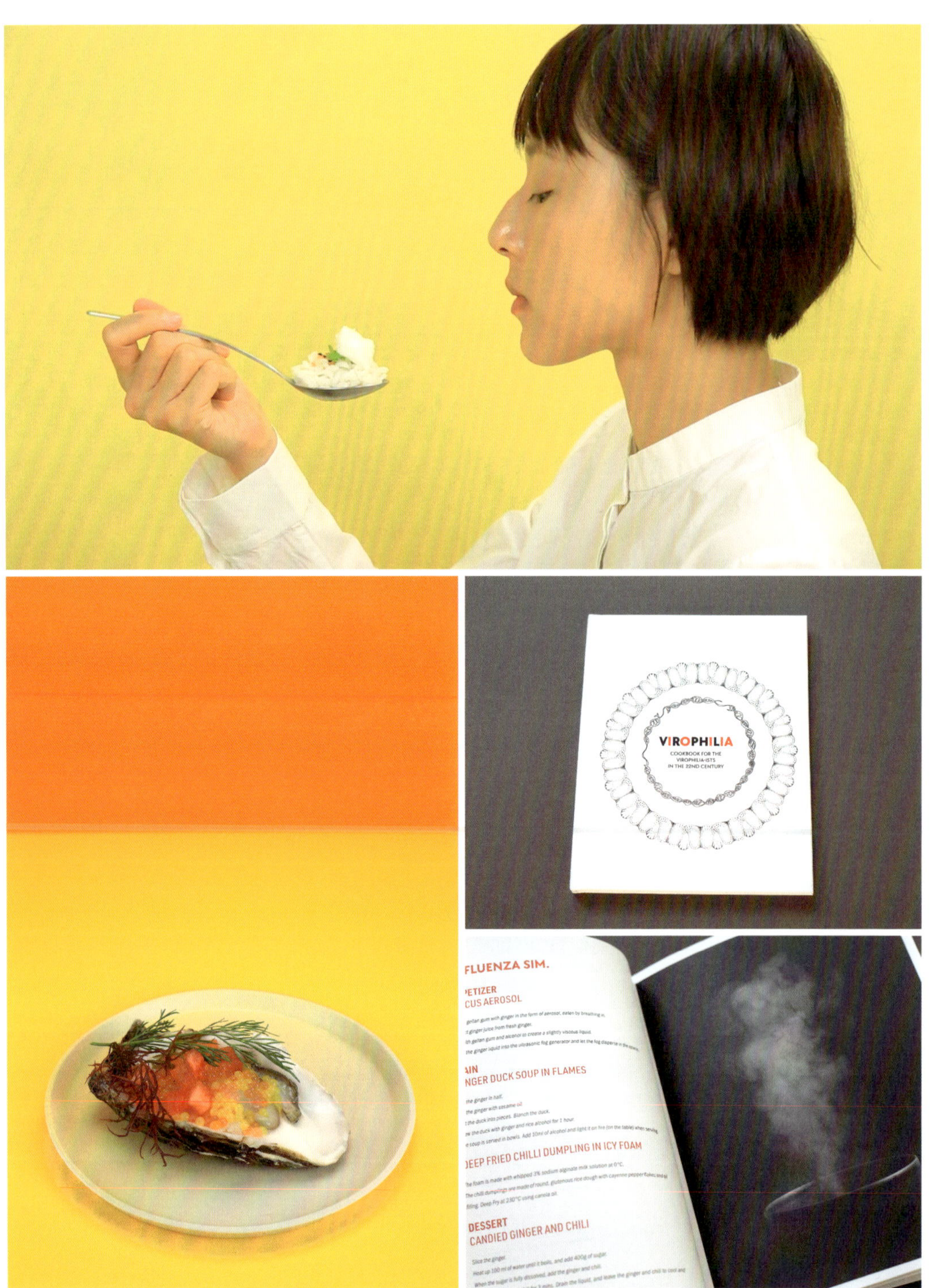
VIROPHILIA
COOKBOOK FOR THE
VIROPHILIA-ISTS
IN THE 22ND CENTURY
FLUENZA SIM.
PETIZER
CUS AEROSOL
MAIN
NGER DUCK SOUP IN FLAMES
DEEP FRIED CHILLI DUMPLING IN ICY FOAM
DESSERT
CANDIED GINGER AND CHILI

Proposals of Collaboration with the Viral Entities
Tame is to Tame, Virophilia

Pei-Ying Lin

Proposals of Collaboration with the Viral Entities is a series of endeavours towards finding a balance between our anthropocentric position and our unavoidable encounter of the viral others.

Tame is to Tame (2016)

Tame is to Tame is a conceptual "dance" between humans and viruses and explores an alternative human-virus relationship in depth. The virus-taming program is built upon virology research and shows people an alternative way to look at the "invisible and inanimate" viruses—which we perceive as enemies—and illustrates how these "agents" can redefine the cultural definition of human and individualism.

The project directly demonstrates the journey of the artist and the scientist and invites the audience to become a virus tamer by going through a collection of tamer's artefacts:

— a manifesto, a poster, and a Norovirus plushie
— laboratory profiles of the very first two virus tamers—the artist and the scientist—and their immunity towards Norovirus that defines the type of tamer they can be
— two scrolls of their encounters with the virus,
— a set of tamer's tea, which helps to reduce physical discomfort if infected
— tamer's exercise and tamer's dance
— a collaborative board game to face different scenarios.

Virophilia (2018–2020)

Can we initiate a further relationship with the viruses—proactively instead of passively? *Virophilia* investigates the possibilities of human-virus encounter in the realm of food culture, via events and performances that open up new discourse and perspectives. It consists of a cookbook, written in the year 2068, which examines retrospectively how humans started to develop cuisines with viruses which extended our sensorial experience, a dinner performance where the participants can experience it physically, and videos that show dining encounters between humans and viruses.

Tame is to Tame collaborators: Miranda de Graaf, Viroscience Lab, Erasmus MC, Yen-An Chen, Hsin Yu Chang, Po-Hao Chi, Min-Shu Huang, Rachel Jui Chi Chang, Ling-Li Chen, Yi-Ling Wu, Li-Wei Chen, FrenchFries.tw
With support from: Bio Art and Design Award, NWO, ZonMW, Viroscience Lab, Erasmus MC, De Ontdekfabriek, MU Artspace

Virophilia collaborators: Toby Kiers, Miranda de Graaf, Rene van der Vlugt, Corina Brussaard, Jos Looije, Ishtar Hsu, Cecile Espinasse, Min-Shu Huang, Yen-An Chen, Li-Ting Chen, Angela Ying-Jung Chen, and all the participants
With support from: AirWG, Waag Society, Mediamatic, 3PackageDeal, Amsterdam Fonds voor de Kunst, Vrije Universiteit Amsterdam

Pei-Ying Lin (TW) is an artist / designer based in Eindhoven (NL). Her main focus is exploring and experimenting science and human society through artistic methods, particularly around building a common discussion ground for different cultural perspectives regarding elements that construct our individual perception of the world. Recently she has been focusing on manipulating the boundary of invisible/visible, living/non-living and finding ways to build tools and methods that facilitate such explorations. She won an Honorary Mention in Hybrid Arts of Ars Electronica 2015, Professional Runner Up in Speculative Concepts of Core 77 Awards 2015, and BioArt and Design Award 2016.

http://peiyinglin.net

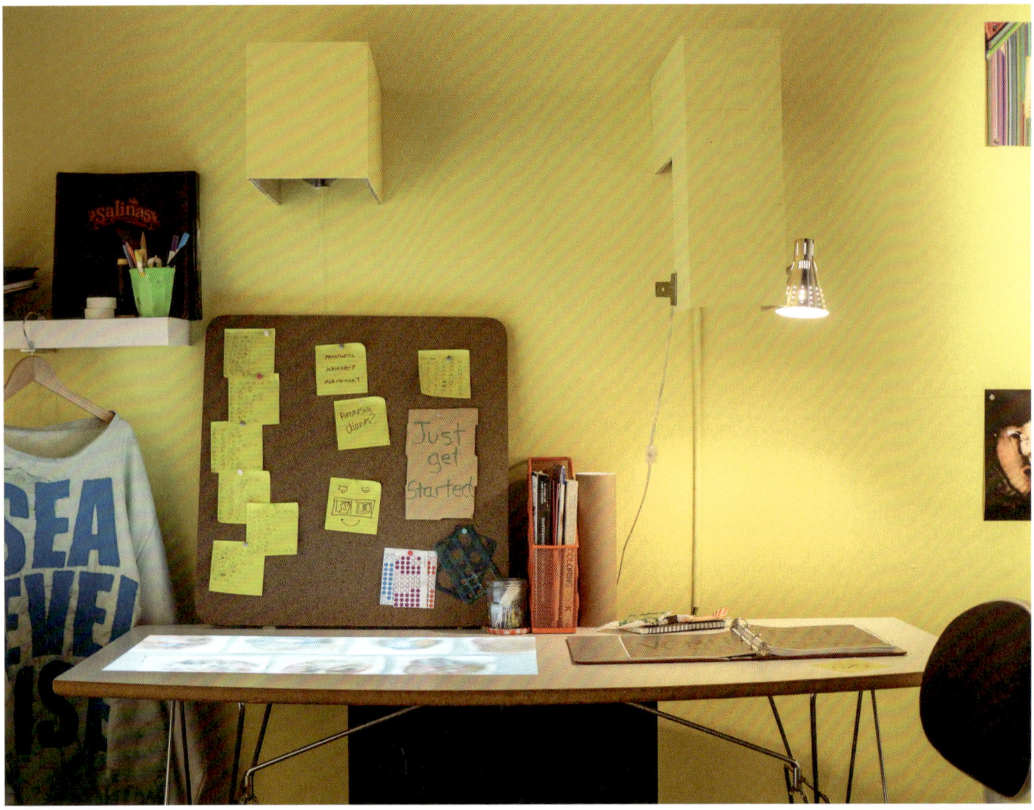

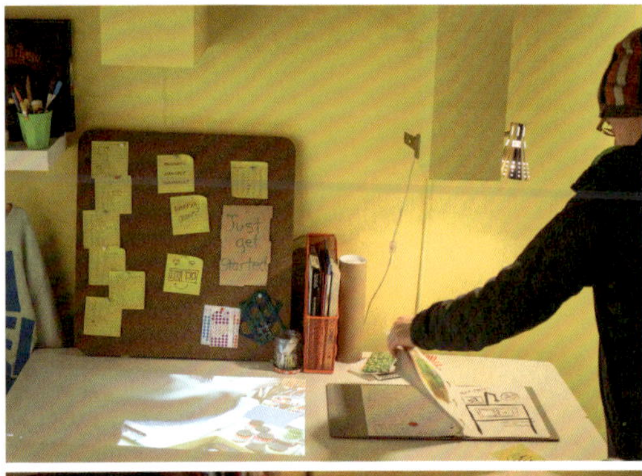

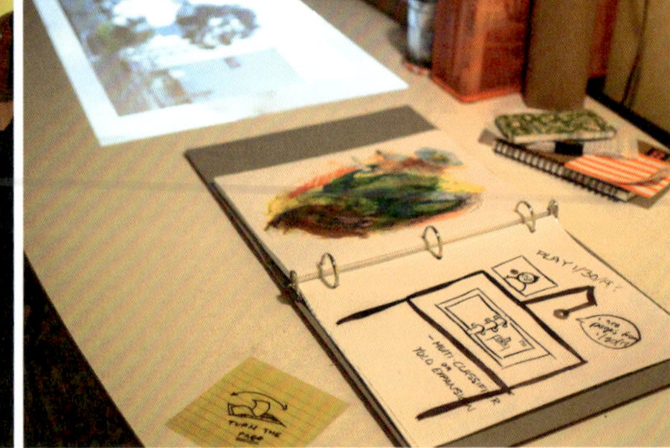

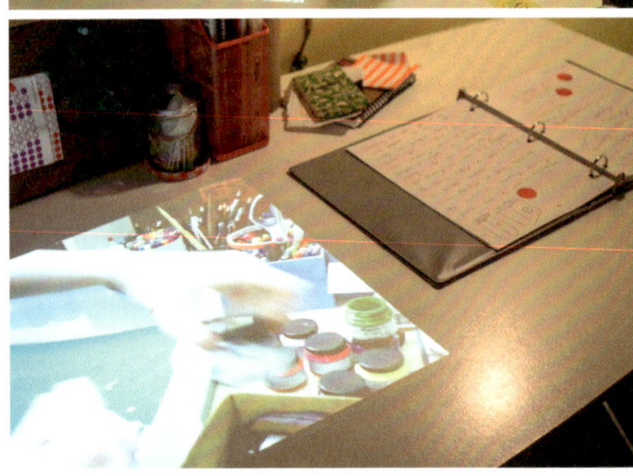

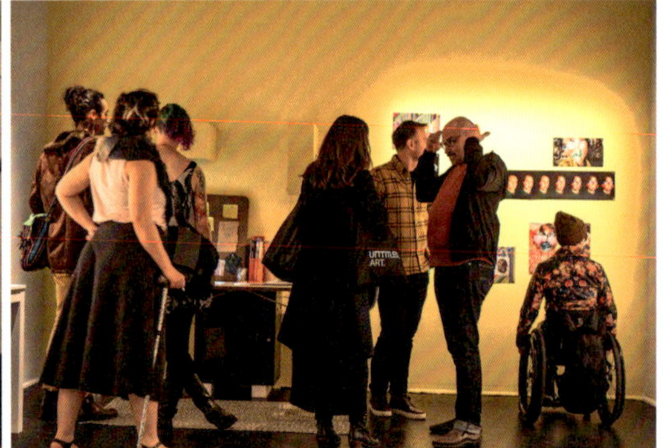

STARTS Prize'20 · Honorary Mention

Prosthetic Memory

M Eifler

Prosthetic Memory is an ongoing experiment in self-augmentation combining handmade journals, daily videos, and a custom AI. With the journal lying flat on a desk, a camera captures its pages. The AI compares this feed to its model, determines which page is showing, and projects an associated video memory on the desk nearby. Created to replace the artist's long-term memory that was damaged by a childhood brain injury, *Prosthetic Memory* explores questions like:

- When memories are external, mediated, and public, what is the difference between how they are experienced by their creator and an audience?
- Do our assumptions, fears, and uses for AI change when data and machine learning models are created by individuals and families on a personal, instead of a corporate scale?

- Given our increasing exposure to algorithmic interventions, how do our identities and perceptions shift when we see ourselves and others through that lens?

The first iteration of *Prosthetic Memory,* captured in the documentation provided, created a bridge between the physical and virtual components of the memory. In upcoming iterations an age-malleable recreation (deep fake) of the artist will appear on a screen above the notebook, reading from its pages, and, using NLP and sentiment analysis, pointing the user to other pages and videos with similar events or feelings.

Collaborator: Steve Sedlmayr

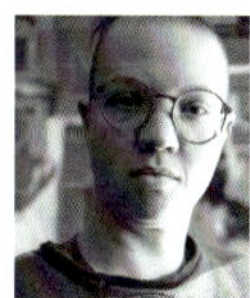

M Eifler (US) is an artist and researcher working in embodied/spatial interaction, speculative interfaces, and computational prosthetics. They have exhibited work or performed at TED in Vancouver, the Exploratorium, SFMoMA, the YBCA, the Wattis Institute in San Francisco, XOXO, Wiensowski & Harbord in Berlin, Laurie M. Tisch Gallery and the Armory Show in New York, Seattle International Film Festival, as well as the Smithsonian Institution and Kennedy Center. During the pandemic they have been honored to contribute to the Harvard Safra Center's Roadmap to Pandemic Resilience team. Eifler graduated from California College of Art in 2011 with an interdisciplinary MFA.

http://www.blinkpopshift.com/2020#/prosthetic-memory

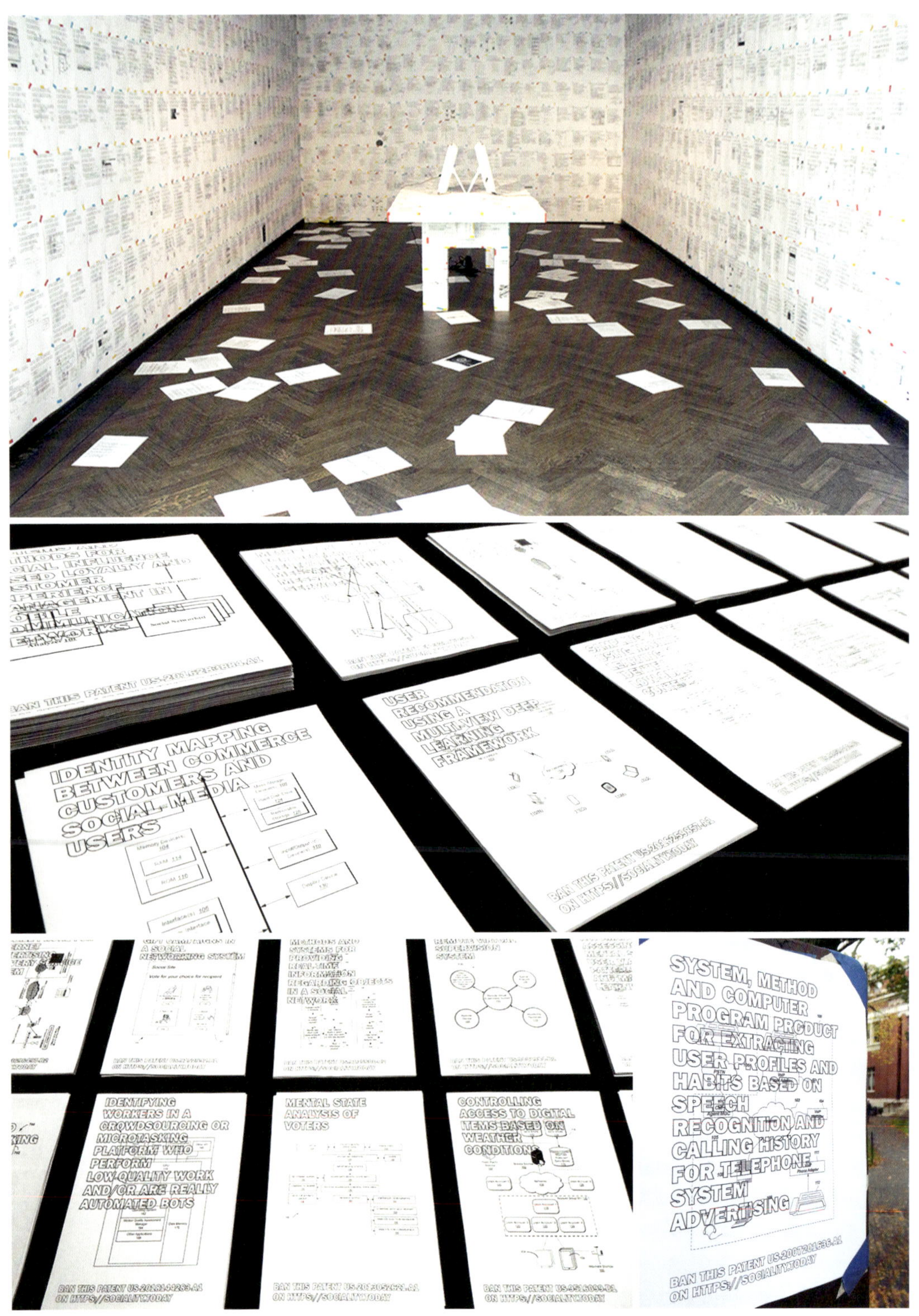
IDENTITY MAPPING
BETWEEN COMMERCE
CUSTOMERS AND
SOCIAL MEDIA
USERS
USER
RECOMMENDATION
USING A
MULTIVIEW DEEP
LEARNING
FRAMEWORK
BAN THIS PATENT US-9-554545-14
ON HTTPS://SOCIALITYTODAY
METHODS AND
SYSTEMS FOR
PROVIDING
REAL-TIME
INFORMATION
REGARDING OBJECTS
IN A SOCIAL
NETWORK
IDENTIFYING
WORKERS IN A
CROWDSOURCING OR
MICROTASKING
PLATFORM WHO
PERFORM
LOW-QUALITY WORK
AND/OR ARE REALLY
AUTOMATED BOTS
MENTAL STATE
ANALYSIS OF
VOTERS
CONTROLLING
ACCESS TO DIGITAL
ITEMS BASED ON
WEATHER
CONDITION
SYSTEM, METHOD
AND COMPUTER
PROGRAM PRODUCT
FOR EXTRACTING
USER PROFILES AND
HABITS BASED ON
SPEECH
RECOGNITION AND
CALLING HISTORY
FOR TELEPHONE
SYSTEM
ADVERTISING
BAN THIS PATENT US-2007204636-A1
ON HTTPS://SOCIALITYTODAY
BAN THIS PATENT US-2020342293-A1
ON HTTPS://SOCIALITYTODAY
BAN THIS PATENT US-2015052472-A1
ON HTTPS://SOCIALITYTODAY
BAN THIS PATENT US-952009-B2
ON HTTPS://SOCIALITYTODAY

Sociality

Paolo Cirio

This artwork documented over twenty-thousand patents of socially manipulative information technology. In *Sociality,* Cirio collected and rated Internet inventions submitted to the U.S. patent office. Subsequently, he invited the public to share, flag, and ban the technologies designed to monitor and manipulate social behaviors. The patent images and data were obtained by Cirio through hacking the Google Patents search engine. Then he rated the patents and created thousands of compositions with images of flowcharts and titles of inventions, which were published on the project's website, *https://Sociality.today.* The visual compositions on the website were printed in the form of posters and a coloring book for informing on devices that enable discrimination, polarization, addiction, deception, and surveillance.

The concept of turning patents into vehicles for regulation aims to exploit intellectual property law as a tool for democratic oversight. This work integrates both the dystopia surrounding technology and the utopia of its participatory governance with flowcharts of patents taking the form of documentary and protest art. With this problematizing piece, Cirio exposed evidence of social manipulation and questioned the ethical, legal, and economic structures of such technological apparatuses. In the exhibition, the public confronts large-scale compositions with hundreds of images of flowcharts that abstractly invoke the complexity and magnitude of such uncanny plans to program people.

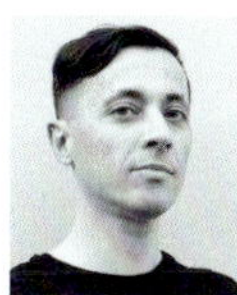

Paolo Cirio (IT) has exhibited in museums and art institutions worldwide. He shows his research and intervention-based works through prints, installations, videos, and public art. Paolo Cirio works with legal, economic, and cultural systems of the information society. He investigates social fields impacted by the Internet, such as privacy, democracy, finance, and intellectual property. He shows his research and intervention-based works through artifacts, photos, installations, videos, and public art. Cirio's art considers how society is affected by the control over information. It embodies the contradictions, ethics, conflicts, and potentials inherent to the social complexity of information society through a critical and proactive approach. Paolo Cirio examines the ethics and aesthetics of working with online piracy, data breach, identity theft, privacy, fake news, algorithms, and hacking.

https://Sociality.today

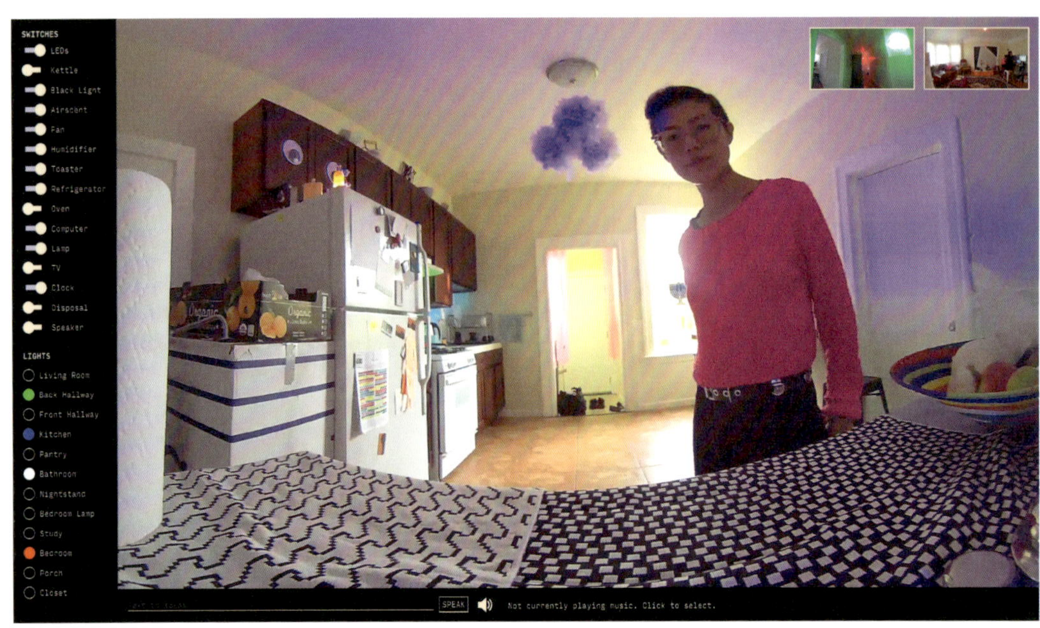

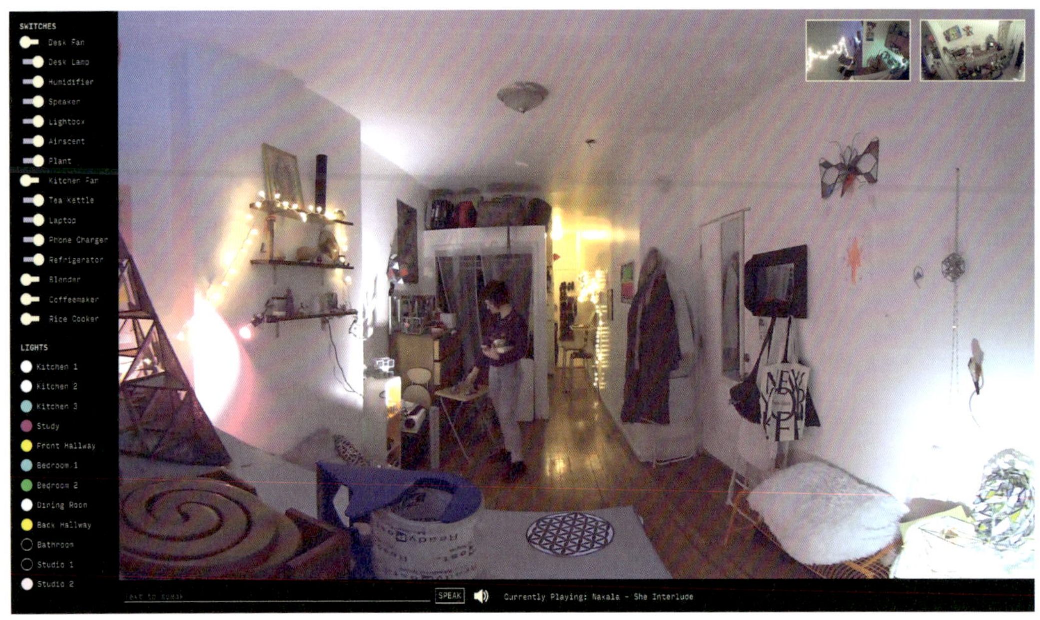

STARTS Prize'20 · Honorary Mention

SOMEONE

Lauren Lee McCarthy

Visitors are invited to act as a human version of Amazon Alexa. For this exhibition, four participants' homes are installed with custom-designed smart devices, including cameras, microphones, switches, lights, and appliances. The gallery contains a command center that resembles a cross between call center and WeWork co-working space, featuring four computer stations. Visitors may hear smart home occupants call out for "Someone"—prompting the visitors to step in as their home automation assistant and respond to their needs. They can peek into the four homes via the laptops, watch over them, and remotely control the devices in their homes. This installation was originally a live remote intelligence portal into four homes across the United States that took place over a two-month duration.

We're sold smart devices that outfit our homes with surveillance cameras, sensors, and automated control offering us convenience, at the cost of loss of privacy and control over our lives and homes. We're meant to think these slick plastic pieces of technology are about utility, but the space they invade is personal. Home is the place where we are first socialized, first watched over, first cared for. What does it mean to have this role assumed by AI? Home is the first site of one's cultural education. Now this is shaped by technology created by a small, homogenous group of developers.

By substituting humans for AI, the role of virtual assistant is re-contextualized. Inhabitants call out for "Someone," invoking visitors as intelligence, complicating the dynamic between audience and performer. Installed simultaneously in multiple homes across the country, we're challenged to consider the scale of the work, and the even more expansive, networked systems that structure society. *SOMEONE* is a meditation on the smart home, the tensions between intimacy vs privacy, convenience vs agency, and the role of human labor in the future of automation.

Artist: Lauren Lee McCarthy
Software and hardware development: Harvey Moon, Josh Billions
Interface software: Lauren Lee McCarthy
Furniture design collaboration and fabrication: Lela Barclay de Tolly
Smart home participant collaborators: Valeria Haedo, Adelle Lin, Amanda McDonald Crowley, Ksenya Samarskaya

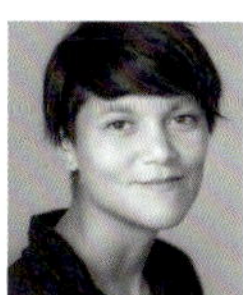

Lauren Lee McCarthy (US) is an LA-based artist examining social relationships in the midst of surveillance, automation, and algorithmic living. She is the creator of p5.js, and Co-Director of the Processing Foundation. Lauren's work has been exhibited at The Barbican Centre, Ars Electronica, Fotomuseum Winterthur, Haus der elektronischen Künste, SIGGRAPH, Onassis Cultural Center, IDFA DocLab, and the Seoul Museum of Art. She's the recipient of a Creative Capital Award, Sundance Fellowship, Eyebeam Residency, and grants from the Knight Foundation, Mozilla Foundation, Google, and Rhizome.

https://lauren-mccarthy.com/SOMEONE

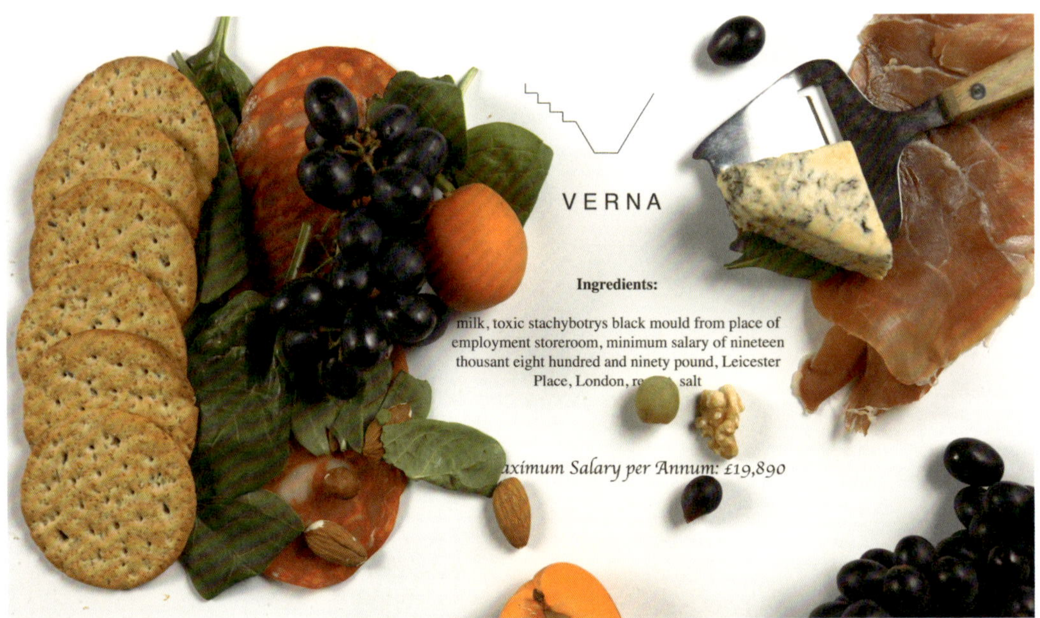

Spoiled Spores

Avril Corroon

Responding to the housing crisis in Ireland and London, *Spoiled Spores* is an installation of up to 25 toxic cheeses made with a culture of toxic black mold sampled from rental accommodation in Dublin and London. Corroon comes from Ireland where the housing crisis is arguably one of the biggest social economic issues facing the country. The cost of purchasing accomodation in Dublin has risen by 90% since 2012, whereas wages have only increased by 18%. Consequently the number of homeless families has increased by 216% since March 2015.

Spoiled Spores examines the extortionately priced housing that tenants are forced to endure and juxtaposes this with the manufacturing of high-end artisanal commodities for middle and rentier class consumers. A poisonous trap for the landlord per-

haps? Participants were found through the artist's extended network of peers and call outs online for those who lived in rental accomodation with damp issues. For a year Corroon scraped numerous forms of mold from dank walls and ceilings in London and later in Dublin. Perfectly aged, these apparently high end luxury cheeses are one of a kind, each with an ingredient list including the rental cost, and uniquely named after corresponding tenants, Katie, Alan, Sophie etc. Upon entering the installation, viewers are hit with the nauseating stench of the festering cheese, which is layed out in industrial fridges that hum like loud baritones. Simultaneously alluring and repelling, scent is used to toy with notions of taste and its relation to class whilst also presenting a bodily communication between the abject truckles and the viewer.

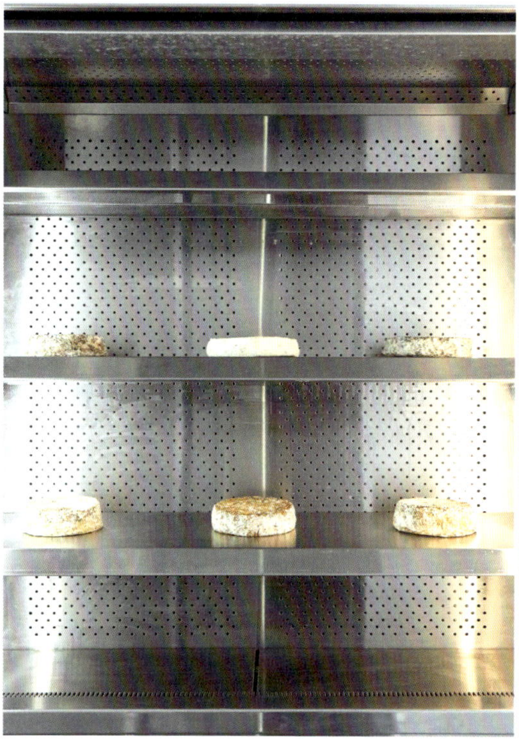

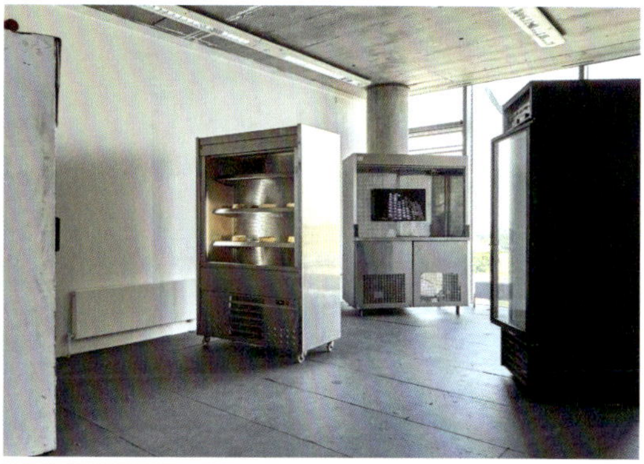

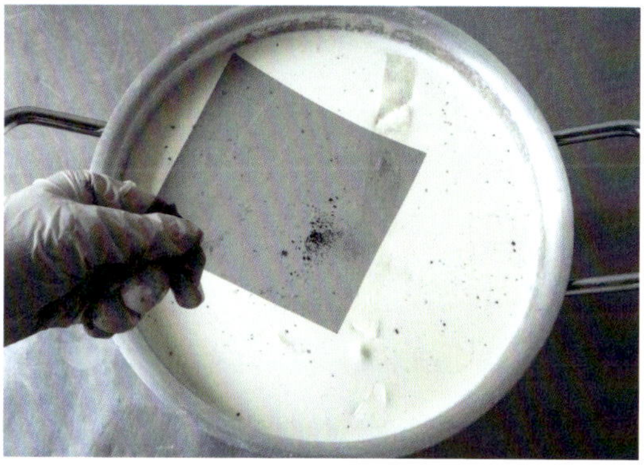

Drawn in by ideas of cheese boards and seasonal condiments, Corroon's narrative short film reveals the production process and the unexpected and deeply disturbing backstory, the provenance of the molds. This adjacency lures us into an apparent cheese mongers, only to reveal a commentary on the living conditions, including her own, where mold samples have been taken as the basis for these supposed Camemberts and Gorgonzolas.

This project was made possible with the participants and many hands:
Alan, Charlie, Donal, Emma, Eimear, Jazbo, Katie, Louis, Ruzha, Ross, Selwen, Stephen and those who wish to remain anonymous to protect their tenancy.

Spoiled Spores was exhibited in 2019 as a solo exhibition of the same name at the LAB Gallery in Dublin, curated by Sheena Barrett. Previously it was exhibited at the 2019 Goldsmiths University MFA Degree Show where it was awarded the Goldsmiths MFA Award with Acme Studios in London.
The film *Spoiled Spores* is in the collection of Arts Council Ireland.
This project was partially supported by Westmeath County Council, Ireland.

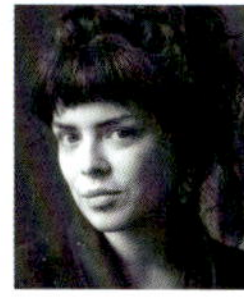

Avril Corroon (IE) works with moving image, performance, sculpture, and food to explore situations where precarious conditions have become every-day. She re-presents these instances in a satirical and absurdist form through juxtaposition and elaborate visual narratives. Such examples include: a video examining "The Landlord" as monster, and covertly filming staff treatment in the service industry where she works. She graduated with an MFA from Goldsmiths University in 2019 and a BA from NCAD in 2014. She has exhibited and screened work in Ireland and London, as well as participated in residencies in the Netherlands and Basque Country.

https://avrilcorroon.com/Spoiled-Spores-1

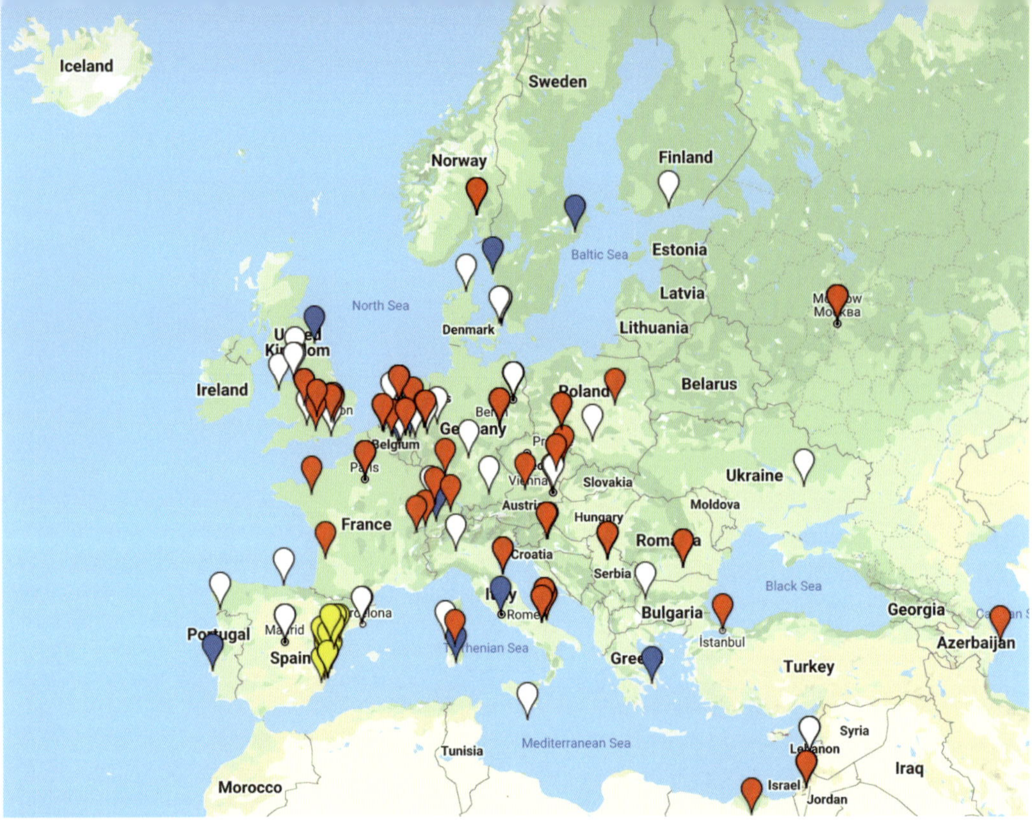

The Wrong Biennale, 4th edition, from November 1st, 2019 to March 1st, 2020. Europe map of embassies, pavilions and routers.

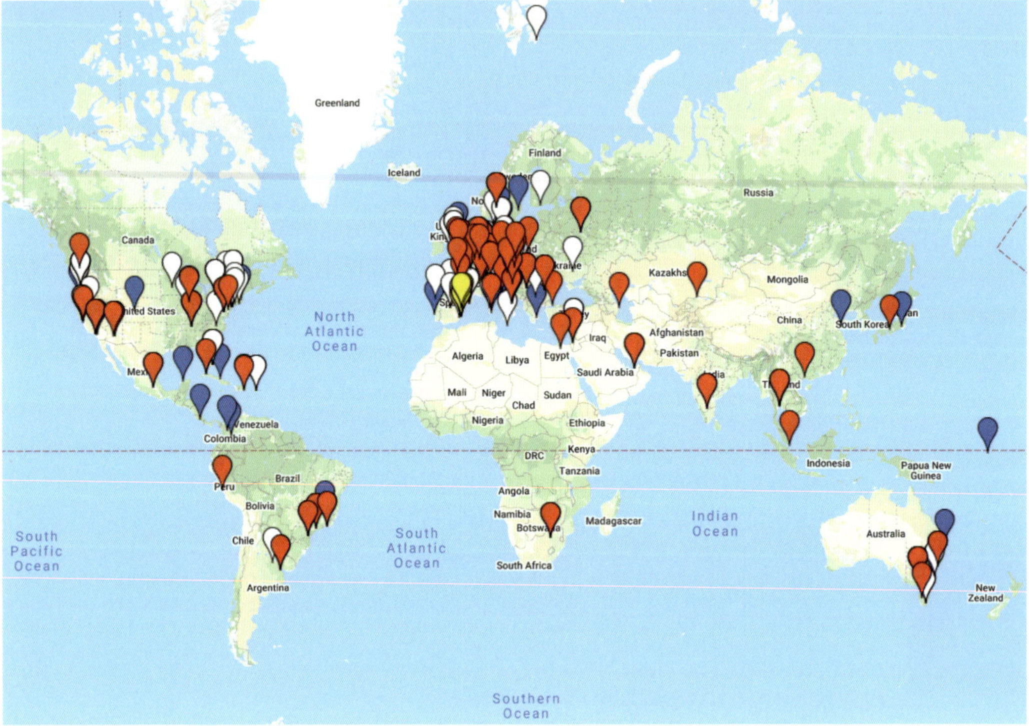

The Wrong Biennale, 4th edition, from November 1st, 2019 to March 1st, 2020. World map of embassies, pavilions and routers.

　　STARTS Prize'20 · Honorary Mention

The Wrong

David Quiles Guilló

The Wrong was born in 2013 as a collaborative effort to create and promote digital art & culture, launching a global art biennale open to participation. *The Wrong Biennale* happens online and offline: Online happens in pavilions—virtual curated spaces in any accessible online media where selected artworks are exhibited. Offline happens in embassies, institutions, art spaces, galleries, and artist-run spaces in cities around the world. An extended team of curators appoint themselves to feature what they like best of the new digital art scene today. Artists also appoint themselves via open calls and routers. Since 2013, more than 5,500 artists and curators have officially participated in *The Wrong Biennale.*

"Counting its viewership in the millions, *The Wrong* just might be the world's largest art biennale—the digital world's answer to Venice."

The New York Times

The 4th edition bloomed from November 1st, 2019 until March 1st, 2020, featuring +2300 artists +210 curators +150 online pavilions +100 embassies +320 events +120 locations around the world, and all over the internet.

In March 2020, following the end of the 4th edition and in the midst of the Covid19 pandemic outbreak, *The Wrong* announces new biennale editions for November 1st, 2021, November 1st, 2023, and November 1st, 2025—and adds two new strains: *The Wrong Website*—an online website featuring a daily feed of digital art & culture links and *The Wrong TV*—an online TV platform live streaming digital art and culture.

"Anyone interested in the field of digital art ought to pay attention to *The Wrong.*"

Christiane Paul, new media curator for
The Whitney Museum of American Art

Curators and artists:
https://biennale.thewrong.org/2019-2020
Team: David Quiles Guilló, Graziela Calfat,
Alejandra Raschkes, Jennifer Talbot
Council: Ben Grosser, Erica Lapadat-Janzen,
Florian Kuhlmann, Guilherme Brandão, Miyö Van Stenis,
Jon Cates, Pablo Hannon, Carla Gannis, Moises Mañas,
Patrick Lichty
With support from: CMCV—Consorci de Museus de la
Comunitat Valenciana, Generalitat Valenciana; SESC
SP—Sao Paulo; SOIS CULTURA awards 2019; CARGO

David Quiles Guilló (ES) is an art entrepreneur, new media powerhouse, awarded creative and full weirdo at large. Curator for contemporary digital art, creative director, artist, writer, editor & publisher, experimental musician, digital poet, creative consultant, cultural programmer, and graphic designer. Founder and director of the critically acclaimed international collaborative projects: *The Wrong* (since 2013), the most compelling digital art biennale ever, *NOVA cultura contemporanea* (2010–2012), a contemporary culture festival, and *ROJO magazine* (2001–2011), a printed visual magazine & exhibition platform to promote creativity and art.

https://thewrong.org

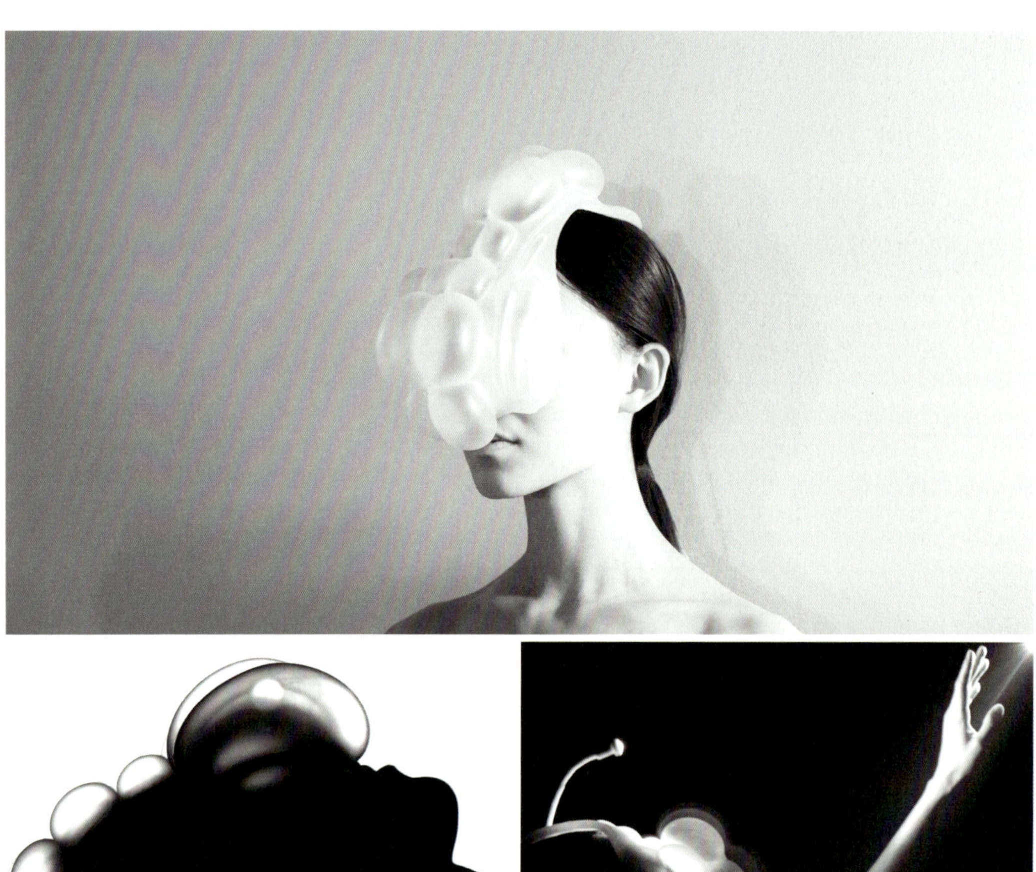

TransVision

Jiabao Li

Through three perceptual machines, *TransVision* questions the habitual ways in which we interpret and understand the visual world intervened by digital media, and how technology mediates the way we perceive reality.

Hyperallergenic Vision
We have observed an increase in allergies and intolerances in modern society. Hypersensitivities are emerging not only medically but also mentally. Digital media reinforce people's tendency to over-react through the viral spread of information and amplification of opinions, making us hypersensitive to our sociopolitical environment. By creating an artificial allergy to the color red, this machine manifests the nonsensical hypersensitivity created by digital media. In nocebo mode, red expands, which is similar to social media's amplification effect; in placebo mode, red shrinks, like our filtered communication landscape where we can unfollow people with different opinions.

   STARTS Prize'20 · Honorary Mention

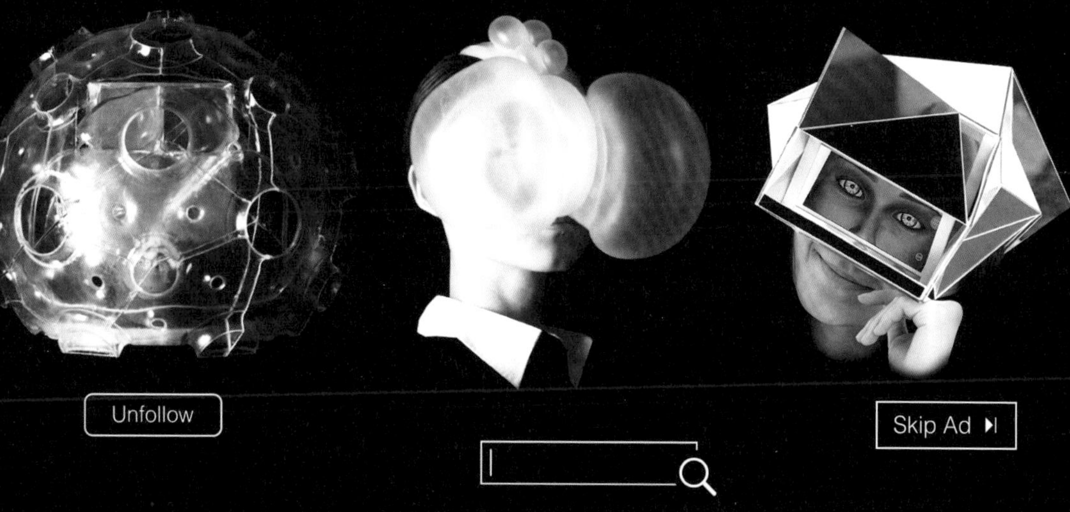

Tactile Vision

Obsessively searching online for one thing is like looking through a pinhole where we build up everything without an overview. This machine helps to make the wearer conscious of how the way we navigate the internet naturally narrows our views of the world. The silicon mask breathes gently when the light is far away, but rapidly when the light gets closer. The wearers can navigate in space and find each other in total darkness with this tactile vision, like a dating App for cave animals. Similar to searching, when you are only looking for one thing, you lose the capacity to see things in context and to therefore make more informed decisions.

Commoditized Vision

Our visual field is packed with so much information that our perception has become a commodity with real estate value. By creating tension between the meditative state and the consumptive state, this machine contemplates how our perception has become part of the value chain in this particular socioeconomic context. You can earn money by looking at advertisements, and spend money to see an ads free world.

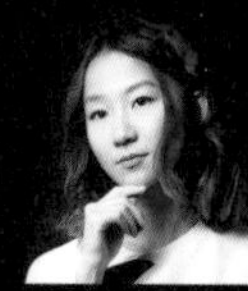

Jiabao Li (CN) works at the intersection of emerging technology, art and design and creates new ways for humans to perceive the world. Her research-based projects range from wearables, projections, drones, and installations to scientific experiments, and they explore how technology is transforming our perception, identity, emotion, and sensation. Jiabao is a recipient of numerous awards and has published and exhibited her work in major artistic and research institutions worldwide. Jiabao graduated with distinction from Harvard Graduate School of Design with a Masters in Design Technology. She is currently a prototyping designer at Apple where she invents and explores new products, interfaces, and technologies.

https://www.jiabaoli.org/transvision

S+T+ARTS
PRIZE '20

NOMINATIONS

aqua_forensic
Underwater Interception of Biotweaking in Aquatocene
Robertina Šebjanič, Gjino Šutić

aqua_forensic illuminates the invisible anthropogenic pharmaceutical pollutants—residues of human consumption. The project combines art/science/citizen science in a "hunt for a monster" and opens the discussion about our solidarity and empathy with waters beyond human perception. The project is presented as an installation, workshop, and public discussion with the intention to create new narratives. The installation represents the research of invisible chemical pollutants (mood controllers, antibiotics, antimycotics, painkillers, hormone pills etc.) and their impact on water habitats. Research was conducted at a residency in 2018 at the Danube river (Linz, AT) and the Adriatic Sea (Dubrovnik, HR). The vast complexity of the water ecosystems, which cover most of the planet, is still a mystery. With pollution we change the oceans inside out—influencing the life of the interconnected ecosystem. It is the result of global socio-technological, (geo)political, and economic usage of the world's waters. *aqua_forensic* is a voyage into the relationship between the microbial seas and humans who are aquaforming the water habitats all around the planet. The question is: How do the oceans experience our impact?

With support from: Ars Electronica within the EMAP/EMARE project, UR Institute (HR), Projekt Atol Institute (SI), Čistoća Dubrovnik, Sektor Institute (SI), The Ministry of Culture of the Republic of Slovenia and The Ministry of Culture of the Republic of Croatia. Co-funded by the Creative Europe Programme of the European Union.
Special thanks to: Miha Godec, Tanja Minarik, Martina Brković, Antonia Merčep, Lovro Martinović, Veronika Liebl, Jessica Galirow, Uroš Veber, Annick Bureaud, Slavko Glamočanin, team of Lokrum nature reserve, Eleonore team, UR Institute team

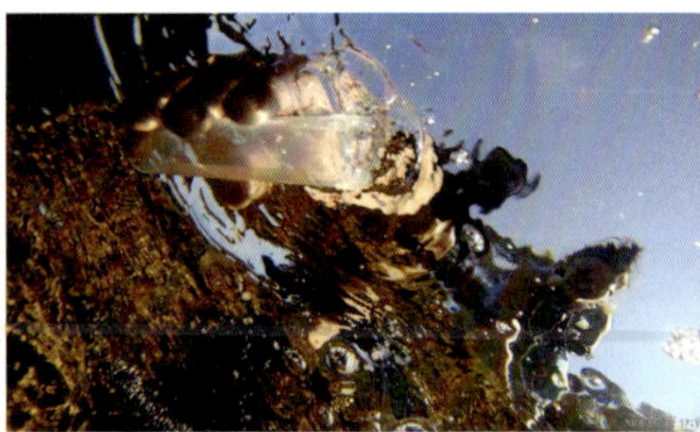

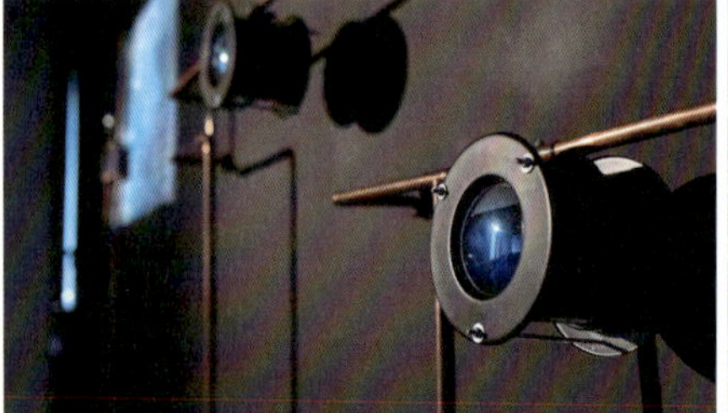

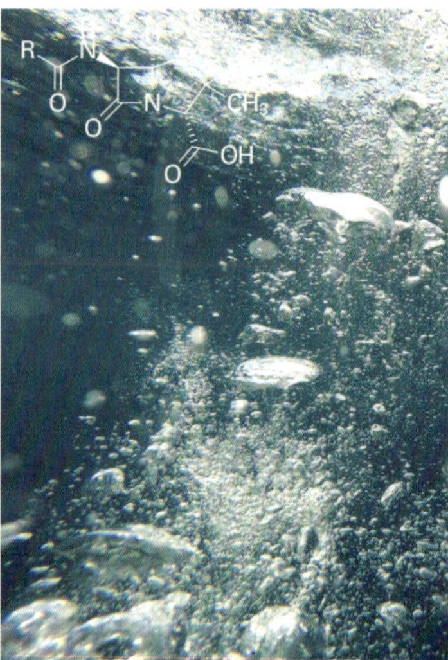

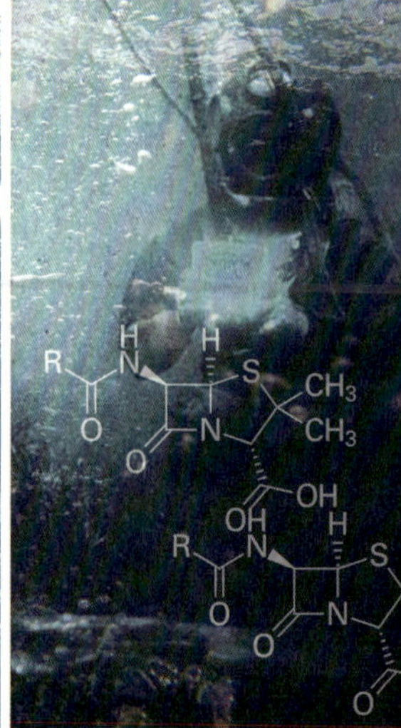

Takashi Terada

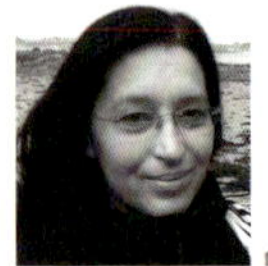
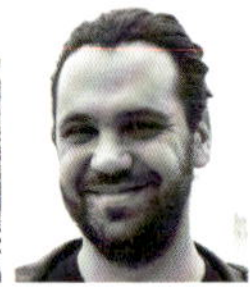

Robertina Šebjanič (SI) is an internationally exhibited and awarded artist. Her research-based work deals with the cultural, (bio)political, and ecological realities of aquatic environments. With her projects she tackles the philosophical questions at the intersection of art, technology and science. **Gjino Šutić** (HR) is a biotechnologist, post-modern intermedia artist, innovator, and educator, and the founder and director of Universal Research Institute & Gen0 Industries. He conducts research in experimental biotechnology, bioelectronics & ecological engineering, postmodern new media art and hybrid art.

https://robertina.net/aqua_forensic

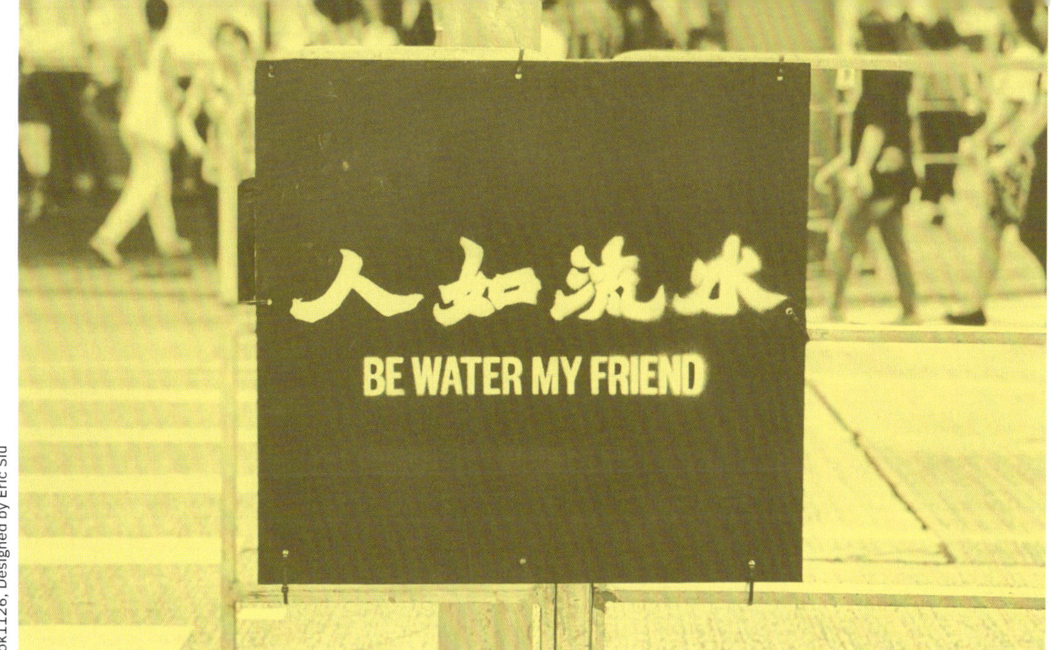

Be Water by Hong Kongers

Dedicated to the Hong Kong protesters by Eric Siu & Joel Kwong

Since the summer of 2019, a tremendous political movement has been happening in Hong Kong. Digital technology plays a key role in the whole movement, and the use of technology is creative, innovative, and pervasive. Digital community functions range from front-line support and crowdsourcing campaigns to protest art, social media (fact-checking and reporting), online petitions, political education, and so on. Protesters use multiple platforms including live-streaming, forums and apps, e-commerce, websites, music, and whatever else seems appropriate in the moment. The philosophy behind this is "Be Water," a saying of martial arts star Bruce Lee, which means to be shapeless, formless, and able to adapt to any situation. Democracy is recognized as a fundamental value and a basic human right throughout most of the world. However, it must be constantly monitored and safeguarded. The protest movement in Hong Kong shows how the "Be Water" strategy allied to digital technology can be a powerful means for citizens to resist attacks on their democratic rights and freedoms. From crowdfunding to global digital activism, Hong Kong protesters were able to alert the world to their struggle. Digital technologies also helped protesters to decentralize power and enabled all individuals to protect and strengthen democracy together. As the saying goes, water doesn't stay still—while technology and science are deemed to be inhumane and cold, they possess hidden potential to flow into new areas of human experience and transform into different states with water-like vitality and capacity. Through this submission, we hope to bring Hong Kongers to the center of art, technology and society, and to provoke a much-needed dialogue about how digital culture shapes our practice of civic responsibility—now and in the future.

All Hong Kong protesters involved in the struggle to safeguard democracy.

Hong Kong protesters. Since the latest pro-democracy movement erupted in 2019, Hong Kong protesters have been following a strategy called "Be Water." With this philosophy, Hong Kongers have recollected the scattered pieces of hope from the Umbrella Movement in 2014 to imagine a new form of protest. Among their many innovations, Hong Kongers have pursued leaderless organization and digital activism, which have captured the world's attention. To continue their movement, Hong Kongers hope to widen global solidarity and let the "Be Water" current flow to the worlds of art and technology. Eric Siu is a media artist born and raised in Hong Kong. Joel Kwong is a media art curator raised and currently based in Hong Kong.

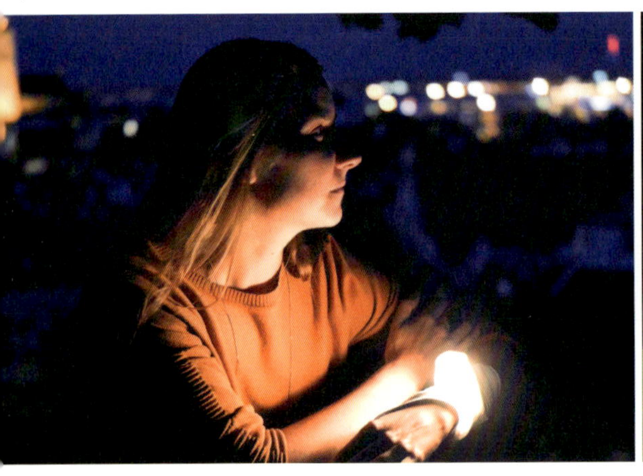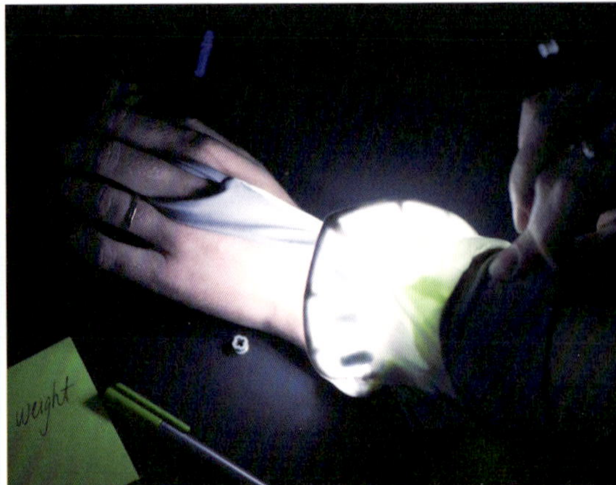

BETAlight

Barbro Scholz with Esther Stühmer, Axel Sylvester, and Tanja Döring

BETAlight is a flexible light source that can be worn on the body and allows the user to adjust its shape, orientation, brightness, and light temperature according to his or her needs. *BETAlight* is not only a wearable light source. It is a concept that allows the user to use light as a material to create personal illuminated spaces—individual room situations can be achieved by placing it somewhere in the room or by wearing it on the body.
Creating a personal light space allows a non-physical space definition that is adaptable and changeable to required lighting situations. It is weightless, only the light source is a physical object. The use of light as a space-defining material is far more subtle than a physically closed space, it provides the opportunity to create a space of retreat by less "loud" means. A personal light space can create positive effects of light on the body by especially selected cold or warm light.
In the device, implemented sensors are used to turn the light on and off, to control the brightness and adjust the light temperature to switch between different light scenarios. The fully textile circuit makes the light source completely flexible, thin, and lightweight. The shell is designed of a textile monomaterial, to allow easy recycling. *BETAlight* combines the best available materials and methods after testing and considering different production and recycling methods. The project was a multidisciplinary collaboration with a strong focus on criteria of sustainability and ethics. Skills from textile-, fashion- and interaction design, computer science, and production expertise were brought together to create a sustainable e-textile light application with natural interaction.

Film: Tarvo Tammeoks
Mentor: Kristi Kuusk
Illustration and print layout: Tatiana van Beelen
This project has received funding in Wearsustain Call2, from the European Union's Horizon 2020 research and innovation programme under grant agreement No 732098

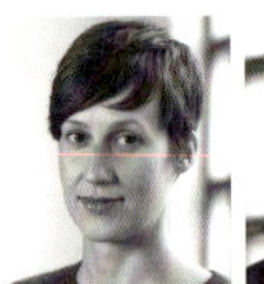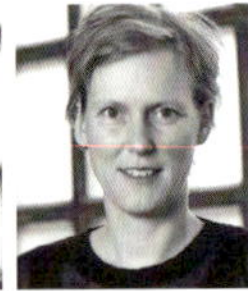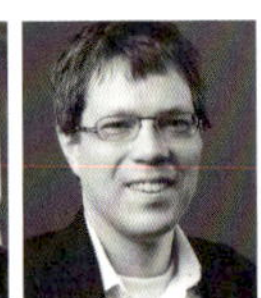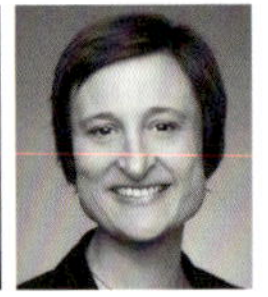

Barbro Scholz (DE) is a textile designer researching the physical and digital materiality of e-textiles design. **Esther Holsten-Stühmer** (DE) is a textile designer interested in clothing as a shell, space, and interaction. Together they are Stühmer|Scholz Design Office working for industry, education and research. **Axel Sylvester** (DE) is a tech enthusiast realizing cross-disciplinary innovation for human needs. **Tanja Döring** (DE) is a researcher in Human-Computer Interaction working at the intersection of materiality and computing.

https://stuhmerscholz.de/betalight

CMD: Experiment in Bio Algorithmic Politics

Michael Sedbon

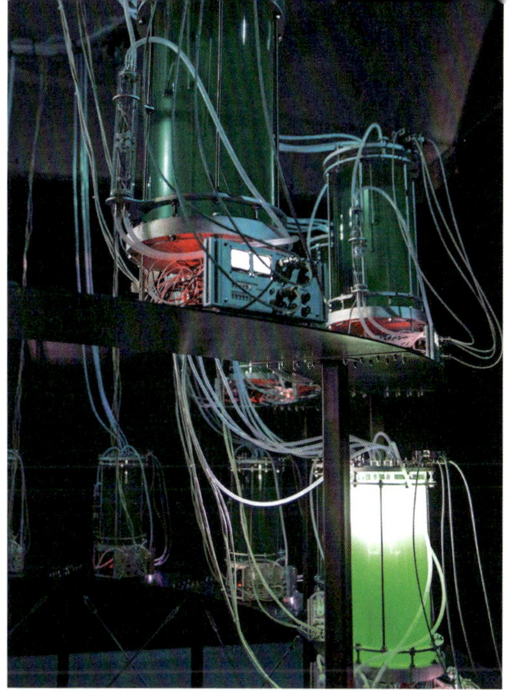

In this installation, two artificial ecosystems are sharing a light source. Access to this light source is granted through a market. Each colony of photosynthetic bacteria can claim access to light thanks to credits earned for their oxygen production. The rules driving the market are optimized through a genetic algorithm. This artificial intelligence is testing different populations of financial systems on these 2 sets of cyanobacteria. The photosynthetic cells and the computer are experimenting with different political systems granting access to this resource, allowing the system to oscillate between collaboration and competition. The genetic algorithm governing the installation pictures the rules of these proto-societies as genes. By breeding populations of societies, new generations of markets arise.

This experimental setup incarnates the need for embracing evolutionary design paradigms for machines and systems while looking at scales going from micro-transistors to planet-size computation, asking how the designs of infrastructures that allow our technologies and ecosystems to interact produce narratives around the concentration of resources and power.

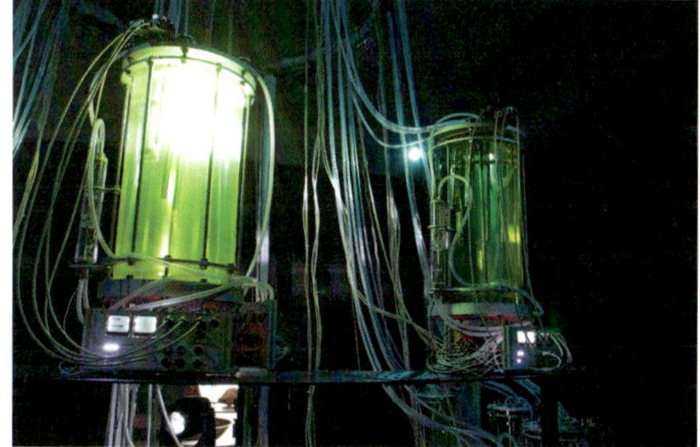

Concept and production: Michael Sedbon
Collaborators: Bio-physics of Photosynthesis and Photosynthesis & Hybrid Forms Lab, Vrije Universiteit Amsterdam; Raoul Frese (VU); MU Hybrid Art House
Technical Support: Sandrine D'Haene, Manu Alfonso Soler; Alexander Lambertz, Mees Dieperink
This project has been produced as part of the Bio Arts and Design Award 2019

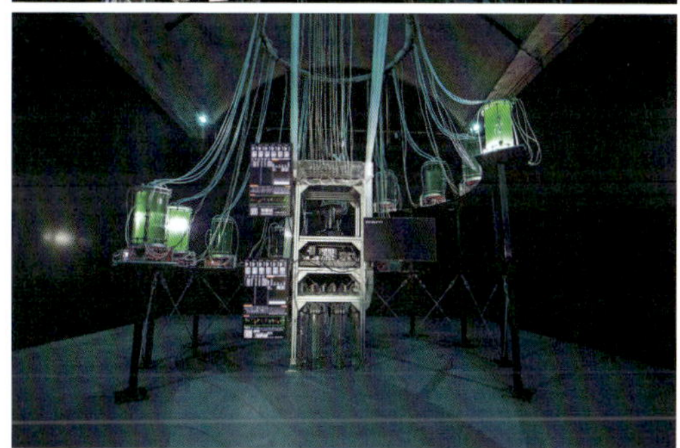

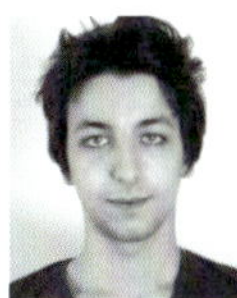

Michael Sedbon's (FR) work explores networked technologies and systems through their convergence with non-human intelligence (plants, bacteria, etc...) in regard to the Infocene problematics, seen as our current cultural era where Information is the force with the greatest impact on human societies and environments. He has built up a practice-based art and design studio enhanced by collaborations with life-science and computing research institutes. He designs and builds biological computers that behave as thought experiments and aim to question technological and scientific cultures.

https://michaelsedbon.com/CMD

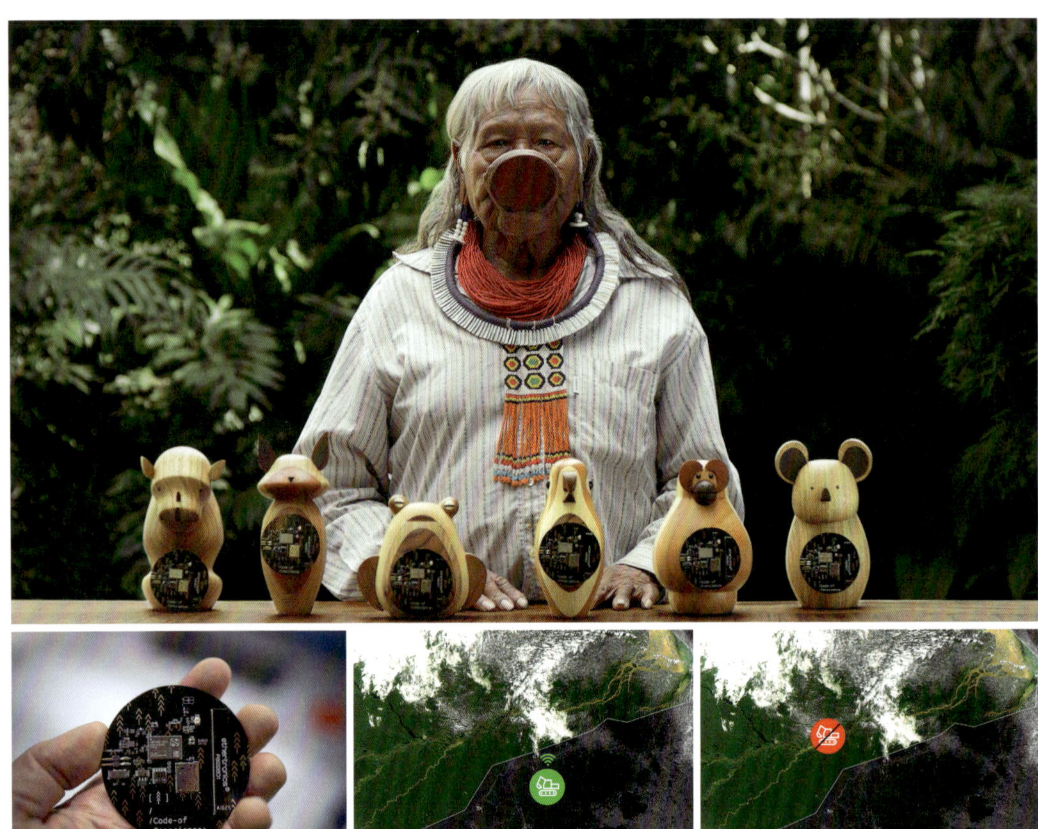

Code of Conscience

Code of Conscience

The *Code of Conscience* is open source software that restricts the use of heavy-duty vehicles in protected land areas. The code uses open source mapping data from the United Nations' World Database on Protected Areas in conjunction with on-vehicle GPS tracking technology to autonomously restrict deforestation crews from entering protected zones. A small, low-cost chip has been developed to equip the code into older, non-GPS models. The software is available for free on *CodeofConscience.org*.

An invitation comprising the *Code of Conscience* chip embedded in a wooden sculpture of an endangered animal was sent to the CEOs of the world's top ten construction equipment manufacturers, urging them to adopt the code for all new machines leaving their factories.

Team:
AKQA: Tim Devine, Hugo Veiga, Pedro Araújo, Daniel Kalil, Adam Grant
Tekt Industries: Matthew Adams

Launched in the second half of 2019 the **Code of Conscience** is a collective of designers, engineers, industrial, and governmental partners, led by Tim Devine, Hugo Vega, and Adam Grant.

https://www.codeofconscience.org

Compression Cradle

Lucy McRae

Compression Cradle envisages a future world where mechanical touch is an antidote for today's "forever connectedness." As people increasingly handle devices more than human flesh, we create opportunities for technology to vie for our affections. How will art, design, and business cater to society's evolving physical and emotional needs? *Compression Cradle* is a machine that affectionately squeezes the body with a sequence of aerated volumes. Through a choreography of touch sensations, this mechanism assists in altering the expression of oxytocin—the hormone released in the brain, responsible for building trust and pair bonding. This immersive artwork is a playful and mechanical antidote to the lack of human touch that will become more extreme in the future. We have gained critical insight into the calming effect *Compression Cradle's* mechanical touch has on autistic people, and research continues on the future of touch, empathy, and the human condition. *Compression Cradle,* like all of Lucy McRae's projects, is deeply committed to a single objective: the preservation of humanity.

Co-commission by Het Nieuwe Instituut and Museum of Applied Arts & Sciences
Artist: Lucy McRae
Creative producer: Alice Parker
Machine fabrication: Machine Histories
Custom soft goods: Anjia Jalac
Studio team: Minah Kim, Fiona Ng & Brendan Ho
Co-curators: Francien Van Westrenen, Angela Rui, Marina Otero, Keinton Butler
Photography: Scottie Cameron, Daria Scagliola
Special thanks to: Keinton Butler, Guus Beumer, Mark Van Veen, Ellen Zoete, Angela Rui, Steven Joyner & Jason Pilarski

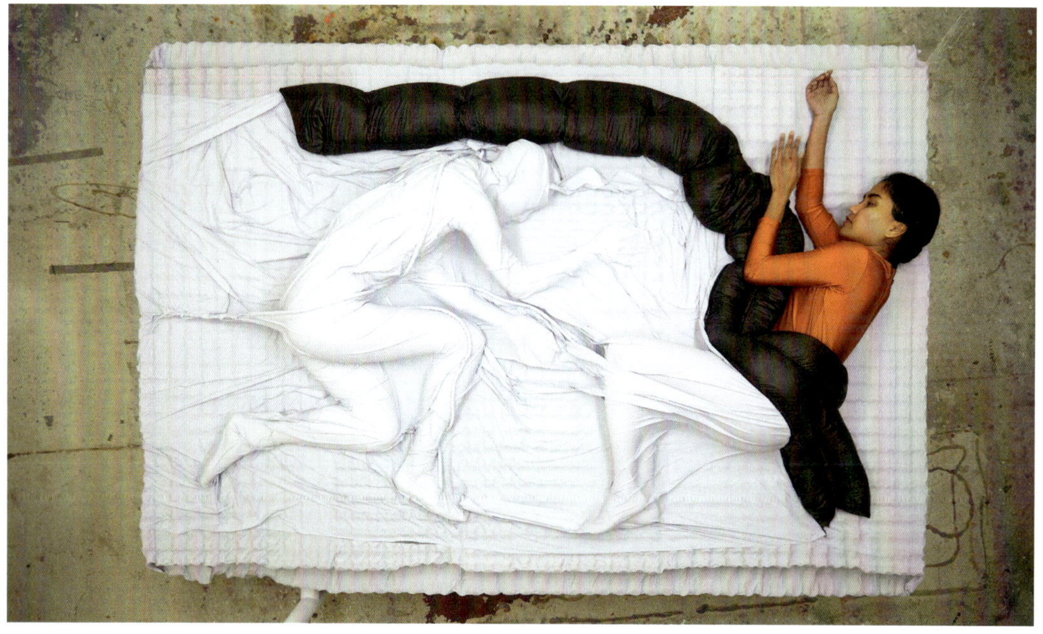

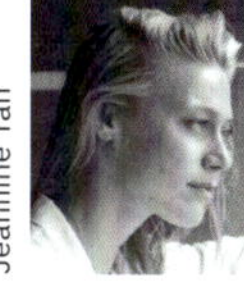

Lucy McRae

Lucy McRae (GB) is a science fiction artist, filmmaker, inventor, and body architect, who works across installation, film, photography, artificial intelligence, and edible technology. Her work speculates on the future of human existence, exploring the limits of the body, beauty, biotechnology, and the self as well as the cultural and emotional impacts science and technology have on redesigning the body. Lucy has exhibited internationally at museums, film festivals, MIT, Ars Electronica, NASA, and science forums and is recognized as a Young Global Leader by the World Economic Forum.

https://www.lucymcrae.net/compression-cradle

CONTAIN / Open Cell
Mobile COVID-19 Emergency Testing Facilities
Open Cell + worldwide contributors

CONTAIN is a decentralized and open-source approach for testing COVID-19. OpenCell has developed mobile COVID-19 testing labs that can be placed at any location needed. Each container is equipped with 5 liquid handling robots and 2 qPCR machines and can provide results in as little as 5 hours. A single lab can be run by a single operator and can process 2,400 tests a day.

The testing involves a procedure called reverse transcription-quantitative polymerase chain reaction (RT-qPCR). In short, it involves extracting viral RNA from a sample and amplifying it to a measurable level so that it is possible to see whether a person is infected with COVID-19. What differentiates OpenCell's labs is the automated RNA extraction protocol using a magnetic-bead method which insulates OpenCell from some of the global demand on RNA extraction kits. Another main benefit of OpenCell's project is that it is open-source. Over 150 volunteers worldwide contributed towards the challenges involved in developing testing capacity. The blueprints and protocols are available to everyone in form of a living document allowing people across the world to contribute and reproduce the project.

OpenCell London + worldwide contributors: Helene Steiner, Kenneth T. Walker, Matthew Donora, Thomas Meany, Anthony Thomas, Manoj Nathwani, Alexander James Philips, Krishma Ramgoolam, Kjara S Pilch, Phil Oberacker, Tomasz Piotr Jurkowski, Rares Marius Gosman, Aubin Fleiss, Alex Perkins, Neil MacKenzie, Davide Danovi

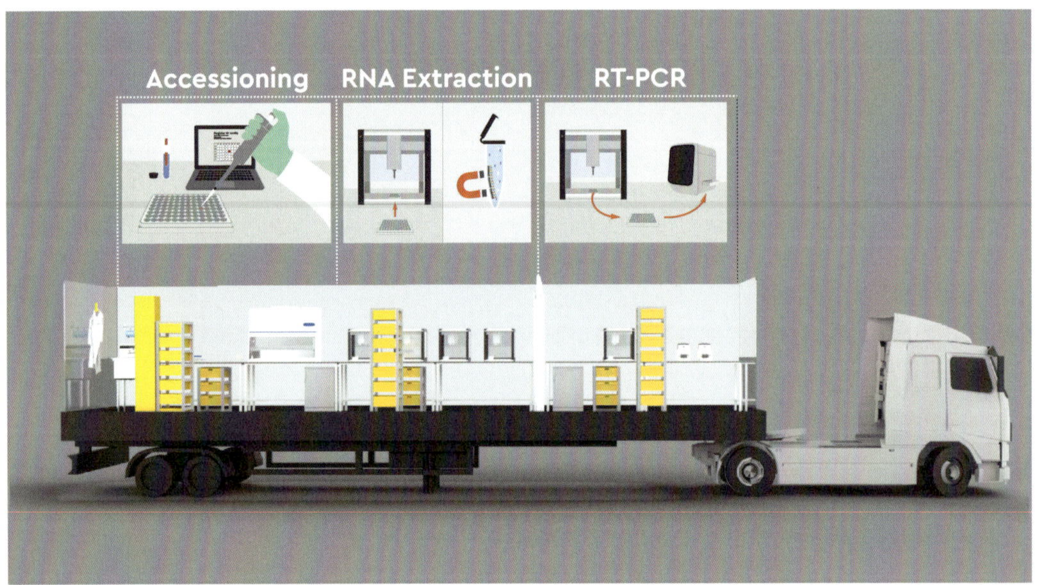

Open Cell (UK) is a lab space consisting of 70 shipping containers in London. OpenCell was founded in June 2018 to provide early-stage biotech startups with affordable lab-space. Laboratories here work on synthetic biology, CRISPR, DNA sequencing, therapeutics, biologics, hardware, bioelectronics, software, biomaterials, bioplastics, and more.

opencell.bio/coronavirus

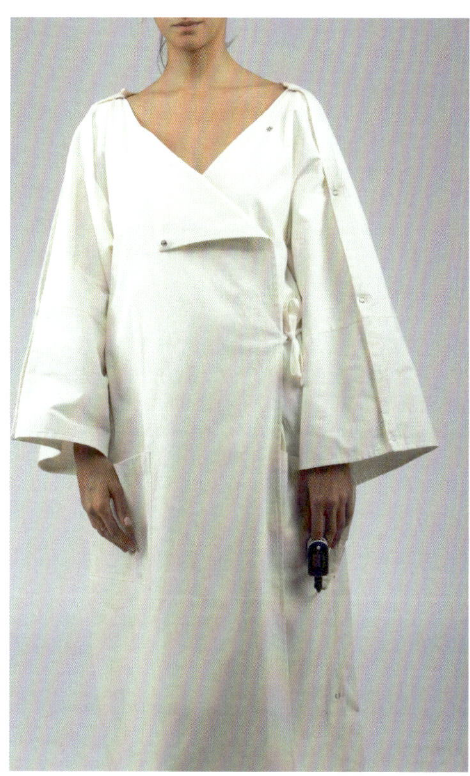
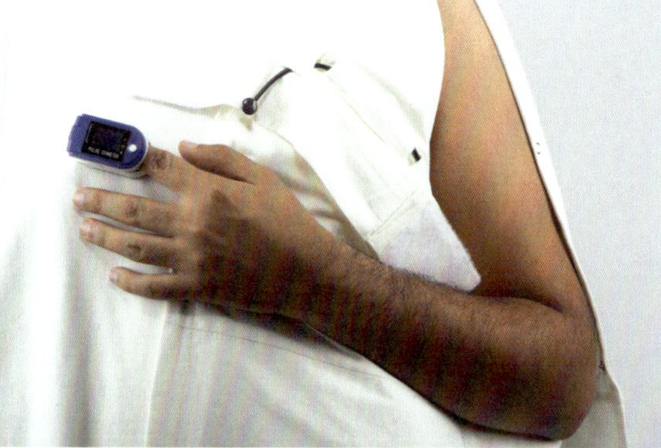
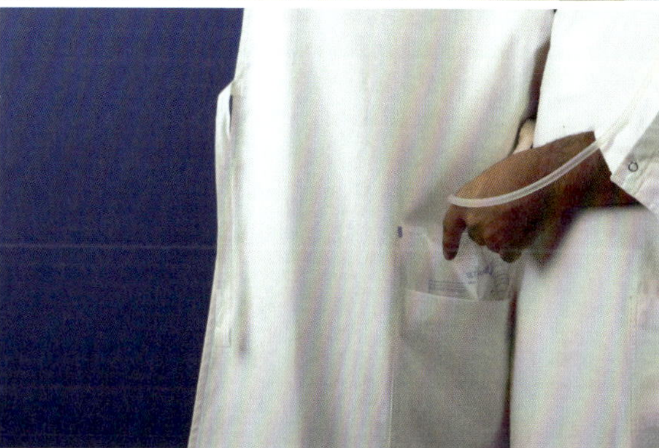

Hale: An Upgrade on Patient Attire

Mariam Ibrahim

Hale: An Upgrade on Patient Attire aims to create a conversation around the potential development of the hospital gown and to predict, using simple solutions, what could potentially become the future of the patient gown. It features a series of garments designed to improve a patient's sense of wellbeing during their hospital stay whilst being supremely functional, allowing easy handling by both patient and doctor, while adhering to strict sanitation requirements. The first is a disposable gown, for use before, during, and immediately after surgery. The second is a launderable gown for stable patients, and the third is a sensor gown, which unobtrusively tracks the patient's blood oxygen level, body temperature, position, and pulse. This information is then relayed on to a web app every 10 to 30 seconds as opposed to the manual monitoring that is exercised in hospitals—taken every 12 hours on average—leaving a gap of unmonitored time in a patient's stay. Thus, using simple devices, it relieves the burden of both societal and diagnostic problems, including restrictive hospital sensors and round-the-clock health surveillance, leading to rapid and more informed diagnoses.

Supervised by Ghalia El-Srakbi
Programming consultant: Mina Habib Hanna

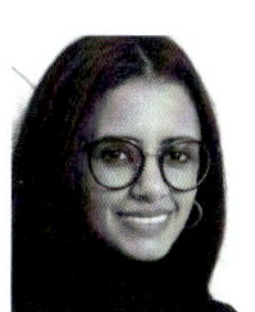

Mariam Ibrahim (1996, Cairo, EG) is based in Cairo since 2015 and completed a Bachelor of Arts in Graphic Design with a minor in Arab & Islamic Civilizations at the American University in Cairo (2019). Mariam is a multi-disciplinary context-driven designer who combines empathy with evidence-based innovation to create experiences that are impactful, scalable, and contextually relevant. Her general focus is design for social impact in relation with aspects of identity, culture, and gender.

https://mariamibrahim.com/hale-an-upgrade-on-patient-attire

Hybrid Living Materials
The Mediated Matter Group

Hybrid Living Materials (HLMs) point to an exciting future for designers at the intersection of biology and technology—the grown and the made—to deliver products that are customized to a particular shape, as well as a specific material, chemical, and even genetic make-up. The HLM platform incorporates engineerable cells into structural materials to bequeath them with unique biological and responsive properties. We interface a digital design platform with engineered bacteria to achieve programmable control of gene expression across the surface of 3D printed objects. We use this technology to create brilliant color and fluorescence patterns on wearable scale objects. With the ability to plan gene expression and 3D geometry in a CAD environment, researchers and designers alike can program biological function into physical objects. HLMs, extended to patterning drugs to medical devices or useful enzymes to building skins, can make a future tailored to both body and environment. This work is published in *Advanced Functional Materials (https://doi.org/10.1002/adfm.201907401)* and has been featured in the London Design Museum, National Gallery of Victoria, and The Museum of Modern Art NY.

Team: Rachel Soo Hoo Smith, Christoph Bader, Sunanda Sharma, Dominik Kolb, Tzu-Chieh Tang, Ahmed Hosny, Felix Moser, James C. Weaver, Christopher A. Voigt, and Prof. Neri Oxman.

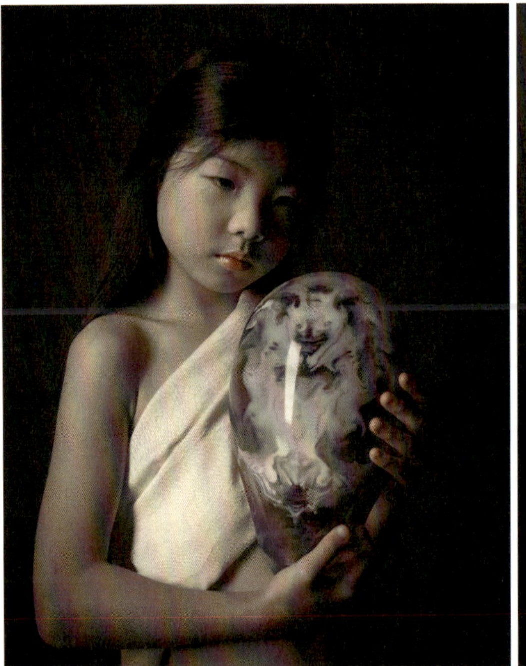
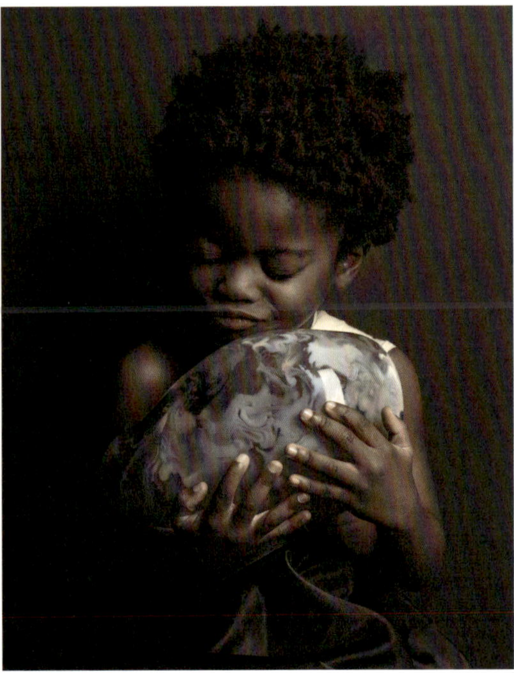

The Mediated Matter Group focuses on Nature-inspired Design and Design-inspired Nature. Our research area, Material Ecology, integrates computational form-finding strategies with biologically inspired fabrication tools and technologies. Our research lies at the intersection of computer science, material engineering, and synthetic biology. We apply ourselves to design across scales with the objective to enhance the relation between natural and man-made environments. We strive to rethink the future of designs that interface the body, the building, and ecology in the bio-digital age.

https://www.media.mit.edu/projects/hybrid-living-materials/overview

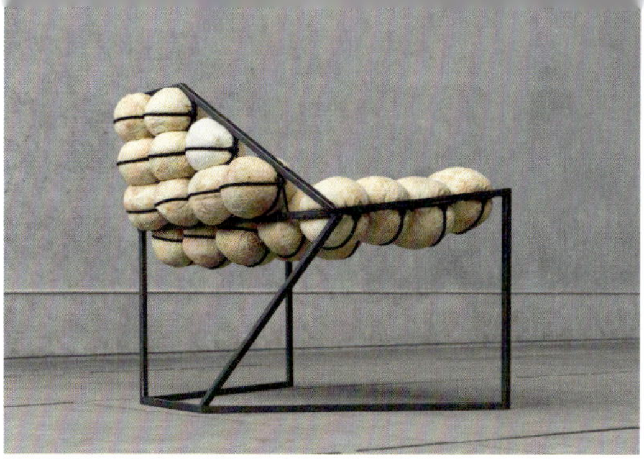

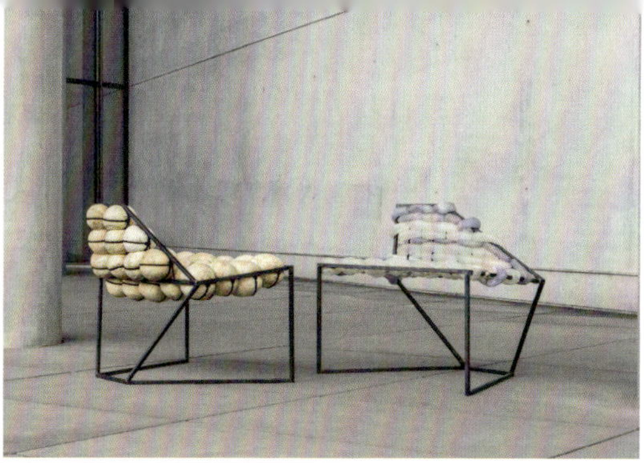

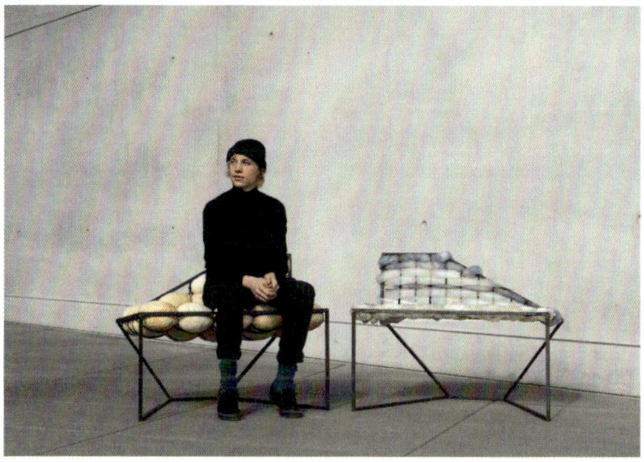

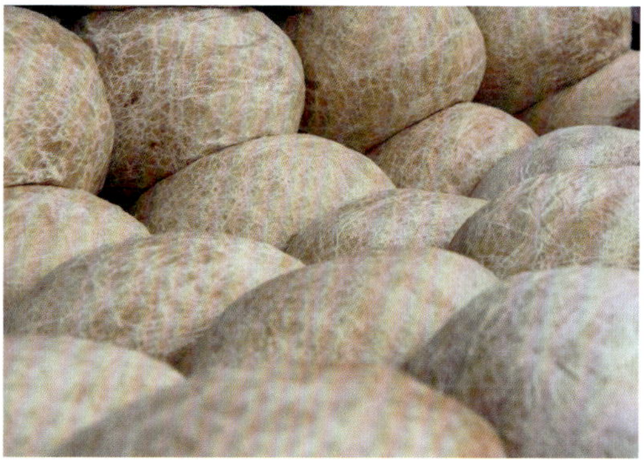

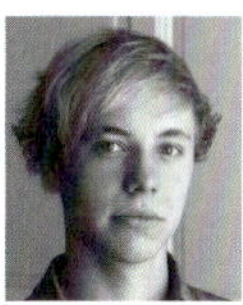

INNER VALUES

Tobias Trübenbacher

Due to livestock farming and industrial food production, the prices for animal products have decreased enormously in the recent past. While just some decades ago farm animals were highly valued and most of their resources were further processed, in present times only the tastiest and easiest to prepare parts of an animal are actually used. Today more than half of an animal goes directly to animal rendering plants after slaughter and thus more or less instantly to the garbage can. Since we never get in contact with the slaughter process, we started to be disgusted by the "by-products" of animals. But are they really nothing more than waste? Is our rejective attitude towards these materials justified and legitimate?

Or shouldn't we, if we really need to kill animals, at least appreciate all of their resources instead? These questions led to the *INNER VALUES* project—seating furniture made of tanned and further processed cattle intestines and pigs' bladders, transformed into soft leather. The chairs boost the former poor reputation of the supposed waste products and infuse it with opposite values. They reveal the true value and unique beauty of these materials.

Design, concept: Tobias Trübenbacher
Video, pictures: Tobias Trübenbacher, Nikolai Marcinowski
With support from: University of Applied Sciences Munich, Prof. Ralph Ammer

Tobias Trübenbacher (DE) is a Berlin-based product designer. After graduating from school, Tobias started studying product design at the University of Applied Sciences in Munich, followed by an internship at Atelier Steffen Kehrle studio. Later Tobias moved to Berlin to continue his studies at the University of the Arts, where he is currently working in the Design and Social Context department of Prof. Ineke Hans. Besides studying, Tobias is presently working for Studio Mark Braun. For three years he has held the *Studienstiftung des deutschen Volkes* scholarship.

http://tobiastruebenbacher.com/ux-portfolio/inner_values

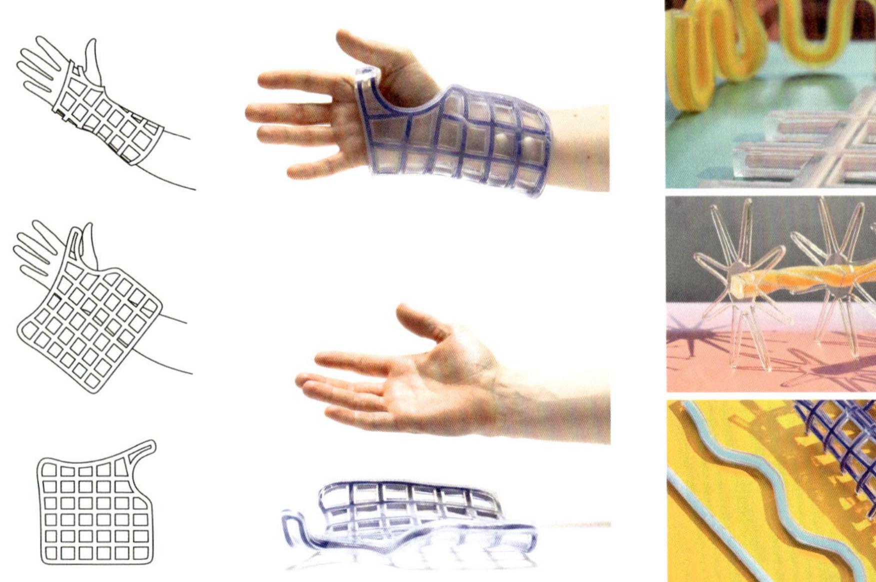

Re:flex

Pierre Azalbert, Benton Ching, Karlijn Sibbel

Re:flex is the result of experiment-driven, multidisciplinary research around materials that can respond to physical stimuli. It draws inspiration from natural organisms which can adapt to changes in their environment by adjusting themselves naturally to new circumstances. By contrast, man-made designs, buildings, and materials are often static and hence incapable of adapting to rapidly changing conditions. *Re:flex* is a novel material which can move and transform in response to heat. It can be deformed into a temporary shape when heated, and frozen in place through cooling down. When heated again, *Re:flex* remembers and returns again to its original shape. This can be easily done with warm water or hot air using common household appliances. As a cross-disciplinary team, we explore the field that lies in-between scientific research and everyday applications of transformative matter. Through material research and design-led experimentation, we craft objects that can twist, bend, twirl, and remember. Using *Re:flex* we develop designs for reusability, adaptability, and body-fitting, the creation of motion, and many other capabilities.

Special thanks to James Fraser who was instrumental in the initial development of *Re:flex*.
Thanks to Imperial College London and the Royal College of Art and thanks to the Dutch Design Foundation and Material Driven for their ongoing support and help in promoting our project.

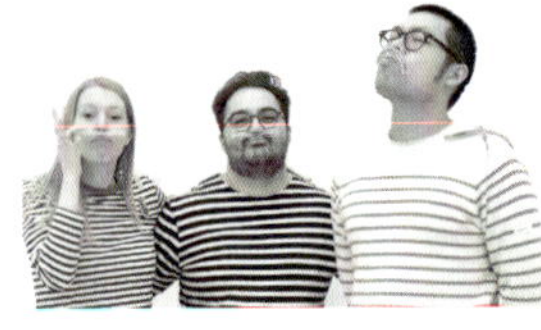

Pierre Azalbert, Benton Ching, Karlijn Sibbel (Multinational) form a multidisciplinary team with a passion for bridging the gap between scientific research and everyday life. They met while taking part in the Innovation Design Engineering masters at the Royal College of Art and Imperial College London. At the heart of their practice is an ethos of accessibility—translating the arcane into the understandable. Their work encompasses the fields of new material development, technological reinterpretation, and immersive experience.

https://www.materialreflex.com

Re³ Glass

Faidra Oikonomopoulou, Telesilla Bristogianni

The *Re³ Glass* project introduces a novel, reversible building system comprising dry-assembled, interlocking cast components out of waste glass. Despite the common notion that glass is 100% recyclable, the majority of everyday discarded glass objects are neither reused nor recycled due to recipe mismatching or contamination. Therefore, *Re³ Glass* explores the redirection of discarded glasses, from Pyrex® trays and artware to mobile phone and computer screens, from the landfill to the building sector. Cavities and notches are introduced to the design, to achieve lightweight yet strong components. Interlocking shapes allow for easy assembly and disassembly, and favor reuse and recyclability. Experiments at the TU Delft Glass Lab with different glass compositions, cooling techniques, and geometries have resulted in a wide range of clear, colored, translucent opaque or marbled glass elements that can be used to form circular, robust, and aesthetically intriguing cast glass structures. In this manner, the project explores the great potential of cast waste glass in the architectural realm, escaping the prevailing two-dimensional and transparent character of the material in the built environment.

Project initiators: Faidra Oikonomopoulou and Telesilla Bristogianni for Delft University of Technology

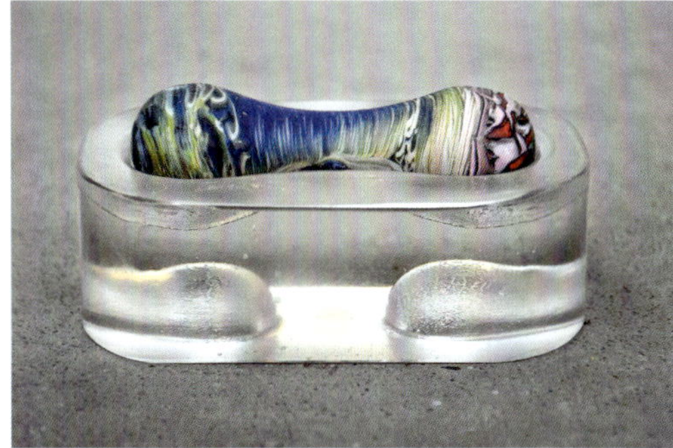

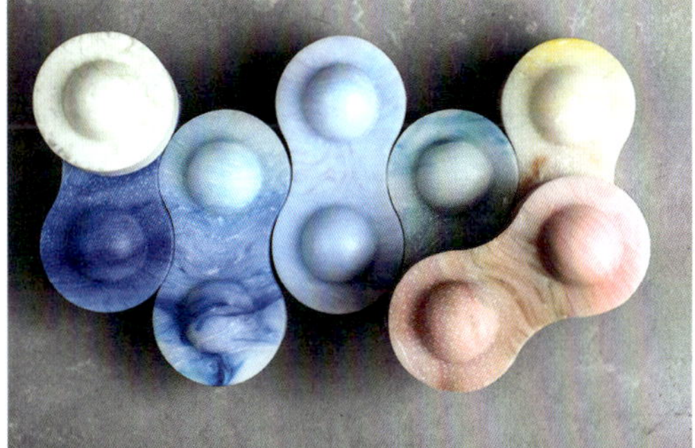

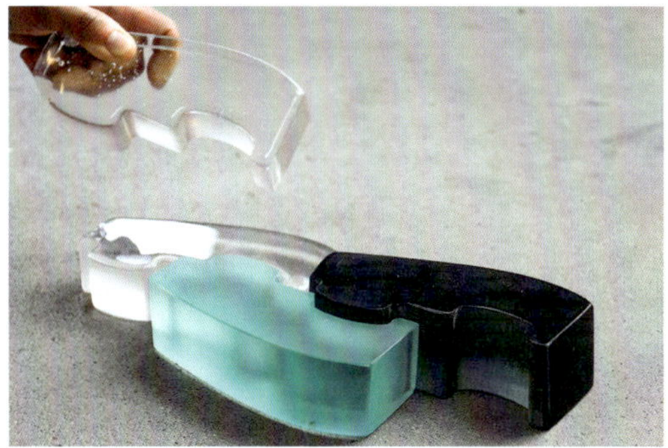

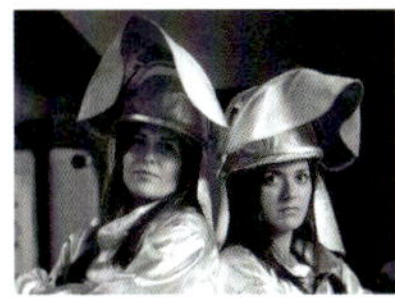

Dr. Faidra Oikonomopoulou (GR) & **Telesilla Bristogianni** (GR), both Architect Engineers (NTUA) and Building Technologists (TU Delft), joined TU Delft in 2014 as researchers focusing on structural applications of cast glass. They were deeply involved in the research and development of the Crystal Houses façade (NL), for which they received multiple awards. Through this project they discovered the architectural potential of cast glass and the involved engineering challenges. This is when they conceived the *Re³ Glass*—a project nominated for the New Material Award 2018 and exhibited at prestigious design exhibitions.

https://www.tudelft.nl/bk/over-faculteit/afdelingen/architectural-engineering-and-technology/organisatie/leerstoelen/structural-design-mechanics/glass-transparency-research-group/research-topics/re3-glass/

Sounding Soil

Marcus Maeder

Sounding Soil began when Marcus Maeder one day, out of sheer curiosity, stuck a self-developed, highly sensitive needle microphone into the ground on an alpine pasture in the Valais/Switzerland. What could be heard was an extremely complex and strange soundscape: sounds of soil animals, roots, and water moving through the pores of the soil. Beyond that, the animals in the darkness of the ground seemed to communicate with each other clearly acoustically. But who is communicating why and how? This led to a research and art project, where six partners and institutions are now working together in an interdisciplinary way. Various works of art have been developed, some of which are participatory in nature: On the one hand, there is the *Sounding Soil* container, which has been on tour since last year. It not only contains recordings of different soils all over Switzerland (including a generative music composition), but also the best recordings of the participants of a Citizen Science project. Brand new is the work *Edaphon Braggio,* which makes it possible to experience the acoustic topography in the soil of a mountain community in the south of Switzerland.

Sounding Soil is carried out as a cooperation between the Zurich University of the Arts (ZHdK)/the Institute for Computer Music and Sound Technology, the Swiss Federal Institute for Forest, Snow and Landscape Research (WSL), the Swiss Soil Monitoring Network (NABO), the Institute for Terrestrial Ecosystems as well as the USYS Transdisciplinary Lab at the Swiss Federal Institute of Technology (ETH) in Zurich, the Research Institute of Organic Agriculture (FiBL) and Biovision Foundation for Ecological Development.
Project Team:
Forest entomology: Martin Gossner, WSL
Project coordinator: Sabine Lerch, Biovision
Artist and principal investigator: Marcus Maeder, ZHdK/ICST
Modelling & monitoring: Michael Müller, NABO/Agroscope
Programming: Ken Gubler, ZHdK
Micro-Engineering: Sébastien Schiesser, ZHdK/ICST
Entomological lab: Doris Schneider Mathys, WSL
Scientific supervision: Michael Stauffacher, ETH –USYS TdLab; Rainer Schulin, ETH – Institute for Terrestrial Ecosystems

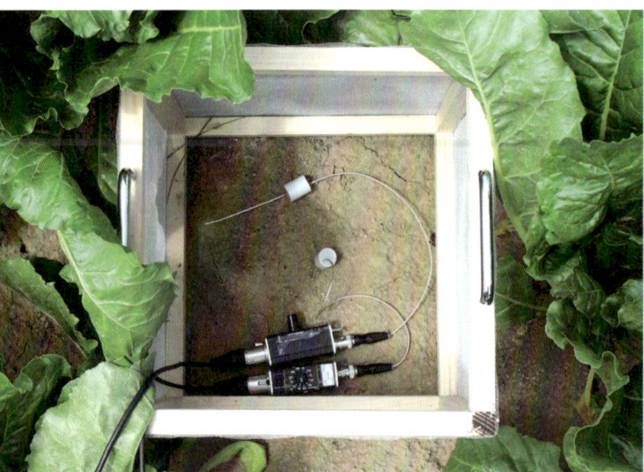

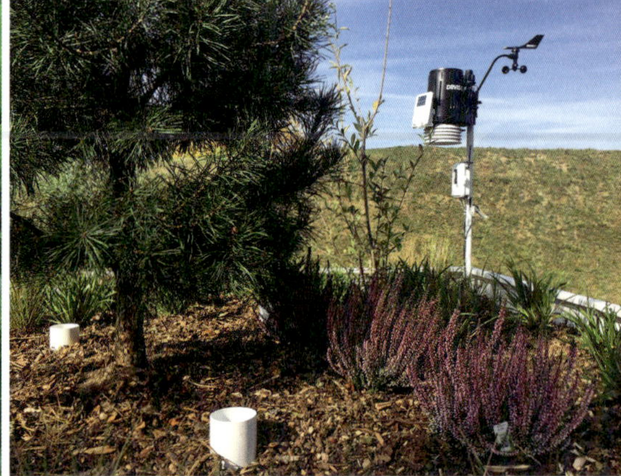

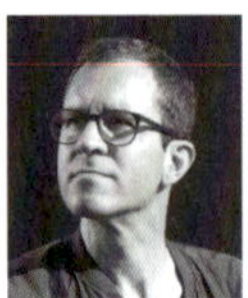

Marcus Maeder (CH) is a sound artist, researcher, and composer of electronic music. Maeder works as a research associate at the Institute for Computer Music and Sound Technology ICST of the Zurich University of the Arts ZHdK. At the ICST, he researches in the fields of data sonification and acoustic ecology. He is particularly interested in the artistic experience of normally imperceptible phenomena in nature, especially processes related to environmental problems and climate change. Maeder's and Roman Zweifel's installation *treelab* was shown at the UN Climate Conference COP 21 in Paris in 2015 at the invitation of the French president François Hollande.

http://www.soundingsoil.ch

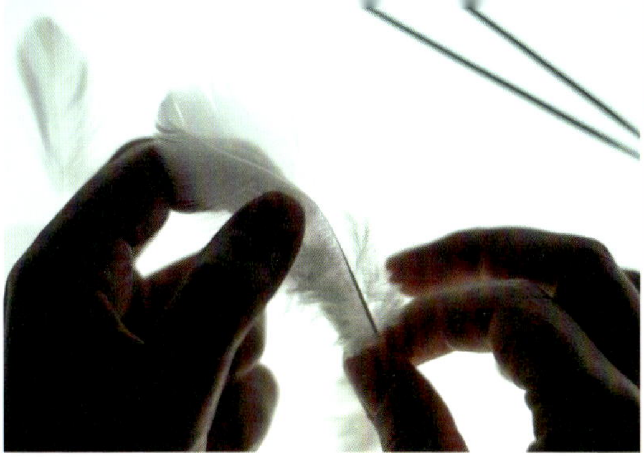

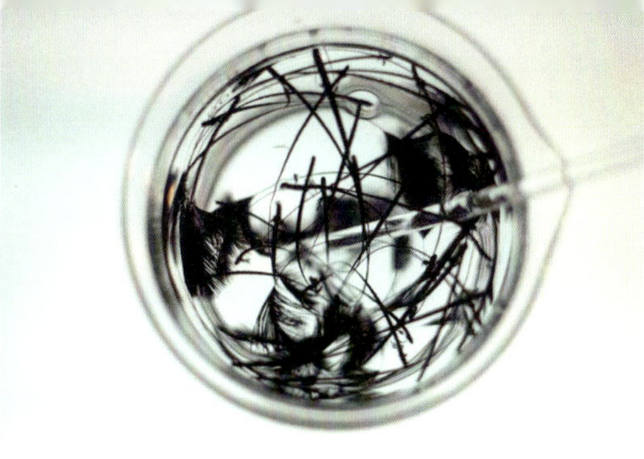

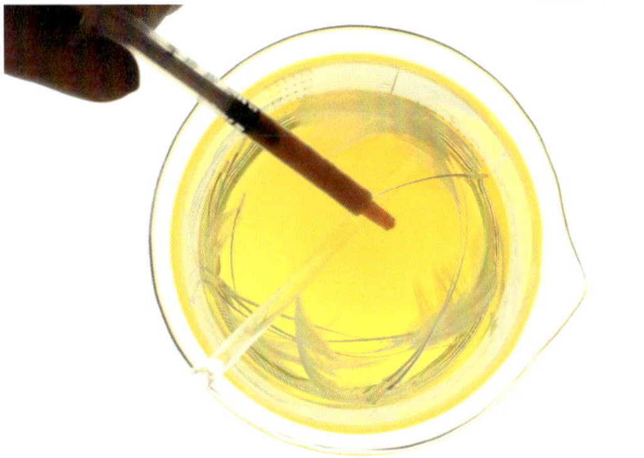

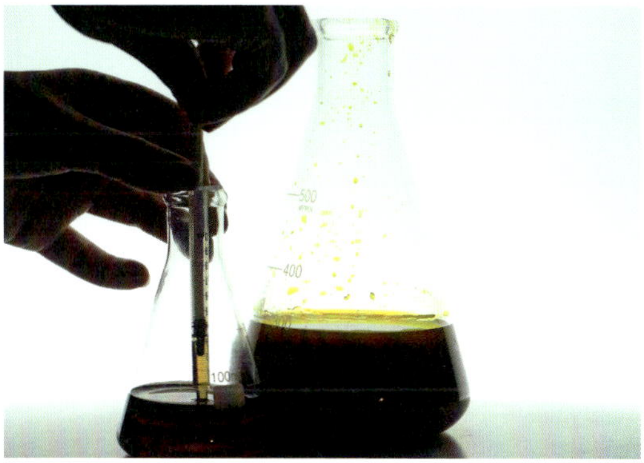

Stymphalian Birds

Audrey Briot

Stymphalian Birds is an art installation in which complex haptic interactions with feathers are sonified in acoustic soundscapes. The project explores the aesthetics and the societal impacts of a hybrid textile at the crossroads of electronics and haute couture. The textile combines traditional handcrafts with digital technologies, chemical processes, and elements created by nature. These four different approaches seamlessly connect traditional featherwork and Lunéville embroidery with state-of-the-art fabrication methods from materials science, which make the feathers electrically conductive and interactive. The combination of electronic circuits and physical transformation of the feathers to give them electrical conductivity will now permit these flexible sensors crafted by nature to detect touch and respond to it by sound.

Stymphalian Birds invites us to reconsider interactions of living beings with their environment, introducing the immediate periphery of the body as an interface. The intention of the project is to demonstrate the ability of cyber organisms to be sentient beings communicating across boundaries.

Materials science advisors: Ana C. Baptista and Cédric Honnet
HCI advisor: Paul Strohmeier
Video and sound edited by Martin Bady

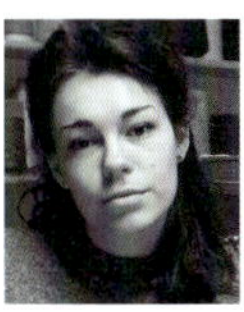

Audrey Briot (FR) is a textile designer, technologist, and researcher. She is cofounder of DataPaulette, a collective and hackerspace dedicated to research in textiles technologies and soft materials. Her work is dedicated to the positive impact of emerging technologies on the preservation of savoir-faire, especially in textiles. She is focusing on non-verbal communication transmitted by textiles, which represent for her an entire culture and even a substitute of writing. In order to do so she relies on anthropological research going back to the Paleolithic. Following this direction she connects machines and computers to make textiles that are memory vectors with added data and interactivity.

https://audreybriot.fr/stymphalian-birds

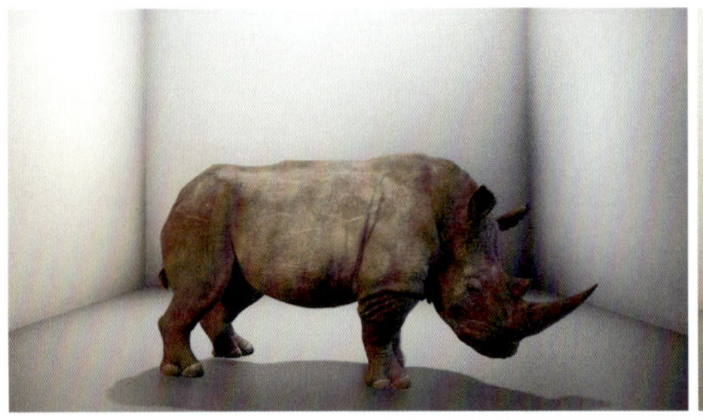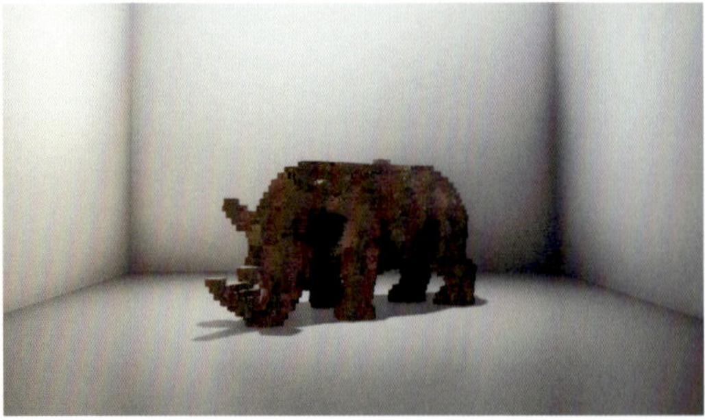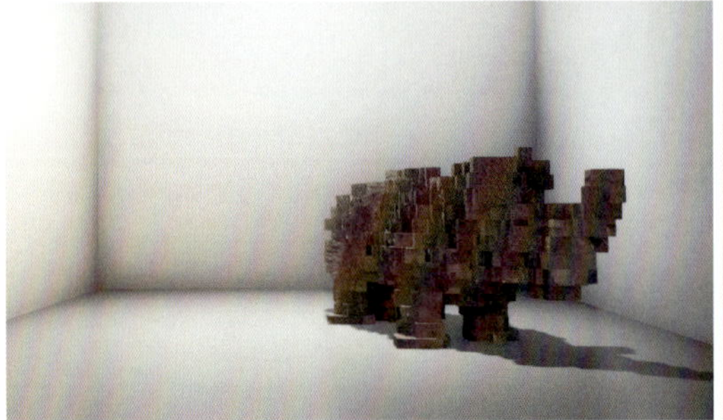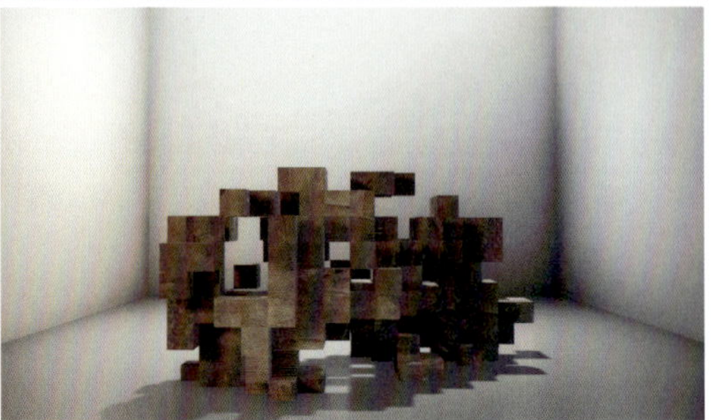

The Substitute

Alexandra Daisy Ginsberg

On March 20, 2018, headlines announced the death of Sudan, the last male northern white rhinoceros *(Ceratotherium simum cottoni)*. We briefly mourned a subspecies lost to the human desire for the imagined life-enhancing properties of its horn, comforted that it might be brought back using biotechnology, albeit gestated by a different subspecies. But would humans protect a resurrected rhino, having decimated an entire species? And would this new rhino be real?

The Substitute explores a paradox: our preoccupation with creating new life forms, while neglecting existing ones. A northern white rhino is digitally brought back to life, informed by developments in the human creation of artificial intelligence (AI). Based on research from AI lab DeepMind, the rhino performs as an artificial agent, an autonomous entity that learns from its environment. A life-size projection, 5m wide, shows the artificial rhino roaming in a virtual world, becoming more "real" as it comprehends the limits of the space. As the artificial rhino habituates to its space, its form and sound toggle from pixelation to lifelike— reminding the viewer that this living, breathing rhino, coming to life without its natural context, is entirely artificial. The experimental data is played on a second screen, showing the path and development of the agent's navigational cells. The rhino's behaviors and sounds are adapted from rare research footage of the last herd, provided by Dr. Richard Policht. Is this rhino, coming to life divorced from its natural context, a better substitute for the real?

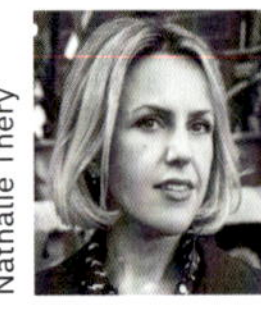

Alexandra Daisy Ginsberg (GB) is an artist examining our fraught relationships with nature and technology. Through subjects as diverse as artificial intelligence, synthetic biology, and conservation, she investigates the human impulse to "better" the world. Daisy is lead author of *Synthetic Aesthetics: Investigating Synthetic Biology's Designs on Nature* (MIT Press, 2014), and in 2017 completed *Better*, her PhD, at the Royal College of Art, interrogating how powerful dreams of "better" futures shape what we design. Daisy exhibits internationally, including at MoMA, the Museum of Contemporary Art, Tokyo, the Centre Pompidou, and the Royal Academy, and her work is in museum and private collections.

https://daisyginsberg.com/work/the-substitute, https://vimeo.com/352678068

The Net Wanderer
A tour of suspended handshakes
Cheng Guo

The Net Wanderer is a research project that explores the connection between the critical network gateways in China and the infrastructure running these gateways. Guo Cheng uses computer network diagnostic tools that track the IP addresses of these nodes as well as specific geographic locations. The project investigates how borders have been constructed to protect cyber-sovereignty, and how it can be observed.

The utopian idea of the Internet was that of a universal space for all, unbound by borders. In reality, networks are intertwined with real-world territoriality, as Guo Cheng shows by taking on the role of a tourist visiting the elusive sites hosting the network infrastructures of the Great Firewall of China (GFW). The installation lets users become virtual firewall tourists, entering websites of choice that, if blocked by the GFW, take them to a game that allows them to submit their usernames. A custom-made wall-mounted machine then engraves the names and scores along with the IP address of a GFW node, while footage on the screen shows Guo Cheng using geolocation data to track the physical location of the firewall's network gateway.

The work was originally commissioned within the Digital Earth fellowship program.

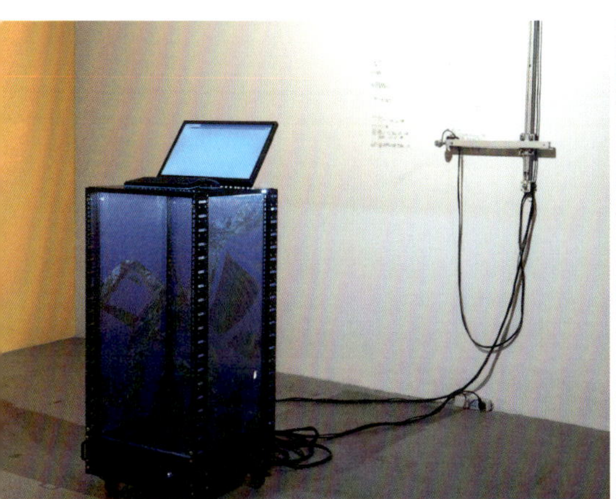

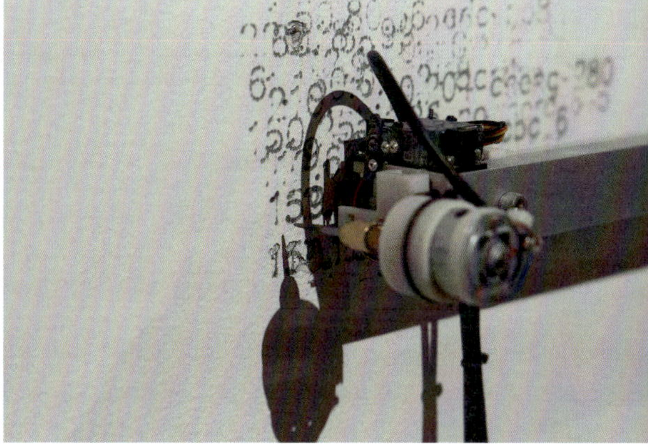

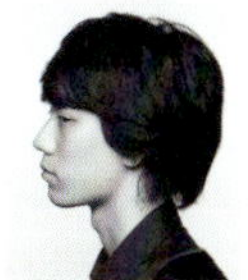

Guo Cheng (CN) is an artist currently based in Shanghai. He graduated from MA Design Products at Royal College of Art (London) and obtained his BE in Industrial Design at Tongji University (Shanghai). His practice mainly focuses on exploring the interrelation between mainstream/emerging technologies and individuals under the context of culture and social life. His recent solo show includes *Down to Earth* (Canton Gallery, Guanshou, 2019), group exhibitions include *The Eternal Network* (exhibition of Transmediale 2020) (HKW, Berlin), *Machines Are Not Alone: A Machinic Trilogy* (Chronus Art Center, Shanghai, 2018), and *The Ecstasy of Time* (HE Xiangning Art Museum, Shenzhen, 2017). He received the Digital Earth Fellowship (2018), Special Jury Prize of Huayu Youth Award (Sanya, 2018), and he was the winner of the BAD Award (The Hague, 2017).

http://www.guo-cheng.net/index.php/projects/the-net-wanderer

Topographie Digitale
DataPaulette

Topographie Digitale is an interactive installation. This landscape uses electrically functionalized and pleated textiles as sensitive surfaces reacting to touch to interact with a video-projected digital clone of this scenery.

The project is an illustration of hybridization between our scientific discovery and traditional craftsmanship as a "creole" technique, a fundamental subject of research for our collective. We have, in this case, collaborated with the pleating specialist Maison Lognon, to investigate the combination of augmenting a textile both with new electrical functionality using in-situ polymerization, as well as the new physical affordances introduced by the patterns and textures of the pleated fabric. The pleated fabric, functionalized by this chemical treatment and the electronic system give birth to a material with a mixed heritage that is both technological and traditional, a prefiguration of a potential emerging craft. The combination of crafts and technologies is an alternative to rethink the place of the digital in our society in a more resilient way.

DataPaulette: Audrey Briot, Martin De Bie, Alice Giordani, and Cédric Honnet
Visualizations: Léon Denise
Material Science: Ana C. Baptista
HCI research: Paul Strohmeier
Physical Computing: Marc Teyssier
With support from: European Research Council (ERC StG Interactive Skin 714797),
Le Signe – National Center of Graphic Design (Chaumont, France)

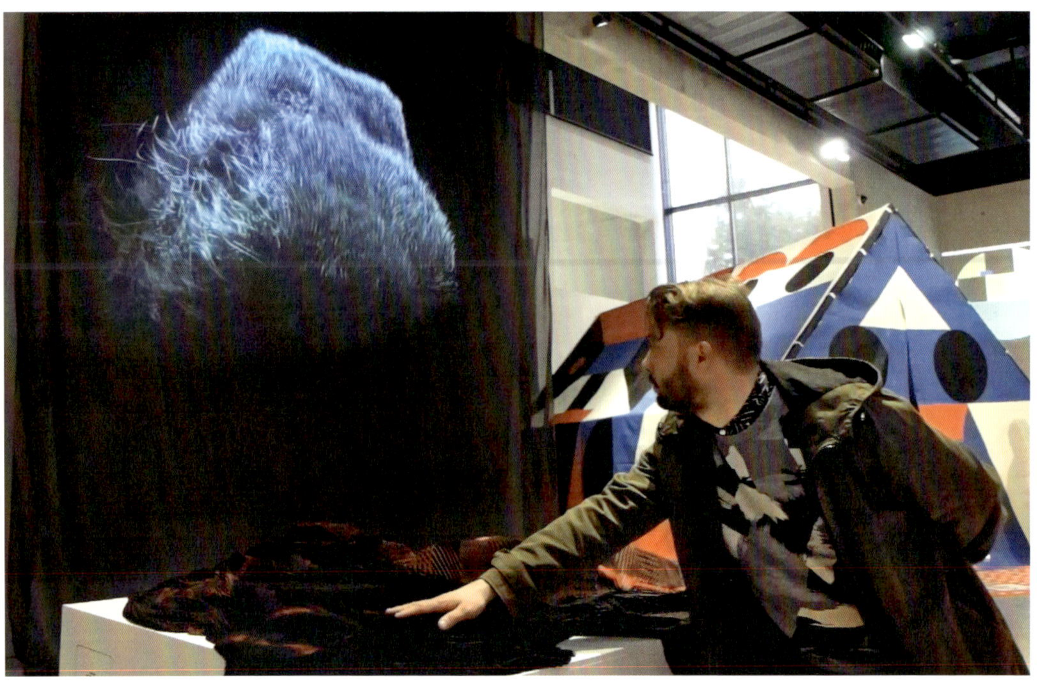

DataPaulette is a multidisciplinary collective, based in Paris, focused on research and development in textiles and digital technologies. Founded in 2014, DataPaulette has taken the form of an independent laboratory, operating as a hackerspace.

datapaulette.org/work/topographie-digitale

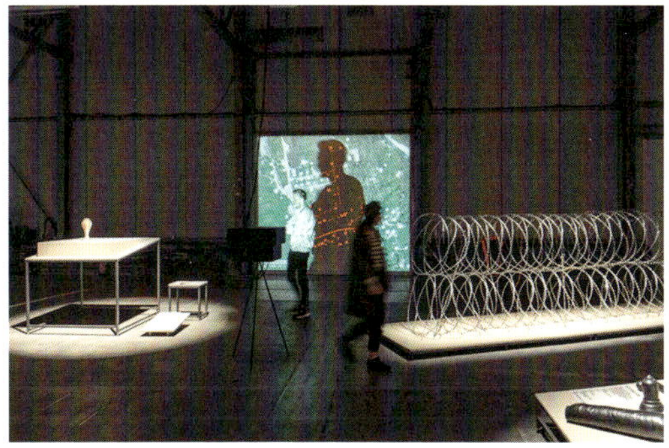

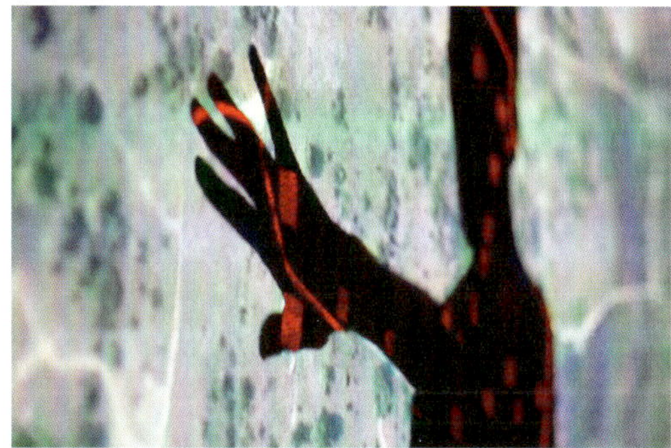

Voicing Borders

Irakli Sabekia

On the Eastern boundary of Europe, razor-wire fence stretches across Georgia. It marks territories occupied by the Russian invasion of 2008. Arbitrarily traced through the country, the line has become the cause of constant violations of human rights. Behind the fence, in an attempt to erase the traces of local communities, whole villages were burned down, demolished, and the remains completely removed from the area, leaving behind empty fields.

Voicing Borders is an installation addressing this situation. An interactive projection of the satellite images allows viewers to engage with them and, using their own shadow against the projected image, to unveil hidden information. Emerging from seemingly empty landscapes, structures and locations of the destroyed villages reveal themselves to the viewers. The second part of the project targets the very weapon of occupation—razor-wire fence. A specially designed radio transmitter

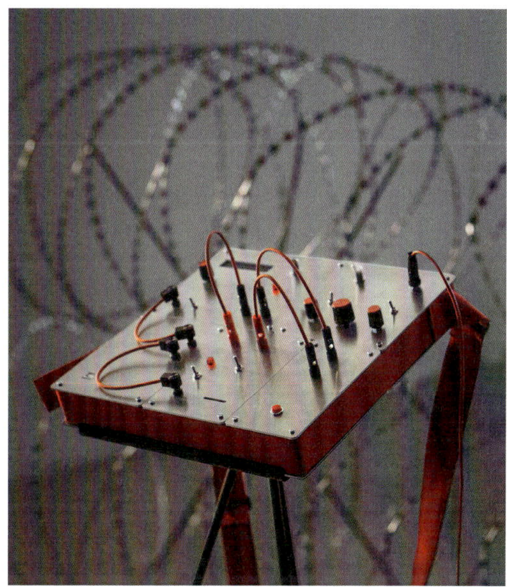

connects to the fence and transforms it into an antenna. Broadcasting through it a simple message in Morse Code, it transmits the names of the disappeared villages and their geographic coordinates, forcing the fence to voice what it's meant to hide.

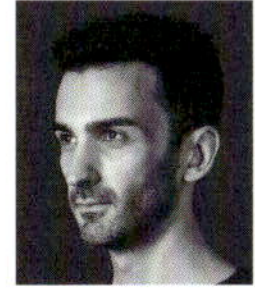

Irakli Sabekia (GE) is a Georgian designer and researcher based in the Netherlands. A recent graduate of the Design Academy Eindhoven, he has a background in sciences and visual communication. His work, frequently in the form of installations, explores the capacity of experience in creating insight. Using it as a tool to enter into a dialogue with the viewer and create a meaningful encounter, which enables not merely new knowledge but rather understanding of the issues that he addresses. By means of material, technology, and audiovisual media, he creates worlds that engage the senses but target the mind.

www.iraklisabekia.com/voicing-borders.html

S+T+ARTS PRIZE '20   JURY

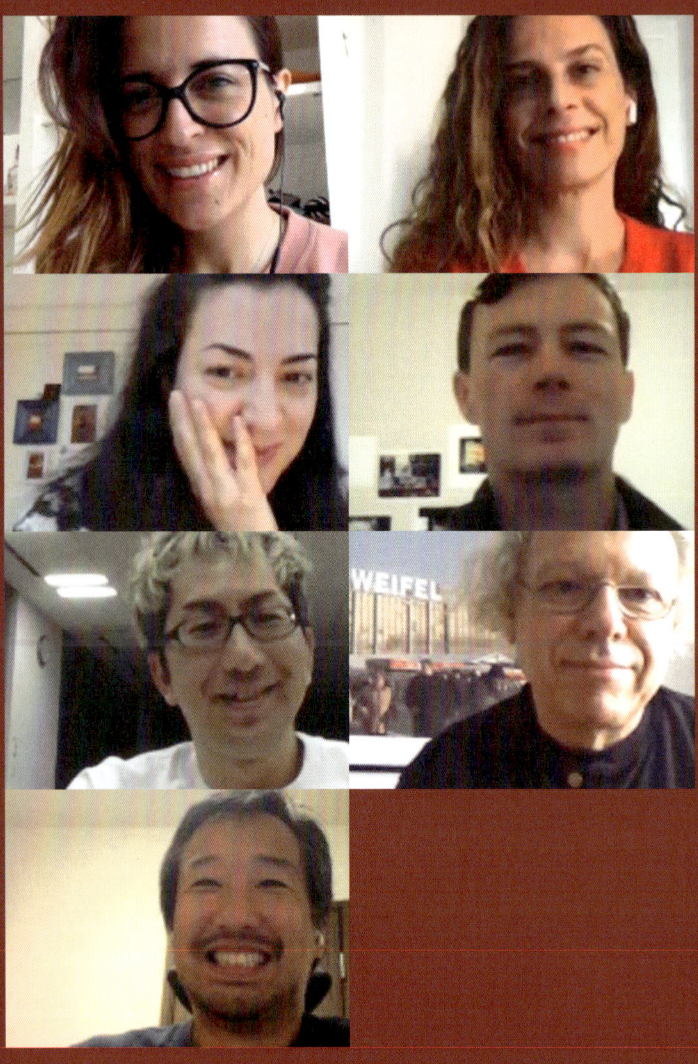

Mara Balestrini, Clara Blume, Francesca Bria, Domhnaill Hernon,
Nobu Ide, Alexander Mankowsky, Kei Shimada

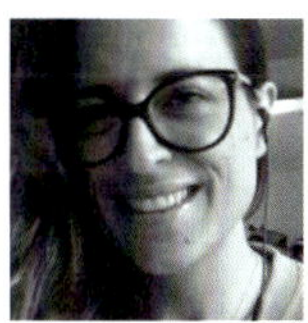

Mara Balestrini (IT) is a Human Computer Interaction (HCI) researcher and a technology strategist. She is currently CEO at the innovation agency Ideas for Change and a co-founder of SalusCoop, the first Spanish cooperative for citizens' health data. Mara's work sits at the intersection of civic technology, design, and Action Research. She has authored over 30 publications on these subjects and coordinated projects such as *Making Sense EU, Bristol Approach,* and *#Data-Futures.* Mara earned a PhD in Computer Science from the Intel Collaborative Research Institute on Sustainable Connected Cities at University College London. Her work has been awarded at ACM CHI, ACM CSCW, Ars Electronica, among others, and featured in international media such as the BBC, *The Guardian, The Financial Times* and *El País.*

Clara Blume (AT), PhD, is Deputy Director and Head of Art, Science, and Technology at Open Austria, the Austrian Consulate and innovation office in Silicon Valley. She curates and promotes artistic 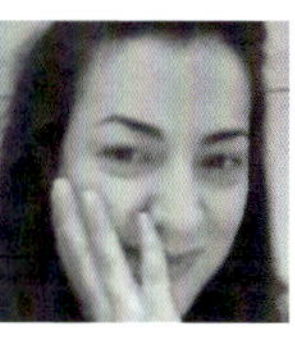 projects at the intersection of art + tech while bridging Austria with the innovation ecosystem in the SF Bay Area. Before, she worked as a professional musician, songwriter, and internationally touring recording artist. Blume has an academic background in fine arts, composition, comparative literature, cultural studies, and history. She is a regular conference speaker and a published author.

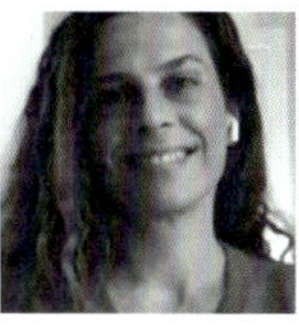

Francesca Bria (IT) is the President of the Italian National Innovation Fund and Honorary Professor at the UCL Institute for Innovation and Public Purpose in London. She is Senior Adviser to the United Nations Human Settlements Programme (UN-Habitat) on digital cities and digital rights. Francesca Bria is leading the *DECODE* project on data sovereignty in Europe and is a member of the European Commission high level expert group, Economic and Societal Impact of Research and Innovation (ESIR). Francesca has a PhD in Innovation and Entrepreneurship from Imperial College London and an MSc in Digital Economy from Birbeck, University of London. She has been teaching in several universities in the UK and Italy and she has advised governments, public, and private organizations on technology and innovation policy, and its socio-economic and environmental impact.

Domhnaill Hernon (IE) is an award-winning technology, innovation and creativity executive. Domhnaill received an undergrad degree in Aeronautical Engineering and a PhD in Aerodynamics 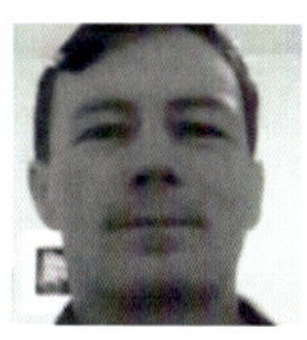 from the University of Limerick and an executive MBA from Dublin City University, Ireland. He previously led R&D organizations and developed and executed strategies to overcome the "innovation valley of death." He is Head of Experiments in Art and Technology (E.A.T.), which is a new initiative he founded to fuse art and engineering/science to develop solutions that humanize technology. Domhnaill' s work has been featured in *Wired Magazine,* Times Square, SXSW, Nasdaq, MWC and Inspirefest, to name just a few, and he advises cultural programs globally.

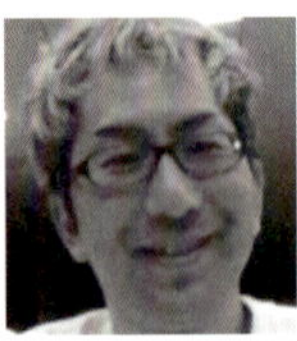 **Nobu Ide** (JP) started his career at Sharp Corporation in 1995, where he spent 18 years. He joined Wacom in 2013 as General Manager of technology marketing to reinforce Wacom's leadership position in digital pen solutions. Promoted to SVP, heading the company's Technology Solution Business Unit in 2015, and to Executive Director in 2017, Nobu drove collaborations with key industry partners across the globe. In April 2018, he assumed the role of Representative Director, President & CEO.

Alexander Mankowsky (DE), born 1957 in Berlin, studied Social Science, Philosophy and Psychology at Freie Universität Berlin. In 1989 he started working in the Daimler research institute in 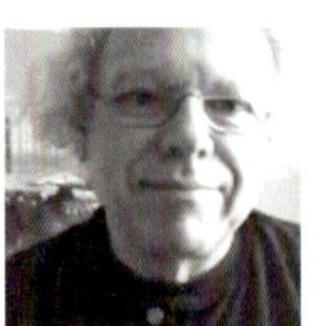 Berlin. The multidisciplinary approach in the institute integrated a wide array of disciplines, from social sciences to artificial intelligence. His current working topics are Futures Studies, focusing on the ever changing culture of mobility, the interdependency of social and technological innovation, and other aspects of envisioning paths into the future.

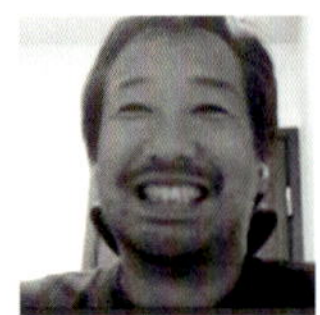 **Kei Shimada** (JP/US) is a Japanese American entrepreneur, angel investor, and currently leader of the Digital Makers Lab at IBM Japan. In his current role, he is leading a group of talented engineers in creating world first, region first, industry first innovative products and solutions through co-creation with external technology partners around the globe. He is also a consultant, advising companies on digital transformation. Kei's strength lies in identifying and solving complex problems. He holds several awards and patents in this field. His other strength lies in creative execution, most recently leading a team to produce the world's first AI classic concert at Ars Electronica in 2019. Kei is one of Japan's most active keynote speakers and has given talks and moderated panels in over 20 countries. His interests include neural technology, next-generation mobility, cooking, and teaching his son to code.

The advisors are renowned international consultants with expertise in this field. They recommend projects and encourage a wide range of potential participants to submit proposals. In addition, they ensure a balance in terms of gender and geographical origin of the participants.

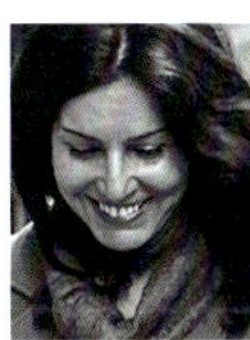

Isabel Berz (ES) is Head of IED REC, the Research and Education Center at the Istituto Europeo di Design, Spain. As fashion designer, researcher and educator, Isabel launched her own fashion label in 1990. In 2004 she was nominated Director of the Fashion School at IED Madrid, and in 2016 she founded IED REC, Research and Education Center in Madrid as an incubator of research at the intersection of Fashion, Design, Craft and Technology. IED REC creates research programs like IED CoDesign Project Las Manuelas, IED Craft Platform and is Partner of the EU COSME Worth Partnership Project and the EU Horizon 2020 Re-FREAM Project.

Amanda Masha Caminals (ES) is co-director and curator of the Mutant Institute of Environmental Narratives (IMNA), the laboratory of Matadero Madrid that fosters artistic practices in connection with 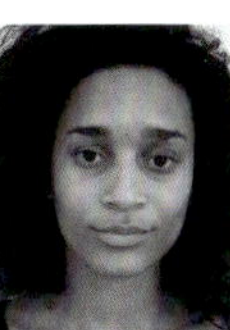 journalism, science and technology as a response to the challenges of the climate crisis. Previous to that, she directed the CITY STATION of the Environmental Health Clinic by artist Natalie Jeremijenko at the Centre for Contemporary Culture of Barcelona (CCCB). She is founder of the organization Translocalia, a network of artists, curators, and designers to plan for the future through art. She holds a BA in Humanities, a degree in History of Art and an MA Hons in Curating Contemporary Art from the Royal College of Art in London.

Beatrice de Gelder (NL) is Professor of Cognitive Neuroscience in the Faculty of Psychology and Neuroscience at Maastricht University in Maastricht, The Netherlands, and a member of the Maastricht 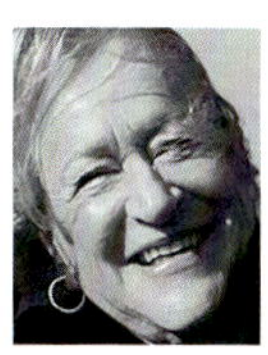 Brain Imaging Centre (M-BIC). Prior to her current assignments, she was a Senior Scientist at the Martinos Center for Biomedical Imaging, Harvard University. She received an MA in Philosophy, an MA in Experimental Psychology, and a PhD in Philosophy from Louvain University in Belgium. Her current research focuses on face and body recognition and, recently, on the neuroscience of art.

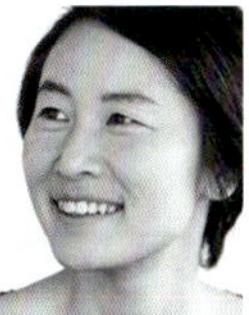

Chiaki Hayashi (JP) is the co-founder and currently the Representative Director of Loftwork Inc. Loftwork successfully produces over 600 projects a year. She manages the operation of the company's creative platform Loftwork.com, which has 25,000 creators registered, FabCafe, which is a cafe with digital fabrication tools, and a material-centered co-working office MTRL. She is currently Japan Liaison to the Director at the MIT Media Lab. She has recently founded "Hidakuma," which aims to rebuild nature and local creativity.

Hiroshi Ishii (JP/US) is the Jerome B. Wiesner Professor of Media Arts and Sciences at the MIT Media Lab. Joining the Media Lab in 1995, he founded the Tangible Media Group to make digital tangible by giving 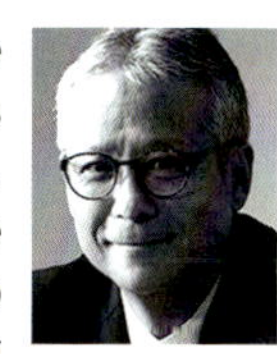 physical and dynamic form to digital information and computation. Here he pursues his visions of *Tangible Bits* (1997) and *Radical Atoms* (2012) that will transcend the current dominant paradigm of Human-Computer Interaction: *Painted Bits* of Graphical User Interfaces. For his visionary work in HCI, he was awarded tenure from MIT in 2001 and the SIGCHI Lifetime Research Award in 2019.

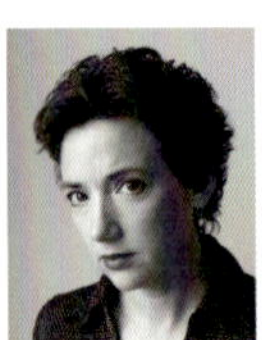

Naomi Kaempfer (US/DE/IL) studied Product Engineering, and Design Management. She established the design and art Manufacturing Platform—a novelty in 2003, which became the renowned *.MGX for Materialise,* and the base for *i.materialise.* From 2008-2011 she was chair professor of "the LAB"—the technology department at the Design Academy, and between 2010-2013, Kaempfer was Design Strategy Expert with Delhaize Group. Kaempfer joined Stratasys in 2014 as Creative Director, Art, Fashion and Design. She explores the possibilities of 3D printing in the creative disciplines, collaborating with designers, artists, museums, art and design institutions etc.. and has set up numerous collections in collaboration with top artists and designers at MoMA, V&A, Pompidou, MET, Smithsonian Cooper Hewitt, and many more.

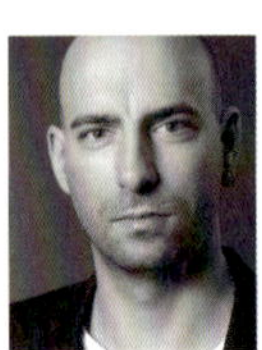

Manuel Kretzer (DE) is Professor for Material and Technology at the Dessau Department of Design, Anhalt University of Applied Sciences. His research aims at the creation of dynamic and adaptive objects with a specific focus on new smart and biological material performance and their combination with advanced digital design and fabrication tools. In 2012 he initiated materiability, a free educational platform that attempts to connect architects, designers, and artists and provides access to novel material developments and technologies.

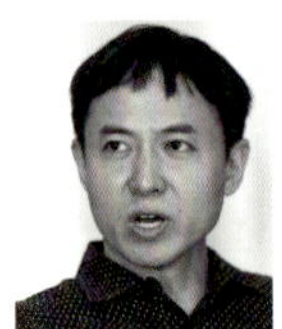

Daehyung Lee (KR) is the Director of Hzone. He currently works as Art Director of CONNECT, BTS, a global initiative developed in collaboration with curators from five major cities—London (Serpentine Galleries), Berlin (Martin Gropius Bau), Buenos Aires (CCK), Seoul (DDP), and New York (Brooklyn Bridge Park). He served as the founding art director of Hyundai Motor Company for six years, connecting Tate, LACMA, MMCA, Bloomberg, and Blue Prize. He curated *Counterbalance: The Stone and the Mountain* at the Korean Pavilion, La Biennale di Venezia 2017. He also served as artistic advisor to Korea Research Fellow 2018–2020, the interdisciplinary playground ZER01NE (2018), Busan Biennale (2014), and Cheongju Craft Biennale (2013). He has been on the jury for the Ars Electronica Festival's STARTS Prize since 2018. He holds an MA in Curatorial Studies from Columbia University in New York and curated *Korean Eye Moon Generation* in 2009 and its nomadic show until 2012 at Saatchi Gallery in London.

Christiane Luible-Bär (AT) is co-leader of the department Fashion & Technology at the University of Art and Design Linz. Her main field of interest is practice-led design research for the field of fashion 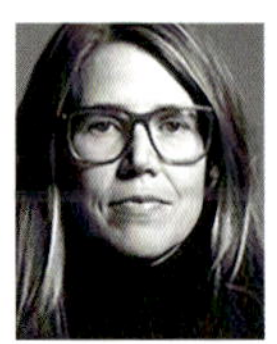 design. At this, she focuses on the 3D modeling and virtual simulation of fashion and the influence of digital media on the process of fashion design. She received several international Design Awards such as the Lucky Strike Junior Design Award. She collaborated on large European clothing research projects and is today responsible for several research projects dealing with fashion and technology.

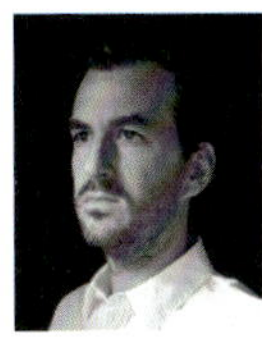

Achim Menges (DE) is an architect in Frankfurt and professor at the University of Stuttgart, where he is founding director of the Institute for Computational Design and Construction (ICD) and director of the Cluster of Excellence Integrative Computational Design and Construction for Architecture (IntCDC). The focus of Achim Menges' practice and research is on the development of integrative design at the intersection of computational design methods, robotic manufacturing, and construction, as well as advanced material and building systems. His design research and projects have received many international awards, been published and exhibited worldwide, and form parts of several renowned museum collections.

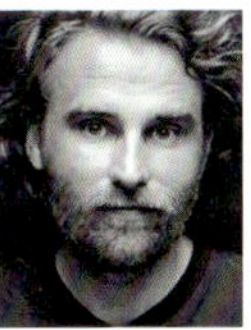

Bastian Schäfer (DE), born in 1980, is a maverick, kitesurfer, TED speaker, father of a boy and a girl, and automotive engineer. After working at Volkswagen Design he entered Airbus in 2006 in different projects for A340, A350, and A380. In 2009 he joined the project team that created the award winning Airbus Concept Cabin with its bionic structure. Bastian Schäfer is the project leader of the Bionic Partition project, where he is focusing on generative design combined with 3D printing technology.

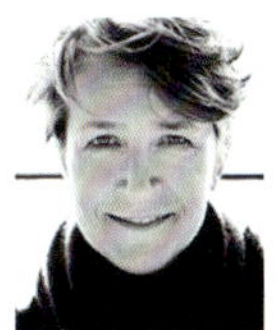

Angelique Spaninks (NL). Combining journalism, criticism, and curating, Angelique Spaninks has developed a generalist, interdisciplinary practice bridging contemporary art, design, digital culture, and bio art & design. Since 2005 she runs MU Hybrid Art House, one of the leading contemporary art institutes in the Netherlands with an outspoken multidisciplinary program as both director and curator. Over the years she has been part of many cultural boards, think tanks, and commissions to help further develop cross cultural practice and policy in the Netherlands and abroad.

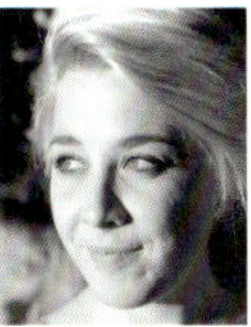

Helene Steiner (AT) is a designer and engineer who works at the interface between technology and science. She co-founded Open Cell with the mission to provide affordable lab space to early-stage start-ups innovating at the intersection of design and biology. She leads the biomaterial platform at the fashion department at the Royal College of Art and was previously a postdoc research fellow in Microsoft Research Cambridge and a visiting research fellow in the Tangible Research group of the MIT Media Lab. She holds an MDes from Bauhaus University, an MA from the Royal College of Art and an MSc from Imperial College London.

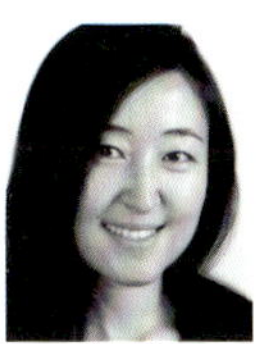

Lining Yao (CN) is an Assistant Professor of Human-Computer Interaction Institute (HCII) at Carnegie Mellon University, School of Computer Science, directing the Morphing Matter Lab *(https://morphingmatter. cs.cmu.edu)*. Morphing Matter Lab develops materials, tools, and applications of adaptive, dynamic, and intelligent morphing matter from nano to macro scales. Research often combines material science, computational fabrication, creative art and design practices. Lining and her lab follow an anti-disciplinary work approach, publishing and exhibiting across science, engineering, design and art. Lining gained her PhD at MIT Media Lab in 2017.

ARS ELECTRONICA 2020
Festival for Art, Technology & Society

Organization
Ars Electronica Linz GmbH & Co KG

Co-CEOs
Markus Jandl (starting 01.09.2020)
Gerfried Stocker,
Diethard Schwarzmair (until 31.08.2020)
Ars-Electronica-Straße 1, 4040 Linz, Austria
Tel: +4373272720
Fax: +4373272722
info@ars.electronica.art

Co-organizer CyberArts Exhibition
OÖ Landes-Kultur GmbH
Managing Director: Alfred Weidinger
OK im OÖ Kulturquartier
Artistic Director: Martin Sturm

Co-organizer Kepler Gardens
Johannes Kepler University Linz
Rector: Meinhard Lukas

Co-organizer Campus
University of Art and Design Linz
Rector: Brigitte Hütter

Artistic Director: Gerfried Stocker
Managing Director: Martin Honzik
Director of European Cooperation,
Finance & Organization: Veronika Liebl
Technical Director: Karl Julian Schmidinger

Head of Festival: Christl Baur
Head of create your world: Hans Christian Merten

Production Team:
Lea Sophia Bernhard, Hortense Boulais-Ifrene, Michael Burgstaller, Alexis Carras, Melinda File, Hannes F. Franks, Petra Freimund, Marion Friedl, Jessica Galirow, Nils Gallist, Anna Grubauer, Jürgen Hagler, Randolf Helmstetter, Markus Hillebrandt, Manuela Hillmann, Ferenc Hirt, Isabella Kartusch, Ruth Köchl, Andrea Kohut, Katharina Kolar, Maria Koller, Veronika Sanna Krenn, Tanja Lepschi, Kristina Maurer, Nives Meloni, Manuela Naveau, Andrew Newman, Michaela Obermayer, Emiko Ogawa, Benjamin Pittertschatscher, Christina Radner, Marco Rainer, Dallas Rockvam, Michael Samhaber, Michael Sarsteiner, Sonja Schachinger, Thomas Schlager, Julian Schmiederer, Armin Seidl, Daina Silina, Karla Spiluttini, Helmut Steinecker, Mauricio Ernesto Suarez Ramos, Nana Thurner, Lukas Traxler, Felix Tröbinger, Jochen Tuch, Edin Turalic, Joschi Viteka, Laura Welzenbach, Michaela Wimplinger, Alexander Wöran, Carla Milena Zamora Campos, Vivian Zech

Press
Christopher Sonnleitner, Joan Bairam, Robert Bauernhansl, Martin Hieslmair, Barbara Hinterleitner, Katia Kreuzhuber, Yazdan Zand

Marketing
Katja Bozic, Agnes Peterseil, Eva Tsackmaktsian, Christine Utz

Prix Ars Electronica 2020

Idea: Hannes Leopoldseder
Conception: Christine Schöpf, Gerfried Stocker
Managing Director: Martin Honzik
Director of European Cooperation,
Finance & Organization: Veronika Liebl
Technical Director: Karl Julian Schmidinger

Head of Prix Ars Electronica: Emiko Ogawa

Production Team: Victoria Absmann, Christl Baur, Marion Friedl, Jürgen Hagler, Veronika Krenn, Andrea Kohut, Katharina Kolar, Kristina Maurer, Hans Christian Merten, Manuela Naveau, Christina Radner, Jutta Schmiederer, Karla Spiluttini, Nana Thurner, Joschi Viteka

Ars Electronica Linz GmbH & Co KG

Co-CEOs
Markus Jandl (starting 1.9.2020), Gerfried Stocker, Diethard Schwarzmair (until 31.08.2020)

Ars Electronica Center
Andreas Bauer, Christoph Kremer, Hassan Abou-Alfadel, Sahel Ahmadzai, Viktoria Aistleitner, Sonja Bailer, Joan Bairam, Reinhard Bengesser, Anastasia Bragina, Sarah Brait, Lisa-Maria Brandstötter, Manuela Bruckner, Esma Cingi, Julia Croton, Moritz Danner, Shirin Darwish, Aline Darwish, Blanka Denkmaier, Reinhart Ebner, Erika Eiter, Lilly Ensinger, Amir-Ali Eshghi, Julia Felberbauer, Katrin Fenninger, Melinda File, Andrea Fröhlich, Philipp Gartlehner, Mitra Gazvini-Zateh, Elisabeth Gerhard, Firas Ghilan, Dominic Gottinger, Marlene Grinner, Melanie Gruber, Nicole Grüneis, Thu Trang Eva Ha, Harald Haas, Birgit Hartinger, Alexandra Heiligenbrunner, Danny Heilmann, Barbara Heinzl, Katherine Heller, Thomas Hillinger, Katharina Hof, Florian Hofer, Sri Rahayu Hofstadler, Gerold Hofstadler, Eva Hofstädter, Fabian Hollinetz, Anca Ignat, Thomas Jannke, David Jentgens, Sabrina Kaselitz, Herwig Kerschner, Sandra Kiendler, Jona Kislinger, Sarka Klafböck, Viktoria Klepp, Karin Knoll, Michael Koller, Thomas Kollmann, Wolfgang Königsmaier, Sabine Leidlmair, Anna Katharina Link, Jakob

Luckeneder, Melanie Ludwig, Kornelia Maier, Ulrike Mair, Clemens Mock, Erika Mondria, Horst Morocutti, Claudia Moser, Silvia Mukherjee, Daniel Murina, Heinrich Niederhuber, Andrea Oberfichtner, Michaela Obermayer, Hana Opresnik, Dietmar Peter, Svetlana Petrovic, Katharina Pilar, Armin Pils, Ulrike Rieseneder, Ezan Riza, Clara Roth, Petra Saubolle-Hofmann, Alina Sauter, Birgitt Schäffer, Mario Schmidhumer, Sarah Schmidt, Lydia Schneeberger, Fabian Schwarz, Thomas Schwarz, Manfred Seifriedsberger, Majd Shukair, Magdalena Sick-Leitner, Minoosh Sorkhkamal Zadeh –Steininger, Martin Spanka, Elisabeth Spöck, Margarethe Stöttner-Breuer, Thomas Straßhofer, Andreas Stürmer, Johannes Stürzlinger, Bhoomesh Tak, Michael Thaler, Thomas Viehböck, Raffaela Vornicu, Manuel Walch, Florian Wanninger, Gregor Woschitz

Ars Electronica Futurelab
Horst Hörtner, Roland Haring, Hideaki Ogawa, Flavia Andessner, Friedrich Bachinger, Sanja Bajakic, Florian Berger, Patrick Berger, Alexandre Bezri, Kerstin Blätterbinder, Birgit Cakir, Arno Deutschbauer, Manuel Dobusch, Samuel Jakob Eckl, Marianne Eisl, Stephan Feichter, Peter Freudling, Matthew Gardiner, Vanessa Graf, Barbara Habringer, Peter Holzkorn, Kyoko Kunoh, Anna Kuthan, Elisabeth Luger, Maria Mayr, Stefan Mittlböck-Jungwirth-Fohringer, Otto Naderer, Nicolas Naveau, Ali Nikrang, Maria Anna Pfeifer, Johannes Pöll, Daniel Rammer, Erwin Reitböck, Clemens Francis Scharfen, Raphael Elias Schaumburg-Lippe, Simon Schmid, Yoko Shimizu, Susanne Teufelauer, Georgios Tsampounaris, Julian Zauner

Ars Electronica Festival / Prix / Exhibitions
Martin Honzik, Veronika Christina Liebl, Karl Schmidinger, Christl Baur, Florina Costamoling, Marion Friedl, Jessica Galirow, Anna Grubauer, Ferenc Hirt, Isabella Kartusch, Andrea Kohut, Katharina Maria Kolar, Veronika Sanna Krenn, Kristina Maurer, Hans Christian Merten, Manuela Naveau, Andrew Newman, Emiko Ogawa, Christina Radner, Michael Samhaber, Karla Spiluttini, Laura Welzenbach, Carla Milena Zamora Campos

Ars Electronica Management Services
Elisabeth Kapeller, Markus Jandl, Isabella Albel-Feicht, Robert Bauernhansl, Patrick Buchinger, Barbara Diesenreither, Johannes Egler, Michaela Frech, Anton Grünwald Belada, Haitham Harwash, Martin Hieslmair, Barbara Hinterleitner, Julia Hofstätter, Sabine Hummelbrunner, Stephan Kobler, Daniela Krassnitzer, Katia Kreuzhuber, Dominic Lengauer, Bernhard Mandl, Florian Miesenberger, Peter J. Nitzschmann, Edith Noska-Neubauer, Humayun Omari, Agnes Peterseil, Beate Prinz, Gabriele Purdue, Gunther Ritz, Christopher Sonnleitner, David Starzengruber, Eva Tsackmaktsian, Michaela Wimplinger

Ars Electronica Solutions
Michael Mondria, Michael Kaiser, Andreas Pramböck, Ina Badics, Chris Bruckmayr, Stefan Dorn, Stefanie Farkashazy, Michaela Fragner, Yvonne Hauser, Alexander Heilinger, Fadil Kujundzic, Harald Moser, Patrick Müller, My Trinh Müller-Gardiner, Robert Pibernig, Sabine Sieberer, Dominik Trichlin, Markus Wipplinger, Karim Zuderell

Ars Electronica International
Amanda Augustin, Lea Sophia Bernhard, Hannes Franks, Manuela Hillmann, Ruth Köchl, Tanja Lepschi, Nives Meloni, Julian Schmiederer, Daina Silina, Mauricio Ernesto Suarez Ramos, Nana Thurner, Alexander Wöran, Yazdan Zand

CYBERARTS Exhibition Team / OÖ Landes-Kultur GmbH:

Genoveva Rückert, Andreas Kurz, Maria Venzl, Martina Rauschmayer, Marlies Stöger

OK Night & Streaming:
Markus Reindl, Jarno Bachheimer
Production Team: Katharina Baldinger-Hackl, Alfred Fürholzer, Martin Haselsteiner, David Kraxberger, Bernhard Kitzmüller, Franz Quirchtmayr, Felix Pöchhacker, Aron Rynda, Andreas Steindl, André Tschinder, Hans-Jörg Weidinger, Simon Wilhelm, Gerhard Wörnhörer

Kunstuniversität Linz — Universität für künstlerische und industrielle Gestaltung

Rector: Brigitte Hütter
Vice-Rectors: Erik Aigner, Karin Harasser, Frank Louis
Team: Christa Sommerer, Manuela Naveau, Sylvia Leitner, Davide Bevilacqua, Julia Nüßlein, Fabricio Lamoncha, Enrique Tomás, Gloria Meynen, Tina Frank, Sander Hofstee, Irene Posch, Anne Nigten, Sofia Braga, Franz Linimayr, Ewald Haider, Markus Decker, Alfred Wollersberger, Christian Forstner, Julia Gschwendtner, Eva Fostl

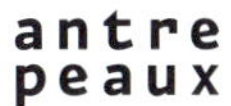

Antre Peaux

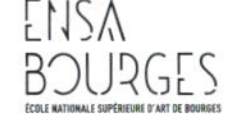

Ecole nationale supérieure d'art (ENSA)

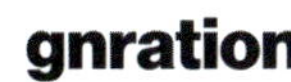

gnration

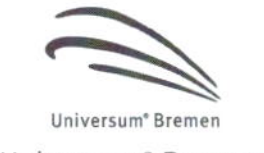

Universum® Bremen

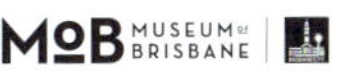

Museum of Brisbane

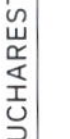

Centre for Fine Arts Brussels (BOZAR)

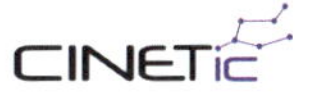

UNATC

CINETic Arts

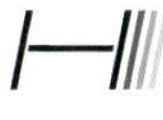

H3 Studio

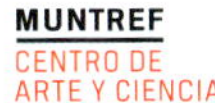

Museo de la Universidad Nacional de Tres de Febrero - Centro de Arte y Ciencia

Universidad Nacional de Tres de Febrero

LatBioLab Latinamerican Bioart Lab

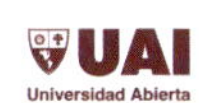

UAI Universidad Abierta Interamericana

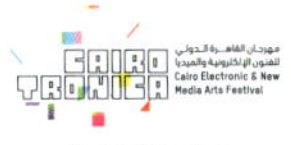

Cairotronica

Space Exploration Initiative

Tangible Media Group

MIT Media Lab

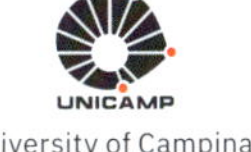

University of Campinas (UNICAMP)

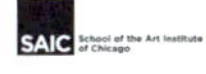

Municipality of Figueira de Castelo Rodrigo

Art & Technology Studies at the School of the Art Institute of Chicago

Cluj Cultural Centr

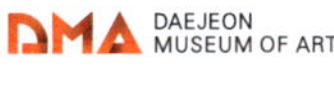

Daejeon Museum of Art

The Clinic for Open Source Arts (COSA)

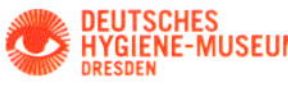

Deutsches Hygiene Museum Dresden

Science Gallery Dublin

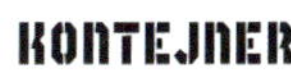

Kontejner

MU Hybrid Art House

Kulturhauptstadt Esch

Aalto University

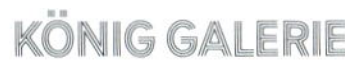

KÖNIG GALERIE

Galerie Liusa Wang

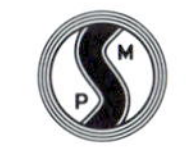

Daata Editions

PSM Gallery

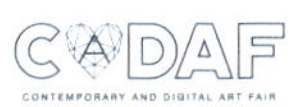

CADAF The Contemporary and Digital Art Fair

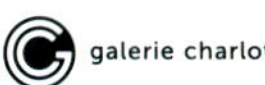

Galerie Charlot

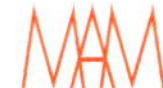

MAM Mario Mauroner Contemporary Art Vienna

VENT gallery

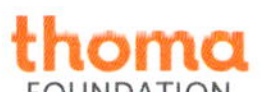

Carl & Marilynn Thoma Art Foundation

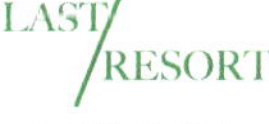

LAST/RESORT

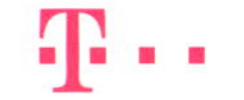

Art Collection Deutsche Telekom

SOUND:FRAME

sound:frame

bitforms

bitforms gallery

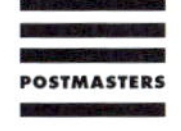

Postmasters Gallery

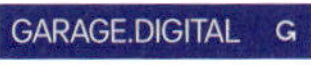

Garage Museum of Contemporary Art

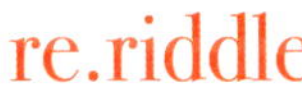

Re.Riddle Gallery

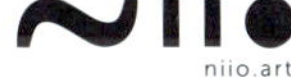

Niio

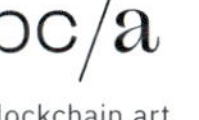

blockchain.art

The WRONG

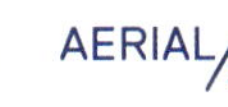

Aerial/Sparks

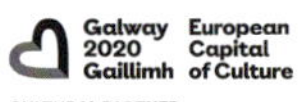

Galway 2020 European
Capital of Culture

GDAŃSK

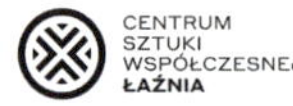

Laznia Center for
Contemporary Art

GIJÓN

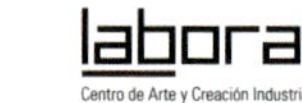

LABoral Centro de Arte y
Creación Industrial

GRANADA

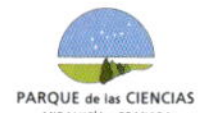

Parque de las Ciencias

GRENOBLE

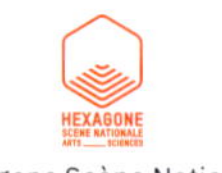

Hexagone Scène Nationale
Arts Sciences

HELSINGØR

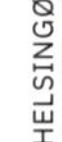

The Culture Yard

HONG KONG

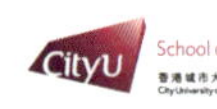

School of Creative Media

HSINCHU

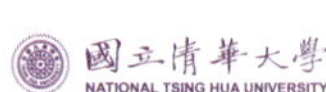

National Tsing Hua
University

JAKARTA

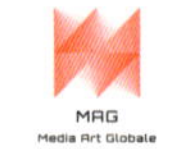

Media Art Globale

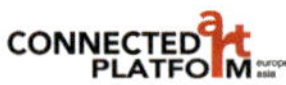

Connected Art Platform
(CAP)

JERUSALEM

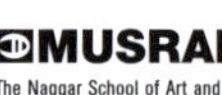

Musrara, Naggar School
of Arts

JOHANNESBURG

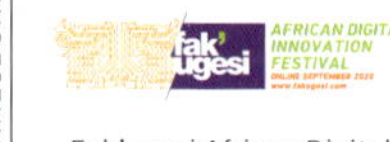

Fak'ugesi African Digital
Innovation Festival

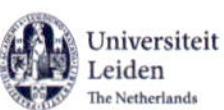

PACE Pan-African
Creative Exchange

LEIDEN

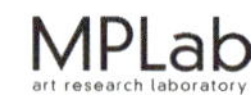

Leiden University

LIEPAJA

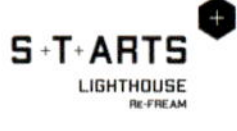

MPLab – Liepaja University
Art Research Laboratory

LIMA

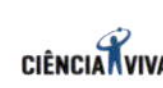

Museo de Arte de Lima –
MALI

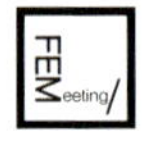

Alta Tecnología Andina –
ATA

LINZ / BERLIN / VALENCIA

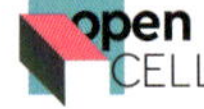

Re-FREAM

LISBON

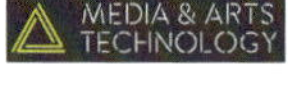

Ciência Viva

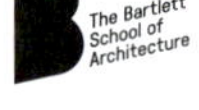

FEMeeting

LIVERPOOL

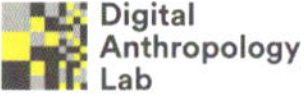

FACT

LONDON

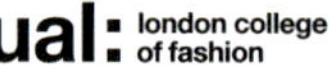

Open Cell

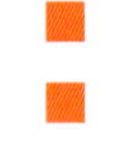

Media and Arts Technology
Centre for Doctoral Training
at Queen Mary University
of London

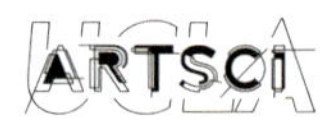

The Bartlett School of
Architecture, University
College London

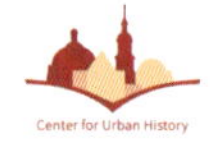

Digital Anthropology Lab

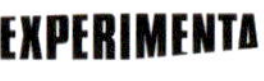

London College of Fashion,
University of the Arts
London

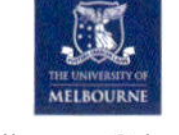

MA Interaction Design
Communication at
the London College of
Communication, University
of the Arts London

LOS ANGELES

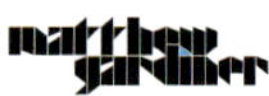

UCLA ArtSci Center

LVIV

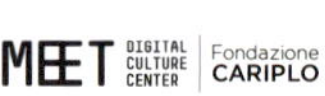

Center for Urban
History of East
Central Europe

MELBOURNE

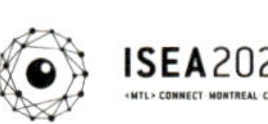

Experimenta

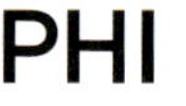

Melbourne School of
Design, The University of
Melbourne

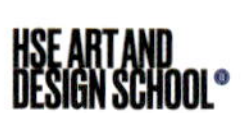

Studio Matthew
Gardiner

MILAN

MEET Digital Culture
Center

MONTREAL

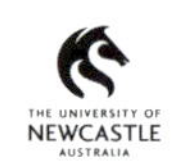

ISEA2020

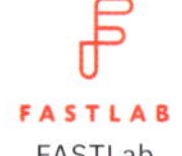

PHI

MOSCOW

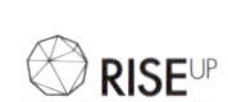

HSE ART AND DESIGN
SCHOOL

NANTES

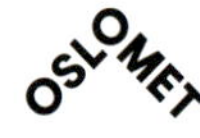

le lieu unique

NEWCASTLE

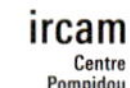

University of Newcastle

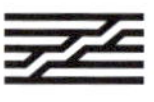

FASTLab

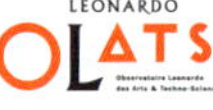

Art Thinking Australia

NIKOSIA

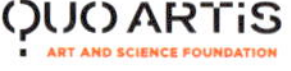

RISE ITICA

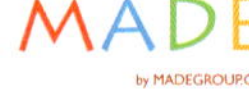

Austrian Embassy
Nicosia

OSLOFJORD

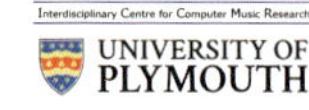

Oslo Metropolitan
University

PARIS

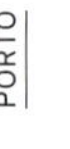

IRCAM

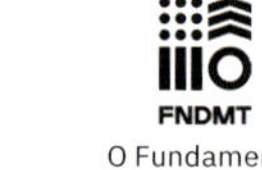

Google Arts &
Culture Lab

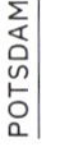

Leonardo/Olats

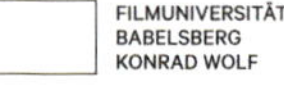

Quo Artis

PAROS

MADE Group

PLYMOUTH

Interdisciplinary Centre for
Computer Music Research
(ICCMR), University of
Plymouth

PORTO

O Fundamento

POTSDAM

Filmuniversität Babelsberg
Konrad Wolf

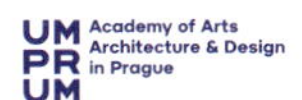

Academy of Arts Prague

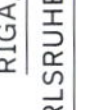

RIXC

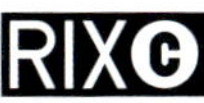

BioDesign Lab HfG

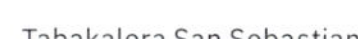

Tabakalera San Sebastian

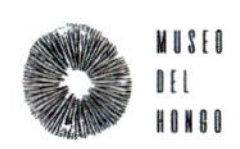

Museo del Hongo

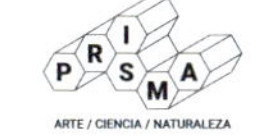

PRISMA: Art, Science, Technology

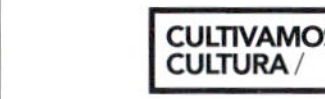

Cultivamos Cultura

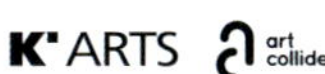

K'ARTS Korea National University of Arts

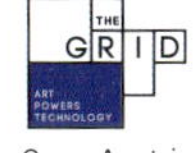

Open Austria

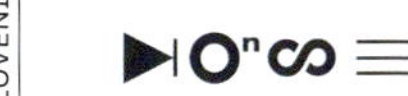

konS – Platform for Contemporary Investigative Art

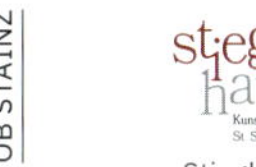

Kur Futurelab

Stieglerhaus

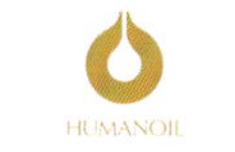

NOBA - Norwegian Bioart Arena

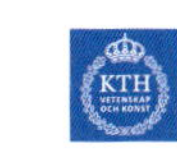

KTH Royal Institute of Technology

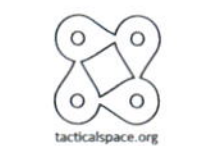

Tactical Space Lab

Kaohsiung Film Archive (KFA)

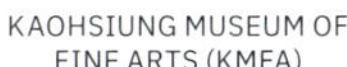

KAOHSIUNG MUSEUM OF FINE ARTS (KMFA)

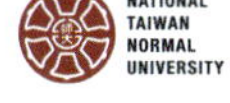

National Taiwan Normal University (NTNU)

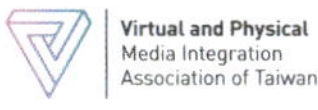

Virtual and Physical Media Integration Association of Taiwan (VPAT)

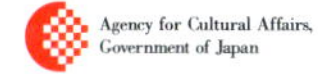

Estonian Academy of Arts

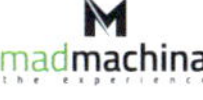

Mad Machina

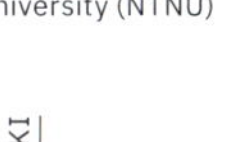

MindSpaces

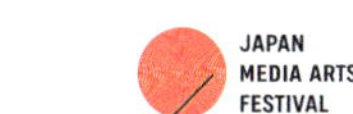

Japan Media Arts Festival

Agency for Cultural Affairs, Government of Japan

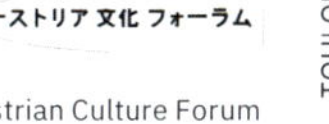

Austrian Culture Forum Tokyo

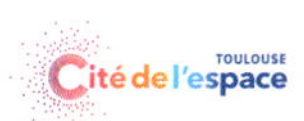

Cité de l'espace

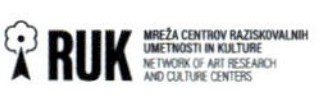

RUK

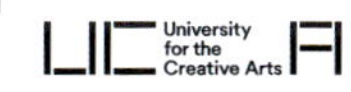

UCA University for the Creative Arts

SERPENTINE

Serpentine Gallery

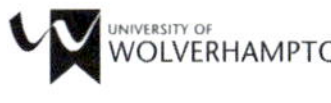

FutureEverything

University of Wolverhampton

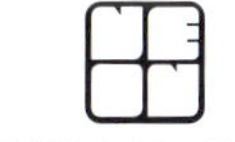

NEoN Digital Arts Festival

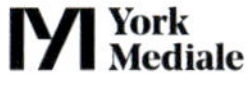

York Mediale

Art In Flux

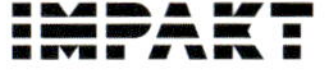

IMPAKT

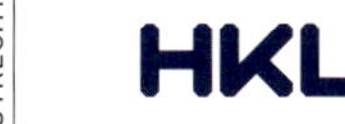

HKU University Of The Arts Utrecht

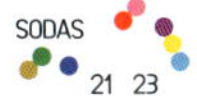

CIA-UV University of Valparaíso Artistic Research Center

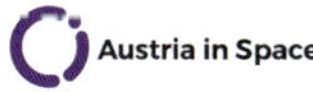

Austria in Space

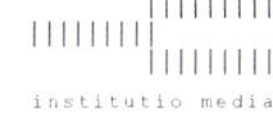

Instituto Media

LTMKS

Letmekoo / LTMKS (Lithuanian Interdisciplinary Artists' Association)

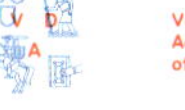
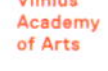

SODAS 21 23

VDA PhAMA (Department of Photography and Media Art at Vilnius Academy of Arts)

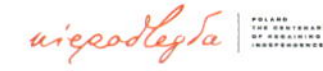
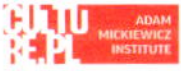

Adam Mickiewicz Institute

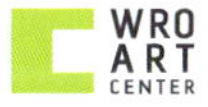

WRO ART CENTER

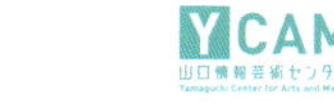

Yamaguchi Center for Arts and Media [YCAM]

COOPERATION PARTNERS

.art
Amnesty International Österreich
Anton Bruckner Privatuniversität
ArtTechLab Amsterdam
Atelierhaus Salzamt
Austrian Council on Robotics and Artificial Intelligence
AWS – Jugend Innovativ
Bruckner Orchester Linz
c3
CoderDojo Linz
Creative Region
Crossing Europe Film Festival Linz
Edinburgh Futures Institute
Europe for Festivals, Festivals for Europe EFFE

FAB Verein zur Förderung von Arbeit und Beschäftigung
Fachhochschule Oberösterreich — Campus Hagenberg
Fachhochschule St. Pölten
FC - Francisco Carolinum
Fraunhofer MEVIS: Institute for Medical Image Computing
Grand Garage
IMZ International Music + Media Centre
Kepler Salon – Verein zur Förderung von Wissensvermittlung
LINZ CENTER OF MECHATRONICS GMBH
Marché du Film – Festival de Cannes
OMAi
Polycular OG

PSNC – Poznan Supercomputing and Networking Center
RIEGL Laser Measurement Systems GmbH
Rotax MAX Dome Linz
ScanLAB Projects
Siemens Healthcare Diagnostics GmbH
Spin Digital Video Technologies GmbH
Stadtpfarrkirche Urfahr
Stadtwerkstatt
ULF - Unabhängiges LandesFreiwilligenzentrum
VALIE EXPORT Center Linz
Visualization Center C
White Castle Games Agency
Zero1

ARS ELECTRONIC RECEIVES SUPPORT FROM

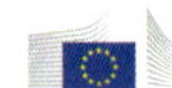
Europäische Kommission Horizon 2020

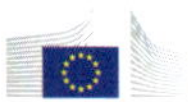
Europäische Kommission

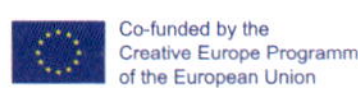
Creative Europe

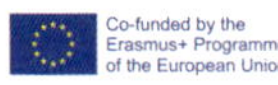
Europäische Union Erasmus+

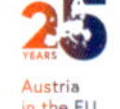
Austria in the EU

Bundesministerium für Kunst, Kultur, öffentlichen Dienst und Sport

Bundesministerium Europäische und internationale Angelegenheiten

Bundesministerium für Bildung, Wissenschaft und Forschung

OeAD-GmbH

KulturKontakt Austria/ OeAD

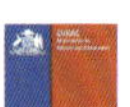
Chile

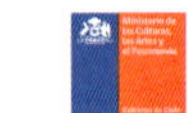
Ministerio de Relaciones Exteriores, Dirección de Asuntos Culturales Chile

Ministerio de las Culturas, las Artes y el Patrimonio Chile

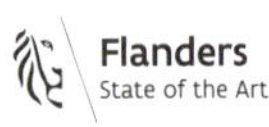
Flanders State of the Art

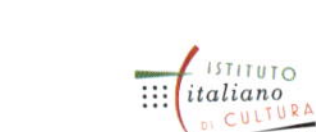
Istituto Italiano di Cultura

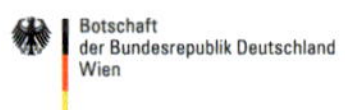
Botschaft der Bundesrepublik Deutschland in Wien

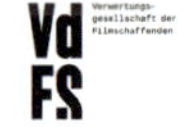
Verwertungsgesellschaft der Filmschaffenden VdFS GenmbH

MOBILITY PARTNER

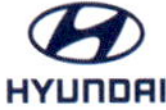
Hyundai Import GmbH

SPONSORS

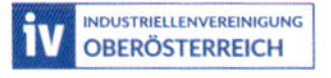
Hakuhodo

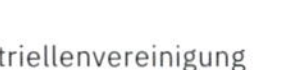
Industriellenvereinigung Oberösterreich

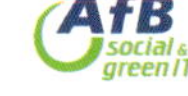
AfB mildtätige und gemeinnützige Gesellschaft zur Schaffung von Arbeitsplätzen für behinderte Menschen mbH

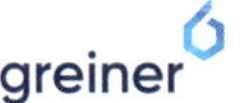
GREINER AG

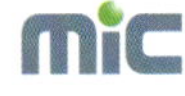
MIC – managing international customs & trade compliance

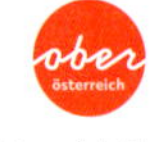
Oberösterreich Tourismus GmbH

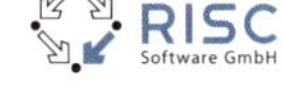
RISC Software GmbH

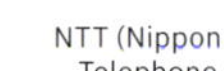
NTT (Nippon Telegraph and Telephone Corporation)

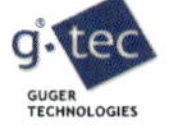
g.tec medical engineering GmbH

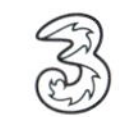 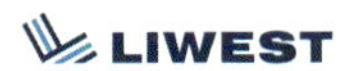 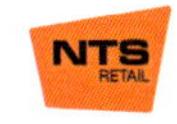 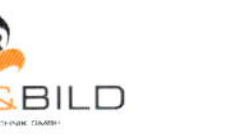

Hutchinson Drei Austria GmbH	Liwest Kabelmedien GmbH	NTS New Technology Systems GmbH	Ton & Bild Medientechnik GmbH	Pädagogische Hochschule OÖ

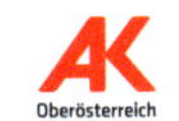 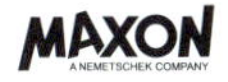 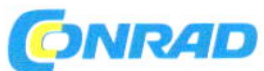 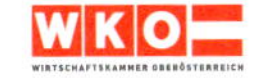 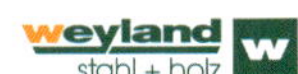

Arbeiterkammer OÖ	MAXON Computer GmbH	Conrad Electronic GmbH & Co KG	WKO Oberösterreich	Weyland GmbH

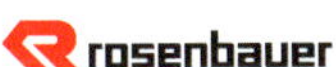 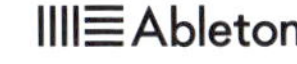 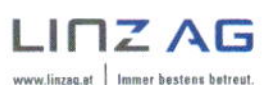 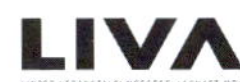 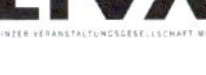

Rosenbauer International AG	Ableton AG	Österreichisches Rotes Kreuz	Linz AG	LIVA

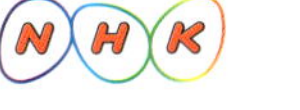 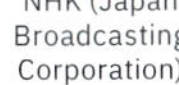 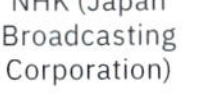  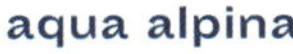 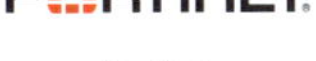

NHK (Japan Broadcasting Corporation)	BIO AUSTRIA	Aruba Networks, Inc.	CCF - Computer Center Feldbach	Fortinet	Triple A Aqua Service GmbH

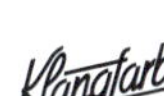 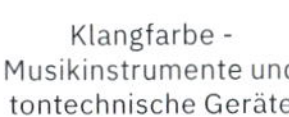 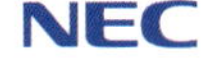 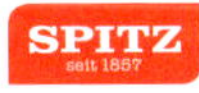 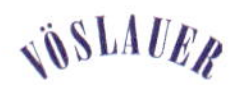 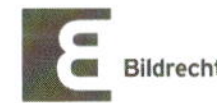

Klangfarbe - Musikinstrumente und tontechnische Geräte Handelsges.m.b.H.	NEC Dispaly Solutions Europe GmbH	S. Spitz GmbH	Vöslauer Mineralwasser GmbH	Bildrecht GmbH

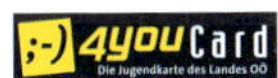 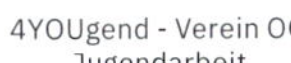 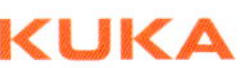 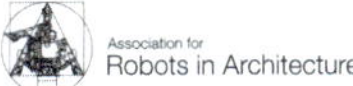 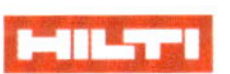 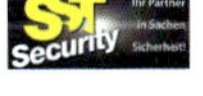 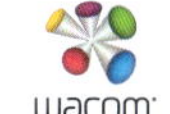

4YOUgend - Verein OÖ Jugendarbeit	KUKA CEE GmbH	Association for Robots in Architecture	Hilti Austria Ges.m.b.H.	S.S.T. Security	Wacom Co., Ltd.

PROJECT PARTNERS

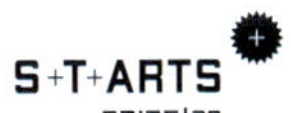 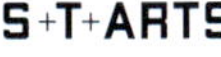 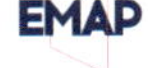 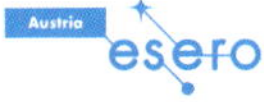 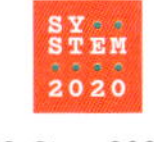

STARTS Prize ´20	STARTS EU	EMAP European Media Art Platform	esero Austria	SyStem 2020

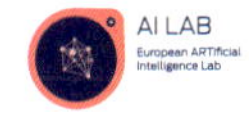  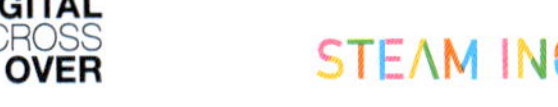 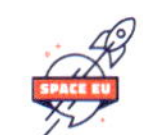 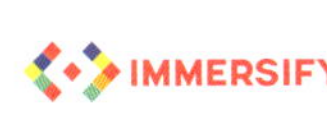 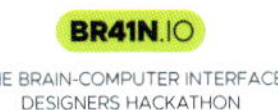

European ARTificial Intelligence Lab	AIxMusic	space EU	IMMERSIFY	BR41N.IO

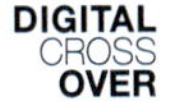 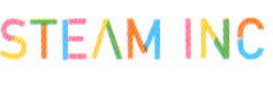 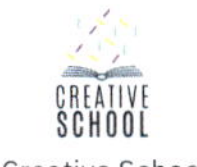 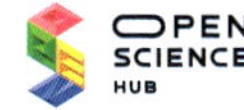

Digital Cross Over	STEAM INC	Creative School	Studiotopia	OSHub

MEDIA PARTNERS

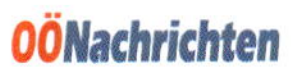 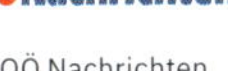 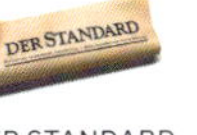 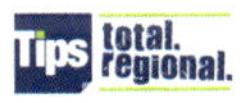 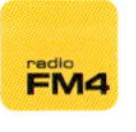 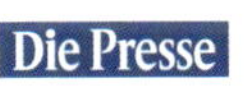 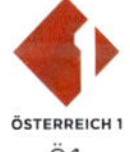

OÖ Nachrichten	DER STANDARD	TIPS	FM4	DIE PRESSE	Ö1

CyberArts 2020

Prix Ars Electronica 2020
Computer Animation · Interactive Art + · Digital Communities
Visionary Pioneers of Media Art · u19—create your world

STARTS Prize'20
Grand Prize of the European Commission honoring Innovation
in Technology, Industry and Society stimulated by the Arts

Editors: Hannes Leopoldseder, Christine Schöpf, Gerfried Stocker

Editing: Jutta Schmiederer
Translations: (German—English): Douglas Deitemyer
Copyediting: Catherine Lewis, Jutta Schmiederer

Graphic design and production: Gerhard Kirchschläger
Typeface: IBM Plex Sans
Printed by: Gutenberg Werbering Gesellschaft m.b.H., Linz
Paper: Claro Bulk, 135 g/m², 300 g/m²
Photos: pp. 184—189; 255—256 Martin Hieslmair, Katia Kreuzhuber, Barbara Hinterleitner

© 2020 Ars Electronica
© 2020 for the reproduced works by the artists, or their legal successors

Published by
Hatje Cantz Verlag GmbH
Mommsenstrasse 27
10629 Berlin
Germany
www.hatjecantz.de
A Ganske Publishing Group company

Hatje Cantz books are available internationally at selected bookstores.
For more information about our distribution partners please visit our homepage at
www.hatjecantz.com.

ISBN 978-3-7757-4761-5

Printed in Austria

Cover illustration:
Front: Miwa Matreyek; *Infinitely Yours*, documentation still: Keida Mascaro; Max Hattler: *Serial Parallels*
Back: Audrey Briot: *Stymphalian Birds;* Andrea Ling: *Design by Decay, Decay by Design,* photo: Ally Schmaling